June 12–13, 2014
Edinburgh, UK

**Association for
Computing Machinery**

Advancing Computing as a Science & Profession

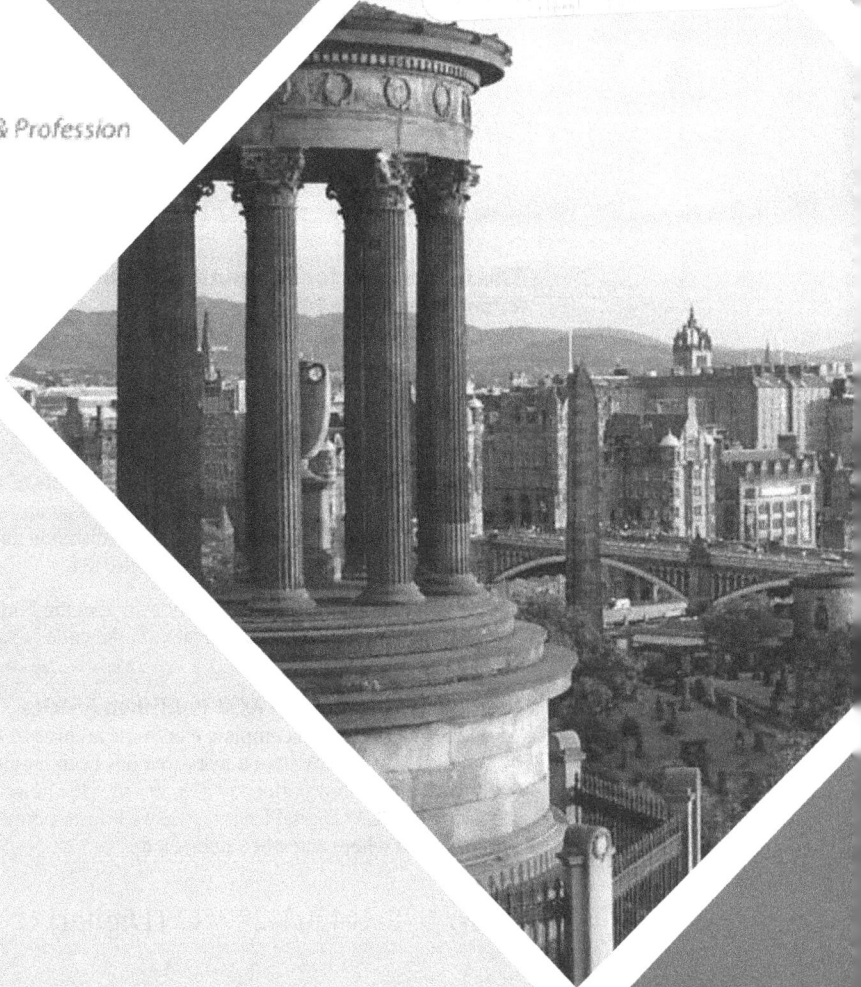

LCTES'14

Proceedings of the 2014 SIGPLAN/SIGBED Conference on

Languages, Compilers and Tools for Embedded Systems

Sponsored by:

ACM SIGPLAN & ACM SIGBED

Association for
Computing Machinery

Advancing Computing as a Science & Profession

The Association for Computing Machinery
2 Penn Plaza, Suite 701
New York, New York 10121-0701

Notice to Past Authors of ACM-Published Articles

ISBN: 978-1-4503-2877-7 (Digital)

ISBN: 978-1-4503-3086-2 (Print)

Additional copies may be ordered prepaid from:

ACM Order Department
PO Box 30777
New York, NY 10087-0777, USA

Phone: 1-800-342-6626 (USA and Canada)
+1-212-626-0500 (Global)
Fax: +1-212-944-1318
E-mail: acmhelp@acm.org
Hours of Operation: 8:30 am – 4:30 pm ET

Printed in the USA

Foreword

It is our great pleasure to welcome you to the *2014 ACM Conference on Languages, Compilers, and Tools for Embedded Systems.* This year's conference continues its tradition of being the premier forum for presentation of research results on leading edge issues in embedded systems.

The call for papers attracted 51 submissions from all over the world. Each paper received at least three reviews. Reviewing was "double-blind," meaning that author identities were withheld from the reviewers. After the reviewing was completed, the PC met for a 5-day long online meeting to deliberate on the papers and to reach consensus on each paper. These deliberations were open to the entire PC, and generated interesting and fruitful discussions on several papers. Finally, the program committee accepted 16 high-quality papers that cover a variety of topics, including worst-case timing analysis, static program analysis, code generation and optimization, and computer architecture.

In addition to the reviewed research papers, the program includes two keynote speeches by renowned researchers, Dr. David Whalley and Dr. Minyi Guo. We encourage attendees to attend the keynote talk presentations. These valuable and insightful talks can and will guide us to a better understanding of the future:

- *Energy Efficient Data Access Techniques,* Dr. David Whalley (Florida State University)

- *Energy Efficient Data Access and Storage through HW/SW Co-design,* Dr. Minyi Guo (Shanghai Jiao Tong University)

Putting together LCTES'*14* was a team effort. We first thank the authors for providing the content of the program. We are grateful to the members of the program committee, who worked very hard in reviewing papers and providing feedback for authors. Finally, we thank our sponsors, ACM SIGPLAN and ACM SIGBED, for their generous support.

We hope that you will find this program interesting and thought-provoking and that the conference will provide you with a valuable opportunity to share ideas with other researchers and practitioners from institutions around the world. Please enjoy the program!

Youtao Zhang
LCTES'14 General Chair
University of Pittsburgh, USA

Prasad Kulkarni
LCTES'14 Program Chair
University of Kansas, USA

Table of Contents

LCTES'14 Organization List..vii

LCTES 2014 Sponsors viii

Session: Keynote Address 1
Session Chair: Prasad A. Kulkarni *(University of Kansas, USA)*

- **Energy Efficient Data Access Techniques**..1
  David Whalley *(Florida State University)*

Session: Code Generation and Optimization
Session Chair: Jean-Pierre Talpin *(INRIA, France)*

- **Efficient Code Generation in a Region-Based Dynamic Binary Translator** 3
  Tom Spink, Harry Wagstaff, Björn Franke, Nigel Topham *(University of Edinburgh)*

- **CASM - Optimized Compilation of Abstract State Machines** 13
  Roland Lezuo, Philipp Paulweber, Andreas Krall *(Vienna University of Technology)*

- **Combinatorial Spill Code Optimization and Ultimate Coalescing**.....................................23
  Roberto Castañeda Lozano, Mats Carlsson *(SCALE, Swedish Institute of Computer Science)*,
  Gabriel Hjort Blindell, Christian Schulte *(SCALE, School of ICT, KTH Royal Institute of Technology)*

Session: Worst Case Timing Analysis

- **Cache-Related Preemption Delay Analysis for FIFO Caches**..33
  Clément Ballabriga, Lee Kee Chong, Abhik Roychoudhury *(National University of Singapore)*

- **How to Compute Worst-Case Execution Time by Optimization Modulo Theory
  and a Clever Encoding of Program Semantics**...43
  Julien Henry, Mihail Asavoae *(VERIMAG / Université Joseph Fourier)*, David Monniaux *(VERIMAG / CNRS)*,
  Claire Maïza *(VERIMAG / Grenoble INP)*

- **WCET-Aware Dynamic Instruction Cache Locking** 53
  Wenguang Zheng, Hui Wu *(The University of New South Wales)*

Session: Search Space Exploration

- **Exploration of Compiler Optimization Sequences Using Clustering-Based Selection**.........63
  Luiz G. A. Martins *(Federal University of Uberlândia)*, Ricardo Nobre *(University of Porto & INESC-TEC)*,
  Alexandre C. B. Delbem, Eduardo Marques *(University of São Paulo)*,
  João M. P. Cardoso *(University of Porto & INESC-TEC)*

- **Partitioning Data-Parallel Programs for Heterogeneous Mpsocs :
  Time and Energy Design Space Exploration**..73
  Kiran Chandramohan, Michael F.P. O'Boyle *(University of Edinburgh)*

Session: Keynote Address 2
Session Chair: Youtao Zhang *(University of Pittsburgh, USA)*

- **Energy Efficient Data Access and Storage Through HW/SW Co-Design** 83
  Minyi Guo *(Shanghai Jiao Tong University)*

Session: Static Analysis and Optimization

- **Exploiting Function Similarity for Code Size Reduction**..85
  Tobias J.K. Edler von Koch, Björn Franke *(University of Edinburgh)*,
  Pranav Bhandarkar, Anshuman Dasgupta *(Qualcomm Innovation Center Inc.)*

- **ASAC: Automatic Sensitivity Analysis for Approximate Computing** 95
  Pooja Roy *(National University of Singapore)*, Rajarshi Ray *(National Institute of Technology, Meghalaya)*,
  Chundong Wang *(Data Storage Institute)*, Weng Fai Wong *(National University of Singapore)*

- **em-SPADE: A Compiler Extension for Checking Rules Extracted from Processor Specifications** 105
  Sandeep Chaudhary, Sebastian Fischmeister, Lin Tan *(University of Waterloo)*

Session: Many-core, GPU, and VLIW

- **VOBLA: A Vehicle for Optimized Basic Linear Algebra** 115
  Ulysse Beaugnon *(INRIA and École Normale Supérieure)*,
  Alexey Kravets, Sven van Haastregt *(ARM)*, Riyadh Baghdadi *(INRIA and École Normale Supérieure)*,
  David Tweed, Javed Absar, Anton Lokhmotov *(ARM)*

- **A Framework to Schedule Parametric Dataflow Applications on Many-Core Platforms** 125
  Vagelis Bebelis *(INRIA / STMicroelectronics)*, Pascal Fradet, Alain Girault *(INRIA)*

- **Improving Performance of Loops on DIAM-Based VLIW Architectures** 135
  Jinyong Lee, Jongwon Lee *(Seoul National University)*,
  Jongeun Lee *(Ulsan National Institute of Science and Technology)*, Yunheung Paek *(Seoul National University)*

Session: Memory Optimization and Management

- **Superoptimization of Memory Subsystems** 145
  Joseph G. Wingbermuehle, Ron K. Cytron, Roger D. Chamberlain *(Washington University)*

- **Lightweight and Block-Level Concurrent Sweeping for JavaScript Garbage Collection** 155
  Hongjune Kim, Seonmyeong Bak, Jaejin Lee *(Seoul National University)*

Author Index

Author Index 165

LCTES 2014 Conference Organization

General Chair: Youtao Zhang *(University of Pittsburgh, USA)*

Program Chair: Prasad Kulkarni *(University of Kansas, USA)*

Publicity Chair: Lei Jiang *(University of Pittsburgh, USA)*

Web Chair: Michael Jantz *(University of Kansas, USA)*

Steering Committee Chair: Bruce Childers *(University of Pittsburgh, USA)*

Program Committee: Jason Agron *(Intel, USA)*
Sebastian Altmeyer *(University of Amsterdam, Netherlands)*
Philip Brisk *(University of California, Riverside, USA)*
Alexandre Chapoutot *(ENSTA Paristech, France)*
Apala Guha *(Indraprastha Institute of Information Technology, India)*
Rajiv Gupta *(University of California, Riverside, USA)*
Stephen Hines *(Google, USA)*
Jason Hiser *(University of Virginia, USA)*
Changhee Jung *(VirginiaTech, USA)*
Mahmut Kandemir *(Pennsylvania State University, USA)*
Kai Lampka *(Uppsala University, Sweden)*
Jaejin Lee *(Seoul National University, Korea)*
Florence Maraninchi *(Grenoble INP, Verimag, France)*
Gayatri Mehta *(University of North Texas, USA)*
Frank Mueller *(North Carolina State University, USA)*
Santosh Pande *(Georgia Tech, USA)*
Abhik Roychoudhury *(National University of Singapore, Singapore)*
Magnus Sjalander *(Uppsala University, Sweden)*
Fabian Scheler *(University Erlangen-Nuremberg, Germany)*
Klaus Schneider *(University of Kaiserslautern, Germany)*
Zili Shao *(Hong Kong Polytechnic University, Hong Kong)*
Aviral Shrivastava *(Arizona State University, USA)*
Greg Stitt *(University of Florida, USA)*
Jean-Pierre Talpin *(INRIA, France)*
Yi Wang *(Uppsala University, Sweden)*
Fang Yu *(National Chengchi University, Taiwan)*
Chengmo Yang *(University of Delaware, USA)*
Heechul Yun *(University of Kansas, USA)*
Haibo Zeng *(McGill University, Canada)*

Sponsors:

Keynote
Energy Efficient Data Access Techniques

David Whalley
Computer Science Department
Florida State University
Tallahassee, FL, United States 32306-4530
whalley@cs.fsu.edu

ABSTRACT
Energy has become a first class design constraint for all types of processors. Data accesses contribute to processor energy usage and can account for up to 25% of the total energy used in embedded processors. Using a set-associative level-one data cache (L1 DC) organization is particularly energy inefficient as load operations access all L1 DC tag and data arrays in parallel to reduce access latency, but the data can reside in at most one way. Techniques that reduce L1 DC energy usage at the expense of degrading performance, such as filter caches, have not been adopted. In this presentation I will describe various techniques we have developed to reduce the energy usage for L1 DC accesses without adversely affecting performance. These techniques include avoiding unnecessary loads from L1 DC data arrays and a practical data filter cache design that not only significantly reduces data access energy usage, but also avoids the traditional execution time penalty associated with data filter caches.

Categories and Subject Descriptors
B.3.2 [Hardware]: Memory structures – *Design styles, Cache memories*

General Terms
Hardware design, execution time improvement, energy efficiency

Keywords
Execution time; energy; memory hierarchy; data cache; speculation

Bio
David Whalley received his PhD in CS from the University of Virginia in 1990. He is currently the E.P. Miles professor of the Computer Science Department at Florida State University (FSU) and is an FSU Distinguished Research Professor. His research interests include low-level compiler optimizations, tools for supporting the development and maintenance of compilers, program performance evaluation tools, predicting execution time, computer architecture, and embedded systems. Some of the techniques that he developed for new compiler optimizations and diagnostic tools are currently being applied in industrial and academic compilers. His research is currently supported by the National Science Foundation. More information about his background and research can be found on his home page, http://www.cs.fsu.edu/~whalley.

LCTES'14, June 12–13, 2014, Edinburgh, UK.
ACM 978-1-4503-2877-7/14/06.
http://dx.doi.org/10.1145/2597809.2602568

Efficient Code Generation in a Region-Based Dynamic Binary Translator

Tom Spink   Harry Wagstaff   Björn Franke   Nigel Topham

Institute for Computing Systems Architecture, School of Informatics, University of Edinburgh
t.spink@sms.ed.ac.uk, h.wagstaff@sms.ed.ac.uk, bfranke@inf.ed.ac.uk, npt@inf.ed.ac.uk

Abstract

Region-based JIT compilation operates on translation units comprising multiple basic blocks and, possibly cyclic or conditional, control flow between these. It promises to reconcile aggressive code optimisation and low compilation latency in performance-critical dynamic binary translators. Whilst various region selection schemes and isolated code optimisation techniques have been investigated it remains unclear how to best exploit such regions for efficient code generation. Complex interactions with indirect branch tables and translation caches can have adverse effects on performance if not considered carefully. In this paper we present a complete code generation strategy for a region-based dynamic binary translator, which exploits branch type and control flow profiling information to improve code quality for the common case. We demonstrate that using our code generation strategy a competitive region-based dynamic compiler can be built on top of the LLVM JIT compilation framework. For the ARM V5T target ISA and SPEC CPU 2006 benchmarks we achieve execution rates of, on average, 867 MIPS and up to 1323 MIPS on a standard X86 host machine, outperforming state-of-the-art QEMU-ARM by delivering a speedup of 264%.

Categories and Subject Descriptors D.3.4 [*Programming Languages*]: Processors—Incremental Compilers

General Terms Design, experimentation, measurement, performance

Keywords Dynamic binary translation; region-based just-in-time compilation; alias analysis

1. Introduction

Dynamic binary translation (DBT) is a widely used technology that makes it possible to run code compiled for a target platform on a host platform with a different instruction set architecture (ISA). With DBT, machine instructions of a program for the target platform are translated to machine instructions for the host platform during the execution of the program. Among the main uses of DBT are *cross-platform virtualisation* for the migration of legacy applications to different hardware platforms (e.g. APPLE ROSETTA and IBM POWERVM LX86 [25] both based on TRANSITIVE's QUICKTRANSIT, or HP ARIES [32]) and the provision of *virtual platforms* for convenient software development for embedded systems (e.g. VIRTUAL PROTOTYPE by SYNOPSYS).

LCTES '14,   June 12–13, 2014, Edinburgh, UK.
Copyright is held by the owner/author(s). Publication rights licensed to ACM.
ACM 978-1-4503-2877-7 /14/06... $15.00.
http://dx.doi.org/10.1145/2597809.2597810

Efficient DBT heavily relies on Just-in-Time (JIT) compilation for the translation of target machine instructions to host machine instructions. Although JIT compiled code generally runs much faster than interpreted code, JIT compilation incurs an additional overhead. For this reason, only the most frequently executed code fragments are translated to native code whereas less frequently executed code is still interpreted. Of central concern are the *size* and *shape* of these translation units presented to the JIT compiler: While smaller code fragments such as individual instructions or basic blocks take less time for JIT compilation, larger fragments such as linear traces or regions comprising control flow offer more scope for aggressive code optimisation [1]. For this reason, many modern DBT systems rely on regions as translation units for JIT compilation and several different region selection schemes have been proposed in the literature [5, 11, 13, 17]. However, it remains an open question as how to efficiently exploit such regions for JIT code generation resulting in improved performance.

Our main contribution is a *complete, region-based* JIT *code generation strategy* considering optimal handling of branch type information and region exits, registration of JIT compiled code in translation caches, continuous profiling and recompilation, region chaining, and host code generation including custom alias analysis. The **key ideas** can be summarised as follows: We collect branch type information during code discovery and profiling and only expose region entries and indirect branch targets, whereas direct branch targets are neither accessible from outside the region nor through the indirect branch target table. This directly improves code quality as unnecessarily exposed branch targets defeat control and data flow analysis. Only identified region entries are registered in the translation cache, we do not allow arbitrary entry to a region. Again, this optimisation aids control and data flow analysis and, thus, ultimately improves performance. In addition, we provide shortcuts for region exits and implement region chaining, improving the transition from one region to another. We continuously profile execution, grow and recompile regions using up-to-date profiling information to include newly discovered blocks and transitions. Finally, we apply a custom alias analysis for host code generation, exploiting knowledge about the structure of the code, which is difficult to uncover using standard alias analysis. Whilst some of these techniques have been investigated before in isolation, we combine them, for the first time, to a complete region-based JIT compilation strategy inside a DBT system.

We have implemented our novel code generation strategy in our multi-threaded DBT system targeting the ARM V5T ISA on a standard 12-core x86-64 host machine. We demonstrate its effectiveness across the SPEC CPU2006 integer benchmarks, where our system achieves an average execution rate of 867 MIPS, and up to 1323 MIPS. This is about 2.64 times faster than state-of-the-art QEMU-ARM.

1.1 Motivating Example

Most DBT systems will use some form of CPU state structure that contains the active state of the register file and any CPU flags – along with other control information. A DBT that works on an instruction-by-instruction basis will usually access this structure for every target instruction being executed, as most instructions will

Listing 1. Example ARM assembly

```
1   BEGIN:  mov r2, #1
2   LOOP:   cmp r0, 0
3           beq END
4           mul r2, r2, r0
5           sub r0, r0, #1
6           b LOOP
7   END:    mov r0, r2
```

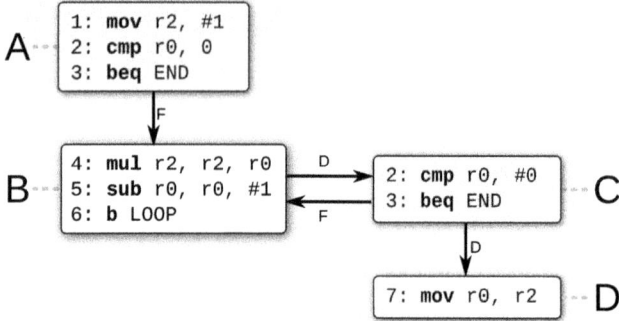

Figure 1. Blocks discovered by the profiler for the example code in Listing 1. An edge labelled **F** denotes a fall-through from a predicated branch, and an edge labelled **D** denotes a direct branch target.

Listing 2. Native code with block addresses taken

```
1   BLOCK_A:
2     movl $1, 8(%edi)
3     movl 0(%edi), %eax
4     test %eax, %eax
5     jz BLOCK_D
6   BLOCK_B:
7     movl 8(%edi), %ecx
8     movl 0(%edi), %eax
9     imul %eax, %ecx
10    movl %ecx, 8(%edi)
11    subl $1, %eax
12    movl %eax, 0(%edi)
13  BLOCK_C:
14    movl 0(%edi), %eax
15    test %eax, %eax
16    jnz BLOCK_B
17  BLOCK_D:
18    movl 8(%edi), %eax
19    movl %eax, 0(%edi)
```

Listing 3. Native code without block addresses taken

```
1   BLOCK_A:
2     movl $1, %ecx
3     movl 0(%edi), %eax
4     test %eax, %eax
5     jz END
6   LOOP:
7     mul %eax, %ecx
8     subl $1, %eax
9     jnz LOOP
10  END:
11    movl %ecx, 0(%edi)
12    movl %ecx, 8(%edi)
```

Figure 2. Host machine code generated using a naïve scheme and using our integrated, region-based code generation methodology.

involve a read or write to one or more registers. However, a DBT that translates on a block-by-block basis (such as [3]) will typically assume that executing a basic block is an atomic operation, and can introduce optimisations that only update the CPU state structure once the entire basic block has been executed. This is because intermediate values from the results of target instructions can be kept in host registers, and re-used throughout the block until the last moment. This important optimisation significantly reduces the amount of reads and writes to memory, and can therefore greatly increase performance.

Traditional region-based DBTs work on a block-by-block basis, and will allow entry to the region via any block that is part of the region, however the consequence of this is that the address of each basic block must be taken, and doing so prevents any kind of *inter-block* optimisation. Whilst *intra-block* optimisations can still be applied, more aggressive *inter-block* optimisations cannot, as guarantees about CPU state must be maintained on entry to each block. In contrast, trace-based DBTs generate inherently linear control-flow graphs, which are only ever entered from the top (the *trace head*) and are usually only exited from the bottom. This enables optimisations to be applied across the entire trace but due to the lack of *interesting* control-flow, they miss out on certain loop optimisations.

The benefit of a region-based DBT is that non-linear control-flow is allowed within the region, which can lead to optimisations that would not be possible with linear control-flow (e.g. loop optimisations), but this benefit is restricted if addresses of individual blocks within the region are taken, e.g. inserted to an indirect branch target table. This limits the ability of the optimiser to keep intermediate values (such as loop induction variables) in host registers, and to defer updating the CPU state structure until an exit point is reached.

The code given in Listing 1 (and the subsequent *control flow graph* (CFG) given in Figure 1), shows a simple ARM function that calculates the factorial of a number, supplied in r0. If native code was to be generated for this sequence, and we allowed entry to the sequence via any block, then each basic block would need to load the values of the registers in use from the register file, and cannot re-use values from a predecessor. Furthermore, at the end of a basic block, the register file must be updated with any changes in register values. This particular problem can pollute native code with unnecessary loads and stores when certain blocks are not actually region entries, and with careful profiling and capturing of CFG edge

information, it can be determined which blocks are internal to the region.

In the example CFG, block A is a region entry, and blocks B, C and D are only branched to by control-flow from other blocks. Two branch fall-through edges exist as $\overrightarrow{AB}$ and $\overrightarrow{CB}$, and two direct branches exist as $\overrightarrow{BC}$ and $\overrightarrow{CD}$. It is important to note that there are two basic blocks (A and C) discovered with overlapping code. This is because (given the input $r_0 \geq 1$) the profiler will discover the fall-through edge $\overrightarrow{AB}$ first, and then discover the direct edge $\overrightarrow{BC}$ that branches inside A, and hence creates a new basic block C containing the latter half of A.

If entry was allowed via any block, target register values would need to be loaded from the CPU state structure in each block – ensuring that the correct register values are used. This would be detrimental in performance, especially in the case of the loop between B and C, as the value of the induction variable in r0 would need to be read from memory in C and written to memory in B, rather than keeping r0 in a host register.

However, if we change the constraints to only allow entry via block A, and keep B, C and D as *region local* blocks, then we can produce an optimised form that loads initial register values into a host CPU register, which is reused throughout the loop, until we exit the code sequence and require that the updated register values are written back in to the CPU state structure.

This difference is clearly demonstrated in Listing 2 and Listing 3, where Listing 2 shows an example of x86 assembly generated for the code sequence described in Listing 1. When every block has its address taken, the block must access memory to request the value of the target machine register from the state structure. In Listing 3, we can see that an optimised form can be generated where host registers are used to track the state of the target machine register, until the very end where the values are written back to memory. This removes all memory accesses from the loop between block B and C, and can exploit host ISA features to generate an extremely efficient loop.

In general, our guiding principle is speculation and optimisation for the common case, i.e. we use profiling information on branch types, region entries, and indirect branch targets immediately for code optimisation even if there is the possibility of later updates of this information, possibly initiating re-compilation.

1.2 Contributions

This paper is not concerned with developing new ways of region selection, but its focus is on a strategy for efficient code generation and optimisation for regions once these have been formed using any of the techniques presented in the literature [5, 11, 13, 17]. Neither do we propose another technique for resolving indirect branches,

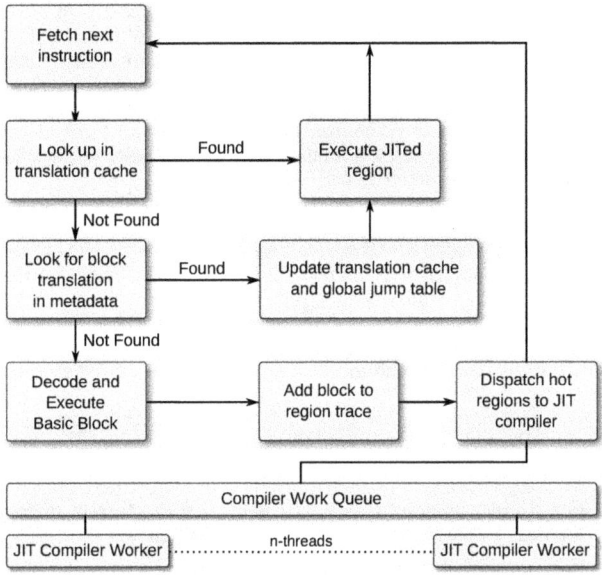

Figure 3. Main execution loop of our retargetable DBT system with decoupled, concurrent JIT compilation threads.

but we show how branch type and control flow information can be exploited on top of any of the existing mechanisms for resolving indirect branches [9, 14, 18, 23, 31]. Overall, we make the following contributions in this paper:

1. We introduce a **complete, region-based JIT code generation strategy** suitable for integration in high-speed DBT systems,

2. we demonstrate how to exploit **branch type profiling information** to enable improved back-end code generation including **loop optimisation**,

3. we introduce light-weight **region chaining**, borrowing concepts from trace chaining, and

4. we develop a new **custom alias analysis** that allows us to more accurately separate independent memory accesses, again enabling improved back-end code generation.

1.3 Overview

The remainder of this paper is structured as follows. In Section 2 we provide the background to our DBT system and, in particular, the region selection scheme used throughout this paper. This is followed by the presentation of our novel code generation strategy in Section 3. We present our empirical evaluation in Section 4 before we discuss related work in Section 5. Finally, we summarise and conclude in Section 6.

2. Background

2.1 DBT System Overview

Figure 3 shows the main execution loop of our DBT, which employs an interpretive component and farm of concurrent JIT compiler threads to achieve maximum speed. We initially begin by running the target program through the interpreter and collect profiling information about the basic blocks by building a region-oriented *control flow graph* (CFG). Once a region has been determined to exceed a certain threshold it will be dispatched to a JIT compiler worker, which will translate the region to native code. This process is asynchronous, and the target program will continue executing in the interpreter. Once the native code has been compiled, it will be made available by registering *region entry points* in block metadata and when the interpreter encounters a registered block, it will update the translation cache and begin executing the native code. Once inside native code, execution will remain there as long as blocks are available to execute. If a block is encountered that has not yet been compiled, control will return to the interpreter

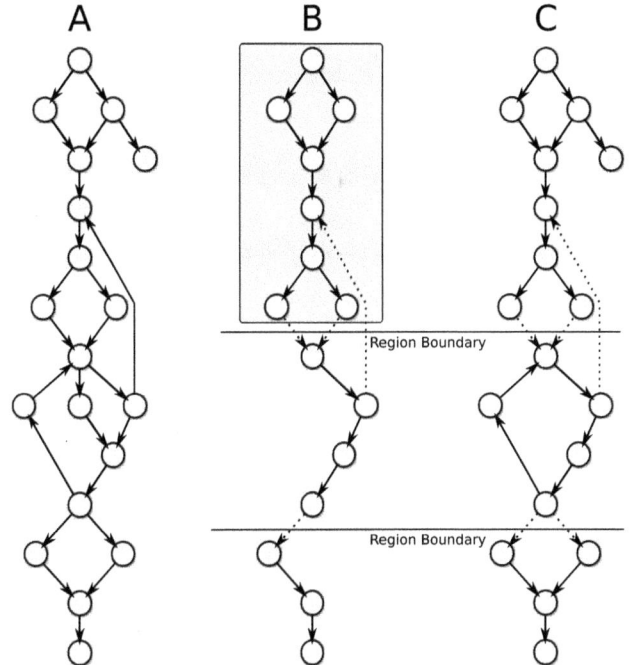

Figure 4. (A) Example of a whole-program control flow graph. (B) Parts of the control flow graph from (A) dynamically discovered after some time of execution, including forced region limits at page boundaries. (C) Additional control flow has been dynamically discovered after some more time executing the program.

and profiling information updated accordingly. Gathering further profiling information about a region may lead to a region becoming eligible for recompilation, which gives rise to progressively optimal code, much like *tiered* or *staged* compilation [20].

2.2 Region Selection

In a DBT system, region selection is concerned with forming the *shape* of translation units, where a region is typically a collection of basic blocks connected by control flow edges. This stage follows code discovery and profiling and it determines the boundaries of a fragment of recently discovered target code, and prepares it for translation into native host code. A number of region selection schemes for use in JIT compilers and DBT systems have been developed, e.g. [5, 11, 13, 17]. The focus of these papers has been on *policies* for region selection, i.e. decisions on how far and for how long to grow a region, but they do not explore code generation strategies for regions. Often regions are distinguished from *traces*, whilst technically traces are degenerate regions they are often treated separately due to their linear shape, i.e. the absence of multiple control flow successors and, in particular, loops.

JIT compilers present in e.g. JAVA VMs would have meta-information about the structure of the program being executed, and could use this information for *method*-based region selection techniques. But, the presence of meta-information is not guaranteed and cannot be relied upon, and indeed is not present in a raw instruction stream, so the DBT must rely on dynamic profiling information to effectively perform region selection [30]. In this paper we use a page based region selection scheme similar to the one presented in [4]. Such a scheme enables efficient MMU emulation and detection of self-modifying code through page protection mechanisms provided by the OS. As shown in Figure 4(B) we start building a dynamic CFG and insert basic blocks and control flow edges between wherever we encounter dynamic control flow. After a certain interval (in terms of blocks executed in the interpreter) we scan the CFG and form regions, depending on the temperature and whether this is above a certain, adaptive threshold. In our scheme page boundaries are also compulsory region boundaries. Regions are then passed to the JIT compiler for code generation, and profiling execution continues, possibly extending the dynamically discovered CFG further (see Figure 4(C)).

3. Methodology

3.1 Overview

Our DBT begins executing a target program by means of an interpreter, which collects profiling information about execution flow as it executes. The interpreter executes basic blocks of instructions at a time, and edge information is collected about these blocks. Metadata structures, which describe regions, are used to track the "temperature" of a region, and when a "hot" region is detected, a *translation work unit* is dispatched to a compiler work queue. An idle JIT compiler worker thread picks up this work unit, and begins compilation. A work unit consists of a list of basic blocks to compile (which represents blocks within one region), the associated control-flow graph connecting those basic blocks together and a list of the blocks which are *region entries*. The compiler then translates each block in turn (on an instruction-by-instruction basis) into LLVM IR. Finally, when each block has been compiled, a *local jump table* (sometimes also referred to as *indirect branch target buffer*) is generated, which contains the addresses of each block that is a *region entry* block and each block that is the target of an indirect jump.

The *region prologue* is a small piece of set-up code common to each *region function*, which loads values that are reused throughout the native code (such as pointers to the various CPU state structures). Following this setup, an indirect branch via the previously generated *local jump table* is performed to begin execution at the desired basic block. A *region function* therefore, contains the translated native code for every block discovered (and marked as hot) in the region, and invoking this function will branch to the block that is to be executed, by accessing the *program counter* from the CPU state structure.

It is important to note that not all basic blocks that have been compiled have their addresses taken and corresponding entries registered in the *local jump table*. This constraint means that non-*region-entry* basic blocks cannot be entered from outside the region. The consequence, and indeed benefit, of not taking addresses of certain basic blocks allows LLVM to be more aggressive during the optimisation, phase – potentially merging basic blocks together and performing inter-block optimisations.

In Figure 4, the control-flow graph labelled *A* describes the *actual* control-flow of the target program, where *B* and *C* show the *discovered* control-flow, along with region boundaries. The shaded portion of *B* is magnified in Figure 5, which shows how blocks within a region are compiled to a region function, and how the function chains to other region functions by means of the *global jump table*.

3.2 Translation Lookup Cache

The *translation lookup cache* is a structure that lives in the execution engine component of the DBT and is used to resolve addresses of basic blocks to native code. In fact, it is a mapping of block addresses to the region function that contains the native translation of a particular block. Only *region entry* blocks are entered in to the translation cache, as it is only possible to branch to *region entry* blocks from the *local jump table*.

3.3 Region Chaining

Chaining is becoming a common feature in trace based JIT compilation systems, such as in the DALVIK VM and TRACEMONKEY. This technique typically involves profiling execution flow between compiled traces, and updating the translated code for hot edge source nodes of inter-trace jumps, to jump directly to the destination translation unit. We extend *trace chaining* to *region chaining*, which deals with hot control flow between regions. This can be the result of hot inter-region edges emerging only after some warmup time, where region selection has already partitioned code into regions, or due to unavoidable region limits such as page boundaries introduced by the region selection scheme (see also Section 2.2).

To simplify code generation we implement a weak form of region chaining, where we keep a *global jump table* of translated regions. It is important to distinguish this from the *translation cache* – the *global jump table* is only a jump table at region/page granularity and is not used when transitioning from the interpreter into native code. Conversely, the *translation cache* contains translation information at basic block granularity and is only used when transitioning from interpreter to native code.

The global jump table contains one entry (initially empty) for each possible region. Each entry consists of a single function pointer. In our case, we have at most one region per page, so the jump table contains $4GB/8KB = 524,288$ entries. These entries are updated when a miss occurs in the *translation cache* described above. Since, when we retranslate a region, we invalidate the translation cache entry for that region, this ensures that the *global jump table* always points to the most up to date translation for each region.

The *global jump table* is used when it is determined that a translated branch might have another region as its destination. This determination is made differently depending on the circumstances:

1. For a direct branch: if the target is outside the current region, then the global jump table is used if the branch is taken.

2. For an indirect branch if no targets within the current region have been encountered so far: the global jump table is used immediately.

3. For an indirect branch, if one or more targets within the current region have been encountered: if the branch resolves to an address within the current region, then the *local jump table* is used, otherwise the *global jump table* is used.

Since the global jump table is initialised with 'empty' entries, the requested entry must be checked before it is used (essentially a null-pointer check). If the requested entry is empty, execution flow leaves translated code.

3.4 Branching

A basic block is defined as a single-entry, single-exit linear code sequence, and as such the *terminating instruction* is always a branch to one or more basic blocks. There are two types of branches that can be made out of a basic block:

- **Direct:** A branch whose destination is known at JIT compilation time, i.e. the destination is a PC-relative or absolute address.

- **Indirect:** A branch whose destination is not known at JIT compilation time, i.e. a branch that uses a register value to calculate the destination.

These two cases can further be classified in to *predicated* and *non-predicated*, which impose additional constraints on the control-flow out of a basic block. When a branch is *predicated*, the fall-through block for the *branch not taken* case can be treated as a *direct* branch.

In Figure 5, each node in the CFG (except for *E*) has been discovered by the profiler, and as such the CFG has been compiled to LLVM IR on a block-by-block basis. Node *E* and the corresponding edge $\overrightarrow{CE}$ have not yet been discovered by the profiler, i.e. they have not yet executed, or have not exceeded the compilation threshold.

Nodes *A* and *F* are *region entries*, and *H* and *I* are the targets of indirect branches. As such, these nodes have their block addresses taken, and a corresponding entry added to the *local jump table*. The other nodes are never accessed by an indirect jump (as far as the current profiling information is concerned) so their block addresses are not taken, and no entry is registered in the *local jump table*.

This leads to the case where native code may be available for a basic block, i.e. it has been compiled, but it is not reachable from outside the region.

3.4.1 Direct Branches

Where we have a direct branch from basic block *A* to *B*, (and *B* has no indirect branch predecessors), we do not have to add the address

Main Execution Loop

From Native Code or Interpreter

Determine block address from PC

Look up block address in translation cache — Found → Invoke region function → To Native Code

Not Found

Look for block translation in metadata — Found → Update translation cache and global jump table

Not Found

To Interpreter

	.
A	r3 Region Function
B	(empty)
C	(empty)
D	(empty)
E	(empty)
F	r3 Region Function
G	(empty)
H	(empty)
I	(empty)

Translation Lookup Cache
Maps Block Address to Region Function Pointer

Native Code

r1 Region Function

r3 Region Function

Region Prologue

Local Jump Table
| &A |
| &F |
| &H |
| &I |

r0	(empty)
r1	Region Function
r2	(empty)
r3	Region Function
r4	(empty)
	.
rn	(empty)

Global Jump Table
Maps Region Index to Region Function Pointer

Translated Region

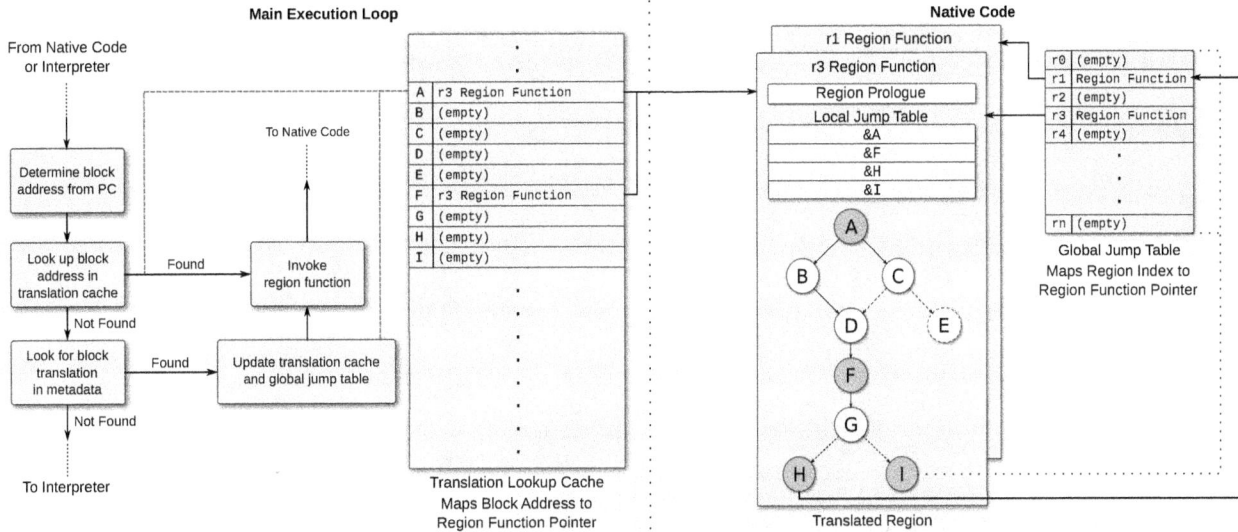

Figure 5. Interaction between regions via the *global jump table* and the internal interactions between basic blocks, either directly or via the *local jump table*. The control flow graph represents the region in the shaded area in Figure 4(B).

of B to the local jump table and instead we can emit LLVM IR to perform a direct branch to B.

There are two approaches that we take when generating the proper control-transfer sequence, and they depend on whether or not the terminating branch is predicated or non-predicated.

For a non-predicated branch, given we know at compile time the jump target, if the target lies outside the region boundary, we generate code to transfer control via the *global jump table* – as shown by node H. This means we chain directly to the region containing the destination block (if available). If the target lies within the region, as shown by node A, then we can check to see if we are compiling that particular block in this work unit, and if so, we can emit LLVM IR that directly branches to it. If the destination block is not in the work unit, then we must return immediately to the interpreter, as a native translation is not available in this round of compilation.

For a predicated branch, the same sequence applies as before, except we first determine whether or not the branch is to be taken. If the branch is not taken, then the fall-through block is directly branched to (if present in the work unit).

3.4.2 Indirect Branches

As we cannot know at JIT compile time what the destination of an indirect branch might be, we have to rely on profiling information to assist in making decisions about how to transfer control from a basic block to a successor. An important point to note is that we can treat a predicated indirect branch instruction as having a single direct edge to the fall-through block, and treat this as in the direct branch case (Section 3.4.1).

If the edge information we receive at compile time contains no edges, then we must transfer control via the *global jump table*. This is demonstrated in Figure 5 as node I, and is because we know that the *local jump table* cannot satisfy our jump (since an entry would only be available if we have encountered that particular edge). Exiting via the *global jump table* is required because the indirect branch may be to a different region. If it turns out that this speculation is incorrect (or if the destination region does not contain a translation for the target block) we return to the interpreter.

If the edge information contains exactly one edge, then we can emit a simple comparison instruction to determine whether or not that edge should be taken. If the edge is correct, we branch directly to that basic block and otherwise fall back to the *global jump table*. Node C (before discovery of E) is an example of this, where we have a single indirect edge $\overrightarrow{CD}$, but have not yet discovered $\overrightarrow{CE}$.

Finally, for a block with multiple indirect successors (such as node G), we emit code to check that the target block lies within the same region, and if so we perform an indirect branch via the *local jump table*. If the target block lies outside the current region, we branch via the *global jump table*.

Other implementations of *local jump tables* are possible, e.g. some of the techniques presented in [9, 14, 18, 23, 31] could act as drop-in replacements, however, we have found our implementation to provide sufficiently low lookup times and high hit rates.

3.5 Region Registration in Translation Caches

Every basic block that is encountered by our DBT has metadata held about it, which describes certain properties about the block, and contains a pointer to the region function containing its implementation, if it has been identified as a region entry. When the execution engine begins executing a block, it looks up the block metadata and checks to see if a native translation exists – if so, the translation cache is updated and native code is entered. Additionally, the *global jump table* is updated with a pointer to the function for the region containing the block. If a region is recompiled, the block metadata will be updated to reflect the new function pointer and the change would propagate through to the translation cache.

3.6 Continuous Profiling and Recompilation

The mixing of instructions and data, and the presence of indirect branching make it impossible to fully and accurately determine the precise control flow of a program from machine code only. Although techniques exist which attempt to extract control flow information from programs statically [22] these often must be extremely conservative and thus DBT systems using them suffer from poor performance.

On the other hand, techniques for extracting control flow information at run time are becoming increasingly effective [20]. These techniques often do not capture all possible control flow paths through a program in their first pass – thus, it is necessary to profile continuously.

We may therefore discover new control flow within regions which we have already translated and compiled. If we do not retranslate the relevant regions when we encounter such control flow at run time we can only evaluate it sub-optimally. For example, we may discover that a block which we previously excluded from the region *local jump table* is in fact a region entry. In this case, we must return to the interpreter to execute this block, since we do not have a translation entry for it.

7

Our technique does not require any special treatment for the retranslation of regions. Instead, the profiling system does not distinguish between already translated and non-translated regions. If previously-untranslated code or control flow is encountered in a translated region, it is executed using the interpreter and profiled. If it is frequently executed and becomes hot, the full region will be retranslated in order to include the new code and control flow.

3.7 Host Machine Code Generation

A *translation work unit* is the unit provided to a JIT compiler worker thread and consists of a list of *basic block descriptors*, along with basic block edge information, representing a particular region. The *basic block descriptors* contain a list of decoded instructions. Each instruction in a block is translated to LLVM IR one-by-one, using a technique similar to [29] and once the instructions have been translated, a *block epilogue* is emitted. This epilogue is generated based on the type of control-flow associated with the block, and essentially contains the IR that transfers control to the next block.

Finally, after all the blocks in the *translation work unit* have been compiled, and the region prologue has been generated, a single LLVM function remains that represents the region just compiled. This function is then passed through the LLVM optimiser, as described in Section 3.7.1.

After the optimisation passes have completed, the LLVM IR is compiled to native machine code using the LLVM JIT compiler interface and when the native code is available, each basic block that is marked as a *region entry* has a pointer to the newly compiled function stored in its metadata.

3.7.1 LLVM Optimisation Passes

During the translation phase, an LLVM module is built containing the function that represents the region being translated. The module also contains helper functions, which are highly amenable to inlining. All the helper functions are marked as internalisable, and an inlining pass is applied. Typically, the helper functions will provide a very small function (such as reading the PC register, or writing to target machine memory), and are easily inlined.

After inlining, the resulting module is subjected to a number of LLVM passes, based on the standard CLANG -O3 optimisation level. The main difference is that instead of using an LLVM provided alias analysis implementation, we use ours as described in Section 3.7.2.

Since we allowed some basic blocks not to be region entry points, this has opened up more scope for aggressive loop optimisation, which yields the full benefit of a region-based JIT. With a trace-based JIT, loop optimisations rarely happen, as traces are inherently linear. However, with our region-based approach, we can perform a significant amount of loop optimisations across the control-flow within a region, which would also not be possible if we allowed entry to the region from any basic block.

3.7.2 Alias Analysis

Alias analysis of pointers is an important phase that enables further program optimisations to reason better about data flow. For example, a *dead store elimination* pass uses pointer aliasing information to determine whether or not a redundant store to a memory location can be eliminated, based on any memory accesses that happen between those stores.

Listing 4 shows how incomplete pointer aliasing information can lead to the optimiser being unable to remove dead stores. The stores on lines 1 and 5 are killed by the store on line 7, but because the optimiser cannot detect that the operations on pointers in lines 2-4 do not alias, it cannot remove the stores. This directly translates to machine code as shown in Listing 5, which is safe (and correct), but in our case not at all optimal.

In the example shown in Figure 6, the problem stems from the alias analysis implementation (quite correctly) being unable to determine whether or not the pointer held in %4 aliases with the constant pointer value 61931224. Assuming that %4 and 61931224 alias is a safe assumption and as such generates safe code. But, armed with the knowledge about the working of our DBT, we know that %4 contains a pointer to a CPU state register,

---

Listing 4. LLVM IR after dead store elimination

```
1  store i32 36076, i32* %4
2  %42 = load i64* inttoptr (i64 61931224 to i64*)
3  %43 = add i64 %42, 6
4  store i64 %43, i64* inttoptr (i64 61931224 to i64*)
5  store i32 36076, i32* %4
6  ...
7  store i32 36092, i32* %4
```

Listing 5. X86 machine code after target lowering

```
1  movl $37076, 60(%r12)
2  addq $6, 61931224
3  movl $37076, 60(%r12)
4  ...
5  movl $36092, 60(%r12)
```

Figure 6. Remaining dead-stores in LLVM IR after optimisation, and resulting X86 machine code due to incomplete alias analysis.

Vendor & Model	DELL™ POWEREDGE™ R610
Number cores	2 × 6
Processor Type	2× Intel© Xeon™ X5660
Clock/FSB Frequency	2.80/1.33 GHz
L1-Cache	2 × 6× 32K Instruction/Data
L2-Cache	2 × 6 × 256K
L3-Cache	2× 12 MB
Memory	36 GB across 6 channels
Operating System	Linux version 2.6.32 (x86-64)

Table 1. DBT Host Configuration.

DBT Parameter	Setting
Target architecture	ARM V5T
Host architecture	x86-64
Translation/Execution Model	Asynch. Mixed-Mode
Tracing Scheme	Region-based [4]
Tracing Interval	30000 blocks
Translation Cache	8192 Entries
JIT compiler	LLVM 3.4
No. of JIT Compilation Threads	10
JIT Optimisation	-O3 & Part. Eval. [29]
Initial JIT Threshold	20
Dynamic JIT Threshold	Adaptive [4]
System Calls	Emulation
Floating Point	Software Emulation ('soft')

Table 2. DBT System Configuration.

and that the constant pointer is an address that does not intersect with the CPU state structure, hence we can say that they do not alias. Providing this guarantee to LLVM's *dead store elimination* optimisation pass enables the pass to remove the redundant stores, and generate better code. The particular example described above is important for region-based compilation, as redundant updates to the CPU state are eliminated, hence reducing the number of memory operations occurring in a particular sequence.

When a loop is involved, keeping target machine register values in host registers instead of constantly reading and writing to the CPU state structure improves performance significantly – but this kind of loop optimisation can only work to its full potential when combined with the *jump table optimisation* technique described in Section 3.4.

4. Experimental Evaluation

4.1 Experimental Methodology

We have evaluated our DBT code generation approach using the SPEC CPU2006 integer benchmark. It is widely used and considered to be representative of a broad spectrum of application domains. We used it together with its *reference* data sets. The benchmarks have been compiled using the GCC 4.6.0 C/C++ cross-

Absolute Performance SPEC CPU2006

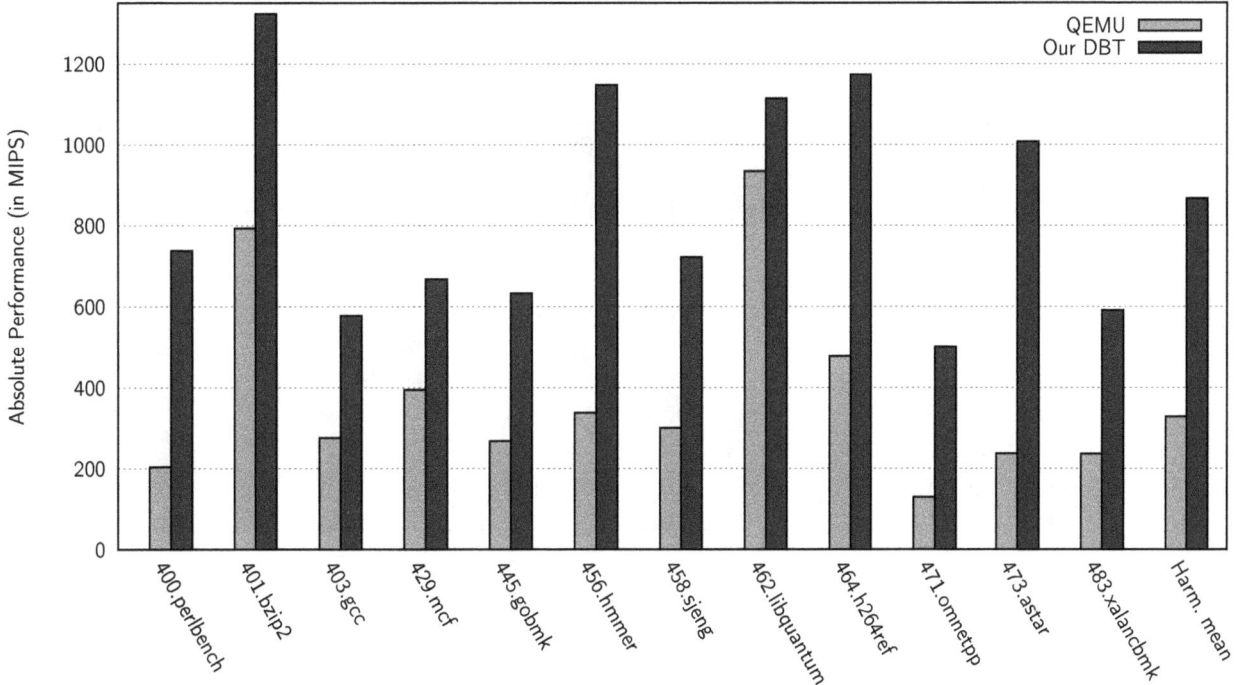

Figure 7. Absolute performance figures (in MIPS) for the *long-running* SPEC CPU2006 integer benchmarks for both QEMU-ARM and our DBT, indicating that the quality of the generated code by our system is superior to the code generated by QEMU-ARM.

compilers, targeting the ARM V5T architecture (without hardware floating-point support) and with -O2 optimisation settings.

We have measured the elapsed real time between invocation and termination of each benchmark in our DBT system using the UNIX time command on the host machine described in Table 1 with our DBT system configured as in Table 2. We used the average elapsed wall clock time across 10 runs for each benchmark and configuration in order to calculate execution rates (using MIPS in terms of target instructions) and speedups. For summary figures we report harmonic means weighted by dynamic target instruction count. For the comparison to the state-of-the-art we use the ARM port of QEMU 1.4.2 as a baseline.

Additionally, we have also evaluated our DBT using the EEMBC-1.1 benchmark suite. These benchmarks are typically shorter running and serve to evaluate the performance of the JIT compiler portion of our DBT. In order to normalise performance to particular duration, we adjusted the iteration count of each benchmark so that it ran for about ten seconds in QEMU, then we invoked the benchmark with the same iteration count in our DBT and measured performance in the same manner as for SPEC.

4.2 Experimental Results for SPEC CPU2006

Figure 7 gives an overview of the absolute performance of QEMU vs. our DBT. In every case, we improve on QEMU, and on average achieve a 2.64x improvement in absolute performance.

The biggest improvement is achieved for 473.astar, which can be attributed to the benchmark responding well to our ability to apply loop optimisations within a region. The relative performance improvement of 473.astar when *region chaining* is enabled is negligible, and so indicates that the majority of time is spent in region local code. Aggressive loop optimisations are performed within this region (where the bulk of the algorithm lies). This explains the excellent performance improvement over QEMU, which performs no such optimisations. This explanation can also be applied to 464.h264ref, which benefits greatly from our ability to optimise loops better than QEMU.

The smallest improvement is for 462.libquantum, which may be due to the benchmark itself being heavy in arithmetic instruc-

tions, but not so much in looping constructs. This particular characteristic explains the excellent performance of QEMU, and hence why we only see a 1.2x improvement in this case. QEMU's block-based optimisations work well here, due to the linear nature of the arithmetic instructions and larger basic block sizes.

Interestingly, the relative performance improvements as optimisations are enabled (shown in Figure 8) of 462.libquantum are similar to that of 473.astar, and the absolute performance of both the benchmarks are within the same area - but 462.libquantum is already fast in QEMU.

4.3 Impact of Optimisations

Figure 8 shows how combinations of the optimisations described in Section 3 affect the relative performance of the DBT. The baseline is using standard LLVM -O3 optimisation and partial evaluation, but without any of our optimisations described in the paper applied.

Overall, the addition of our custom alias analysis improves every benchmark, except for 429.mcf. On average this gives a 1.32x performance improvement, but it is the combination of all our strategies that yield the best result. *Jump table optimisation* on its own does not give rise to a significant performance improvement, but responds well when combined with alias analysis. This may be due to the fact that the most interesting optimisation to apply across basic blocks is to remove dead stores and to keep host registers live with frequently used values (potentially from the CPU state structure). Without the precise aliasing information this kind of optimisation is not possible to do effectively, and so the combination of both *jump table optimisation* and *custom alias analysis* give rise to the best performance improvements.

473.astar remains at baseline performance when the *region chaining* optimisation is applied, and this may be due to the majority of execution being spent in region-local code. It has an absolute performance figure of > 1000 MIPS, which indicates fast running code, but the benefits of *region chaining* are minimal, due to the lack of inter-region control-flow.

403.gcc is a particularly control-flow heavy benchmark, and responds well to the combination of all the optimisations together.

9

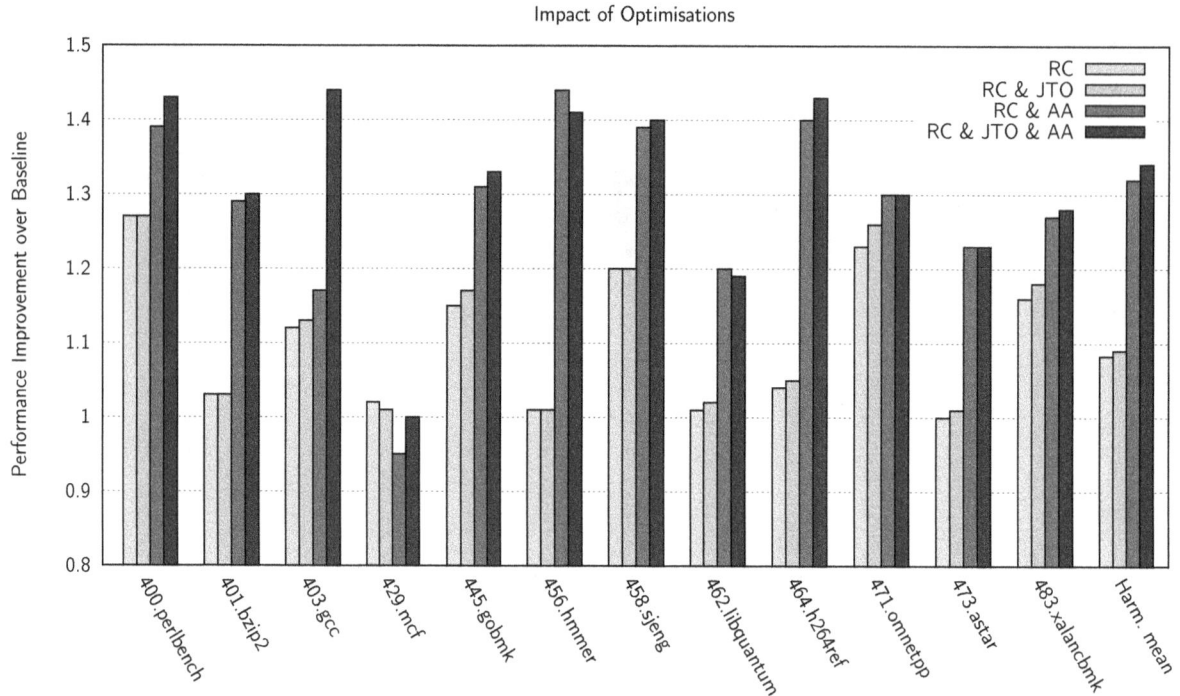

Figure 8. Breakdown of performance impact of different optimisations. Baseline is standard LLVM -O3 and partial evaluation [29] at JIT compilation time. Additional region chaining (RC), jump table optimisation (JTO) and alias analysis (AA) complement each other.

Also of interest is the 429.mcf benchmark, which does not consistently improve in performance like the majority of the other benchmarks. Despite this, 429.mcf is more than 1.5 times faster in our DBT system than in QEMU.

4.4 JIT Compilation Performance

The execution time of the SPEC CPU2006 benchmarks with their reference data sets is dominated by the time spent executing native code, whereas the fraction accounted for JIT compilation time is small. For such long-running benchmarks *code quality* is paramount and this where our region based code optimisations outperform simpler basic block or trace based schemes. However, JIT compilation time is still important for shorter-running applications, or programs that exhibit phased behaviour and, hence, exercise the JIT compiler more heavily. To evaluate JIT compilation performance of our DBT system we have run additional, smaller benchmarks, where time for JIT compilation constitutes a larger portion of the overall time (see Figure 9). In every case, we beat QEMU in absolute execution performance, but as in the SPEC results, our relative performance improvements vary greatly. As can be seen, the most significant result here is that we execute fft00 at a rate of 6138 MIPS compared to QEMU's 3897.95. However, this only shows a modest relative performance gain of 1.5x, where as idctrn01 outperforms QEMU by 2.85x. We can attribute these variances again to the characteristics of individual benchmarks in the suite, where we can say that in the benchmarks which are amenable to loop optimisations, i.e. contain more intra-region loops, we show a greater *relative* performance improvement. Overall, these results demonstrate that even for shorter-running applications where JIT compilation latency plays a greater role than absolute code quality our system is highly competitive despite its use of larger translation units and aggressive code optimisations.

5. Related Work

5.1 Region based DBT Systems

Region based JIT compilation has been used for some time in JAVA virtual machines, e.g. [26, 27], but has only been considered more recently for DBT systems [4, 19, 21]. The reason for this late adop-

tion of region based policies has been presumably the increased latency for compilation and optimisation of larger regions, which has only been addressed recently with the introduction of decoupled, latency-hiding JIT task farms [4]. The bulk of the work in this field has focused on region selection, though, and less on code generation and optimisation for dynamically discovered regions. In [19] large translations units, i.e. regions, are introduced for dynamic binary translation and region selection policies based on strongly connected components, control flow graph fragments and OS pages are compared. A refined page based region selection scheme is developed in [4] and combined with a parallel JIT compilation task farm. Specific optimisations for a DBT system, which compiles target- to host code via JVM bytecode, are considered in [21].

5.2 Code Generation and Optimisation in DBT Systems

Most DBT systems appear to have adopted a code generation strategy operating on individual basic blocks or linear traces of basic blocks. For example, QEMU uses such an approach using its own *tiny code generator* (TCG) and additional block chaining, translation caching and lazy condition evaluation [3]. DYNAMO [2] is a dynamic optimisation system, i.e. the input is an executing native instruction stream. DYNAMO uses an interpreter for initial execution until a "hot" instruction sequence is identified. At that point, DYNAMO generates an optimised version of the trace into a software code cache. DYNAMO treats backward branches as trace delimiters, i.e. traces are by definition linear. After translation it emits an optimised single-entry, multi-exit, contiguous sequence of instructions for each trace. Trace optimisation in DYNAMO considers branch types, but is generally less aggressive than our scheme, which utilises additional loop optimisations. DYNAMORIO [6] is a successor of DYNAMO. DYNAMORIO operates on two kinds of code sequences: basic blocks and traces. Both have linear control flow, with a single entrance and potentially multiple exits, but no internal join points. Optimisations are restricted to the linear control flow present in traces. The single-entry multiple-exit format simplifies analysis algorithms, but limits the scope of optimisations that can be applied. STRATA [12] is a retargetable DBT system offering additional uses for dynamic instrumentation and optimisation. Different fragment selection policies [13] have been evalu-

Absolute Performance EEMBC

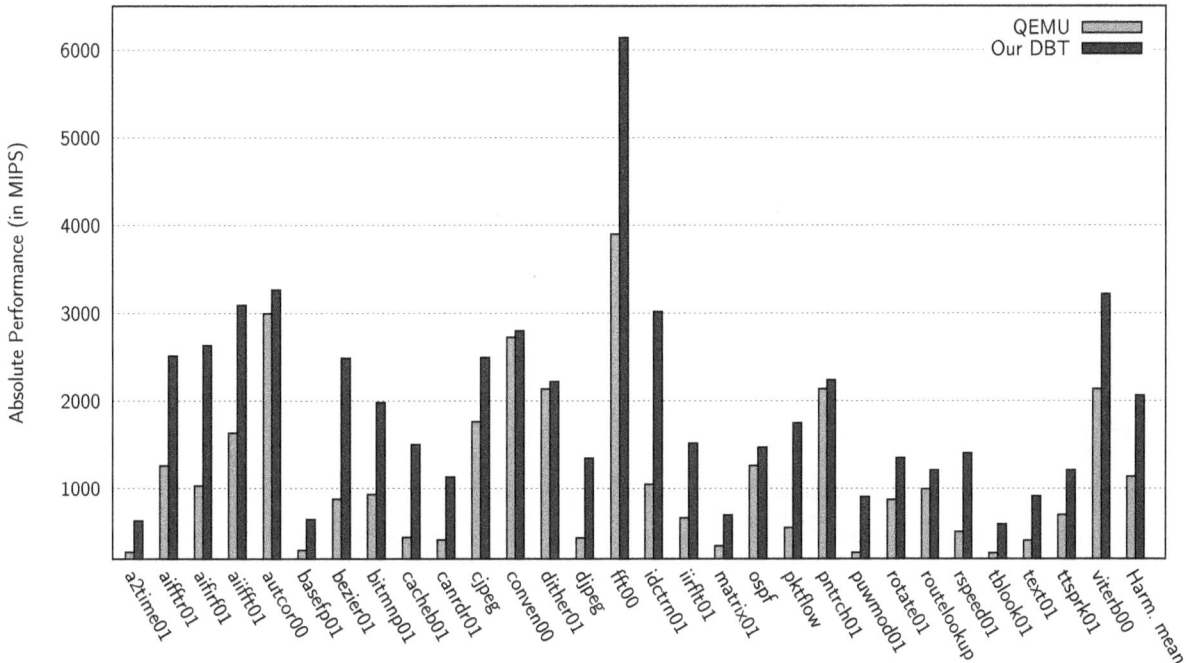

Figure 9. Absolute performance figures (in MIPS) for the *shorter-running* EEMBC benchmarks for both QEMU-ARM and our DBT, indicating that JIT startup time and compilation performance of our DBT is more than competitive with QEMU-ARM despite aggressive code optimisations applied by our system.

ated for STRATA, however, all of these have in common that they are linear traces, possibly spanning branch or function call boundaries. STRATA uses chaining of traces to avoid overheads associated with returning to the main execution loop after every native trace. An ARM port of STRATA considers architecture-specific optimisations, e.g. relating to the exposed PC [24]. The optimisations performed by UQDBT – a machine-adaptable dynamic binary translator – are discussed in [8, 28]. This tool uses an algorithm for finding hot paths using edge weight profiles, and optimises code in a machine-independent way, based on hot path information. Whilst units of translation in UQDBT are basic blocks, for its hot path (re)optimisation it groups hot basic blocks and their connecting control flow edges into regions. The paper focuses primarily on newly discovered hot paths and locality transformations, but does not provide a complete code generation strategy. A particular aspect of code generation in DBT systems, namely recovery of jump table case statements, is discussed in [7]. Alias analysis for DBT systems is considered in [10], but unlike our approach this requires runtime checks.

5.3 DBT Systems Using LLVM for JIT Compilation

A parallel and concurrent JIT compilation task farm for use in DBT systems is presented in [4]. The JIT compiler is based on the LLVM framework, which is used for translation of paged regions of target instructions to host instructions. The paper discusses a particular region selection scheme and parallel JIT compilation, but provides no details of the actual code generation approach used. LNQ [16] extends QEMU with an LLVM based JIT compiler, but does not consider code regions for translation. It uses linear traces instead. HQEMU [15] is a multi-threaded dynamic binary translator, which extends QEMU with multiple instances of the LLVM compiler for JIT compilation. Similar to our system HQEMU builds on top of LLVM, but it only operates on linear traces and does not support region-based compilation. Unfortunately, direct performance comparisons are hampered as the paper only reports relative improvements over an unusual baseline, which we were unable to verify or repeat.

6. Summary & Conclusions

In this paper we have developed a novel, integrated approach to JIT code generation within region-based DBT systems. We exploit branch type information, introduce region chaining, develop selective region registration in translation caches, add on continuous profiling and recompilation, and finally include custom alias analysis to enable aggressive code optimisations, which would not be possible in a JIT scheme based on linear traces. We demonstrate the efficiency of our region-based JIT code generation approach using the SPEC CPU2006 benchmarks compiled for the ARM V5T ISA, which our DBT system translates on-the-fly to the host machine's X86 ISA. In comparison to state-of-the-art QEMU-ARM we achieve an average speedup of 2.64, and up to 4.25 for individual benchmarks. We show that each of the techniques developed in this paper on their own contributes to increased code quality, but it is the particular combination of code generation steps that results in performance improvements greater than the sum of its parts.

References

[1] J. Aycock. A brief history of just-in-time. *ACM Comput. Surv.*, 35(2): 97–113, June 2003. ISSN 0360-0300. . URL http://doi.acm.org/10.1145/857076.857077.

[2] V. Bala, E. Duesterwald, and S. Banerjia. Dynamo: a transparent dynamic optimization system. In *Proceedings of the ACM SIGPLAN 2000 Conference on Programming Language Design and Implementation*, PLDI '00, pages 1–12, New York, NY, USA, 2000. ACM. ISBN 1-58113-199-2. . URL http://doi.acm.org/10.1145/349299.349303.

[3] F. Bellard. QEMU, a fast and portable dynamic translator. In *Proceedings of the Annual Conference on USENIX Annual Technical Conference*, ATEC '05, pages 41–41, Berkeley, CA, USA, 2005. USENIX Association. URL http://dl.acm.org/citation.cfm?id=1247360.1247401.

[4] I. Böhm, T. J. Edler von Koch, S. C. Kyle, B. Franke, and N. Topham. Generalized just-in-time trace compilation using a parallel task farm in a dynamic binary translator. In *Proceedings of the 32nd ACM SIGPLAN Conference on Programming Language Design and Implementation*, PLDI '11, pages 74–85, New York, NY, USA, 2011. ACM. ISBN 978-1-4503-0663-8. . URL http://doi.acm.org/10.1145/1993498.1993508.

[5] D. Bruening and E. Duesterwald. Exploring optimal compilation unit shapes for an embedded just-in-time compiler. In *In Proceedings of the 2000 ACM Workshop on Feedback-Directed and Dynamic Optimization FDDO-3*, pages 13–20, 2000.

[6] D. Bruening, T. Garnett, and S. Amarasinghe. An infrastructure for adaptive dynamic optimization. In *Proceedings of the international symposium on Code Generation and Optimization: Feedback-directed and Runtime Optimization*, CGO '03, pages 265–275, Washington, DC, USA, 2003. IEEE Computer Society. ISBN 0-7695-1913-X. URL http://dl.acm.org/citation.cfm?id=776261.776290.

[7] C. Cifuentes and M. V. Emmerik. Recovery of jump table case statements from binary code. In *Proceedings of the 7th International Workshop on Program Comprehension*, IWPC '99, pages 192–, Washington, DC, USA, 1999. IEEE Computer Society. ISBN 0-7695-0179-6. URL http://dl.acm.org/citation.cfm?id=520033.858247.

[8] C. Cifuentes and M. V. Emmerik. UQBT: Adaptive binary translation at low cost. *IEEE Computer*, 33(3):60–66, 2000.

[9] B. Dhanasekaran and K. Hazelwood. Improving indirect branch translation in dynamic binary translators. In *Proceedings of the ASPLOS Workshop on Runtime Environments, Systems, Layering, and Virtualized Environments*, RESoLVE'11, pages 11–18, 2011.

[10] B. Guo, Y. Wu, C. Wang, M. J. Bridges, G. Ottoni, N. Vachharajani, J. Chang, and D. I. August. Selective runtime memory disambiguation in a dynamic binary translator. In *Proceedings of the 15th International Conference on Compiler Construction*, CC'06, pages 65–79, Berlin, Heidelberg, 2006. Springer-Verlag. ISBN 3-540-33050-X, 978-3-540-33050-9. . URL http://dx.doi.org/10.1007/11688839_6.

[11] D. Hiniker, K. Hazelwood, and M. D. Smith. Improving region selection in dynamic optimization systems. In *Proceedings of the 38th Annual IEEE/ACM International Symposium on Microarchitecture*, MICRO 38, pages 141–154, Washington, DC, USA, 2005. IEEE Computer Society. ISBN 0-7695-2440-0. . URL http://dx.doi.org/10.1109/MICRO.2005.22.

[12] J. D. Hiser, N. Kumar, M. Zhao, S. Zhou, B. R. Childers, J. W. Davidson, and M. L. Soffa. Techniques and tools for dynamic optimization. In *Proceedings of the 20th International Conference on Parallel and Distributed Processing*, IPDPS'06, pages 279–279, Washington, DC, USA, 2006. IEEE Computer Society. ISBN 1-4244-0054-6. URL http://dl.acm.org/citation.cfm?id=1898699.1898797.

[13] J. D. Hiser, D. Williams, A. Filipi, J. W. Davidson, and B. R. Childers. Evaluating fragment construction policies for SDT systems. In *Proceedings of the 2nd International Conference on Virtual Execution Environments*, VEE '06, pages 122–132, New York, NY, USA, 2006. ACM. ISBN 1-59593-332-8. . URL http://doi.acm.org/10.1145/1134760.1134778.

[14] J. D. Hiser, D. Williams, W. Hu, J. W. Davidson, J. Mars, and B. R. Childers. Evaluating indirect branch handling mechanisms in software dynamic translation systems. In *Proceedings of the International Symposium on Code Generation and Optimization*, CGO '07, pages 61–73, Washington, DC, USA, 2007. IEEE Computer Society. ISBN 0-7695-2764-7. . URL http://dx.doi.org/10.1109/CGO.2007.10.

[15] D.-Y. Hong, C.-C. Hsu, P.-C. Yew, J.-J. Wu, W.-C. Hsu, P. Liu, C.-M. Wang, and Y.-C. Chung. HQEMU: a multi-threaded and retargetable dynamic binary translator on multicores. In *Proceedings of the Tenth International Symposium on Code Generation and Optimization*, CGO '12, pages 104–113, New York, NY, USA, 2012. ACM. ISBN 978-1-4503-1206-6. . URL http://doi.acm.org/10.1145/2259016.2259030.

[16] C.-C. Hsu, P. Liu, C.-M. Wang, J.-J. Wu, D.-Y. Hong, P.-C. Yew, and W.-C. Hsu. LnQ: Building high performance dynamic binary translators with existing compiler backends. In *Proceedings of the 2011 International Conference on Parallel Processing*, ICPP '11, pages 226–234, Washington, DC, USA, 2011. IEEE Computer Society. ISBN 978-0-7695-4510-3. . URL http://dx.doi.org/10.1109/ICPP.2011.57.

[17] C.-C. Hsu, P. Liu, J.-J. Wu, P.-C. Yew, D.-Y. Hong, W.-C. Hsu, and C.-M. Wang. Improving dynamic binary optimization through early-exit guided code region formation. In *Proceedings of the 9th ACM SIGPLAN/SIGOPS International Conference on Virtual Execution Environments*, VEE '13, pages 23–32, New York, NY, USA, 2013. ACM. ISBN 978-1-4503-1266-0. URL http://doi.acm.org/10.1145/2451512.2451519.

[18] N. Jia, C. Yang, J. Wang, D. Tong, and K. Wang. SPIRE: improving dynamic binary translation through SPC-indexed indirect branch redirecting. In *Proceedings of the 9th ACM SIGPLAN/SIGOPS International Conference on Virtual Execution Environments*, VEE '13, pages 1–12, New York, NY, USA, 2013. ACM. ISBN 978-1-4503-1266-0. . URL http://doi.acm.org/10.1145/2451512.2451516.

[19] D. Jones and N. Topham. High speed CPU simulation using LTU dynamic binary translation. In *Proceedings of the 4th International Conference on High Performance Embedded Architectures and Compilers*, HiPEAC '09, pages 50–64, Berlin, Heidelberg, 2009. Springer-Verlag. ISBN 978-3-540-92989-5. . URL http://dx.doi.org/10.1007/978-3-540-92990-1_6.

[20] R. Joshi, M. D. Bond, and C. Zilles. Targeted path profiling: Lower overhead path profiling for staged dynamic optimization systems. In *Proceedings of the International Symposium on Code Generation and Optimization: Feedback-Directed and Runtime Optimization*, CGO '04, pages 239–, Washington, DC, USA, 2004. IEEE Computer Society. ISBN 0-7695-2102-9. URL http://dl.acm.org/citation.cfm?id=977395.977660.

[21] M. Kaufmann and R. G. Spallek. Superblock compilation and other optimization techniques for a Java-based DBT machine emulator. In *Proceedings of the 9th ACM SIGPLAN/SIGOPS International Conference on Virtual Execution Environments*, VEE '13, pages 33–40, New York, NY, USA, 2013. ACM. ISBN 978-1-4503-1266-0. . URL http://doi.acm.org/10.1145/2451512.2451521.

[22] J. Kinder, F. Zuleger, and H. Veith. An abstract interpretation-based framework for control flow reconstruction from binaries. In *Proceedings of the 10th International Conference on Verification, Model Checking, and Abstract Interpretation*, VMCAI '09, pages 214–228, Berlin, Heidelberg, 2009. Springer-Verlag. ISBN 978-3-540-93899-6. . URL http://dx.doi.org/10.1007/978-3-540-93900-9_19.

[23] T. Koju, X. Tong, A. I. Sheikh, M. Ohara, and T. Nakatani. Optimizing indirect branches in a system-level dynamic binary translator. In *Proceedings of the 5th Annual International Systems and Storage Conference*, SYSTOR '12, pages 5:1–5:12, New York, NY, USA, 2012. ACM. ISBN 978-1-4503-1448-0. . URL http://doi.acm.org/10.1145/2367589.2367599.

[24] R. W. Moore, J. A. Baiocchi, B. R. Childers, J. W. Davidson, and J. D. Hiser. Addressing the challenges of DBT for the ARM architecture. In *Proceedings of the 2009 ACM SIGPLAN/SIGBED Conference on Languages, Compilers, and Tools for Embedded Systems*, LCTES '09, pages 147–156, New York, NY, USA, 2009. ACM. ISBN 978-1-60558-356-3. . URL http://doi.acm.org/10.1145/1542452.1542472.

[25] E. Stahl and M. Anand. A comparison of PowerVM and x86-based virtualization performance. Technical Report WP101574, IBM Techdocs White Papers, 2010.

[26] T. Suganuma, T. Yasue, and T. Nakatani. A region-based compilation technique for a Java just-in-time compiler. In *Proceedings of the ACM SIGPLAN 2003 Conference on Programming Language Design and Implementation*, PLDI '03, pages 312–323, New York, NY, USA, 2003. ACM. ISBN 1-58113-662-5. . URL http://doi.acm.org/10.1145/781131.781166.

[27] T. Suganuma, T. Yasue, and T. Nakatani. A region-based compilation technique for dynamic compilers. *ACM Trans. Program. Lang. Syst.*, 28(1):134–174, Jan. 2006. ISSN 0164-0925. . URL http://doi.acm.org/10.1145/1111596.1111600.

[28] D. Ung and C. Cifuentes. Optimising hot paths in a dynamic binary translator. *SIGARCH Comput. Archit. News*, 29(1):55–65, Mar. 2001. ISSN 0163-5964. . URL http://doi.acm.org/10.1145/373574.373590.

[29] H. Wagstaff, M. Gould, B. Franke, and N. Topham. Early partial evaluation in a JIT-compiled, retargetable instruction set simulator generated from a high-level architecture description. In *Proceedings of the Annual Design Automation Conference*, DAC '13, pages 21:1–21:6, New York, NY, USA, 2013. ACM. ISBN 978-1-4503-2071-9. . URL http://doi.acm.org/10.1145/2463209.2488760.

[30] J. Whaley. Partial method compilation using dynamic profile information. In *Proceedings of the 16th ACM SIGPLAN Conference on Object-Oriented Programming, Systems, Languages, and Applications*, OOPSLA '01, pages 166–179, New York, NY, USA, 2001. ACM. ISBN 1-58113-335-9. . URL http://doi.acm.org/10.1145/504282.504295.

[31] L. Yin, J. Haitao, S. Guangzhong, J. Guojie, and C. Guoliang. Improve indirect branch prediction with private cache in dynamic binary translation. In *International Conference on High Performance Computing and Communication and International Conference on Embedded Software and Systems (HPCC-ICESS)*, pages 280–286, 2012. .

[32] C. Zheng and C. Thompson. PA-RISC to IA-64: transparent execution, no recompilation. *Computer*, 33(3):47 –52, Mar. 2000.

CASM - Optimized Compilation of Abstract State Machines *

Roland Lezuo

Vienna University of Technology
Institute of Computer Languages
Vienna, Austria
roland.lezuo@tuwien.ac.at

Philipp Paulweber

Vienna University of Technology
Institute of Computer Languages
Vienna, Austria
p.paulweber@gmail.com

Andreas Krall

Vienna University of Technology
Institute of Computer Languages
Vienna, Austria
andi@complang.tuwien.ac.at

Abstract

In this paper we present CASM, a language based on Abstract State Machines (ASM), and its optimizing compiler. ASM is a well-defined (formal) method based on algebraic concepts. A distinct feature of ASM is its combination of parallel and sequential execution semantics. This makes it an excellent choice to formally specify and verify micro-architectures. We present a compilation scheme and an implementation of a runtime system supporting efficient execution of ASM. After introducing novel analysis techniques we present optimizations allowing us to eliminate many costly operations.

Benchmark results show that our baseline compiler is 2-3 magnitudes faster than other ASM implementations. The optimizations further increase the performance of the compiled programs up to 264%. The achieved performance allows our ASM implementation to be used with industry-size applications.

Categories and Subject Descriptors D3.4 [*Programming Languages*]: Processors – compilers, optimization, code generation

Keywords ASM, compilation, optimization, redundancy elimination, parallelism

1. Introduction

ASM is a formal method well suited to formalize semantics of micro-processors [24], programming languages [16] and instruction set simulators [18]. Formal specifications are a precondition for thorough verification of safety-critical embedded systems. We intensively use our ASM implementation (CASM) in a compiler verification project [17] as the formal foundation for the required proofs. Precise machine models for various micro-processors commonly used in embedded systems have been developed. These CASM models can be used to synthesize instruction set simulators. Available tools for ASM have the major drawback that they do not perform well enough to handle industry-size applications. In this paper we introduce an optimizing CASM compiler and present two effective optimizations. Ultimately the compiler is applied to a CASM formalization of the MIPS instruction set to synthesize compiled simulations for industry-size applications.

The remainder of the paper is structured as follows: In section 2 we introduce other implementations of ASM. Section 3 gives an overview of the CASM language and the most important features influencing the compilation. An overview of the CASM compiler is given in section 4 and section 5 describes the optimizations. We report on the performance in section 6. Section 7 discusses future work and section 8 finally concludes the paper.

2. Related Work

ASMs were introduced by Gurevich (originally named evolving algebras) in the Lipari Guide [12]. Core concepts of ASMs are the algebraic state and rules, which describe exactly how the state is changed by means of *updates* applied to the state. Evaluation of a rule itself is side-effect free, a concept introduced in functional programming.

The ideas of ASMs were further developed by Gurevich and others at Microsoft Research resulting in a powerful specification language called AsmL [14]. AsmL is designed to be simple, precise, executable, testable, inter operable, integrated, scalable and analyzable. The language is statically typed, supports object oriented features, has call-by-value semantics and supports exceptions. An efficient compiler for .NET has been developed and the language has been fully integrated into the .NET framework and the Microsoft development environment [5]. The tool environment comprehends *parameter generation* for providing method calls with parameter sets, *finite state machine* generation from an ASM, *sequence generation* for deriving test sequences and *runtime verification* for testing if an implementation performs conforming to the model. The tool environment around AsmL is the most advanced currently available.

One of the most performance critical issues in ASMs is the problem of partial updates. Gurevich and Tillmann discussed the problem in detail and showed how concurrent data modifications can be implemented efficiently [13]. Similar problems occur in version control systems on software merging [20]. Techniques which work only on the delta (the differences) of the data sets inspire optimizations on efficient update implementation in ASMs.

Castillo describes the ASM Workbench in [9]. Similar to CASM he added a type system to his language. The ASM Workbench is implemented in ML[1] in an extensible way. Castillo describes an interpreter and a plugin for a model checker, which allows

---

* This work is partially supported by the Austrian Research Promotion Agency (FFG) under contract 827485, *Correct Compilers for Correct Application Specific Processors* and Catena DSP GmbH.

---

[1] http://en.wikipedia.org/wiki/Standard_ML

to translate certain restricted classes of abstract state machines to models for the SMV[2] model checker.

Schmid describes compiling ASM to C++ [23]. The compiler uses the ASM Workbench language as input. He proposes a double buffering technique avoiding implementing update sets at all. This approach is limited to parallel execution semantics only, though. CASM uses a so called *pseudo state* (more details are in section 4.3.3) to implement *update sets* efficiently.

Schmid also introduced AsmGofer in [22]. AsmGofer is an interpreter for an ASM based language. It is written in the Gofer[3] language (a subset of Haskell) and covers most of the features described in the Lipari guide. The author notes however that the implementation is aimed at prototype modeling and too slow for performance critical applications.

Anlauff introduces XASM, a component based ASM language compiled to C [3]. The novel feature of XASM is the introduction of a component model, allowing implementation of reusable components. XASM supports *functions* implemented in C using the *extern* keyword. CASM does not feature modularization, but can be extended using C code as well. XASM was used as the core of the gem-mex system, a graphical language for ASMs.

Farahbod designed CoreASM, an extensible ASM execution engine [10]. The CoreASM project is actively maintained and has a large user base. The CASM language is inspired by the CoreASM language, but over time they have diverged significantly.

Praun, Schneider and Gross presented an algorithm for load elimination in the presence of side-effects, concurrency and precise exceptions [21]. Even the most conservative variant without side-effect and concurrency analysis can eliminate up to 55% of the loads and whole program analysis in an ahead-of-time Java compiler can increase the reduction up to 70%. Barik and Sarkar achieve performance improvements up to a factor of 1.76 in a just-in-time compiler for the parallel language X10 in the Jikes RVM applying interprocedural load elimination [4]. Our optimizations also aim at redundancy elimination in concurrent (parallel execution) context. ASM's partial updates can be treated in a similar way as side-effects. This work demonstrates the high levels of redundancy elimination possible in such systems.

3. The CASM Language

This section gives a brief description of ASM based programming languages in general and highlights features specific to CASM. An excellent introduction to the formal semantics of ASM languages is given by Börger and Schmid in [7]. More details on the CASM language can be found in [19].

3.1 Semantics of ASM Based Languages

The core concepts of ASM are the state and the transactional semantics of language statements. Based on algebraic concepts the *state* of the machine is modeled using *functions*. The *function* is a mathematical object and has a domain and a range. A null-ary *function* is, roughly speaking, a global variable in C-like languages. N-ary functions can best be thought of as hash-maps. In contrast to C-like languages, *functions* are always defined on their whole domain. *Functions* take the special value *undef* on arguments for which no value has been defined explicitly. The name of a *function* together with concrete arguments is called a *location*.

Statements of an ASM language are evaluated using the current *state* of the machine (defined by the total of its *functions*). The effects of each statement (called an *update*) will affect the *next* state however. All statements of a block are executed in parallel and their

[2] http://www.cs.cmu.edu/~modelcheck/smv.html

[3] http://web.cecs.pdx.edu/~mpj/goferarc/index.html

```
function x :  -> Int initially { 2 }                    1
function y :  -> Int initially { 3 }                    2
                                                        3
rule swap =                                             4
{                                                       5
  x := y                                                6
  y := x                                                7
}                                                       8
```

Listing 1. Swapping of two Values (Parallel Semantics)

```
function t :  -> Int initially { undef }                1
function x :  -> Int initially { 2 }                    2
function y :  -> Int initially { 3 }                    3
                                                        4
rule swap =                                             5
{                                                       6
 {|                                                     7
    t := x                                              8
    x := y                                              9
    y := t                                              10
 |}                                                     11
   print t                                              12
}                                                       13
```

Listing 2. Swapping of two Values (Sequential Semantics)

updates are *merged* (union) into a so called *update set*. Applying the resulting *update set* to the global machine state is called a *step* of the machine.

Listing 1 shows a code snippet swapping the contents of two null-ary functions utilizing the parallel execution semantics (denoted by braces) of CASM. The *update set* produced by the first update statement (line 6) is the set { x=3 }. The second update statement (line 7) is evaluated using the same state as the first one, so it produces the update { y=2 }. When leaving the block the updates are merged into the *update set* { x=3, y=2 }.

Parallel updates to the same *location* (non-empty set intersection) are a runtime error (a so called *inconsistent update*). CASM aborts the execution but we plan to invoke an error handler provided by the user in a future version.

TurboASM [11] extend ASM with the concept of sequential composition. Statements in a block using sequential execution semantics (denoted {| and |} in CASM) apply their updates before the subsequent statement is evaluated. The updates produced by each of the statements can overwrite each other in the resulting *update set*. When leaving the sequential block the original state (the one valid when entering the block) is restored. The intermediate states only exist temporarily (not the *update set* though). The rationale for this behavior is that the machine makes a *virtual step* after each statement in a sequential block.

Listing 2 illustrates this behavior. Inside the block with sequential execution semantics the values of the functions *x* and *y* are swapped using a temporary (function). Because of the sequential block the update in line 10 is evaluated in an intermediate state where the update to *t* (line 8) has been applied. The update set produced by the whole block therefore is { t=2, x=3, y=2 }. The changes have not been committed to the global machine state though. The `print` statement in line 12 will see the initial value *undef* when reading the function *t*.

Procedures are called *rules* in ASM. A distinct *rule* (top-level) is invoked on program startup. When the top-level rule returns the machine makes a *step* (and applies the *update set* to the machine state). The top-level rule will then repeatedly be executed until the program explicitly terminates.

3.2 CASM Specifics

The CASM language is statically typed (to ease programming a type inference system is implemented). Basic types are integer, sub range integer, float, rational, reference to rule and string. Custom types can be constructed using enumerations, tuples and lists. All *functions* and rule arguments must be explicitly typed. CASM performs no implicit type conversions. Builtins are used to convert boolean and enumeration types to integer representations. Integers can also be converted to boolean and enumeration types (for which a range check is performed). Variables (bindings created by *let* rules) may be typed explicitly but if they are not, their types will be inferred.

The original ASM specifies call-by-name semantics for rule invocation (procedure call). Call-by-name can be compiled using thunks [6], but doing so is not very efficient. We introduce a CASM specific *call* rule implementing call-by-value semantics.

The common control-flow statements, *i.e.* if-then-else, case, direct and indirect (using rule references) subroutine invocation (*call* rule) are available. As all state is global in CASM the only variables are values (expressions) bound to names (*let* rule).

CASM offers a set of built-in functions to operate on lists and stacks and can be extended with custom C functions. All built-ins must be side-effect free though.

3.3 Loops

Due to CASM's transactional semantics a loop counter can not be implemented. Commonly known loop constructs are therefore not part of the language. One way to express iterated execution is to utilize the property that the top-level rule will be executed repeatedly. This also solves the loop counter issue as after each iteration of the top-level rule the *update set* is applied to the state, which allows to model a loop counter. The semantics of the *forall* rule (*forall var in range*) is that the body is executed for each value (assigned to *var*) of the *range* in parallel.

The other way to implement a loop is by means of the *iterate* rule which sequentially composes the result of the loop body until the *update set* of a single iteration is empty. Iterate basically searches the fix-point of its body.

3.4 Notes for Implementors

The key issues to deal with when implementing an ASM language are: infinite domains for functions, n-ary functions, transactional and parallel semantics, intermediate and temporary states. One needs to implement a *lookup* mechanism for *locations* which is relative to the current state. *Updates* have set semantics. They need to be *merged* and must be checked for *inconsistency*. On the other hand the language is side-effect free.

4. The CASM Implementation

We developed a CASM interpreter and a CASM to C source-to-source compiler. Both the interpreter and the compiler are implemented in C++ and share the frontend and some parts of the runtime system.

4.1 Frontend

The abstract syntax tree (AST) is built using a Yacc parser. Type inference is performed on the AST using *apriori* known types (*functions*, built-ins, arguments) and propagates them through the AST. For all untyped variables *inferred* types are calculated. When a fix-point is reached the computed types are checked for completeness and consistency. The only difficulties are arising from the special value *undef* (which is compatible to all types) and empty list constants (as the type of the list element is undetermined). The typed AST can either be interpreted by a recursive AST interpreter

(CASM-i) or can be compiled. In the remainder of this section we describe the compiler.

4.2 Backend

The typed AST is used by the code generator to emit low-level C code (source-to-source translation). For each rule of the CASM program a distinct compile unit is emitted which allows parallel compilation. The emitted code is designed to allow good optimizations by a C compiler.

Code generation is (with exception of *lookups* and *updates*, see 4.3.4) straight forward. For each CASM rule the compiler emits a C function, which is split when the compile unit becomes too large. CASM control-flow constructs (i.e. *if*, *case* and *call*) are mapped to their C counterparts. The *forall* and *iterate* rules are translated to corresponding C loops. All iterations of a *forall* loop are considered to be executed in parallel, while the iterations of an *iterate* rule behave like being executed in sequential execution mode. The code generator adds a surrounding block with appropriate semantics (if needed) and merges the updates produced by each iteration accordingly.

CASM variables (i.e. let rule and rule arguments) are mapped to (scoped) local variables. Expression trees are translated in post-order fashion (this is possible as CASM is side-effect free). The temporaries are stored in local variables called *registers*. Each register has a unique name derived from a numbering of the AST nodes. Our assumption is that the C compiler will be able to very efficiently compile such code.

4.3 Runtime

This section describes the implementation of an efficient runtime system for an ASM language. This section also motivates the optimizations.

4.3.1 Dynamic Memory Allocation

Only *functions* and updates need to be allocated dynamically. Due to the transactional semantics of ASM languages the life-span of an update is exactly one *step* of the machine. A pre-allocated memory pool is used to store updates until a *step* is made and all updates are committed to the function storage. This pool can simply be reused in subsequent steps (dump-allocation). The runtime therefore has virtually no memory management overheads.

4.3.2 Storage for CASM Functions

Set operations are necessary to properly implement *functions*. All *locations* not explicitly defined otherwise have the special value *undef* (demanding an *is-element-of* set operation). A distinct hash-map (with linear probing) is used as storage for each *function*. The function arguments are concatenated to form the key. Each slot of the map has two special properties, *undef* and *branded*. The *undef* property is set if the *location* has the special value *undef*. An update may set a previously defined *location* to *undef*, so such *locations* need to be tracked explicitly. A slot is *branded* when its corresponding *location* is accessed for the first time. (*Branding* allows to use other default values than *undef*, CASM supports this feature). The runtime uses the slot's address, which must be guaranteed to be stable, as a unique identifier.

After each *step* of the machine the hash-map can safely be enlarged should the load factor have become too large. In the rare case that during a single *step* the hash-map would overflow, additional memory is allocated. In-between the next machine *step* the hash-map is resized and the overflow memory gets merged.

If a sub range integer type is used for the domain of a CASM function, an array is used as *function* storage instead of a hash-map (for reasonable sizes of the domain). An additional bit is needed to keep track of the special value *undef*.

```
{
    stmt₁
    {| stmt₂ ; stmt₃ |}
    {| stmt₄ ; stmt₅ |}
}
```

Listing 3. Interleaving PAR/SEQ

4.3.3 Updates and Pseudo States

Due to the interleaving of parallel and sequential execution semantics the state used to evaluate a statement and the state affected by its updates are in general not equal [11]. Listing 3 illustrates the problem. $stmt_1$ and the sequential blocks containing $stmt_2$ and $stmt_4$ are in a parallel block. Therefore they are evaluated under the same state S_0, their updates however are applied to different states. While updates produced by $stmt_1$ are applied to the S_0, updates produced by $stmt_2$ are used to create a *temporary* state S_1. The sequential composition with $stmt_3$ may modify updates produced by $stmt_2$ and only the resulting update set will be applied to S_0. The same situation arises with $stmt_4$ and $stmt_5$. As e.g. $stmt_4$ may contain a nested parallel block a tree-like structure of states is created. The nesting of update sets is very similar to nested transactions in software transactional memory (STM) [1]. The major difference is that an STM transaction aborts when reading an object for which a commit is pending while in ASM read access can never fail. Multiple updates to the same *location* in a parallel context is a runtime error (*inconsistent update*) in CASM.

Our assumption is that the number of updated *locations* (in a single ASM step) is much smaller than the whole state of the program. We therefore do not duplicate the state but keep track of all updates produced so far in a data structure called *update set*. When looking up a *location* the runtime has to query the *update set* for updates affecting the current state (due to sequential execution semantics).

We use the notation of *pseudo state* to keep track of updates affecting the current state. The *pseudo state* is a counter which is increased (at runtime) when a block with *different* execution semantics is entered. When a block is left (and control-flow returns into a block with *different* execution semantics) the *update set* is merged into the *update set* of the surrounding block. This is a serialization of the (partial) parallel execution semantics of ASM. Initially the system starts in parallel execution state, so *pseudo state* 0 denotes a block with parallel execution semantics. When entering a block with sequential semantics *pseudo state* will be increased to 1. By construction this counter is odd when executing a block with sequential execution semantics and even when in parallel mode.

The *update set* is implemented as a hash-map. The keys are 64 bit values, the lower 16 bits are the *pseudo state* of the block the update originates from, the remaining bits are the lower bits of the slot used to store the *location*. (This limits the number of nested states to 65536. The number of locations is limited to 2 to the power of 48. The maximum memory utilization of CASM therefore is 256 TiB, which is sufficient for any realistic application.)

Additionally the slots in the *update set* are forming a linked list with the latest update being the head. This property is used when merging update sets. Figure 1 shows the update set data structure.

4.3.4 Lookup and Update

A lookup for a specific *location* first needs to query the *functions* storage to acquire the address of the slot. This address and the current *pseudo state* are used to query the *update set* for any updates to this location which may be visible in the current state. By construction of the *update set* the corresponding keys can be efficiently calculated using the current key. The sequential states

lookup: $\mathcal{O}(\#ps)$, merge: $\mathcal{O}(\#updates)$, insert&collision: $\mathcal{O}(1)$

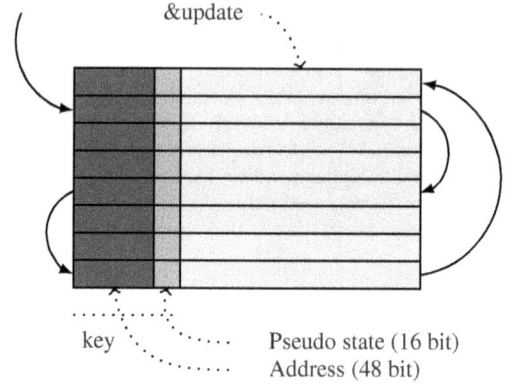

Figure 1. Update Set

are all odd numbered *pseudo states* with a number that is lower than the current one. The complexity of this operation is linear in the number of active *pseudo states* (dynamic nesting depth of parallel and sequential blocks).

An update also needs to query the functions storage to acquire the address of the slot corresponding to the location. This address and the current *pseudo state* form the key for the *update set*. If the slot in the *update set* already contains a value the further behavior depends on the current *pseudo state*. In sequential execution mode (odd pseudo state) the value will be overwritten, in parallel mode an *inconsistent update* error is triggered. The complexity of the *inconsistency* check is constant.

4.3.5 Merging of Update Sets

When leaving a block (with *different* execution semantics) the list property of the *update set* is exploited to efficiently merge all updates into the surrounding *update set*. The list is traversed backwards until the first update not belonging to the current update set is found (encoded in the lower 16 bits of the key). All updates are removed from the *update set* and re-inserted with the *pseudo state* part of their key reduced by one. Merging of *update sets* produced by sequential blocks may trigger inconsistent update errors as they are re-inserted into an *update set* with parallel execution semantics. The complexity of merging is linear in the size of the *update set* to be merged.

5. The Optimizing Compiler

In this section we describe the analyses and transformations performed by the optimizer. The optimizer is divided into multiple passes. Analyses only identify and mark opportunities while the transformations actually perform the changes.

5.1 Lookup and Update Elimination

The hash-maps used to implement the *update set* and *functions* are obviously very expensive in terms of performance. In this section we describe two optimizations called *lookup elimination* and *update elimination* that aim to reduce the number of hash-map operations. The first observation is that lookups from a parallel execution context will always retrieve the same value (for same *locations*). In such situations only the first lookup needs to query the function storage and the *update set* to retrieve the value. The second observation is that, in sequential execution context, updates and lookup behave like local variables in the language C.

16

```
{                              {
    if X(3) = 3 then               local X_3 = X(3) in
        skip                           if X_3 = 3 then
    if X(3) = 4 then                       skip
        skip                           if X_3 = 4 then
}                                          skip
                               }
```

Table 1. Redundant Lookup and its Elimination

```
                               local L_1 = foo in
{|                             {|
    X(4) := foo                    X(4) := L_1
    if X(4) > 0 then               if L_1 > 0 then
        skip                           skip
|}                             |}
```

Table 2. Preceded Lookup and its Elimination

```
{|                             {|
    X(5) := foo
    X(5) := bar                    X(5) := bar
|}                             |}
```

Table 3. Redundant Update and its Elimination

The idea is to introduce so called *local locations*. That is a rule-local storage which will be used by optimized lookup and update code. Once fetched, the *local location* can be used by subsequent lookups without the overheads of a hash-map. Table 1 illustrates the basic idea (*local* is not a valid CASM keyword).

Another pattern which allows the elimination of a lookup arises from updates (to the same location) preceding the lookup in a sequential context. In this case the value to be retrieved is known already and can be propagated instead of performing an expensive lookup. We call this pattern a *preceded lookup* for an example see table 2.

Update elimination tries to reduce the number of updates stored in the *update set*. If a specific *location* is updated multiple times in a sequential context, only the last update will be committed to the state. All preceding updates can safely be omitted. See table 3 for an example.

5.2 PAR/SEQ Control Flow Graph

We use an extension to the control flow graph (CFG) called the PAR/SEQ CFG to capture the nested parallel and sequential execution semantics. The nodes of this CFG are the instructions as they will be generated by the code generator, therefore it captures the semantics of the serialized statements. *Forall* rule bodies are executed in parallel leaving *iterate* as the only loop construct. We currently treat *iterate* as a black-box, like a *call*, hence our PAR/SEQ CFG is cycle free.

First we describe the generation of the PAR/SEQ CFG and discuss its properties later.

The PAR/SEQ CFG is generated from the AST representation of a single rule. Each node has a unique label, a type (e.g. IF, UPDATE, expression), the execution context (parallel or sequential) and its state nesting depth. The state nesting depth is a simple counter which is increased when entering a block and decreased when leaving (very similar to *pseudo states* described in 4.3.3). Our extension is to add synthetic nodes into the CFG when entering or leaving a block and when the control-flow of if-then-else merges. The state nesting depth of the synthetic nodes is the state nesting depth of the containing block.

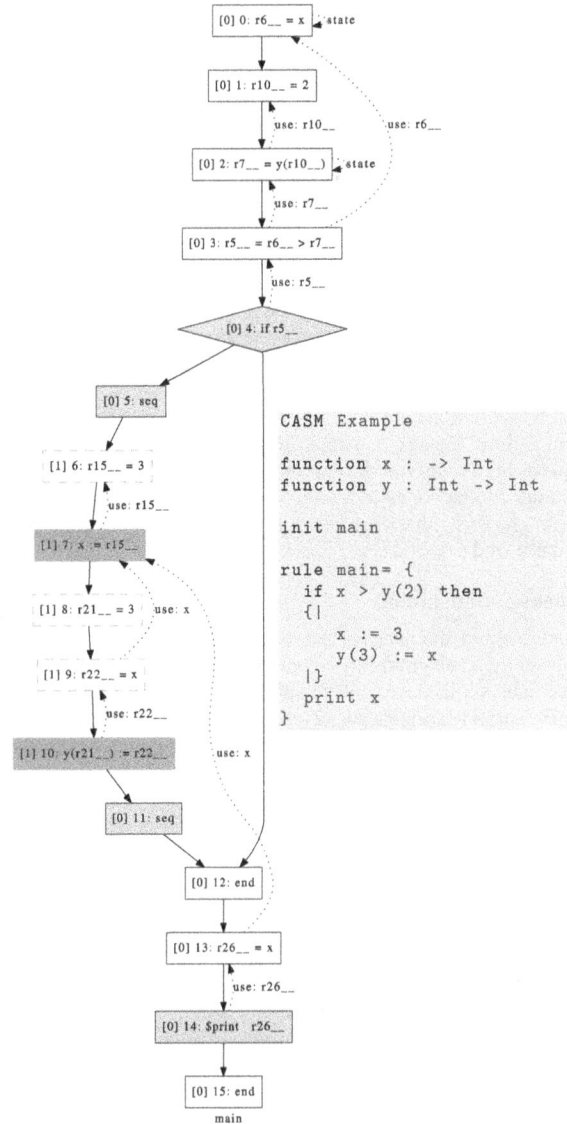

Figure 2. PAR/SEQ CFG (with use/def)

In figure 2 the PAR/SEQ CFG generated by the compiler and the corresponding CASM program is shown. Nodes filled with color correspond to CASM statements and white nodes result from expressions. Blue encodes parallel execution semantics and green is sequential. The nodes are labeled with their state nesting depth (in square brackets) followed by a unique id and their content. Examples for synthetic nodes are nodes number 5, 11 and 12. Results of the use/def analysis are shown as well and will be explained later.

5.3 PAR/SEQ Use/Def Analysis

We use a modified version of the classic use/def analysis called PAR/SEQ Use/Def to identify and categorize state lookups. It is based on the results of a state-unaware reaching-definition analysis [2]. Variables can be treated very simply (CASM is side-effect free, variables are bound and never updated). A lookup is the occurrence of a *function* name on the right side of an expression node. For each lookup its local definitions are considered. If there is no local definition the (expensive) hash-map operation must be performed, we call this a *state-lookup*. The occurrence is marked as such.

```
1  function x :  -> Int
2
3  rule foo =
4
5  {|
6    print x   // 1 lookup
7    x := x+1  // 1 redundant update , 1 redundant lookup
8    x := x*x  // 1 update , 2 preceded lookups
9  |}
```

Listing 4. Original Source

```
1  function x :  -> Int
2
3  rule foo =
4  local L_1 = x in          // 1 lookup
5    {|
6      print L_1
7      local L_2 := L_1+1 in
8        x := L_2*L_2         // 1 update
9    |}
```

Listing 5. After Optimization

If there is exactly one definition we mark the lookup as *local-lookup*. Such lookups are candidates for the lookup elimination pass.

Multiple definitions are not analyzed any further. At the point the control-flow merges a virtual node performing a *pseudo-definition* of the *location* will be added by the lookup elimination pass (similar to phi nodes in SSA). Multiple subsequent lookups to the same *location* therefore see only one definition and can be further optimized.

5.4 Lookup Elimination

For a *local-lookup* the decisive question is: what is the execution semantics of the inner-most block containing the definition **and** the use? The analysis discovers all paths in the PAR/SEQ CFG and records the state nesting depth of each node. The nice property is that the node with the smallest number is their common inner-most block (called *common state*). This property holds because the synthetic nodes act like virtual instructions ensuring that each path of the CFG goes through its containing block. In a way this encodes the least common dominator into each path.

If the *common state* has parallel execution semantics the effects of the definition is not visible. These kinds of lookups are marked as *state-lookup* which are handled separately. If the *common state* is sequential and there is only one path in the CFG the *location* is promoted to a local one. We call this pattern a *preceded lookup* and the transformation is shown in table 2.

For each *location* marked as *state-lookup* the number of occurrences in a rule is counted. If there are more than 2 occurrences the *location* is speculatively promoted to a local one and the lookup is hoisted to the outer-most block possible. The scope of variables used to calculate the *location* are boundaries for hoisting. This transformation is speculative because a lookup from a rarely executed path can be moved to a more frequently executed one.

5.5 Update Elimination

Updates in the same sequential block are considered for elimination. The nodes of each sequential block of a rule are traversed backwards and updates to *locations* are recorded. When there are multiple updates to the same *location* all but the last one are removed. The generic pattern is shown in table 3.

5.6 An Example

We want to illustrate the effects of theses optimizations on a small example. Listing 4 shows a small CASM rule which prints the value of the function x and afterwards updates it to the value $(x + 1)$ to the power of 2. For printing the value a lookup is performed (line 6). This lookup is the very first lookup of that *location* in this rule, so it can't be eliminated. In line 7 the value of x is increased by one. Again a lookup is performed, but this one is redundant and can be eliminated. The function x is then updated to contain the incremented value. This update is followed by another one and can therefore be eliminated. In line 8 finally the square is calculated and x is updated to the new value. To calculate the square value

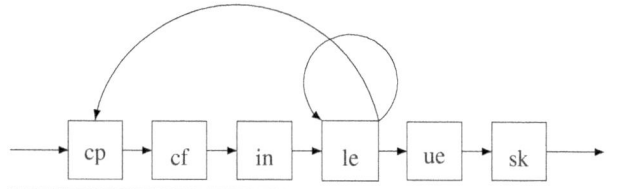

Figure 3. Compiler Passes

x is looked up twice. Theses lookups are preceded ones, as x was updated in line 7.

The optimizing compiler rewrites the source as given in listing 5 (though this isn't valid CASM syntax). The only lookup of x is now performed in line 4. This value (L_1) is used for printing (line 6) and to compute another *local location* (L_2) in line 7. This *local location* is used to eliminate the preceded lookups in line 8. Line 7 does not update x any more. The update to the *local location* does not involve the *update set* and is therefore a very cheap operation. In line 8 the two lookups are replaced by usage of the local location L_2, which does not involve *update set* operations.

In this small example the number of lookups was reduced from 4 to 1 and the number of updates from 2 to 1.

5.7 Supporting Optimizations

Lookup and update elimination strongly depend on i) exact analysis results for *all* paths ii) *locations* to be known at compile time, which is achieved by inlining.

The semantics of the *call* rule allows inlining by replacing the invocation with the AST tree of the inlined rule. Rule arguments must be evaluated (call-by-value) which can be achieved by adding *let* nodes to the AST. Maybe the names of an inlined rule's local variables (*let*) need to be renamed.

Because the CASM language is side-effect free, the analysis framework is able to perform constant folding for all built-ins. Using C macros we are even able to reuse the implementation in the analysis framework. Due to constant propagation a lot of dead code is identified and is removed as well.

Figure 3 gives an overview of the schedule of all transformations. Constant propagation (cp) and constant folding (cf) are executed before the inliner (in) is invoked. They may resolve indirect calls so the inliner is more effective. Afterwards lookup elimination (le) is performed until a fix point is reached. The reason for iterating lookup elimination is that the added *pseudo-definitions* may enable further optimizations. Elimination of *preceded lookups* may have propagated constants and therefore a fix point of those 4 optimizations is searched. Finally update elimination (ue) is performed and lookups, which have been hoisted to the beginning of the rule, are sunk (sk) to the least common dominator of all their (remaining) uses.

18

6. Evaluation

6.1 Baseline Compiler

In this section we evaluate the quality of the baseline compiler. For this purpose we compare it to other available implementations of ASM based languages, namely CoreASM and AsmL. CoreASM is an interpreter written in Java while the AsmL language is compiled to .NET code. A small suite of programs each stressing a different implementation detail of ASM languages has been implemented for each language.

The *bubblesort* program (a very naive implementation of the well known sorting algorithm) performs many steps with small update sets. It aims to benchmark the effectiveness of applying update sets to ASM functions. *Fibonacci* uses dynamic programming to calculate the well known numbers. It benchmarks rule invocation (recursive) and has a moderate size of the update set. *Quicksort* (the sorting algorithm) makes heavy use of sequential execution, although the update sets are very small. The *sieve* program is an implementation of Eratosthenes' famous prime number sieve. This program heavily stresses the implementation of the update set, everything is executed sequentially producing large update sets. The benchmark program *gray* calculates Gray codes for a given word length. It is the program with the most output and a mix of sequential execution, rule invocation and numeric operations. *Trivial* is the trivial program, immediately exiting without any operation. It is used to measure startup overheads of the various implementations.

The performance of the various implementations varies a lot. We use small data sets for the interpreters and larger sets for the compilers to have measurable execution times.

For benchmarking we use the CASM compiler (rev. 1a092c) and gcc 4.7.2 (as shipped with Ubuntu 12.10). We do not perform any CASM specific optimizations and disable optimizations of the C compiler (-O0 flag). The CASM interpreter (CASM-i) is the same version as the compiler.

The CoreASM engine version used is 1.5.6-beta using the command line driver Carma 0.7.3 (latest release). We executed CoreASM using Java 1.7 with the 64 bit Server VM (23.7-b01).

Microsoft's AsmL implementation compiles to .NET code and is freely available on `http://asml.codeplex.com/`. We downloaded version 80132 and followed their build instruction using Visual Studio C# 2005 Express Edition.

The benchmarks involving small data sets were executed on a Core i7-Q820 @ 1.73 GHz with 8 GiB memory under 64 bit Ubuntu 12.10. For the large data sets a dual boot system (Core i7-2600k @ 3.4 GHz, 8GiB memory) using 64 bit Windows 7 Enterprise SP1 and 64 bit Ubuntu 13.10 was used. We report on the average of 10 runs and started the AsmL binary once before the benchmark to exclude overheads induced by the .NET framework [4].

Our own implementation of a CASM interpreter (CASM-i) is designed to have very low startup times and is used to execute small programs only. It is used in the compiler verification project. The baseline compiler is a magnitude faster than the interpreter (up to 60 times) which is a good indicator that the baseline compiler performs well.

When it comes to performance CoreASM is clearly inferior to the other implementations. Programs compiled by our compiler perform up to 2500 times better and even our interpreter is one order of magnitude faster. The focus of CoreASM are high level models though.

The AsmL results are varying a lot. For *fibonacci* performance is on par with the CASM compiler (still 35% slower, though). But *fibonacci* is also the benchmark putting the least pressure on

[4] `http://msdn.microsoft.com/en-us/library/cc656914(v=vs.110).aspx`

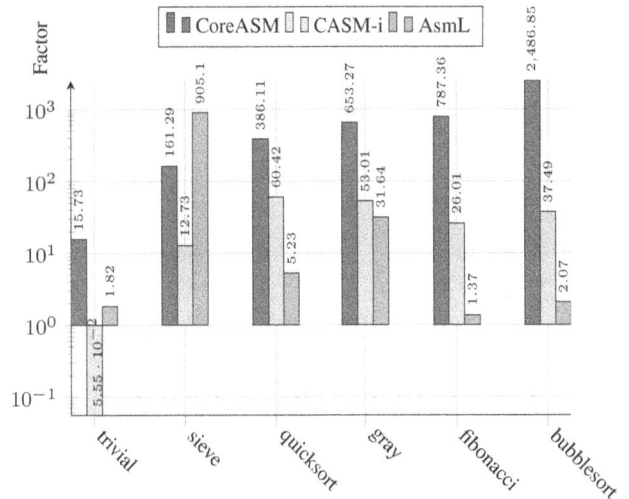

Figure 4. CASM relative Performance (Compiler as Baseline, smaller is better, log-scale)

ASM specifics. It uses mostly recursive function invocation with a comparably small update set. *Bubblesort* is slower by a moderate factor of 2 while *sieve* is slower by a factor of 900. A detailed examination showed that AsmL has quadratic runtime for increased sizes of the sieve. The main difference in the two programs is that *bubblesort* executes a large number of machine steps each with a small update set, while *sieve* exactly executes one step. The update set produced by *sieve* is quite large (the whole array) and a lot of updates need to be merged sequentially. This indicates that AsmL is not optimized for this case and agrees with the observed behavior of *quicksort* (small sequential update sets) and *gray* (moderate sized sequential update sets). Overall the performance of AsmL compiled programs is significantly lower than programs compiled by the CASM compiler.

Figure 4 shows the relative performance (with CASM compiler being the baseline) of the 4 implementations, please note the logarithmic scaling of the y axis. Numeric values are found in table 4. The CASM baseline compiler is by far the best performing ASM implementation.

6.2 Optimizing Compiler

In this section we evaluate the effectiveness of lookup and update elimination and investigate the scalability of the CASM compiler. We compare the performance data of our baseline compiler with the optimizing version. The other ASM implementations are simply not capable of executing programs of the desired size.

6.2.1 The Application

To create a large realistic benchmark we translate binary MIPS programs into a CASM representation and compile them to native code (that is a kind of compiled simulation). A Python script performs a very simple basic block analysis and a CASM rule is emitted for each identified basic block of the program. We add a semantic model of the MIPS architecture originally developed for compiler verification and provide a top-level executing the program's basic blocks. The basic structure of a program generated this way is presented in listing 6.

The benchmark programs are taken from the well known MiBench [15] suite. As our optimizations perform aggressive inlining we only want to optimize the kernel of the applications to

	trivial	small data sets					large date sets				
		sieve	quicksort	gray	fibonacci	bubblesort	sieve	quicksort	gray	fibonacci	bubblesort
CASM	0.0865	0.0857	0.0842	0.0882	0.0854	0.0859	0.0822	0.586	0.7702	3.0436	2.5458
AsmL	0.1292						74.39	3.0628	24.3702	4.1752	5.2748
CASM-i	0.0048	0.10	0.0212	0.2287	0.0107	0.0466	1.05	35.41	40.83	79.17	95.43
CoreASM	1.3604	13.82	32.51	57.61	67.24	213.62					

Table 4. Execution Time CoreASM, AsmL, CASM

```
enum FieldValues = { FV_RT, FV_IMM, FV_RS, ...
function BLOCK : -> Int
function GPR : Int -> Int

function (static) PARG: Int * FieldValues -> Int
  initially {
    [0x80001000,FV_RT] -> 28,
    [0x80001000,FV_IMM] -> 32769,
    [0x80001000,FV_RS] -> 0,
    ...

function (static) BASICBLOCK: Int -> RuleRef
  initially {
    0 -> @bb_0,
    701 -> @bb_701,
    ...

rule andi(addr : Int) =
let rs = PARG(addr, FV_RS) in
let rt = PARG(addr, FV_RT) in
let imm = PARG(addr, FV_IMM) in
  call write_reg
    (rt, BVand(32, GPR(rs), BVze( 16, 32,imm)))

rule bb_0 =
{|
  BLOCK:=630
  call bb_call(@lui, 0x80001000)
  call bb_call(@bb_bltzal, 0x80001004)
  call bb_call(@addiu, 0x80001008)
|}

rule run_program =
{|
    call (BASICBLOCK(BLOCK))
    if trapped then
      program(self) := undef
|}
```

Listing 6. Compiled Simulation in CASM

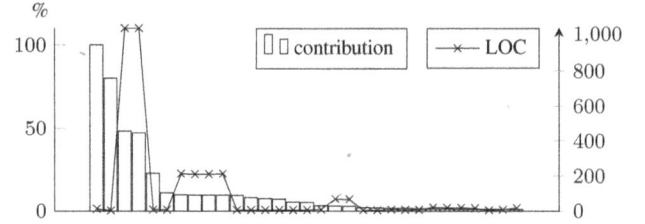

Figure 5. Rule Contribution and Size - Rijndael

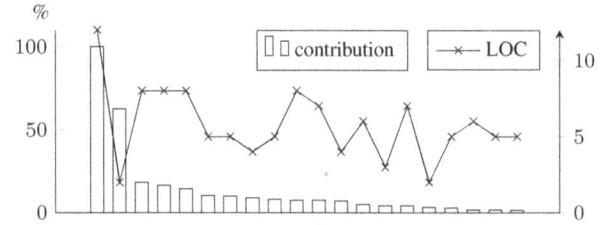

Figure 6. Rule Contribution and Size - Dijkstra

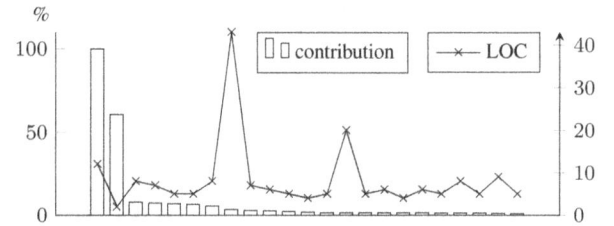

Figure 7. Rule Contribution and Size - Patricia

keep the increase in code size small. Our code generator can instrument the code to collect profiling information measuring the total execution time of each CASM rule (including time spent in invoked rules). Applying a simple heuristic all rules contributing at least 1% to the total runtime have been selected for optimization. Our assumption is that the effects on code size by inlining are small but the achieved effect (in terms of performance gains) large.

Lookup and update elimination work best on large rules so their impact should be high if the frequently executed rules are large and low for small rules. Figure 5 depicts the contribution of a rule's execution time to total program execution time (bars) and their size in LOC (crosses) for the rijndael program. (The rule contributing 100% to total program execution time is the top-level rule, the second bar is a dispatching rule. All further bars correspond to basic blocks or instructions.) Note that two of the most contributing rules each have 1000 LOC. We expect to see a high impact of lookup and update elimination for the rijndael program. Figure 7 on the other hand shows that the patricia program has many small rules and the first large rule does not contribute much to total execution time. A high impact can not be expected. Figure 6 shows the same diagram for the dijkstra program. Medium sized

rules with moderate contribution. We expect our optimizations to have an impact for this program.

6.2.2 Results

We use 3 configurations of our compiler in this evaluation. Baseline is without CASM specific optimizations and without optimizations of the C compiler (-O0). The configuration titled *O0* has CASM specific, but no C compiler optimizations (-O0). *O3* has CASM and full C compiler optimizations (-O3). The benchmarks were executed on Xeon E5504 @ 2.00GHz with 8GiB memory (on the Infragrid cluster [5]). We used gcc 4.4.7 on a Red Hat Enterprise Linux Server release 6.4 for compilation. Due to the shared nature of the cluster we report on the best of 10 runs here. MiBench's small data sets have been used for all but the search benchmark.

Table 5 lists for each benchmark program the total number of rules and the number of rules optimized as well as the total number

---

[5] http://hpc.uvt.ro/infrastructure/infragrid/

	rules		optimizations		
	opt	total	cp	lookup	update
basicmath	30	4097	1440	236	22
bf	43	1226	8060	889	451
crc	17	3501	416	56	7
dijkstra	20	5455	494	52	1
patricia	23	5864	761	150	0
qsort	21	5393	720	65	1
rawcaudio	38	3293	656	65	1
rawdaudio	29	3293	656	65	1
rijndael	32	3431	42452	4394	2864
search	28	3239	2086	274	5
sha	26	3291	2840	381	3
susan	29	5337	7570	1192	224
toast	23	7812	6803	885	53
untoast	40	7812	1840	264	17

Table 5. CASM Optimizations

		total LOC C		binary MiB	
	C files	w/o opt	full opt	w/o opt	full opt
basicmath	4104	531769	+1357	29	35
bf	1233	179890	+10369	9.1	11
crc	3508	419546	+679	24	29
dijkstra	5462	691294	+866	38	46
patricia	5871	694523	+622	39	48
qsort	5400	641228	+1328	36	44
rawcaudio	3300	402138	+901	23	27
rawdaudio	3300	402138	+946	23	27
rijndael	3438	524481	+49198	26	32
search	3246	419649	+4660	23	28
sha	3298	408628	+5506	23	28
susan	5344	727943	+10029	28	46
toast	7819	972261	+10903	53	64
untoast	7819	972261	+3401	53	64

Table 7. Generated Output Statistics

		w/o opt	full opt
	LOC casm	sec	sec
basicmath	136871	8.16	18.10
bf	48693	3.67	50.06
crc	109625	3.50	4.24
dijkstra	208337	5.78	6.73
patricia	180455	5.60	7.57
qsort	165011	5.08	6.60
rawcaudio	106716	3.23	4.69
rawdaudio	106716	3.30	4.10
rijndael	149435	4.82	218.23
search	122043	3.18	5.62
sha	104539	3.25	8.42
susan	187091	5.46	50.19
toast	261206	7.22	45.78
untoast	261206	7.50	10.18

Table 6. CASM Compiler Statistics (compile time)

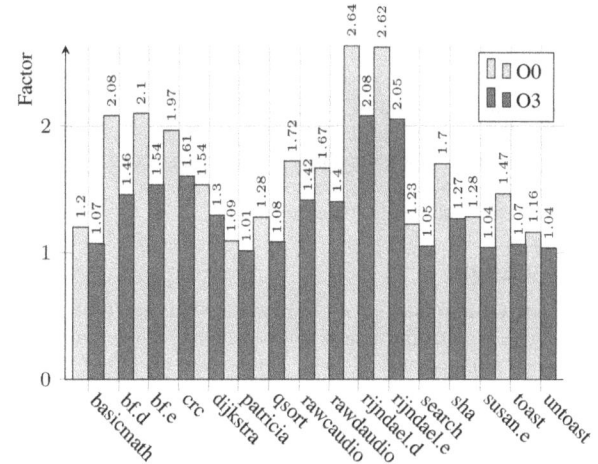

Figure 8. Impact of CASM Optimizations

of optimizations performed. We report on the number of constant propagations (cp), lookup eliminations and update eliminations. As expected we see a large number of optimizations performed in the rijndael program. Although patricia is doing well in numbers the effects do not materialize due to the disadvantageous distribution of block contribution to the total runtime.

In table 6 the size of the test programs in LOC and the compilation times with and without optimizations are listed.

In table 7 we summarize the output produced by the CASM compiler. Generally we are generating a single C file for each rule but are merging smaller rules to reduce the number of files. For rijndael we see the by far largest increase in code size with moderate 10%. The increase in the size of the binary is approximately 20%.

To assure that the observed behavior is not solely due to optimizations of the C compiler we report on the effects of compiling optimized CASM programs with and without compiler optimizations. Figure 8 shows the relative impact of CASM optimizations with and without optimizations by the C compiler. The relative performance is clearly decreased but our optimizations still account for a factor of 2 (rijndael) to at least 1% for patricia. (On a side note: by using well-known compiled simulation techniques (e.g. [8]) the size of the basic blocks can be enlarged from which our compiler would profit immediately.) In figure 9 the overall speedup factors for the applications are shown along with absolute performance data. The speedup is relative from the non-optimized version to the fully optimized one. We are able to achieve factors 6

and above here. For rijndael (factor 5.44) more than 50% of this speedup is due to CASM optimizations (the rest is due to the C compiler).

The MHz value relates the total number of simulated MIPS instructions to the absolute runtime of the programs We are able to achieve simulation speeds above 3 MHz which is an impressing result. The numbers also indicate that the performance without optimizations would be approximately 500 kHz. Search and susan show very low performance here. This is due to the very short execution time of these two programs (5 and 4 seconds). The startup time of the programs is approximately 1 second (the initial memory state of the MIPS programs (data section) is initialized by a CASM rule producing updates) therefore a significant reduction of simulation speed is expected.

The experimental data show a huge performance increase achieved by the CASM compiler. A speedup of more than factor 6 can be achieved. We showed that the C code generated by the CASM compiler can be very efficiently optimized. Our novel optimizations lookup elimination and update reduction can increase program performance up to 264%. This shows that they are highly effective.

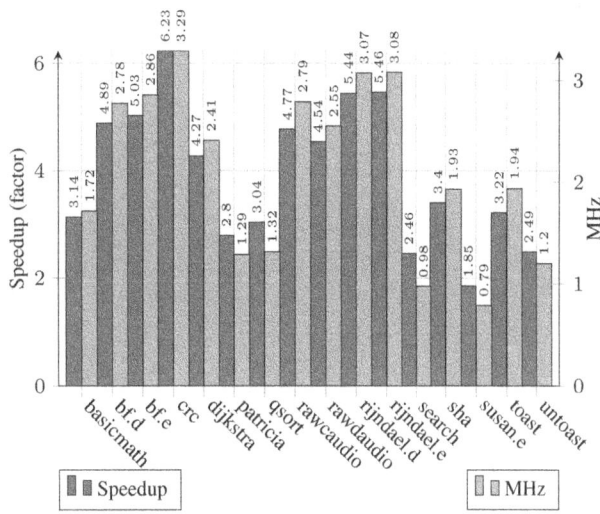

Figure 9. Improvements and Total Performance

7. Future Work

We are currently working on an inter-procedural analysis framework to reduce the amount of inlined code. Also the scope of the update elimination should be increased from sequential block scope to whole rule scope. Due to the highly effective constant propagation and constant folding we also see a large potential in implementing common subexpression elimination.

8. Conclusion

In this paper we introduced the Abstract State Machine based language CASM. We described the implementation of the runtime system and the compilation to C code. The novel PAR/SEQ Control Flow Graph representation and PAR/SEQ Use/Def Analysis based on it were presented. We then discuss how these data structures can be used to eliminate expensive runtime operations of ASM implementations. In a thorough evaluation we demonstrated that our baseline compiler alone outperforms other available implementations (including Microsoft's AsmL compiler) by 2-3 orders of magnitude. Finally we demonstrate the effectiveness of our code-generation achieving an overall speedup of up to factor 6. Our novel optimizations lookup and update elimination contribute up to 264% to the overall performance gain.

References

[1] K. Agrawal, J. T. Fineman, and J. Sukha. Nested parallelism in transactional memory. In *Proceedings of the 13th ACM SIGPLAN Symposium on Principles and Practice of Parallel Programming*, PPoPP '08, pages 163–174, New York, NY, USA, 2008. ACM. ISBN 978-1-59593-795-7. .

[2] A. V. Aho, M. Lam, R. Sethi, and J. Ullman. *Compilers: Principles, Techniques, & Tools*. Addison-Wesley, 2007. ISBN 978-0321547989.

[3] M. Anlauff. XASM- An Extensible, Component-Based Abstract State Machines Language. In Y. Gurevich, P. Kutter, M. Odersky, and L. Thiele, editors, *Abstract State Machines - Theory and Applications*, volume 1912 of *Lecture Notes in Computer Science*, pages 69–90. Springer Berlin Heidelberg, 2000. ISBN 978-3-540-67959-2. .

[4] R. Barik and V. Sarkar. Interprocedural load elimination for dynamic optimization of parallel programs. In *Parallel Architectures and Compilation Techniques, 2009. PACT'09. 18th International Conference on*, pages 41–52. IEEE, 2009.

[5] M. Barnett, W. Grieskamp, L. Nachmanson, W. Schulte, N. Tillmann, and M. Veanes. Towards a tool environment for model-based testing

with AsmL. In *Formal Approaches to Software Testing, FATES 2003, volume 2931 of LNCS*, pages 264–280. Springer, 2003.

[6] J. Bergin and S. Greenfield. Teaching parameter passing by example using thunks in C and C++. *SIGCSE Bull.*, 25(1):10–14, Mar. 1993. ISSN 0097-8418. .

[7] E. Börger and J. Schmid. Composition and submachine concepts for sequential ASMs. In *Computer Science Logic (Proceedings of CSL 2000), volume 1862 of LNCS*, pages 41–60. Springer-Verlag, 2000.

[8] F. Brandner, N. Horspool, and A. Krall. DSP Instruction Set Simulation. In S. S. Bhattacharyya, E. F. Deprettere, R. Leupers, and J. Takala, editors, *Handbook of Signal Processing Systems*, pages 945–974. Springer New York, 2013. ISBN 978-1-4614-6858-5. .

[9] G. D. Castillo. The ASM workbench - A tool environment for computer-aided analysis and validation of abstract state machine models. In *Proceedings of the 7th International Conference on Tools and Algorithms for the Construction and Analysis of Systems*, TACAS 2001, pages 578–581, London, UK, UK, 2001. Springer-Verlag.

[10] R. Farahbod, V. Gervasi, and U. Glässer. CoreASM: An extensible ASM execution engine. *Fundamenta Informaticae*, 77:1–33, 2007.

[11] N. G. Fruja and R. F. Stärk. The hidden computation steps of Turbo Abstract State Machines. In *Abstract State Machines — Advances in Theory and Applications, 10th International Workshop, ASM 2003*, pages 244–262. Springer-Verlag, 2003.

[12] Y. Gurevich. *Evolving algebras 1993: Lipari guide*, pages 9–36. Oxford University Press, Inc., New York, NY, USA, 1995.

[13] Y. Gurevich and N. Tillmann. Partial updates. *Theoretical Computer Science*, 336(2):311–342, 2005.

[14] Y. Gurevich, B. Rossman, and W. Schulte. Semantic essence of AsmL. *Theor. Comput. Sci.*, 343(3):370–412, Oct. 2005. ISSN 0304-3975. .

[15] M. R. Guthaus, J. S. Ringenberg, D. Ernst, T. M. Austin, T. Mudge, and R. B. Brown. Mibench: A free, commercially representative embedded benchmark suite. In *Proceedings of the Workload Characterization, 2001. WWC-4. 2001 IEEE International Workshop*, WWC '01, pages 3–14, Washington, DC, USA, 2001. IEEE Computer Society. ISBN 0-7803-7315-4. .

[16] J. K. Huggins and W. Shen. The static and dynamic semantics of C, 2000.

[17] R. Lezuo. *Scalable Translation Validation*. PhD thesis, Vienna University of Technology, 2014.

[18] R. Lezuo and A. Krall. Using the CASM language for simulator synthesis and model verification. In *Proceedings of the 2013 Workshop on Rapid Simulation and Performance Evaluation: Methods and Tools*, RAPIDO '13, pages 6:1–6:8, New York, NY, USA, 2013. ACM. ISBN 978-1-4503-1539-5. .

[19] R. Lezuo, G. Barany, and A. Krall. CASM: Implementing an Abstract State Machine based Programming Language. In S. Wagner and H. Lichter, editors, *Software Engineering 2013 Workshopband, 26. Februar - 1. März 2013 in Aachen*, volume 215 of *GI Edition - Lecture Notes in Informatics*, pages 75–90, February 2013. ISBN 978-3-88579-609-1. (6. Arbeitstagung Programmiersprachen (ATPS'13)).

[20] T. Mens. A state-of-the-art survey on software merging. *Software Engineering, IEEE Transactions on*, 28(5):449–462, 2002.

[21] C. Praun, F. Schneider, and T. Gross. Load elimination in the presence of side effects, concurrency and precise exceptions. In L. Rauchwerger, editor, *Languages and Compilers for Parallel Computing*, volume 2958 of *Lecture Notes in Computer Science*, pages 390–404. Springer Berlin Heidelberg, 2004. ISBN 978-3-540-21199-0. .

[22] J. Schmid. Introduction to AsmGofer, 2001. URL http://www.tydo.de/AsmGofer.

[23] J. Schmid. Compiling abstract state machines to C++. *Journal of Universal Computer Science*, 7(11):1068–1087, 2001.

[24] J. Teich, P. W. Kutter, and R. Weper. Description and simulation of microprocessor instruction sets using ASMs. In *Proceedings of the International Workshop on Abstract State Machines, Theory and Applications*, ASM '00, pages 266–286, London, UK, 2000. Springer-Verlag. ISBN 3-540-67959-6.

Combinatorial Spill Code Optimization
and Ultimate Coalescing

Roberto Castañeda Lozano   Mats Carlsson

SCALE, Swedish Institute of Computer Science,
Sweden
{rcas,matsc}@sics.se

Gabriel Hjort Blindell   Christian Schulte

SCALE, School of ICT, KTH Royal Institute of
Technology, Sweden
{ghb,cschulte}@kth.se

Abstract

This paper presents a novel combinatorial model that integrates global register allocation based on ultimate coalescing, spill code optimization, register packing, and multiple register banks with instruction scheduling (including VLIW). The model exploits alternative temporaries that hold the same value as a new concept for ultimate coalescing and spill code optimization.

The paper presents Unison as a code generator based on the model and advanced solving techniques using constraint programming. Thorough experiments using MediaBench and a processor (Hexagon) that are typical for embedded systems demonstrate that Unison: is robust and scalable; generates faster code than LLVM (up to 41% with a mean improvement of 7%); possibly generates optimal code (for 29% of the experiments); effortlessly supports different optimization criteria (code size on par with LLVM).

Unison is significant as it addresses the same aspects as traditional code generation algorithms, yet is based on a simple integrated model and robustly can generate optimal code.

Categories and Subject Descriptors   D.3.4 [*Programming Languages*]: Processors—compilers, code generation, optimization; D.3.2 [*Programming Languages*]: Language Classifications—constraint and logic languages; I.2.8 [*Artificial Intelligence*]: Problem Solving, Control Methods, and Search—backtracking, scheduling

Keywords   spill code optimization; ultimate coalescing; combinatorial optimization; register allocation; instruction scheduling

1. Introduction

Register allocation and instruction scheduling are essential aspects of generating assembly code during compilation. They are particularly relevant for embedded processors such as Qualcomm's *Hexagon* or Recore Systems' *Xentium* with additional challenges such as very long instruction word (VLIW) capabilities and irregular register banks. This paper presents a novel combinatorial model and Unison as a code generator using the model. The model is formally expressed by variables and relations (constraints) between

LCTES '14,   June 12–13, 2014, Edinburgh, United Kingdom.
Copyright © 2014 ACM 978-1-4503-2877-7/14/06. . . $15.00.
http://dx.doi.org/10.1145/2597809.2597815

variables. Unison uses constraint programming as a combinatorial optimization technique to solve the model and thereby generates potentially optimal assembly code for a given input function and processor architecture. Unison addresses all major subproblems of integrated register allocation and instruction scheduling. This approach overcomes significant limitations of previous work while being scalable and robust (wrt. different input functions) and produces better assembly code than traditional algorithms.

Today's compilers typically generate assembly in stages: instruction selection is followed by register allocation and instruction scheduling. Each stage commonly executes a heuristic algorithm as taking optimal decisions is considered to be computationally infeasible. By design, both staging and heuristic algorithms compromise the quality of the generated code. Moreover, heuristic algorithms are difficult to adapt to new architectural features and frequent processor revisions, particularly for embedded processors. Using instead a combinatorial model simplifies the construction of compilers while generating potentially optimal code.

Existing combinatorial models of register allocation and instruction scheduling predefine which instructions access each *temporary* (program variable) and thus do not support the substitution of temporaries that hold the same value. This is a significant limitation that precludes two essential optimizations: *spill code optimization* (remove unnecessary memory access instructions inserted during register allocation) and *ultimate coalescing* (remove unnecessary register-to-register copy instructions considering the value of each temporary). This paper introduces *alternative temporaries* as an approach that supports the substitution of temporaries and thus enables spill code optimization and ultimate coalescing.

Approach.   This paper assumes functions in Static Single Assignment (SSA) form after instruction selection as input. SSA functions are transformed to Linear SSA (LSSA) where each temporary is live in a single *basic block* and extended with optional copy instructions to support register allocation as in [3]. LSSA functions are augmented with *alternative temporaries*, a novel abstraction that supports the substitution of temporaries and enables spill code optimization and ultimate coalescing.

LSSA functions with alternative temporaries are transformed into combinatorial problems according to a formal model of register allocation and instruction scheduling which is parameterized with respect to a generic processor description. The model captures all major subproblems of global register allocation, including: spill code optimization and ultimate coalescing; multiple register banks; and register packing, where several small temporaries can be assigned to the same register. These subproblems are integrated with instruction scheduling and bundling for VLIW processors. The single model reflects the trade-off between interdependent register allocation and instruction scheduling decisions.

The combinatorial register allocation and instruction scheduling problems are solved using constraint programming [17], a technique that exploits the structure of the combinatorial model. Solutions to the combinatorial problems can be optimized accurately for different criteria such as speed, code size, or energy consumption. A presolving phase is introduced to increase robustness. Experiments on compiling medium-size MediaBench functions for Hexagon, a typical Digital Signal Processor (DSP), show that the introduced approach generates better code than existing combinatorial approaches and the LLVM code generator, and that the approach scales despite a significant growth of the solution space.

Contributions. The paper introduces a program representation and combinatorial model of register allocation and instruction scheduling that use the new concept of alternative temporaries to enable spill code optimization and ultimate coalescing. It shows presolving techniques that exploit the structure of the combinatorial model to increase robustness. Extensive experiments provide insight into the benefits and current limitations of the approach using Hexagon as a real-world DSP. The experiments demonstrate that the approach is robust, scales up to medium-size functions, adapts easily to different optimization criteria, and yields better code than previous combinatorial approaches and heuristic algorithms where LLVM is used as an example.

In the context of combinatorial optimization, the results are surprising. While the introduction of alternative temporaries leads to a combinatorial problem which is exponentially harder to solve, the approach is demonstrated to be scalable and robust while producing significantly better code.

Plan of the paper. Section 2 explains the necessary background. Alternative temporaries are introduced in Section 3, followed by the combinatorial model in Section 4. Unison as the code generator is discussed in Section 5. Section 6 contains the experimental evaluation. Related work is discussed in Section 7, and the paper concludes with Section 8.

2. Background

This section provides background information on combinatorial optimization, the program representation used in this paper, and the main aspects of register allocation.

2.1 Combinatorial Optimization

Register allocation and instruction scheduling are computationally hard combinatorial optimization problems. They can be solved by problem-specific heuristic algorithms (typically leading to suboptimal solutions) or by general combinatorial optimization techniques (potentially leading to optimal solutions). The latter amounts to *modeling* the problem and *solving* the resulting model with some combinatorial optimization technique.

A *combinatorial model* consists of *variables* (typically ranging over integers or Booleans), *constraints* expressing relations among the variables, and an *objective function* to define preferred solutions. A *solution* is a variable assignment satisfying all constraints of the model and an *optimal solution* minimizes (or maximizes) the value of the objective function. A combinatorial model serves as a template for an *instance*, which takes problem parameters into account resulting in a complete problem description.

Solving applies combinatorial optimization techniques to find solutions of an instance. Example techniques include constraint programming, integer programming, Boolean satisfiability solving, and local search. This paper uses *constraint programming* [17] as a modern combinatorial optimization technique. Constraint programming solvers interleave *constraint propagation* and *search* to find solutions. Constraint propagation discards values for variables

(that is, partial assignments) that cannot be part of any solution. When no further propagation is possible, search tries several alternatives on which constraint propagation and search are repeated. Constraint propagation is essential to reduce the search space.

Constraint programming can capture and exploit explicit structure existing in many combinatorial models. Structure is captured by *global constraints* that express problem-specific relations among several variables. Global constraints offer two benefits: they ease modeling (as will become clear in Section 4) by capturing common patterns in problems, and enable strong propagation that leads to a drastically reduced search space.

2.2 Input Program

Instruction set. This paper assumes input functions for which Hexagon V4 instructions have been selected. Hexagon V4 is a DSP included in Qualcomm's Snapdragon system-on-chip for mobile devices [15]. Hexagon provides two typical embedded processor features: VLIW capabilities and different-width registers. VLIW processors exploit instruction-level parallelism by executing statically scheduled *bundles* of instructions in parallel. Hexagon bundles contain up to four 32-bit instructions. The register file includes 32 general-purpose registers (R0...R31) of 32 bits each which can be accessed as 16 registers (R1:0...R31:30) of 64 bits.

Control-flow graphs, operations, and temporaries. Functions are represented by their control-flow graph (CFG) in Static Single Assignment (SSA) form. A basic block (*block* for short) in the CFG consists of *operations* and *temporaries*. Operations use and define temporaries and are implemented by processor instructions. Temporaries are storage locations holding values corresponding to program variables after instruction selection. For example, an operation implemented by the Hexagon instruction abs that defines temporary t' as the absolute value of a used temporary t is denoted as $t' \leftarrow$ abs t. For clarity, examples in the paper only show instructions and temporaries that are relevant to the discussion.

Static Single Assignment form. SSA is a program form where temporaries are statically defined once. This form uses ϕ-*functions* at the join points of the CFG to merge definitions of the same temporary. This paper refers to SSA in its conventional form [19].

Liveness and interference. A *program point* is located between two consecutive statements. A temporary t is *live* at a program point if t holds a value that might be used in the future. The *live range* of a temporary t is the set of program points where t is live. The *basic definition of interference* states that two temporaries interfere if their live ranges overlap. The *ultimate notion of interference* by Chaitin *et al.* [4] additionally requires that the values of interfering temporaries differ. This refinement is essential for optimizing register allocation as is explained in Section 2.3.

Preassignments. Architectural constraints and application binary interfaces (ABIs) predetermine the registers to which certain temporaries must be assigned. A temporary t that is *preassigned* to a register r is denoted by $t \triangleright r$.

Example. Figure 1 shows the CFG of the factorial function in SSA form which is used as running example in the paper. The figure shows the purpose of ϕ-functions: for example, $t_{10} \leftarrow \phi(t_3, t_7)$ assigns t_{10} to either t_3 or t_7, depending on whether block b_3 is entered from b_1 or b_2. For readability, Hexagon register-to-register transfer (tfr), immediate transfer (tfri), load (ldw), store (stw), multiply (mul), indirect jump (jump), and conditional direct jump (jump if, jump ifn) instructions are shown in a simplified syntax. The top operation in b_1 and the bottom operation in b_3 define and use, respectively, the temporaries that are live on the function boundaries and are preassigned by the ABI: return address $t_1 \triangleright$R31, argument $t_2 \triangleright$R0, and return value $t_{10} \triangleright$R0.

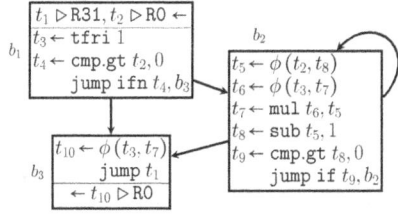

Figure 1. Factorial function in SSA with Hexagon instructions.

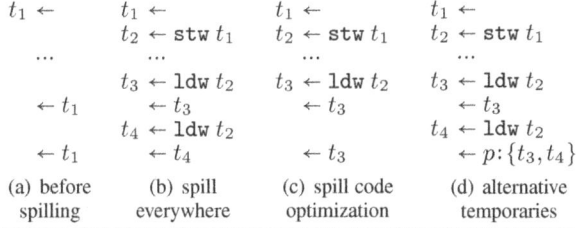

(a) before spilling	(b) spill everywhere	(c) spill code optimization	(d) alternative temporaries

Figure 2. Spill code optimization.

2.3 Register Allocation

Register allocation assigns temporaries to either processor registers or memory. To reduce the number of memory accesses, registers are reused by non-interfering temporaries.

Spill code optimization. In general, optimal register utilization does not guarantee the availability of enough processor registers and some temporaries must be *spilled* (that is, stored in memory). Spilling a temporary requires the insertion of store and load instructions to move its value to and from memory. The selection and placement of these instructions has considerable impact on the efficiency of the generated code. In a *spill-everywhere* model, a load instruction is inserted immediately before each use of the spilled temporary. *Spill code optimization* reduces the cost of a spill by reusing the spilled temporary defined by a single load instruction.

Figure 2 shows an example where the temporary t_1 with two consecutive uses from Figure 2(a) is spilled to a new, memory-allocated temporary t_2 using a store instruction (`stw`) and reloaded using load instructions (`ldw`). In Figure 2(b) a load is inserted before each use, following the spill-everywhere model. In Figure 2(c), spill code optimization is performed to supply the two consecutive uses by the same load. Figure 2(d) is discussed in Section 3.

Coalescing. The input program may contain temporaries related by *copies* (operations that replicate the value of a temporary into another). Copy-related temporaries that do not interfere can be *coalesced* (assigned to the same register) in order to discard the corresponding copies and thereby improve efficiency and reduce code size. *Ultimate coalescing* considers all copy-related temporaries as candidates for coalescing: copy-related temporaries never interfere as they hold the same value.

The example in Figure 3 copies the value of t_1 into t_2 using a register-to-register transfer instruction (`tfr`). Using basic interference in Figure 3(a), t_1 and t_2 cannot be coalesced since their live ranges overlap. Using ultimate interference in Figure 3(b), t_1 and t_2 are coalesced into t_1 and the copy is discarded. Figure 3(c) is discussed in Section 3.

Packing. Each temporary t has a certain bit width (hereafter just called *width*) which is determined by t's source data type. Many processors allow temporaries of small widths to be assigned to different parts of a physical register of larger width. For example, the Hexagon processor combines pairs of 32-bits registers (R3, R2) into 64-bit registers (R3:2). Packing non-interfering temporaries into the same physical register is key to improving register utilization.

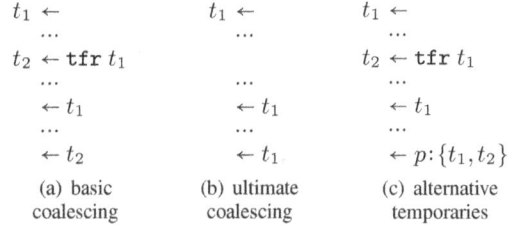

(a) basic coalescing	(b) ultimate coalescing	(c) alternative temporaries

Figure 3. Coalescing.

Scope. *Local* register allocation deals with one block at a time, spilling all temporaries that are live at block boundaries. *Global* register allocation considers entire functions, yielding better code as temporaries can be kept in the same register across blocks.

2.4 Program Transformations

The combinatorial model described in Section 4 is based on a dedicated program representation for input functions. This representation uses the Linear Static Single Assignment form (LSSA) extended with copies as described by Castañeda et al. [3, Section 3] (note that they define *operation* and *instruction* reversely to this paper).

Linear Static Single Assignment form. Linear Static Single Assignment form (LSSA) is stricter than SSA in that each temporary is only defined and used within one block. The relation that two temporaries in different blocks correspond to the same temporary in SSA is captured by a *congruence* between temporaries. The local scope of LSSA temporaries leads to simple live ranges which is exploited in Section 4. This property also enables a decomposition scheme that can be exploited for robust code generation [3, Section 7]. LSSA is constructed from SSA by splitting each temporary t whose live ranges span multiple blocks $b_1, b_2, \ldots, b_n$ into a set of congruent local temporaries $t_{b_1} \equiv t_{b_2} \equiv \cdots \equiv t_{b_n}$. *Delimiter operations* are inserted at the boundaries of each block to define and use its live-in and live-out temporaries. These operations are not part of the generated code.

Copies. The LSSA program is extended with copies similarly to Appel and George's approach [1]. These operations are required to implement LSSA congruences and to handle spilling, multiple register banks, and preassignments.

A copy $t_d \leftarrow t_s$ replicates the value of the temporary t_s into the temporary t_d. To allow t_s and t_d to be assigned to different types of locations such as registers or memory, the copy can be implemented by alternative instructions $\{\perp, i_1, i_2, \ldots, i_n\}$ where the instruction i_j depends on the location types to which t_s and t_d are assigned. Copies implemented by the null instruction $\perp$ are discarded, otherwise they are *active* and must appear in the generated assembly code.

The copy insertion points and their alternative instructions depend on the processor. For example, Hexagon programs are extended with copies of the form $t_k \leftarrow \{\perp, \texttt{tfr}, \texttt{stw}\}\, t_s$ after the definition of t_s in a register and $t_d \leftarrow \{\perp, \texttt{tfr}, \texttt{ldw}\}\, t_k$ before the use of t_d in a register, for all temporaries t_s, t_d not pre-assigned to a reserved register such as the return address register R31. Figure 5(a) shows the example given in Figure 2(b) where loads and stores are extended as copies that can be implemented by alternative instructions.

Example. Figure 4 shows the factorial function from Figure 1 in LSSA form extended with copies. Temporary t_1, whose live range spans all blocks in Figure 1, is split into the congruent local temporaries t_1, t_7, and t_{18} in Figure 4. The global relation between LSSA temporaries is solely captured by the congruences displayed on the arcs.

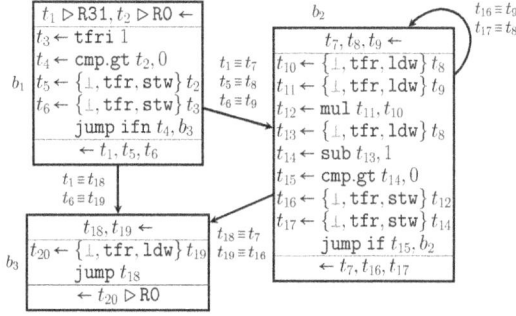

Figure 4. Function in LSSA extended with copies.

3. Alternative Temporaries

The program representation described in Section 2 yields a register allocation model that suffers from the limitations of spill-everywhere and basic coalescing [3, Section 6]. For example, optimizing the spill code in Figure 2(b) requires substituting the temporary t_3 for t_4 in the second use. Basic interference precludes ultimate coalescing as same-value temporaries cannot substitute each other. For example, coalescing temporaries t_1 and t_2 in Figure 3(a) requires substituting t_1 for t_2. In both cases, the program representation lacks the flexibility to substitute temporaries.

Alternative temporaries extend the capabilities of combinatorial register allocation by enabling spill code optimization and ultimate coalescing. This is achieved by augmenting the program representation with *operands* as use and definition ports in operations. Congruences, preassignments, and operation uses and definitions are lifted from temporaries to operands. Temporaries hold the values transferred among operations by *connecting* to the corresponding def- and use-operands. For example, the operation $t' \leftarrow \mathtt{abs}\ t$ is transformed to $p' : t' \leftarrow \mathtt{abs}\ p : t$ where p and p' are operands connected to the temporaries t and t'. Operands can be connected to alternative temporaries that hold the same value to determine how the value is transferred among the corresponding operations. For example, if a second temporary t'' holds the same value as t, the operation above is transformed to $p' : t' \leftarrow \mathtt{abs}\ p : \{t, t''\}$ where either t or t'' can be connected to p. Examples in the paper omit operand identifiers when possible, for example as $t' \leftarrow \mathtt{abs}\ \{t, t''\}$.

Alternative temporaries enable the substitution of temporaries. For example, Figure 2(d) shows the alternative temporaries needed to optimize the spill code. If operand p is connected to temporary t_3, then t_4 is not used and the second load operation is discarded. As for the ultimate coalescing example, Figure 3(c) shows the alternative temporaries required to coalesce t_1 and t_2. If operand p is connected to temporary t_1, then t_2 is not used and the copy is discarded. In both cases, the proper temporary connections yield the intended results shown in Figures 2(c) and 3(b).

Construction. A program with alternative temporaries is constructed by replacing each occurrence of a temporary t with an operand p and a set of alternative temporaries that hold the same value as t and can thus be connected to p. This set can be effectively approximated by all temporaries that are copy-related to t. Figure 5(b) shows the alternative temporaries that correspond to the example given in Figure 5(a). This and all subsequent code examples are linearized for presentation purposes; no ordering among operations is imposed. For example, the second load operation in Figure 5(b) could actually be scheduled before the first one in the generated assembly code.

Discarding invalid connections. In the most general form, an operand that replaces a temporary t can be connected to any temporary that holds the same value as t. For example, operand p_1 in Figure 5(b) replaces an occurrence of t_2 in Figure 5(a) and can thus

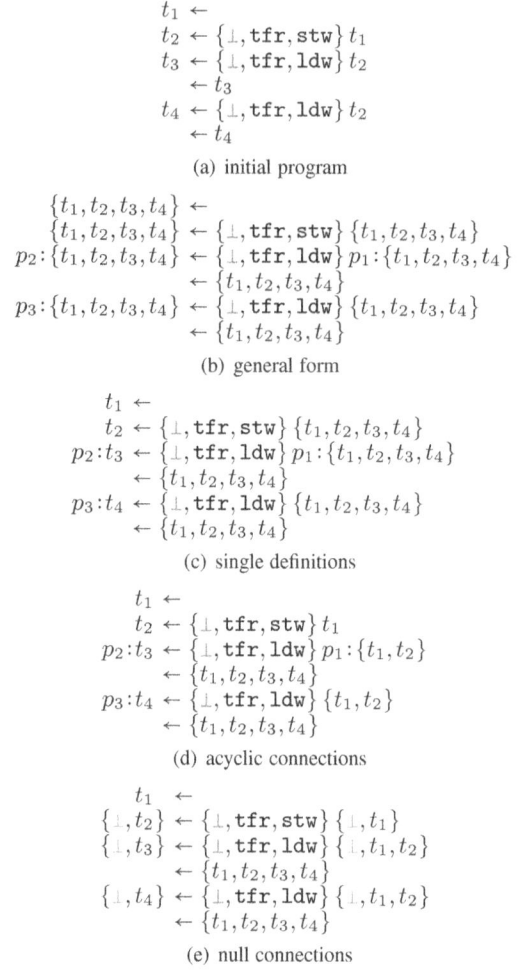

$$t_1 \leftarrow$$
$$t_2 \leftarrow \{\bot, \mathtt{tfr}, \mathtt{stw}\}\ t_1$$
$$t_3 \leftarrow \{\bot, \mathtt{tfr}, \mathtt{ldw}\}\ t_2$$
$$\leftarrow t_3$$
$$t_4 \leftarrow \{\bot, \mathtt{tfr}, \mathtt{ldw}\}\ t_2$$
$$\leftarrow t_4$$

(a) initial program

$$\{t_1, t_2, t_3, t_4\} \leftarrow$$
$$\{t_1, t_2, t_3, t_4\} \leftarrow \{\bot, \mathtt{tfr}, \mathtt{stw}\}\ \{t_1, t_2, t_3, t_4\}$$
$$p_2 : \{t_1, t_2, t_3, t_4\} \leftarrow \{\bot, \mathtt{tfr}, \mathtt{ldw}\}\ p_1 : \{t_1, t_2, t_3, t_4\}$$
$$\leftarrow \{t_1, t_2, t_3, t_4\}$$
$$p_3 : \{t_1, t_2, t_3, t_4\} \leftarrow \{\bot, \mathtt{tfr}, \mathtt{ldw}\}\ \{t_1, t_2, t_3, t_4\}$$
$$\leftarrow \{t_1, t_2, t_3, t_4\}$$

(b) general form

$$t_1 \leftarrow$$
$$t_2 \leftarrow \{\bot, \mathtt{tfr}, \mathtt{stw}\}\ \{t_1, t_2, t_3, t_4\}$$
$$p_2 : t_3 \leftarrow \{\bot, \mathtt{tfr}, \mathtt{ldw}\}\ p_1 : \{t_1, t_2, t_3, t_4\}$$
$$\leftarrow \{t_1, t_2, t_3, t_4\}$$
$$p_3 : t_4 \leftarrow \{\bot, \mathtt{tfr}, \mathtt{ldw}\}\ \{t_1, t_2, t_3, t_4\}$$
$$\leftarrow \{t_1, t_2, t_3, t_4\}$$

(c) single definitions

$$t_1 \leftarrow$$
$$t_2 \leftarrow \{\bot, \mathtt{tfr}, \mathtt{stw}\}\ t_1$$
$$p_2 : t_3 \leftarrow \{\bot, \mathtt{tfr}, \mathtt{ldw}\}\ p_1 : \{t_1, t_2\}$$
$$\leftarrow \{t_1, t_2, t_3, t_4\}$$
$$p_3 : t_4 \leftarrow \{\bot, \mathtt{tfr}, \mathtt{ldw}\}\ \{t_1, t_2\}$$
$$\leftarrow \{t_1, t_2, t_3, t_4\}$$

(d) acyclic connections

$$t_1 \leftarrow$$
$$\{\bot, t_2\} \leftarrow \{\bot, \mathtt{tfr}, \mathtt{stw}\}\ \{\bot, t_1\}$$
$$\{\bot, t_3\} \leftarrow \{\bot, \mathtt{tfr}, \mathtt{ldw}\}\ \{\bot, t_1, t_2\}$$
$$\leftarrow \{t_1, t_2, t_3, t_4\}$$
$$\{\bot, t_4\} \leftarrow \{\bot, \mathtt{tfr}, \mathtt{ldw}\}\ \{\bot, t_1, t_2\}$$
$$\leftarrow \{t_1, t_2, t_3, t_4\}$$

(e) null connections

Figure 5. Step-by-step construction of alternative temporaries.

be connected to any of the same-value temporaries $\{t_1, t_2, t_3, t_4\}$. However, many of the potential combinations of connections in this form are invalid. For example, the def-operands p_2 and p_3 in Figure 5(b) cannot be connected to the same temporary t since that would define t twice. Likewise, the operands p_1 and p_2 cannot be connected to the same temporary since that would create a *connection cycle* where an operation uses its own definition. Such invalid connections are discarded to simplify the program representation as well as the combinatorial model in Section 4. The discarding process consists of two steps:

(1) *Single definitions* selects, for each temporary t, a single def-operand to which t can be connected. Figure 5(c) illustrates how enforcing single definitions prevents multiple definitions of the same temporary. For example, the two def-operands p_2 and p_3 in Figure 5(c) cannot be connected to the same temporary as is permitted in Figure 5(b). Enforcing single definitions discards some valid combinations such as connecting p_2 to t_4 and p_3 to t_3 in Figure 5(b). However, for each valid combination that is discarded a structurally equivalent permutation remains in the program representation. For example, connecting p_2 to t_3 and p_3 to t_4 is structurally equivalent to the combination mentioned above since t_3 and t_4 are interchangeable in all potential connections with use-operands.

(2) *Acyclic connections* discards combinations of temporary connections potentially leading to *connection cycles*. In a connection cycle, an operation o uses a temporary that depends on o's own

26

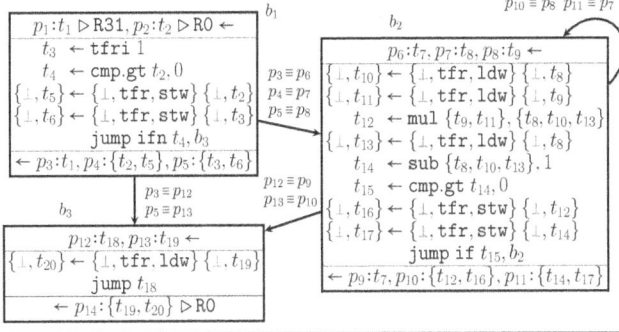

Figure 6. Function with alternative temporaries.

definition:

$$t_1 \leftarrow t_0;\ t_2 \leftarrow t_1;\ \ldots;\ t_n \leftarrow t_{n-1};\ t_0 \leftarrow t_n$$

Figure 5(d) illustrates how acyclic connections are enforced. For example, the operand p_1 in Figure 5(d) cannot be connected to temporary t_3 to create a cycle as is permitted in Figure 5(c). Enforcing acyclic connections preserves temporaries as alternatives in the operations where they originally appear. For example, temporary t_2 appears as a use of the second copy in Figure 5(a) and thus the potential connection of operand p_1 to t_2 is preserved in Figure 5(d). This property maintains the support gained by copy extension to handle problems such as spilling or preassignments.

Null connections. After invalid connections are discarded, null connections (denoted as $\bot$) are inserted as alternatives for copy operands to indicate that their corresponding copies can be discarded. A temporary potentially defined by a copy is *live* iff the copy is active as explained in Section 2.4. Figure 5(e) shows the final result after the insertion of null connections.

Example. Figure 6 shows the factorial function from Figure 4 augmented with alternative temporaries. For example, the second use-operand of the sub operation in block b_2 can be connected to three alternative temporaries: t_8, t_{10}, and t_{13}. These temporaries hold the same value since they are copy-related. The arc labels and delimiter operations illustrate how congruences and preassignments are lifted from temporaries to operands.

To summarize, alternative temporaries enable combinatorial spill code optimization and ultimate coalescing. The program representation includes operands as use and definition ports in operations. Alternative connections between operands and temporaries control the route followed by values among operations.

4. Combinatorial Model

This section incrementally describes the integrated combinatorial model for register allocation and instruction scheduling. The model introduces variables and constraints that capture alternative temporaries and enable spill code optimization and ultimate coalescing.

The combinatorial model is parameterized with respect to a program with alternative temporaries and a processor description. A program is described by the following parameters: a set of blocks B, operations O, operands P, and temporaries T; the function operands(o) that gives the operands of operation o; the function temps(p) that gives the temporaries that can be connected to operand p; and the predicate use(p) that indicates whether p is a use operand. Parameters that describe the processor and additional program parameters are introduced as needed.

4.1 Register Allocation

A solution to the register allocation problem corresponds to an assignment of the register allocation variables that satisfies Constraints 1-8 below. The register allocation variables are: a_o and i_o for each operation o to indicate whether o is *active* and which *instruction* implements it; l_t and r_t for each temporary t to indicate whether t is *live* and to which *register* it is assigned; and y_p for each operand p to indicate which *temporary* is connected to it.

The temporary connection variables and their related Constraints 1-4 are the essential improvements over the model presented by Castañeda *et al.* [3]. Each new y_p variable indicates which temporary is connected to the operand p among a set of alternative temporaries temps(p). Through these variables the combinatorial model can leverage the optimization opportunities enabled by the program representation with alternative temporaries. Although a new dimension of decision variables is introduced which yields an exponential growth of the solution space, the new model scales equally to that of Castañeda *et al.* as shown in Section 6.

Alternative temporaries and active operations. A temporary t is live iff it is used (that is, connected to some use-operand p):

$$l_t \iff \exists p \in P : (\text{use}(p) \wedge y_p = t) \quad \forall t \in T \quad (1)$$

The *single definitions* step in the construction of alternative temporaries forces each temporary t to be connectable to exactly one def-operand. The operation that contains this operand is given by definer(t) and is active iff t is live:

$$a_{\text{definer}(t)} \iff l_t \quad \forall t \in T \quad (2)$$

Active operations are connected to temporaries and are implemented by non-null instructions:

$$a_o \iff y_p \neq \bot \quad \forall o \in O,\ \forall p \in \text{operands}(o) \quad (3)$$

$$a_o \iff i_o \neq \bot \quad \forall o \in O \quad (4)$$

Unified register array and instruction selection. The combinatorial model is based on a unified register array where its elements can be either processor registers from different banks or a practically infinite number of *memory registers* (representing memory locations on the runtime stack) [3, Section 4.1]. In this abstraction memory registers form a *register class* in the same way as the rest of register subsets that are interchangeable for some instruction.

Instructions access their operands in certain register classes as determined by the processor. The processor parameter class(i, p) gives the register class of operand p if its operation is implemented by instruction i. The instruction that implements an operation determines the register class to which its operands are allocated:

$$r_{y_p} \in \text{class}(i_o, p) \quad \forall o \in O,\ \forall p \in \text{operands}(o) \quad (5)$$

Register assignment and packing. Register assignment maps non-interfering temporaries to registers. The combinatorial model captures register assignment according to the basic definition of interference. It relies on alternative temporaries to avoid solutions where same-value temporaries are simultaneously live, effectively delivering ultimate coalescing. This yields a simple geometric representation of register assignment that can be exploited by existing global constraints in constraint programming.

Local register assignments can be projected onto a rectangular area as described by Castañeda *et al.* [3, Section 4.1] and illustrated by the figure to the left. The horizontal dimension represents the registers in the unified register array, and the vertical dimension represents time in clock cycles. Each live temporary t yields a rectangle with width$(t) = 1$ (the width is later redefined for register packing). The top and bottom coordinates of t reflect the live start (ls_t) and end (le_t) cycles, which correspond to the issue cycles of t's definer and last user. The horizontal coordinate represents the register

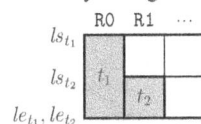

27

to which the temporary is assigned. For register allocation in isolation, live ranges are given as program parameters. For the model extended with instruction scheduling these are variables that depend on the computed schedule as described in Section 4.2.

In this representation, two live temporaries (for example, t_1 and t_2 above) interfere iff their rectangles overlap vertically. The non-overlapping rectangles constraint disjoint2 [17] forces such interfering temporaries to be assigned to different registers:

$$\text{disjoint2}(\{\langle r_t, r_t + \text{width}(t) \times l_t, ls_t, le_t\rangle : t \in T(b)\}) \quad \forall b \in B \quad (6)$$

where the program parameter $T(b)$ gives the temporaries in block b.

As Section 2 explains, certain operands are preassigned to registers. The temporaries connected to such operands are preassigned to the corresponding registers:

$$r_{y_p} = \mathbf{r} \quad \forall p \in P : p \triangleright \mathbf{r} \quad (7)$$

Register packing is readily captured by this representation as explained by Castañeda *et al.* Registers are decomposed into register *atoms*. An atom is the minimum part of a physical register that can be referenced by an operation (for example, R5 in Hexagon). Each column in the unified register array corresponds to an atom, where atoms representing different parts of a larger register are adjacent. $\text{width}(t)$ is redefined as a processor parameter giving the number of atoms that temporary t occupies. The variable r_t represents the first of the atoms to which t is assigned. Enforcing non-interference among live temporaries assigned to the same register (Constraint 6) thus becomes isomorphic to rectangle packing.

Global Register Allocation. In LSSA with alternative temporaries, blocks are solely related by operand congruences, which leads to a direct extension of the local problem [3, 20]. The program parameter $p \equiv q$ indicates that operands p and q are congruent. Congruent operands are assigned to the same register:

$$r_{y_p} = r_{y_q} \quad \forall p, q \in P : p \equiv q \quad (8)$$

4.2 Instruction Scheduling and Bundling

An *issue cycle* variable c_o is defined for each operation o. A solution to the instruction scheduling problem corresponds to an assignment of the issue cycle variables that satisfies Constraints 9-12 below. Instruction bundling for VLIW processors such as Hexagon is captured by interpreting sets of operations issued in the same cycle as bundles. The live start (ls_t) and end (le_t) of a temporary t are variable in the integrated register allocation and instruction scheduling problem, as they depend on the issue cycle of the definer and users of t. More specifically, the live range of a temporary t starts at the issue cycle of its definer:

$$l_t \implies ls_t = c_{\text{definer}(t)} \quad \forall t \in T \quad (9)$$

and ends with the last issue cycle of its users:

$$l_t \implies le_t = \max_{o \in \text{users}(t)} c_o \quad \forall t \in T \quad (10)$$

where $\text{users}(t)$ gives the operations that contain a use-operand connected to t.

If a temporary t is not used and hence not live (Constraint 1) its live start and end variables are unconstrained. This does not compromise the correctness of the model since these variables only matter if t is live (Constraint 6).

Precedences. The processor parameter $\text{lat}(\mathbf{i})$ gives the latency with which instruction $\mathbf{i}$ defines its resulting temporaries. An operation that uses a temporary t can only be issued after the issue cycle plus the latency of the definer of t:

$$a_o \implies c_o \geq c_{\text{definer}(y_p)} + \text{lat}(i_{\text{definer}(y_p)})$$
$$\forall o \in O, \forall p \in \text{operands}(o) : \text{use}(p) \quad (11)$$

Processor resources. Operations share limited processor resources such as functional units and data buses. They are described by the following processor parameters: a set of resources R; the functions $\text{con}(\mathbf{i}, \mathbf{r})$ and $\text{dur}(\mathbf{i}, \mathbf{r})$ that give the units of a resource $\mathbf{r}$ consumed by instruction $\mathbf{i}$ and the cycles during which $\mathbf{r}$ is consumed; and the function $\text{cap}(\mathbf{r})$ that gives the capacity of resource $\mathbf{r}$ in number of units. The capacity of each processor resource cannot be exceeded at any issue cycle. This structure is naturally captured as a task-resource model with a cumulative constraint [17] for each block and processor resource. Each cumulative constraint includes a task for each operation o in the block where the consumption and duration are zero if o is implemented by the null instruction:

$$\text{cumulative}(\{\langle c_o, \text{con}(i_o, \mathbf{r}), \text{dur}(i_o, \mathbf{r})\rangle : o \in O(b)\}, \text{cap}(\mathbf{r}))$$
$$\forall b \in B, \forall \mathbf{r} \in R \quad (12)$$

where the program parameter $O(b)$ gives the operations in block b.

4.3 Optimization criteria

Code generation typically aims at solutions that are as good as possible for some optimization criterion such as speed, code size, or energy consumption. Traditional heuristic algorithms embed such optimization criteria implicitly into decisions. For example, traditional list scheduling [16] issues operations as early as possible under the implicit assumption that this yields compact schedules. Unlike heuristic algorithms, the model captures different optimization criteria accurately and unambiguously in a generic minimization objective function:

$$\sum_{b \in B} \text{weight}(b) \times \text{cost}(b)$$

where $\text{weight}(b)$ and $\text{cost}(b)$ give the weight and estimated cost of block b. Note that also non-linear objective functions are possible but for the purpose of this paper linear functions are sufficient. To optimize for speed, $\text{weight}(b)$ is set to $\text{freq}(b)$ (a program parameter giving the estimated execution frequency of block b), and $\text{cost}(b)$ is defined as $\max_{o \in O(b):a_o} c_o$. To optimize for code size, $\text{weight}(b)$ is disregarded and $\text{cost}(b)$ is defined as $\sum_{o \in O(b)} \text{con}(i_o, \text{bits})$, where the processor resource bits represents the bits with which instructions are encoded. Optimization criteria such as energy consumption can be modeled analogously.

4.4 Limitations

While the introduced combinatorial model captures a wide array of register allocation and instruction scheduling subproblems (as demonstrated in Section 7), it still exhibits some limitations to be addressed in the future.

Unpredictable processor features like cache memories lead to instruction latencies which are unknown at compilation time. As is common in combinatorial approaches, the introduced model assumes the best-case for such latencies and relies on pipeline stalling to handle worse cases. This assumption may underestimate the contribution of unknown latencies to the objective function.

The introduced model does not permit to move operations across blocks, which limits the amount of exploitable instruction-level parallelism. Existing combinatorial models of global instruction scheduling could be integrated with our approach [14, 22].

In some cases it is beneficial to recompute (that is, *rematerialize*) a reused value rather than occupying a register until its later use, or spilling. The model does not currently support rematerialization, but alternative temporaries may allow its incorporation following the approach of Goodwin and Wilken [10].

28

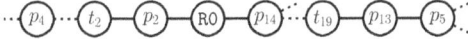

Figure 7. Subgraph of the connection graph G for Figure 6.

5. Code Generator

This section describes *Unison*, a constraint-based code generator for the model introduced in Section 4 that features robust and scalable optimization by using presolving and decomposition techniques that exploit properties of the program representation. Unison is implemented on top of the constraint programming system Gecode [9].

Presolving. Presolving techniques reformulate combinatorial problems to boost the robustness of the solving process. Unison uses an array of dedicated presolving techniques, including: generating *implied constraints* (logically redundant constraints that improve propagation), computing lower bounds by solving *problem relaxations* where some constraints are excluded, and detecting and removing redundant solutions to avoid unnecessary search.

A common approach to generate implied constraints is by negating *nogoods* – combinations of variable assignments that cannot hold together. This paper introduces *connection nogoods* as a particularly effective presolving technique. A connection nogood is a conjunction of connections of the form $y_p = t$. The generation process consists of two steps:

(1) A *connection graph* G (Figure 7 shows an example) is constructed from a LSSA function with alternative temporaries. G contains a node for each operand, temporary, and pre-assigned register, and two classes of edges: *must-connect* edges (solid) relating congruent operands, operands and registers in preassignments, and operands and temporaries whose connection is forced by single-alternatives; and *may-connect* edges (dotted) relating operands with the temporaries that may be connected to them.

(2) Nogoods are derived by analyzing G as follows. Two distinct nodes *interfere* if both of them are either registers, or use- or def-operands of the same operation. For example, p_4 and p_5 in Figure 7 interfere since both are use-operands of the bottom delimiter operation of b_1. Interfering nodes cannot be transitively connected. Suppose that there is a path in G between two interfering nodes that crosses k may-connect edges $(p_1, t_1), \ldots, (p_k, t_k)$. Then the problem has no solution if the operands and temporaries in all k may-connect edges in the path are connected. This derives $y_{p_1} = t_1 \wedge \ldots \wedge y_{p_k} = t_k$ as a connection nogood.

For example, in Figure 7 there is a path between p_4 and p_5 that crosses the may-connect edges (p_4, t_2) and (p_{14}, t_{19}), yielding the nogood $y_{p_4} = t_2 \wedge y_{p_{14}} = t_{19}$.

Problem decomposition. Unison exploits properties of LSSA to decompose the problem as introduced in Castañeda *et al.* [3], which increases its scalability and gives it *anytime behavior* – solutions are found in increasing quality as code generation runs.

LSSA temporaries are live in single blocks and only indirectly related to temporaries from other blocks by congruences on *global* operands. Global operands belong to the delimiter operations inserted during LSSA construction. For example, the global operands in Figure 6 are $\{p_1, p_2, \ldots, p_{14}\}$. The register variables of these operands are related by congruence constraints in the combinatorial model (Constraint 8). Once these variables are assigned, the rest of the register allocation and instruction scheduling problem can be solved independently for each block.

Unison exploits this observation to proceed iteratively as shown by Figure 8: (1) A SSA function is transformed to LSSA, extended with copies, and augmented with alternative temporaries; (2) the function is translated into a problem according to the model introduced in Section 4 and presolved with the techniques introduced above; (3) a *global problem* is solved by assigning the register vari-

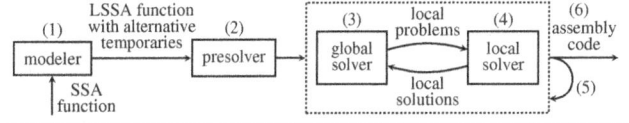

Figure 8. Architecture of the *Unison* code generator.

able r_{y_p} of each global operand p such that all constraints are satisfied. Search in the global solver is arranged in two phases: *global allocation* and *global assignment*, under a global time limit. Global allocation selects a register class (possibly memory) for each set of congruent global operands G in decreasing size of G. A cost-benefit analysis determines the register class to which the selected set G is allocated first. The benefit component estimates the saved spilling overhead, while the cost component is based on an estimate of the increased register pressure. This analysis is parameterized with an *aggressiveness* factor to guide the allocation towards either the benefit or the cost component. Global assignment selects a particular register from the register class allocated to each set G; (4) a *local problem* is solved for each block b by assigning its remaining variables such that all but the congruence constraints are satisfied and $\text{cost}(b)$ is minimized. A *search portfolio* is used to increase the robustness of the local solver, where up to five complementary search strategies are applied sequentially until an optimal local solution is found or a local time limit is reached. All search strategies are arranged in multiple phases, typically starting with the active (a_o), instruction (i_o) and temporary (y_p) variables; following with the issue cycle variables (c_o); and finishing with the register variables (r_t). (5) the solutions to the global and local problems are combined into a full solution s and a new iteration is run from (3), increasing the aggressiveness of the global solver and constraining future solutions to be better than s according to the objective function in Section 4.3; and (6) when optimality is proven or a time limit is reached, assembly code is generated according to the last full solution (which, by construction, is the best one found).

6. Experimental Evaluation

This section presents experimental results on different characteristics of Unison: code quality improvements; the impact of using alternative temporaries and presolving techniques; scalability and runtime behavior; and using different optimization criteria.

Setup. As input for the experiments we use MediaBench, a benchmark suite widely employed in embedded compiler research [13]. Ten medium-size functions (from 25 to 1000 instructions) are sampled from each signal-processing application included in the benchmark suite (jpeg, mpeg, gsm, g721, epic, adpcm), with the exception of adpcm where only five functions are available. The purpose of sampling is to shorten the runtime of the experimental evaluation while conserving a set of functions that is representative of the benchmark. Cluster sampling is applied on each application by randomly selecting a function from each cluster, computed by a 10-means analysis. Functions are clustered by size (in number of input LLVM operations) and register pressure (approximated as the fraction of temporaries spilled by LLVM's register allocator).

Each function is compiled and optimized using the LLVM 3.3 compiler infrastructure with the -O3 flag, and Hexagon V4 instructions are selected using LLVM's instruction selector. Due to limitations in the current interface between our prototype and LLVM, certain low-level CFG and alias analysis optimizations in LLVM are disabled to ensure an accurate comparison. However, these optimizations are all orthogonal to the combinatorial model itself; in fact, disabling them is disadvantageous to the constraint-based approach which has more potential to leverage instruction-level parallelism by considering the full solution space. The following flags, prefixed with `-disable-`, are used: `post-ra`, `tail-duplicate`, `branch-fold`, `block-placement`, `phi-elim-edge-splitting`, and `hexagon-cfgopt`.

The evaluation uses the number of execution cycles (*cycles* for short) of a generated assembly function as a measure of its quality. This number is estimated statically according to the speed criterion defined in Section 4.3; lack of post-code-generation support and limited access to Hexagon development tools prevent us from measuring the actual number of execution cycles. The execution frequency freq is estimated by LLVM's code generator.

The global and local solvers in Unison are implemented on top of the constraint programming system Gecode 4.2.1. On each function Unison runs for ten iterations (the decision for this number will become clear when discussing the runtime behavior). Every iteration has a global time limit of $7 * i$ ms, where i is the number of operations in the function, and a local time limit of 25 s. The experiments are run with a single thread on a Linux machine equipped with an Intel Xeon E5607 2.27 GHz processor and 24 GB of RAM. All results are averaged over 10 repetitions. The maximum coefficient of variation for the average solving time and code quality (speed or code size) for all functions is 1.6% and 0.3%, respectively.

Code quality compared to traditional approaches. We compare the quality of the code generated by Unison with that of the code generated by LLVM as a representative of traditional, staged approaches. LLVM solves register allocation and local instruction scheduling by priority-based coloring [6] and list scheduling [16]. Global instruction scheduling is not yet available in LLVM.

The results indicate that our approach delivers code of significantly better quality than LLVM for the MediaBench sample. Figure 11(a) shows the cycle improvement using our approach over LLVM for each of the 55 functions. Unison improves code quality for 39 functions (up to 40.9%), and produces inferior code for 7 functions (down to −7.0%), yielding a geometric mean (GM) improvement of 7.1%. Optimal solutions are found for 16 functions.

The best cases typically correspond to functions that contain large blocks and multiple function calls. Unison can efficiently handle the former by advanced VLIW bundling and the latter by integrated handling of ABI preassignments, packing, and spill code optimization. Three of the worst cases (for `run_length_decode_zeros`, `decode_mcu`, and `decode_mcu_AC_first`) are affected by the lack of rematerialization in the combinatorial model, as discussed in Section 4.4. This limitation explains why Unison's solution for `run_length_decode_zeros` is optimal but worse than LLVM's. The remaining inferior cases are due to incomplete communication between the global and the local solver of the decomposition introduced in Section 5.

Impact of alternative temporaries on code quality. Alternative temporaries allow the generation of better code by enabling spill code optimization and ultimate coalescing. To measure this benefit we compare the cycles of optimal solutions found for the model with alternative temporaries against those found for the model without from Castañeda *et al.* [3].

The comparison demonstrates that alternative temporaries have indeed a positive impact on code quality. Figure 9 shows the cycle improvement given by the model with alternative temporaries, for the functions solved to optimality. In the cases indicated with vertical dots only a lower bound of the improvement could be computed. The use of alternative temporaries improves code quality for 16 out of the 26 functions solved to optimality (up to 10.8%), yielding a GM improvement of 2.2%. No solution is worse, which confirms the hypothesis that using alternative temporaries can only improve code quality.

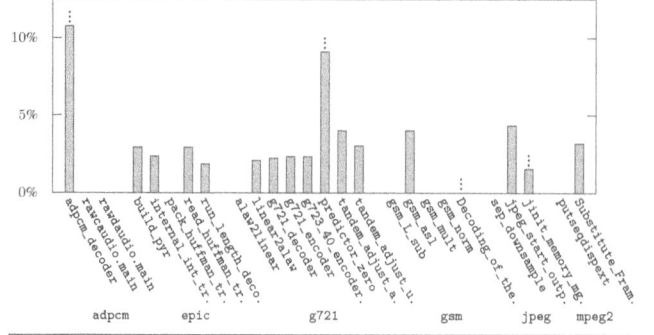

Figure 9. Cycle improvement over the model from Castañeda *et al.* for optimal solutions. Vertical dots indicate lower bounds.

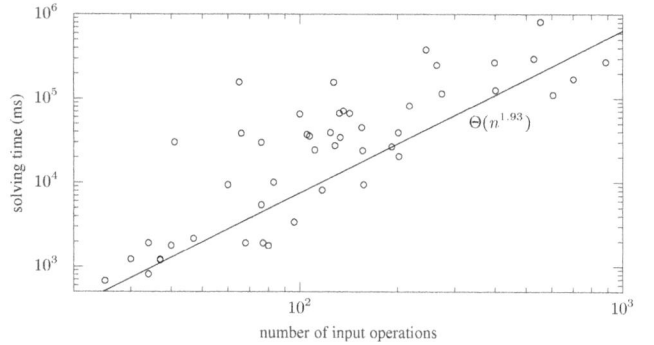

Figure 10. Time to reach LLVM code quality vs. input size.

Impact of presolving on robustness. Section 5 introduces presolving techniques to make code generation more robust. To measure the impact of these techniques we compare the results obtained in the first experiment (*code quality compared to traditional approaches*) with a similar experiment where presolving is disabled.

The results confirm that the presolving techniques are indeed essential for Unison's robustness: without them, 6 out of the 55 functions cannot be solved at all, and the code quality of the solved functions decreases drastically. The number of functions for which Unison improves code quality drops from 39 to 28 (up to 40.9% for `predictor_zero`) and the number of inferior cases grows from 7 to 15 (down to −40.4% for `g723_40_encoder`). The GM improvement over LLVM decreases considerably, from 7.1% down to 0.2%. Also, only 8 optimal solutions can be found.

Scalability. To quantify the scalability of Unison we measure the solving time to generate code that is on par with LLVM in terms of cycles. For each function, Unison iterates until the solution quality is at least as good as that of LLVM. The 7 functions which cannot reach the baseline quality are excluded from the experiment.

The measurements demonstrate that Unison is scalable. Figure 10 shows the solving time to generate as good code as LLVM. The figure reveals an average computational complexity that is approximately quadratic in the number of input operations – a least square analysis gives $\Theta(n^{1.93})$. This scalable behavior is due to the combination of decomposition, presolving, and time limits.

A similar figure is presented by Castañeda *et al.* which suggests that their code generator can handle functions approximately four times larger, but they measure the number of operations after the input is extended with copies, a process that inflates the size by an average factor of 3.1. Furthermore, they only report results for MIPS32 – a simple, single-issue processor. In other words, even with spill code optimization and ultimate coalescing our model scales as well as the model of Castañeda *et al.* Compared to LLVM, however, Unison is still orders of magnitude slower.

30

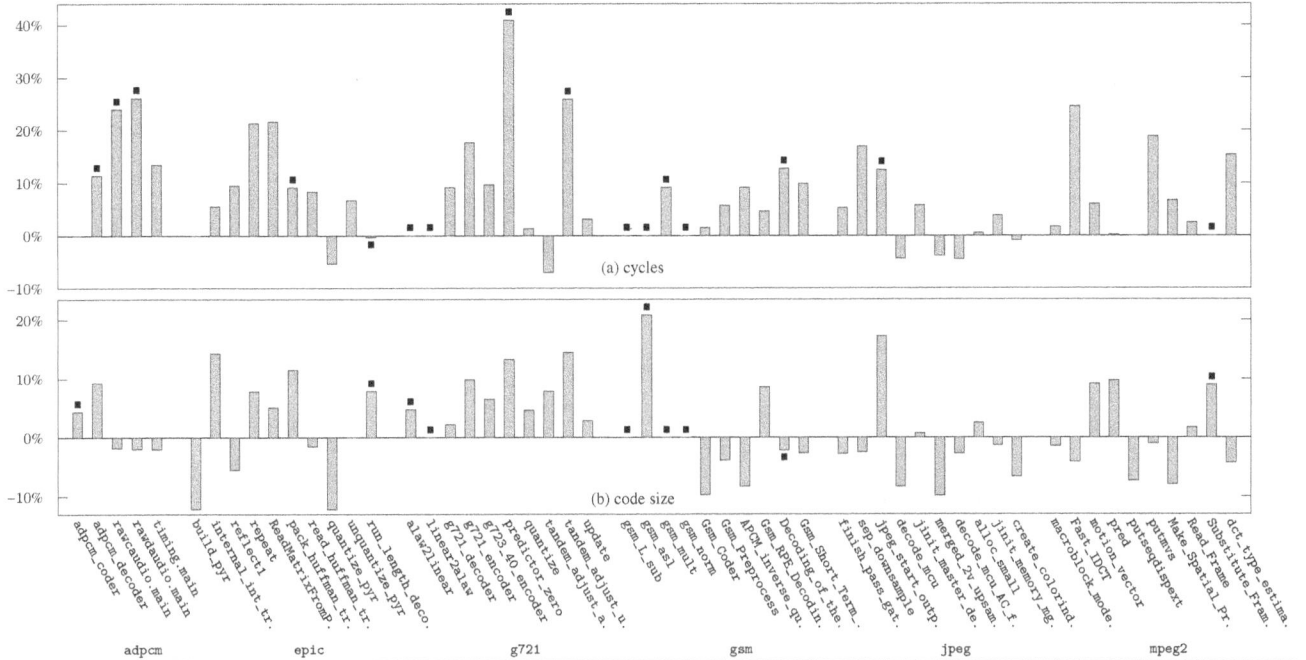

Figure 11. Cycle and code size improvement over LLVM. Negative bars means that results are worse, and ■ indicates optimal solutions.

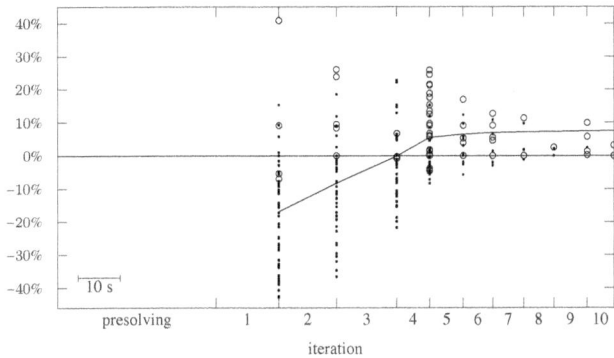

Figure 12. Cycle improvement over LLVM per iteration. In every iteration a dot corresponds to the best solution found per function. When a function cannot be improved further by Unison, the last solution is indicated by a circle in the iteration it was found. The curve shows the cycle improvement across all functions. The horizontal range is proportional to the average time of each iteration.

Runtime behavior. To study how Unison behaves as it runs, we measure the time spent and its quality improvement over LLVM for each iteration. The results indicate that Unison has a reasonable anytime behavior, in which each iteration progressively delivers better code. Figure 12 demonstrates this runtime behavior. Three stages can be identified in an average run of Unison: first, presolving together with the first iteration deliver an initial solution (taking 39.9% of the total runtime). This delay is mostly due to presolving; then, iterations two to four drastically improve the code quality (7.4% in average, taking 27.0% of the total runtime); finally, the code quality appears to converge, and the remaining iterations only improve the code quality marginally (0.4% in average, taking the remaining 28.3% of the runtime). This convergent behavior motivates running ten iterations for the experiments.

Impact of different optimization criteria on robustness. The combinatorial model can be easily adjusted to optimize for different criteria, as described in Section 4.3. To study the robustness

of Unison for different optimization criteria, we switch to code size optimization and compare the size of the code generated by Unison with that of the code generated by LLVM. The LLVM intermediate optimizer and code generator are run with the flags -Oz and -O2, respectively. The latter is chosen as the highest optimization level that does not trade larger code size for higher speed since LLVM's code generator does not support explicit code size optimization.

The results demonstrate that Unison robustly adapts to different optimization criteria. Figure 11(b) shows the size improvement using our approach over LLVM for each function. Unison is already competitive with LLVM even though no effort has been invested in tuning it for code size optimization. Among the 55 functions our approach improves code size for 25 functions (up to 20.8%), and produces larger code size for 25 functions (down to −12.2%), yielding a slight GM improvement of 1.2%. Optimal solutions are found for 10 functions. As above, `Decoding_of_the_coded_Log_Area_Ratios` is optimal because Unison's model does not include rematerialization.

7. Related Work

There is a significant body of research on solving the three main code generation problems (instruction selection, register allocation, and instruction scheduling) with combinatorial optimization techniques, both with integrated models and in isolation. Table 1 summarizes the characteristics of the most prominent approaches that handle register allocation. The approaches are classified into three groups: those which also integrate instruction scheduling and selection (top), instruction scheduling only (middle); or solve register allocation in isolation (bottom).

Among the integrated approaches (top and middle), only those of Wilson *et al.* [20], Castañeda *et al.* [3], and this paper support global register allocation. The three approaches handle it by constraints that assign related, inter-block temporaries to the same register. Furthermore, this paper is the first integrated approach that features ultimate coalescing and, together with Castañeda *et al.*, the only integrated approach that features register packing.

approach	TC	SO	CO	GL	RP	MB	RM	SC	SL
Wilson [20]	IP	-	basic	✓	-	-	-	✓	✓
Gebotys [8]	IP	✓	-	-	-	✓	-	✓	✓
Bashford [2]	CP	✓	basic	-	-	✓	-	✓	✓
Eriksson [7]	IP	-	-	-	-	✓	-	✓	✓
Chang [5]	IP	✓	-	-	-	-	-	✓	-
Kästner [11]	IP	-	-	-	-	-	-	✓	-
Nagarakatte [14]	IP	✓	-	-	-	-	-	✓	-
Castañeda [3]	CP	-	basic	✓	✓	✓	-	✓	-
(this paper)	**CP**	✓	**ultimate**	✓	✓	✓	-	✓	-
Goodwin [10]	IP	✓	basic	✓	✓	-	✓	-	-
Appel [1]	IP	✓	-	✓	-	-	-	-	-
Scholz [18]	PBQP	-	ultimate	✓	✓	-	-	-	-
Krause [12]	DP	✓	basic	✓	✓	-	✓	-	-

Table 1. Related combinatorial approaches: *TeChnique (Integer, Constraint, Partitioned Boolean Quadratic, and Dynamic Programming), Spill code Optimization, COalescing, GLobal register allocation, Register Packing, Multiple register Banks, ReMaterialization, instruction SCheduling, and instruction SeLection.*

Isolated register allocation approaches (bottom) exploit knowledge about the selected instructions and the computed schedule to formulate simpler models and capture more subproblems than the integrated ones. For example, Scholz and Eckstein's model derives constraints from temporary interferences [18], which is only possible if an instruction schedule is assumed. It is worth noticing that this paper only lacks rematerialization to match the features of the isolated approaches. All other integrated approaches provide at least two features less than their isolated counterparts.

The combinatorial model introduced in this paper builds on the work by Castañeda *et al.* by incorporating spill code optimization and ultimate coalescing, while retaining the original robustness for medium-size functions. Furthermore, while Castañeda *et al.* demonstrate the capabilities of their approach on a simple MIPS32 processor this paper reports results for Hexagon, a more challenging processor with VLIW capabilities and different-width registers.

The concept of alternative temporaries is related to the idea of *alternative implementations* by Wilson *et al.* [20]. Alternative implementations consist of groups of operations among which the integer programming solver must choose one for execution. This abstraction is exploited to generate spill code and register-to-register copies, and to select array addressing instructions. Unfortunately, the publications by Wilson *et al.* [20, 21] do not provide enough detail to determine to which extent *alternative temporaries* and *alternative implementations* are related.

8. Conclusion and Future Work

This paper has introduced a program representation and combinatorial model of register allocation and instruction scheduling that use alternative temporaries to enable spill code optimization and ultimate coalescing. The model is shown to be scalable and robust while matching, for the first time, the features of traditional heuristic approaches. Thorough experiments on a real-world DSP demonstrate that the approach can be easily adapted to different optimization criteria and generates better code than heuristics and previous combinatorial approaches.

Future work. There is considerable future work towards combinatorial code generation. A first step is to address the limitations identified in Section 4.4. Furthermore, the runtime behavior can be improved by integrating different solving techniques, including randomization and search restarts for robustness, large neighborhood search for scalability, and computation of stronger bounds with integer programming for shorter solving time.

Acknowledgments

This research has been partially funded by LM Ericsson AB and the Swedish Research Council (VR 621-2011-6229). The authors are grateful for helpful comments from Frej Drejhammar, Peter A. Jonsson, Ingo Sander, and the anonymous reviewers.

References

[1] A. W. Appel and L. George. Optimal spilling for CISC machines with few registers. *SIGPLAN Not.*, 36:243–253, May 2001.

[2] S. Bashford and R. Leupers. Phase-coupled mapping of data flow graphs to irregular data paths. *Design Automation for Embedded Systems*, pages 119–165, Mar. 1999.

[3] R. Castañeda Lozano, M. Carlsson, F. Drejhammar, and C. Schulte. Constraint-based register allocation and instruction scheduling. In *CP*, volume 7514 of *LNCS*, pages 750–766. Springer, 2012.

[4] G. J. Chaitin, M. A. Auslander, A. K. Chandra, J. Cocke, M. E. Hopkins, and P. W. Markstein. Register allocation via coloring. *Computer Languages*, 6(1):47–57, 1981.

[5] C.-M. Chang, C.-M. Chen, and C.-T. King. Using integer linear programming for instruction scheduling and register allocation in multi-issue processors. *Computers Math. Applic.*, 34:1–14, Nov. 1997.

[6] F. Chow and J. Hennessy. Register allocation by priority-based coloring. *SIGPLAN Not.*, 19(6):222–232, June 1984.

[7] M. V. Eriksson, O. Skoog, and C. W. Kessler. Optimal vs. heuristic integrated code generation for clustered VLIW architectures. In *SCOPES*, 2008.

[8] C. H. Gebotys. An efficient model for DSP code generation: Performance, code size, estimated energy. In *ISSS*, pages 41–47. IEEE, 1997.

[9] Gecode Team. Gecode: generic constraint development environment. www.gecode.org, 2006.

[10] D. W. Goodwin and K. D. Wilken. Optimal and near-optimal global register allocations using 0-1 integer programming. *Software – Practice and Experience*, 26:929–965, Aug. 1996.

[11] D. Kästner. PROPAN: A retargetable system for postpass optimisations and analyses. In *LCTES*, volume 1985 of *LNCS*, 2001.

[12] P. K. Krause. Optimal register allocation in polynomial time. In *CC*, volume 7791 of *LNCS*, pages 1–20. Springer, 2013.

[13] C. Lee, M. Potkonjak, and W. H. Mangione-Smith. MediaBench: A tool for evaluating and synthesizing multimedia and communications systems. In *MICRO-30*, pages 330–335. IEEE, 1997.

[14] S. G. Nagarakatte and R. Govindarajan. Register allocation and optimal spill code scheduling in software pipelined loops using 0-1 integer linear programming formulation. In *CC*, volume 4420 of *LNCS*, pages 126–140. Springer, 2007.

[15] *Hexagon V4 Programmer's Reference Manual*. Qualcomm Technologies, Inc., Aug. 2013.

[16] B. R. Rau and J. A. Fisher. Instruction-level parallel processing: history, overview, and perspective. *J. Supercomput.*, 7:9–50, May 1993.

[17] F. Rossi, P. van Beek, and T. Walsh. *Handbook of Constraint Programming*. Elsevier, 2006.

[18] B. Scholz and E. Eckstein. Register allocation for irregular architectures. *SIGPLAN Not.*, 37:139–148, June 2002.

[19] V. Sreedhar, R. Ju, D. Gillies, and V. Santhanam. Translating out of static single assignment form. In *SAS*, volume 1694 of *LNCS*, pages 849–849. Springer, 1999.

[20] T. Wilson, G. Grewal, B. Halley, and D. Banerji. An integrated approach to retargetable code generation. In *ISSS*, pages 70–75. IEEE, 1994.

[21] T. Wilson, G. Grewal, S. Henshall, and D. Banerji. An ILP-based approach to code generation. In *Code Generation for Embedded Processors*, pages 103–118. Springer, 2002.

[22] S. Winkel. Optimal versus heuristic global code scheduling. In *MICRO-40*, pages 43–55. IEEE, 2007.

Cache-Related Preemption Delay Analysis for FIFO Caches

Clément Ballabriga   Lee Kee Chong   Abhik Roychoudhury

National University of Singapore

{clementb,cleekee,abhik}@comp.nus.edu.sg

Abstract

Hard real-time systems are typically composed of multiple tasks, subjected to timing constraints. To guarantee that these constraints will be respected, the Worst-Case Response Time (WCRT) of each task is needed. In the presence of systems supporting preemptible tasks, we need to take into account the time lost due to task preemption. A major part of this delay is the Cache-Related Preemption Delay (CRPD), which represents the penalties due to cache block evictions by preempting tasks. Previous works on CRPD have focused on caches with Least Recently used (LRU) replacement policy. However, for many real-world processors such as ARM9 or ARM11, the use of First-in-first-out (FIFO) cache replacement policy is common.

In this paper, we propose an approach to compute CRPD in the presence of instruction caches with FIFO replacement policy. We use the result of a FIFO instruction cache categorization analysis to account for single-task cache misses, and we model as an Integer Linear Programming (ILP) system the additional preemption-related cache misses. We study the effect of cache related timing anomalies, our work is the first to deal with the effect of timing anomalies in CRPD computation. We also present a WCRT computation method that takes advantage of the fact that our computed CRPD does not increase linearly with respect to the preemption count. We evaluated our method by computing the CRPD with realistic benchmarks (e.g. drone control application, robot controller application), under various cache configuration parameters. The experimentation shows that our method is able to compute tight CRPD bound for benchmark tasks.

Categories and Subject Descriptors   D.2.4 [*Software Engineering*]: Software/Program Verification

Keywords   CRPD; FIFO caches; WCRT; timing anomalies

1. Introduction

In real time systems, the execution time of a real time program must be *predictable* and *consistent* to ensure reliability and safety of the system. The Worst Case Execution Time (WCET) of a program is a bound on the maximum execution time of the program over all possible executions. WCET analysis is used to bound the WCET of a program to verify that all required timing constraints are met. The micro-architecture on which the program executes is a significant factor in WCET analysis, as a program can have different execution time depending on the underlying hardware. Thus, the timing bound obtained from WCET analysis is significantly improved by modeling the underlying micro-architecture components such as caches, pipeline and branch predictor.

Conventionally WCET analysis assumes an *uninterrupted* sequential execution of the program being analyzed. However, in reality many real time systems run in a *multi-tasking* environment, in which different programs (or tasks) are scheduled to run concurrently. For system with *pre-emptive priority scheduling*, a task can be interrupted by another task which has a higher priority to run. Therefore, it is impractical to assume that a program is always allowed to run uninterrupted. There could be an additional delay imposed on a running task due to interruption by another task. This delay is caused by changes to the micro-architectural states of the system by the interrupting task. For example, the interrupting task may replace some cache blocks in the caches. Caches are small but fast memories, used to bridge the performance gap between a processor and the main memory. Set-associative caches are divided into fixed-size *sets*. Each set can hold up to A different blocks from the main memory (A is called the cache associativity level). When a block needs to be added to a cache set that is already full , a *replacement policy* is used to determine the evicted block. Caches are at least an order of magnitude faster than the main memory, thus the changes to cache content due to an interrupting task is a major factor in the delay caused by the interruption. This delay is known in the literature as *Cache Related Preemption Delay* (CRPD). CRPD analysis techniques have been proposed to put a bound on CRPD.

In this paper we will concentrate on obtaining the bound on CRPD for set-associative caches with *First-In First-Out* (FIFO) replacement policy. Traditionally, CRPD analysis bounds the additional cache misses introduced by preemptions through the following two factors: (i) number of cache blocks introduced by the preempting task (i.e. Evicting Cache Block or ECB), and (ii) number of cache blocks that may be reused by the preempted task after preemption (i.e. Useful Cache Block or UCB). Existing work on CRPD analysis focus on caches with Least Recently Used (LRU) replacement policy. A study [4] shows that these factors cannot safely bound CRPD cost for FIFO caches, due to the presence of *unbounded timing effect* for FIFO caches. A single evicted memory block from cache due to preemption can cause unbounded number of additional cache misses after the preemption. Thus, the concepts of ECB and UCB cannot be used to safely bound CRPD cost for FIFO caches. These concepts do not work for FIFO caches because they try to bound the number of additional concrete cache misses. Instead, our CRPD analysis relies on information from the underlying cache analysis for computing WCET. We utilize *static phase detection* [7] technique to obtain the set of memory blocks that are categorized as *always hit* in the cache assuming no preemption. We solve the maximum number of additional cache misses introduced by the *always hit* blocks as an *integer linear programming* (ILP)

LCTES '14,   June 12–13, 2014, Edinburgh, United Kingdom.
Copyright © 2014 ACM 978-1-4503-2877-7/14/06. . . $15.00.
http://dx.doi.org/10.1145/2597809.2597814

problem, given a bound on the total number of preemptions. Our analysis is safe as we conservatively introduce miss penalty for all memory blocks not classified as *always hit*.

We also studied the possible effects of *timing anomalies* on CRPD analysis in general. Existing CRPD analysis techniques assume an underlying micro-architecture model that is free from timing anomalies. However, such assumption may render the CRPD analysis unsound, as the worst-case delay is underestimated. In this work, we studied three types of timing anomalies exhibited by out-of-order processors or FIFO caches [13]. We take these timing anomalies into consideration in our CRPD analysis and show that our analysis is safe in the presence of these timing anomalies. To the best of our knowledge, ours is the first work on CRPD analysis that explicitly handles architectures exhibiting timing anomalies.

We implemented our FIFO CRPD analysis in Chronos [11], an open source WCET analysis tool. We have tested our analysis method on several subject programs, and compare the results with a state-of-the-art approach. The state-of-the-art approach to handle CRPD analysis with FIFO instruction caches is by computing the CRPD assuming LRU replacement policy, and bound the value for FIFO policy using the concept of *relative competitiveness* [16]. Our experimental results show that, when compared to current CRPD analysis technique for FIFO caches, we are able to compute significantly tighter bound on CRPD cost for all subject programs.

2. Background

FIFO caches CPU caches are generally small in size and they can be filled up with memory blocks rapidly and frequently. There needs to be a *replacement policy* to decide the exact memory blocks that should be discarded (*i.e.* replaced by newly inserted memory blocks) when a cache set is full. *First-In First-Out* or FIFO is one such replacement policies. FIFO caches are used in CPU architectures such as ARM9 and ARM11.

In general, FIFO caches always replace a memory block that has been in the cache set the longest, as shown in Figure 2 (this figure assumes that all represented blocks are mapped to the same set).

$$[d, c, b, a] \xrightarrow{e} [e, d, c, b] \xrightarrow{a} [a, e, d, c] \xrightarrow{a} [a, e, d, c]$$

Figure 2: Effect of a memory sequence *eaa* on a cache set for FIFO policy. First memory access e causes a cache miss, and block a is evicted since it is the first memory block inserted in the cache set. Similarly for the second memory access a, block b is replaced. There is no change to the cache state when there is a cache hit (as shown by the third memory access).

Timing anomalies In general, timing anomaly describes a counter-intuitive observation, in which a local worst case timing behaviour does not entail a global worst case timing behaviour. Certain micro-architectural features exhibit timing anomalies. For example, a cache hit can cause a higher execution time than a cache miss in a processor with out-of-order execution [13]. This may affect the soundness of WCET analysis that models the underlying hardware.

Work in [12] and [5] shows that FIFO caches exhibit timing anomaly due to *unbounded timing effect*. With FIFO caches, if some memory block access in a program results in a cache miss, then the cache miss outcome will not necessarily lead to the maximal cache miss count for the overall program. An example is shown in Figure 1. Let us consider that we have a 2-way FIFO instruction cache. Here, the first access to c is a cache miss in the general case (*i.e.* the initial cache state does not contain any block from the example). In this case, the overall cache miss count is 5. However, if we alter the initial cache state to make sure that the first access to c is a cache hit, the overall cache miss count is increased to 6.

3. Methodology

In this section, we present our method for CRPD computation in the presence of FIFO caches. Our method seeks to return a bound on the number of additional cache misses for a task T_0, which is preempted by another task up to MPC (Maximum Preemption Count) times. We assume that the preempting task shares cache sets with T_0. The CRPD of T_0 is simply the maximum number of additional cache misses (caused by preemption) multiplied by the cache miss penalty. Our method uses concepts from *static phase detection* [7], which is an approach to statically categorize FIFO instruction cache accesses without considering preemption. We shall briefly describe static phase detection, then we shall explain how our analysis can use the information produced by static phase detection to compute CRPD.

3.1 Static phase detection

Static phase detection is a method to statically categorize each instruction as *always hit*, *always miss*, or *not classified*, in the presence of an instruction cache with FIFO replacement policy. The analysis works by detecting *phases* in instruction cache accesses.

Let B be a set of memory blocks that are mapped to the same cache set, and let $|B|$ be the number of pairwise different blocks in B. A B-phase is an access sequence such that *(i)* $|B| \leq A$ (A being the cache associativity) and *(ii)* all blocks in B and only the blocks from B are accessed (*i.e.* a block can be accessed more than once in the phase, as long as all blocks from B are accessed). After exactly $|B|$ B-phases, it is guaranteed that all the blocks from B are loaded in the cache. Therefore, subsequent accesses to blocks in B are guaranteed to be cache hits.

This allows us to categorize some instructions in a program as *always hit*, if those instructions will always be cache hits during runtime. Let I be an instruction in the program. For all paths in the control flow graph (CFG) leading to I, if the cache accesses immediately preceding I can be partitioned into $|B|$ B-phases where B contains I's cache block, then I is classified as *always hit*. Conversely, if there exists a path leading to I that cannot be partitioned into $|B|$ B-phases where B contains I's cache block, then execution along this path can lead to a cache miss when I's cache block is accessed. In this case, I is categorized as *not classified*.

3.2 Phase content

Static phase detection does not consider the effect of task preemption. Any instruction that is classified as *always hit* by static phase detection may cause cache misses in case of preemption. The goal of our analysis is to bound the number of cache misses occurring in *always hit* instructions due to preemption. We do not take into account cache misses occurring in instructions classified as *always miss* or *not classified* under the assumption that those cache misses will already be taken into account in the computation of WCET.

Since an *always hit* instruction has, on all incoming paths, an access sequence that can be partitioned into $|B|$ B-phases, cache misses can occur if a preemption disrupt these access sequences. Thus, the first step of our analysis is to compute the *phase content* for all *always hit* instructions.

DEFINITION 3.1. *(Phase content). The phase content of an instruction I, denoted as $PC(I)$, is the minimal set of instructions such that for any path p from the program entry point to I, there exists a sub-path p' leading to I that contains only instructions from $PC(I)$, and whose access sequence can be partitioned into $|B|$ B-phases where B contains I's cache block.*

If a preemption occurs at any instruction in $PC(I)$, the preemption may disrupt the access sequence leading to instruction I in a way that causes cache misses for I. An example is shown in Figure 3. We consider a FIFO cache with an associativity of 2. In the

$$[?, ?] \xrightarrow{\mathbf{a}} [a, ?] \xrightarrow{\mathbf{c}} [c, a] \xrightarrow{\mathbf{a}} [c, a] \xrightarrow{\mathbf{b}} [b, c] \xrightarrow{\mathbf{c}} [b, c] \xrightarrow{\mathbf{a}} [a, b] \xrightarrow{\mathbf{b}} [a, b] \xrightarrow{\mathbf{c}} \quad \text{total : 5 misses}$$

$$[c, ?] \xrightarrow{\mathbf{a}} [a, c] \xrightarrow{\mathbf{c}} [a, c] \xrightarrow{\mathbf{a}} [a, c] \xrightarrow{\mathbf{b}} [b, a] \xrightarrow{\mathbf{c}} [c, b] \xrightarrow{\mathbf{a}} [a, c] \xrightarrow{\mathbf{b}} [b, a] \xrightarrow{\mathbf{c}} \quad \text{total : 6 misses}$$

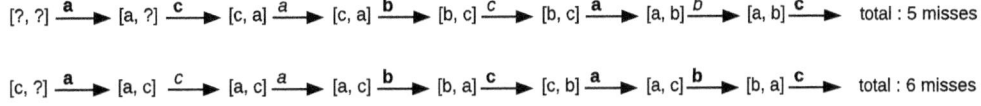

Figure 1: FIFO cache timing anomaly example. For the memory access sequence at the bottom, the entry cache state causes a cache hit for the first access to c, but this causes the overall cache miss count to be greater than the memory access sequence on top.

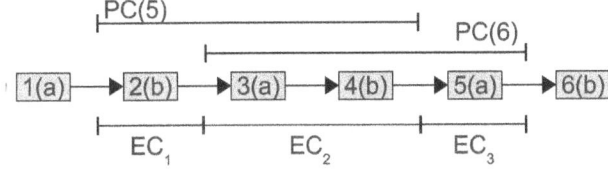

Figure 3: Phase contents and equivalence classes

figure, the nodes of the CFG are *l-blocks*. An *l-block* is a maximal sequence of instructions such that each instruction is in the same basic block, and mapped to the same cache block. As with basic blocks, it is possible to connect *l-blocks* using edges to represent the control flow. Each *l-block* in the figure is labeled with $x(y)$, where x refers to the node number and y refers to the mapped cache block set. *l-blocks* 5 and 6 are classified as *always hit*, because they are executed after two phases containing cache blocks $[a, b]$. The figure shows the phase contents for *l-blocks* 5 and 6. If a preemption occurs in the code delimited by $PC(5)$ (resp. $PC(6)$), an additional cache miss may occur in *l-block* 5 (resp. *l-block* 6).

3.3 Equivalence classes

Let us define PC^{-1} as follows:

$$I' \in PC^{-1}(I) \Leftrightarrow I \in PC(I')$$

In other words, if a preemption occurs at instruction I, it may cause additional misses for instructions in the set $PC^{-1}(I)$. Let us define the equivalence relation $\sim$, as follows:

$$I \sim I' \Leftrightarrow PC^{-1}(I) = PC^{-1}(I')$$

Let SI be the set of all instructions in a program, and let $(SI/\sim) = \{EC_1, ..., EC_N\}$ be the set of N equivalence classes defined by the equivalence relation $\sim$. We also define $PC^{-1}(EC_k)$ as the result of applying $PC^{-1}()$ function to any instruction in EC_k.

To bound the maximum number of additional cache misses due to preemption, we first need to bound, for each equivalence class $EC_k \in (SI/\sim)$, the number of preemptions occurring inside it (*i.e.* occurring at an instruction in that equivalence class). We only need to bound the preemption count for each equivalence class, and not for each individual instruction. This is based on the observation that if two instructions I_1 and I_2 are in the same equivalence class EC_1, then $PC^{-1}(EC_1) = PC^{-1}(I_1) = PC^{-1}(I_2)$. This means that a preemption occurring at either I_1 or I_2 will have the same effect on the additional cache misses. Then, the bound for additional cache misses of each *always hit* instruction can be expressed as a function of the preemption count for each equivalence class.

Figure 3 shows the partitioning of the CFG according to the equivalence classes. In this example, the equivalence classes $\{EC_1, EC_2, EC_3\}$ are computed based on the phase contents for *l-blocks* 5 and 6 only. A preemption occurring in EC_1 (resp. EC_3) may add one cache miss for *l-block* 5 (resp *l-block* 6), and a preemption occurring in EC_2 may add one cache miss for both *l-blocks* 5 and 6.

3.4 ILP formulation

We bound the additional cache miss count using an ILP system. We make use of the ILP system computed by the main WCET analysis (containing, for example, the structural constraints derived from the program CFG), and we add additional CRPD-related constraints to it. We first describe how to bound the preemption count for each equivalence class, and then we show how to express the bounds on the number of cache misses for each *always hit* instruction.

For each equivalence class $EC_k \in (SI/\sim)$, an ILP variable ec_k is created. This variable represents the number of times a preemption occurs at an instruction contained in the equivalence class EC_k. The ec_k variables are bounded as follows:

$$\sum_{k \in [1;n]} ec_k \leq MPC$$

MPC is the maximum preemption count of the preempting task. MPC is a parameter of the analysis, and is considered a constant from the point of view of the ILP system.

For each *always hit* instruction I_k, an ILP variable xpm_k is created to represent the number of cache misses (due to preemption) for I_k. xpm_k is created only if the cache set containing I_k is also used by the preempting task (otherwise the preempting task cannot evict the cache block containing I_k). Instruction I_k may cause cache miss only if a preemption occurs at an instruction from an equivalence class EC_k such that $I_k \in PC^{-1}(EC_k)$. Thus, the number of cache misses for I_k can be bounded using the bounds on the maximum preemption count in each equivalence class:

$$xpm_k \leq \sum_{\forall j / I_k \in PC^{-1}(EC_j)} ec_j$$

Each xpm_k variable must also be bounded by the execution count of the basic block containing I_k. This can be achieved by the constraint $xpm_k \leq x_k$, where x_k represents the execution count of the basic block. We assume that x_k already exists in the ILP system computed by the main WCET analysis.

Finally, the maximum number of additional cache misses due to preemption is found by solving the following objective function:

$$maximize \sum_{\forall k / I_k \in SI} xpm_k$$

We will show a simple example using the CFG in Figure 3. The additional cache misses due to preemption for *l-blocks* 5 and 6 are represented by ILP variables xpm_5 and xpm_6 respectively. Equivalence classes ec_1 and ec_2 contribute additional cache misses for *l-block* 5, while equivalence classes ec_2 and ec_3 contribute additional cache misses for *l-block* 6. The total preemption count in all equivalence classes is bounded by the maximum preemption count, MPC (set to 1 in this case). Thus, we have the following ILP constraints :

$$xpm_5 \leq ec_1 + ec_2$$
$$xpm_6 \leq ec_2 + ec_3$$
$$ec_1 + ec_2 + ec_3 \leq 1$$

Maximizing the number of additional cache misses ($xpm_5 + xpm_6$) with an ILP solver yields the following result:

$$ec_1 = 0,\ ec_2 = 1,\ ec_3 = 0,\ xpm_5 = 1,\ xpm_6 = 1$$

It shows that the preemption should occur in equivalence class EC_2 to cause maximum additional cache miss count (two additional misses; one for *l-block* 5 and one for *l-block* 6).

3.5 Computing the WCRT

In this section, we will show how to get the Worst-Case Response Time (WCRT) of a task, based on our CRPD computation method. We assume a *fixed-priority preemptive scheduling* of a set of periodic tasks with possibility of nested preemptions. The ILP system constructed in section 3.4 can be used to compute the CRPD between two tasks for any number of preemptions, based on the MPC parameter. Let us define:

$$crpd(T_i, T_j, n) = addmiss(T_i, T_j, n) \times penalty$$

$crpd(T_i, T_j, n)$ is the estimated CRPD when task T_j preempts task T_i for n preemptions (the n parameter is optional, and defaults to 1 if omitted). $addmiss(T_i, T_j, n)$ is the bound on the additional cache misses for n preemptions of T_i by T_j (as computed using the ILP system, while setting MPC to n). $penalty$ bounds the increase in execution time when a cache miss occurs.

Traditionally, CRPD is computed for one preemption, and then this result is multiplied with the preemption count in the WCRT computation formula. However, that may be pessimistic, since although we have $n \times crpd(T_i, T_j) \geq crpd(T_i, T_j, n)$, in the general case we do not have $n \times crpd(T_i, T_j) = crpd(T_i, T_j, n)$. This is because there is a finite number of program points where a preemption can cause a large number of cache misses. Once these program points are taken by preemptions, additional preemptions cannot contribute as much to the CRPD.

In this paper, we discuss on the WCRT computation of a task using two approaches - *Fixed CRPD approach* and *Iterative approach*. In the former approach, we will have to run the CRPD computation only once (for one preemption). In the latter approach, we have to iteratively re-compute the CRPD each time the maximum preemption count is updated, during the fixed-point calculation. Each approach has its advantages and drawbacks, as discussed in the next subsections.

3.5.1 Fixed CRPD approach

In this approach, we compute the CRPD for one preemption, and use the result as it is done traditionally to compute the WCRT. The following equation computes the WCRT of task T_i, $WCRT_{Ti}$ until a fixed-point is reached:

$$WCRT_{Ti} = WCET_{Ti}$$
$$+ \sum_{\forall j \in hp(i)} \left\lceil \frac{WCRT_{Ti}}{PERIOD_{Tj}} \right\rceil (WCET_{Tj} + \gamma_{Ti,Tj}) \quad (1)$$

In Equation (1), $WCET_{Ti}$ is the computed WCET of task T_i. $\left\lceil \frac{WCRT_{Ti}}{PERIOD_{Tj}} \right\rceil$ bounds the number of preemptions by task T_j on task T_i, where $PERIOD_{Tj}$ is the period of task T_j. $hp(i)$ contains the set of tasks with higher priority than task T_i. Without considering nested preemption, we can simply define $\gamma_{Ti,Tj} = crpd(T_i, T_j)$. If nested preemptions are possible, then this is incorrect, because if task T_j preempts a task T_k which in turn preempts task T_i, then the CRPD of T_j preempting T_k is not taken into account. To solve this problem, we define γ function as such :

$$\gamma_{Ti,Tj} = crpd(T_i, T_j) + \sum_{\forall k / k \in hp(i) \wedge j \in hp(k)} crpd(T_k, T_j)$$

This approach has the advantage of being fast (we have to perform the CRPD computation only once), and easily adaptable to existing WCRT computation formula. Its main drawback is the introduction of pessimism.

3.5.2 Iterative approach

It is possible to take into account the real preemption count at each step of the fixed-point WCRT computation. With an iterative approach, the WCRT of each task is computed in order of decreasing priority. For each task, the maximum preemption count (MPC) by higher-priority tasks is computed, and is fed to the ILP system. This (intermediate) CRPD enables us to refine the maximum preemption count, and this process is repeated until a fixed-point is reached. Thus, this method gives a tighter result.

The main drawback of this approach is the analysis time, because we have to solve an ILP system at each step of the fixed-point WCRT computation. To mitigate this issue while still maintaining a relatively tight CRPD bound, it is possible to use a *hybrid approach*. The main idea is to use the iterative approach until some arbitrary time limit is reached. This will produce a temporary (underestimated) CRPD, since the analysis is not finished. Then, from this temporary value, we can compute the final (safe) CRPD bound in a non-costly way.

To describe this last step, we make the following observation: an increase in the maximum preemption count, $MPC_{increase}$, leads to an increase in the $CRPD$, $CRPD_{increase}$. As the maximum preemption counts get higher, the ratio $\frac{CRPD_{increase}}{MPC_{increase}}$ decreases (or remains equal). Because of this, the following property holds for all M (where M is the preemption count):

$$crpd(T_0, T_1, M + 1) - crpd(T_0, T_1, M) \leq$$
$$crpd(T_0, T_1, M) - crpd(T_0, T_1, M - 1)$$

Let M_1 be the maximum preemption count obtained when the time limit is reached. Based on the observation made above, for any M_2 greater than M_1, the following property holds :

$$crpd(T_0, T_1, M_2) - crpd(T_0, T_1, M_1) \leq$$
$$(crpd(T_0, T_1, M_1 + 1) - crpd(T_0, T_1, M_1)) \times (M_2 - M_1)$$

Therefore, once the iterative analysis has reached the time limit, it is possible to bound $crpd(T_0, T_1, M_2)$ for any M_2 greater than M_1, by the following value:

$$crpd(T_0, T_1, M_1) +$$
$$(crpd(T_0, T_1, M_1 + 1) - crpd(T_0, T_1, M_1)) \times (M_2 - M_1)$$

This allows us to compute the final WCRT by fixed-point iteration without having to solve a costly ILP system at each step. The computed WCRT will be tighter than the one computed with fixed CRPD approach, but less tight than the one computed with fully iterative approach. This hybrid approach is described in Algorithm 1.

3.6 Scalability

The ILP constraint generation described in section 3.4 produces a large number of constraints and variables, which causes a large ILP computation time. Ideally we want to decrease the number of ILP constraints and variables. The following observation can be made: for any *l-block* (recall that an *l-block* is a maximal sequence of instructions such that each instruction is in the same basic block, and in the same cache block) containing the sequence of instructions $(I_1, I_2, ..., I_n)$, the effect on cache misses will be the same if a preemption occurs in $[I_2; I_n]$, independently of the exact instruction. The reason for this is illustrated in Figure 4. In l-block 2, the instructions I_2 through I_5 are guaranteed to be cache hits, since the cache block is loaded in I_1. If a preemption occurs at any of these instructions and evicts the cache block, it will result in one

Algorithm 1 Iterative hybrid computation

1: $TL \leftarrow$ task list ordered by decreasing priority
2: **for** $i \in TL$ **do**
3:     $WCRT_i \leftarrow WCET_i$
4:     $change \leftarrow true$
5:     $flag \leftarrow false$
6:     **while** $change \wedge (WCRT_i \leq deadline_i)$ **do**
7:         **for** $j \in hp(i)$ **do**
8:             $MPC_{i,j} \leftarrow \lceil \frac{WCRT_i}{PERIOD_j} \rceil$
9:             **if** $flag$ **then**
10:                 $\gamma_{i,j} \leftarrow \gamma0_{i,j} + R \times (MPC_{i,j} - MPC0_{i,j})$
11:             **else**
12:                 $\gamma_{i,j} \leftarrow crpd(i, j, MPC_{i,j})$
13:             **end if**
14:         **end for**
15:         **if** $(time\ is\ up) \wedge \neg flag$ **then**
16:             **for** $j \in hp(i)$ **do**
17:                 $\gamma0_{i,j} \leftarrow \gamma_{i,j}$
18:                 $MPC0_{i,j} \leftarrow MPC_{i,j}$
19:                 $R \leftarrow crpd(i, j, MPC_{i,j} + 1) - \gamma0_{i,j}$
20:             **end for**
21:             $flag \leftarrow true$
22:         **end if**
23:         **for** $j \in hp(i)$ **do**
24:             $S_\gamma \leftarrow \sum\limits_{\forall k / k \in hp(i) \wedge j \in hp(k)} \gamma_{k,j}$
25:             $\gamma'_{i,j} \leftarrow MPC_{i,j} \times WCET_j + S_\gamma$
26:             $WCRT_i' \leftarrow WCET_i + \sum\limits_{\forall j \in hp(i)} \gamma'_{i,j}$
27:         **end for**
28:         $change \leftarrow (WCRT_i = WCRT_i')$
29:         $WCRT_i \leftarrow WCRT_i'$
30:     **end while**
31: **end for**

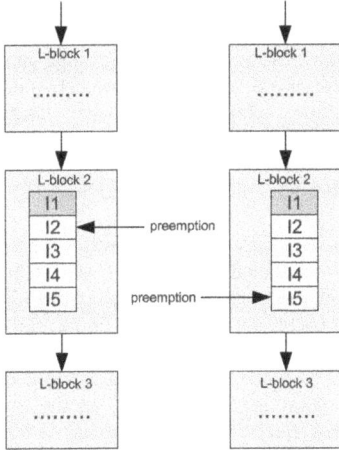

Figure 4: Preemption point equivalence

preemption-related miss, regardless of the specific instruction that is executing when the preemption occurs.

Based on this observation, it is possible to generate, for each l-block L_k, only two xpm variables: variable xpm_1 for the first instruction I_1 of the l-block, and variable xpm_2 for the second instruction I_2. Both variables are constrained by the expression $xpm_I \leq \sum_{\forall k / I \in PC^{-1}(EC_k)} ec_k$ as described in Section 3.4. Ad-

ditionally, variable xpm_1 is bounded by $xpm_1 \leq x_k$ (where x_k represents the execution count of l-block L_k, which is equal to the execution count of the basic block containing L_k). On the other hand, variable xpm_2 is bounded by $xpm_2 \leq x_k \times |instr(k) - 1|$, where $instr(k)$ is the set of instructions in the l-block L_k. This constraint represents the fact that variable xpm_2 counts additional cache misses not only for instruction I_2, but also for all instructions in the l-block except for I_1. This amounts to $|instr(k) - 1|$ instructions. As such, the maximum additional misses for these instructions is $|instr(k) - 1|$ each time l-block L_k is executed.

3.7 Handling timing anomalies

In this section, we will discuss three timing anomalies related to caches that may affect the safety of CRPD analysis in general. We shall refer to these timing anomalies as *Anomaly 1*, *Anomaly 2* and *Anomaly 3*. *Anomaly 1* and *Anomaly 2*, as mentioned in [13], may occur in the presence of an out-of-order processor. Mainly, a cache hit or miss may cause unexpected timing delay in the execution of instructions in the pipeline. *Anomaly 3* came from work in [3], which show that FIFO caches exhibit *domino effect*, in which a change in the cache state could potentially cause an unbounded timing delay. Thus, if an additional cache hit or miss is introduced due to preemption, a safe CRPD analysis should consider these unexpected timing delays. We also propose some solutions to handle the identified anomalies. It should be noted that the solutions are in general applicable to any CRPD analysis, with certain assumptions on the WCET analysis technique that is being used. We first state the necessary assumptions.

Assumptions about the WCET analysis Let us assume that a task T is defined as its control flow graph, $G_T = (B, E)$, where $B = \{LB_1, ..., LB_n\}$ is the set of *l-blocks* in task T, and E is the set of edges representing control flow between two l-blocks. Task T is then represented by an ILP system having a variable c_n (execution count) for each l-block $LB_n \in B$. For each l-block, two variables exists: th_n and tm_n, representing respectively the maximum execution time of that l-block in case of cache hit or cache miss. The ILP variables ch_n and cm_n represent the number of cache hits and misses, respectively, for l-block n. For each l-block n, an ILP constraint $ch_n + cm_n = c_n$ is generated. The $WCET$ and MC functions, to compute respectively the WCET of the task, and its total cache miss count (preemption-related or not), are defined as follows:

DEFINITION 3.2. *(WCET). The result $WCET(T)$ is defined as the maximized objective function $\sum_{\forall k \leq n} th_k \times ch_k + tm_k \times cm_k$, for the ILP system generated for task T.*

DEFINITION 3.3. *(MC). The miss count, noted $MC(T)$ is defined as the maximized objective function $\sum_{\forall k \leq n} cm_k$, for the ILP system generated for task T.*

For each of the three timing anomalies, we first give an example that illustrates the anomalous behaviour, then we proceed to propose a solution to handle the anomaly.

Anomaly 1: Miss penalties can be higher than expected The cache analysis used in WCET computation usually take cache misses into account by adding a fixed miss penalty for each miss. Simply making this miss penalty equal to the memory latency behind the cache can lead to WCET underestimation. Lundqvist et al. proved in [13] that in some cases, replacing a cache hit by a cache miss can increase the execution time by an amount greater than the memory latency.

Figure 5 shows an example, assuming a processor similar to the one used in the example in Figure 6. The cache miss while fetching instruction A causes instruction B to be scheduled later, after

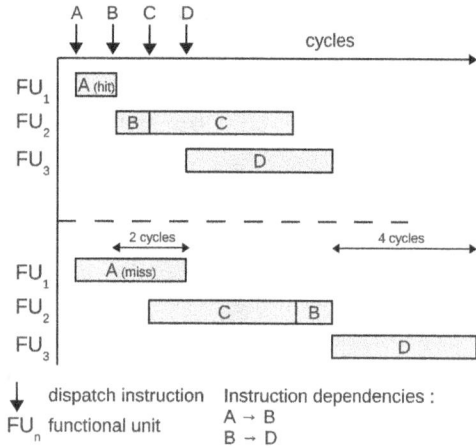

Figure 5: Miss penalty greater than memory latency

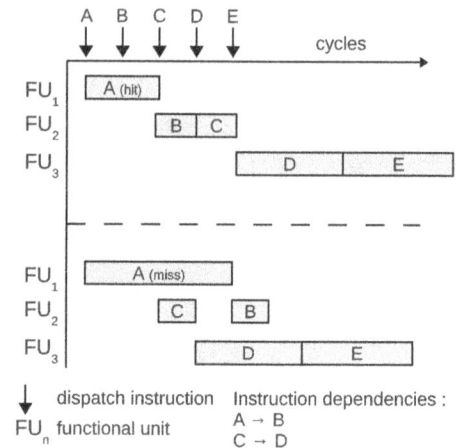

Figure 6: Hit resulting in longer time

instruction C. Since instruction D depends on B, the execution is delayed by 4 cycles (compared to the cache hit scenario), while the memory latency is only 2 cycles.

In order to avoid WCET underestimation due to this anomaly, we need to compute correctly the miss penalty for each potential cache miss. A sound way to do that is to compute the th_n and tm_n values for each *l-block* using a pipeline analysis approach (*e.g.* the *execution graph* method [10]). Then, the penalty is computed as shown in Definition 3.4 to avoid the problem described above. This penalty should be a sound over-approximation, since computing the exact th_n and tm_n values is generally infeasible.

DEFINITION 3.4. *(penalty). The miss penalty, penalty(T) is defined for a specific task T, as:*

$$penalty(T) \geq max(tm_n - th_n | n \in [1; N])$$

Anomaly 2: Cache hits can result in worst case timing The majority of cache-related analysis for WCET computation assume that, if the hit/miss classification of a memory access cannot be determined, the case leading to the WCET is the cache miss. Unfortunately, it has been shown by Lundqvist et al. [13] that it is not always true. In some cases, specifically in the presence of processors with out-of-order execution, replacing a cache miss by a cache hit can increase the execution time of an instruction sequence.

An example is shown in Figure 6, assuming an out-of-order execution processor, and an instruction sequence using three functional units. In this example, a cache miss while fetching the instruction A (shown in the lower half of the figure) causes instruction C to be scheduled earlier. Since instruction D depends on C, this causes the execution of the instruction sequence to finish one cycle earlier compared to the cache hit case. This effect can lead to unsafe CRPD analysis. For example, let us consider a preempted task, containing a l-block LB_k classified as *always miss*. A preemption can load the cache block of LB_k into the cache, causing cache hit for LB_k. Traditionally, CRPD analysis attempt to bound additional cache misses, but does not consider any additional cache hits due to preemption. If the execution time for LB_k is greater in case of cache hits, this effect will not be captured by the CRPD analysis, potentially leading to an unsafe WCET.

There is a trivial way to prevent WCET underestimation in this case, and another, more sophisticated way. The trivial way is to consider all *always miss* as *not classified* in the WCET analysis prior to the CRPD computation. This allows us to modify (without

any impact on the computed WCET) tm_n for each l-block as such:

$$tm_n \leftarrow max(tm_n, th_n) \qquad (2)$$

By doing this, we guarantee that tm_n is the worst possible time for the *l-block* n (including the scenario presented in Figure 6).

The other way is to include lost time due to additional cache hits in the CRPD computation. To do that, we define the *hit penalty* as $max(0, tm_n - th_n)$, and compute the maximum additional cache hits in the same way we computed the bound on the additional cache misses. This is done by modifying our CRPD analysis so that the phase content, $PC(I)$ is computed for each *always miss* instruction I (instead of *always hit*), and if a preemption occurs at an instruction in $PC(I)$, then I can cause cache hits. We did not implement the latter method as it makes a difference only for *l-blocks* showing a greater execution time for cache hits. That is quite rare in our observation, so the increase in precision is negligible.

Anomaly 3: Impact on WCET may not be bounded (Domino effect) In LRU caches, the effect of a change in cache state is *bounded*, because after any sequence of (at least) A different blocks mapping to the same cache set (on a A-way cache), the whole set is filled with blocks belonging to this sequence. As shown by C. Berg et al. [3], this is not true with FIFO caches. With FIFO caches, a cache state alteration can have unbounded repercussions in subsequent accesses.

Figure 7 shows an example with a 2-way set-associative FIFO cache. The edges are labeled with the concrete cache states at that program point, with the most recently loaded block located on the left. For the CFG on the left side of the figure, for even iteration numbers, accesses to a and c are hits; while for odd iteration numbers, accesses to b are hits, so there is 1.5 cache misses on average per loop iteration. For the CFG on the right, an access to block x is added. Each cache block access in the loop is now a cache miss. The additional access to block x adds, on average, 1.5 cache misses per loop iteration, and this effect is unbounded (except, of course, by the maximum loop iteration count).

This problem does not occur in our CRPD analysis, since the cache blocks involved in the domino effect would be categorized as *not classified* by the static phase detection step. However, this observation is not sufficient to ensure that this effect can be safely ignored in the general case. To handle the problem in the general case, we make the following observation: when dealing with WCET computation, we are assuming that no infinite path exists in the program. This is guaranteed by additional flow constraints, such as loop bounds. When computing the effect of a preemption on the

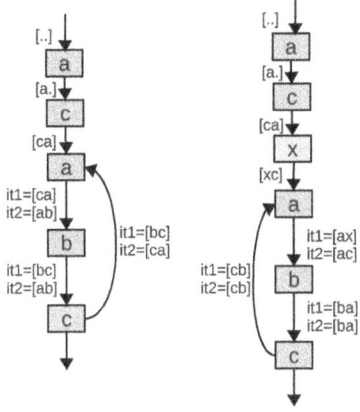

Figure 7: FIFO cache domino effect

miss count, we must take these constraints into account, in order to get a bounded result. The effect of a preemption on the miss count is captured by *addmiss* (defined in Definition 3.7), which allows us to ensure a bounded effect.

CRPD soundness We proceed to present a proof to guarantee the safety of our CRPD analysis. We have defined $WCET(T)$ in Definition 3.2. Let us further introduce $WCETPR(T_0, T_1, p)$ as the WCET of task $T0$ subject to cache interference due to preemption by task $T1$ at program point p, as defined in Definition 3.5. Let us also define $addmiss(T_0, T_1)$ in Definition 3.7, as the bound on the additional cache misses due to preemption of T_0 by T_1. Our concept of program path in a CFG is defined in Definition 3.6.

DEFINITION 3.5. *(WCETPR and MCPR). $WCETPR(T0, T1, p)$ is the computed WCET of task $T0$, such that the cache classification analysis is performed on the CFG $G_{T0,T1,p}$. This CFG results from the merging of the CFGs of $T0$ (preempted task) and $T1$ (preempting task), connected with call/return edges at program point p. Only the cache classification analysis is computed on $G_{T0,T1,p}$. The main WCET analysis is performed on $T0$ alone. The function $MCPR(T0, T1, p)$ is defined in a similar way for the miss count (recall that $MC(T)$ is defined in Definition 3.3).*

DEFINITION 3.6. *(path). A program path in a task T is defined as a function associating an execution count to each node in the CFG of T. The functions $WCET$, $WCETPR$, MC, and $MCPR$ are enhanced to accept a path as the last (optional) parameter. The effect of this optional path parameter is the creation of ILP constraints $\forall n, path(LB_n) = c_n$. We also note $path \in T$ if path is a valid path for the task T.*

DEFINITION 3.7. *(addmiss). $addmiss(T_0, T_1)$ is defined as:*

$$max(MCPR(T_0, T_1, p, path) - MC(T_0, path) | path \in T_0)$$

In other words, it is the maximum additional cache miss counted by the ILP solution, for any possible path through task T_0, and for any possible program point for preemption by task T_1. This does not represent the maximum number of additional concrete misses, but instead it is the difference of miss count as determined by the analysis. Since addmiss() is computed from the result of the ILP system, it takes into account the various flow control constraints that are needed to ensure that no infinite path exists within the program. Therefore, an implementation of addmiss() compatible with this definition will always yield a finite and safe bound on the number of additional cache misses, even in the presence of unbounded domino effect.

The following lemma states that the CRPD is sound if a preemption does not change the worst-case path for the preempted task.

LEMMA 3.1. *Let T_0 be a preempted task, and T_1 a preempting task. Then $\forall path \in T_0$:*

$$\forall p, WCETPR(T_0, T_1, p, path) \leq$$
$$WCET(T_0, path) + addmiss(T_0, T_1) \times penalty(T_0)$$

PROOF. Let $\sum_{\forall k \leq n} th_k \times ch'_k + tm_k \times cm'_k$ be the objective function for computing $WCETPR(T_0, T_1, p, path)$, and let $\sum_{\forall k \leq n} th_k \times ch_k + tm_k \times cm_k$ be the objective function for computing $WCET(T_0, path)$. ch'_k and cm'_k represent the number of cache hits and misses, respectively, for a l-block k in case of preemption. Therefore, $WCETPR(T_0, T_1, p, path) - WCET(T_0, path)$ is equal to the difference of the maximized objective functions:

$$\sum_{\forall k \leq n} th_k \times (ch'_k - ch_k) + tm_k \times (cm'_k - cm_k)$$

Since the worst-case path is unchanged by the preemption, we have $\forall k, c'_k = c_k$, and so the above can be rewritten as:

$$\sum_{\forall k \leq n} (cm'_k - cm_k) \times (tm_k - th_k)$$

We need to make the following assumption :

$$\forall n, th_n \leq tm_n \tag{3}$$

Therefore, we have :

$$\sum_{\forall k \leq n} (cm'_k - cm_k) \times (tm_k - th_k) \leq \sum_{\forall k \leq n} (cm'_k - cm_k) \times penalty(T_0)$$

$$\sum_{\forall k \leq n} (cm'_k - cm_k) \times penalty(T_0) \leq addmiss(T_0, T_1) \times penalty(T_0)$$

Recall that $penalty(T_0)$ is defined in Definition 3.4.

The following theorem states that the CRPD is sound even if the preemption changes the worst-case path.

THEOREM 3.2. *Let T_0 be a preempted task, and T_1 a preempting task. Then:*

$$\forall p, WCETPR(T_0, T_1, p) \leq WCET(T_0) +$$
$$addmiss(T_0, T_1) \times penalty(T_0)$$

PROOF. Let p be any program point in T_0, and let $wcpath$ be the worst-case path for $WCETPR(T_0, T_1, p)$. Then, the following properties are true:

1. $WCET(T_0, wcpath) \leq WCET(T_0)$, since adding a path constraints to an ILP system can never increase the result.

2. $\forall p, WCETPR(T_0, T_1, p) \leq WCETPR(T_0, T_1, p, wcpath)$, since $wcpath$ is the path with the highest WCET

3. $\forall p, WCETPR(T_0, T_1, p, wcpath) \leq WCET(T_0, wcpath) + addmiss(T_0, T_1) \times penalty(T_0)$, from Lemma 3.1

Therefore from (1), (2) and (3), we have $\forall p, WCETPR(T_0, T_1, p) \leq WCET(T_0) + addmiss(T_0, T_1) \times penalty(T_0)$.

This result enables us to guarantee that a CRPD analysis will be safe even in the presence of timing anomalies, provided that some conditions are respected. Indeed, it is not tied to any specific CRPD computation method, and can be applied to any existing CRPD analysis, as long as these propositions are true:

1. The CRPD computed for the preemption of the task T_0 by T_1 is a bound on $addmiss(T_0, T_1) \times penalty(T_0)$.

Task	Size	Task	Size
senddataautopilot	300	altitudecontrol	1496
chedkfailsafe	1116	climbcontrol	6104
checkmega128value	648	stabilisation	3600
testppm	7876	radiocontrol	3600
Fly-by-wire		Autopilot	

Table 1: Code size (in bytes) of tasks in Papabench *fly-by-wire* and *autopilot* modules

Task	Size
encode (adpcm)	5716
decode (adpcm)	5240
reset (adpcm)	1104
clblock (compress)	2016
output (compress)	1372
Mälardalen benchmarks	

Task	Size
remote	944
balance	27580
trackandmove	6704
Robot control	

Table 2: Code size (in bytes) of tasks in Mälardalen benchmarks and robot control application

2. *penalty* and *addmiss* are compatible with the definitions found in Definition 3.4 and Definition 3.7.

3. Assumption (3) must be true. This is easily accomplished by disabling the *may* cache analysis, and altering tm_n values as described in Equation 2.

Timing anomalies with our FIFO CRPD analysis In our approach, we do not do the *may* cache analysis, and our *penalty* is computed as defined in Definition 3.4. Furthermore, since our FIFO CRPD analysis uses an ILP system to bounds the number of additional cache misses due to preemption for any possible path and preemption point, this result bounds $addmiss(T_0, T_1)$, therefore the proof described above applies to our analysis as well.

4. Experimental results

In this section, we give experimental results for our method by analyzing a set of representative benchmarks. We implemented our CRPD analysis framework on top of Chronos [11], an open source WCET analysis tool. We extended Chronos to support ARM architecture and all of our chosen benchmarks are compiled as ARM binaries. In our analysis, we model a single ARM926EJ-S processor core with a level 1 instruction cache that supports FIFO replacement policy. We run our analysis for different instruction cache configurations (associativity level, number of sets, and cache block size). We use three types of benchmarks: *PapaBench* [15], *Malardalen* benchmarks [8], and a robot control application [6].

For each benchmark, we compute the bound on the additional cache misses due to a single preemption for each *task set* consisting of two tasks: a low priority task, and a high priority task. We assume a *fixed-priority preemptive scheduling* of tasks. The list of the analyzed task sets is defined in Table 3. Both the tasks in a task set will run in the same processor core. We compute the preemption cost (in term of additional cache misses) with our method, and compare it to the preemption cost computed with the *relative competitiveness* method [16]. We also plot the average number of additional cache misses against the number of preemptions, to attempt to determine the advantage of using the iterative $CRPD$ computation, as opposed to computing the $CRPD$ for one preemption and multiplying it by the preemption count.

4.1 Benchmarks

PapaBench PapaBench is a real-time benchmark based on the control application of a drone called Paparazzi. It has two modules: *fly-by-wire*, and *auto-pilot*. Each module contains several tasks, which are large enough for the needs of our experiments.

Mälardalen benchmarks The Mälardalen benchmarks are a set of programs designed to evaluate WCET analysis methods. Most Mälardalen programs are too small to be interesting for our experiments, so we used two of the largest programs in the Mälardalen benchmarks, *compress* and *adpcm*.

Robot Control Application This benchmark is a real-life robot controller application. This software contains several tasks, such

Set	Low-priority	High-priority
1	senddataautopilot	checkfailsafe
2	senddataautopilot	checkmega128values
3	senddataautopilot	testppm
4	testppm	checkfailsafe
5	testppm	checkmega128values
6	testppm	senddataautopilot

(a) PapaBench (fly-by-wire)

Set	Low-priority	High-priority
7	altitudecontrol	climbcontrol
8	altitudecontrol	radiocontrol
9	altitudecontrol	stabilisation
10	climbcontrol	altitudecontrol
11	climbcontrol	radiocontrol
12	climbcontrol	stabilisation

(b) PapaBench (auto-pilot)

Set	Low-priority	High-priority
13	encode (adpcm)	decode
14	reset (adpcm)	encode
15	clblock (compress)	output

(c) Mälardalen benchmarks

Set	Low-priority	High-priority
16	remote	balance
17	remote	trackandmove
18	trackandmove	balance

(d) Robot control application

Table 3: Task sets definition

as *navigation* task, and *balance* task (to ensure that the robot does not fall). The tasks are preemptible (*balance* task has the highest priority), and sufficiently large for our experiments.

Table 1 shows the code size (in bytes) for the PapaBench tasks. Table 2 shows the code size (in bytes) for the tasks from the *Mälardalen* benchmarks and the robot control application.

4.2 Results

For each task set, the bound on the number of additional cache misses (the misses already present without preemption are not counted) for a single preemption is computed for each cache configuration. The cache configuration parameters include the associativity level (from 1 to 4), the cache block size (from 16 to 32) and the set count (from 16 to 64). The results are shown for Papabench in Figure 8 and Figure 9 (for *fly-by-wire* and *autopilot* modules respectively). The results for the Mälardalen benchmarks and the robot control application are shown in Figure 10 and Figure 11 respectively. The task sets referenced are defined in Table 3.

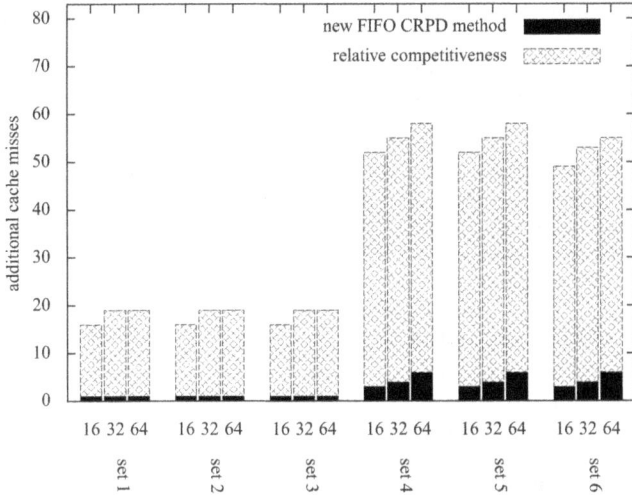

Figure 8: Papabench (fly-by-wire) experimental results

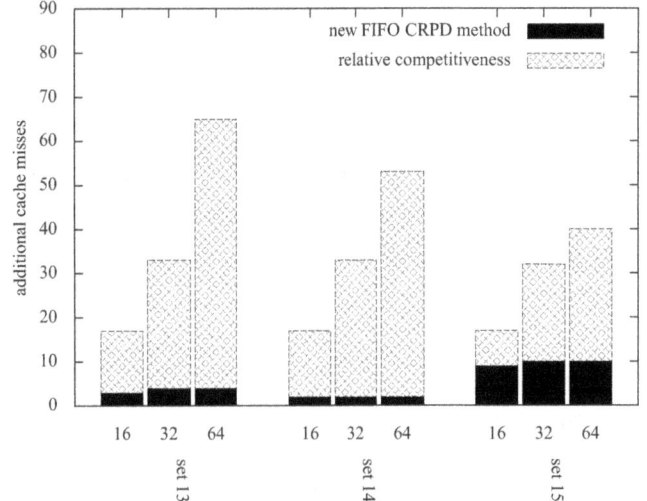

Figure 10: Mälardalen experimental results

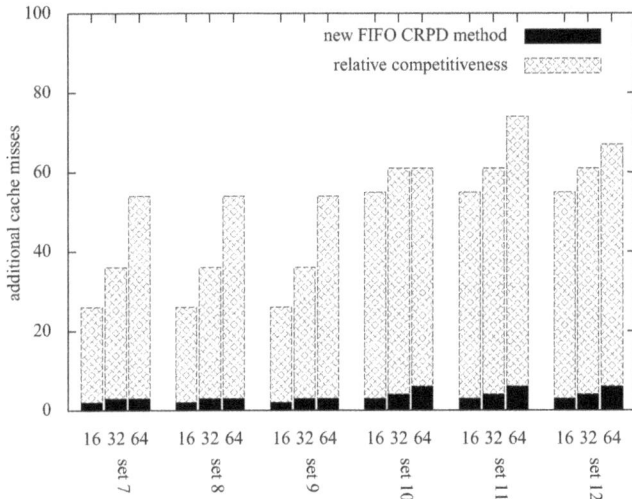

Figure 9: Papabench (auto-pilot) experimental results

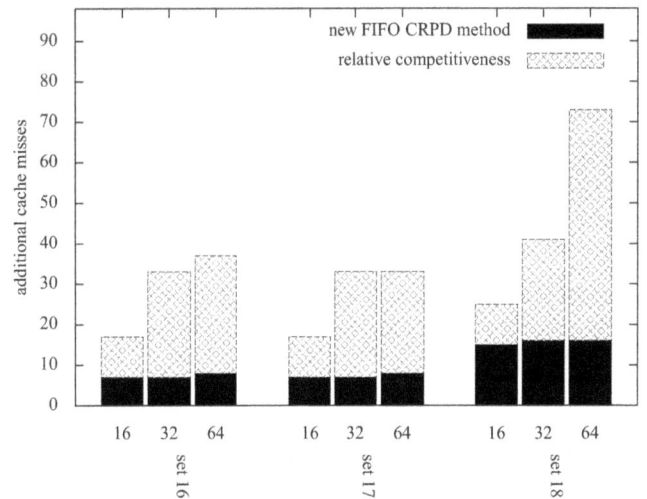

Figure 11: Robot experimental results

We display results only for each different set count, while averaging the results over the other parameters (cache block size, and associativity level), because we observe that the results are primarily influenced by the cache set count. The associativity level has little effect on the results, since increasing the number of ways for FIFO caches only increases the maximum length of phases to detect in the static phase detection analysis, however those longer phases happen rarely in programs. The number of additional cache misses increases with cache set count, as more cache sets allow for more blocks to be in the cache at the same time, whicah are potentially evicted by a preemption. The cache block size has little effect on the additional cache miss count on average, because while it allows for a greater amount of data in the cache, it does not affect the maximum count of blocks that can be in the cache.

The results show that the new approach introduces far less pessimism, compared with the approach based on relative competitiveness. This gap between the two methods can be attributed to two main causes. First, since the relative competitiveness based approach handles FIFO caches by assuming a LRU cache with a lower associativity level, and that the resulting miss count must be multiplied (by a factor depending on the associativity level), it is reasonable to expect a high miss count. Additionally, our approach

counts additional cache misses due to preemption only for blocks that were previously *always hit*, thus limiting the double-counting of cache miss significantly.

Sensitivity to number of preemptions As mentioned previously in Section 3, our method can be used either at each iteration in the WCRT computation (in order to compute the exact number of added cache misses for each preemption count), or it can be used to compute the additional misses for one preemption, and multiply that number by the preemption count at each iteration of the WCRT computation. The second method is faster (because we do not need to repeat the computation at each step of the iteration), but it is also more pessimistic: while the number of preemption increases, less and less additional cache misses are caused by each preemption.

This effect is shown in Figure 12. We see that for a low number of preemptions (*i.e.* less than 200), there is not much difference in tightness between the two approaches (note that the preemption count is the maximum number of preemptions each time the preempted task is activated, not the total preemption count). As the preemption count goes up, the difference between the two methods increases. This threshold increases with the preempted task size (since it increases the number of program points where a preemption could generate a lots of additional misses).

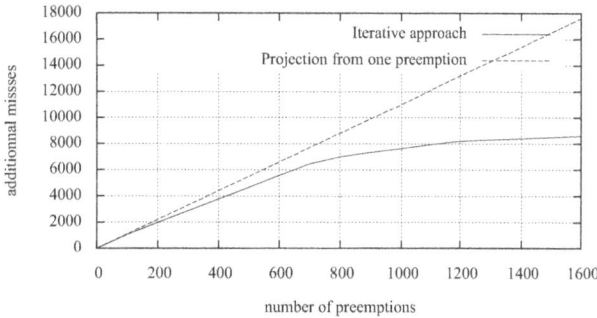

Figure 12: Iterative approach vs. standalone CRPD

5. Related work

There has been extensive research focusing on CRPD analysis on LRU caches. Traditionally, CRPD is computed by analyzing *(i)* the preempted task [1, 9], *(ii)* the preempting task [19], or *(iii)* both the preempted and preempting tasks [2, 14, 17, 18]. The concept of *useful cache block* (UCB) is introduced by [9] for analyzing the preempted task. UCB is computed for the preempted task, and represents the cache blocks that are in use by the preempted task that could cause cache misses if evicted by the preempting task. On the other hand, the set of *evicting cache block* (ECB) is computed for the preempting task, and represents the cache blocks that may be evicted by the preempting task. The notion is that a cache set unused by the preempting task will not cause any eviction of cache blocks used by the preempted task in the same cache set. Several approaches combine ECB and UCB to compute the CRPD. An article by S. Altmeyer et al. [2] gives an overview of these methods, and shows the strengths and weaknesses of each approach.

C. Burguière et al. [4] have performed a study of other replacement policies (including Pseudo-LRU and FIFO), in the context of the CRPD. This study finds that in FIFO caches, the bound on the number of additional misses due to a preemption cannot be expressed in terms of UCB and ECB. C. Berg [3] shows that some non-LRU cache replacement policies (including FIFO, among others) exhibit *domino effect*. This means that for FIFO instruction caches, an additional cache miss somewhere in a program can modify the cache state, thus causing further misses later in the program, which in turn can cause even further misses, and so on. As shown in [3], this effect has a potentially *unbounded* length (except, of course, by the length of the program execution). This fact largely contributes to the infeasibility of the CRPD computation on FIFO caches using UCB and ECB, as presented in [4].

A work-around for this problem has been proposed in [16] by using the concept of *relative competitiveness*. *Relative competitiveness* of cache replacement policies allows us to express the bound on the number of cache misses for a given access sequence and replacement policy, in terms of the bound under a different replacement policy. Applied to the CRPD computation for FIFO caches, computation on relative competitiveness enables us to express the CRPD for a FIFO cache as a function of the CRPD for a LRU cache of lower associativity level, and so we can apply the methods described previously (*i.e.* UCB/ECB analysis) to compute the CRPD for FIFO caches. The main drawback with this method is the high over-estimation of cache miss count.

6. Conclusion

We have proposed an approach to handle CRPD in the presence of an instruction cache with a FIFO replacement policy. Our analysis computes the additional cache misses due to task preemption in a safe way, while avoiding the double-counting of cache misses

already taken into account by the underlying FIFO cache categorization method. We have also proposed a set of properties that a CRPD analysis must satisfy in order to be safe in presence of timing anomalies, and we shown that our analysis does satisfy these properties. Finally, we presented a method to use our CRPD analysis in the context of WCRT computation, in a way that handles diminishing CRPD contributions as the preemption count increases, providing tight bounds. We evaluated our analysis on realistic benchmarks by modeling a real-life ARM processor. The results show that our approach provides tight CRPD bounds in comparison to the state-of-the-art approach.

Acknowledgments

This work was partially supported by A*STAR Public Sector Funding Project Number 1121202007 - "Scalable Timing Analysis Methods for Embedded Software".

References

[1] S. Altmeyer and C. Burguiere. A new notion of useful cache block to improve the bounds of cache-related preemption delay. In *ECRTS*, 2009.

[2] S. Altmeyer, R. I. Davis, and C. Maiza. Cache related pre-emption delay aware response time analysis for fixed priority pre-emptive systems. In *RTSS*, 2011.

[3] C. Berg. Plru cache domino effects. In *WCET*, 2006.

[4] C. Burguiere, J. Reineke, and S. Altmeyer. Cache-related preemption delay computation for set-associative caches - pitfalls and solutions. In *WCET*, 2009.

[5] F. Cassez, R. R. Hansen, and M. C. Olesen. What is a timing anomaly? In *WCET*, 2012.

[6] L. K. Chong, C. Ballabriga, V.-T. Pham, S. Chattopadhyay, and A. Roychoudhury. Integrated timing analysis of application and operating systems code. In *RTSS*, 2013.

[7] D. Grund and J. Reineke. Precise and efficient FIFO-replacement analysis based on static phase detection. In *ECRTS*, 2010.

[8] J. Gustafsson, A. Betts, A. Ermedahl, and B. Lisper. The mälardalen wcet benchmarks: Past, present and future. In *WCET*, 2010.

[9] C.-G. Lee, H. Hahn, Y.-M. Seo, S. L. Min, R. Ha, S. Hong, C. Y. Park, M. Lee, and C. S. Kim. Analysis of cache-related preemption delay in fixed-priority preemptive scheduling. *IEEE Trans. Comput.*, 47(6), 1998.

[10] X. Li, A. Roychoudhury, and T. Mitra. Modeling out-of-order processors for wcet analysis. *Real-Time Systems*, 34(3), 2006.

[11] X. Li, Y. Liang, T. Mitra, and A. Roychoudhury. Chronos: A timing analyzer for embedded software. *Science of Computer Programming*, 2007.

[12] T. Lundqvist. *A WCET Analysis Method for Pipelined Microprocessors with Cache Memories*. PhD thesis, Chalmers University of Technology, 2002.

[13] T. Lundqvist and P. Stenström. Timing anomalies in dynamically scheduled microprocessors. In *RTSS*, 1999.

[14] H. S. Negi, T. Mitra, and A. Roychoudhury. Accurate estimation of cache-related preemption delay. In *CODES+ISSS*, 2003.

[15] F. Nemer, H. Cassé, P. Sainrat, J.-P. Bahsoun, and M. De Michiel. Papabench: a free real-time benchmark. In *WCET*, 2006.

[16] J. Reineke and D. Grund. Relative competitive analysis of cache replacement policies. In *LCTES*, 2008.

[17] J. Staschulat and R. Ernst. Scalable precision cache analysis for real-time software. *ACM TECS*, 6(4), 2007.

[18] Y. Tan and V. J. Mooney. Integrated intra- and inter-task cache analysis for preemptive multi-tasking real-time systems. In *SCOPES*, 2004.

[19] H. Tomiyama and N. D. Dutt. Program path analysis to bound cache-related preemption delay in preemptive real-time systems. In *CODES*, 2000.

How to Compute Worst-Case Execution Time by Optimization Modulo Theory and a Clever Encoding of Program Semantics*

Julien Henry   Mihail Asavoae   David Monniaux   Claire Maïza

Univ. Grenoble Alpes, VERIMAG, F-38000 Grenoble, France
CNRS, VERIMAG, F-38000 Grenoble, France
First-Name.Last-Name@imag.fr

Abstract

In systems with hard real-time constraints, it is necessary to compute upper bounds on the worst-case execution time (WCET) of programs; the closer the bound to the real WCET, the better. This is especially the case of synchronous reactive control loops with a fixed clock; the WCET of the loop body must not exceed the clock period.

We compute the WCET (or at least a close upper bound thereof) as the solution of an *optimization modulo theory* problem that takes into account the semantics of the program, in contrast to other methods that compute the longest path whether or not it is feasible according to these semantics. Optimization modulo theory extends satisfiability modulo theory (SMT) to maximization problems.

Immediate encodings of WCET problems into SMT yield formulas intractable for all current production-grade solvers — this is inherent to the DPLL(T) approach to SMT implemented in these solvers. By conjoining some appropriate "cuts" to these formulas, we considerably reduce the computation time of the SMT-solver.

We experimented our approach on a variety of control programs, using the OTAWA analyzer both as baseline and as underlying microarchitectural analysis for our analysis, and show notable improvement on the WCET bound on a variety of benchmarks and control programs.

Categories and Subject Descriptors D.2.8 [*Software Engineering*]: Metrics—Performance measures; C.3 [*Computer Systems Organization*]: Special-Purpose and Application-Based Systems—Real-Time and Embedded Systems; D.2.4 [*Software Engineering*]: Software/Program Verification—Validation

Keywords WCET; Optimization Modulo Theory; Bounded Model Checking; Craig Interpolants

* This work was partially funded by grant W-SEPT (ANR-12-INSE-0001) from the French *Agence nationale de la recherche* and grant STATOR from the European Research Council.

1. Introduction

In embedded systems, it is often necessary to ascertain that the worst-case execution time (WCET) of a program is less than a certain threshold. This is in particular the case for synchronous reactive control loops (infinite loops that acquire sensor values, compute appropriate actions and update, write them to actuators, and wait for the next clock tick) [7]: the WCET of the loop body ("step") must be less than the period of the clock.

Computing the WCET of a program on a modern architecture requires a combination of low-level, microarchitectural reasoning (regarding pipeline and cache states, busses, cycle-accurate timing) and higher-level reasoning (program control flow, loop counts, variable pointers). A common approach is to apply a form of abstract interpretation to the microarchitecture, deduce worst-case timings for elementary blocks, and reassemble these into the global WCET according to the control flow and maximal iteration counts using integer linear programming (ILP) [38, 40].

One pitfall of this approach is that the reassembly may take into account paths that cannot actually occur in the real program, possibly overestimating the WCET. This is because this reassembly is mostly driven by the control-flow structure of the program, and (in most approaches) ignores semantic conditions. For instance, a control program may (clock-)enable certain parts of the program according to modular arithmetic with respect to time:

```
if (clock % 4==0) { /* A */ }
/* unrelated code */
if (clock % 12==1) { /* B */ }
```

These arithmetic constraints entail that certain combinations of parts cannot be active simultaneously (sections A and B are mutually incompatible). If such constraints are not taken into account (as in most approaches), the WCET will be grossly over-estimated.

The purpose of this article is to take such *semantic constraints* into account, in a fully automated and very precise fashion. Specifically, we consider the case where the program for which WCET is to be determined contains only loops for which small static bounds can be determined (but our approach can also be applied to general programs through summarization, see section 8). This is very commonly the case for synchronous control programs, such as those found in aircraft fly-by-wire controls [37]. Programs of this form are typically compiled into C from high-level data-flow synchronous programming languages such as SIMULINK[2], LUSTRE or SCADE[3] [7].

[2] SIMULINK™ is a block diagram environment for multidomain simulation and model-based design from The Mathworks.

[3] SCADE™ is a model-based development environment dedicated to critical embedded software, from Esterel Technologies, derived from the academic language LUSTRE.

We compute the WCET of such programs by expressing it as the solution of an *optimization modulo theory* problem. Optimization modulo theory is an extension of *satisfiability modulo theory* (SMT) where the returned solution is not just any solution, but one maximizing some objective; in our case, solutions define execution traces of the program, and the objective is their execution time.

Expressing execution traces of programs as solutions to an SMT problem is a classical approach in *bounded model checking*; typically, the SMT problem includes a constraint stating that the execution trace reaches some failure point, and an "unsatisfiable" answer means that this failure point is unreachable. In the case of optimization, the SMT solver has to disprove the existence of solutions greater than the maximum to be returned — in our case, to disprove the existence of traces of execution time greater than the WCET. Unfortunately, all currently available SMT solvers take unacceptably long time to conclude on naive encodings of WCET problems. This is because all these solvers implement variants of the DPLL(T) approach [27], which has exponential behavior on so-called "diamond formulas", which appear in naive encodings of WCET on sequences of if-then-elses.

Computing or proving the WCET by direct, naive encoding into SMT therefore leads to intractable problems, which is probably the reason why, to our best knowledge, it has not been proposed in the literature. We however show how an alternate encoding, including "cuts", makes such computations tractable. Our contributions are:

1. The computation of worst-case execution time (WCET), or an over-approximation thereof, by optimization modulo theory. The same idea may also be applicable to other similar problems (e.g. number of calls to a memory allocator). Our approach exhibits a worst-case path, which may be useful for targeting optimizations so as to lower WCET [41].

2. The introduction of "cuts" into the encoding so as to make SMT-solving tractable, without any change in the code of the SMT solver. The same idea may extend to other problems with an additive or modular structure.

In section 2, we recall the usual approach for the computation of an upper bound on WCET. In section 3, we recall the general framework of bounded model checking using SMT-solving. In section 4, we explain how we improve upon the "normal" SMT encoding of programs so as to make WCET problems tractable, and in section 5 we explain (both theoretically and practically) why the normal encoding results in intractable problems. In section 6 we describe our implementation and experimental results. We present the related work in section 7, we discuss possible extensions and future works in section 8, and then, in section 9 we draw the conclusions.

2. Worst-Case Execution Time

Let us first summarize the classical approach to static timing analysis (for more detail, read e.g. [38, 40]). Figure 1 shows the general timing analysis workflow used in a large part of WCET tools including industrial ones such as AiT[4] or academic ones such as OTAWA[5] [2] or CHRONOS[6] [29]. For the sake of simplicity, we shall restrict ourselves to mono-processor platforms with no bus-master devices except for the CPU.

The analysis considers the object code. The control flow graph is first reconstructed from the binary. Then, a *value analysis* (e.g. abstract interpretation for interval analysis) extracts memory addresses, loop bounds and simple infeasible paths [19]; such an analysis may be performed on the binary or the source files (in the lat-

---

[4] http://www.absint.com/ait/

[5] http://www.otawa.fr

[6] http://www.comp.nus.edu.sg/~rpembed/chronos/

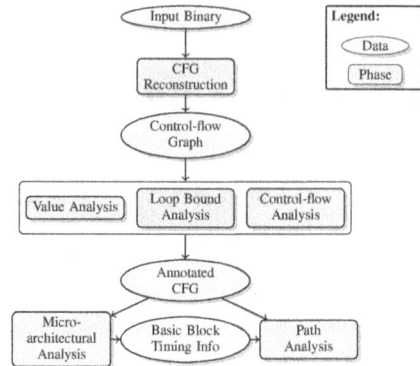

Figure 1. WCET analysis workflow

ter case, it is necessary to trace object code and low-level variables to the source code, perhaps using the debugging information provided by the compiler). This semantic and addressing information help the micro-architectural analysis, which bounds the execution time of basic blocks taking into account the whole architecture of the platform (pipeline, caches, buses,...)[18, 35]. The most popular method to derive this architecture analysis is abstract interpretation with specific abstract domains. For instance, a pipeline abstraction represents sets of detailed pipeline states, including values for registers or buffers [18]; while a cache abstraction typically tracks which value may or must be in each cache line [35].

The last step of the analysis uses the basic block execution time and the semantic information to derive the WCET, usually, in the "implicit path enumeration technique" (IPET) approach, as the solution of an integer linear program (ILP) [30]. The ILP variables represent the execution counts (along a given trace) of each basic block in the program. The ILP constraints describe the structure of the control flow graph (e.g. the number of times a given block is entered equals the number of times it is exited), as well as maximal iteration counts for loops, obtained by value analysis or provided by the user. Finally, the execution time to be maximized is the sum of the basic blocks weighted by their local worst-case execution time computed by the microarchitectural analysis.

The obtained worst-case path may however be *infeasible* semantically, for instance, if a condition tests $x < 10$ and later the unmodified value of x is again tested in a condition $x > 20$ along that path. This is because the ILP represents mostly syntactic information from the control-flow graph. This weakness has long been recognized within the WCET community, which has devised schemes for eliminating infeasible worst-case paths, for instance, by modifying the control-flow graph before the architecture analysis [33], or by adding ILP constraints [19, 21]. Infeasible paths are found via pattern matching of conditions [21] or applying abstract execution [19]; these methods focus on paths made infeasible by numeric constraints. These approaches are limited by the expressiveness of ILP constraints as used in IPET: they consider only "conflict conditions" (exclusive conditional statements: "if condition a is true then condition b must be false").

On a loop-free program, the ILP approach is equivalent to finding the longest path in the control-flow graph, weighted according to the local WCET of the basic blocks. Yet, again, this syntactic longest path may be infeasible. Instead of piecemeal elimination of infeasible paths, we propose encoding the set of feasible paths into an SMT formula, as done in bounded model-checking; the success of SMT-solving is based on the ability of SMT solvers to exclude whole groups of spurious solutions by learning lemmas.

```
/* S */
if (b) {
  x = x + 2; /* C */
} else {
  x = x + 3; /* D */
}
assert(x >= 10);
```

First-order encoding:
$((b \wedge x_2 = x_1 + 2) \vee (\neg b \wedge x_2 = x_1 + 3)) \wedge x_2 \geq 10$

Or, if the logic language comprises the "if then else" operator:
$ite(b, x_1 + 2, x_1 + 3) \geq 10$

If one wants to record the execution trace finely:
$(C \Leftrightarrow S \wedge b) \wedge (D \Leftrightarrow S \wedge \neg b) \wedge$
$(C \Rightarrow x_2 = x_1 + 2) \wedge (D \Rightarrow x_2 = x_1 + 3) \wedge x_2 \geq 10$

Figure 2. Encoding of a simple program into a first-order logic formula

Loop-free programs without recursion may seem a very restricted class, but in safety-critical control systems, it is common that the program consists in one big infinite control loop whose body must verify a WCET constraint, and this body itself does not contain loops, or only loops with small static bounds (say, for retrieving a value from an interpolation table of known static size), which can be unrolled. Such programs typically eschew more complicated algorithms, if only because arguing for their termination or functional correctness would be onerous with respect to the stringent requirements imposed by the authorities. Complicated or dynamic data structures are usually avoided [30, ch. II]. This is the class of programs targeted by e.g. the Astrée static analyzer [14].

Our approach replaces the path analysis by ILP (and possibly refinement for infeasible paths) by optimization modulo theory. The control-flow extraction and micro-architectural analysis are left unchanged, and one may thus use existing WCET tools. In this paper we consider a simple architecture (ARMv7), though we plan to look into more complicated ones and address, for example, persistency analyses for caches, like in [25].

3. Using Bounded Model Checking to Measure Worst-Case Execution Time

Bounded model checking is an approach for finding software bugs, where traces of length at most n are exhaustively explored. In most current approaches, the set of feasible traces of length n is defined using a first-order logic formula, where, roughly speaking, arithmetic constraints correspond to tests and assignments, control flow is encoded using Booleans, and disjunctions correspond to multiple control edges. The source program may be a high-level language, an intermediate code (e.g. Java bytecode, LLVM bitcode [22, 28], Common Intermediate Language...) or even, with some added difficulty, binary executable code [8].

The first step is to unroll all loops up to statically determined bounds. Program variables and registers are then mapped to formula variables (implicitly existentially quantified). In an imperative language, but not in first-order logic, the same variable may be assigned several times: therefore, as in compilation to *static single assignment* (SSA) form, different names have to be introduced for the same program variable, one for each update and others for variables whose value differs according to where control flows from (Fig. 2). If the source program uses arrays or pointers to memory, the formula may need to refer not only to scalar variables, but also to *uninterpreted functions* and *functional arrays* [27]. Modern SMT-solvers support these datatypes and others suitable for the

analysis of low-level programs, such as bit-vectors (fixed-width binary arithmetic). If constructs occur in the source program that cannot be translated exactly into the target logic (e.g. the program has nonlinear arithmetic but the logic does not), they may be safely over-approximated by nondeterministic choice. Details on "conventional" first-order encodings for program traces are given in the literature on bounded model checking [11] and are beyond the scope of this article.

Let us now see how to encode a WCET problem into SMT. In a simple model (which can be made more complex and realistic, see section 8), each program block i has a fixed execution time $t_i \in \mathbb{N}$, and the total execution time T is the sum of the execution times of the blocks encountered in the trace. This execution time can be incorporated into a "conventional" encoding for program traces in two ways:

Sum encoding If Booleans $\chi_i \in \{0,1\}$ record which blocks i were reached by the execution trace τ, then

$$T(\tau) = \left(\sum_{i|\chi_i=true} t_i \right) = \left(\sum_i \chi_i t_i \right) \quad (1)$$

Counter encoding Alternatively, the program may be modified by adding a time counter as an ordinary variable, which is incremented in each block. The resulting program then undergoes the "conventional" encoding: the final value of the counter is the execution time.

An alternative is to attach a cost to transitions instead of program blocks. The sum encoding is then done similarly, with Booleans $\chi_{i,j} \in \{0,1\}$ recording which of the transitions have been taken by an execution trace τ.

$$T(\tau) = \left(\sum_{(i,j)|\chi_{i,j}=true} t_{i,j} \right) = \left(\sum_{(i,j)} \chi_{i,j} t_{i,j} \right) \quad (2)$$

The problem is now how to determine the WCET $\beta = \max T(\tau)$. An obvious approach is binary search [36], maintaining an interval $[l,h]$ containing β: take a middle point $m := \lceil \frac{l+h}{2} \rceil$, test whether there exists a trace τ such that $T(\tau) \geq m$; if so, then set $l := m$ (or set $l := T(\tau)$, if available) and restart, else set $h := m - 1$ and restart; stop when the integer interval $[l,h]$ is reduced to a singleton. l and h may be respectively initialized to zero and a safe upper bound on worst-case execution time, for instance one obtained by a simple "longest path in the acyclic graph" algorithm.

4. Adding Cuts

Experiments with both sum encoding and counter encoding applied to the "conventional" encoding of programs into SMT were disappointing: the SMT solver was taking far too much time. In particular, the last step of computing WCET, that is, running the SMT-solver in order to disprove the existence of traces longer than the computed WCET, was agonizingly slow even for very small programs. In section 5 we shall see how this is inherent to how SMT-solvers based on DPLL(T) — that is, all current production-grade SMT-solvers — handle the kind of formulas generated from WCET constraints; but let us first see how we worked around this problem so as to make WCET computations tractable.

4.1 Rationale

A key insight is that the SMT-solver, applied to such a naive encoding, explores a very large number of combinations of branches (exponential with respect to the number of tests), thus a very large number of partial traces $\tau_1, \ldots, \tau_n$, even though the execution time

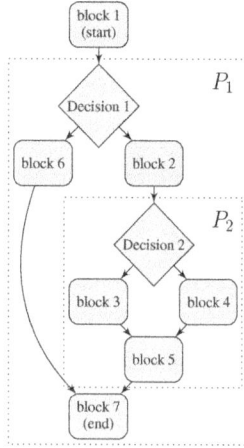

Figure 3. Two portions P_1 and P_2 of a program obtained as the range between a node with several incoming edges and its immediate dominator

of these partial traces is insufficient to change the overall WCET (section 5 will explain this insight in more detail, both theoretically and experimentally).

Consider the control-flow graph in Fig. 3; let $t_1, \ldots, t_7$ be the WCET of blocks $1 \ldots 7$ established by microarchitectural analysis (for the sake of simplicity, we neglect the time taken for decisions). Assume we have already found a path from start to end going through block 6, taking β time units; also assume that $t_1 + t_2 + \max(t_3, t_4) + t_5 + t_7 \leq \beta$. Then it is useless for the SMT-solver to search for paths going through decision 2, because none of them can have execution time longer than β; yet that is what happens if using a naive encoding with all current production SMT-solvers (see section 5). If instead of 1 decision we have 42, then the solver may explore 2^{42} paths even though there is a simple reason why none of them will increase the WCET.

Our idea is simple: to the original SMT formula (from "counter encoding" or "sum encoding"), conjoin constraints expressing that the total execution time of some portions of the program is less than some upper bound (depending on the portion). This upper bound acts as an "abstraction" or "summary" of the portion (e.g. here we say that the time taken in P_2 is at most $\max(t_3, t_4) + t_5$, and the hope is that this summary is sufficient for the SMT-solver in many cases. There remain two problems: how to select such portions, and how to compute this upper bound.

Note that these extra constraints are implied by the original formula, and thus that conjoining them to it does not change the solution set or the WCET obtained, but only the execution time of the analysis. Such constraints are often called "cuts" in operation research, thus our terminology.

4.2 Selecting portions

The choice of a portion of code to summarize follows source-level criteria: for instance, a procedure, a block, a macro expansion. If operating on a control-flow graph, a candidate portion can be between a node with several incoming edges and its *immediate dominator*, if there is non trivial control flow between the two (Fig. 3).[7] On structured languages, this means that we add one

---

[7] A *dominator* D of a block B is a block such that any path reaching B must go through D. The *immediate dominator* of a block B is the unique $I \neq B$ dominator of B such that I does not dominate any other dominator $D \neq B$ of B. For instance, the immediate dominator of the end of a cascade of if-then-else statements is the beginning of the cascade.

constraint for the total timing of every "if-then-else" or "switch" statement (recall that loops are unrolled, if needed into a cascade of "if-then-else"). This is the approach that we followed in our experimental evaluation (section 6).

Let us however remark that these portions of code need not be contiguous: with the sum encoding, it is straightforward to encode the fact that the total time of a number of instruction blocks is less than a bound, even though these instructions blocks are distributed throughout the code. This is also possible, but less easy, with the counter encoding (one has to encode an upper bound on the sum of differences between starting and ending times over all contiguous subsets of the portion). This means that it is possible to consider portions that are semantically, but not syntactically related. For instance, one can consider for each Boolean, or other variable used in a test, a kind of "slice" of the program that is directly affected by this variable (e.g. all contents of if-then-elses testing on this variable) and compute an upper bound for the total execution time of this slice — in the example in the introduction where the execution of two portions A and B depend on a variable clock, we could compute an upper bound on the total time of the program sliced with respect to clock, that only contains the portions A and B. Implementing this "slicing" approach is part of our future work.

4.3 Obtaining upper bounds on the WCET of portions

Let us now consider the problem of, given a portion, computing an upper bound on its WCET. In the case of a contiguous portion, an upper bound may be obtained by a simple syntactic analysis: the longest syntactic path is used as a bound (even though it might be unfeasible). This approach may be extended to non-contiguous portions. Let us denote by P the portion. For each block b, let t_b be the upper bound on the time spent in block b (obtained from microarchitectural analysis), and let w_b be an unknown denoting the worst time spent inside P in paths from the start of the program to the beginning of b. If $b_1, \ldots, b_k$ are the predecessors of b, then $w_b = \max(w_{b_1} + t_{b_1} \cdot \chi_P(b_1), \ldots, w_{b_k} + t_{b_k} \cdot \chi_P(b_k))$ where $\chi_P(x)$ is 1 if $x \in P$, 0 otherwise. This system of equations can be easily solved in (quasi) linear time by considering the w_b in a topological order of the blocks (recall that we consider loop-free programs). Another approach would be to recursively call the complete WCET procedure on the program portion, and use its output as a bound.

The simpler approach described above gave excellent results in most benchmarks, and we had to refine the cuts with the SMT-based procedure for only one benchmark (see section 6).

4.4 Example

Let us now see a short, but complete example, extracted from a control program composed of an initialization phase followed by an infinite loop clocked at a precise frequency. The goal of the analysis is to show that the WCET of the loop body never exceeds the clocking period. For the sake of brevity, we consider only a very short extract of the control program, implementing a "rate limiter"; in the real program its input is the result of previous computation steps, but here we consider that the input is nondeterministic within $[-10000, +10000]$. The code run at every clock tick is:

```
// returns a value between min and max
extern int input(int min, int max);
void rate_limiter_step() {
        int x_old = input(-10000,10000);
        int x = input(-10000,10000);
        if (x > x_old+10)
                x = x_old +10;
        if (x < x_old -10)
                x = x_old -10;
        x_old = x;
}
```

46

This program is compiled to LLVM bitcode,[8] then bitcode-level optimizations are applied, resulting in a LLVM control-flow graph (Fig. 4 left). From this graph we generate a first-order formula including cuts (Fig. 4 right). Its models describe execution traces along with the corresponding execution time *cost* given by the "sum encoding". Here, costs are attached to the transitions between each pairs of blocks. These costs are supposed to be given. Section 6.3 will describe in full details how we use the OTAWA tool to derive such precise costs for each transitions.

The SMT encoding of the program semantics (Fig. 4 right) is relatively simple since the bitcode has an SSA form: The $ite(b, x, y)$ construct is an *if-then-else* statement and is equal to x if b is true, otherwise is equal to y. In our encoding, SMT variables starting with letter x refer to the LLVM SSA-variables, there is one Boolean b_i for each LLVM BasicBlock, and one Boolean t_i_j for each transition. Each transition t_i_j have a cost c_i_j given by OTAWA. For instance, the block `entry` is given the Boolean b_0, the block `if.then` is given the Boolean b_1, and the transition from `entry` to `if.then` is given the Boolean t_0_1 and has a cost of 15 clock cycles. The cuts are derived as follows: `if.end` has several incoming transitions and its immediate dominator is `entry`. The longest syntactic path between these two blocks is equal to 21. The cut will then be $c\_0\_1 + c\_1\_2 + c\_0\_2 \leq 21$. There is a similar cut for the portion between `if.end` and `if.end6`. Finally, we can also add the constraint $cost \leq 43$ since it is the cost of the longest syntactic path. While this longest syntactic path has cost 43 (it goes both through `if.then` and `if.then4`), our SMT-based approach shows there is no semantically feasible path longer than 36 clock cycles.

4.5 Relationship with Craig interpolants

A *Craig interpolant* for an unsatisfiable conjunction $F_1 \wedge F_2$ is a formula I such that $F_1 \Rightarrow I$ and $I \wedge F_2$ is unsatisfiable, whose free variables are included in the intersection of those of F_1 and F_2.

In the case of a program $A; B$ consisting of two portions A and B executed in sequence, the usual way of encoding the program yields $\phi_A \wedge \phi_B$ where ϕ_A and ϕ_B are, respectively, the encodings of A and B. The free variables of this formula are the inputs $i_1, \ldots, i_m$ and outputs $o_1, \ldots, o_n$ of the program, as well as all temporaries and local variables. Let $t_1, \ldots, t_p$ be the variables live at the edge from A to B; then the input-output relationship of the program, with free variables $i_1, \ldots, i_m, o_1, \ldots, o_n$ is F:

$$\exists t_1, \ldots, t_p (\exists \ldots \phi_A) \wedge (\exists \ldots \phi_B)$$

Let us now assume additionally that o_1 is the final time and t_1 is the time when control flow from A to B (counter encoding). The SMT formulas used in our optimization process are of the form $F \wedge t_1 \geq \beta$. The cut for portion A is of the form $t_1 \leq \beta_A$, that for portion B of the form $o_1 - t_1 \leq \beta_B$. Then, if the cut for portion A is used to prove that $F \wedge t_1 \geq \beta$ is unsatisfiable, then this cut is a Craig interpolant for the unsatisfiable formula $(\phi_A) \wedge (\phi_B \wedge t_1 \geq \beta)$ (similarly, if the cut for portion B is used, then it is an interpolant for $\phi_B \wedge (\phi_A \wedge t_1 \geq \beta)$). Our approach may thus be understood as preventively computing possible Craig interpolants so as to speed up solving. The same intuition applies to the sum encoding (up to the creation of supplementary variables).

5. Intractability: Diamond Formulas

Let us now explain why the formulas without cuts result in unacceptable execution times in the SMT-solvers.

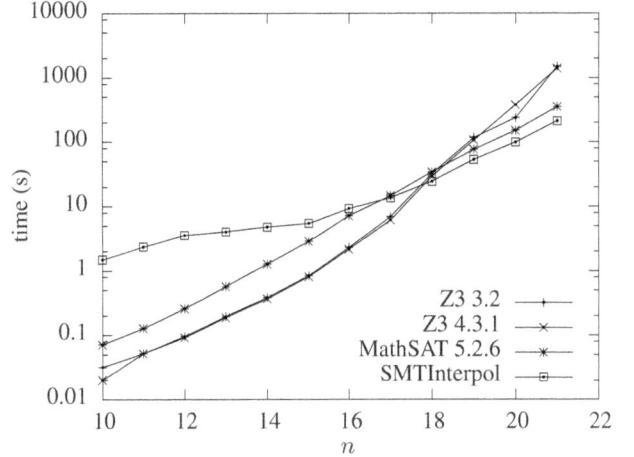

Figure 5. Intractability of diamond formulas obtained from timing analysis of a family of programs with very simple functional semantics. Execution times of various state-of-the-art SMT-solvers on Formula 4, for $m = 5n$ (the hardest), showing exponential behavior in the formula size n. The CPU is a 2 GHz Intel Core 2 Q8400.

Consider a program consisting in a sequence of n fragments where the i-th fragment is of the form:

```
if (b_i) { /* block of cost x_i */
    /* time cost 2, not changing b_i */
} else {
    /* time cost 3, not changing b_i */
}
if (b_i) { /* block of cost y_i */
    /* time cost 3 */
} else {
    /* time cost 2 */
}
```

The $(b_i)_{1 \leq i \leq n}$ are Booleans. A human observer easily concludes that the worst-case execution time is $5n$, by analyzing each fragment separately.

Using the "sum encoding", the timing analysis is expressed as

$$T = \max \left\{ \sum_{i=1}^{n} x_i + y_i \ \middle| \ \bigwedge_{i=1}^{n} (x_i = ite(b_i, 2, 3)) \wedge (y_i = ite(b_i, 3, 2)) \right\} \quad (3)$$

Given a bound m, an SMT-solver will have to solve for the unknowns $(b_i), (x_i), (y_i)_{1 \leq i \leq n}$ the constraint

$$((b_1 \wedge x_1 = 2 \wedge y_1 = 3) \vee (\neg b_1 \wedge x_1 = 3 \wedge y_1 = 2)) \wedge \ldots$$
$$((b_n \wedge x_n = 2 \wedge y_n = 3) \vee (\neg b_n \wedge x_n = 3 \wedge y_n = 2)) \wedge$$
$$x_1 + y_1 + \cdots + x_n + y_n \geq m \quad (4)$$

In the "DPLL(T)" approach (see e.g. Kroening and Strichman [27] for an introduction), SMT is implemented as a combination of a SAT solver,[9] which searches within a Boolean state space (here, amounting to $b_1, \ldots, b_n \in \{0, 1\}^n$, but in general arithmetic or

---

[8] LLVM (http://www.llvm.org/) [28] is a compilation framework with a standardized intermediate representation (bitcode), into which one can compile with a variety of compilers including GCC (C, C++, Ada...) and CLANG (C, C++).

[9] Almost all current SAT solvers implement variants of *constraint-driven clause learning* (CDCL), a major improvement over DPLL (Davis, Putnam, Logemann, Loveland), thus the terminology. None of what we say here, however, is specific to CDCL: our remarks stay valid as long as the combination of propositional and theory reasoning proceeds by sending clauses constructed from the predicates syntactically present in the original formula to the propositional solver.

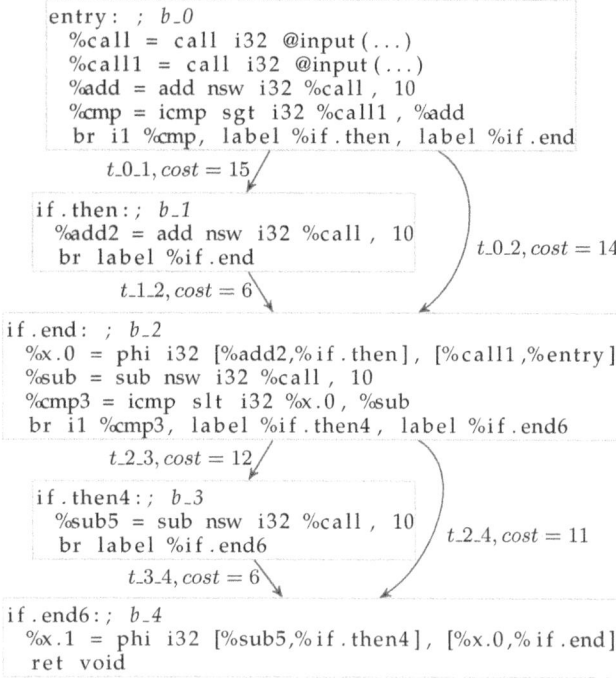

```
entry: ; b_0
  %call = call i32 @input(...)
  %call1 = call i32 @input(...)
  %add = add nsw i32 %call, 10
  %cmp = icmp sgt i32 %call1, %add
  br i1 %cmp, label %if.then, label %if.end
```
$t\_0\_1, cost = 15$

```
if.then:; b_1
  %add2 = add nsw i32 %call, 10
  br label %if.end
```
$t\_1\_2, cost = 6$
$t\_0\_2, cost = 14$

```
if.end: ; b_2
  %x.0 = phi i32 [%add2,%if.then], [%call1,%entry]
  %sub = sub nsw i32 %call, 10
  %cmp3 = icmp slt i32 %x.0, %sub
  br i1 %cmp3, label %if.then4, label %if.end6
```
$t\_2\_3, cost = 12$

```
if.then4:; b_3
  %sub5 = sub nsw i32 %call, 10
  br label %if.end6
```
$t\_3\_4, cost = 6$
$t\_2\_4, cost = 11$

```
if.end6:; b_4
  %x.1 = phi i32 [%sub5,%if.then4], [%x.0,%if.end]
  ret void
```

$$
\begin{aligned}
&-10000 \leq x\_call \leq 10000 \\
\wedge\ &-10000 \leq x\_call1 \leq 10000 \\
\wedge\ &x\_add = (x\_call + 10) \\
\wedge\ &t\_0\_1 = (b\_0 \wedge (x\_call1 > x\_add)) \\
\wedge\ &t\_0\_2 = (b\_0 \wedge \neg(x\_call1 > x\_add)) \\
\wedge\ &b\_1 = t\_0\_1 \\
\wedge\ &x\_add2 = (x\_call + 10) \\
\wedge\ &t\_1\_2 = b\_1 \\
\wedge\ &b\_2 = (t\_0\_2 \vee t\_1\_2) \\
\wedge\ &b\_2 \Rightarrow (x\_x.0 = ite(t\_1\_2, x\_add2, x\_call1)) \\
\wedge\ &x\_sub = (x\_call - 10) \\
\wedge\ &t\_2\_3 = (b\_2 \wedge (x\_x.0 < x\_sub)) \\
\wedge\ &t\_2\_4 = (b\_2 \wedge \neg(x\_x.0 < x\_sub)) \\
\wedge\ &b\_3 = t\_2\_3 \\
\wedge\ &x\_sub5 = (x\_call - 10) \\
\wedge\ &t\_3\_4 = b\_3 \\
\wedge\ &b\_4 = (t\_2\_4 \vee t\_3\_4) \\
\wedge\ &b\_4 \Rightarrow (x\_x.1 = ite(t\_3\_4, x\_sub5, x\_x.0)) \\[4pt]
\wedge\ &b\_0 = b\_4 = true\ ;\ \text{search for a trace from entry to if.end6}
\end{aligned}
$$

timing
$$
\begin{aligned}
\wedge\ &c\_0\_1 = ite(t\_0\_1, 15, 0)\ ;\ t\_0\_1 \text{ has cost 15 if taken, else 0} \\
\wedge\ &c\_0\_2 = ite(t\_0\_2, 14, 0) \\
\wedge\ &c\_1\_2 = ite(t\_1\_2, 6, 0) \\
\wedge\ &c\_2\_3 = ite(t\_2\_3, 12, 0) \\
\wedge\ &c\_2\_4 = ite(t\_2\_4, 11, 0) \\
\wedge\ &c\_3\_4 = ite(t\_3\_4, 6, 0) \\
\wedge\ &cost = (c\_0\_1 + c\_0\_2 + c\_1\_2 + c\_2\_4 + c\_3\_4)
\end{aligned}
$$

cuts
$$
\begin{aligned}
\wedge\ &(c\_0\_1 + c\_1\_2 + c\_0\_2) \leq 21\ ;\ \text{between entry and if.end} \\
\wedge\ &(c\_3\_4 + c\_2\_4 + c\_2\_3) \leq 22\ ;\ \text{between if.end and if.end6} \\
\wedge\ &cost \leq 43
\end{aligned}
$$

Figure 4. LLVM control-flow graph of the rate_limiter_step function, and its encoding as an SMT formula with cuts.

other theory predicates are also taken into account) and a decision procedure for conjunctions of atomic formulas from a theory T.[10] Once $b_1, \ldots, b_n$ have been picked, Formula 4 simplifies to a conjunction

$$x_1 = \alpha_1 \wedge y_1 = \beta_1 \wedge \ldots \wedge x_n = \alpha_n \wedge y_n = \beta_n$$
$$\wedge\ x_1 + y_1 + \cdots + x_n + y_n \geq m \quad (5)$$

where the α_i, β_i are constants in $\{2, 3\}$ such that for each i, $\alpha_i + \beta_i = 5$. Such a formula is satisfiable if and only if $m \leq 5n$.

Assume now $m > 5n$. All combinations of $b_1, \ldots, b_n$ lead to unsatisfiable constraints, thus Formula 4 is unsatisfiable. Such an exhaustive exploration is equivalent to exploring 2^n paths in the control flow graph, computing the execution time for each and comparing it to the bound. Could an SMT-solver do better? SMT-solvers, when exploring the Boolean state space, may detect that the current Boolean choices (say, $b_3 \wedge \neg b_5 \wedge b_7$) lead to an arithmetic contradiction, without picking a value for all the Booleans. The SMT-solver extracts a (possibly smaller) contradiction (say, $b_3 \wedge \neg b_5$), adds the negation of this contradiction to the Boolean constraints as a *theory clause*, and restarts Boolean solving. The hope is that there exist short contradictions that enable the SMT-solver to prune the Boolean search space. Yet, in our case, there are no such short contradictions: if one leaves out *any* of the conjuncts in Formula 5, the conjunction becomes satisfiable. Note the asymmetry between proving satisfiability and unsatisfiability: for satisfiability, one can always hope that clever heuristics will lead to one solution, while for unsatisfiability, the prover has to close all branches in the search.

The difficulty of Formula 4 or similar "diamond formulas" is well-known in SMT circles. It boils down to the SMT-solver working exclusively with the predicates found in the original formulas, without deriving new useful ones such as $x_i + y_i \leq 5$. All state-of-the-art solvers that we have tried have exponential running time in n when solving Formula 4 for $m = 5n$ (Fig. 5)[11]; the difficulty increases exponentially as upper bound on the WCET to be proved becomes closer to the actual WCET.

There have been proposals of alternative approaches to DPLL(T), where one would directly solve for the numeric values instead of solving for Booleans then turning theory lemmas into Boolean constraints [5, 12, 13, 17, 31]; but no production solver implements them.[12] This is the reason why we turned to incorporating cuts into the encoding.

6. Implementation and Experimental Results

We experimented our approach for computing the worst-case execution time on benchmarks from several sources, referenced in Table 1. nsichneu and statemate belong to the Mälardalen WCET benchmarks set [20][13], being the largest of the set (w.r.t. code size). cruise-control and digital-stopwatch are generated from SCADE™ designs. autopilot and fly-by-wire come from the Papabench benchmark [34] derived from the Paparazzi free software suite for piloting UAVs (http://paparazzi.enac.fr/). tdf and miniflight are industrial avionic case-studies.

---

[10] We leave out improvements such as *theory propagation* for the sake of simplicity. See [27] for more details.

[11] A special version of MathSAT 5, which was kindly made available to us by the authors [36], implements the binary search approach internally. It suffers from the same exponential behavior as noted in the figure: in its last step, it has to prove that the maximum obtained truly is maximum.

[12] Dejan Jovanovic was kind enough to experiment with some of our formulas in his experimental solver [17], but the execution time was unacceptably high. We stress that this field of workable alternatives to DPLL(T) is still new and it is too early to draw conclusions.

[13] http://www.mrtc.mdh.se/projects/wcet/benchmarks.html

6.1 Description of the Implementation

We use the infrastructure of the PAGAI static analyzer [22][14] to produce an SMT formula corresponding to the semantics of a program expressed in LLVM bitcode.

A limitation is that, at present, PAGAI considers that floating-point variables are real numbers and that integers are unbounded mathematical integers, as opposed to finite bit-vectors; certainly an industrial tool meant to provide sound bounds should have accurate semantics, but this limitation is irrelevant to our proof-of-concept (note how the bitvectors from functional semantics and the timing variables are fully separated — their combination would therefore not pose a problem to any SMT-solver implementing a variant of the Nelson-Oppen combination of procedures [27, ch. 10]).

Using the LLVM optimization facilities, we first apply some standard transformation to the program (loop unrolling, function inlining, SSA) so as to obtain a single loop-free function; in a manner reminiscent of bounded model checking. Once the SMT formula is constructed, we enrich it with an upper timing bound for each basic block.

Finally, we conjoin to our formula the cuts for the "sum encoding", i.e., constraints of the form $\sum_{i \in S} c_i \le B$, where the c_i's are the cost variables attached to the basic blocks. There is one such "cut" for every basic block with several incoming edges: the constraint expresses an upper bound on the total timing of the program portion comprised between the block and its immediate dominator (Fig. 3). The bound B is the weight of the maximal path through the range, be it feasible or infeasible (a more expensive method is to call the WCET computation recursively on the range).

We use Z3 [16] as an SMT solver and a binary search strategy to maximize the *cost* variable modulo SMT.

The encoding of program semantics into SMT may not be fully precise in some cases. Whenever we cannot precisely translate a construct from the LLVM bitcode, we abstract it by nondeterministic choices into all the variables possibly written to by the construct (an operation referred to as havoc in certain systems); for instance, this is the case for loads from memory locations that we cannot trace to a specific variable. We relied on the LLVM mem2reg optimization phase to lift memory accesses into SSA (single static assignment) variables; all accesses that it could not lift were thus abstracted as nondeterministic choice. We realized that, due to being limited to local, stack-allocated variables, this phase missed some possible liftings, e.g. those of global variables. This resulted in the same variable from the program to be analyzed being considered as several unrelated nondeterministic loads from memory, thereby breaking dependencies between tests and preventing infeasible paths from being discarded. We thus implemented a supplemental lifting phase for global variables. It is however possible that our analysis still misses infeasible paths because of badly abstracted constructs (for instance, arrays), and that further improvements could bring even better results (that is, upper bounds on the WCET that would be closer to the real WCET).

Furthermore, some paths are infeasible because of a global invariant of the control loop (e.g. some Booleans a and b activate mutually exclusive modes of operations, and $\neg a \lor \neg b$ is an invariant); we have not yet integrated such invariants, which could be obtained either by static analysis of the program, either by analysis of the high-level specification from which the program is extracted [1].

Our current implementation keeps inside the program the resulting formulas statements and variables that have no effect on control flow and thus on WCET. Better performance could probably be obtained by slicing away such irrelevant statements.

Benchmark name	LLVM #lines	LLVM #BB
statemate	2885	632
nsichneu	12453	1374
cruise-control	234	43
digital-stopwatch	1085	188
autopilot	8805	1191
fly-by-wire	5498	609
miniflight	5860	745
tdf	2689	533

Table 1. Table referencing the various benchmarks. LLVM #lines is the number of lines in the LLVM bitcode, and LLVM #BB is its number of Basic Blocks.

6.2 Results with bitcode-based timing

The problem addressed in this article is not architectural modeling and low-level timing analysis: we assume that worst-case timings for basic blocks are given by an external analysis. Here we report on results with a simple timing basis: the time taken by a LLVM bitcode block is its number of instructions; our goal here is to check whether improvements to WCET can be obtained by our analysis with reasonable computation costs, independently of the architecture.

As expected, the naive approach (without adding cuts to the formula) does not scale at all, and the computation has reached our timeout in all of our largest benchmarks. Once the cuts are conjoined to the formula, the WCET is computed considerably faster, with some benchmarks needing less than a minute while they timed out with the naive approach.

Our results (Table 2, first part) show that the use of bounded model checking by SMT solving improves the precision of the computed upper bound on the worst-case execution time, since the longest syntactic path is in most cases not feasible due to the semantics of the instructions. As usual with WCET analyzes, it is difficult to estimate the absolute quality of the resulting bound, because the exact WCET is unknown (perhaps what we obtain is actually the WCET, perhaps it overestimates it somewhat).

On the autopilot software, our analysis reduces the WCET bound by 69.7%. This software has multiple clock domains, statically scheduled by the periodic_task() function using switches and arithmetic constraints. Approaches that do not take functional semantics into account therefore consider activation patterns that cannot occur in the real system, leading to a huge overestimation compared to our semantic-sensitive approach.

6.3 Results with realistic timing

The timing model used in the preceding subsection is not meant to be realistic. We therefore experimented with realistic timings for the basic blocks, obtained by the OTAWA tool [2] for an ARMv7 architecture. The results are given in Table 2 (second half).

The difficulty here is that OTAWA considers the basic blocks occurring in binary code, while our analysis considers the basic blocks in the LLVM bitcode. The LLVM blocks are close to those in the binary code, but code generation slightly changes the block structure in some cases. The matching of binary code to LLVM bitcode is thus sometimes imperfect and we had to resort to one that safely overestimates the execution time. Fig. 6 gives an overview of the general workflow for deriving the appropriate costs of LLVM basic blocks. The alternative would be to generate the SMT formulas not from LLVM bitcode, but directly from the binary code; unfortunately a reliable implementation needs to address a lot of open questions, and as such, it falls into our future plans.

While the nsichneu benchmark is fully handled by our approach when using bitcode-based timing, it is much harder when

---

[14] http://pagai.forge.imag.fr

49

Benchmark name	WCET bounds			Analysis time (in seconds)		#cuts
	syntactic/OTAWA	max-SMT	diff	with cuts	without cuts	
Bitcode-based timings (in number of LLVM instructions)						
statemate	997	951	4.6%	118.3	$+\infty$	143
nsichneu	9693	5998	38.1%	131.4	$+\infty$	252
cruise-control	123	121	1.6%	0.1	0.1	13
digital-stopwatch	332	302	9.0%	1.0	35.5	53
autopilot	4198	1271	69.7%	782.0	$+\infty$	498
fly-by-wire	2932	2792	4.7%	7.6	$+\infty$	163
miniflight	4015	3428	14.6%	35.8	$+\infty$	251
tdf	1583	1569	0.8%	5.4	343.8	254
Realistic timings (in cycles) for an ARMv7 architecture						
statemate	3297	3211	2.6%	943.5	$+\infty$	143
nsichneu* (1 iteration)	17242	<13332**	22.7%	3600**	$+\infty$	378
cruise-control	881	873	0.9%	0.1	0.2	13
digital-stopwatch	1012	954	5.7%	0.6	2104.2	53
autopilot	12663	5734	54.7%	1808.8	$+\infty$	498
fly-by-wire	6361	5848	8.0%	10.8	$+\infty$	163
miniflight	17980	14752	18.0%	40.9	$+\infty$	251
tdf	5789	5727	1.0%	13.0	$+\infty$	254

Table 2. *max-SMT* is the upper bound on WCET reported by our analysis based on optimization modulo theory, while *syntactic/OTAWA* is the execution time of longest syntactic path (provided by Otawa when using realistic timings). *diff* is the improvement brought by our method. The analysis time for *max-SMT* is reported with and without added cuts; $+\infty$ indicates timeout (1 hour). #cuts is the number of added cuts. In the second part, *) nsichneu has been simplified to one main-loop iteration (instead of 2), and has been computed with cuts refinement as described in subsection 6.3. **) Computation takes longer than 1 hour. A safe bound of 13332 is already known after this time.

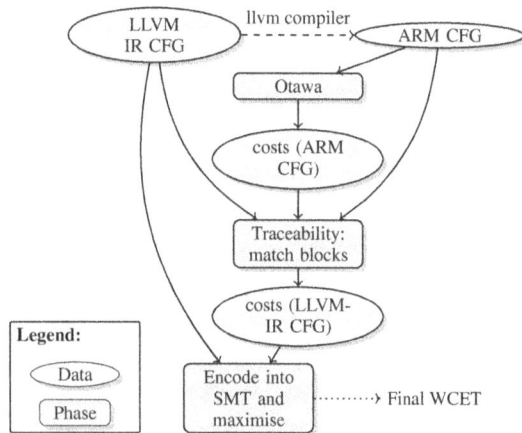

Figure 6. General workflow for deriving timings using OTAWA.

using the realistic metric. We had to improve our implementation in two ways: 1. We extract cuts for larger portions of the program: we take the portions from our previous cuts (between merge points and their immediate dominators) and derive new cuts by recursively grouping these portions by two. We then have cuts for one half, one quarter, etc. of the program. 2. Instead of directly optimising the total cost variable of the program, we successively optimize the variables expressing the "cuts" (in order of portion size). This allows to strengthen the cuts with smaller upper bounds, and helps the analysis of the bigger portions. In this benchmark, all the biggest paths are unfeasible because of inconsistent semantic constraints over the variables involved in the tests. Better cuts could be derived if we were not restricted to contiguous portions in the implementation. The computation time is around 6.5 hours to get the exact WCET (13298 cycles), but we could have stopped after one hour and get a correct upper bound of 13332 cycles, which is already very close to the final result.

7. Related Work

The work closest to ours is from Chu and Jaffar [10]. They perform symbolic execution on the program, thereby unrolling an exponentially-sized execution tree (each if-then-else construct doubles the number of branches). This would be intolerably expensive if not for the very astute subsumption criterion used to fold some of the branches into others already computed. More specifically, their symbolic execution generalizes each explored state S to a first-order formula defining states from which the feasible paths are included in those starting from S; these formula are obtained from *Craig interpolants* extracted from the proofs of infeasibility.

In our approach, we also learn formula that block infeasible paths or paths that cannot lead to paths longer than the WCET obtained, in two ways: the SMT-solver learns blocking clauses by itself, and we feed "cuts" to it. Let us now attempt to give a high-level view of the difference between our approach and theirs. Symbolic execution [6] (in depth-first fashion) can be simulated by SMT-solving by having the SMT-solver select decision literals [27] in the order of execution of the program encoded into the formula; in contrast, general bounded model checking by SMT-solving will assert predicates in an arbitrary order, which may be preferrable in some cases (e.g. if $x \leq 0$ is asserted early in the program and $x + y \geq 0$ very late, after multiple if-then-elses, it is useful to be able to derive $y \geq 0$ immediately without having to wait until the end of each path). Yet, an SMT-solver based on DPLL(T) does not learn lemmas constructed from new predicates, while the approach in [10] learns new predicates on-the-fly from Craig interpolants. In our approach, we help the SMT-solver by preventively feeding "candidate lemmas", which, if used in a proof that there is no path longer than a certain bound, act as Craig interpolants, as explained in subsection 4.5. Our approach therefore leverages both out-of-order predicate selection and interpolation, and, as a consequence, it seems to scale better.

Two recent works — Biere et al. [4] and its follow-up Knoop et al. [26] — integrate the WCET path analysis into a counterexample guided abstraction refinement loop. As such, the IPET approach using ILP is refined by extracting a witness path for the maximal time, and testing its feasibility by SMT-solving; if the path is infeasible, an additional ILP constraint is generated, to exclude the spurious path. Because this ILP constraint relates all the conditionals corresponding to the spurious witness path, excluding infeasible paths in this way exhibits an exponential behavior we strove to avoid. Moreover, our approach is more flexible with respect to (1) the class of properties which can be expressed, as it is not limited by the ILP semantics and (2) the ability to incorporate non-functional semantics (which is unclear whether [4] or [26] can).

Metzner [32] proposed an approach where the program control flow is encoded into a model along with either the concrete semantics of a simple model of instruction cache, or an abstraction thereof. The WCET bound is obtained by binary search, with each test performed using the VIS model-checker[15]. Huber and Schoeberl [24] proposed a similar approach with the model-checker UPPAAL.[16] In both cases, the functional semantics are however not encoded, save for loop bounds: branches are chosen nondeterministically, and thus the analysis may consider infeasible paths. Dalsgaard et al. [15] encode into UPPAAL precise models of a pipeline, instruction cache and data cache, but again the program is modeled as "data insensitive", meaning that infeasible paths are not discarded except when exceeding a loop bound.

Holsti [23] considers a loop (though the same approach can also be applied to loop-free code): the loop is sliced, keeping only instructions and variables that affect control flow, and a global "timing" counter T is added; the input-output relation of the loop body is obtained as a formula in linear integer arithmetic (Presburger arithmetic); some form of *acceleration* is used to establish a relation between T, some induction variables and some inputs to the program. Applied to loop-free programs, this method should give exactly the same result as our approach. Its main weakness is that representations of Presburger sets are notoriously expensive, whereas SMT scales up (the examples given in the cited article seem very small, taking only a few lines and at most 1500 clock cycles for the entire loop execution); also, the restriction to Presburger arithmetic may exclude many programs, though one can model constructs outside of Presburger arithmetic by nondeterministic choices. Its strong point is the ability to precisely deal with loops, including those where the iteration count affects which program fragments are active.

8. Extensions and Future Work

The "counter encoding" is best suited for code portions that have a single entry and exit point (in which case they express the timing difference between entry and exit). In contrast, the "sum encoding" may be applied to arbitrary subsets of the code, which do not in fact need to be connected in the control-flow graph. One may thus use other heuristic criteria, such as usage of related variables.

A model based on worst-case execution times for every block, to be reassembled into a global worst-case execution time, may be too simplistic: indeed, the execution time of a block may depend on which blocks were executed beforehand, or, for finer modeling, on the value of pointer variables (for determining cache status).

A very general and tempting idea, as suggested earlier in MDD-based model-checking [32], in symbolic execution and bounded model checking by [9, 10], in combined abstract interpretation and SAT-solving [3] is to integrate in the same analysis both the non-functional semantics (e.g. caches) and the functional semantics; in our case, we would replace both the micro-architectural analysis (or part of it) and the path analysis by a single pass of optimization

modulo SMT. Because merely encoding the functional semantics and a simplistic timing model already led to intractable formulas, we decided to postpone such micro-architectural modeling until we had solved scalability issues. We intend to integrate such *non-functional* aspects into the SMT problem in future work.

Detailed modeling of the cache, pipeline, etc. may be too expensive to compute beforehand and encode into SMT. One alternative is to iteratively refine the model with respect to the current "worst-case trace": to each basic block one attaches an upper bound on the worst-case execution time, and once a worst-case trace is obtained, a trace analysis is run over it to derive stronger constraints. These constraints can then be incorporated in the SMT encoding before searching for a new longest path.

We have discussed obtaining a tight upper bound on the worst-case operation time of the program from upper bounds on the execution times of the basic blocks. If using lower bounds on the worst-case execution times of the basic blocks, one may obtain a lower bound on the worst-case execution time of the program. Having both is useful to gauge the amount of over-approximation incurred. Also, by applying minimization instead of maximization, one gets bounds on best-case execution time, which is useful for some scheduling applications [39].

On a more practical angle, our analysis is to be connected to analyses both on the high level specification (e.g. providing invariants) and on the object code (micro-architectural timing analysis); this poses engineering difficulties, because typical compilation framework may not support sufficient tracing information.

Our requirement that the program should be loop-free, or at least contain loops with small constant bounds, can be relaxed through an approach similar to that of Chu and Jaffar [10]: the body of a loop can be summarized by its WCET, or more precisely by some summaries involving the cost variables and the scalar variables of the program. Then, this entire loop can be considered as a single block in an analysis of a larger program, with possibly overapproximations in the WCET, depending on how the summaries are produced.

9. Conclusion

We have shown that optimization using satisfiability modulo theory (SMT) is a workable approach for bounding the worst-case execution time of loop-free programs (or programs where loops can be unrolled). To our knowledge, this is the first time that such an approach was successfully applied.

Our approach computes an upper bound on the WCET, which may or may not be the actual WCET. The sources of discrepancy are 1) the microarchitectural analysis (e.g. the cache analysis does not know whether an access is a hit or a miss), 2) the composition of WCET for basic blocks into WCET for the program, which may lose dependencies on execution history[17], 3) the encoding of the program into SMT, which may be imprecise (e.g. unsupported constructs replaced by nondeterministic choices).

We showed that straightforward encodings of WCET problems into SMT yield problems intractable by all current production-grade SMT-solvers ("diamond formulas"), and how to work around this issue using a clever encoding. We believe this approach can be generalized to other properties, and lead to fruitful interaction between modular abstraction and SMT-solving.

From a practical point of view, our approach integrates with any SMT solver without any modification, which makes it convenient for efficient and robust implementation. It could also integrate various simple analyses for introducing other relevant cuts.

---

[15] http://vlsi.colorado.edu/~vis/

[16] http://www.uppaal.org/

---

[17] This does not apply to some simple microcontroller architectures, without cache or pipeline states, e.g. Atmel AVR[TM] and Freescale[TM] HCS12.

While our redundant encoding brings staggering improvements in analysis time, allowing formerly intractable problems to be solved under one minute, the improvements in the WCET upper bound brought by the elimination of infeasible paths depend on the structure of the program being analyzed. The improvement on the WCET bound of some industrial examples (18%, 55%…) is impressive, in a field where improvements are often of a few percents. This means that, at least for certain classes of programs, it is necessary to take infeasible paths into account. At present, certain industries avoid using formal verification for WCET because it has a reputation for giving overly pessimistic over-estimates; it seems likely that some of this over-estimation arises from infeasible paths.

Our approach to improving bounds on WCET blends well with other WCET analyses. It can be coupled with an existing micro-architectural analysis, or part of that analysis may be integrated into our approach. It can be combined with precise, yet less scalable analyzes [23, 26] to summarize inner loops; but may itself be used as a way to summarize the WCET of portion of a larger program.

References

[1] M. Asavoae, C. Maiza, and P. Raymond. Program semantics in model-based WCET analysis: A state of the art perspective. In C. Maiza, editor, *WCET 2013*, volume 30 of *OASICS*, pages 32–41. Schloss Dagstuhl - Leibniz-Zentrum fuer Informatik, 2013.

[2] C. Ballabriga, H. Cassé, C. Rochange, and P. Sainrat. OTAWA: An open toolbox for adaptive WCET analysis. In *SEUS*, volume 6399 of *LNCS*, pages 35–46. Springer, 2010.

[3] A. Banerjee, S. Chattopadhyay, and A. Roychoudhury. Precise micro-architectural modeling for WCET analysis via AI+SAT. In *IEEE Real-Time and Embedded Technology and Applications Symposium (RTAS)*, pages 87–96. IEEE Computer Society, 2013.

[4] A. Biere, J. Knoop, L. Kovács, and J. Zwirchmayr. The Auspicious Couple: Symbolic Execution and WCET Analysis. In *WCET*, volume 30 of *OASIcs*, pages 53–63. IBFI Schloss Dagstuhl, 2013. URL http://drops.dagstuhl.de/opus/volltexte/2013/4122.

[5] N. Bjørner, B. Dutertre, and L. de Moura. Accelerating lemma learning using joins - DPLL(⊔), 2008. Appeared as short paper in LPAR 2008, outside of proceedings.

[6] C. Cadar and K. Sen. Symbolic execution for software testing: Three decades later. *Commun. ACM*, 56(2):82–90, Feb. 2013.

[7] P. Caspi, P. Raymond, and S. Tripakis. Synchronous programming. In *Handbook of Real-Time and Embedded Systems*, chapter 14. Chapman & Hall / CRC, 2008.

[8] S. Chaki and J. Ivers. Software model checking without source code. *Innovations in Systems and Software Engineering*, 6(3):233–242, 2010. ISSN 1614-5046. .

[9] S. Chattopadhyay and A. Roychoudhury. Scalable and precise refinement of cache timing analysis via path-sensitive verification. *Real-Time Systems*, 49(4):517–562, 2013.

[10] D.-H. Chu and J. Jaffar. Symbolic simulation on complicated loops for WCET path analysis. In *EMSOFT*, pages 319–328, 2011. ISBN 978-1-4503-0714-7. .

[11] L. Cordeiro, B. Fischer, and J. Marques-Silva. SMT-based bounded model checking for embedded ANSI-C software. *IEEE Trans. Software Eng.*, 38(4):957–974, 2012.

[12] S. Cotton. *On Some Problems in Satisfiability Solving*. PhD thesis, Université Joseph Fourier, Grenoble, 2009.

[13] S. Cotton. Natural domain SMT: A preliminary assessment. In *FORMATS*, volume 6246 of *LNCS*, pages 77–91. Springer, 2010.

[14] P. Cousot et al. The Astrée analyzer. In *ESOP*, volume 3444 of *LNCS*, pages 21–30. Springer, 2005.

[15] A. Dalsgaard, M. Olesen, M. Toft, R. Hansen, and K. Larsen. META-MOC: Modular execution time analysis using model checking. In *WCET*, pages 113–123, 2010.

[16] L. M. de Moura and N. Bjørner. Z3: An efficient SMT solver. In *TACAS*, volume 4963 of *LNCS*, pages 337–340. Springer, 2008.

[17] L. M. de Moura and D. Jovanovic. A model-constructing satisfiability calculus. In *VMCAI*, volume 7737 of *LNCS*, pages 1–12. Springer, 2013.

[18] J. Engblom and B. Jonsson. Processor pipelines and their properties for static wcet analysis. In *EMSOFT*, volume 2491 of *LNCS*, pages 334–348. Springer, 2002.

[19] J. Gustafsson, A. Ermedahl, C. Sandberg, and B. Lisper. Automatic derivation of loop bounds and infeasible paths for WCET analysis using abstract execution. In *RTSS*, 2006.

[20] J. Gustafsson, A. Betts, A. Ermedahl, and B. Lisper. The Mälardalen WCET benchmarks – past, present and future. In *WCET*, volume 15 of *OASICS*, pages 136–146. IBFI Schloss Dagstuhl, 2010.

[21] C. Healy and D. Whalley. Automatic detection and exploitation of branch constraints for timing analysis. *IEEE Trans. on Software Engineering*, 28(8), Aug. 2002.

[22] J. Henry, D. Monniaux, and M. Moy. Pagai: A path sensitive static analyser. *Electr. Notes Theor. Comput. Sci.*, 289:15–25, 2012.

[23] N. Holsti. Computing time as a program variable: a way around infeasible paths. In *WCET*, volume 08003 of *Dagstuhl Seminar Proceedings*. IBFI Schloss Dagstuhl, 2008.

[24] B. Huber and M. Schoeberl. Comparison of implicit path enumeration and model checking based wcet analysis. In *WCET*, volume 10 of *OASICS*. IBFI Schloss Dagstuhl, 2009. URL http://drops.dagstuhl.de/opus/volltexte/2009/2281.

[25] B. K. Huynh, L. Ju, and A. Roychoudhury. Scope-aware data cache analysis for WCET estimation. In *IEEE Real-Time and Embedded Technology and Applications Symposium*, pages 203–212, 2011.

[26] J. Knoop, L. Kovács, and J. Zwirchmayr. WCET squeezing: on-demand feasibility refinement for proven precise WCET-bounds. In *RTNS*, pages 161–170, 2013.

[27] D. Kroening and O. Strichman. *Decision Procedures*. Springer, 2008.

[28] C. Lattner and V. S. Adve. LLVM: A compilation framework for lifelong program analysis & transformation. In *CGO*, pages 75–88. IEEE Computer Society, 2004.

[29] X. Li, Y. Liang, T. Mitra, and A. Roychoudhury. Chronos: A timing analyzer for embedded software. *Science of Computer Programming*, 69(1–3):56–67, 2007.

[30] Y.-T. S. Li and S. Malik. Performance analysis of embedded software using implicit path enumeration. *IEEE Trans. on Computer-Aided Design of Integrated Circuits and Systems*, 16(12):1477–1487, 1997.

[31] K. L. McMillan, A. Kuehlmann, and M. Sagiv. Generalizing DPLL to richer logics. In *CAV*, volume 5643 of *LNCS*, pages 462–476. Springer, 2009.

[32] A. Metzner. Why model checking can improve WCET analysis. In *CAV*, pages 334–347, 2004.

[33] H. Negi, A. Roychoudhury, and T. Mitra. Simplifying WCET analysis by code transformations. In *WCET*, 2004.

[34] F. Nemer, H. Cassé, P. Sainrat, J. P. Bahsoun, and M. D. Michiel. Papabench: a free real-time benchmark. In *WCET*, volume 4 of *OASICS*. IBFI Schloss Dagstuhl, 2006.

[35] J. Reineke. *Caches in WCET Analysis: Predictability - Competitiveness - Sensitivity*. PhD thesis, University of Saarland, 2009.

[36] R. Sebastiani and S. Tomasi. Optimization in SMT with $\mathcal{LA}(\mathbb{Q})$ cost functions. In *IJCAR*, volume 7364 of *LNCS*, pages 484–498. Springer, 2012.

[37] J. Souyris, V. Wiels, D. Delmas, and H. Delseny. Formal verification of avionics software products. In A. Cavalcanti and D. Dams, editors, *Formal Methods (FM)*, volume 5850 of *LNCS*, pages 532–546. Springer, 2009. ISBN 978-3-642-05088-6. .

[38] H. Theiling, C. Ferdinand, and R. Wilhelm. Fast and precise WCET prediction by separated cache and path analyses. *Int. J. of Time-Critical Computing Systems*, 18:157–179, 2000.

[39] R. Wilhelm. Determining bounds on execution times. In *Handbook on Embedded Systems*, chapter 14. CRC Press, 2006.

[40] R. Wilhelm et al. The worst-case execution-time problem - overview of methods and survey of tools. *ACM Trans. Embedded Comput. Syst.*, 7(3), 2008.

[41] W. Zhao, W. C. Kreahling, D. B. Whalley, C. A. Healy, and F. Mueller. Improving WCET by applying worst-case path optimizations. *Real-Time Systems*, 34(2):129–152, 2006.

WCET-Aware Dynamic Instruction Cache Locking

Wenguang Zheng

School of Computer Science and Engineering
The University of New South Wales
wenguangz@cse.unsw.edu.au

Hui Wu

School of Computer Science and Engineering
The University of New South Wales
huiw@cse.unsw.edu.au

Abstract

Caches are widely used in embedded systems to bridge the increasing speed gap between processors and off-chip memory. However, caches make it significantly harder to compute the WCET(Worst Case Execution Time) of a task. To alleviate this problem, cache locking has been proposed. We investigate the I-cache locking problem, and propose a WCET-aware, min-cut based dynamic instruction cache locking approach for reducing the WCET of a single task. We have implemented our approach and compared it with the two state-of-the-art cache locking approaches by using a set of benchmarks from the MRTC benchmark suite. The experimental results show that our approach achieves the average improvements of 41%, 15% and 7% over the partial locking approach for the 256B, 512B and 1KB caches, respectively, and 7%, 18% and 17% over the longest path based dynamic locking approach for the 256B, 512B and 1KB caches, respectively.

Categories and Subject Descriptors   B.3.3 [*Performance Analysis and Design Aids*]: Worst-case analysis

Keywords   Worst-case execution time; dynamic instruction cache locking; minimum cut

1.   Introduction

Caches (I-cache and D-cache) are effective to bridge the speed gap between processors and off-chip memory. With the utilization of caches, the execution time of a task can be significantly reduced. Caches are managed by hardware. For each memory access, it is difficult to know at compile time if the corresponding data or instruction is already in the cache. Therefore, caches make it significantly harder to compute the WCET of a task. Cache locking is an effective technique to remedy the unpredictability of caches. If an instruction or data is locked into the cache, it will not be replaced. The access time of each locked instruction or data is always one cycle. As a result, cache locking makes it significantly easier to compute the WCET of a task. Furthermore, cache locking can reduce the WCET of a task as we can lock the contents on the longest paths to reduce the access times of those contents.

There are two types of cache locking, static cache locking and dynamic cache locking. Static cache locking assumes that the live ranges of the locked contents span the entire task. Therefore, the locked contents of a task remain locked during the entire execution of the task. As a result, the contents mapped to the same location in a cache cannot be locked simultaneously, resulting in low cache utilization. Dynamic cache locking considers the live ranges of the locked contents. Different contents can be locked into the same location of a cache as long as their live ranges do not overlap, leading to more efficient cache utilization than static cache locking.

For static cache locking, the major task is to select the contents to be locked into a cache. For dynamic cache locking, there are two additional tasks, determining when to load and lock the selected contents, and when to unlock them. Typically, the locked contents can be unlocked when their live ranges end. To reduce the WCET of a task, we need to select the contents on the longest path to be locked into the cache. The longest path may change after some contents on the longest path are locked into the cache. For this reason, the previous cache locking approaches iteratively select the contents on the longest path to be locked into the cache. However, selecting contents on a single longest path may not minimize the WCET of a task.

In this paper, we investigate the WCET-aware, dynamic I-cache locking problem for a single task. The unit of contents for locking is a memory block entirely mapped to a cache line. Our objective is to select a set of memory blocks of a task and find a loading point for each memory block selected such that the task's WCET is minimized after the memory blocks selected are loaded and locked at the loading points. We make the following major contributions.

1. We propose a min-cut based, dynamic cache locking approach. Unlike all the previous cache locking approaches that consider the longest path only, our approach considers a subgraph that contains not only the longest path, but also all the paths whose lengths are close to that of the longest path, and select a minimum set of memory blocks of instructions to be locked into the cache.

2. We propose an efficient technique for determining a good loading point for each memory block selected as the locked cache contents, further reducing the WCET of a task.

3. We have implemented our approach and compared it with the two state-of-the-art cache locking approaches, the partial locking approach proposed in [6] and the longest path based dynamic locking approach proposed in [15], by using a set of benchmarks from the MRTC benchmark suite [8]. The experimental results show that our approach achieves the average improvements of 41%, 15% and 7% over the partial locking approach for the 256B, 512B and 1KB caches, respectively, and 7%, 18% and 17% over the longest path based dynamic locking approach for the 256B, 512B and 1KB caches, respectively.

The rest of this paper is organized as follow. Section 2 gives a brief survey of the related work. Section 3 presents a motivational

LCTES '14,   June 12–13, 2014, Edinburgh, UK.
Copyright © 2014 ACM 978-1-4503-2877-7 /14/06... $15.00.
http://dx.doi.org/10.1145/2597809.2597820

example. Section 4 describes the system model and key definitions. Section 5 proposes our algorithm for selecting memory blocks of a single loop as locked I-cache contents. Section 6 presents our approach to loop nests. Section 7 shows the experimental results and analyses, and Section 8 concludes this paper.

2. Related Work

Cache locking problems have been extensively studied, and various approaches have been proposed.

Many cache locking approaches have been proposed to reduce the WCET or the ACET (Average Case Execution Time) of a single task. [13] proposes instruction cache locking algorithms that aim at minimizing the ACET of a task. It uses a PEFT (Probability Execution Flow Tree) to model a task. [1] proposes an approach to reduce the ACET of a task. A cost-benefit model is constructed to determine which memory addresses should be locked in order to reduce the ACET. [10] uses the temporal reuse profile to construct the cost-benefit model, and locks the memory blocks with the largest miss rate to reduce the ACET.

[19] studies the D-cache locking problem. It combines D-cache locking with the static cache analysis to estimate the precise worst cache memory performance. [7] proposes a static I-cache locking approach that aims at minimizing the WCET by iteratively reducing the longest path length. It uses an EFG (Execution Flow Graph) to model the possible execution paths, and selects the instructions on the current longest path with the largest benefit to be locked in the cache. [11] studies the static I-cache locking problem. It formulates the problem using an EFT (Execution Flow Tree) and a linear programming model. For a subset of the problems with certain properties, it proposes polynomial time optimal algorithms. Furthermore, it proves that the general problem is NP-Hard. [14] proposes an ILP (Integer Linear Programming) based, static I-cache locking algorithm for minimizing the WCET of a single task. [6] points out that full cache locking may cause more cache misses which would have a negative effect on WCET reduction. It proposes a partial I-cache locking mechanism to lock a part of I-cache. [16] proposes a dynamic I-cache locking approach. It partitions a program into a set of regions. For each regions, there is a loading point. [15] presents two dynamic I-cache locking algorithms. One is a greedy algorithm, and the other is a genetic algorithm. A cost function is used for each pre-header of loops to determine the whether this loop pre-header should be selected as a loading point. However, the cost function is not clearly defined. [5] compares static and dynamic cache locking using genetic algorithm. It point outs that static cache locking is more predictable, and dynamic cache locking shows better improvement in most cases.

A number of approaches have been proposed to integrate task scheduling and cache locking. [17] studies static I-cache locking for multitask real-time systems. It proposes two algorithms, one aiming at minimizing the CPU utilization and the other attempting to minimize the interferences between tasks. [3] proposes a genetic algorithm for the problem of selecting instructions to be locked into the I-cache to reduce the response time of multitasks. [12] combines cache locking with task assignment to reduce the WCETs of a set of tasks on a multiprocessor system with two levels of caches. It applies cache locking to both I-cache and D-cache by using the algorithms proposed in [11] and [19] to reduce the WCET for each task. Then, it optimizes the task assignment considering the locked cache size. [4] proposes a dynamic I-cache locking approach for multitask systems. It uses the response time analysis approach proposed in [18] for the schedulability test, and combines the schedulability analysis with cache locking using a genetic algorithm to improve the performance of the I-cache on a multitasking, preemptive real-time system.

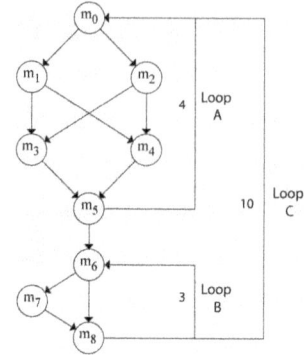

Figure 1. motivation example

3. An Motivational Example

In this section, we use an example to compare the state-of-the-art approaches to the WCET-aware I-cache locking problem and illustrate the key ideas of our approach. Consider a task whose CFG is shown in Figure1. The task consists of three loops. loop A and loop B are nested in loop C. The numbers of iterations of loop A, loop B and loop C are 4, 3, 10, respectively. For simplicity, we make the following assumptions.

1. The I-cache is fully associative and has 4 cache lines which can store 4 memory blocks.

2. Each basic block is exactly one memory block.

3. If a basic block is in the I-cache, its execution time is 1. Otherwise, it is 30.

3.1 Static Full Cache Locking

Consider the approach proposed in [7] which iteratively finds the longest path and selects the memory block with the largest benefit on the longest path as the locked cache contents. Before cache locking, there are four longest paths. Obviously, the nodes of loop A have larger benefits because of its larger number of iterations. The four basic blocks m_0, m_1, m_3, m_5 may be subsequently selected as the locked cache contents, resulting in a WCET of $120 + (62 * 4 + 90 * 3) * 10 = 5300$.

3.2 Longest Path Based Dynamic Cache Locking

Using the longest path based dynamic cache locking approach proposed in [15], the selected contents are loaded and locked at the pre-headers of loop A and loop B. For loop A, m_0, m_1, m_4, m_5 may be subsequently selected as the locked cache contents as they have the largest frequencies on the current longest paths. When loop A terminates, all the cache lines occupied by its memory blocks can be released. So, the entire loop B can be locked. The memory blocks m_0, m_1, m_4, m_5 will be fetched and locked 10 times at the preheader of loop A, and the three memory blocks of loop B will also be fetched and locked 10 times at the pre-header of loop B. The times taken to fetch and lock the selected memory blocks of loop A and loop B are 30*4*10=1200 and 30*3*10=900, respectively. Therefore the WCET of the task is $(62*4+30*4)*10+(3*3+3*30)*10 = 4670$.

3.3 Partial Cache Locking

Using the partial cache locking approach proposed in [6], m_0 and m_6 may be selected as the locked cache contents. The other two cache lines are kept free so that the memory accesses to m_7 and m_8 will be hit after the first cache misses. For loop A, each iteration will cause 3 cache misses. For loop B, there are only two cache

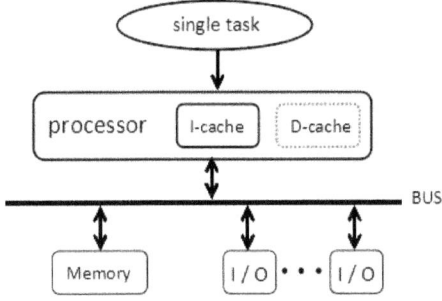

Figure 2. System model

misses during the execution of the task. Since only two memory blocks are locked, the time spent on fetching and locking these two memory blocks is 2*30= 60. Hence, the WECT of the task is 60 +(91*4+(3*2+(1+30+30))*10= 4370.

3.4 Optimal Solution

In order to find the optimal solution, we need to use a dynamic approach so that after loop A terminates, all the cache lines occupied by it can be released. This is done by loading and locking all the selected memory blocks at the preheaders of loops A and B. Furthermore, we need to select a minimum number of basic blocks as the locked cache contents. In this case, the minimum number of basic blocks can be computed by finding three minimum node cuts of the control flow graphs of loop A and loop B without back edges. For loop A, the three minimum node cuts are either $\{m_0\}$, $\{m_1, m_2\}$, $\{m_5\}$ or $\{m_0\}$, $\{m_3, m_4\}$, $\{m_5\}$. For loop B, all the three basic blocks can be locked. Therefore, the WCET of the optimal solution is (33*4+30*4+3*3+30*3)*10= 3510.

4. System Model and Definitions

The target processor has an I-cache and a D-cache as shown in Figure 2. The I-cache is an n-way set associative cache with the following parameters, the cache line size l, the associativity n, and the cache size s. Therefore, the number of sets is equal to $s/(l*n)$. Each set has a set number between 0 and $k-1$, where k is equal to $s/(l*n)$. We don not consider the D-cache locking problem. If an instruction is in the I-cache, it takes one cycle to fetch the instruction. Otherwise, it takes w cycles. The unit for locking is a cache line.

The main memory is partitioned into memory blocks such that each memory block is mapped to exactly one cache line. Thus, each basic block of a task is mapped to one or more sets of the I-cache.

A task is represented by the weighted CFG (Control Flow Graph) where each node denotes a basic block, each node weight is the execution time of the corresponding basic block, and each edge represents the control dependency between the two nodes. We assume that each path of a CFG is feasible.

Given a loop, a weighted DAG is constructed by removing all the back edges from the CFG of the loop. Given a weighed DAG and a path P, the length of P is the sum of the weights of all the nodes on P.

Given a weighted DAG G and an integer x, the x-spanning graph $G(x)$ is a subgraph of G where the length of each path is larger than x. The x-spanning graph of a weighted DAG G can be computed in $O(e)$ time as shown in Algorithm 1, where e is the number of edges in G.

Given an x-spanning graph $G(x)$, the y-projection graph $G(x, y)$ is a subgraph of $G(x)$ satisfying the following constraint.

ALGORITHM 1: $x - SpanningGraph(G, x)$

input : G: a weighted DAG
   x: an integer
output: The x-spanning graph $G(x)$ in which each path
   length is greater than x
$G(x) = G$;
/*compute the length $a(v)$ of the longest path to each node v*/
for *each node v in topological order* **do**
  if $indegree(v) = 0$ **then**
    $a(v) = w(v)$;
    /* $w(v)$ is the node weight of v */
  else
    $a(v) = w(v)+\max\{a(u) : u$ *is a parent of v in G*$\}$;

/*compute $b(v)$ for each node v where $b(v)$ is x - longest path length form v to a sink node*/
for *each node in G in reverse topological order* **do**
  if $outdegree(v) = 0$; **then**
    $b(v) = x$;
  else
    $b(v) = \min\{b(u) - w(u) : u$ *is a child of v*$\}$;
  if $b(v) > a(v)$ **then**
    delete v and all the edges incident on v from $G(x)$;

return $G(x)$;

ALGORITHM 2: $y - ProjectionGraph(G(x), y)$

input : $G(x)$: an x-spanning graph
   y: a set number
output: The y-projection graph $G(x, y)$ of $G(x)$
$G(x, y) = G(x)$;
for *each node v in G(x, y)* **do**
  if *all the memory blocks of v have been selected as the cache contents or v has no memory block mapped to the set y* **then**
    for *each parent v_i and each child v_j of v* **do**
      if *the edge (v_i, v_j) does not exist in G(x, y)*
      then
        Add (v_i, v_j) to $G(x, y)$;
    delete v and all the edges incident on v from $G(x, y)$;

return $G(x, y)$;

- For each node of $G(x, y)$, its corresponding basic block has a memory block mapped to the set y and the memory block has not been selected as the locked cache contents.

The algorithm for constructing the y-projection graph $G(x, y)$ is shown in Algorithm 2. Its time complexity is $O(e)$, where e is the number of edges in $G(x)$.

For each loop nest, we define a loop nest tree as follows. A loop nest tree is a tree where each node denotes a loop, and each edge (v_i, v_j) denotes that v_j is immediately nested in v_i.

5. I-Cache Locking for A Single Loop

Before presenting our approach to dynamic I-cache locking for a whole task, we consider a single loop and propose a min-cut based algorithm for selecting the memory blocks of the loop as the locked cache contents.

Given a single loop L, our algorithm aims at finding a minimum set of memory blocks of the loop such that the WCET of the loop is minimized after the set of memory blocks are locked into the I-cache. Our algorithm works as follows.

1. Create a weighted DAG G' by removing the back edges of the CFG of the loop.

2. For each set y, find a minimum set of memory blocks of the loop that are mapped to the set y, and select them as the locked cache contents.

Let c be the time taken to fetch one memory block from the off-chip memory. To find the minimum set of memory blocks for each set y, our algorithm repeats the following steps until the set y has no enough free space for the selected memory blocks.

1. Find the longest path length l_{max} of G'

2. Construct the x-spanning graph of G', where x is $l_{max} - c$.

3. Construct the y-projection graph of the x-spanning graph.

4. Find a minimum node cut C of the y-projection graph.

5. If the size of C is not less than the number of iterations of the loop, discard C. Otherwise, do the following.

   - If the number of free cache lines of set y is not less than the size of C, for each basic block B_i in C, select a memory block M_i with the largest execution time among all the memory blocks of B_i that have not been selected as the locked cache contents, recalculate the execution times of B_i and all the basic blocks affected, and update their corresponding node weights in the y-projection graph.

The details of our algorithm are shown in pseudo code in Algorithm 3. Next, we use an example to show how our algorithm works. Consider a DAG G shown in Figure 3 that represents a single iteration of a loop. For ease of descriptions, we assume that there are two sets in the I-cache, each set has two cache lines, and each node (basic block) is exactly one memory block of instructions. The execution time of each basic block is 1 if it is locked into the I-cache. Otherwise, it is 30. All the circle nodes are mapped to set 0, and all the square nodes are mapped to set 1. Now, we show how our algorithm selects locked cache contents for set 0. Based on the assumptions, the longest path length of the DAG G is 180. and x is set to 150. In the first iteration, $G(150)$, the 150-spanning graph, is constructed as shown in Figure 4. Based on $G(150)$, the 0-projection graph $G(150, 0)$ of $G(150)$ is constructed as shown in Figure 5. In $G(150, 0)$, $\{v_6\}$ is a minimum node cut. Thus, v_6 is selected as the locked contents and its weight is changed from 30 to 1. Now, the longest path length of G becomes 151. In the second iteration, the 121-spanning graph, $G(121)$, is constructed as shown in Figure 6. The 0-projection graph of $G(121)$ is constructed as shown in Figure 7. A minimum node cut of $G(121, 0)$ is $\{v_1\}$. So, v_1 is selected as the locked cache contents and its weight is changed from 30 to 1 as shown in Figure 8. Now, the longest path length of the DAG G is reduced to 122. The same selection process is applied on square nodes to find the locked cache contents for set 1.

6. Cache Locking for Loop Nests

In this section, we present our approach to the WCET aware, dynamic I-cache locking problem for a whole task. Our approach ignores all the basic blocks that are not inside a loop, and considers individual loop nests. For each loop nest, all its memory blocks selected as the cache contents are loaded and locked into the I-cache at the preheaders of the loops of the loop nest. Hence, the

---

ALGORITHM 3: $SingleLoopLocking(G, k, n)$

input : G: the weighted CFG of a loop
k: the total number of sets in the I-cache
$n[]$: an array where $n[i](i = 0, 1, \cdots, k - 1$ stores the number of cache lines available in the set i

output: $A[]$: an array where $A[i]$ $(i = 0, 1, \cdots, k - 1)$ stores the set of memory blocks of the loop to be locked into the set i of the I-cache

$G' = G$;
remove all the back edges from G';
for *each set $y(y = 0, 1, \cdots, k - 1)$* **do**
  $size = 0$;
  /* $size$ is the number of memory blocks of the loop that have been selected as the locked cache contents of the set y so far */
  $A[y] = \emptyset$;
  while $size < n[y]$ **do**
    calculate the longest path length l_{max} of G';
    $x = l_{max} - c$;
    $G'(x) = x - SpanningGraph(G', x)$;
    $G'(x, y) = y - ProjectionGraph(G'(x), y)$;
    if $G'(x, y) = \emptyset$ **then**
      | **break**;
    else
      | compute the minimum node cut C of $G'(x, y)$;
      | **if** *$size(C)$ is less than the number of iterations of the loop* **then**
      | | $size = size + size(C)$;
      | | **if** $size \leq n[y]$ **then**
      | | | **for** *each node $v_i \in C$* **do**
      | | | | select a memory block M_i with the largest execution time among all the memory blocks that have not been selected as the locked cache contents;
      | | | | $A[y] = A[y] \cup \{M_i\}$;
      | | | | recalculate the execution times of v_i and all the other nodes affected; updates their corresponding node weights in $G'(x, y)$;
      | **else**
      | | **break**;
  $n[y] = n[y] - size$;
return A ;

---

live range of each basic block of a loop nest does not go beyond the loop nest. After the live range of a memory block ends, the cache line storing this memory block can be reused.

We introduce a special instruction *fetch* for loading contiguous memory blocks into the I-cache and locking them. When a cache line is already locked, *fetch* can still load a memory block into it. Therefore, no *unlock* instruction is needed. In order not to disrupt the mapping between basic blocks and memory blocks, we insert a procedure call instruction at the preheader of each loop. The instruction calls the corresponding loading procedure which is placed at the end of the task. The loading procedure contains a sequence of *fetch* instructions for loading the memory blocks selected into the I-cache and locking them. The program point of a call to a loading procedure is called the loading point of each memory block to be loaded and locked into the I-cache by the loading procedure. Ini-

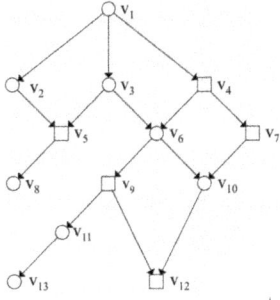

Figure 3. A DAG G

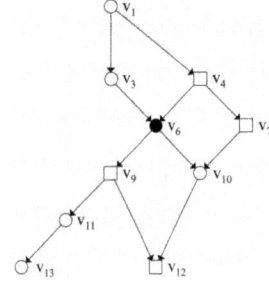

Figure 6. $G(121)$

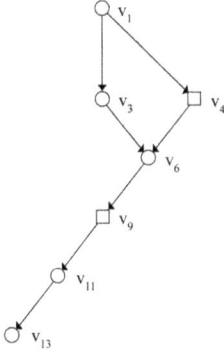

Figure 4. $G(150)$, 150-spanning graph of G

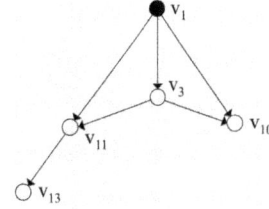

Figure 7. $G(121, 0)$

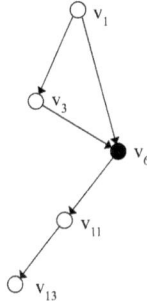

Figure 5. $G(150, 0)$, 0-projection graph of $G(150)$

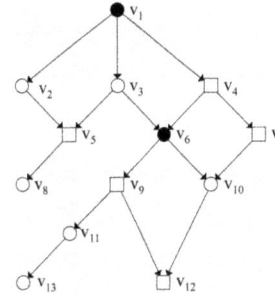

Figure 8. The DAG G after locking $v6$ and $v1$

tially, each loading procedure is empty. After applying our I-cache locking algorithm, a sequence of *fetch* instructions will be added to each loading procedure. If no *fetch* instruction is added to a loading procedure, the corresponding call will be replaced by a *nop* instruction.

Our approach processes each loop nest sequentially. For each loop nest, all its loops are processed in reverse topological order of the loop nest tree, i.e., starting with an inner-most loop and working toward the out-most loop. For a leaf loop in the loop nest tree, our approach applies Algorithm 3 to select a set of memory blocks of the loop as the locked cache contents. Then, the entire loop reduces into two blocks, a preheader block and a loop block. The preheader block contains a call to the loading procedure for this loop, and its weight is the execution time of the loading procedure plus the execution time of the call. The loop block represents the entire loop and its weight is the worst case execution time of the loop after locking all the selected memory blocks into the cache. For a non-leaf loop in the loop nest tree, our approach finds a good loading point for each loop to reduce the WCET as much as possible.

Initially, the loading point of all the selected memory blocks of each loop is at its preheader. Our approach may move the loading points of some selected memory blocks of a loop to the preheader of one of its outer loops in order to decrease the WCET of the loop nest. Notice that after moving the loading point of a selected memory block to the preheader of an outer loop, its live range will increase. Therefore, a loading point motion typically occurs when the I-cache has enough space to store the selected memory blocks of a loop and its inner loops. After moving the loading points for a set of selected memory blocks, our approach applies Algorithm 3 to select a set of memory blocks of the loop as the locked cache contents providing that the cache still has free space. Then, the entire loop reduces into two blocks, a preheader block and a loop block as before.

To facilitate descriptions, we introduce the following notation.

- $S(L_i)$: a set of the selected memory blocks which are fetched and locked at the preheader of L_i.

Given a loop nest L, our approach works as follows.

1. Construct the loop nest tree of L.

2. For each loop L_i in reverse topological order of the loop nest tree, do the following.

   - If L_i is a leaf node in the loop nest tree, perform the following tasks.

57

ALGORITHM 4: *loopNestLocking(L, k, s)*

input : L: a loop nest
  k: the number of sets in the I-cache
  s: the set size
output: A set of memory blocks selected as the locked cache contents and a set of loading points
var $n[]$: an array where $n[i](i = 0, 1, \cdots, k-1)$ stores the number of cache lines available in the set i

construct a loop nest tree T of L;
for *each loop L_i in reverse topological order of T* **do**
  if *L_i is a leaf node in T* **then**
      for $j = 0, 1, \cdots, k-1$ **do**
        $\lfloor\ n[j] = s;$
      $A = SingleLoopLocking(L_i, k, n);$
      $S(L_i) = \cup_{j=0:k-1} A[j];$
      shrink the subgraph representing L_i into a preheader block node and a loop block node, and set the node weights of the preheader block node and the loop block node to the execution time of the loading procedure and the WCET of L_i, respectively;
  else
      construct the DAG $G(L_i)$;
      $S(L_i) = \emptyset;$
      for *each set $y(y = 0, 1, \cdots, k-1$* **do**
          construct the y-projection graph $G_y(L_i)$;
          find the maximum size s_{max} of the space in the set y used by the selected memory blocks of any child of L_i in T;
          $s_y = s - s_{max};$
          /* Move loading points from the preheaders of the inner loops of L_i into the preheader of L_i to further reduce the WCET of L_i */
          while $s_y \geq 0$ **do**
              find the longest path in $G_y(L_i)$;
              on the longest path, find a selected memory block B with the maximum accumulated execution time that is mapped to the set y and in $\{S(L_j) : L_j$ is a child of L_i in T $\}$;
              assume B is in $S(L_r)$;
              $S(L_r) = S(L_r) - \{B\};$
              $S(L_i) = S(L_i) \cup \{B\};$
              update the weights of the nodes affected;
              find the new maximum size s'_{max} of the space in the set y used by any child of L_i in T;
              if $s'_{max} = s_{max}$ **then**
                $\lfloor\ s_y = s_y - 1;$
              $s_{max} = s'_{max};$
      for $j = 0, 1, \cdots, k-1$ **do**
        $\lfloor\ n[j] = s_j;$
      $A = SingleLoopLocking(L_i, k, n);$
      $S(L_i) = S(L_i) \cup \cup_{j=0:k-1} A[j];$
      shrink the subgraph representing L_i into a preheader block node and a loop block node, and set the node weights of the preheader block node and the loop block node to the execution time of the loading procedure and the WCET of L_i, respectively;

for *each L_i in the loop nest* **do**
  add *fetch* instructions to the loading procedure of L_i to load and lock the selected memory blocks into the I-cache;

```
for  (i = 0; i < 10; i + +)          /*Loop 1,  L₁*/
{
    for  (i = 0; i < 20; i + +)       /*Loop 2,  L₄*/
    {
        if  (x > y)
          {...;}
        else
          {...;}
    }
    for  (i = 0; i < 20; i + +)       /*Loop 3,  L₂*/
    {
        for  (i = 0; i < 50; i + +)   /* Loop 4,  L₃*/
        {
            if  (x > y)
              {...;}
            else
              {...;}
        } ,}
    }
}
```

Figure 9. A loop nest

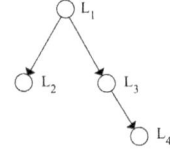

Figure 10. The loop nest tree of the loop nest in Figure9

(a) Select a set of the memory blocks of L_i as the locked cache contents by using Algorithm 3.

(b) Shrink the subgraph representing L_i in the CFG of the loop nest into a preheader block node and a loop block node, and set the node weights of the preheader block node and the loop block node to the execution time of the loading procedure and the WCET of L_i, respectively.

Otherwise, do the following.

(a) Construct the weighted DAG $G(L_i)$ of the loop L_i.

(b) For each set $y(y = 0, 1, \cdots, k-1)$, do the following.

  i. Construct the y-projection graph $G_y(L_i)$ of $G(L_i)$.

  ii. Keep finding a selected memory block with the highest impact on the WCET of L_i and move its loading point to the preheader of L_i until the set y has no more free space as follows.

  A. Find the longest path of $G_y(L_i)$.

  B. On the longest path, find a selected memory block B with the maximum accumulated execution time in L_i among all the selected memory blocks that are mapped to the set y and loaded at the preheaders of the children of L_i in the loop nest tree. The accumulated execution time of a memory block is its execution time multiplied by its total number of executions in L_i.

  C. Move the loading point of B to the preheader of L_i, update the weights of the nodes affected in $G_y(L_i)$, and adjust the size of the free space of the set y.

(c) Select a set of the memory blocks of L_i as the locked cache contents by using Algorithm 3.

(d) Shrink the subgraph representing L_i into a preheader block node and a loop block node, and set the node weights of the preheader block node and the loop block node to the execution time of the loading procedure and the WCET of L_i, respectively.

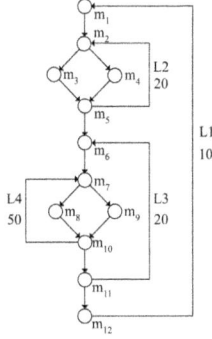

Figure 11. The CFG of the loop nest in Figure9

Figure 12. Loading points of the loop nest

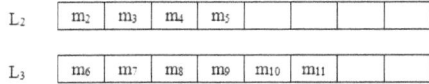

Figure 13. The locked contents at the preheaders of L_2 and L_3

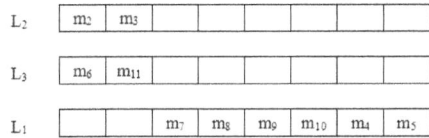

Figure 14. The final locked contents at the preheaders of L_1, L_2 and L_3

The details of our algorithm are shown in Algorithm 4. Next we use an example to show our approach works. Consider the loop nest shown in Figure 9. Its loop nest tree is shown in Figure 10. For ease of descriptions, we make the following assumptions. 1) The number of sets of the I-cache is one. 2) The associativity n is 8. 3) Each basic block is mapped to exactly one memory block. 4) If a basic block is in the I-cache, its execution time is 1. Otherwise, it is 30. Our approach starts with L_4. It will select all the 4 basic blocks m_7, m_8, m_9, m_{10} as the locked cache contents and put their loading points at the preheader of L_4. When processing

Table 1. The benchmarks

Benchmark	Code size (Bytes)	Description
cnt	2880	counts non-negative numbers in matrix
crc	5168	Cyclic redundancy check computation on 40 bytes of data
edn	10563	Finite Impulse Response (FIR) filter calculations
malmult	3737	Matrix multiplication of two 20x20 matrices
qurt	4898	Root computation of quadratic equations
adpcm	8289	Adaptive pulse code modulation algorithm
fir	13881	Finite impulse response filter (signal processing algorithms) over a 700 items long sample

L_3, our approach will move the loading points of m_7, m_8, m_9, m_{10} to the preheader of L_3. Then, it will select m_6 and m_{11} as locked contents of L_3. Similarly, our approach will select m_2, m_3, m_4 and m_5 of L_2 and put their loading points at the preheader of L_2. The selection results of locked contents for L_2 and L_3 are shown in Figure 13. When processing L_1, our approach will move the loading points of m_4, m_5, m_7, m_8, m_9, and m_{10} to the preheader of L_1 as shown in Figure 14. All the three loading points are shown in Figure 12, where each loading point is a call to its corresponding loading procedure that contains the instructions for fetching and locking all the memory blocks selected. Notice that after the loading points of m_4, m_5, m_7, m_8, m_9, and m_{10} are moved to the preheader of L_1, their live ranges extend to entire L_1, overlapping with the live ranges of m_2, m_3, m_6 and m_{11}.

7. Experimental Results

We have implemented our approach and compared it with the two state-of-the-art approaches, the partial locking approach proposed by Ding et al. [6] and the longest path based dynamic cache locking approach proposed by Puaut [15].

7.1 Setup

The benchmarks, as shown in Table 1, are taken from the MRTC benchmark suite [8]. SimpleScalar PISA instruction set [2] is used to compile benchmarks. We use Chronos [9], a WCET analysis tool, to compute the WCETs. Since we focus on the instruction cache, we switch off the pipeline model and branch prediction. We use two different associativities 2 and 4, two different cache line sizes 32B and 64B, 3 different cache sizes 256B, 512B and 1KB. The miss latency is 30 cycles and the hit latency is 1 cycle. For each benchmark, we use different cache configurations to compute its WCETs by using our approach and its WCETs by using the partial locking approach and the longest path based dynamic cache locking approach.

7.2 Our Approach vs. Partial Locking

The improvements of our approach over the partial locking approach are shown in Figures 15-17 where the horizontal axis and the vertical axis denote the benchmarks and the improvements of our approach over the partial locking approach, respectively.

59

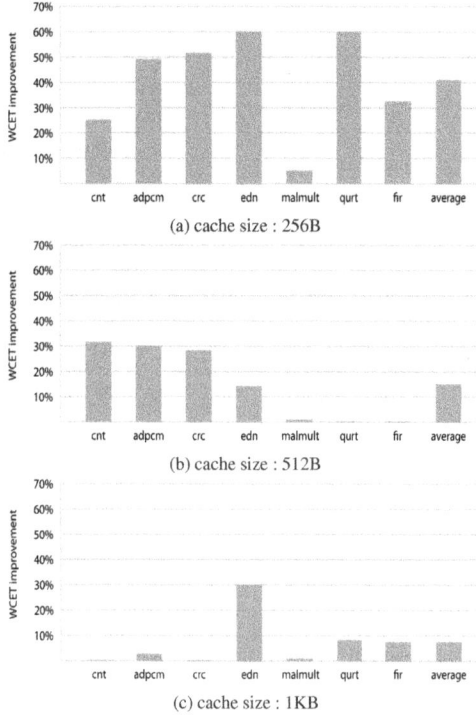

Figure 15. WCET improvements of our approach over the partial locking approach (4-way set associative cache, 32B cache lines)

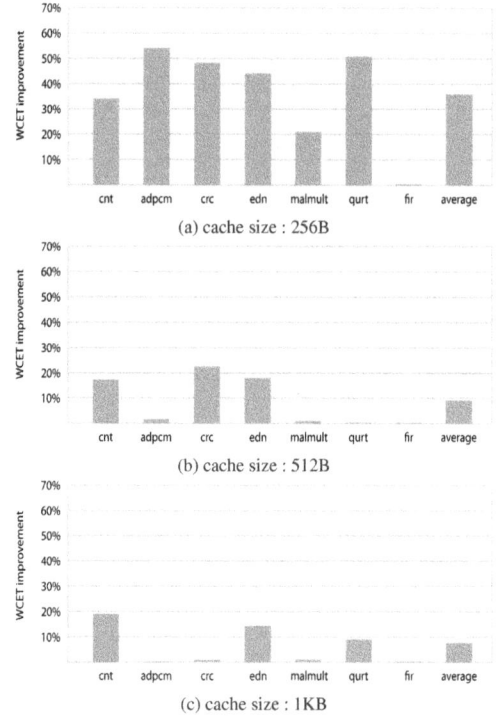

Figure 16. WCET improvements of our approach over the partial locking approach (2-way set associative cache, 32B cache lines)

For the 4-way set associative cache with a cache line size of 32B, the average improvements of our approach are 41%, 15% and 7% for the 256B cache, the 512B cache and the 1KB cache, respectively. For the 2-way set associative cache with a cache line size of 32B, the improvements are 37%, 9% and 7% for the 256B cache, the 512B cache and the 1KB cache, respectively. The improvement for the 2-way set associative cache with a cache line size of 64B are 39%, 17% and 7% for the 256B cache, the 512B cache and the 1KB cache, respectively.

Compared with the partial locking approach, our approach performs much better for the small caches. The reason is as follows. In our approach, many memory blocks have disjoint live ranges and thus can be locked to the same cache lines. In contrast, in the partial locking approach, all the memory blocks have overlapping live ranges and consequently cannot share cache lines.

On average, the improvement of our approach over the partial locking approach decreases as the cache size increases, especially for some benchmarks with a small code size, such as *cnt*. The key reason is that more cache lines are available so that more memory blocks can be loaded and locked into the cache when the cache size increases.

Our approach achieves dramatic improvements for the benchmarks which contain many sequentially executed, non-nested loops such as *edn*. Obviously, the live ranges of those loops do not overlap. Therefore, the memory blocks of those loops can share cache lines.

For the benchmarks contained many deeply nested loops such as *malmult*, our approach makes less improvement. The key reason is that in our approach, a lot of time is spent on loading and locking the selected memory blocks.

The experimental results also show that, with a fixed cache line size, the improvement of our approach decreases as the associativity of the I-cache decreases. The key reason is that in our approach,

fewer memory blocks can be loaded and locked into a set due to its decreased size.

Furthermore, with a fixed associativity, the improvement of our approach increases as the cache line size increases for most benchmarks.

Overall, there are two major reasons that our approach performs significantly better than the partial locking approach. Firstly, our approach uses dynamic cache locking so that memory blocks with disjoint live ranges can be loaded and locked into the same cache line, resulting in more efficient utilization of the I-cache. Secondly, our approach selects a minimum number of memory blocks by using the min-cut algorithm.

7.3 Our Approach vs. Longest Path Based Dynamic Locking

The improvements of our approach over the longest path based dynamic locking approach are shown in Figures 18-20. Our approach achieves the average improvements of 7%, 18% and 17% for the 4 way set associative cache with a size of 256B, 512B, and 1KB, respectively. For the 2-way set associative cache with a cache line size of 32B, the improvements are 7%, 16% and 16% for 256B, 512B and 1KB, respectively. The improvements for the 2-way set associative cache with a cache line size of 64B are 7%, 15% and 16% for 256B, 512B and 1KB, respectively.

Our approach performs much better for the benchmarks containing many deeply nested loops such as *malmult*. The reason is that our approach moves some loading points to the preheaders of outer loops to reduce the the execution frequency of the *fetch* instructions. For such benchmarks, the improvement increases as the cache size increases. The reason is that more selected memory blocks can be loaded and locked at the preheaders of outer loops.

For the benchmarks such as *edn* which contain many sequentially executed small non-nested loops, our approach achieves less improvements. The key reason is that each *fetch* instruction is ex-

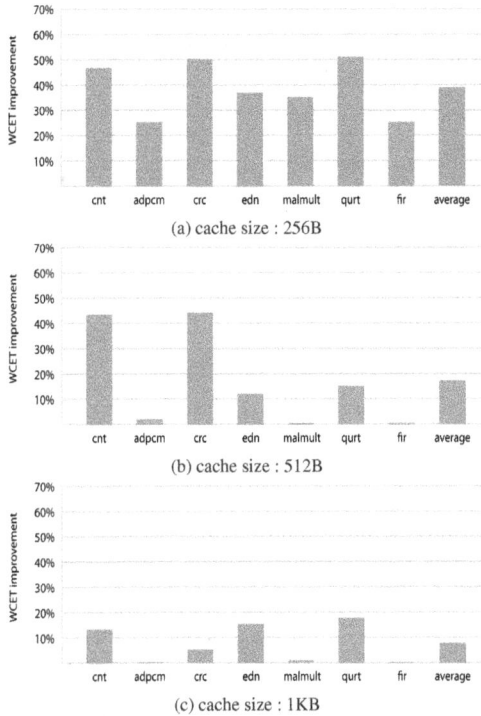

Figure 17. WCET improvements of our approach over the partial locking approach (2-way set associative cache, 64B cache lines)

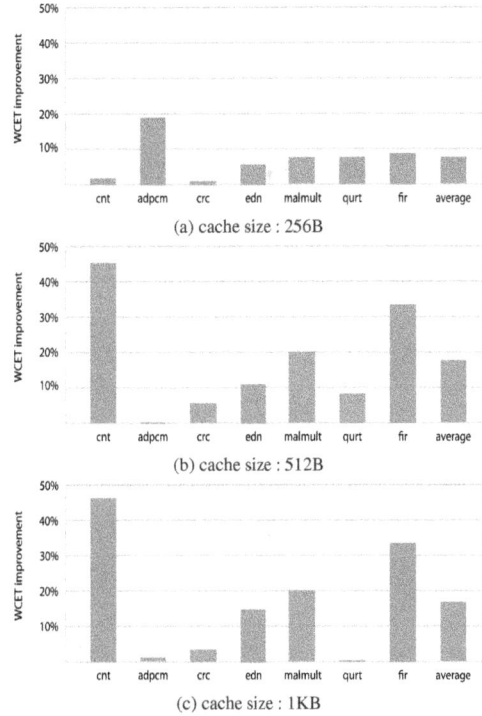

Figure 18. WCET improvements of our approach over the longest path based dynamic locking approach (4-way set associative cache, 32B cache lines)

ecuted only once and the costs on loading and locking memory blocks are nearly the same as the longest path based dynamic locking approach.

For the benchmarks containing large sequential non-nested loops, the improvement dependents on the structure of the CFG of the benchmark. Our approach have a dramatic improvement in some benchmarks such as *fir*, or a slight improvement in some benchmarks such as *adpcm*.

With a fixed cache line size, the improvement of our approach slightly decreases as the associativity of the I-cache decreases due to the reason that fewer memory blocks can be loaded and locked into a set. With a fixed associativity of the I-cache, the improvement of our approach remains similar as the cache line size increases.

Overall, our approach has two major advantages compared with the longest path based dynamic locking approach. Firstly, our approach uses a more effective algorithm for determining the loading points of the selected memory blocks to further reduce the WECT of a loop nest. Secondly, our approach makes more effective selections of locked cache contents by using the min-cut based algorithm.

8. Conclusion

We investigate the problem of selecting memory blocks of the instructions of a single task as the locked contents and determining their loading points to minimize the WCET of the task. We propose a dynamic cache locking approach. Our approach considers the live range of each memory block. When the live range of a memory block ends, the cache line it occupies can be reused. Our approach selects a minimum set of memory blocks of each loop as the locked cache contents to reduce the WCET of the loop as much as possible by finding minimum node cuts of the weighted DAG of the loop that contains not only the longest path, but also the paths whose lengths are close to the longest path length. Therefore, our

approach makes more efficient use of the I-cache than the previous approaches. Furthermore, our approach can find good loading points for the selected memory blocks to further reduce the WCET of a task. We have implemented our approach and compared it with the two state-of-the-art cache locking approaches, the partial locking approach proposed in [6] and the dynamic locking approach proposed in [15], by using a set of benchmarks from the MRTC benchmark suite. The experimental results show that our approach achieves the average improvements of 41%, 15% and 7% over the partial locking approach for the 256B, 512B and 1KB caches, respectively, and 7%, 18% and 17% over the longest path based dynamic locking for the 256B, 512B and 1KB caches, respectively.

To conclude this paper, we propose two open problems. One open problem is to extend our approach to the D-cache locking problem. As each variable has its own live range, it is very challenging to propose a fast, efficient dynamic D-cache locking heuristic for selecting variables as the D-cache contents to effectively reduce the WCET of a task. The other one is to integrate our approach with task scheduling. Tasks may pre-empt each other. If a task T_i is pre-empted by a task T_j, the cache lines locked by T_i cannot be used by T_j. Therefore, pre-emptions have a significant impact on the performance of cache locking. A good cache locking approach needs to take both task scheduling and cache locking into account simultaneously.

References

[1] K. Anand and R. Barua. Instruction cache locking inside a binary rewriter. In *Proceedings of the 2009 International Conference on Compilers, Architecture, and Synthesis for Embedded Systems (CASES)*, pages 185–194. ACM, 2009.

[2] D. Burger and T. M. Austin. The simplescalar tool set, version 2.0. *ACM SIGARCH Computer Architecture News*, 25(3):13–25, 1997.

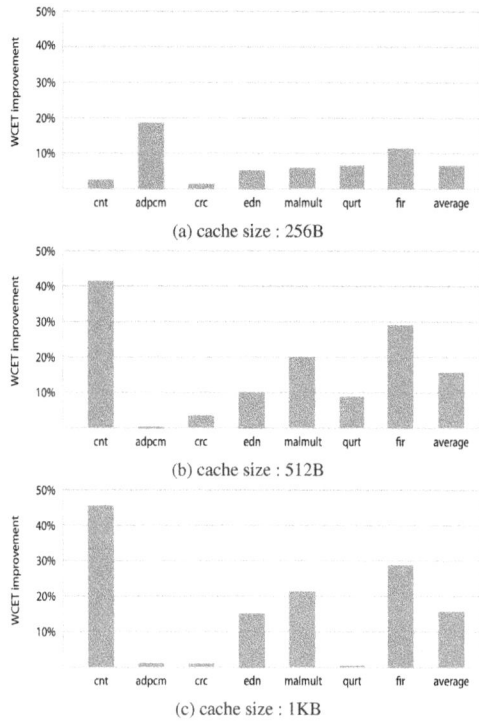

(a) cache size : 256B

(b) cache size : 512B

(c) cache size : 1KB

Figure 19. WCET improvements of our approach over the longest path based dynamic locking approach (2-way set associative cache, 32B cache lines)

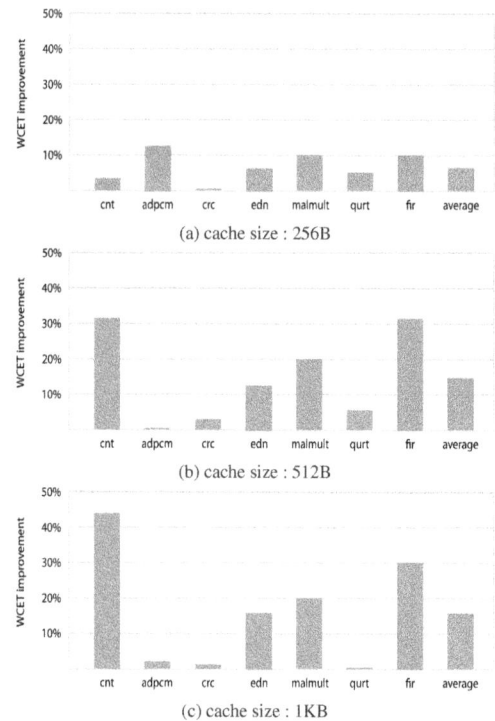

(a) cache size : 256B

(b) cache size : 512B

(c) cache size : 1KB

Figure 20. WCET improvements of our approach over the longest path based dynamic locking approach (2-way set associative cache, 64B cache lines)

[3] A. M. Campoy, A. Ivars, and J. Busquets-Mataix. Using genetic algorithms in content selection for locking-caches. In *Proceedings of the International Symposium on Applied Informatics*, pages 271–276, 2001.

[4] A. M. Campoy, A. P. Ivars, and J. Busquets-Mataix. Dynamic use of locking caches in multitask, preemptive real-time systems. In *Proceedings of the 15th Triennial World Congress of the International Federation of Automatic Control*, 2002.

[5] A. M. Campoy, A. Perles, F. Rodriguez, and J. Busquets-Mataix. Static use of locking caches vs. dynamic use of locking caches for real-time systems. In *Proceedings of Canadian Conference on Electrical and Computer Engineering*, volume 2, pages 1283–1286. IEEE, 2003.

[6] H. Ding, Y. Liang, and T. Mitra. Wcet-centric partial instruction cache locking. In *Proceedings of the 49th Design Automation Conference (DAC)*, pages 412–420. IEEE, 2012.

[7] H. Falk, S. Plazar, and H. Theiling. Compile-time decided instruction cache locking using worst-case execution paths. In *Proceedings of the 5th IEEE/ACM International Conference on Hardware/Software Codesign and System Synthesis*, pages 143–148. ACM, 2007.

[8] J. Gustafsson, A. Betts, A. Ermedahl, and B. Lisper. The mälardalen wcet benchmarks: Past, present and future. In *WCET*, pages 136–146, 2010.

[9] X. Li, Y. Liang, T. Mitra, and A. Roychoudhury. Chronos: A timing analyzer for embedded software. *Science of Computer Programming*, 69(1-3):56–67, 2007. http://www.comp.nus.edu.sg/~rpembed/chronos.

[10] Y. Liang and T. Mitra. Instruction cache locking using temporal reuse profile. In *Proceedings of the 47th Design Automation Conference (DAC)*, pages 344–349. ACM, 2010.

[11] T. Liu, M. Li, and C. J. Xue. Minimizing wcet for real-time embedded systems via static instruction cache locking. In *Proceedings of the*

15th IEEE Real-Time and Embedded Technology and Applications Symposium (RTAS), pages 35–44. IEEE, 2009.

[12] T. Liu, Y. Zhao, M. Li, and C. J. Xue. Task assignment with cache partitioning and locking for wcet minimization on mpsoc. In *Proceedings of the 39th International Conference on Parallel Processing (ICPP)*, pages 573–582. IEEE, 2010.

[13] T. Liu, M. Li, and C. J. Xue. Instruction cache locking for embedded systems using probability profile. *Journal of Signal Processing Systems*, 69(2):173–188, 2012.

[14] S. Plazar, J. C. Kleinsorge, P. Marwedel, and H. Falk. Wcet-aware static locking of instruction caches. In *Proceedings of the 10th International Symposium on Code Generation and Optimization (CGO)*, pages 44–52. ACM, 2012.

[15] I. Puaut. Wcet-centric software-controlled instruction caches for hard real-time systems. In *Proceedings of the 18th Euromicro Conference on Real-Time Systems*, pages 10–pp. IEEE, 2006.

[16] I. Puaut and A. Arnaud. Dynamic instruction cache locking in hard real-time systems. In *Proceedings of the 14th International Conference on Real-Time and Network Systems*, 2006.

[17] I. Puaut and D. Decotigny. Low-complexity algorithms for static cache locking in multitasking hard real-time systems. In *Proceedings of the 23rd IEEE Real-Time Systems Symposium (RTSS)*, pages 114–123. IEEE, 2002.

[18] J. Staschulat, S. Schliecker, and R. Ernst. Scheduling analysis of real-time systems with precise modeling of cache related preemption delay. In *Proceedings of 17th Euromicro Conference on Real-Time Systems*, pages 41–48. IEEE, 2005.

[19] X. Vera, B. Lisper, and J. Xue. Data cache locking for higher program predictability. In *ACM SIGMETRICS Performance Evaluation Review*, volume 31, pages 272–282. ACM, 2003.

Exploration of Compiler Optimization Sequences Using Clustering-Based Selection

Luiz G. A. Martins

Faculty of Computing, Federal Univ. of
Uberlândia, Uberlândia, Brazil
gustavo@facom.ufu.br

Ricardo Nobre

Faculty of Engineering, Univ. of Porto
INESC-TEC, Porto, Portugal
ricardo.nobre@fe.up.pt

Alexandre C. B. Delbem

Inst. of Math. and Computer Science,
Univ. of São Paulo, São Carlos, Brazil
acbd@icmc.usp.br

Eduardo Marques

Inst. of Math. and Computer Science,
Univ. of São Paulo, São Carlos, Brazil
emarques@icmc.usp.br

João M. P. Cardoso

Faculty of Engineering, Univ. of Porto
INESC-TEC, Porto, Portugal
jmpc@acm.org

Abstract

Due to the large number of optimizations provided in modern compilers and to compiler optimization specific opportunities, a Design Space Exploration (DSE) is necessary to search for the best sequence of compiler optimizations for a given code fragment (e.g., function). As this exploration is a complex and time consuming task, in this paper we present DSE strategies to select optimization sequences to both improve the performance of each function and reduce the exploration time. The DSE is based on a clustering approach which groups functions with similarities and then explore the reduced search space provided by the optimizations previously suggested for the functions in each group. The identification of similarities between functions uses a data mining method which is applied to a symbolic code representation of the source code. The DSE process uses the reduced set identified by clustering in two ways: as the design space or as the initial configuration. In both ways, the adoption of a pre-selection based on clustering allows the use of simple and fast DSE algorithms. Our experiments for evaluating the effectiveness of the proposed approach address the exploration of compiler optimization sequences considering 49 compilation passes and targeting a Xilinx MicroBlaze processor, and were performed aiming performance improvements for 41 functions. Experimental results reveal that the use of our new clustering-based DSE approach achieved a significant reduction on the total exploration time of the search space (18× over a Genetic Algorithm approach for DSE) at the same time that important performance speedups (43% over the baseline) were obtained by the optimized codes.

Categories and Subject Descriptors D.3.4 [*Programming Languages*]: Processors-compilers, optimization

LCTES '14, June 12–13, 2014, Edinburgh, UK.
Copyright © 2014 ACM 978-1-4503-2877-7 /14/06... $15.00.
http://dx.doi.org/10.1145/2597809.2597821

General Terms Performance, Measurements, Algorithms

Keywords Phase-ordering problem; design space exploration; clustering; compilers

1. Introduction

Modern compilers include a large number of optimizations that interact with each other and with the input code in complex ways [1]. Traditionally, standard compilers adopt optimization levels that are selectable through a simple set of compiler parameters. The particular optimizations for each optimization level are chosen to improve the performance of a representative set of programs. However, several authors have shown that the choice of optimizations, and their order of application (sequence of passes), can have a significant impact on performance and it is platform and application dependent [2][3]. A straightforward, but usually not viable approach for exploring sequences of compiler optimizations, is to test all possible combinations of K optimizations from a list of N possible compiler passes to choose from. Therefore, developers typically use their expertise to engage in a labor intensive source code modification process and to test multiple compiler alternatives, aiming at achieving satisfactory optimization sequences for a specific target application or function. A Design Space Exploration (DSE) scheme is desirable to find the optimization sequence that results in the best performance for a given code fragment (or function), considering the target processor and the set of optimizations supported by the compiler. However, stringent time-to-market requirements in embedded systems usually impose restrictions with respect to DSE execution time and thus might be important to speedup the DSE process.

In this paper, we present a new DSE approach based on software code clustering to search for optimization sequences aiming at performance improvements of code fragments (e.g., functions). In our DSE approach, we employ simple search algorithms which use a clustering method to select a set of the potential compiler optimizations. We explore here the following search algorithms alternatives: random sampling, clean, inclusion, and a genetic algorithm (GA). The purpose is to provide alternatives able to speedup the exploration time without compromising the level of optimization achieved. In this context, our clustering method allows the choice of a reduced set of the optimizations which are then used in the DSE process striving to improve performance. The clustering process can reveal similar patterns among software codes, giving important insights for determining potential groups of optimizations. The identification of similarities is performed from a symbolic encoding, named DNA of the program [4], and using a data mining approach proposed in [5]. The usage of the DNA encoding aims at identifying the main code structures, such as loops, operations and other programming constructs, that may be related to specific optimizations. The data mining approach is used to detect highly correlated groups of functions extracting potential clusters hidden in the DNA representations. Our clustering approach is based on a set of reference functions for which the near-optimal sequences of compiler optimizations have been previously determined. Each new function is then added to those reference functions and clustering is applied. The set of optimizations used for the functions belonging to the cluster where the new function belongs is then the input to a DSE approach aiming at determining the best sequence of optimizations. Here, we describe four simple algorithms and two hybrid variations to explore the best compiler optimization sequences for a given function. The experimental results shown that the employment of our approach significantly reduces the execution time of the DSE without significant speedup reductions when compared to the speedups achieved by close to optimum sequences of optimizations. Experiments were performed considering different DSE strategies. The purpose of these experiments was to evaluate the effectiveness of our clustering-based selection of optimizations, as well as to determine the trade-off between DSE execution time and performance improvements on optimized code for the DSE strategies presented.

The rest of this paper is organized as follows. Section 2 presents the compilation environment used in this work to develop the DSE schemes. Section 3 depicts our clustering-based approach to select compiler optimizations and introduces the fundamentals of the techniques used for source code representation and for data mining. The algorithms employed in our DSE approach are described in Section 4. Section 5 presents the experiments performed to evaluate our approach and the results. Section 6 reviews related work on the topic of determining sequences of compiler optimizations. Finally, Section 7 presents some conclusions and briefly describes ongoing and future work.

2. DSE Infrastructure

Our experiments were run on top of an integrated compilation environment developed in the context of the REFLECT FP7 project [6]. The environment includes ReflectC, a compiler controlled by LARA aspects/strategies. It is based on CoSy (COmpiler SYstem) [7], an industrial compiler which supports a large number of optimizations. Figure 1 shows the LARA-based compilation flow used in this work.

LARA [8] is a domain-specific aspect-oriented language that effectively provides the implementation of DSE strategies able to control and guide complete toolchains (e.g., compiler and simulator), as well as to evaluate the optimization alternatives based on feedback information reported during the exploration. LARA strategies define specific compiler optimizations that best suit the mapping of an application to the target processor (e.g., Xilinx MicroBlaze). A top-level aspect implements the DSE algorithm relying on the LARA outer-loop mechanism (represented by dashed lines in Figure 1), while other aspects are responsible for guiding the ReflectC compiler, in the process of generating a solution, and for evaluation of the resulting codes. The modularity of the DSE infrastructure requires only the aspect that encapsulates the execution of the tools in the toolchain to be modified when using a different compiler. This integrated and unified view also allows to program and easily apply different DSE strategies.

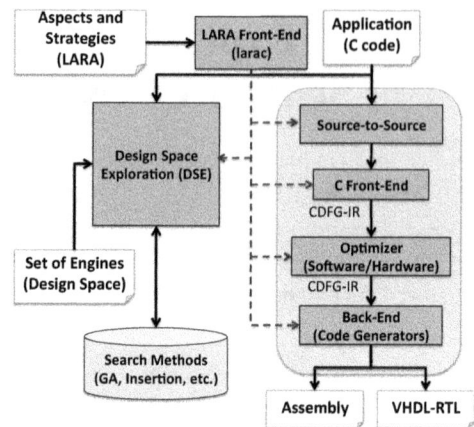

Figure 1. LARA based Design Flow.

A CoSy based toolchain built around LARA abstracts the developer from the interaction with all used mapping tools while effectively guiding the DSE flow process in the exploration of alternative optimizations sequences targeting the target processor. The CoSy based compiler exposes full control of the order of optimizations (herein named as engines), and optional tuning of those engines, to the LARA weaver. Although we focus on the MicroBlaze processor, a weaver integrated in the ReflectC compiler provides other code generators including a CoSy based VHDL generator. Basically, the weaver is responsible for executing the LARA specifications expressing compilation engines to be applied. Table 1 shows the 49 CoSy compilation engines (including analysis, optimizations and lower passes) used in our experiments. We manually selected these engines based on their apparent importance. Intentionally our DSE approach randomly selects optimization engines without grouping them by any order or compilation stage. More details about the CoSy engines can be found in [7].

Table 1. CoSy optimization engines used in DSE.

cse	loopive	funceval	ifconvert	markconvert
misc	looprev	loopfuse	loopbcount	ckfstrength
alias	promote	loophoist	loopcanon	loopstrength
cache	tailrec	lowerpfc	loopguard	hwloopcreate
rodata	vshrink	lrrename	setpurity	loopinvariant
vprop	vstrength	mvpostop	setrefobj	lowerboolval
demote	copyprop	noreturn	blockmerge	lowerbitfield
conevun	constprop	strength	chainflow	scalarreplace
exprprop	dismemun	tailmerge	loopremove	condassigncreate
globcse	domorder	algebraic	loopscalar	

3. Clustering-based Engines Selection

Source code has characteristics that make the direct use of typical clustering methods difficult, mainly related to their dependence of the code features for mining [5]. To address this problem, we initially translate the source code to a symbolic representation, referred to as DNA of a program [4], and employ a variation of the data mining method proposed in [5]. This data mining method is based on clustering techniques and allows to find patterns in codes with independence of the code size or programming language. The data mining approach combines three different algorithms to generate the clusters with reference benchmarks and the new function (target). First, it computes a distance matrix by using the Normalized Compression Distance (NCD) [9] for each pair of DNA code.

A phylogenetic reconstruction algorithm, named Neighbor Joining or NJ [10], constructs a tree topology from that matrix. Then, an ambiguity-based clustering algorithm detects highly correlated groups of functions, extracting potential clusters hidden in the tree topology. Subsequently, the distinct passes used in optimization sequences for the clustered reference functions are included in the design space employed in DSE. The exploration can thus be performed using any search method implemented in the compiler environment, such as Genetic Algorithms [11] and Insertion [12].

Figure 2 illustrates the selection process of optimizations based on clustering and using the DNA representation. This process is responsible to output the set of engines used in Figure 1 using function's granularity as an example. The techniques employed in this process are described as follows.

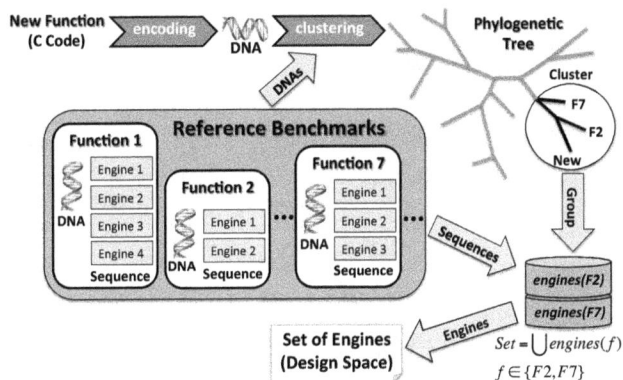

Figure 2. Selection of compiler engines based on clustering.

3.1 DNA encoding

The effect of a compiler optimization is highly dependent on the code being compiled. Therefore, the identification of code patterns can expose similarities among programs and it may aid to determine potential sequences of optimizations. However, data mining schemes to identify such patterns over source code can be very complex tasks, as they may need to deal with many files, numerous lines of code and varying code structures [4]. Most pattern-mining research [13][14] relies on high similarity levels that hamper the identification of code patterns with subtle differences, but that possible share the same optimization strategy.

We employ a DNA encoding due to its capability to highlight main program structures according to the transformation rules specified, allowing to identify approximate patterns from the source code. The DNA is a symbolic representation proposed in [4], where programs elements (e.g., operators and loops) are encoded in a string of symbols, similarly with Genetics. The translation is based on transformation rules and generates lossy intermediate representations. According to the transformation rules used, this representation may reflect with higher or lower degree the sequence of tokens that identifies each program function. Here, we use the same transformation rules set employed in [5]. According to the authors, these rules set emphasize the similarities in the loop body operations. However, other transformation rules, possibly more complex, can be also applied. In particular, transformation rules aware of datatypes can be also used.

Figure 3 illustrates five hypothetical examples of loop structures, the simple transformation rules employed and the corresponding DNA representations. As shown, the DNA representation used in this paper is fully based on syntax-oriented transformation rules. The idea is to acquire if this simple approach achieves an efficient clustering. The impact of using other transformation rules

(semantically based and possibly including also data-dependence information) is planned for future work.

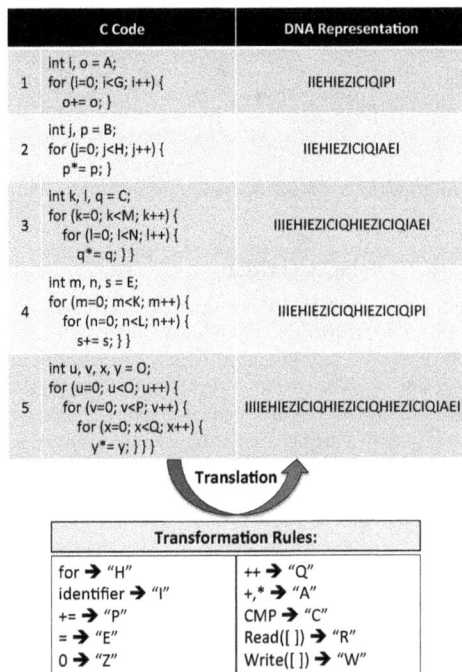

Figure 3. Instances of the DNA encoding.

3.2 Normalized Compression Distance

The Normalized Compression Distance (NCD) is a compression-based metric proposed in [9], whose properties are based on Kolmogorov complexity theory [15]. The basic idea is that two objects are considered close if one can be significantly compressed using the information in the other. Therefore, the distance $NCD(x; y)$ for each pair of functions (x and y) is the improvement due to compressing y using x as reference and compressing y from scratch, expressed as the ratio between the bit-wise length of the two compressed versions. It can be calculated as follows [9]:

$$NCD(x;y) = \frac{C(xy) - min(C(x); C(y))}{max(C(x); C(y))} \quad (1)$$

where $C(\star)$ is the length of the compressed version of the file $\star$, xy is the file resulting from the concatenation of x and y.

The NCD metric does not require any knowledge about the features of the data analyzed to find relationships. Such feature independence enables the NCD-based algorithm to deal with several types of program data at code level, including (but not limited to) the source codes and intermediate representations (as DNA). It also enables one to extract information from codes at different levels of abstraction [4].

The algorithm computes the NCD metric from the DNA code, generating the matrix corresponding to the considered functions (references and target). For example, Table 2 presents the distance matrix obtained from the DNA encoding of Figure 3. It shows for example that codes 2 and 3 (using their DNA representations) are the most similar according to NCD metrics, while codes 1 and 5 are the most different.

Many compressors can be used in NCD computation. In this work, we adopted the *bzlib* compressor for calculating the distance matrices. This selection was based on previous experiments, where

Table 2. NCD matrix from DNA representation

DNA	1	2	3	4	5
1	0	0.29	0.36	0.21	0.40
2	0.29	0	0.20	0.34	0.31
3	0.36	0.20	0	0.28	0.25
4	0.21	0.34	0.28	0	0.35
5	0.40	0.31	0.25	0.35	0

the *bzib* compressor achieved the best clustering for a number of tests.

3.3 Neighbor Joining Algorithm

The Neighbor Joining (NJ) [10] is a simple and computationally efficient algorithm for constructing phylogenetic trees. The algorithm output is an unrooted tree structure which describes the relationships among objects. The tree topology is defined by consecutively joining pairs of neighbors. This tree is iteratively constructed, as illustrated in Figure 4, starting from a star-like tree, where all objects (leaf nodes) are connected through one interior node. At each iteration, a new pair of neighbors are connected by an intermediate node and the distance matrix is recalculated considering this new node. The algorithm provides a tree topology that enables determining recursively clusters composed by other clusters. Finally, as NJ does not depend on any type of a priori knowledge about the problem domain, it is an interesting algorithm for identifying hierarchical similarities among software codes [5].

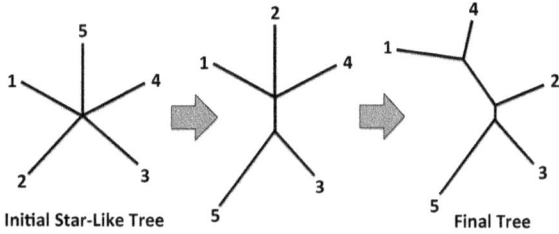

Figure 4. Phylogenetic tree construction using Neighbor Joining.

3.4 Ambiguity-based Clustering

Given a phylogenetic tree, it is important to verify the existence of subtrees with high degree of independence in the phylogeny. Thus, a hierarchical clustering algorithm is employed to extract potential clusters hidden in the tree topology.

Unlike the original approach presented in [5], where the Fast Newman algorithm (FN) [16] was used, we adopt a clustering method inspired by the measure of ambiguity of tree structures. FN is an algorithm from complex networks analysis that focuses on discovering clusters in a large-scale networks. On the other hand, the ambiguity-based approach responses better to small networks. In a first stage, we expect to deal with a small number of reference benchmarks, making the ambiguity-based approach more appropriate. However, possibly when considering a large set of reference functions, we may switch to the Fast Newman approach.

Tree ambiguity can be defined from the ambiguity between two leaf nodes. Leaves i and j of a tree T are ambiguous, if there are two or more internal nodes (ancestors) between them in T, i.e., internal nodes in the unique path from i to j. In other words, both nodes (i and j) are not tightly similar, since they require more than one intermediate node, to counterbalance their differences in relation to other leaf nodes (that compose a third momentum affecting the equilibrium between i and j). The ambiguity of T (or tree ambiguity) is the accumulated ambiguities involving all

the pairs of leaves of T. This definition can result in imprecise evaluation of the reliability of a tree. Any tree with three nodes has ambiguity equal to one. Moreover, any tree with more than one leaf and with an odd number of leaves has at least ambiguity equal to one. For larger trees (with at least some hundreds of leaves), this additional ambiguity may be irrelevant when comparing the reliability of clustering trees. However, it must be avoided when evaluating small trees, like those used in our environment.

We bypass this problem using the concept of strong ambiguity. Basically, two leaf nodes are strong ambiguous if there are three or more internal nodes (ancestors) between them. Our clustering approach employs measures of strong ambiguity to separate the functions into groups. Therefore, a new input function to be compiled is joined to all functions reachable by a couple of intermediate nodes. Figure 5 shows the clustering over the phylogenetic tree built from the five examples of DNAs in Figure 3, and considering the last one (example 5) as the input function.

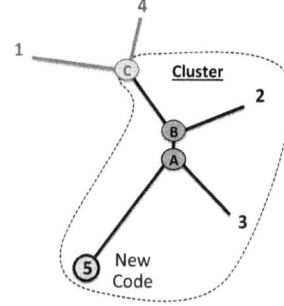

Figure 5. Strong Ambiguity-based Clustering.

In this case, example 5 (input function) is joined to example 3 by an internal node (A), and to example 2 through the path formed by two internal nodes (A and B), and to examples 1 and 4 through the path formed by three intermediate nodes (A, B and C). Considering the strong ambiguity concept, the third internal node (node C) is the boundary of the cluster. Therefore, example 5 was clustered with all leaf nodes apart by a path with up to two internal nodes (nodes A and B), i.e., examples 3 and 2.

The number of internal nodes considered can be also modified for tuning the strength of a relationship to establish a cluster. In this paper, we extended the original boundary condition (three internal nodes) when the input function is clustered with just one reference function.

4. DSE Strategies

In this paper, a number of DSE strategies were programmed and applied using our LARA based environment. These strategies differ with respect to the technique and the design space employed in the search of the best optimization sequence for a given function. A brief description of each DSE strategy is given as follows.

4.1 Genetic Algorithm and Random Sampling

A standard Genetic Algorithm (GA) [11] was used to explore the search space for finding the optimal sequence of optimizations for each function. Basically, a GA consists in generating an initial population of random solutions with a subsequent iterative evolution of their individuals, determined by their evaluation and ranking. Each evolutionary step, called generation, involves the selection of the parent solutions (i.e., pairs of compilation sequences in our experiments); the application of the genetic operators (crossover and mutation); evaluation of children solutions (new solutions generated by operators); and the reinsertion operator (to decide the survivors for the next generation). This iterative process is performed until achieving the maximum number of generations or if 15 subsequent generations do not result in latency improvement.

All tests used the same GA configuration, which was empirically chosen. The GA runs over 100 generations, each one with a population size of 300 individuals. Each individual (chromosome) is a point in the search space (compiler optimization sequence) represented as an array with variable size corresponding to the sequence length. Each position of the array (gene) may store an optimization pass, indicating its order of employment in the compiler. During the generation of the initial population, we applied a uniform distribution to the sequence length in order to guarantee similar quantities for all possible sizes (1 to 16). Previous experiments using longer sequences shown insignificant improvements. The individuals generated are thus evaluated and ranked according to their fitness function. Here, the number of clock cycles associated with the resultant code generated after applying the optimization sequence represented by individual coding is used as fitness. In each generation, a uniform crossover operator was defined with 60% of probability for applying crossover to a pair of individuals. A simple tournament selection ($Tour = 3$) was used for parent solutions selection. A mutation rate of 40% was applied over the population of new solutions generated by crossover. Three types of mutation operators were developed: including a new pass to a point randomly chosen of the compilation sequence; removing the optimization placed in any point of the sequence; and changing the order of two passes of the sequence. All operators have the same probability of occurrence and the choice between them is totally random. Only one mutation is applied over each individual selected to be mutated. The elitism reinsertion strategy keeps the best optimization sequences (parents and children) in population at the end of each generation.

Initially, the GA-based approach was performed in both full and reduced spaces. However, in our exploratory experiments we observed that the generation of initial population was sufficient to reach the best compiler sequences for the reduced search space. In fact, the number of optimizations available on pruned space is relatively small (13 on average), thus 300 samples, even randomly generated, are able to achieve good results from that optimizations set. In addition, it is a filtered subset of optimizations usually covering only the potential optimizations for the code under compilation. For our experiments, there was none performance improvement during evolution and DSE was finalized at the 15th generation (stopping criterion). Therefore, a *random sampling* algorithm was used for the exploration of the reduced optimizations space. This process has exactly the same steps used in the generation of the initial population of the GA approach.

4.2 Insertion Algorithm

The *Insertion* algorithm is an iterative greedy algorithm presented in [12], which incrementally includes new optimizations to a sequence. The *insertion*'s pseudocode is presented in Algorithm 1.

The algorithm starts by acquiring the performance of the input function without optimizations. Then, the algorithm traverses the search space of optimizations sequentially, in a predefined order, building a solution by inserting one optimization at a time and verifying the resultant performance of the optimized code. If an improvement occurs, the optimization is included in the current solution. Otherwise, it is discarded and the next optimization in the sequence is tested. In full DSE, the sequence order is arbitrarily defined. In reduced DSE (i.e., optimized), the sequence order is defined in relation to the proximity among the functions in the phylogenetic tree.

In both approaches (full and reduced DSE), when testing the insertion of a new optimization, the algorithm evaluates the opti-

---

Algorithm 1: *Insertion* METHOD

Input: Number of iterations (N), search space (S) and input function (F)
Output: Best compiler optimization sequence ($bestSeq$)

```
 1  currSeq ← {}
 2  currFit ← evaluate(F, currSeq)
 3  refFit ← currFit
 4  for i ← 1 to N do
 5      bestSeq ← currSeq
 6      bestFit ← currFit
 7      for e ← 1 to size(S) do
 8          for pos ← 0 to size(currSeq) do
 9              newSeq ←
                    putEngine(S(e), currSeq(pos + 1))
10              newFit ← evaluate(F, newSeq)
11              if newFit < bestFit then
12                  bestSeq ← newSeq
13                  bestFit ← newFit
14          if bestFit > currFit then
15              currSeq ← bestSeq
16              currFit ← bestFit
17      if currFit < refFit then
18          refFit ← currFit
19      else
20          break
21  return bestSeq
```

---

mization in all possible positions of the current sequence, aiming at achieving the best sequence. Since the optimizations are processed in the same order they appear in the search space, the approach results can be influenced by the arrangement used. For minimizing this problem, it is necessary to traverse the search space a number of times. The number of iterations is an input of the algorithm. The employment of a small number of iterations may increase the dependence between sequence order and results, limiting the coverage of the search space. On the other hand, a high number of iterations increases the execution time of the DSE process. Here, we adopted 3 iterations for both approaches (full and reduced space), since higher values did not provide better results in our experiments. The algorithm also stops when there is no improvement between iterations.

4.3 Clean Algorithm

The *clean* algorithm is also an iterative greedy approach, which incrementally removes optimizations from the current sequence. However, unlike the previous one, this algorithm starts from the sequence formed by all optimizations of the search space. In each iteration, an optimization is removed from the current sequence in order to verify its effect on performance. The removal of optimizations is done sequentially, i.e., from the first until the last one (N-th pass). If there is not a performance decrease, the optimization is definitely removed from the sequence. Otherwise, the compiler engine is kept in its position and the next engine is evaluated. Therefore, the algorithm execution involves $N + 1$ simulations of the input function, where N is the length of the search space. Algorithm 2 shows the pseudocode of the *clean* algorithm.

Since the *clean* algorithm does not allow changing the order of optimizations, its results are strongly influenced by the optimizations arrangement in the initial sequence. In our experiments this

---

Algorithm 2: *Clean* METHOD

    Input: Engines in search space (S) and input function (F)
    Output: Best compiler optimization sequence ($bestSeq$)

1 $bestSeq \leftarrow S$
2 $bestFit \leftarrow evaluate(F, bestSeq)$
3 $pos \leftarrow 1$
4 **while** $pos \leq size(bestSeq)$ **do**
5     $newSeq \leftarrow removeEngine(bestSeq(pos))$
6     $newFit \leftarrow evaluate(F, newSeq)$
7   **if** $newFit \leq bestFit$ **then**
8         $bestSeq \leftarrow newSeq$
9         $bestFit \leftarrow newFit$
10   **else**
11       $pos \leftarrow pos + 1$

12 **return** $bestSeq$

---

approach was only performed over the reduced search space, where the sequence order is defined based on the proximity among the functions in the phylogenetic tree. That is, we adopt the same optimization sequence of the closest reference function, including the distinct (new) passes found in the optimization sequences of the other functions in the cluster.

4.4 Hybrid Approaches

During the experiments, we observed that the joining between *insertion* and *clean* algorithms improves the effectiveness of the exploration, approximating the performance to the one resulted in GA-based DSE with full search space. Basically, we use a single iteration of the *insertion* algorithm based on full search space in order to deal with optimizations that are not present in the reduced space. It also allows the reordering of the optimizations, bypassing the problem identified in the *clean* algorithm. Instances of two hybrid approaches are shown in Figure 6.

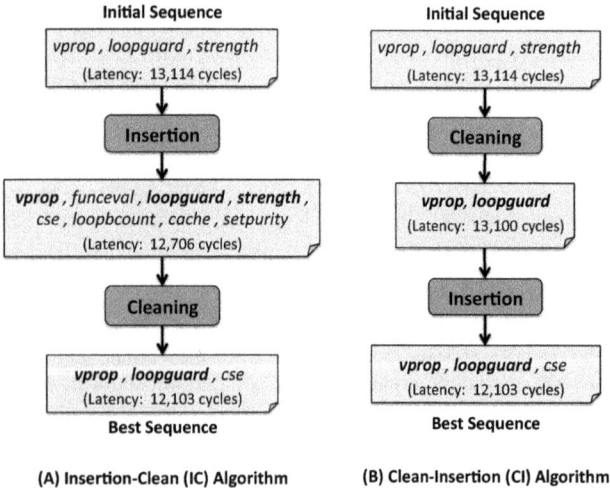

Figure 6. Hybrid DSE strategies.

The *clean-insertion* (CI) algorithm adopts as input the subset of the optimizations generated through the clustering-based selection method. The *clean* algorithm is performed over this reduced set in order to remove all superfluous optimizations, reducing the sequence length. This output sequence is then used as initial sequence for the *insertion* algorithm. Since the insertion process starts from

a promising non-empty point of the search space, the optimal sequence can be achieved through inclusion of fewer optimizations from the full optimizations set. In practice, the use of all optimizations in the *insertion* algorithm allows the exploration of neighbor regions to the original subspace. Finally, the inclusion of a new optimization can make other unnecessary. Therefore, the *clean* algorithm should be performed again. Given that it is a simple and fast algorithm, its execution does not affect the performance of this approach.

The *insertion-clean* (IC) algorithm also uses the reduced subset as input (initial sequence). However, this approach starts by including new optimizations in the initial sequence before cleaning. The basic idea is that redundant passes can be combined with new optimizations improving the latency of the program. On the other hand, this approach often deals with larger optimization sequences, where there are more positions for testing a given pass. Therefore, its execution time is excessively larger than the CI approach and the latencies were similar.

5. Experimental Results

The DSE strategies evaluated in this paper were implemented and executed using LARA. The objective was to achieve sequences of optimizations targeting a Xilinx MicroBlaze processor (a RISC architecture) for 41 functions from image [17] and DSP [18] benchmark repositories from Texas Instruments (TI). We applied a variety of algorithms to explore the optimizations space, providing distinct accuracies and execution times, aiming at validating the utility of the clustering-based optimization selection approach in the DSE process. These strategies basically differ with respect to the technique employed in the search of the best optimization sequence for a given function.

DSE strategies using *insertion* and Genetic Algorithms (GA) were executed on the full optimizations set, whereas approaches based on random sampling, and algorithms for cleaning and engine insertion were executed on a reduced search space. The experiments without optimization selection, named Full DSE, were performed using a total of 49 CoSy engines in search space (see Table 1). Given that a maximum sequence length of 16 compiler passes (empirically chosen from previous experiments) was adopted in the experiments, the number of potential sequences in the search space is in the order of 50^{16} (49 passes + non-optimization state), preventing an exhaustive exploration.

The executions with our clustering-based selection approach are identified as Reduced DSE. It was performed using a subset of optimizations (13 optimizations on average) chosen from the similarity between the target function and reference functions. During the clustering we considered 11 reference functions [17]–[19]: *adpcm* (*coder* and *decoder*), *autocorrelation*, *bubble sort*, *dotprod*, *fdct*, *fibonacci*, *max*, *min*, *pop count* and *sobel*. This reference group is a set of the functions previously used in other context [5] and was intentionally kept as it represents functions with different characteristics. Note that the impact on our DSE approach of different reference functions is planned for future work.

The results obtained from the reduced subset were compared with those achieved with the *insertion* and GA-based DSE over full optimizations space. Considering that a GA with carefully set parameters generally results on values close to optimal [20][21], the speedups achieved by the GA-based DSE with full optimizations space are used as goal for the other strategies. Figure 7 shows the best speedups achieved with the DSE strategies using a single algorithm. These speedups were calculated with respect to execution clock cycles achieved by the functions without optimizations.

As expected, the use of the DSE strategy based on GA using the full optimization space achieved the best speedups. On the other hand, the *insertion* algorithm with a pruned space obtained the

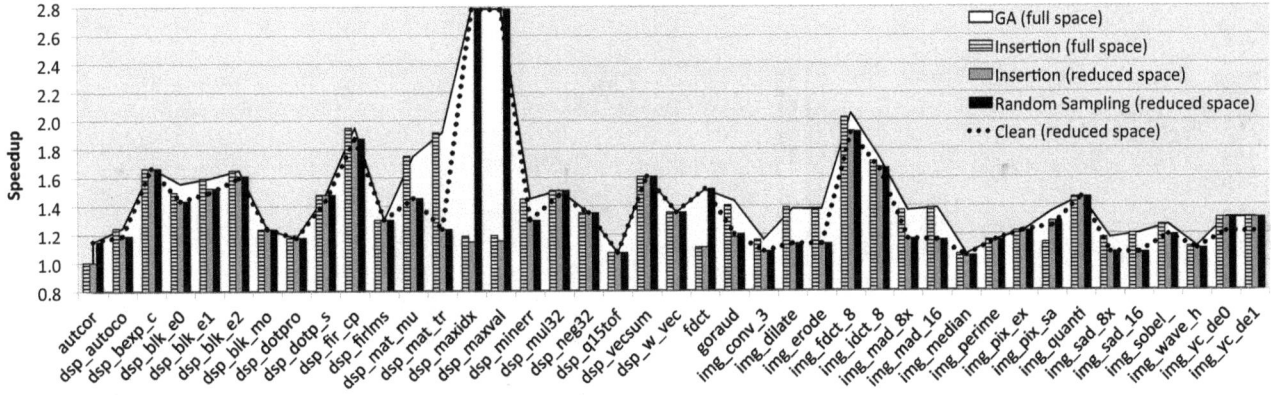

Figure 7. Speedups obtained for each benchmark using single algorithm-based DSE strategies in full and pruned space.

worst results. The *insertion* algorithm presented a similar behavior for full and reduced sets. For instance, both approaches were not able to determine the best sequences of optimizations for the functions dsp_maxidx and dsp_maxval. As expected, the exploration with full space achieved better speedups than when applied in the pruned optimizations set. The *clean* algorithm is the simplest and fastest approach used in this paper. However, its achieved speedups are very close to the random sampling and full *insertion* methods, and only different in about 0.08 to GA-based algorithm.

Such as the approach used in [1], we also searched the best single optimization sequence for our 11 reference functions. During this process, each potential optimization sequence was evaluated over all functions, and a geometric mean was calculated from their speedups considering the performance of the original code (without optimizations). The "best overall sequence" was applied over the functions analyzed in order to validate the representativity level of the reference set. Furthermore, we implemented two mixed approaches joining the *clean* and *insertion* algorithms, considering the behavior observed from the individual algorithms. The purpose of these hybrid approaches was to overcome the limitations of the original algorithms, providing a more effective exploration of the search space. The best speedups (hybrid approach and overall sequence) were compared with the GA-based DSE strategies, as shown in Figure 8.

In general, the hybrid approaches achieved speedups very close to those achieved by the GA-based DSE. The adoption of the "best overall sequence" also achieved good speedups, although its values are slightly worse than the other ones (for example, when exploring optimization sequences for the img_conv_3 function). Such observation is corroborated through observation of the geometric means of the best speedups achieved for each DSE strategy, as outlined in Figure 9. The speedups achieved by the "best overall sequence" confirm the good representativity of the reference set adopted.

Basically, the approaches can be clustered into 3 groups according to their geometric mean values. The first group is formed by GA (44%), *clean-insertion* and *insertion-clean* (both hybrid approaches with 43%). The intermediate group comprises the *insertion* algorithm with full space (36%), *random sampling* (36%), *clean* algorithm (35%), and best overall sequence (34%). The last group is formed by the *insertion* algorithm with a pruned space (28%). Note that the difference between the geometric mean speedups of the groups is around 0.16.

Figure 10 presents the size of the initial search space explored by the hybrid approaches, as well as the number of optimizations contained in their near-optimal sequences achieved by GA and hybrid approaches (CI and IC algorithms) for each function evaluated.

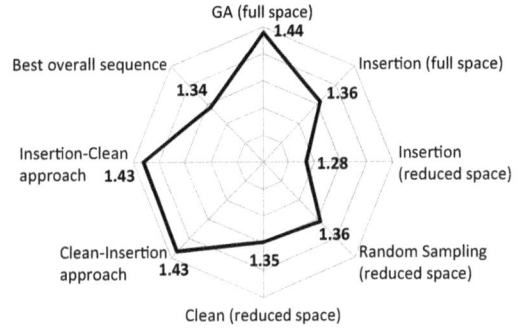

Figure 9. Geometric means of the best speedups according to the DSE strategies.

Generally, the final sequences are smaller than the size of initial space, except for img_dilate, img_fdct_8 and img_idct_8, and the "best overall sequence" formed by 16 optimizations. Also, the final compilation sequences resulted in each algorithm (GA, IC and CI) are very similar for most functions. In fact, hybrid algorithms had performance similar to the GA approach.

Therefore, the reduction in terms of speedup may be acceptable, especially when considering the gains in DSE execution time, as shown in Figure 11. There are large differences of DSE execution times between the GA-based approach and other DSE strategies. Although the GA-based approach achieves always equal or better optimization sequences, it also spends more execution time during DSE. Among the algorithms based on pruned space, the *clean* algorithm is the fastest and *random sampling* is the slowest.

Figure 12 presents the average of the execution time of each DSE strategy in relation to input functions. As can be observed, significant improvements were achieved with respect to the execution time when comparing DSE in full and reduced spaces. The GA-based exploration over full space took on average 6,500 seconds, whilst random sampling, insertion and clean approaches using pruned search spaces took about 458, 127 and 23 seconds, i.e., gains around $14\times$, $51\times$ and $286\times$, respectively. Considering the hybrid approaches, the DSE execution time gains over the GA-based approach were approximately $18\times$ and $4\times$ for the *clean-insertion* and the *insertion-clean* algorithms, respectively.

6. Related Work

It is a common practice to apply the same set of optimizations in a fixed order on each program when targeting a given archi-

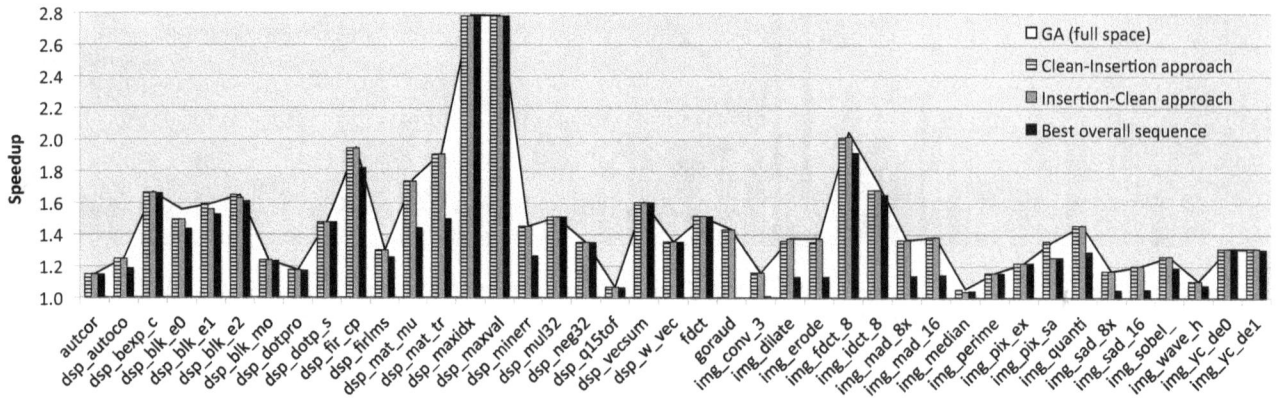

Figure 8. Speedups achieved for each benchmark using hybrid algorithm-based DSE strategies and an overall optimization sequence.

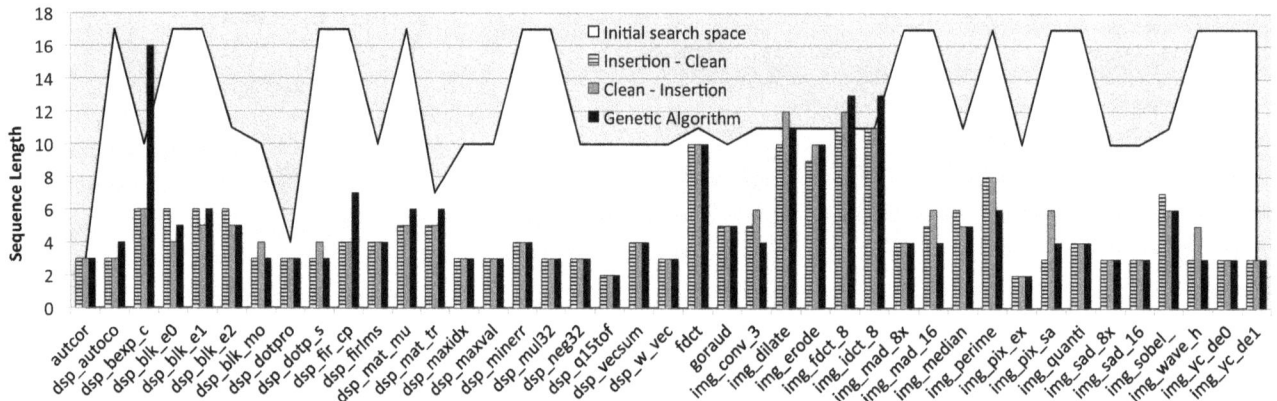

Figure 10. Sequence lengths in the initial search space and in the final optimization sequences in relation to the search algorithm used and the function evaluated.

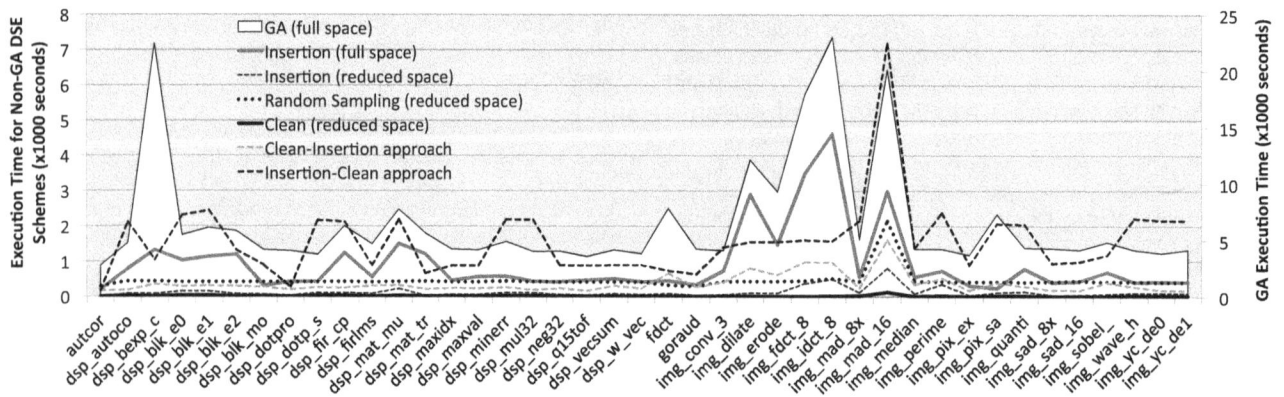

Figure 11. Execution time of the DSE strategies obtained for each benchmark evaluated in full or pruned space

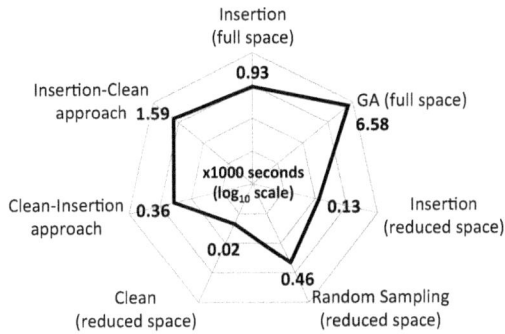

Figure 12. Execution time average of the DSE strategies.

tecture/platform. However, different code fragments may require a specific ordering of optimizations to obtain the best performance for a given platform [1]. Compilers for embedded computing systems are more dependent on code transformations and optimizations as the computer architectures used have typically more constraints related to memory size and organization, processor speed, and may have high-levels of customization such as the ones allowed by the use of FPGAs [22]. For this kind of systems, non-trivial compiler sequences are usually needed to achieve the required results. Given the large number of compiler optimizations, a vast Design Space Exploration (DSE) may exist and the research of techniques to efficiently and effectively search this space is a hot topic of research.

The exploration of compiler sequences for typical general purpose processors has been addressed in [2], but has been typically focused on a limited number of simple compiler optimizations. In [12], the authors analyzed the impact of compiler optimizations on the quality of the FPGA-based hardware generated by a High Level Synthesis (HLS) process. Based on this analysis, they proposed an iterative HLS-directed approach, which executes profiling during the optimization process to discard damaging optimizations to the generated hardware quality.

The identification of compiler sequences generally relies on developers expertize or iterative compilation [3]. Machine-learning techniques, such as Genetic Algorithms (GAs), have been commonly employed to search for the best optimization sequences for specific applications. Randomized search algorithms have been also used to identify suitable compilation sequences [23]. A system called COLE is presented in [3]. It uses a multi-objective evolutionary algorithm based on SPEA2 [24] to automatically find pareto optimal optimization settings for the *gcc* compiler. The work in [20] uses several machine learning algorithms to find the best sequence of optimization passes, observing that search techniques such as GAs achieve gains very close to best performance. This work was extended in [25] where they compare the ability of GA-based and function-level searches to find the best optimization sequences for their VPO compiler. The reuse methodology proposed in [26] uses generic programming to incorporate user-defined optimizations into the compiler.

An approach based on a number of code features has also revealed interesting results and acceptable accuracy to predict the impact of hardware compilation for a number of benchmarks [27]. The method proposed in [28] uses a form based on the characteristics of the code to identify a number of loop transformations, such as loop unrolling, loop skewing, and loop distribution. Recent research has proposed novel feature-vector based heuristic techniques to quickly customize sequences for individual functions during JIT (Just In Time) compilation [1][21]. In [29], a predictive model based on logistic regression uses the features extracted of

the function to derive customized optimization sequences. Support vector machines are employed in [30] to derive function-specific optimization sequences for the IBM JVM (Java Virtual Machine). These approaches reveal that the use of analytical models and cost functions based on certain code features may allow good predictors and may truly contribute to the identification of compiler sequences when considering hardware and/or software compilation. Our work is orthogonal to previous research, since pruning of the search space can be seen as a separate task of the exploration process. Generally, it is used as an important initial step of DSE strategies.

Several techniques have been used to reduce the space of potential candidate solutions. For instance, the identification of corner cases of the search space can be done by probing the design space or by worst-case analytical methods, such as the network calculus [31] for the network processing domain, and the event-stream based methods for the real-time embedded domain [32]. A statistical analysis of the effect of compiler options is used in [33] to prune the search space and find a single compiler optimization sequence for a set of programs that performs better than the standard settings used in *gcc*. In [34], the authors use machine learning techniques to limit the search space, increasing the speed of iterative optimizations. This methodology is able to indicate, for a given program, the areas of the solution space where the search should be focused. Moreover, it is independent of the solution-space, the search algorithm and the compiler/optimizer used. PEAK, an automated performance tuning system is presented in [35]. It uses three heuristic algorithms to select good compiler optimization settings. It performs a previous space pruning through the withdrawal of transformations with negative performance effects to speedup the search. In [36], a gcc-based framework (Milepost GCC) is used to automatically extract program features and learn the best optimizations across programs and architectures. Their framework uses machine learning techniques to correlate the new program with the closest one seen earlier to apply a customized and potentially more effective optimization combination. Although this approach is close to our approach, our method does not need any training and is based on clustering and simple DSE schemes. The main idea is that the code patterns extracted by clustering can aid in the appropriate selection of optimizations, which can be used in DSE strategies to conduct/suggest efficient optimization sequences.

7. Conclusions

The selection of the sequence of compiler optimizations can have a significant impact on performance and it is platform and application dependent. Therefore, the adoption of a efficient Design Space Exploration (DSE) scheme to aid embedded system developers is of a paramount importance. This paper presented a DSE approach which uses a clustering-based selection method for reducing the number of optimizations used during the exploration of optimization sequences. We analyzed different DSE algorithm alternatives to employ our clustering-based approach. Experiments shown that the use of our approach results in a significant reduction of the search space and makes feasible the use of simple DSE algorithms. For instance, approaches based on the *clean* algorithm resulted in good trade-off between program optimization achievements (performance improvements) and DSE execution time. Particularly, the performance improvements achieved are comparable to close to optimal compilation sequences provided by a Genetic Algorithm (GA) using the full optimizations set. When compared to the results achieved by a DSE strategy using a GA and targeting a Xilinx MicroBlaze processor, our approach using the simplest and fastest algorithm (*clean* algorithm) allowed significant reductions of DSE execution time (around $286\times$) at the same time that it achieved performance improvements only 9% below the ones provided by GA, guaranteeing speedups of 35% over the baseline for the 41 benchmarks used in the experiments. The *clean-insertion* algorithm resulted in speedups similar to those found by the GA approach (43%) with a 18× faster DSE execution time (364 seconds compared to 108 minutes of GA).

Ongoing work is focusing on probabilistic heuristics that explore each clustering-based set of optimizations and on exploring sequences of compiler optimizations in the context of hardware generation targeting FPGAs. For future work, we plan to compare our DSE approach to other machine learning approaches. We also intend to investigate the impact of the C to DNA representation transformation rules and the set of reference functions used by the clustering process.

Acknowledgments

This work has been partially supported by FCT (Portuguese Science Foundation) under research grants SFRH/BD/82606/2011, and FEDER/ON2 and FCT project NORTE–07–124–FEDER–000062. LGAM has a scholarship granted by CAPES (process: 0352/13-6) which made possible a 1-year visiting period to FEUP and his contribution to the work presented in this paper. The FEUP authors acknowledge the CoSy license and technical support provided by ACE Associated Compiler Experts bv, The Netherlands.

References

[1] S. Kulkarni and J. Cavazos, "Mitigating the compiler optimization phase-ordering problem using machine learning", *ACM Int. Conf. on Object Oriented Programming Systems Languages and Applications (OOPSLA'12)*, pp.147-162, 2012.

[2] L. Almagor , et al., "Finding effective compilation sequences", *2004 ACM SIGPLAN/SIGBED Conf. on Languages, Compilers, and Tools for Embedded Systems*, vol. 39, pp. 231-239, Jun. 2004.

[3] K. Hoste and L. Eeckhout, "Cole: compiler optimization level exploration", *6th Int. Symp. on Code Generation and Optimization (CGO'08)*, pp.165-174, 2008.

[4] A. Sanches and J. M. P. Cardoso, "On Identifying Patterns in Code Repositories to Assist the Generation of Hardware Templates", *20th Int. Conf. on Field Programmable Logic and Applications (FPL'10)*, pp. 267-270, 2010.

[5] A. Sanches, J. M. P. Cardoso and A. C. B. Delbem, "Identifying Merge-Beneficial Software Kernels for Hardware Implementation", *Int. conf. on Reconfigurable Computing and FPGAs (ReConFig'11)*, pp.74-79, 2011.

[6] J. M. P. Cardoso et al., *Compilation and Synthesis for Embedded Reconfigurable Systems: An Aspect-Oriented Approach*. Springer, 2013.

[7] "ACE CoSy Compiler Development System", Available: http://www.ace.nl/compiler/cosy.html, (accessed in 18/10/2012).

[8] J. M. P. Cardoso, et al., "LARA: an aspect-oriented programming language for embedded systems", *11th ACM Int. Conf. on Aspect-Oriented Software Development (AOSD'12)*, pp.179-190, 2012.

[9] A. R. Cilibrasi and A. P. Vitanyi, "Clustering by compression", *IEEE Trans. Information Theory.*, vol. 51, no. 4, pp. 1523-1545, 2005.

[10] J. Felsenstein, *Inferring phylogenies*. Sinauer Associates, Inc, 2003.

[11] D. E. Goldberg, "Genetic Algorithms in Search, Optimization and Machine Learning", 1st ed., Addison-Wesley Longman, 1989.

[12] Q. Huang, et al., "The Effect of Compiler Optimizations on High-Level Synthesis for FPGAs", *IEEE Int. Symp. on Field-Programmable Custom Computing Machines (FCCM'13)*, pp. 89-96, 2013.

[13] T. Wheeler, and J. Kececioglu, "Multiple alignment by aligning alignments", *15th ISCB Conf. on Intelligent Systems for Molecular Biology, Bioinformatics*, vol. 23, no. 13, pp. i559-i568, 2007.

[14] C. K. Roy, J. R. Cordy, and R. Koschke, "Comparison and Evaluation of Code Clone Detection Techniques and Tools: A Qualitative Approach", *Science of Computer Programming.*, vol. 74, no. 7, pp. 470-495, 2009.

[15] M. Li and P. M. B. Vitanyi, *An introduction to Kolmogorov complexity and its applications*. 2nd ed. Springer-Verlag, 1997.

[16] M. Newman, *Networks: An Introduction*. Oxford Univ. Press, 2010.

[17] Texas Instruments, "TMS320C64x Image/Video Processing Library", 2003.

[18] Texas Instruments, "TMS320C64x DSP Library: Programmer's Reference", 2003.

[19] M. R. Guthaus, et al., "MiBench: A free, commercially representative embedded benchmark suite", *IEEE Int. Workshop of the Workload Characterization (WWC-4)*, pp.3-14, 2001.

[20] P. A. Kulkarni, D. B. Whalley and G. S. Tyson, "Evaluating heuristic optimization phase order search algorithms", *IEEE Int. Symp. on Code Generation and Optimization (CGO'07)*, pp.157-169, 2007.

[21] Michael R. Jantz and Prasad A. Kulkarni, "Performance potential of optimization phase selection during dynamic JIT compilation", *9th ACM SIGPLAN/SIGOPS Int. Conf. on Virtual Execution Environments (VEE '13)*, pp.131-142, 2013.

[22] J. M. P. Cardoso, P. Diniz, and M. Weinhardt, "Compiling for Reconfigurable Computing: A Survey", *ACM Computing Surveys*, vol. 42, no.4, pp.1-65, 2010.

[23] K. D. Cooper, et al., "Exploring the structure of the space of compilation sequences using randomized search algorithms", *Journal of Supercomputing*, vol. 36, no. 2, pp.135-151, 2006.

[24] E. Zitzler and M. Laumanns and L. Thiele, "SPEA2: Improving the Strength Pareto Evolutionary Algorithm", *Swiss Federal Inst. of Technology - Computer Engineering and Networks Lab. (technical report)*, 21 pages, 2001.

[25] P. A. Kulkarni, M. R. Jantz, and D. B. Whalley, "Improving both the performance benefits and speed of optimization phase sequence searches", *ACM SIGPLAN/SIGBED Conf. on Languages, Compilers, and Tools for Embedded Systems (LCTES'10)*, pp.95-104, 2010.

[26] J. J. Willcock, A. Lumsdaine and D. J. Quinlan, "Reusable, generic program analyses and transformations", *8th Int. Conf. on Generative Programming and Component Engineering (GPCE'09)*, pp.5-14, 2009.

[27] R. J. Meeuws, C. Galuzzi and K. L. M. Bertels, "High Level Quantitative Hardware Prediction Modeling using Statistical methods", *Int. Conf. on Embedded Computer Systems: Architectures, Models, and Simulations (SAMOS'10)*, pp.140-149, 2011.

[28] O.S. Dragomir, "K-loops: Loop Transformations for Reconfigurable Architectures", *PhD Thesis*, TU Delft, Faculty of Elektrotechniek, Wiskunde en Informatica, Delft, Netherlands, 2011.

[29] J. Cavazos and M. F. P. O'Boyle, "Method-specific dynamic compilation using logistic regression", *ACM Int. Conf. on Object-Oriented Programming Systems, Languages, and Applications (OOPSLA'06)*, pp.229-240, 2006.

[30] R. Sanchez, et al., "Using machines to learn method-specific compilation strategies", *Int. Symp. on Code Generation and Optimization (CGO'11)*, pp. 257-266, 2011.

[31] J. Y. Le Boudec and P. Thiran, "Network Calculus: A Theory of Deterministic Queuing Systems for the Internet", Springer-Verlag, 2001.

[32] K. Richter, et al., "Bottom-up performance analysis of HW/SW platforms", *Design and Analysis of Distributed Embedded Systems (DIPES'02)*, pp.173-183, IFIP, vol. 91, 2002.

[33] M. Haneda, P. M. W. Knijnenburg and H. A. G. Wijshoff, "Optimizing general purpose compiler optimization", *2nd Conf. on Computing frontiers (CF'05)*, pp.180-188, 2005.

[34] F. Agakov, et al., "Using Machine Learning to Focus Iterative Optimization", *Int. Symp. on Code Generation and Optimization, (CGO'06)*, pp. 295-305, 2006.

[35] Z. Pan and R. Eigenmann, "PEAK: a fast and effective performance tuning system via compiler optimization orchestration", *ACM Trans. on Programming Languages and Systems*, vol. 30, no. 3, pp.1-17, 2008.

[36] G. Fursin, et al., "Milepost GCC: machine learning enabled self-tuning compiler", *Int. Journal of Parallel Programming*, vol. 39, no. 3, pp.296-327, Springer, 2011.

Partitioning Data-parallel Programs for Heterogeneous MPSoCs : Time and Energy Design Space Exploration

Kiran Chandramohan

School of Informatics, University of Edinburgh
Kiran.Chandramohan@ed.ac.uk

Michael F.P. O'Boyle

School of Informatics, University of Edinburgh
mob@inf.ed.ac.uk

Abstract

Multiprocessor System-on-Chips(MPSoCs) are now widely used in embedded devices. MPSoCs typically contain a range of specialised processors. Alongside the CPU, there are microcontrollers, DSPs and other hardware accelerators. Programming these MP-SoCs is difficult because of the difference in instruction-set architecture (ISA) and disjoint address spaces. In this paper we consider MPSoCs as a target for individual benchmarks. We examine how data-parallel programs can be optimally mapped to heterogeneous multicores for different criteria such as performance, power and energy. We investigate the partitioning of seven benchmarks taken from DSPstone, UTDSP and Polybench suites. Based on design space exploration we show that the best partition depends on compiler optimization level, program, input size and crucially optimization criteria. We develop a straightforward approach that attempts to select the best partitioning for a given program. On average it achieves speedups of 2.2x and energy improvements of 1.45x on the OMAP 4430 platform.

Categories and Subject Descriptors D.3.4 [*Programming Languages*]: Processors–Code generation

Keywords spmd, data-parallel, heterogeneous processor, partitioning

1. Introduction

Many of the embedded systems available today are based on MP-SoCs. The processors employed are diverse and consist of devices such as CPUs, DSPs, micro controllers and GPUs. The OMAP[16] from TI, Snapdragon[23] from Qualcomm and Tegra[26] from NVIDIA are examples of popular MPSoCs in the mobile embedded systems market.

In general-purpose computing there has also been a recent cautious move to heterogeneous manycore systems where diversity is currently less extreme. Typically, GPGPUs are used as programmable accelerators and there is variation in CPU microarchitecture while maintaining the same ISA eg. ARM's big.LITTLE [2].

In fact, energy and power have been the driving force behind this gradual convergence of the two communities. The embedded world has lead in system diversity and it is likely that tomorrow's general-purpose heterogeneous manycore platforms will resemble the MPSoCs of today

The design of embedded MPSoCs has been largely application driven with specialised units such as ASICs and DSPs targeting media decoding or digital signal applications. Embedded applications developers have traditionally been expert programmers where the cost of porting and tuning can be amortised across many shipped devices. Because of this, the programming models supported by MPSoCs typically tend to be application driven and change from platform or generation to the next. As embedded MP-SoCs become used for different purposes than they were initially designed for and enter the mainstream, the complexity of programming them becomes an increasingly important issue. Future platforms will have higher levels of parallelism and contain increasing specialised cores. What we would like is to ease the programming burden needed to exploit increasing levels of diversity.

This paper proposes the use of an SPMD model of computation for data-parallel programs and explores the mapping of such applications to the highly heterogeneous TI OMAP platform. This platform has different memory domains, has multiple operating systems, specialised processors with different ISAs and local compilers and rudimentary systems software support. It is a difficult programming target.

We first develop a framework that allows an SPMD compiler model to map down to such a hardware platform. We then explore the mapping space and show that the best mapping depends on the metric involved. By using a highly accurate energy measurement, we show that the best mapping varies depending on whether, time, energy, EDD or power is the optimisation goal. It also depends on the level of code optimisation available and whether power gating is available. It is frequently believed [6] that running the fastest is best for energy. Since heterogeneous multicores provides opportunities for energy-delay tradeoffs, we show in fact that this property no longer holds. We develop a partitioning approach that, when applied to a set of benchmarks, gives on average a 2.2x speedup over sequential execution time and reduces energy consumption by 1.45x on average.

This paper makes the following contributions:

- Develops a framework to map data parallel programs to highly heterogeneous systems

- Provides a detailed energy evaluation methodology

- Explores a partitioning design space and shows its dependency on optimization goal: energy vs time.

- Develops and evaluates a partitioning approach that is within 10% of the best across benchmarks and optimization criteria.

LCTES '14, June 12–13, 2014, Edinburgh, UK.
Copyright © 2014 ACM 978-1-4503-2877-7 /14/06... $15.00.
http://dx.doi.org/10.1145/2597809.2597822

```
for(int k=0;k<N;k++)                         for(int k=0;k<N;k++)
{                                            {
   #pragma omp parallel for                     call_barrier(1) ;
   for(int i=0;i<N;i++)                          for(int i=start_indx;i<end_indx;i++)
     for(int j=0;j<N;j++)                          for(int j=0;j<N;j++)
       path[i][j]=path[i][j]<path[i][k]+path[k][j]?     path[i][j]=path[i][j]<path[i][k]+path[k][j]?
                  path[i][j]:path[i][k]+path[k][j];                 path[i][j]:path[i][k]+path[k][j];
}                                            }
```

(a) OpenMP FloydWarshall

(b) SPMD FloydWarshall

Figure 1: Programming Model

2. Motivation

MPSoCs have the potential for high performance but are hard programming targets. Consider Figure 1a which shows a simple data parallel program, floydwarshall, which we wish to map to the OMAP4430 platform shown in Figure 5, a typical MPSoC platform. The processors have different ISAs, do not share a common address space and even support different operating systems.

Currently, due to programming complexity, programmers are discouraged from exploiting the full potential of the platform; instead running the program on the A9 core or possibly the DSP.

We, however, are interested in using all of the processing element based on a data partitioning approach. In Figure 1a the floydwarshall program has a parallel middle loop which is equivalent to partitioning the path array on the first index e.g. by rows. Applying this partitioning to the original program, gives the code shown in Figure 1b.

This is the local code that each processor will run. The local loop bounds of i are restricted so that only local data is written to. This means that the cores run the same code with different $start\_indx_p$ and end_indx_p depending on the amount of data allocated to them. Here $p \in \{A9_1, A9_2, M3_1, M3_2, DSP\}$. A barrier synchronisation is inserted in line 3 due to the cross processor flow dependence from path[k][j] to path[i][j].

Once we have generated the local programs, the key issue is determining the amount of data to be allocated to each processor and hence its workload. Figure 2 and 3 show the runtime and energy for various partitioning policies relative to sequential execution on the A9. A naive partitioning approach *hom* partitions data uniformly across all cores, *freq* partitions across cores in proportion to their clock frequency, *iter* is the partitioning scheme developed in this paper and *best* is the best partitioning found by exhaustive search. The *best* policy is not realistic but provides a useful upper-bound on performance.

Time If the programmer were to select the DSP or even the M3, then this will lead to slowdown relative to the A9. In Figure 2, the DSP is 5x times slower than just running the code on the A9. Surprisingly, running on the M3 is faster than the DSP but still 4x times slower than on the A9. If we now consider data partitioning across all processors, then *hom* gives the worst performance, 2x times slower than the A9. The *freq* approach is a little better but still slower. Our *iter* scheme is able to nearly achieve the 2x speedup available from exhaustive search, the *best* scheme.

Energy If we now look at energy, a different pattern emerges. The programmer selecting the DSP as their target results in worse energy efficiency than the A9. On the other hand the M3 would give 2x improvement, though this is at the cost of much slower execution, The *hom* and *freq* policies continue to give poor outcomes with 2x as much energy used as the A9 baselines. Our approach however achieves the same level of energy efficiency as the M3 and *best* schemes i.e. 2x less energy than the baseline. Thus our approach is able to achieve significant improvements regardless of the metric of interest.

This example shows that even when we overcome the difficulties of different processors and operating systems, determining the right partitioning is a difficult task for heterogeneous systems. Methods used in homogeneous systems such as uniform partitioning are ineffective. The next sections describe the SPMD model in more detail and describe how this can be mapped to the challenging OMAP platform.

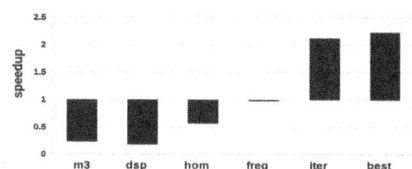

Figure 2: Execution time speedup relative to sequential execution on the A9. The M3 and DSP alone are significantly slower. Equal partitioning, hom and frequency based partitioning perform poorly. Selecting the right partition gives 2x speedup

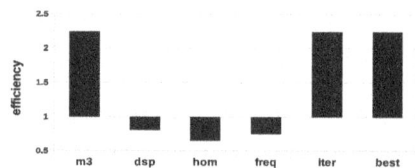

Figure 3: Energy relative to sequential execution on the A9. The M3 alone is significantly more energy efficient than the A9. The DSP alone is less efficient. Equal partitioning, hom and frequency based partitioning perform poorly. Selecting the right partition gives 2x improved energy performance

3. Programming Model

In this section we describe how data parallel programs can be partitioned and mapped using an SPMD model of computation. This is followed by a description of the OMAP programming model and how we are able to map an SPMD model on to it.

3.1 Data Parallelism and SPMD

Data Parallelism Throughout this paper we focus on data parallel programs. These are programs where individual elements of a data structure can be independently computed. They are normally found in array based programs with corresponding parallel loops. Such programs are frequently found in embedded applications. We are not concerned in how the data parallelism is determined. This can either be performed by the programmer who inserts a parallel pragma or determined by automatic parallelisation. Instead we focus on how this potential parallelism can be mapped to a heterogeneous system.

SPMD The SPMD (single program, multiple data) model of parallelism is well known and used in a variety of settings. Unified Parallel C (UPC)[30], Co-Array Fortran[22], and Titanium[31] are a few examples. It consists of a set of parallel tasks which can be either processes or threads that run the same program but operate on independent sections of an array. The array is partitioned

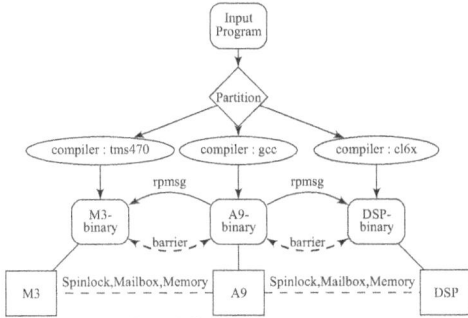
Figure 4: Partitioning a program

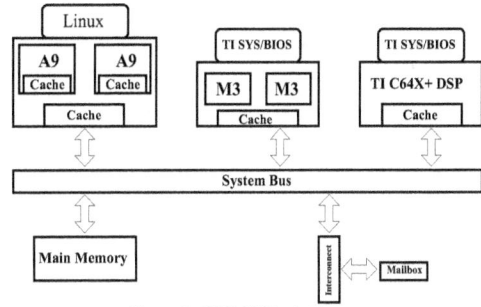
Figure 5: OMAP4 block diagram

across processors such that each processor works on a separate array section. We consider the case when each task is implemented as a separate thread. The set of threads is fixed throughout the entire program execution and typically corresponds to the number of processing elements. The threads are forked off at the start of execution and only join at the end, unlike traditional fork/join parallelism. Synchronization is inserted whenever there is a cross-processor dependence which is achieved by the use of barriers.

Data Partitioning The key issue is how to partition the data. This can be broken into 2 separate stages (i) which dimensions of the data to partition, (ii) how many elements of each dimension to allocate processor. The first stage has been considered by a number of researchers [1]. In this paper we restrict ourselves to just 1 dimensional partitioning. We consider each dimension in turn and determine the most parallel dimension, i.e. partitioning along this dimension incurs the least amount of synchronisation. If there is more than one candidate, we select row partitioning as rows are contiguous in 'C'. The second stage depends on the performance and energy consumptions of the processor. We consider a number of different policies in section 4.

Computation Partitioning Once the data is partitioned, we need to determine the computation to be performed by each processor. We use the local write rule, each thread only writes to its local data, placing a constraint on the the thread's local loop bounds. Figure 1b shows an example of such loop bounds. One important consequence of this mapping rule is that there are no remote-writes and all output dependence's are by definition within a processor.

Synchronisation Synchronisation is needed whenever there is cross-processor dependence i.e. the source of a dependence is in a different thread to the sink. As there are no output-dependences, only flow and anti-dependences need be considered. Furthermore, if a read access is aligned on a partition to a write access, it too is guaranteed to be local. In Figure 1b, the read of path[i][k] is local as it has the same reference on the partitioned 1st dimension [i], i.e it is aligned. The reference path[k][j] is remote as it has a different reference [k] on the partitioned dimension. Once we have the cross-processor dependence graph, barriers are inserted at the highest lexical level that covers the dependence. For more details on optimizing barrier placement see [13].

3.2 The OMAP model

Hardware The TI OMAP4430[17] is a typical mobile applications MPSoC consisting of various subsystems including general purpose processors, a programmable multimedia engine plus graphics and image accelerators. Figure 5 shows the components of the OMAP4430 relevant to this paper. A dual core ARM Cortex-A9 provides general purpose computing. Both processors share a common L2 cache and address space. There are two smaller ARM Cortex-M3s available for smaller and lower power tasks.

Both share a common L1 cache and are responsible for controlling the graphics and image accelerators. There is also distinct programmable multimedia engine based on a TI mini-C64X+ DSP. The PowerVR GPU cannot be currently programmed however, and is not considered in our study.

Operating System The ARM Cortex-A9 cores are configured to run as a Symmetric Multiprocessing system with Ubuntu Linux as the Operating System. In contrast the M3s and DSPs run a TI RTOS called SYS/BIOS. The M3s are configured to run the RTOS in SMP fashion and hence the RTOS is also called SMP/BIOS. Programming the OMAP requires managing not only different address spaces but different operating systems.

The communication between the remote processors(M3s and DSP) and the A9s is managed using an Inter Processor Communication Protocol(IPC) called Syslink. This IPC framework was developed by TI to offload processor-intensive tasks to hardware accelerators/remote processors. The new version of Syslink is called Remote Processor Messaging(RPMsg)[25]. RPMsg works by sending and receiving messages through shared memory. The notification of messages is performed via a Mailbox interrupt mechanism.

Mapping applications to the OMAP therefore currently requires decomposing programs into tasks that fit the IPC model.

3.3 Mapping SPMD programs to OMAP

Figure 4 summarises the partitioning and mapping of an SPMD program onto the OMAP architecture. Each local program is compiled by the processor's host compiler. The resulting binaries are executed by each processor which synchronizes via a spinlock library. There are four main issues to consider i) thread management ii) data partitioning iii) sharing memory and iv) synchronization each of which is described below

3.3.1 Threads

We use the pthread library for parallel programming which offers a fine control over parallelism One thread is created for each A9 cores. One thread for the M3 and another for the DSP. There are in fact two M3 cores; this is handled in the m3 SYSBIOS where we create two threads for computation. The threads for m3 and DSP call remote procedure calls with addresses of the partitioned arrays as arguments. These remote procedure call activates the remote processors and they perform their computation.

3.3.2 Shared memory

The address of the processors are by default distinct. We use dmabuf[24] and some special properties of graphics memory addresses to overcome this. Memory is allocated in the Linux kernel side by creating a GEM buffer object. This can be memory mapped and used from the user space. Using the dmabuf API, physical addresses corresponding to this memory are obtained and propagated to the DSP or M3 using RPMsg/Syslink. This address will be in the tiler/dmm region which is setup with 1:1 physical to virtual mapping, so this can be used as the virtual address on the m3/DSP side.

3.3.3 Synchronization

Barriers are constructed using shared memory and the OMAP hardware spinlock. We built a Linux kernel driver to access the hardware spinlock and provide an A9 user space interface. The SYSBIOS also provides limited access to the spinlock. The barrier is made reverse sensing so that it can be repeatedly used. For A9 and M3, which have more than one thread running, pthread barriers and a local barrier is constructed using semaphores for synchronization respectively.

3.4 Code Generation

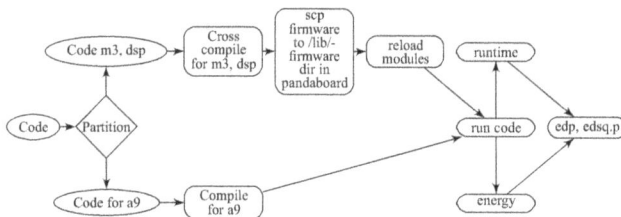

Figure 6: Code generation and runtime

Once the partitioning is decided, code is generated for the A9, M3 and DSP processors. We compile with gcc for A9s. The A9 code initiates the threads for all the processors. For the M3 and DSP a cross compilation is done using tools available as part of TI Code Composer studio. Details of the compilers used are in table 1. For these remote processors the program is compiled along with the SYSBIOS operating system and made into binary firmwares called *tesla-dsp.xe64T* and *ducati-m3-core0.xem3*. These binaries are placed in the directory */lib/firmware/* on the Linux machine. Some modules are reloaded to boot this firmware on the M3 and DSP processors. During this process, some shared memory location is agreed upon for exchanging messages between A9 and the remote processors(M3,DSP) for the Syslink protocol. When the program is run, connections are opened to the A9 and M3 processors and the threads for M3 and DSP make remote procedure calls to execute the code on those processors.

Processor	Cortex A9	Cortex M3	C64X+ DSP
Vendor	ARM	ARM	TI
Frequency	1GHz	200 MHz	466 MHz
Compiler	gcc 4.6.3	CCS tms470	CCS cl6x
OS	Ubuntu 12.04-3	SMP/BIOS	SYS/BIOS

Table 1: Frequency and Compiler details

3.4.1 Runtime

At runtime each program performs the following steps: 1) Allocate buffers for the arrays that have to be partitioned in the program with dmabuf. 2) Open connection to remote processors with Syslink. 3) Attach the allocated buffers to the remote processors and find physical addresses for these buffers so that they can be passed on to the remote processors. 4) Create threads for a9, m3 and DSP. While the a9 threads does the work locally, m3 and DSP threads will use Syslink to make remote procedure calls so that the work will be done on the remote processors. The remote procedures does cache synchronization before and after execution. 5) Wait for threads to join. 6) Detach buffers from the remote processors. 7) Close connection to the remote processors with Syslink. 8) Deallocate the buffers.

Figure 6 shows the complete code-generation and runtime workflow of our approach.

4. Partitioning Policies

In this section we look at four partitioning policies that are used in our experiments. Partitioning policies divide the data among all the cores for processing. The intuition behind these partitioning policies are provided. We also give the formulas that are used to compute the size of the partitions. In these formulas (part) is the function which computes the size of partition of a core.

1. **hom** This is the partitioning we would have intuitively used on a homogeneous multicore processor. Partitioning is uniformly performed for all the cores. We have 5 cores in the OMAP4430 SoC viz. two A9s, two M3s and one DSP. So if the datasize is *size* then we assign all the cores the same partition as follows.

$$part(a9) = part(m3) = part(dsp) = \frac{size}{5} \quad (1)$$

2. **freq** This method tries to capture the heterogeneity by using the clock frequency of the cores to guide the partitioning decision. The clock frequencies of each processor is given in Table 1. Each core is assigned a partition which is in proportion to its frequency compared to the others. Hence in this partitioning method the A9 cores always gets the largest share followed by the DSP and the M3 cores. The intuition behind this method is that faster clock frequencies leads to faster execution and hence lower runtime and energy. The partitions for each core is made as per the following formula. In the formula, $proc \in A9_1, A9_2, M3_1, M3_2, DSP$, *core_freq* is the frequency of *core*, and 2866 is the sum of the frequencies of all the cores.

$$part(core) = (size) * \frac{core\_freq}{2866} \quad (2)$$

3. **unip** We know that certain types of programs are better suited to some processors than others. With the uni processor policy we run the program sequentially on each processor separately and use the information gained from that to guide the partition decision. The information gained is different for runtime and one of the energy cases. For runtime, we first determine the throughput of each processor defined as the ratio of the amount of computation to the time taken for each processor. This is roughly analogous to FLOPS. Once we have found each processor's throughput, a simple way to partition is to assign data partitions to each processor in proportion to its throughput . If m is the throughput of m3 relative to a9 and n is the throughput of DSP relative to the a9 and *size* is the size of the total work to be partitioned, the partitions for the A9, M3 and DSP are given by the following formula.

$$part(a9) = \frac{size}{1 + m + n}$$
$$part(m3) = m * partition(a9)$$
$$part(dsp) = n * partition(a9) \quad (3)$$

Using this partitioning each processor will roughly finish at the same time, reducing load imbalance and execution time. This approach comes at the cost of a single run per processor.

When considering idle energy, we employ the same method as for runtime since running faster will ideally lead to lower idle power consumption. When there is no idle power then running fast is no longer important. In this method we allocate all the work to the the most efficient processor, the one which consumes the least energy for 1 unit of work.

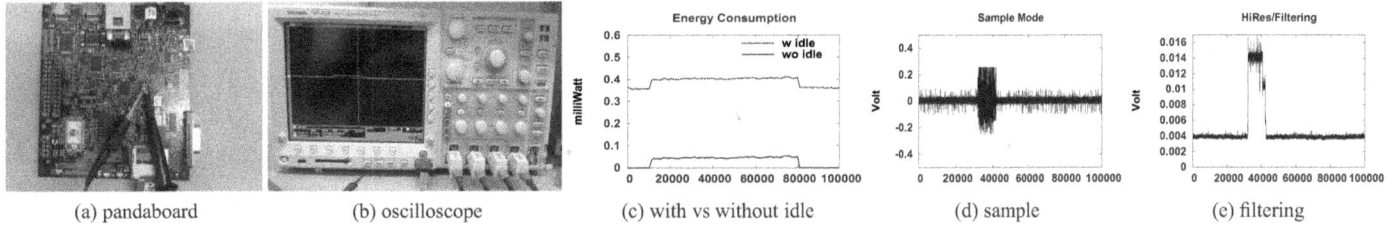

| (a) pandaboard | (b) oscilloscope | (c) with vs without idle | (d) sample | (e) filtering |

Figure 7: Board and Oscilloscope

4. **iter** This is the policy we propose in this paper. It is a simple extension to the *unip* policy. We first use *unip* to determine a starting partition. We then evaluate this partition on each processor in turn. This will give a new throughput value as execution time is not always linear with respect to amount of work. This approach is applied iteratively a maximum of 3 times and hence is more expensive than *unip*.

5. **best** This is the best partitioning policy which gives the best possible partitioning for various optimizing criteria. This policy is implemented by performing a design space exploration for runtime, energy and EDP. Since an exhaustive exploration of all the partitions for all the benchmarks will have too many points to measure we sample at discrete points which are multiples of a fixed quantity that varies with benchmarks. This provides a useful upper bound for our evaluation.

5. Metrics

We are particularly interested in how mapping is effected by different metrics such as time and energy and how to accurately measure these.

5.1 Energy

Energy is the sum of power over time. Measuring power and hence energy is highly non-trivial. This section describes in detail the methodology used to accurately measure power and discusses how it should be accounted for.

Power consumption is found by measuring the current consumed by the processor and multiplying by the supply voltage. The OMAP system is mounted on the Pandaboard which is driven by a supply voltage of 4.2V. However, we cannot measure the current consumption directly from the whole board supply since it is very noisy and hence is not accurate enough to distinguish between partition decisions. Also we would like to know the individual consumption of each processor. Hence we measure each processor's power consumption separately. We also have to measure the power consumed by memory. For this we concentrate on five power rails that supply power i.e. VCORE1 for the A9, VCORE2 for the DSP, VCORE3 for the M3, V1V29 for memory interface and VMEM for the memory. To measure the current we find a resistor in the path of these power rails and measure the voltage drop across the resistor and divide by the resistance. Since the resistors are attached to the board and are very small, pins are soldered to the resistors so that readings can be taken easily. This method is described in detail by Jos [20].

Power variation This approach gives a good insight into the power consumption. However in programs with phases, synchronization and heterogeneous loops the power consumption varies during the execution of an application. Hence we need to continuously monitor the voltage. For this purpose an oscilloscope is used and readings are taken every millisecond. Figure 7a shows the pandaboard with probes attached to one pair of pins to take energy measurements. Figure 7b shows the oscilloscope with a measurement of the processor to which the probes are attached in Figure 7a. The resistance is measured using a digital multimeter. For our experiments a Tektronix MSO4104 oscilloscope and Agilent 34410A digital Multimeter is used. Figure 7d shows a voltage reading from the oscilloscope in the regular sampling mode for the A9 processor when running the floydwarshall benchmark. As can be seen, there is significant noise in the measurement. This can be overcome using either post-filtering using software or using the High Resolution measurement mode of the oscilloscope. Figure 7e shows the same measurement after filtering. All the rails are measured separately and summed up to find the total power/energy consumption. We measure energy consumption in two different ways.

5.1.1 With idle energy

Processors dissipate energy even when they are idle. This idle energy is included in the calculation. This is the energy that we get directly during measurement. The presence of idle energy introduces new dynamics into the partitioning decisions. If there was no idle energy, the only aim for reducing energy would have been to run everything on the most efficient processor. But if we include idle energy the program should ideally also run quickly, since less runtime means less idle energy dissipation.

5.1.2 Without idle energy

Idle energy is removed from the energy consumption in this calculation. Considering this energy is important because the idle energy of a processor is not just the static energy but it also includes energy consumed by other parts of the board. Measuring without idle energy can give a fairer reflection of each components energy contribution. For example, the VCORE3 M3's power supply) provides power not only to the M3 but also to GPIO, UART, L3 interconnect etc. Hence the M3 has a higher static power allocated to it than other processors and hence there is dissipation of energy even when the system is idle but switched ON. This will result in an unfair comparison since other processors have a lower idle energy allocated to them as they have less additional devices on their power rails. Figure 7c shows the energy consumption of the M3 processor with and without idle energy when the floydwarshall benchmark is run entirely on the M3 processor. The dashed line is with idle energy and the solid line is for without idle energy. In both cases the processor starts in the idle state and when the program starts running we see a transition to a higher state of energy consumption. In the without idle energy case we can see that when the processor is in the idle state the idle energy is almost zero. But in the with idle energy case there is almost 0.3milliWatt power dissipation extra.

Which energy metric to use? As we are physically unable to account for energy used by additional devices on some individual power lines, we present results for both with and without idle energy in the remainder of this paper.

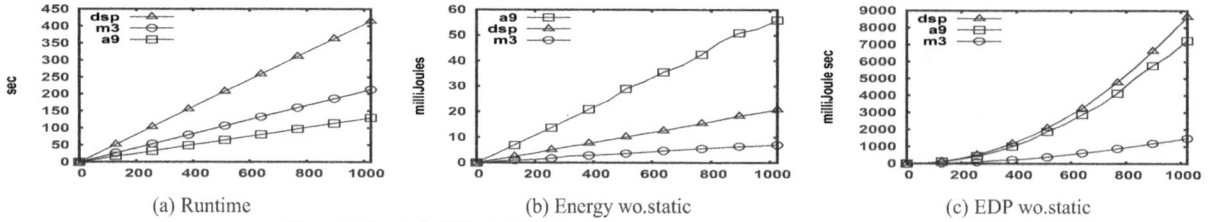

(a) Runtime   (b) Energy wo.static   (c) EDP wo.static

Figure 8: Unoptimized Matrix Multiplication Benchmark : runtime, energy, edp without idle energy

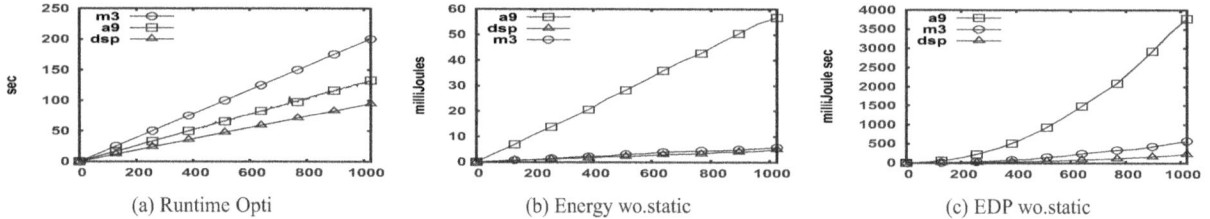

(a) Runtime Opti   (b) Energy wo.static   (c) EDP wo.static

Figure 9: Optimized Matrix Multiplication Benchmark : runtime, energy, edp without idle energy

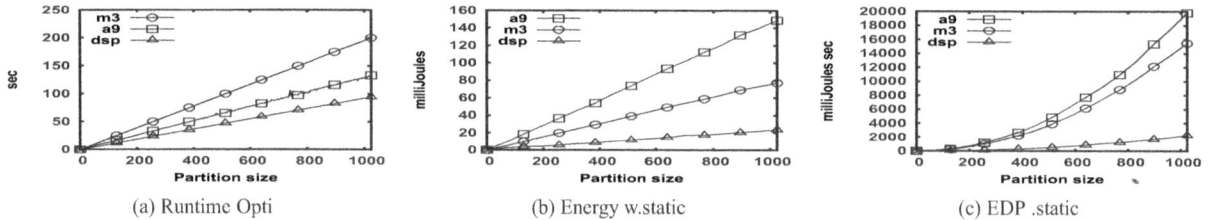

(a) Runtime Opti   (b) Energy w.static   (c) EDP .static

Figure 10: Optimized Matrix Multiplication Benchmark : runtime, energy, edp with idle energy

5.1.3 Runtime and EDP

Runtime is measured separately for each core and for the entire system. Runtime is measured by using the *gettimeofday* system call. Calls are made to this function before and after the execution and the runtime is the difference of the times. All the runtime measurements are made on the A9 side. EDP is measured by computing the product of Runtime and Energy.

6. Experimental Setup

Here we briefly describe the benchmarks used throughout the evaluation. Details of the hardware platform have been provided in section 3.2.

6.1 Benchmarks

Benchmark	Short Name	Suite	Size
Matrix Multiplication	mxm	DSPstone	1024
Dotproduct	dotp	DSPstone	2048
Edgedetect	edge	UTDSP	2048
Histogram	hist	UTDSP	4096
Doitgen	dgen	Polybench	64
Regdetect	regd	Polybench	64
FloydWarshall	flwl	Polybench	512

Table 2: Benchmarks

The benchmarks that we consider are taken from DSPstone[29], UTDSP[3] and polybench[12]. These benchmarks are parallelized and then used for our experiments.

All the benchmarks used are integer based. While ARM Cortex-A9 processor supports floating point, the Cortex M3 does not support floating points and the TI C64x+ DSP supports fixed point. Hence in the latter two cases, floating point is emulated. Table 2 shows the name of the benchmark, short name used in the diagrams

the suite it belongs to and the default size of the arrays that are partitioned in these benchmarks. Matrix Multiplication multiplies two matrices and stores the result in a third matrix. Dotproduct multiples two vectors and stores the result in a third vector. Edgedetect is an edge detection algorithm for images, it contains some convolutions and application of a threshold. Histogram computes the histogram of an image and uses the histogram to make a grayscale mapping and finally uses the mapping to create the output image. Doitgen is a multiresolution analysis kernel and it contains some matrix operations. Regdetect is a regularity detection algorithm for 2D images. FloydWarshall is the all pair shortest path algorithm which we have discussed before in the Background section..

7. Matrix Multiplication Case Study

In this section we study one benchmark, Matrix Multiplication (*mxm*), in detail before presenting the results for all benchmarks in section 8. We first compare the performance of *mxm* on each distinct processor before evaluating partitioning across processors.

7.1 Individual Processor

Figures 8 to 10 show the performance of *mxm* for runtime, energy and EDP for varying scenarios, in each case N=1024

7.1.1 Default optimization level

Initially we use the default compiler flags for each processor's compiler: O2 for gcc and O3 for the TI compilers. The results are shown in Figure 8(a). Here the A9 is clearly the fastest processor followed surprisingly by the the M3 and then the DSP. For energy without idle power, the relative performance changes. The M3 is the best processor followed by the DSP and then the A9 as shown in Figure 8b. In terms of EDP, the M3 is the best processor followed by the A9 and DSP as shown in Figure 8c.

78

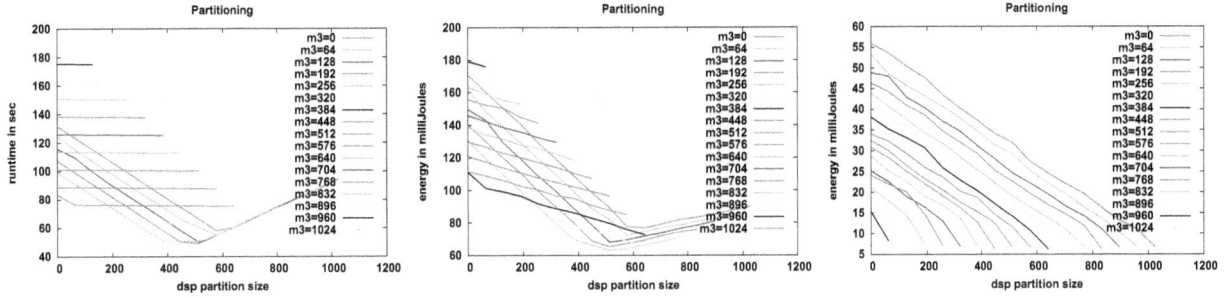

(a) Time: Best DSP=512, M3=192, A9=320   (b) With idle. Best DSP=512, M3=256, A9=256   (c) Without idle. Best DSP=640, M3=384, A9=0

Figure 11: Matmul exploration: Best partitions give more than double runtime and energy (with idle) performance relative to just using A9. If idle energy is discarded the improvement is more than 8 fold.

This shows that processors behave differently for different optimizing criteria. While the A9 is the fastest, it is also the worst for energy.

7.1.2 Effect of Optimizations

The runtime performance of the DSP is surprising since it should perform well for *mxm*. The compile logs indicated that the loop was not software pipelined due to memory dependences The compiler thinks that pointers to array parameters can alias and generated a conservative schedule. We therefore added the *restrict* keyword to these pointers which significantly improved the performance of the DSP. No significant improvement was observed with the M3 or A9 since they lack the hardware to gain from this information. Figure 9a shows the performance after optimization. Now the DSP is the fastest followed by the A9 and M3. For energy (without idle) the DSP and M3 are very similar while the A9 is inefficient as can be seen from Figure 9b. Overall for EDP, DSP is the now the best processor rather than the worst followed by M3 and A9 as shown in Figure 9c.

This shows that the best processor performance depends on backend compiler optimizations.

7.1.3 With Idle Energy

The above results do not consider idle energy and focus only on a processor's dynamic energy consumption. In reality processors dissipate energy even when they are idle and this has to be factored in during measurement. Figure 10 shows the results including idle energy. Here we find that the M3 has a significantly larger amount of idle energy than before. The DSP has the least energy followed by the M3 and A9 as shown in Figure 10b. Runtime is unaffected by how we calculate energy, so overall for EDP, the DSP is the best processor followed by the M3 and DSP as shown in Figure 10c.

This shows that when determining which processor is the best for energy it also depends on how energy is measured. If only dynamic energy is considered then the M3 and DSP are competitive, but if idle energy is also considered then the DSP is the best by a large margin.

7.2 Partitioning

This section considers the platform performance when *mxm* is partitioned across all cores. It first explores the design space of different partition sizes and then explores the power-runtime tradeoff when partitioning.

7.2.1 Exploration

The results of a detailed exploration results are graphically given in Figure 11 for the input size N=1024 and DSP enabled backend

optimizations. In each graph, the x-axis denotes the amount of data allocated to DSP and each curve represents the amount of data allocated to the M3. The y-axis represents runtime, energy with idle power and energy without idle power respectively. In Figure 11a we see the best runtime of 48.92s is achieved when half the data(512 rows) is allocated to the DSP and the M3 has 192 rows allocated to it. The A9 has the remaining 320 rows allocated to it. If all the data were to be allocated to the A9, i.e. M3=DSP=0, then the 2 threads of the A9 would take 131s - more than twice as long. In the case of energy with idle power we see a similar shaped trade-off graph. Again the DSP has 512 rows allocated to it. This time the best energy result of 63 mJ is obtained when the M3 has slightly more work allocated to it, 256 rows. Allocating all work to the A9 would more than double the the energy used to 170 mJ. In the case of without idle energy we see a different trend. As we do not account for increasing idle energy, we see monotonic behavior. The best partition is when the DSP has the most work allocated to it, 640 rows, the remainder being allocated to the M3. No work is scheduled to the A9 as it is too energy hungry. This results in just 6 mJ compared to massive 55 mJ if the default approach of allocating to the A9 is employed.

7.2.2 Power Runtime Tradeoff

Figure 12a shows the tradeoff between power and runtime an important consideration in thermally constrained mobile devices. The figure shows considerable oscillations between 0.6-0.76milliWatt and 0.1-0.2milliWatt. The 0.6-0.7milliWatt range represents those configurations which use the A9 processor and those in the range 0.1-0.2 mW have the A9 switched off. From this figure we can see that power and runtime are not simply correlated. If there is power constraints we should avoid configurations with high power consumption.

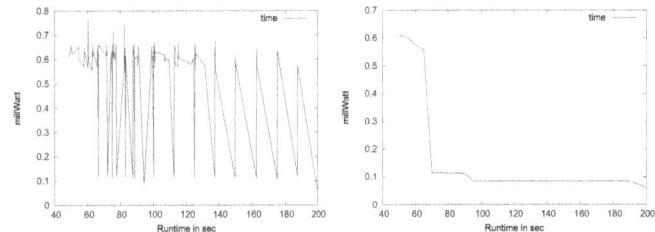

(a) Power-Time Tradeoff   (b) Power-Time Tradeoff Pareto

Figure 12: power runtime tradeoff

Figure 12b shows the tradeoff-curve Pareto frontier. When allowing increased runtime, we keep the best power configuration

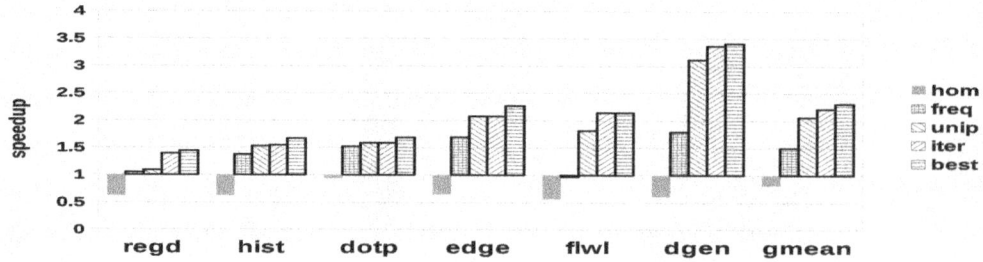

Figure 13: Results of partitioning policies for runtime : All policies except *hom* give performance improvements. *iter* is the best policy with 2.2x speedup just short of the 2.3x achievable by exhaustive search of *best*. *unip* is competetive with *iter* on most benchmarks.

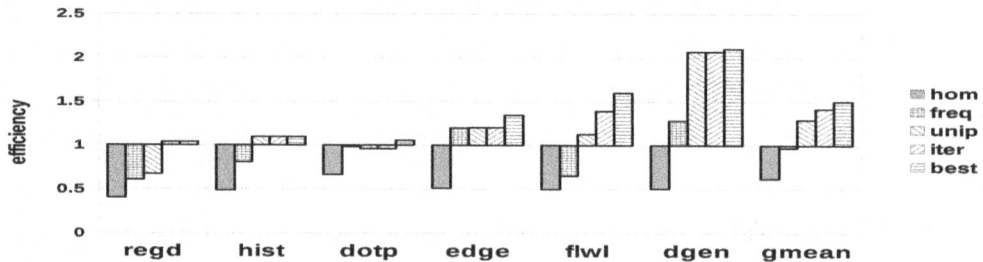

Figure 14: Results of partitioning policies for metric energy with idle. *unip* gives a slowdown on *regd* and is not competitive for *flwl* compared to *iter*. On average *unip* gives an overall energy improvement of 1.3x compared to 1.45x of the *iter* scheme. *iter* approaches the efficiency of the *best* policy. *hom* and *freq* policies are inefficient compared to the sequential execution on A9.

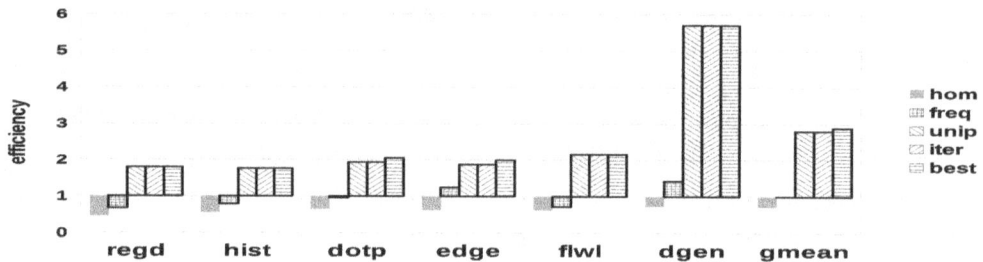

Figure 15: Results of partitioning policies for metric energy without idle. *iter* leads to almost a 3-fold energy improvement on average over sequential execution on A9 and is within 8% of *best*. Partitions of *hom* leads to degradations in all cases. On average *freq* gives no improvement at all.

seen so far. When the runtime is around 65 seconds there is a configuration which has only the M3 and DSP running and hence results in a low power state of around 0.1mW. The next lowest around the 95 second mark is when the DSP is used alone. Finally the configuration with the lowest power consumption is when the M3 alone is used resulting in runtime of around 200 seconds. This graph gives us a method to pick the best configuration for power for a given runtime budget.

8. Partitioning Policy Results

This section evaluates the various partitioning policies described in Section 4 across the benchmark suite for different optimization criteria.

8.1 Runtime

Figure 13 shows the runtime performance of the partitioning decisions as speedups over sequential execution on the A9. The uniform allocation policy *hom* performs uniformly poorly across all benchmarks. It slows down *dotp* the least but gives an average slowdown of 0.7. The frequency based approach *freq* is better, again performing relatively well on *dotp*. However, it slows down on *flwl* and has

an average speedup of just 1.5x. The other schemes that require runs on each processor perform better. The *unip* policy gives an average 2.1x speedup across benchmarks and is competitive with our *iter* approach, particularly on edge. Overall *iter* is the best policy with 2.2x speedup just short of the 2.3x achievable by trying all partitions. It performs particularly well relative to the the other policies on *regd*.

8.2 Energy

Here we examine energy usage with and without idle for each policy. across the benchmarks.

8.2.1 With Idle

When there is idle power it is often best for the processors to run as fast as possible. Figure 14 shows the results for each policy.

The *hom*, and *freq* policies give the same partition decisions here as when optimizing for runtime. The *hom* policy is uniformly poor with an average 0.4x the energy efficiency of running sequentially on the A9. Compared to runtime performance, the *hom* policy actually performs, on average, even worse for energy. Overall it is slightly less efficient than running sequentially on the A9.

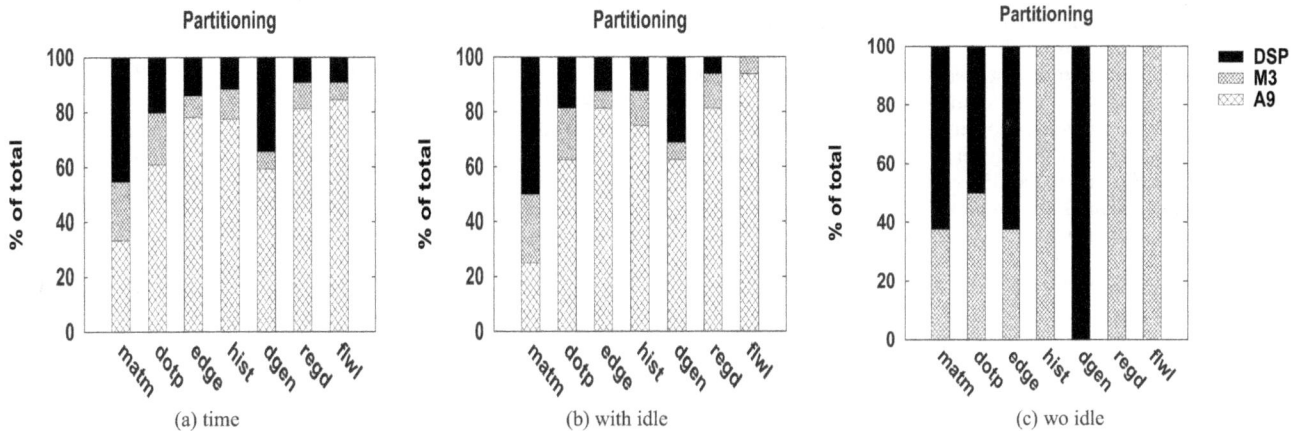

Figure 16: Partitioning overview of all benchmarks for runtime, energy with and without idle. Partitioning is different for each benchmark. A9 gets the major share for runtime in all benchmarks except matm. But for energy without idle, A9 gets no share at all due to its high dynamic energy. The partitioning is similar for metrics runtime and energy with idle.

Both *unip* and *iter* approach the performance of the *best* exhaustive scheme. However, *unip* again performs badly on *regd* leading to on overall energy improvement of 1.3x compared to 1.45x of the *iter* scheme.

8.2.2 Without Idle

When there is no idle power to consider then running fast is no longer important. Figure 15 shows the results for partitioning policies for metric energy without idle. As we can see from the figure, the results are poor for *hom* and *freq*. This happens because these policies allocate a significant amount of computation to the A9 processor which consumes a large amount of dynamic energy. Both *unip* and *iter* have almost identical performance. Only 0 to 8 percentage worse off than the best partition found by a exhaustive search *best*. On average this leads to almost a 3-fold energy improvement over sequential execution over the A9.

8.3 Analysis of Results

In this section we examine the partitioning decisions that lead to best performance.

The best partitions for each metric for runtime is plotted in Figure 16a. As can be seen from the figure, the best partitions are different for different benchmarks. In percentage terms, the data partition size on A9 varies from around 33% to 84%; the M3 has between 6% to 21% of the data allocated to it while the data allocated to the DSP varies from 9% to 45%.

Benchmarks such as *mxm* and *dgen* have three or more loop nests where there is little or no synchronization. There is also significant instruction level parallelism and hence the DSP performs well. resulting in a large computation allocation to the DSP. There is less parallelism available in benchmarks such as *flwl*, *regd* and *hist* due to dependences requiring synchronisation. The M3 receives the most data on the *dotp* benchmark. This is probably due to the other processors being less able to exploit either their better memory hierarchy or internal parallelism. It is the program's properties that dictate the partition size that should be allocated to each processor.

The best partitions for energy with idle are plotted in Figure 16b. As we can see the with-idle partitioning is similar to the runtime partitioning with small changes in the contribution of M3.

The best partitions for energy without idle are plotted in Figure 16c. The partitions are completely different from the others. The A9 is excluded due to its high dynamic energy. While the en-

tire data is allocated to the M3 for *regd*, *hist* and *flwl* benchmarks, it is completely allocated to the DSP for *dgen*. For the other benchmarks it is a mix of M3 and DSP. While there is no idle energy considered there is energy expended in the memory system and splitting between the M3 and DSP helps these benchmarks to run faster and hence result in lower memory energy consumption.

This shows that the best partitioning for each benchmark and each criteria is different. There is no one size fits all solution for all benchmarks/criteria and hence all the fixed partitioning policies fail to give satisfactory performance.

9. Related Work

There is a large amount of related work in this area. Here we just refer to those closest to the work presented in this paper.

Loop Partitioning : Bodin et.al[7] and Agarwal et.al[1] present theoretical frameworks for automatically partitioning parallel loops to minimize cache coherency traffic on shared-memory multiprocessors. While we also perform partitioning of parallel loops our focus is on minimizing runtime, Energy, EDP etc. Since the caches in our setting are not coherent, we are not concerned about cache coherence traffic.

Partitioning : MAPS[11] deals with programming for MP-SoCs. This paper describes the MAPS system which extracts parallelism from sequential applications and generates code for MP-SoCs. This framework is mostly focussed on streaming and coarse-grained parallelism whereas ours deals with data-parallel programs.

Energy Performance tradeoff : Yuki et.al [28] states that for most machines of today running as fast as possible is best in terms of energy and this observation holds for all machines where the dynamic energy is comparable to the static energy. This work is done for homogeneous processors. This is similar to our observation also when measuring energy with a large amount of idle energy.

Using heterogeneity for efficiency Kundu et.al[10] discusses how performance/energy can be improved by partitioning work between an ARM processor and DSP. Experiments are done using OMAP3 SoC on a beagleboard for a single application. In this work we have looked at more applications, applications including synchronization, and also the variability in the best partitions. Reflex [6] performs simple tasks on low-power microcontrollers. To simplify programming they use a Distributed Shared Memory. They report code simplification and power consumption improvements on an OMAP4 and a custom platform for sensing applications. Our work differs from this in that we use static partitioning, barriers for improving programmability and use of data-parallel programs. The work in [27] considers single-ISA AMP processors and shows improvement in performance and energy using synergies between the heterogeneous processors and virtual machine service. Our work is different from this, our work uses multiple-ISA architecture and considers static partitioning of data-parallel programs. Some work have considered offloading a particular type of work to the remote co-processor for efficiency. The work in [5] have offloaded machine learning to the DSP co-processor.

Co-processor Offloading : Some recent work by Ravi.et.al[15] looks at offloading some work to be done on a co-processor. In one of the techniques they discuss,sub-offload, they move a portion of a loop to a co-processor for better performance. We don't have a co-processor view of the other processors.

Scheduling Tasks : Some people have worked on scheduling Tasks at runtime rather than static partitioning. Michel et.al [14] uses ILP to decide the best mapping of tasks for energy efficiency.

10. Conclusion and Future Work

This paper has developed a framework for partitioning data parallel programs for heterogeneous processors that addresses access to shared resources and synchronization. It describes a method for accurately measuring runtime and energy consumption of programs and used this to evaluate different partitioning policies. We show from our design space exploration that the best partitions change with optimization, benchmarks and optimization criteria. This paper presents a simple partitioning approach that is within 10% of the best partitioning scheme across all optimization criteria On average we achieve a 2.2x speedup and a 1.45X energy improvement. Future work will port this framework to other platforms and perform a larger scale evaluation.

Acknowledgments

We would like to thank Robert Clark of Redhat, Suman Anna of Texas Instruments, and Jos van Eijndhoven of VectorFabrics for helpful discussions while setting up the framework. We would also like to thank members of the Compiler and Architecture Design Group at Edinburgh University, especially, Bjoern Franke, and Oscar Almer for their kind help.

References

[1] Agarwal, A., Kranz, D.A., and Natarajan, V., "Automatic partitioning of parallel loops and data arrays for distributed shared-memory multiprocessors," Parallel and Distributed Systems, IEEE Transactions on , Vol.6, No.9, pp. 943-962, Sep 1995

[2] ARM big.LITTLE, http://goo.gl/aL4f4L

[3] C.G. Lee and M. Stoodley, UTDSP Benchmark Suite, 1992, http://goo.gl/PE5wjg

[4] Ceng, J. et.al, MAPS: An integrated framework for MPSoC application parallelization, Design Automation Conference, Jun 2008, pp. 754-759

[5] Chenguang Shen, Supriyo Chakraborty, Kasturi Rangan Raghavan, Haksoo Choi, and Mani B. Srivastava. 2013. Exploiting processor heterogeneity for energy efficient context inference on mobile phones. In Proceedings of the Workshop on Power-Aware Computing and Systems (HotPower '13). ACM, New York, NY, USA, Article 9

[6] F. X. Lin, Z. Wang, R. LiKamWa, and L. Zhong, Reflex: using low-power processors in smartphones without knowing them. In Proceedings of the ACM International Conference on Architectural Support for Programming Languages and Operating Systems(ASPLOS XVII), ACM, March 2012

[7] Francois Bodin, and Michael O'Boyle, A Compiler Strategy for Shared Virtual Memories, Languages, Compilers and Run-Time Systems for Scalable Computers, 1996.

[8] Frederica Darema, David A. George, V. Alan Norton, and Gregory F. Pfister, A single-program-multiple-data computational model for EPEX/FORTRAN, Parallel Computing, 1988, vol 7-1,pp. 11-24

[9] Khokhar, A.A. and Prasanna, V.K. and Shaaban, M.E. and Wang, C.-L., "Heterogeneous computing: challenges and opportunities", Computer, Vol. 26, No. 6, pp. 18-27, Jun 1993

[10] Kundu, T.K. and Paul, K., Improving Android Performance and Energy Efficiency, 24th International Conference on VLSI Design (VLSI Design), Jan 2011, pp 256-261

[11] Leupers, R. and Castrillon, J., MPSoC programming using the MAPS compiler, Design Automation Conference (ASP-DAC), pp. 897-902, Jan 2010

[12] Louis-Noel Pouchet, Polybench Benchmark suite, Ohio State University, 1992, http://www.cse.ohio-state.edu/ pouchet/software/polybench/

[13] MFP O'Boyle, L Kervella, F Bodin, Synchronization minimization in a SPMD execution model, Journal of parallel and distributed computing, 1995, 29(2)

[14] Michel Goraczko, Jie Liu, Dimitrios Lymberopoulos, Slobodan Matic, Bodhi Priyantha, and Feng Zhao. 2008. Energy-optimal software partitioning in heterogeneous multiprocessor embedded systems. In Proceedings of the 45th annual Design Automation Conference (DAC '08). ACM, New York, NY, USA, 191-196

[15] Nishkam Ravi, Yi Yang, Tao Bao, and Srimat Chakradhar. Semi-automatic restructuring of offloadable tasks for many-core accelerators. In Proceedings of SC13: International Conference for High Performance Computing, Networking, Storage and Analysis (SC '13). ACM, New York, NY, USA, Article 12

[16] OMAP SoC, TI, http://www.ti.com/lsds/ti/omap-applications-processors/technologies.page

[17] OMAP4430, http://www.ti.com/product/OMAP4430

[18] Pandaboard, http://pandaboard.org

[19] Pandaboard Manual, http://goo.gl/yGz7u6

[20] Power Measurement in OMAP4, http://goo.gl/TH2Y5R

[21] Rakesh Kumar, Dean M. Tullsen, Norman P. Jouppi, and Parthasarathy Ranganathan, "Heterogeneous Chip Multiprocessors," Computer, Vol. 38, No. 11, pp. 32-38, Nov. 2005

[22] Robert Numrich and John Reid. Co-Array Fortran for Parallel Programming. Tech. rep. RAL-TR-1998-060. Rutherford Appleton Laboratory, 1998

[23] Snapdragon SoC, Qualcomm, http://www.qualcomm.com/snapdragon

[24] Sumit Semwal, DMA Buffer Sharing API Guide, http://lwn.net/Articles/489703/

[25] Syslink/rpmsg, http://omappedia.org/wiki/Category:RPMsg

[26] Tegra SoC, Nvidia, http://www.nvidia.com/object/tegra.html

[27] Ting Cao, Blackburn, S.M., Tiejun Gao, and McKinley, K.S., The Yin and Yang of power and performance for asymmetric hardware and managed software, 39th Annual International Symposium on Computer Architecture, Jun 2012, pp. 225-236

[28] Tomofumi Yuki and Sanjay Rajopadhye, Folklore Confirmed: Compiling for Speed = Compiling for Energy, The 26th International Workshop on Languages and Compilers for Parallel Computing, 2013

[29] V. Zivojnovic et.al, DSPstone: A DSP-Oriented Benchmarking Methodology, Proc. of ICSPAT'94 - Dallas, Oct. 1994

[30] William W. Carlson, Jesse M. Draper and David E. Culler, Introduction to UPC and Language Specification, Tech. Report CCS-TR-99157, 1999

[31] Yelick, Semenzato, Pike, Miyamoto, Liblit, Krishnamurthy, Hilfinger, Graham, Gay, Colella, and Aiken, Titanium: A High-Performance Java Dialect, International Workshop on Java for High-Performance Network Computing, Stanford, California, 1998

Energy Efficient Data Access and Storage through HW/SW Co-design

Minyi Guo
Shanghai Jiao Tong University, Shanghai, China
guo-my@cs.sjtu.edu.cn

ABSTRACT

Massive energy consumption has become a major factor for the design and implementation of datacenters. This has led to numerous academic and industrial efforts to improve the energy efficiency of datacenter infrastructures. As a result, in state-of-the-art datacenter facilities, over 80% of power is now consumed by servers themselves. Historically, the processor has dominated energy consumption in the server. However, as processors have become more energy efficient, their contribution has been decreasing. On the contrary, energy consumed by data accesses and storage is growing, since multi- and many-core severs are requiring increased main memory bandwidth/capacity, large register file and large-scale storage system. Accordingly, energy consumed by data accesses and storage approaching or even surpassing that consumed by processors in many servers. For example, it has been reported that main memory contributes to as much as 40–46% of total energy consumption in server applications. In this talk, we present our continuing efforts to improve the energy efficiency of data accesses and storage. We study on a series of approaches with hardware-software cooperation to save energy consumption of on-chip memory, register file, main memory and storage devices for embedded systems, multi- and many-core servers, respectively. Experiments with a large set of workloads show the accuracy of our analytical models and the effectiveness of our optimizations.

Categories and Subject Descriptors

C.5.m [Computer system implementation]: *Miscellaneous*

Keywords

Energy consumption; Embedded systems; Main memory; Storage devices; Register file;

Bio

Minyi Guo is now a chair professor of Shanghai Jiao Tong University, China. He is also the head of the Department of Computer Science and Engineering at Shanghai Jiao Tong University, China. Before 2009, he was a professor at the University of Aizu, Japan. Dr. Guo is serving as an associate editor of IEEE Transactions on Computers and IEEE Transactions on Parallel and Distributed Systems. His research interests include automatic parallelization and data-parallel languages, bioinformatics, compiler optimization, high-performance computing, and pervasive computing. He has published more than 200 papers in major conferences and journals in these areas. He is a senior member of the IEEE, a member of the ACM, IEICE and IPSJ.

LCTES'14, June 12–13, 2014, Edinburgh, UK.
ACM 978-1-4503-2877-7/14/06.
http://dx.doi.org/10.1145/2597809.2602569

Exploiting Function Similarity for Code Size Reduction

Tobias J.K. Edler von Koch   Björn Franke

Institute for Computing Systems Architecture
School of Informatics
University of Edinburgh
t.v.koch@ed.ac.uk, bfranke@inf.ed.ac.uk

Pranav Bhandarkar   Anshuman Dasgupta

Qualcomm Innovation Center Inc.
Austin, Texas
pranavb@quicinc.com, adasgupt@quicinc.com

Abstract

For cost-sensitive or memory constrained embedded systems, code size is at least as important as performance. Consequently, compact code generation has become a major focus of attention within the compiler community. In this paper we develop a pragmatic, yet effective code size reduction technique, which exploits *structural similarity* of functions. It avoids code duplication through merging of similar functions and targeted insertion of control flow to resolve small differences. We have implemented our purely software based and platform-independent technique in the LLVM compiler framework and evaluated it against the SPEC CPU2006 benchmarks and three target platforms: INTEL X86, ARM based QUALCOMM KRAIT^{TM}, and QUALCOMM HEXAGON^{TM} DSP. We demonstrate that code size for SPEC CPU2006 can be reduced by more than 550KB on X86. This corresponds to an overall code size reduction of 4%, and up to 11.5% for individual programs. Overhead introduced by additional control flow is compensated for by better I-cache performance of the compacted programs. We also show that identifying suitable candidates and subsequent merging of functions can be implemented efficiently.

Categories and Subject Descriptors   D.3 [*Programming Languages*]: Processors—Code Generation;   D.3 [*Programming Languages*]: Processors—Compilers

General Terms   Design, experimentation, measurement, performance

Keywords   Function similarity, function merging, code size

1. Introduction

A large number of embedded processors are deployed in cost-sensitive, but high-volume markets where even modest savings of unit cost can lead to a substantial overall cost reduction. Highly integrated systems-on-chip (SoC) serve these markets and provide embedded processors as part of a more complex system integrated with other components such as memories and various peripheral devices on the same chip. Of all components, memories typically occupy the largest fraction of the chip area and, hence, contribute most to the overall cost. Among embedded memories, flash storage plays a prominent role as non-volatile memory that needs to be large enough to store the full image of the binary executable. As a consequence, any reduction in code size translates directly to equivalent savings of die area and, eventually, unit cost. For example, a 40nm-fabricated ARM CORTEX-M4 will be approximately 0.04mm^2 in size [1]. At the same technology node the effective unit cell size of a multi-level NAND Flash memory is about 0.0098μm^2 [28]. For this example, a hypothetical 1MB code size reduction for a piece of firmware translates into an area equivalent of 0.056mm^2, which is larger than the size of the ARM core's silicon real estate and represents a significant saving for a high-volume SoC.

Existing approaches to compact code generation either rely on hardware support or are purely software based. Among the schemes that require architectural support, e.g. [3, 5], only those, which introduce an additional, compact instruction set architecture (ISA) [19, 21] have found widespread use, e.g. in form of the compact THUMB ISA complementing regular 32-bit ARM instructions. Software only approaches to compact code generation can be broadly classified into two categories: (a) Those that carefully control and limit code expansion through conservative use of transformations, which can increase code size such as loop unrolling or function inlining, and (b), those that actively seek to reduce code size through better ISA utilization (e.g. addressing modes) or reduction of redundancy. Elimination of duplicate functions [30] is an example of such an optimization reducing code redundancy.

In this paper we develop a novel space-saving code transformation, which extends standard elimination of duplicate functions and makes it available to a wider range of functions. Rather than restricting ourselves to eliminating *exact* duplicates, we introduce the notion of *structural similarity* of functions, which enables us to *merge* similar functions. The **key idea** is that two (or more) similar functions are merged into a single function augmented with appropriate control flow to handle the differences, while the original functions can be eliminated and, thus, code size is reduced by nearly a half (for two merged functions).

We have implemented similarity based function merging in the popular LLVM compiler framework and evaluated it against the SPEC CPU2006 benchmarks and three target platforms: INTEL X86, ARM based QUALCOMM KRAIT^{TM}, and QUALCOMM HEXAGON^{TM} DSP. Across the benchmarks we observe total code size reductions of ~550KB, ~330KB and ~500KB, respectively. For individual benchmarks we achieve code size reductions of up to 11.5%. Whilst our new transformation inserts additional control flow, which potentially introduces pipeline inefficiencies, the measured performance impact on the SPEC benchmarks is largely compensated for by improved I-cache utilization, resulting in the same overall performance level as before function merging.

LCTES '14,   June 12–13, 2014, Edinburgh, UK.
Copyright is held by the owner/author(s). Publication rights licensed to ACM.
ACM 978-1-4503-2877-7 /14/06. . . $15.00.
http://dx.doi.org/10.1145/2597809.2597811

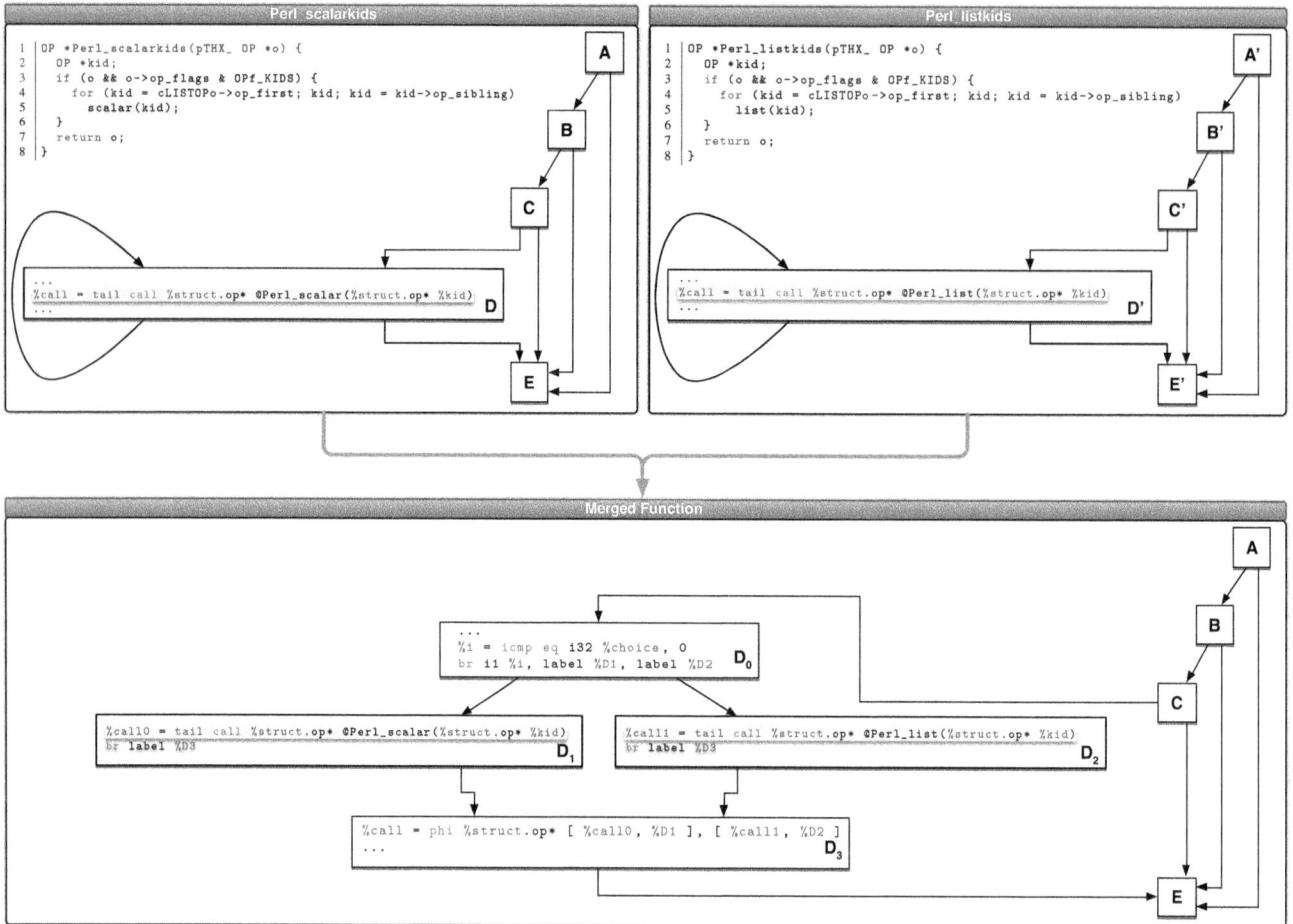

Figure 1: Motivating example: Merging of two functions from the `perlbench` benchmark, which have isomorphic control flow graphs and differ in only one function call instruction (**D** vs **D'**). Similarity based function merging creates a unified function and inserts additional control flow (D_0) to select the right call (D_1 or D_2) and fixes the resulting SSA representation (D_3).

1.1 Motivating Example

Consider the motivating example in Figure 1. We show the source code of two functions from the SPEC CPU2006 `perlbench` benchmark, `Perl_scalarkids` and `Perl_listkids`. The two functions contain identical code except for the function call in line 5 (highlighted in yellow). During compilation, both functions result in nearly identical intermediate representations (IRs) that again only differ in one instruction. Their control flow graphs – shown below the source code – have exactly the same structure. Consequently, the resulting machine code of the two functions will contain significant portions of duplicate code due to the high degree of similarity between them.

Our proposed technique *merges* these two, highly similar functions into a single one by combining code from both and inserting conditional constructs to select the correct instructions in places where they differ. The original functions are replaced by small *thunks* (wrapper functions) that call the merged function with an additional argument to select the correct path. As a result, code size can be reduced significantly.

In the present example, the original two functions result in 2×64 bytes $= 128$ bytes of machine code on the INTEL X86 platform. After merging, we obtain a combined function of size 80 bytes and thunks of size 2×16 bytes. The resulting total code size of 112 bytes is thus **12.5%** smaller.

Why do such similar functions exist in actual software code? There are a number of distinct reasons. Firstly, the nature of industrial-scale software projects can lead to inefficient forms of code reuse by copy-and-paste rather than abstraction. Secondly, lack of explicit support for templates in languages such as C often causes developers to write redundant code for different data types (as is the case in our motivating example). Even in C++, the use of templates can result in the generation of highly similar code [18].

While some of these factors could be remedied manually by careful software engineering or intricate code wizardry, this may come at the expense of a loss of readability, maintainability, or abstraction. Our function merging technique is entirely transparent to the user and hence requires no compromise on any of these important aspects of software development.

Even if functions are dissimilar in the original program code, interprocedural compiler optimizations, such as global constant propagation, may make them more similar and can thus open up opportunities for redundant code elimination.

How prevalent are similar functions in software code? The SPEC CPU2006 benchmark suite contains 15,324 pairs of functions (including generated template code) that share more than 70% equivalent instructions in their compiler intermediate representations. This indicates that there is indeed significant scope for the application of our technique.

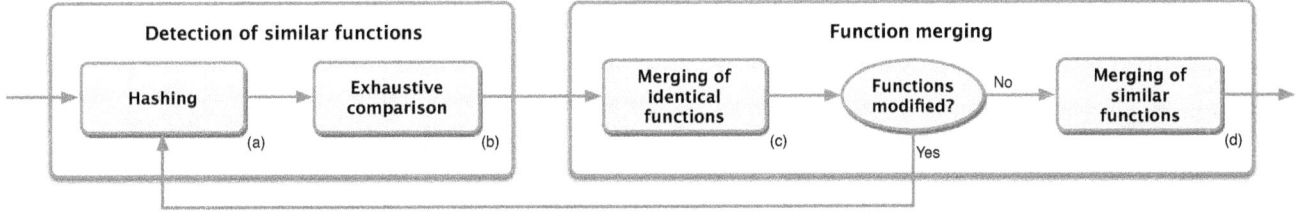

Figure 2: Overview of the function merging algorithm: (a) Functions are sorted into hash buckets; (b) Functions in each bucket are compared on a pairwise basis; (c) Identical functions are merged, and call sites updated; (d) Remaining similar functions are merged.

1.2 Contributions

In this paper we make following contributions:

1. We develop a novel, platform-independent code optimization technique aiming at reducing code size by **merging structurally similar functions**,

2. we introduce a set of **parameters**, which can be used for machine-specific adaptation and fine-tuning of function merging, and

3. we **evaluate** our **LLVM implementation** of code size aware merging of similar functions against the SPEC CPU2006 benchmark suite across three platforms: INTEL X86, ARM based QUALCOMM KRAIT[TM], and the QUALCOMM HEXAGON[TM] DSP.

1.3 Overview

The remainder of this paper is structured as follows. In Section 2 we introduce our novel function merging optimizations. This is followed in Section 3 by an evaluation against standard benchmarks and two target platforms. In Section 4 we discuss the body of related work, before we summarize and conclude in Section 5.

2. Methodology: Function Merging

Our function merging algorithm consists of several steps, shown in Figure 2: the *detection* of similar functions; the merging of *identical* functions; and the merging of the remaining *similar* functions. In the following sections, we will describe each of the steps in detail.

2.1 Detecting Similar Functions

For the detection of similar functions, we introduce a notion of *structural* similarity for functions, which is powerful enough to warrant effective operation, but at the same time avoids the complexities of dealing with full-scale topological similarity of functions [26].

Two functions are structurally similar if both their function signatures and control flow graphs (CFGs) are equivalent. Functions have equivalent **signatures** if they agree in the number, order, and types of their arguments as well as their linkage type and other compiler-specific properties. **CFGs** are equivalent iff there is a directed edge-preserving bijection between the two graphs (graph isomorphism). We further stipulate that the number of instructions in corresponding **basic blocks** of the isomorphic CFGs must be equal. Corresponding **instructions** must have the same result type but may differ in their opcodes and the number and type of inputs.

Detecting structurally similar functions implies a comparison of all functions in a given module. This has an upper bound of $O(n^2)$ comparisons. However, there exist approximations to the aforementioned criteria that can be computed relatively fast and hence make this an ideal application scenario for a hashing-based approach. This avoids comparison of functions that have no chance

Input :
  F_1, F_2: functions to compare
Output:
  NOTMERGEABLE if functions cannot be merged,
  Ratio of equivalent instructions otherwise.
Result :
  Q_1, Q_2: work queues of basic blocks
  T: map of corresponding objects in the two functions
  S: table of instruction pairs marked as equivalent or differing

1 **Procedure** *compare_functions*:
2   **if** $size(F_1.BBs) \neq size(F_2.BBs) \lor size(F_1.Args) \neq size(F_2.Args)$ **then**
3   **return** NOTMERGEABLE
4   **for** $i \leftarrow 0:size(F_1.Args)$ **do**
5   **if not** *type_equivalent($F_1.Args[i], F_2.Args[i]$)* **then**
6   **return** NOTMERGEABLE
7   T.mark_corresponding(F_1.Args[i], F_2.Args[i])
8   **end**
9   Q_1.enqueue(F_1.entry) Q_2.enqueue(F_2.entry)
10 **while not** $Q_1.empty \land$ **not** $Q_2.empty$ **do**
11     $BB_1 \leftarrow Q_1.pop()$ $BB_2 \leftarrow Q_2.pop()$
12   **if** *(seen(BB_1) $\lor$ seen(BB_2)) $\land$* **not** *T.corresponding(BB_1, BB_2)* **then**
13   **return** NOTMERGEABLE
14   **if** *seen(BB_1)* **then**
15   **continue**
16   **if** $size(BB_1) \neq size(BB_2) \lor size(BB_1.Succs) \neq size(BB_2.Succs)$ **then**
17   **return** NOTMERGEABLE
18   T.mark_corresponding(BB_1, BB_2)
19   Q_1.enqueue(BB_1.Succs) Q_2.enqueue(BB_2.Succs)
20   **foreach** $I_1 \in BB_1, I_2 \in BB_2$ **do**
21   **if not** *type_equivalent($I_1.result, I_2.result$)* **then**
22   **return** NOTMERGEABLE
23   T.mark_corresponding(I_1, I_2)
24   **if** $I_1.opcode = I_2.opcode \land inputs\_equivalent(I_1, I_2)$ **then**
25   S.mark_equivalent(I_1, I_2)
26   **else**
27   S.mark_differing(I_1, I_2)
28   **end**
29 **end**
30 **return** count_equivalent(S)/count_total(S)

Algorithm 1: Comparison of two functions by lockstep traversal of their control flow graphs.

of being structurally similar, e.g. because they have a different number of basic blocks.

The detection of similar functions is therefore done in two steps: we first build a hash table of all functions, and then only compare the functions that end up in the same bucket.

A clever selection of factors for the hash function can significantly reduce the number of functions per bucket resulting from realistic code. Examples for such factors are the number of basic blocks in the function, the number and types of arguments, and the number of instructions in the first basic block, among others.

The actual comparison of functions is then performed on a pairwise basis by traversing the two CFGs in lock-step, starting from the entry block, and thus comparing both functions block-by-block and instruction-by-instruction. The procedure is shown in Algorithm 1. In the process, we record which pairs of corresponding instructions are equivalent and which ones differ.

Two instructions are *equivalent* if they have not only the same result type, but additionally match in

1. their opcodes,
2. the number and types of their inputs, and
3. if the inputs are corresponding objects (basic blocks, instructions, arguments in corresponding locations in the two CFGs).

Otherwise, the two instructions are marked as *differing*. Requirements 2. and 3. are what is checked by the *inputs_equivalent* function in line 24.

2.1.1 Parameterization

Even if two functions are structurally similar, it may not be *profitable* to merge them. This is firstly the case if the functions are very small. The insertion of additional control flow would be disproportionate in relation to the size of the original functions. We therefore require functions to have a fixed minimum number of instructions before considering them for merging. Furthermore, functions that have a large number of dissimilar instructions should also not be merged with each other as this would also inflate code size due to excessive control flow. We introduce a simple similarity measure for a pair of functions – the percentage of equivalent instructions among the instructions of the two functions – which can then be used as a tunable threshold to decide when merging should be attempted.

2.2 Merging Functions

Having compared all functions, we then merge those that exceed a user-defined similarity threshold. This is carried out in two steps by first merging identical functions and then merging the remaining similar functions.

2.2.1 Merging Identical Functions

Functions with a similarity measure of 100% are identical and can thus be trivially merged. We delete all redundant copies of a function and update their call sites in the module to point to just one single copy. If a redundant copy of the function is externally visible or has its address taken, we replace it with a thunk (wrapper function) that calls the remaining copy of the function.

Updating call sites across the module modifies other functions that are unrelated to the identical functions being merged. In fact, it may make those more similar or even identical to other functions in the module. We therefore discard any previous comparison results for modified functions and re-compare them to the remaining functions in their respective buckets.

The process of merging identical functions, updating call sites, and re-comparing the modified functions is iterated until a fixpoint is reached.

2.2.2 Merging Similar Functions

In the final stage, we merge similar functions that are not identical but have a sufficient number of equivalent instructions to likely make them profitable to merge, as determined by the similarity threshold. Instructions are equivalent if they have the same opcode and inputs (see Section 2.1 for details). While functions are compared on a pairwise basis, our technique is able to merge any number of functions.

We begin by ordering all remaining pairs of functions by their similarity measure, which expressed the percentage of equivalent instructions for a given function pair. Let $\mathcal{S}(X,Y)$ denote the similarity measure of the pair (X,Y), and let **b** stand for the similarity threshold required for merging. First, we select the most similar function pair (A,B). Then we find the set of functions

$$\mathbb{B} = \{B\} \cup \{B' \mid \mathcal{S}(A,B') = s, s \geq \mathbf{b}, \nexists X.\mathcal{S}(X,B') > s\}$$

and finally, merge A with all functions in $\mathbb{B}$. In other words, A is merged with any function that is similar to it as long as that function is not itself more similar to another.

To merge a function A with a set of functions $\mathbb{B}$, we first make a copy of A with an additional integer argument s. We then insert control flow equivalent to a switch statement wherever there are differences between A and the functions in $\mathbb{B}$ to allow the caller to select the correct instruction to execute by the value of the argument s. Finally, A and all functions in $\mathbb{B}$ are replaced by thunks that call the new merged function with the appropriate values of s.

As the last step in the merging of A and $\mathbb{B}$, we remove all pairs involving A or any of the functions in $\mathbb{B}$ from consideration as they have now been merged and cannot be modified further.

This process is repeated until there are no more function pairs left to merge.

2.3 LLVM Implementation

We have implemented merging of similar function in the LLVM framework. LLVM is an extensible, modular, open-source compiler infrastructure providing a range of frontends, such as CLANG for C/C++, and backends for a multitude of hardware architectures. Our technique is implemented as a module optimization pass in the middle-end which operates on the abstraction level of a platform-neutral, low-level intermediate representation. It is thus both *language-* and *target-independent*.

Function merging is run as a late optimization pass after all other target-independent optimizations have been applied. This is done for two reasons: firstly, our experiments show that function merging can benefit from other optimizations that result in increasing similarity of functions; and secondly, our technique is a relatively aggressive transformation that will hamper the effectiveness of other analyses and optimizations if they were to be run afterwards.

LLVM's IR employs a typed *static single assignment form* (SSA) that has to be maintained by the merging process. While the typed nature of this representation greatly facilitates a wide range of analyses and transformations, it can hamper function merging in cases where different IR-level types do not actually translate into different types on the architectural level. For instance, pointers are represented as separate types depending on which type of value they point to. On the architectural level, all pointers in the same memory space are simply integers of a certain size. The difference only becomes relevant when a pointer is dereferenced.

To solve this issue, we introduce the concept of *pointer-pointer-integer equivalence* at the IR level. During function merging, we treat all pointers in the same memory space – irrespective of the type of the value pointed to – and integers of the same size as identically typed except when the difference is of actual importance, such as when a pointer is dereferenced. Wherever this is the case, the affected value is locally typecast back to the original type to maintain correctness. These additional casts will not affect code size, because they translate into *no-ops* during target lowering.

By using this approach, we are in particular able to merge functions generated by C++ template instantiations for both pointers

Processor & Model	INTEL CORE I3 2100
ISA	INTEL X86-64
Number cores	2
Clock/FSB Frequency	3.10/1.33 GHz
L1-Cache	32KB Instruction/Data
L2-Cache	256KB
L3-Cache	3MB
Memory	4 GB across 2 channels
OS	Scientific Linux 6.4
Processor & Model	QUALCOMM KRAIT™ 400
ISA	ARM V7A
Number cores	4
Clock Frequency	1.70GHz
Extensions	Pipelined VFP V4 and 128-bit wide NEON
OS	Arch Linux Kernel 3.10
Processor & Model	QUALCOMM HEXAGON™ QDSP6 V5
ISA	HEXAGON™ QDSP6 V5
Number cores	3
Clock Frequency	600MHz
Pipeline	in-order dispatch of up to 5 instructions to 4 execution units per clock cycle[7]
Multithreading	barrel temporal multithreading

Table 1: Detailed Specifications of the Target Platforms.

and integer types of the same size. This is one of the reasons quoted for the phenomenon of C++ template bloat [18].

3. Empirical Evaluation

3.1 Experimental Setup

For our evaluation we have chosen three popular target platforms, representing general-purpose and high-performance systems (INTEL X86), mobile systems (QUALCOMM KRAIT™) and embedded DSP systems (QUALCOMM HEXAGON™). KRAIT™ is an ARM based CPU included in various SNAPDRAGON™ SoCs, whereas HEXAGON™ is a multithreaded VLIW DSP found also in the SNAPDRAGON™ SoC. Specific details of the target systems are listed in Table 1.

We evaluate both the code size and performance impact of our optimization using the SPEC CPU2006 benchmark suite. We use the complete set of C/C++ integer and floating point benchmarks on all three platforms.[1] Even though we primarily target embedded systems, the use of an embedded benchmark suite, such as EEMBC, would not be adequate to evaluate high-level code size optimizations such as ours; this is because such benchmark suites mainly consist of algorithmic *kernels* with small numbers of functions. Our technique aims to optimize *entire* embedded applications (e.g. firmwares, mobile device applications, libraries) that can easily reach millions of lines of code. Hence SPEC is a closer approximation to the complexity of such targets.

We have compiled the benchmarks using the CLANG/LLVM 3.3 compiler framework, with and without our similarity based function merging pass, and enabling -Os optimizations as a code size aware baseline. Our optimization is applied on a per-module basis. We measure code size using the *binutils* size tool and report the size of the text section. Performance measurements have been performed on actual INTEL X86 and QUALCOMM KRAIT™ hard-

---

[1] perlbench cannot be compiled without modification on HEXAGON™ due to missing implementations of certain system calls. povray and omnetpp crash on KRAIT™ due to a known problem with SPEC in certain ARM environments even in the baseline configuration without function merging.

ware under conditions of light system load and taking the median running time of three runs of each benchmark. We use the reference input data set.

3.2 Code Size Reduction

Figure 3 shows the code size reductions achieved using our technique on the three evaluation platforms. We obtain a reduction in total code size of **3.9%**, **2.6%**, and **3.8%** on X86, KRAIT™, and HEXAGON™ respectively, for the SPEC CPU2006 benchmark suite. For individual benchmarks, the results range from a marginal code size increase by 0.21% for libquantum to a significant reduction by 12% for dealII on X86. These improvements translate into total code size savings of ~550KB, ~250KB and ~500KB, on the three evaluation platforms respectively.

Since our technique operates at the platform-independent IR level, the results are on a similar order of magnitude across all three platforms. The differences are mainly due to the idiosyncrasies of the underlying instruction set architectures (CISC vs. VLIW vs. compact RISC) and platform-specific compiler backends, which at times respond very differently to the insertion of additional control flow. The particular implementation of system libraries, such as the C++ STL, also has an impact as some code originates from header files.

It is notable that benchmarks implemented in C++, such as dealII and xalancbmk, respond particularly well to function merging. Further investigation reveals that this is largely due to template use which provides ample opportunities for the merging of both identical and similar functions. This can also be observed with omnetpp where the templatization is manual rather than using C++ language features but nonetheless has the same effect.

gcc on the other hand contains large, automatically generated source files, such as the infamous insn-attrtab [23], that exhibit a significant degree of redundancy. Again, we are able to eliminate such code duplication by merging functions.

A number of benchmarks, like bzip2, libquantum, lbm, and astar, show no improvement. These are relatively compact algorithmic benchmarks that provide little scope for the application of our technique.

As our optimization is applied on a per-module basis, it thus performs best on the larger benchmarks that in most cases also consist of larger compilation units.

3.3 Performance Impact

The primary goal of similar function merging is to reduce code size. In some embedded use cases, this goal has strict priority over other optimization objectives such as performance. Nevertheless, it is important to understand the impact of the optimization on benchmark execution times in order to judge its applicability in the general case.

In Figure 5, we show the speedup achieved by applying our technique to the SPEC CPU2006 benchmarks on the X86 and KRAIT™ platforms.

The experiments show a geometric mean slowdown of **0.33%** after applying similar function merging across the benchmark suite. The results range from a 2.15% speedup in the case of mcf to a 2.76% slowdown with dealII. Five of the benchmarks exhibit speedups, while another five remain unchanged.

If we compare speedups to code size improvements, we can see a mixed picture. The dealII and xalancbmk benchmarks, for which code size was reduced by more than 3%, show a performance decrease of above 2%. With omnetpp and gcc, on the other hand, significant reductions in code size do not translate into similar changes in performance, which remains virtually unchanged. Small changes in code size may have a disproportionate effect in performance. This is the case particularly with mcf, where a small

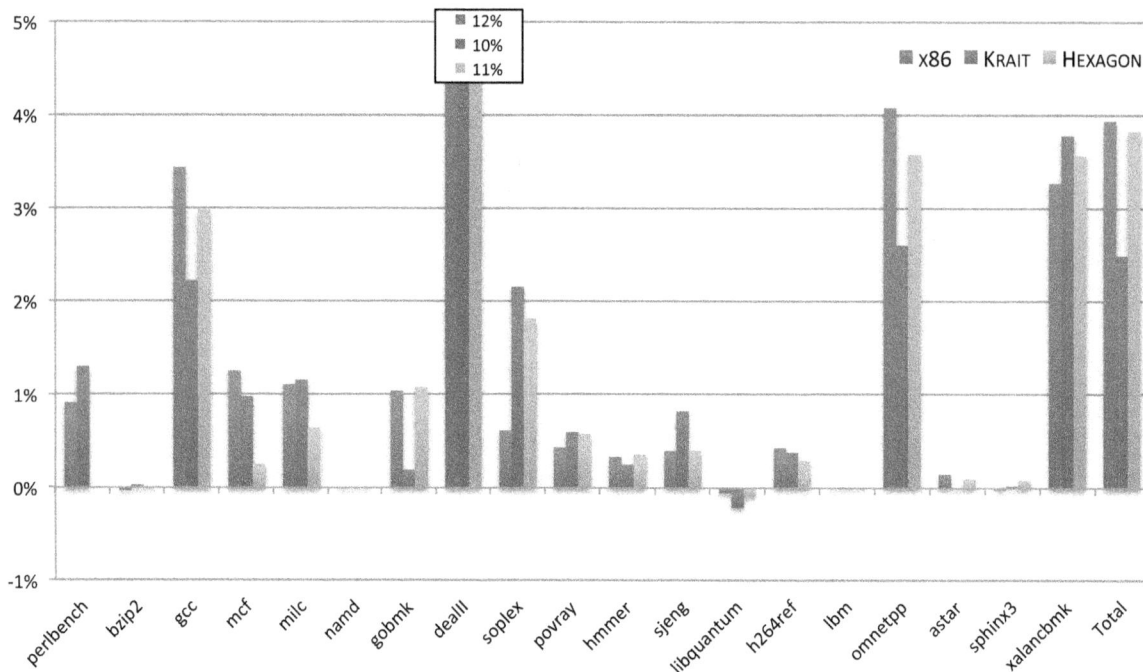

Figure 3: Code size reduction of the SPEC CPU2006 benchmarks achieved using similarity-based function merging on three different hardware platforms. Values > 0% represent a reduction in code size, values < 0% an increase in code size ("higher is better"). Total refers to the combined code size of the entire benchmark suite.

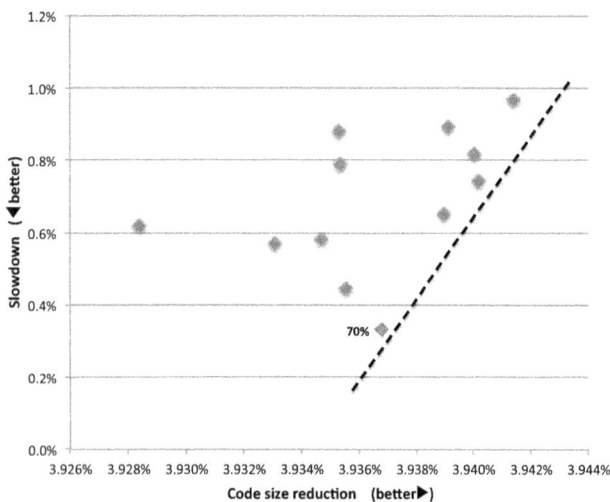

Figure 4: Effect of varying the function similarity threshold on code size and performance for SPEC CPU2006 on X86. Individual points represent different settings of the threshold. Performance is shown as slowdown (lower is better), code size as total code size reduction (higher is better). The dashed line represents the Pareto frontier.

reduction in code size leads to > 2% increase in performance; and namd, where a similarly small code size reduction decreases performance by more than 2%.

There are two main factors involved in determining performance in relation to code size improvements: instruction cache per-

formance; and the 'heat' of the functions optimized. More compact code translates into better I-cache hit ratios that may compensate for the additional control flow inserted by function merging to some extent and even improve performance in some cases. Optimization of 'cold', infrequently executed code by merging has a very limited impact on performance, but may significantly reduce code size. On the other hand, introducing additional control flow into 'hot' code, such as frequently executed loop nests, often has a disproportionately negative effect as is the case with some of the benchmarks.

Overall, however, the majority of the performance results can be considered to be within measurement error. Given the significant code size savings achieved using our technique, such small slowdowns – on average about 0.33% for X86 – are likely to be tolerable in common application scenarios.

3.4 Parameter Tuning

The similar function merging algorithm is guided by a tunable parameter, the function similarity threshold, which is used as an indicator of whether merging is likely to be profitable. If a pair of functions has a percentage of equivalent instructions above this threshold, they are considered for merging. As our evaluation in the previous two sections illustrates, function merging not only has an effect on code size but also on performance.

In Figure 4, we therefore show the impact of varying the function similarity threshold on both of these quantities. As is evident from the results, there is no one setting of the threshold parameter that results in both minimum slowdown and maximum code size reduction. The setting that achieves the highest code size reduction also leads to the most slowdown, while the threshold value with the least slowdown achieves a code size result that is slightly worse than other parameter settings.

The question of selecting the best function similarity threshold value thus becomes one of *Pareto* optimality. Points located on the

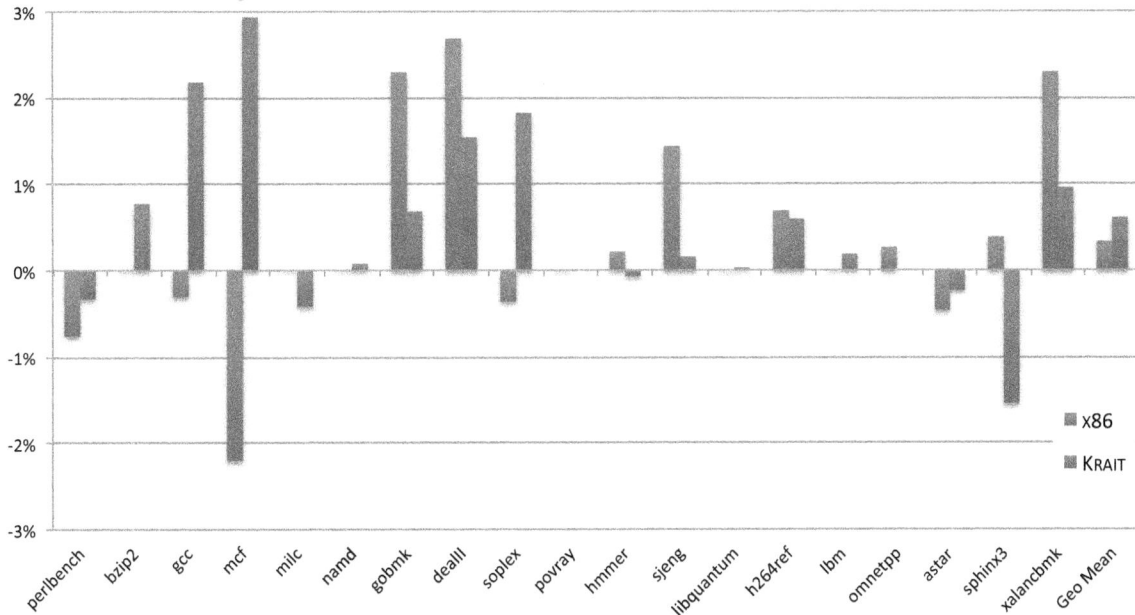

Figure 5: Performance impact due to similarity-based function merging for the SPEC CPU2006 benchmarks on the X86 and KRAIT^{TM} platforms, where values > 0% represent slowdown and values < 0% speedups ("lower is better").

Pareto frontier are acceptable choices reflecting the user's preference for either higher code size savings or better performance.

It is notable, though, that the variation in code size reduction (within a 0.014% range) is much smaller than that of the slowdown (within a 0.8% range). Due to the low variation in the code size measurement, we hence pick the threshold value on the frontier that results in the least performance degradation. This threshold for Pareto-optimal function similarity is set to 70% for both X86 and KRAIT^{TM} in our experimental evaluation.

3.5 Breakdown of Merging Opportunities

As our experiments show, the effectiveness of function merging varies significantly among the SPEC CPU2006 benchmarks. While this is not surprising – SPEC benchmarks were designed to cover a broad range of application categories and their source codes have widely varying characteristics [34] – the performance of our algorithm on individual benchmarks warrants closer investigation.

In Table 2, we show a breakdown of how many functions could be eliminated using function merging for each benchmark on X86. We count functions at the compiler IR level, adding numbers from all compilation units in each benchmark. The *total functions* count represents the total number of functions our algorithm has to process; it also includes functions we eventually do not consider for merging, for instance because they are too small, as well as functions included from header files.

The results show that our optimization can eliminate a total of **6215 functions** across the entire benchmark suite. This represents around **6.8%** of all functions.

As expected, there is some correlation between the number of functions eliminated and the code size reduction achieved by our optimization. For instance, we eliminate 18.8% of dealII's functions and consequently also achieve a large code size reduction. On the other hand, with omnetpp, the number of eliminated functions is small (2.1% of its functions) but the decrease in code size sig-

Benchmark	Total Functions	Eliminated Functions		
		Identical	Similar	Total
perlbench	4772	8	88	96
bzip2	153	0	0	0
gcc	11689	95	208	303
mcf	69	0	1	1
milc	618	0	2	2
namd	245	0	0	0
gobmk	3961	131	243	374
dealII	16014	1733	1276	3009
soplex	3318	20	117	137
povray	4042	31	49	80
hmmer	1402	3	8	11
sjeng	386	0	6	6
libquantum	240	0	1	1
h264ref	1159	3	20	23
lbm	48	0	0	0
omnetpp	5784	57	67	124
astar	208	0	1	1
sphinx3	1049	2	2	4
xalancbmk	35721	612	1431	2043
Total	90878	2695	3520	6215

Table 2: Statistics on the application of our technique to the SPEC CPU2006 benchmarks. *Total functions* refers to the number of functions present in the benchmarks before function merging is applied; *eliminated functions* are those that could subsequently be merged with other functions using our technique and hence were either replaced by thunks or removed entirely.

nificant since the size of the functions being merged is relatively large.

91

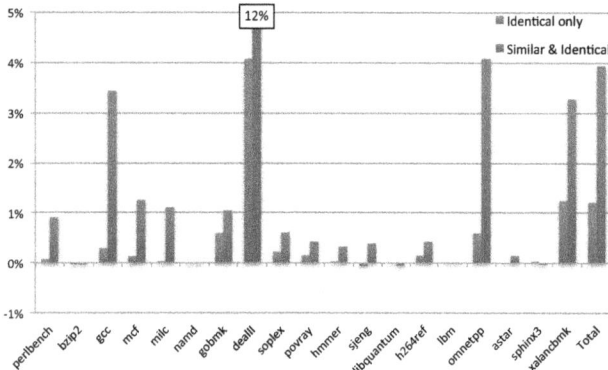

Figure 6: Code size reduction when merging a) identical functions only, and b) merging both identical and similar functions on x86.

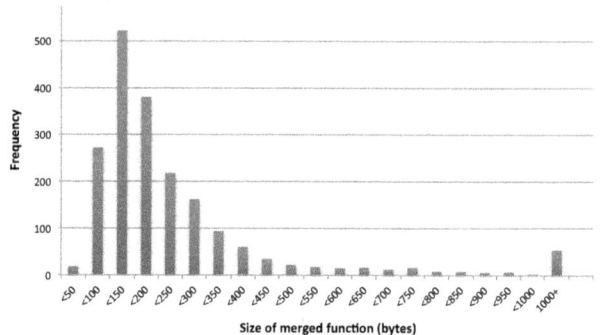

Figure 7: Distribution of sizes of the merged functions resulting from the application of our technique across the SPEC CPU2006 benchmark suite.

mcf, sjeng, and sphinx3 are interesting in that both the number of functions eliminated and the resulting code size reductions are small, but the performance impact disproportionately high with noticeable variance between architectures. This suggests that we merge functions in highly sensitive 'hot' portions of the code where small changes can have an amplified effect on performance. It remains future work to investigate ways of controlling this undesirable performance impact, though.

3.5.1 Identical vs. similar functions

Table 2 also shows that we merge approximately 30% more *similar* functions than *identical* functions across the benchmark suite. In Figure 6, we compare the code size reduction resulting from only merging identical functions to the reduction achieved by our complete technique that also merges similar functions.

We can see that the code size impact of these two stages of our algorithm is very different. While merging of identical functions reduces code size to some extent especially for C++ benchmarks (dealII, omnetpp, and xalancbmk), it has a rather small impact on the remaining benchmarks. Even though a number of identical functions can be merged, their size tends to be relatively small. The total reduction for the entire SPEC code base is thus only about 1.2%.

After enabling similar function merging, on the other hand, the effect of function merging increases dramatically. The overall reduction in code size more than triples and leads to the results discussed in previous sections.

3.5.2 Size of merged functions

Figure 7 shows a histogram of the sizes of the merged functions resulting from the application of our optimization across all benchmarks. Smaller functions in the range of 50 bytes to 400 bytes make up the bulk of merged functions indicating that similar functions are typically small. Nonetheless, there is a long tail of larger functions with sizes reaching up to 11KB. The largest instance is a pair of functions from the gcc benchmark (*pent_np_unit_conflict_cost* and *pent_np_unit_blockage*), which each have 2580 LLVM instructions of which only 6 differ.

3.6 Speed of Optimization

We now turn to the impact of our optimization on *compilation* time. The similar function merging algorithm is dominated by the complexity of function comparison, which has a $O(n^2)$ worst case complexity (see Section 2.1). Even though we apply our algorithm at a

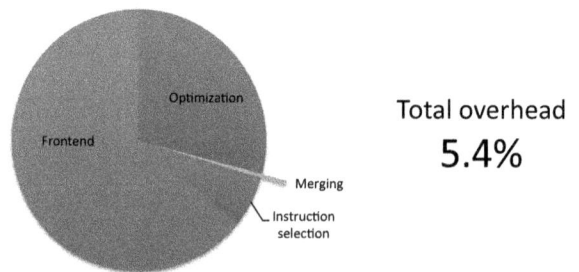

Figure 8: Compilation time impact of function merging, showing the time spent in function merging as a share of the overall compilation time across all SPEC CPU2006 benchmarks. Overhead is the total increase in compilation time for the entire benchmark suite when function merging is applied.

per-module level, some of the compilation units in the benchmarks suite are large (above 100 functions).

We measured both the overall increase in compilation time for the SPEC CPU2006 benchmark suite, as well as the share of time spent in our optimization pass. An overview of the results is shown in Figure 8.

We spend less than 1% of compilation time in function merging, making it a relatively inexpensive pass in relation to other optimization passes. The overall compilation time increases by 5.4% when function merging is applied which is mainly due to its impact on other parts of the compiler, such as instruction selection and register allocation.

Two factors are critical for the performance of the pass: firstly, we see the benefit of the use of a hash table to avoid the comparison of functions that would have no chance of being merged (e.g. due to different signatures); secondly, our fairly restrictive requirements on structural similarity between functions appear to meet a 'sweet spot' where the analysis remains tractable while still achieving good code size improvements.

4. Related Work

Code compaction, especially for embedded systems, has been an active research area for several years. Generally, we can distinguish between purely software based schemes, typically implemented as an additional compiler pass, and hardware-assisted schemes, which expose additional architectural features and often require specialized compiler support for their operation.

4.1 Compilation Schemes

Good surveys of code-size reduction methods, though slightly outdated, can be found in [15] and [2]. Elimination of duplicate functions, i.e. *exactly* identical functions, has previously been implemented in linkers [31] as well as the LLVM compiler. However, these approaches are unable to merge *similar* functions. Identification and elimination of duplication in source code using slicing techniques has been discussed in [24]. A broader comparison and evaluation of code clone detection techniques and tools has been presented in [29]. Again, these approaches are all restricted to processing strictly identical code regions.

Link-time binary rewriting techniques can be used for program compaction [13], for example in the DIABLO tool [33]. Elimination of duplicated code is one of the standard optimization applied by this tool, among several others that contribute to global code and data compaction [11]. Post-pass whole-program optimization [10] has also been reported to include elimination of duplicated code across linked binary executables. Our implementation of the similarity-based function merging transformation presented in this paper is limited to individual translation units, but this is not a conceptual limit and could be extended to cover the whole program.

Code factoring [27] is a code size aware transformation that hoists code blocks common to several basic blocks to their control flow dominator. Code factoring has been implemented in the GCC compiler and operates on single functions. It does not seek to exploit the potential offered by similar functions.

In [6] a generic technique is presented that aims at identifying code sequences that appear repeatedly in a program and replacing them with a single copy of the recurring sequence. This technique is not limited to single-entry single-exit regions, but is capable of compacting matching single-entry multiple-exit regions. However, this technique still requires exact matches of the regions to be merged.

A scheme for reducing the size of a program's code segment, using pattern-matching techniques to identify and coalesce together repeated instruction sequences is shown in [8]. The paper goes beyond the use of textual identity, which limits the applicability of the suffix-tree approach taken in the work, and introduces an abstract register notation. This enables the technique to work for a limited class of similar, but not lexically identical, blocks. Similarity is defined on instructions, i.e. two instructions are called similar if they only differ in their register operands. In this current paper we introduce a notion of similarity of functions, which enables us to merge entire functions, rather than only basic blocks.

Statistical tuning of compiler optimizations with the goal of achieving code size reductions through customized optimization configurations is subject of [22]. A preprocessing stage to code compression is discussed in [16]. First, a program is partitioned into regions of high auto-correlation, which are then rescheduled such as to increase their prediction probability for a given compression engine. Another software only code compression scheme, utilizing profiling information, is presented in [14].

[12] develops a technique for low-level C++ code reuse. The techniques enabling reuse of code of whole procedures at the binary level share some of the ideas with our work. For example, for regions of code that differ in their types conditional control flow is introduced to handle each type individually. Our technique, however, is platform- and language-independent and can be integrated as a generic optimization with a compiler framework, rather than relying on a link-time binary rewriter and specific idioms produced by a C++ compiler.

Outlining of specific functions can contribute to code size reductions [25, 35], but it introduces function call overhead, which in many cases outweighs its benefit.

4.2 Hardware-assisted Schemes

A standard hardware scheme for compact code generation is the provision of an alternative, compact ISA. For example, many ARM cores provide 16-bit THUMB or THUMB2 instructions alongside their 32-bit ARM ISA. Various papers have addressed code generation for such compact ISAs, e.g. [21], sometimes integrated with simultaneous register allocation [19].

A number of different dictionary-based code compression schemes have been discussed in the literature, e.g. [3, 5, 9, 32], however, such techniques have not yet found wide-spread use, possibly due to the hardware overhead (and cost) involved.

4.3 Function Similarity

The concept of similarity of functions plays an important role in software security and malware analysis [4]. A heuristic method for the detection of isomorphisms between the sets of functions in two similar, but differing versions of the same executable file has been investigated in [20], where it has been used to analyze patches to security vulnerabilities. A notion of graph based structural similarity somewhat similar to the one presented in this paper has been introduced in [17], where two executables represented by two graphs A and B are analyzed for similarity, using incremental growth starting from "fixpoints" (or "anchors"), which are known to represent to the same item in both executables.

5. Summary & Conclusions

In this paper we have developed a pragmatic, yet effective approach to code size reduction exploiting similarity of functions. We introduce and formalize the new concept of structural similarity of functions before we show how sufficiently similar functions can be merged. Additional control flow is introduced to the resulting function to resolve and handle the differences present in the original functions. While our function merging transformation is platform-independent, it comprises a set of parameters that can be used for platform-specific fine-tuning. We have implemented this novel optimization using the LLVM compiler framework and evaluated it against the SPEC CPU2006 benchmarks and three target platforms, where we have observed code size reductions by, on average, 4% across all benchmarks and up to 11.5% for individual programs. This translates into > 550KB of code size savings across the entire SPEC CPU2006 benchmark suite. We have shown that this constitutes a significant improvement over existing techniques that only consider merging of strictly identical functions.

5.1 Future Work

Future work will investigate a refined model of structural similarity of functions. Where our current approach requires two or more functions to share isomorphic control flow graphs and only permits differences local to a basic block (although several such local differences per qualifying function are possible), we believe greater benefit can be gained from a more relaxed similarity model, which enables merging of functions with similar, but not strictly isomorphic, control flow graphs. An improved cost model would also be able to throttle merging within deeply nested loops, where additional control flow may harm performance. Similarly, function merging followed by loop unswitching could be used to selectively move the inserted control flow out of the body of a 'hot' loop at the expense of slightly reduced code size savings. We expect an even greater benefit from similarity based function merging when used across translation units, for example as part of the LLVM link time optimization (LTO) stage, which greatly enhances the scope for identifying similar functions.

References

[1] ARM Ltd. ARM CORTEX M-4 specification, 2013. URL http://www.arm.com/products/processors/cortex-m/cortex-m4-processor.php.

[2] A. Beszédes, R. Ferenc, T. Gyimóthy, A. Dolenc, and K. Karsisto. Survey of code-size reduction methods. *ACM Comput. Surv.*, 35(3): 223–267, Sept. 2003.

[3] P. Brisk, J. Macbeth, A. Nahapetian, and M. Sarrafzadeh. A dictionary construction technique for code compression systems with echo instructions. In *Proceedings of the 2005 ACM SIGPLAN/SIGBED Conference on Languages, Compilers, and Tools for Embedded Systems*, LCTES '05, pages 105–114, New York, NY, USA, 2005. ACM.

[4] S. Cesare and Y. Xiang. Malware variant detection using similarity search over sets of control flow graphs. In *2011 IEEE 10th International Conference on Trust, Security and Privacy in Computing and Communications*, TrustCom, pages 181–189, 2011.

[5] S. Chandar, M. Mehendale, and R. Govindarajan. Area and power reduction of embedded DSP systems using instruction compression and re-configurable encoding. *J. VLSI Signal Process. Syst.*, 44(3): 245–267, Sept. 2006.

[6] W.-K. Chen, B. Li, and R. Gupta. Code compaction of matching single-entry multiple-exit regions. In R. Cousot, editor, *Static Analysis*, volume 2694 of *Lecture Notes in Computer Science*, pages 401–417. Springer Berlin Heidelberg, 2003.

[7] L. Codrescu, W. Anderson, S. Venkumanhanti, M. Zeng, E. Plondke, C. Koob, A. Ingle, R. Maule, and R. Talluri. Qualcomm HEXAGON DSP: An architecture optimized for mobile multimedia and communications. In *Proceedings of the IEEE HotChips Symposium on High-Performance Chips, (HotChips 2013)*, Aug. 2013.

[8] K. D. Cooper and N. McIntosh. Enhanced code compression for embedded RISC processors. In *Proceedings of the ACM SIGPLAN 1999 Conference on Programming Language Design and Implementation*, PLDI '99, pages 139–149, New York, NY, USA, 1999. ACM.

[9] M. L. Corliss, E. C. Lewis, and A. Roth. The implementation and evaluation of dynamic code decompression using DISE. *ACM Trans. Embed. Comput. Syst.*, 4(1):38–72, Feb. 2005.

[10] B. De Bus, D. Kästner, D. Chanet, L. Van Put, and B. De Sutter. Postpass compaction techniques. *Commun. ACM*, 46(8):41–46, Aug. 2003.

[11] B. De Sutter, B. De Bus, K. De Bosschere, and S. Debray. Combining global code and data compaction. In *Proceedings of the ACM SIGPLAN Workshop on Languages, Compilers and Tools for Embedded Systems*, LCTES '01, pages 29–38, New York, NY, USA, 2001. ACM.

[12] B. De Sutter, B. De Bus, and K. De Bosschere. Sifting out the mud: low level C++ code reuse. In *Proceedings of the 17th ACM SIGPLAN Conference on Object-Oriented Programming, Systems, Languages, and Applications*, OOPSLA '02, pages 275–291, New York, NY, USA, 2002. ACM.

[13] B. De Sutter, B. De Bus, and K. De Bosschere. Link-time binary rewriting techniques for program compaction. *ACM Trans. Program. Lang. Syst.*, 27(5):882–945, Sept. 2005.

[14] S. Debray and W. Evans. Profile-guided code compression. In *Proceedings of the ACM SIGPLAN 2002 Conference on Programming Language Design and Implementation*, PLDI '02, pages 95–105, New York, NY, USA, 2002. ACM.

[15] S. K. Debray, W. Evans, R. Muth, and B. De Sutter. Compiler techniques for code compaction. *ACM Trans. Program. Lang. Syst.*, 22(2):378–415, Mar. 2000.

[16] M. Drinić, D. Kirovski, and H. Vo. Code optimization for code compression. In *Proceedings of the International Symposium on Code Generation and Optimization: Feedback-Directed and Runtime Optimization*, CGO '03, pages 315–324, Washington, DC, USA, 2003. IEEE Computer Society.

[17] T. Dullien and R. Rolles. Graph-based comparison of executable objects. In *Proceedings of the Symposium sur la Securite des Technologies de l'Information et des Communications*, 2005.

[18] B. Eckel. *Thinking in C++, Vol. 2*, chapter 5. Pearson Education, 2003. ISBN 0130353132.

[19] T. J. Edler von Koch, I. Böhm, and B. Franke. Integrated instruction selection and register allocation for compact code generation exploiting freeform mixing of 16- and 32-bit instructions. In *Proceedings of the 8th Annual IEEE/ACM International Symposium on Code Generation and Optimization*, CGO '10, pages 180–189, New York, NY, USA, 2010. ACM.

[20] H. Flake. Structural comparison of executable objects. In U. Flegel and M. Meier, editors, *DIMVA*, volume 46 of *LNI*, pages 161–173. GI, 2004.

[21] A. Halambi, A. Shrivastava, P. Biswas, N. D. Dutt, and A. Nicolau. An efficient compiler technique for code size reduction using reduced bit-width ISAs. In *DATE*, pages 402–408. IEEE Computer Society, 2002.

[22] M. Haneda, P. M. W. Knijnenburg, and H. A. G. Wijshoff. Code size reduction by compiler tuning. In *Proceedings of the 6th International Conference on Embedded Computer Systems: Architectures, Modeling, and Simulation*, SAMOS'06, pages 186–195, Berlin, Heidelberg, 2006. Springer-Verlag.

[23] R. Jenkins. GCC Bug 29442: insn-attrtab has grown too large. http://gcc.gnu.org/bugzilla/show_bug.cgi?id=29442, October 2006.

[24] R. Komondoor and S. Horwitz. Using slicing to identify duplication in source code. In *Proceedings of the 8th International Symposium on Static Analysis*, SAS '01, pages 40–56, London, UK, UK, 2001. Springer-Verlag.

[25] R. Komondoor and S. Horwitz. Eliminating duplication in source code via procedure extraction. *Dept. of Computer Sciences, Univ. of Wisconsin-Madison, Tech. Rep. 1461*, 2002.

[26] I. Kupka. On similarity of functions. *Topology Proceedings*, 36:137–187, 2010.

[27] G. Lóki, A. Kiss, J. Jász, and A. Beszédes. Code factoring in GCC. In *Proceedings of the 2004 GCC Developers' Summit*, pages 79–84, June 2004.

[28] Y. Park, J. Choi, C. Kang, C. Lee, Y. Shin, B. Choi, J. Kim, S. Jeon, J. Sel, J. Park, K. Choi, T. Yoo, J. Sim, and K. Kim. Highly manufacturable 32Gb multi-level NAND Flash memory with $0.0098 \mu m^2$ cell size using TANOS (Si-Oxide-Al2O3-TaN) cell technology. In *International Electron Devices Meeting*, IEDM'06, pages 1–4, 2006.

[29] C. K. Roy, J. R. Cordy, and R. Koschke. Comparison and evaluation of code clone detection techniques and tools: A qualitative approach. *Sci. Comput. Program.*, 74(7):470–495, May 2009.

[30] R. M. Stallman and the GCC Developer Community. *GNU Compiler Collection Internals*, 2013.

[31] S. Tallam, C. Coutant, I. L. Taylor, X. D. Li, and C. Demetriou. Safe ICF: Pointer safe and unwinding aware identical code folding in gold. In *GCC Developers Summit*, 2010.

[32] M. Thuresson and P. Stenstrom. Evaluation of extended dictionary-based static code compression schemes. In *Proceedings of the 2nd Conference on Computing Frontiers*, CF '05, pages 77–86, New York, NY, USA, 2005. ACM.

[33] L. Van Put, D. Chanet, B. De Bus, B. De Sutter, and K. De Bosschere. DIABLO: a reliable, retargetable and extensible link-time rewriting framework. In *Proceedings of the Fifth IEEE International Symposium on Signal Processing and Information Technology*, pages 7–12, 2005.

[34] D. Ye, J. Ray, C. Harle, and D. Kaeli. Performance characterization of SPEC CPU2006 integer benchmarks on x86-64 architecture. In *2006 IEEE International Symposium on Workload Characterization*, pages 120–127, 2006.

[35] P. Zhao and J. N. Amaral. Function outlining and partial inlining. In *Proceedings of the 17th International Symposium on Computer Architecture on High Performance Computing*, SBAC-PAD '05, pages 101–108, Washington, DC, USA, 2005. IEEE Computer Society.

ASAC: Automatic Sensitivity Analysis for Approximate Computing

Pooja Roy[1], Rajarshi Ray[2], Chundong Wang[3], Weng-Fai Wong[1]

School of Computing, National University of Singapore[1], Singapore
National Institute of Technology, Meghalaya[2], India
Data Storage Institute[3], A*STAR, Singapore
{poojaroy@comp.nus.edu.sg, raj.ray84@gmail.com, wangc@dsi.a-star.edu.sg, wongwf@comp.nus.edu.sg}

Abstract

The approximation based programming paradigm is especially attractive for developing error-resilient applications, targeting low power embedded devices. It allows for program data to be computed and stored approximately for better energy efficiency. The duration of battery in the smartphones, tablets, etc. is generally more of a concern to users than an application's accuracy or fidelity beyond certain acceptable quality of service. Therefore, relaxing accuracy to improve energy efficiency is an attractive trade-off when permissible by the application's domain. Recent works suggest source code annotations and type qualifiers to facilitate safe approximate computation and data manipulation. It requires rewriting of programs or the availability of source codes for annotations. This may not be feasible as real-world applications tend to be large, with source code that is not readily available.

In this paper, we propose a novel *sensitivity analysis* that *automatically* generates annotations for programs for the purpose of approximate computing. Our framework, *ASAC*, extracts information about the sensitivity of the output with respect to program data. We show that the program output is sensitive to only a subset of program data that we deem critical, and hence must be precise. The rest of the data can be computed and stored approximately. We evaluated our analysis on a range of applications, and achieved a 86% accuracy compared to manual annotations by programmers. We validated our analysis by showing that the applications are within the acceptable QoS threshold if we approximate the non-critical data.

Categories and Subject Descriptors D.1.2 [*Programming Techniques*]: - Automatic Programming; D.2.5 [*Software Engineering*]: Testing and Debugging - Code inspection and walk-throughs, Error handling and recovery

Keywords approximate computing, power-aware computing, automatic programming, sensitivity analysis

1. Introduction

Approximate computing is a new programming paradigm that allows programs to trade-off accuracy of internal program data in favour of lower energy consumption. It is especially appealing to low-power embedded devices where energy efficiency is of serious concern. Further, there are many applications targeted to smartphones, tablets, etc. that are capable of tolerating inaccuracy while maintaining the desired quality of service (QoS). Many recent works have shown this to be a promising trade-off for current and future embedded platforms [2, 9, 12, 16, 23, 27].

In general, many programs contain specific parts that contribute to the correctness of the output and others that do not. A correct output usually lies within a Quality of Service range of the application. The parts of a program that do not affect the output beyond a tolerable extent are deemed *approximable*, while parts that are important are *non-approximable*. Depending on the application, the ratio between these two parts can vary significantly. The presence of approximable data in a program is the mainstay of the approximate computing paradigm. The non-approximable program data can be computed and stored in a high power mode, while the approximable regions in a low power mode [9]. Applications allowing such behaviour are called *error-tolerant*. Error-tolerance of applications running on devices prone to soft-errors is well studied [13, 15, 26]. However, in this new paradigm, instead of mitigating the errors, a controlled degradation of QoS due to the errors is allowed.

The challenge is how to discover the distinct approximable and non-approximable parts of a program *automatically*, so that adapting this approximation based programming paradigm is easier. Recent works have proposed source code annotations and type-qualifiers for programmers to indicate whether a variable (data) is error resilient, in other words, approximable [16, 23]. However, this implies rewriting or annotating source codes. This may be easily accomplished for small programs, but is difficult or infeasible for complex programs and legacy softwares. Other works have shown that program approximations can be achieved through algorithmic choices, runtime decision making frameworks, and on the architectural or device level [1, 2, 6, 25]. The provision of algorithmic choices too is the programmer's responsibility and the application is compiled using all the versions of a procedure. This is not only difficult when dealing with large applications having large numbers of procedures, it also inflates size of executables. Such consequences impede the usage of these solutions for embedded devices.

In this paper, we propose "ASAC" - *Automatic Sensitivity analysis for Approximate Computing*, a framework to *automatically* discover approximable data from a program. The main component of this framework is a specialized sensitivity analysis using statistical methods. Sensitivity analysis of parameters of mathematical mod-

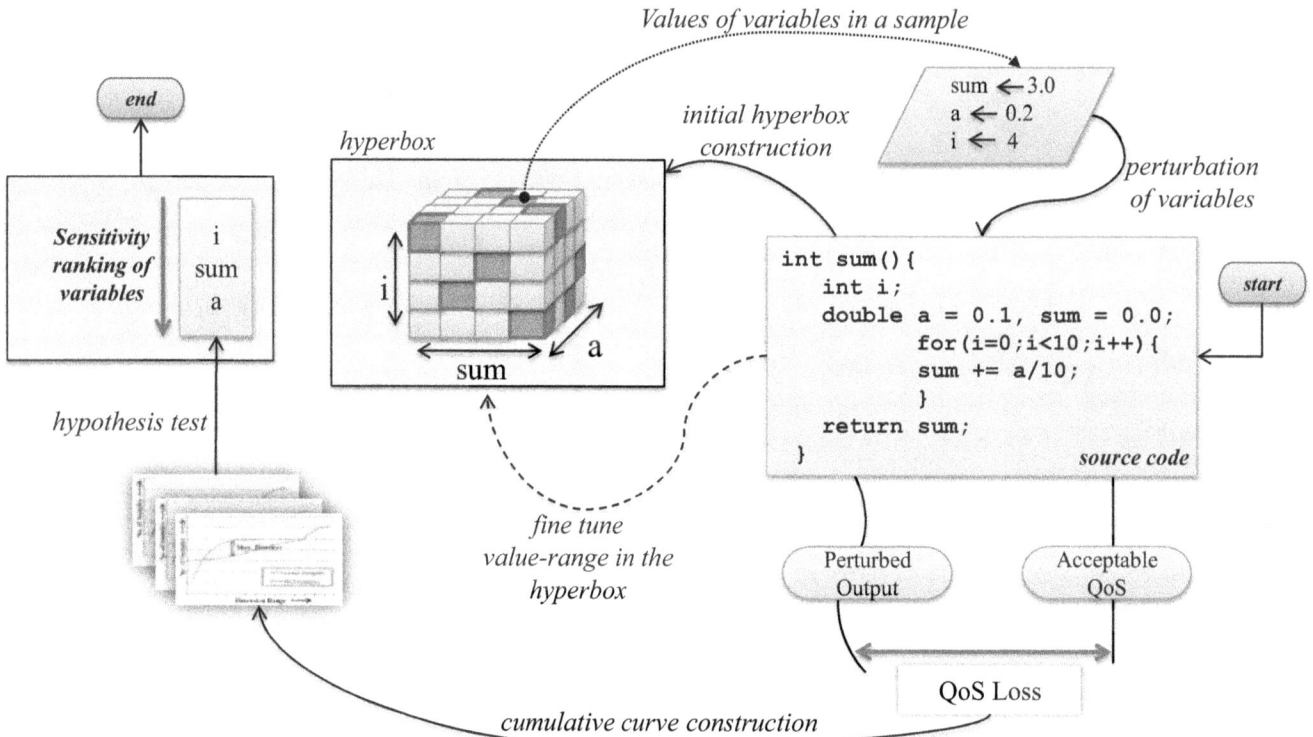

Figure 1: Overview of "ASAC" framework. Each box represents a step and the arrows are the dataflow between them. There is a information flow from Sampler back to the Hyperbox Construction to facilitate further optimization in range analysis.

els using statistical methods is known in literature [20]. Our contribution in this paper is the use of statistical methods for sensitivity analysis of program data. It consists of a random sampler and a hypothesis tester. The main idea of the analysis is to systematically perturb variables and then observe the resultant output sensitivity. Using the outputs from the probes, ASAC applies a hypothesis tester to check against a correct output, which by definition is one fulfilling an acceptable QoS threshold. The hypothesis test generates scores for each variable that ranks the variable's contribution to the output of the program. Based on the scores, the variables are classified as approximable or non- approximable.

ASAC is fully automatic and alleviates the programmer's involvement. With minor modification, it can also be applied to programs where the source code is not available. A direct application of this framework can be as a feedback system to a compiler, providing information about how the program's may be approximated. Moreover, ASAC can be used as a black-box tester to gain insight about the sensitivity of program output against program data. This would be valuable information for platforms susceptible to soft-errors, where instead of allowing the approximation, the sensitivity of the variables can be used as a metric to decide which data should be protected. We evaluated our analysis against a 'gold' standard where a programmer has made type-qualifier based annotations to programs to facilitate approximation [23]. We achieve 86% accuracy in determining approximable data with respect to this manually annotated baseline (MAB). In addition, to show the scalability and generality of our analysis, we apply it to bigger and more complex programs from MiBench and SPEC2006 benchmark suites. Our contributions in this paper are summarized as follows :

- The first automated software analysis that allows approximate computing based programming paradigm.

- A framework to discover program data that can be approximated without compromising the QoS of a given application.

- A black-box analysis that can test programs and order the variables in terms of their contribution to the correctness of the final output.

The rest of the paper is organized as follows: after a brief overview and motivation in Section 2, we will describe our framework in Sections 3 and 4. The evaluation of our analysis is presented in Section 5. Related works are explored in Section 6 and we conclude our paper in Section 7.

2. Overview

In this section we present a brief overview of our framework, ASAC. Our motivation for this work is twofold. The first is to alleviate the existing burden placed on the programmer in facilitating approximate computing. We aim to automatically analyze a program and identify data that can be approximated. In scenarios where annotating programs without programmer's knowledge is considered unsafe, ASAC can serve as the suggestive framework for annotating bigger and more complex programs. Programmers can then fine-tune ASAC's analysis results to obtain the final partitioning. In any case, it is obviously expensive, time consuming, and in some scenarios, infeasible to identify approximable and non-approximable data, and annotate the application completely manually. Moreover, for legacy softwares and other programs that has undergone significant changes over many versions, it may be difficult to understand the implications of approximated variables and their effect globally. Therefore, an automated analysis is indispensable for approximate computing in the large.

Our second motivation is to study the error-resilience of internal program data i.e. program variables, etc. Error-resilient program transformations has been well studied. However, all the existing works focus on approximating different components such as procedure approximation, input data approximation, control- flow based approximation etc. [4, 25]. Other works have studied the error-resilience of data in architectural components such as the arithmetic units, register files, etc. [6, 14]. Here, we are proposing a framework to analyse and approximate internal program data while maintaining an acceptable QoS according to the application.

The key idea is to systematically perturb the program variables and to observe its effect on program output. By quantifying the sensitivity of the output to the perturbations, we can discern program variables in terms of their contributions to the output. A variable that does not contribute to the correctness of the output or the functionality of the program beyond a certain extent is not considered as critical, and therefore can be approximated. Conversely, critical variables cannot be approximated and must be precise.

Figure 1 illustrates ASAC consisting of 3 main stages, namely *discovery*, *probe* and *testing*. In discovery stage, we extract the variables of a program along with the range of values that each can assume during the execution. The cartesian product of the variable range intervals defines an n-dimensional hyperbox. This hyperbox is the sample space for the statistical experiments performed by the sensitivity analysis module. Each dimension represents a variable and the corresponding edge of the hyperbox is the range of that variable. Therefore, the total number of dimensions in the hyperbox is determined by the number of variables in the program.

At the subsequent probe stage, we first divide the hyperbox into smaller hyperboxes of equal sizes. We select a subset of these smaller hyperboxes, the *samples*, and choose a number of points from among them. Each of these points are n-tuple coordinates containing the values of each variable at that point. These points are passed to the program and the values are forcefully assigned (perturbed) to corresponding variables during the execution by means of binary instrumentation. Due to the intrusion, the program output can be expected to be deviated from the correct output. Our aim is to measure this incorrectness. According to the difference between the QoS threshold of the application and the perturbed outputs, we mark each such sample as "good" (pass) or "bad"(fail).

Next, in the testing stage, a cumulative distribution curve is obtained by plotting the number of good or bad samples against the range of each dimension of hyperbox. The two curves undergo a hypothesis test that generates the maximum distance between them. A large distance between the curves means that the program output is very sensitive to the variable representing that dimension of the hyperbox. Conversely, a smaller distance implies the opposite. Each of the stages are described in details in the following sections.

3. Automated Analysis

In this section, we will describe the three stages in detail. First, we explain two main concepts integral to the discovery stage - range analysis and hyperbox construction. Range analysis is well studied. It is commonly used to detect integer overflows, etc. However, here we apply range analysis to estimate the values that a variable can assume during program's execution.

Definition *For each variable V_i in program under analysis, let value(V_i) be the value that V_i can assume during program execution. Then, range$(V_i) = [R_{i1}, R_{i2}]$, where $R_{i1} \leq value(V_i) \leq R_{i2}$. If $R_{i1} = \pm\infty$ or $R_{i2} = \pm\infty$, range(V_i) is given by the datatype of V_i.*

Algorithm 1 Range Analysis
___
Input:
1: Program P, QoS Threshold Q
Output:
2: $R[n]$, where n $\leftarrow$ no. of variables in P

3: Initialize $rangeOf(V_i) = \emptyset \; \forall \; V_i$ in P
4: **for** each variable V_i in P **do**
5:    **if** $rangeof(V_i) = \emptyset$ **then**
6:       $var \leftarrow V_i$
7:       $R_i[2] \leftarrow$ RANGE_ANALYSIS(var) /* standard widening & narrowing operator based */
8:       **if** $R_i[0] \vee R_i[1] = \infty$ **then**
9:          **if** DATATYPE(var) = int_32 **then**
10:             $R_i[0] \leftarrow -32767$ /* standard data */
11:             $R_i[1] \leftarrow 32767$ /* range for int type */
12:          **else if** DATATYPE(var) = float **then**
13:             $R_i[0] \leftarrow 0$ /* dummy range */
14:             $R_i[1] \leftarrow 1$ /* that will shrink over runs */
15:          **else**
16:             /* handle all datatypes similarly */
17:          **end if**
18:       **end if**
19:    **end if**
20: **end for**
21: **return** $R_i[]$

Variables	Datatype	Initial Range	Tuned Range
LineSadBlk0	double	[1 , 1]	[0.0 , 780.0]
P_A	int	[2048 , 2048]	[128 , 128]
P_E	int	[-32768 , 32767]	[34 , 244]
D_dis1	double	[1 , 1]	[-15.0 , 177.0]

Table 1: Ranges of some variables in H.264

This value range is essential for the construction of the hyperbox. We employ widening and narrowing operators based dataflow analysis to calculate the value ranges of the variables [22]. Algorithm 1 gives a pseudo-code description of our range analysis. In cases where the analysis is unable to generate a finite value range, we fine-tune the range based on the data type of the variable (line 9-12). For floating-point variables, we assume a dummy starting range of zero (line 13-14).

In order to extract the real value range, we have a information loop back (see Figure 1) from the sampler to hyperbox construction which makes it easy to get narrow and precise value-ranges from the profile runs of the program. Therefore, even if the dataflow analysis generates an infinite range for a variable, it is soon mitigated. This is shown in Table 1 with the examples of some of the variables in H.264. After calculating the ranges of the variables, we can construct the hyperbox.

Definition *An n-dimensional hyperbox $\mathbb{H}$ is the cartesian product of the range intervals of each of the n variables.*
$\mathbb{H} = [R_{11}, R_{12}] \times [R_{21}, R_{22}] \times \ldots \times [R_{n1}, R_{n2}]$, where $[R_{i1}, R_{i2}]$ is the range of variable (V_i).

Figure 2 shows a conceptual diagram of hyperboxes. Each dimension represents a variable and thus with n variables it will have $n - dimensions$. The starting and ending point of each dimension is R_1 and R_2 of each variable i.e. the range. As the value range of a variable can narrow or widen over runs, the hyperbox may also shrink and grow. The shaded areas are called *samples*.

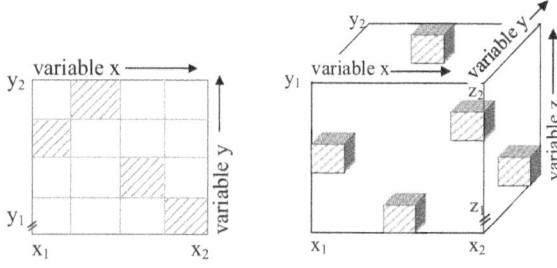

Figure 2: Example of 2 dimensional and 3 dimensional hyper-boxes. A 2-variable program would generate a 2-D hyperbox and similarly, a 3-variable program would generate a 3-D hyperbox as shown.

These are small hyperboxes obtained by discretizing the edges, and selecting only a subset from among them. Discretization provides a finite sampling space from the original hyperbox which has infinitely many sample points. The finite sample space can then be sampled using any statistical sampler. In our framework, we have used the *Latin Hyperbox Sampling* (LHS) algorithm [17]. LHS ensures that the sampling is bias free and with a fairly well coverage of the sample space.

As shown in Figure 2, the 2-D hyperbox is discretized into equal sized grids, and only one sample from each row and column are qualified to be in the subset. For n-dimension, LHS selects only a subset of the samples based on their positioning. The complexity of this method depends on two factors - n, number of variables, i.e. the dimension of the hyperbox, and the constant k i.e. the discretization parameter. Empirically, the number of samples to be selected from a hyperbox can be defined as follows -

$$\text{Number of samples} = \left(\prod_{n=0}^{(k-1)} (k-n) \right)^{n-1}$$

Next, in the first step of the probe stage, we choose m uniformly random points from each sampled hyperboxes. We will present a study of the effects of the constants in a later section. Each of these points are an n-tuple coordinate, where n is the number of variables in the program. For example, a point m_i from a sample s_i has the coordinates $(m_{i_1}, m_{i_2}, ... m_{i_n})$, where m_{i_1} is the value of variable V_1 at the point m_i. The points can be represented as a vector of real numbers. We use these vectors to introduce perturbation in the program execution by passing the values dynamically with an instrumentation tool. We call a program execution with the perturbed values a *probe run*. As the hyperbox was originally constructed by the value ranges of the variables, the perturbation for each variable lies within the range of values the variable is expected to assume during executions.

Definition *Let P_i be a vector of the outputs of all the probe runs of sample S_i, f_{obj} be an objective function, and θ is a constant threshold. If $f_{obj}(P_i) \geq \theta$ then designate P_i to be a "good" sample, else mark it as a "bad" sample. We define the objective function as*

$$f_{obj} = \left(\sum_{j=0}^{j=k} \omega(P_i) \right) / k$$

where $\omega(P_i) = 1$ if $P_i \geq T_{qos}$, otherwise $\omega(P_i) = 0$. T_{qos} is the QoS threshold for the application given by the user.

Algorithm 2 illustrates the detailed steps involved in the construction of hyperbox and how points from among the samples

---

Algorithm 2 Hyperbox Construction & Sampling

Input:
1: $Range[n][2]$, where n is no. of variables in program
2: k, discretization factor
Output:
3: $Vector[n][k]$, containing the values to be passed to program for perturbed run
4: **procedure** HYPERCUBE(Range[n][2],n)
5:     Initialize $H \leftarrow \emptyset$
6:     Initialize $dim = n$
7:     **for** $i = 0$ to dim **do**
8:         $H[i].leftdiagonal \leftarrow Range[i][0]$
9:         $H[i].rightdiagonal \leftarrow Range[i][1]$
10:    **end for**
11: **end procedure**

12: **procedure** LATIN HYPERCUBE SAMPLING(H[n],dim,k)
13:    **for** $i = 0$ to k **do**
14:        **for** $j = 0$ to dim **do**
15:            $L = H[j].leftdiagonal$
16:            $U = H[j].rightdiagonal$
17:            $Interval\_Size = (U - L)/k$
18:            $Interval_Val = $ CHOOSERANDOM(i,j)
19:            $LowLim = Interval\_Val * Interval\_Size$
20:            $T[0][0] \leftarrow L + LowLim$
21:            $T[0][1] \leftarrow L + LowLim + Interval\_Size$
22:            $Sample[i][j] \leftarrow Sample[i][j] \cap$ HYPER-CUBE(T[1][2],j)
23:        **end for**
24:    **end for**
25:    **return** $Sample^T$
26: **end procedure**

---

are chosen. First, a hyperbox is built using the preliminary value ranges obtained from the range analysis (line 3-10). For each variable represented by a particular dimension (edge) of the hyperbox, the edge is discretized into k intervals (line 13-17). Therefore, we have $dim * k$ number of smaller hyperboxes after this step, where dim is the total number of variables and k is the discretization constant. A subset of these smaller hyperboxes are chosen using LHS to have a fair coverage of the ranges (line 18-22). The samples represent the set of values to be passed to the program in the probe runs. The perturbed outputs from all the probe runs are partitioned into two classes - "good" or "bad", based on the QoS threshold of the application.

Figure 3: This graph is an example of how the CDFs are plotted and the hypothesis test's computes the distance metric using them. The two curves are plotted from the cumulative number of samples that are marked "good" and "bad" based on the QoS.

From all the samples marked as either good or bad (0 or 1), we construct a cumulative curve for each dimension of the hyperbox. The number of good samples is counted, and plotted against the range of that dimension. Similarly, a second curve is obtained by counting the samples marked as bad. These two curves are regarded as two cumulative distributions obtained from the perturbed program runs.

Definition *Let Sen_i denote the sensitivity score for a variable V_i. Let $f_{good}V_i$ and $f_{bad}V_i$ be the two cumulative distribution function (CDF) for variable V_i. Then, $Sen_i = max_x|f_{good}V_i(x) - f_{bad}V_i(x)|$, where x is a point in the value range of the variable V_i at which the CDFs are calculated.*

Intuitively, the distance between the two curves denotes the contribution of this variables towards the program output. We apply the *Kolmogorov-Smirnov* hypothesis test [20] to calculate the maximum distance between the two curves. This is called the d-statistics, and it translates to the sensitivity ranking: the higher the distance, the higher is the sensitivity of the output to this variable, and vice-versa. Figure 3 shows an example of the cumulative curves, and the maximum distance between them. A detailed step-by-step description of the generation of the sensitivity scores is given in Algorithm 3. First, the program probe step is detailed in lines 3-15. The procedure receives the vector of values from the hyperbox as input and runs the program by forcefully assigning these values to the variables. Each program run produces a result that is stored to be compared for QoS at a later stage. In this procedure, the hypercube is also updated with fine-tuned range of the variables. Next, in the hypothesis test procedure, an error is calculated from the obtained result and the original result of the program (line 18). This error is used to mark a sample as good or bad. Following this marking, considering all the samples from the hyperbox, a cumulative graph is plotted against each dimension (lines 27-33). Two curves are obtained for each dimension of the hyperbox and they are passed to the KS-Test for the distance metric (line 35).

4. Optimizations

4.1 Discretization Constant

Our proposed analysis has one tunable parameter, the discretization constant, k. This determines the size of the samples for each dimension in the hyperbox. In other words, all the value ranges of the variables are divided up using this constant k so as to reduce the value space (see Algorithm 2). The completion time of the analysis is affected by this parameter. A larger value will cause the analysis to take a longer time to complete because the hyperbox is divided into smaller grids. However, the sensitivity scores obtained from the analysis is not affected by the value of k as shown in Table 2. Thus, we can conclude that the sensitivity of program output with respect to its variables is a characteristic of the program. For our evaluation, we tested with $k = 10, 50, 100, 200$.

Figure 4 shows the total time taken by ASAC to complete its analysis. As shown, when $k \leq 100$, ASAC takes longer time to rank the variables. Table 2 shows the percentage of total variables marked as approximate with two different k values. The percentages for $k = 5$ and $k = 200$ are same as that for $k = 10$ and $k = 100$, respectively. The difference between $k = 10$ and $k = 100$ is attributed to the fine tuning of the ranges of the variables. As the percentages are averaged over 20 runs, different program paths will result in different fine-tuning of the variable ranges. Nonetheless, the difference of percentage of variables marked as approximate shows no significant variation over the values of k as shown in Table 2.

There is another constant m, which determines how many points will be chosen from within one sample to perturb the program. We

---

Algorithm 3 Sensitivity Ranking

Input:
1: $Vector[n][k]$, containing the values to be passed to program for perturbed run
2: Q, QoS Threshold
Output:
3: $SenScores[n]$, sensitivity scores for variables
4: **procedure** PROGRAM PROBE(Vector[n][k])
5:     Initialize $Values[n] \leftarrow \emptyset$
6:     Initialize $dim = n$
7:     **for** $j = 0$ to k **do**
8:         **for** $i = 0$ to dim **do**
9:             $Values[i] \leftarrow Vector[i][j]$
10:         **end for**
11:         $Output[j] \leftarrow$ program executed with $Values[]$
12:         Update hypercube
13:     **end for**
14:     **return** Output[]
15: **end procedure**

16: **procedure** HYPOTHESIS TEST(Output[],Q)
17:     **for** $i = 0$ to k **do**
18:         $err =$ GETERRORFUNCTION(Output[i])
19:         **if** $err \leq Q$ **then**
20:             $Good[i][] = Values[]$
21:         **else**
22:             $Bad[i][] = Values[]$
23:         **end if**
24:     **end for**
25:     **for** $i = 0$ to dim **do**
26:         $j \leftarrow R_i[0]$
27:         **while** $j \neq R_i[1]$ **do**
28:             **if** $j \in Good[i][]$ **then**
29:                 $C_{good}[j]++$
30:             **else if** $j \in Bad[i][]$ **then**
31:                 $C_{bad}[j]++$
32:             **end if**
33:             $j += Interval_{size}$
34:         **end while**
35:         $SenScores[i] \leftarrow$ KS_TEST(C_{good}, C_{bad})
36:     **end for**
37: **end procedure**

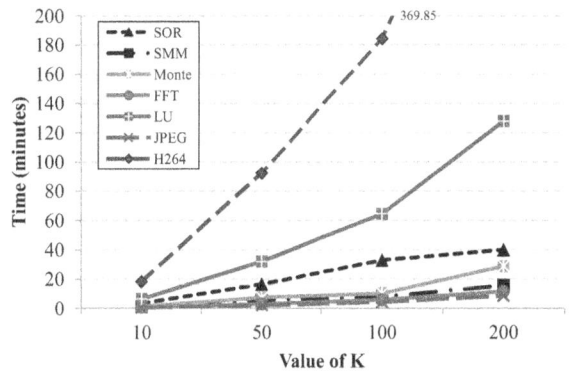

Figure 4: Total time (in minutes) taken by ASAC to produce the variable rankings with varied values of the parameters k while $m = 2$.

observe an interesting trend in the relationship between k and m. As the samples are small in size with a high value of k, increasing the value of m, i.e. choosing many points within a narrow range, results in passing similar values for probing. Therefore, the value of this constant m has no significant impact on the variable ranking when k is high. Nonetheless, a high value of both k and m will translate to higher running time for our analysis.

When k is small, the value of m has an impact on the variables' ranking. A small value of k and m will result in sampling a few representatives from a large hyperbox causing poor coverage of the sample space. This behaviour is accentuated in bigger programs, such as JPEG and H.264. However, it is important to have perturbations with values of variables that are uniformly distributed over its range. Therefore, for our experiments we used $m = 5$ and $k = 100$.

4.2 Perturbation Points

In the probe stage of our framework, we force variables to assume values chosen from the hyperbox. We use the dynamic instrumentation tool PIN [19] to inject the values at runtime. There are two important issues that we would like to discuss here.

First, it is a challenge to identify program points where the variables are perturbed. For example, if a perturbation is introduced at a point where a variable is first *used* after being *defined*, then the effect on output will be different than if the perturbation is introduced at a later point. In the former, the error might propagate and accumulate, resulting in a large deviation from correct output. On the other hand, the error might get masked by further arithmetic operations on the variables [25]. In our implementation, we introduce the perturbations at the first usage of a variable after it is defined. Nonetheless, it would be interesting to study the effects of the perturbation at other program points.

The second challenge is in injecting error into loop structures. It is difficult to force values into loop variables because of its iterative nature. Our aim is to perturb a variable to see the effect on the output. However, if the loop factor is high, then injecting the perturbation at every iteration becomes too aggressive. Instead we chose to perturb only a subset (25%) of the loop iterations. This technique is analogous to the concept of *loop-perforation* [27].

| Bench-marks | Total Decls | Data Approximable(%) | | | |
| | | $k = 2$ | | $m = 5$ | |
		$m = 2$	$m = 10$	$k = 10$	$k = 100$
SOR	28	28	28	28	28
SMM	29	27	27	27	27
Monte	15	33	33	33	33
FFT	85	32	35	36	35
LU	150	6	9	9	10
JPEG	1174	6	10	11	11
H.264	11857	7	15	16	16

Table 2: Percentage of variables marked as approximable by ASAC with different values of k and m.

4.3 Instrumentation & Testing

ASAC involves ranking the variables using their identifiers, i.e. names, which are not easily accessible after the code generation, especially at runtime. Therefore, it is difficult to pass the perturbation values to the program during the probe runs.

To force a sample value into a program, we implemented a compile-time pass that will inject additional code at the appropriate program point in the code to read the value to be forced into a variable from a file, and perform the write of that value into the variable. We also found that for larger applications, it was easier to use the PIN tool to inject such values - provided they are not bound to registers - into variables using their virtual addresses. In the actual implementation, we used a combination of both.

In the testing and evaluation of ASAC, we adapted the *bitflip error model* used by many prior works [3, 4, 14] to introduce errors into the application. A bitflip error essentially means that one or more bits within a data toggles one or more times during execution of the program, inducing an error. We used the same two techniques described above except that in the testing and evaluation, instead of forcing a targeted variable to take a certain value, we choose a (uniformly) random bit among the 16 lower bits of its current, and toggle it. There are many other error models available in literature, we chose bitflip because it is fairly simple to understand and model. Nonetheless, more complicated error models could also be used.

5. Evaluation

We evaluated ASAC against a manually annotated baseline (MAB) that uses type-qualifiers [23]. The authors of that paper kindly provided us with benchmarks from SciMark2 [21] that had such annotations made. We also apply ASAC to two benchmarks from SPEC2006 [28] and MiBench [11] to test its scalability. To measure the QoS loss due to approximation, we defined the error metric for each application, shown in Table 3. For FFT, LU and SOR, we use the mean squared error between the correct answer and the approximated output to quantify the degradation. For applications like SparseMatMult and MonteCarlo, we measure the normalized difference i.e. 0 if the approximated output is equal to correct output and 1 if not. For JPEG and H.264, we use the signal-to-noise ratio (SNR). The error estimation module as well as the QoS threshold is deemed to be provided by the user for our analysis. This makes it easy and portable.

Application	Benchmark	Error Metric	LOC
SOR	SciMark2	Mean Square Error	36
SparseMatMult	SciMark2	Normalized difference	38
MonteCarlo	SciMark2	Normalized difference	59
FFT	SciMark2	Mean Square Error	168
LU	SciMark2	Mean Square Error	283
JPEG	MiBench	SNR	30781
H.264	SPEC2006	SNR	46190

Table 3: Description of all the benchmarks used for evaluation.

Comparison with Manually Annotated Baseline (MAB). Table 4 shows the detailed comparison of ASAC with MAB. We shall examine the *precision, recall and accuracy* metrics of these experiments.

Precision measures how frequent a variable marked by ASAC to be approximable is also annotated as approximable in the MAB. Empirically it is defined as -

$$\frac{tp}{tp+fp}$$

where 'tp' and 'fp' are the 'true positive' and 'false positive' in Table 4, respectively. The former are those variables found to be 'approximable' in both ASAC and MAB. The latter are variables that ASAC declared to be 'approximable' but were annotated as 'non- approximable' in MAB. ASAC achieved a precision of 75%. The 25% loss in precision is due to the fact that our framework is more optimistic in marking variables as approximable.

Benchmarks	True Positive(tp)	False Positive(fp)	False Negative(fn)	True Negative(tn)	Precision	Recall	Accuracy
SOR	5	0	1	2	0.83	1.00	0.88
SMM	1	0	1	6	0.50	1.00	0.88
Monte	2	0	1	2	0.67	1.00	0.80
FFT	15	2	2	12	0.88	0.88	0.87
LU	7	1	1	5	0.88	0.88	0.86
				Average	0.75	0.95	0.86

Table 4: Comparison of *ASAC* with "EnerJ" [23].

Recall measures the robustness of our analysis. It is the complement of the percentage of variables our analysis mistakenly classifies a variable as non-approximable while MAB has annotated it as approximable, defined as follows -

$$\frac{tp}{tp+fn}$$

where 'fn' is 'false negative', variables that are marked as 'non-approximable' as ASAC but annotated as 'approximable' by MAB. These are the cases where our analysis fails to exploit approximable variables. Our analysis shows a high recall value of 95%. Finally, **accuracy** is a metric that combines precision and recall, and quantifies how much can we match the classification by MAB. It is defined as -

$$\frac{tp+tn}{tp+tn+fp+fn}$$

where 'tn' are the 'true negatives', i.e., the variables that both ASAC and MAB agree are non-approximable.

We achieve a high accuracy of 86%, using ASAC's fully automatic approach. The accuracy can be improved further by optimizations discussed in Section 4.

Error Measurement. In order to quantify the error due to approximation of program data, we evaluated different levels of error injection: two levels in JPEG, and three levels for H.264. First, in the Mild injection, errors are injected to only 50% of the variables marked as approximable. This half is chosen from the lower ranked variables (lower sensitivity scores) among those that are marked as approximable. Bitflip errors were injected into these variables during runtime.

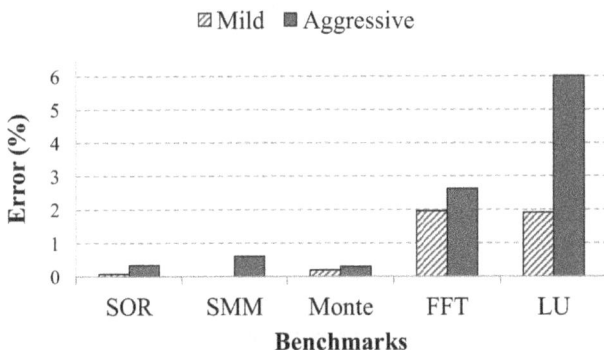

Figure 5: Percentage of error after approximating program data. The two bars are different error percentage after approximating either one-third or all the data that are classified as approximable by ASAC.

Second, in the Aggressive injection, errors are injected to all the variables identified as approximable. For H.264 that has a large number of variables, we created one more level of inject - Medium. For this benchmark, we chose the lowest scored one-third as the Mild injection, 60% for Medium and 100% (all) for Aggressive. Figure 5 shows the error percentages for the SciMark2 applications under Mild and Aggressive error injection. Figure 6 shows the result when Mild and Aggressive error injections were applied to the JPEG benchmark. We applied error injection to the encode and decode steps separately to show the effect of error accumulation. In the Figure 6(e) the errors are aggravated as it takes Figure 6(d) as its input which already contained the errors injected in encode step. Therefore, the Aggressive approximation for decode step is actually more severe than what it would have been if taken in isolation. Table 5 shows the approximation results for all the Mild, Medium and Aggressive applied to H.264.

H.264	SNR_Y	SNR_U	SNR_V	BitRate
Correct	36.67	40.74	42.31	149.62
Mild	36.69	37.64	37.65	146.6
Medium	34.05	36.92	36.79	147.12
Aggressive	29.78	32.89	32.99	146.03

Table 5: H.264 Approximation Results

Further Studies on JPEG and H.264. As we do not have manual annotations for JPEG and H.264 benchmarks, we studied the effect of injecting errors into the variables that ASAC has marked as non- approximable. Essentially, there were two scenarios. First, when Aggressive error injection was applied to those variables deemed non-approximable (i.e., precise), the output of the JPEG benchmark was a corrupted image file, while the H.264 benchmark simply terminated pre-maturely with segmentation fault. This is because ASAC marks all pointers and memory addresses as non-approximable, hence an Aggressive error injection into memory addresses naturally resulted in crashes. Next, we tried to inject errors only into variables that ASAC has marked as non-approximable and are not memory addresses. Figure 7 shows the encode and decode outputs of JPEG. It clearly shows that ASAC is able to correctly mark not only approximable data, but also non-approximable data. For H.264, even a Mild error injection into non-pointer variables led to the application crashing.

6. Related Works

Emerging complex embedded devices generally face strict energy constraints. Users want to run a huge variety of application on their smartphones, tablets, etc. and expect a longer battery life. One way to achieve this is to trade-off the QoS.

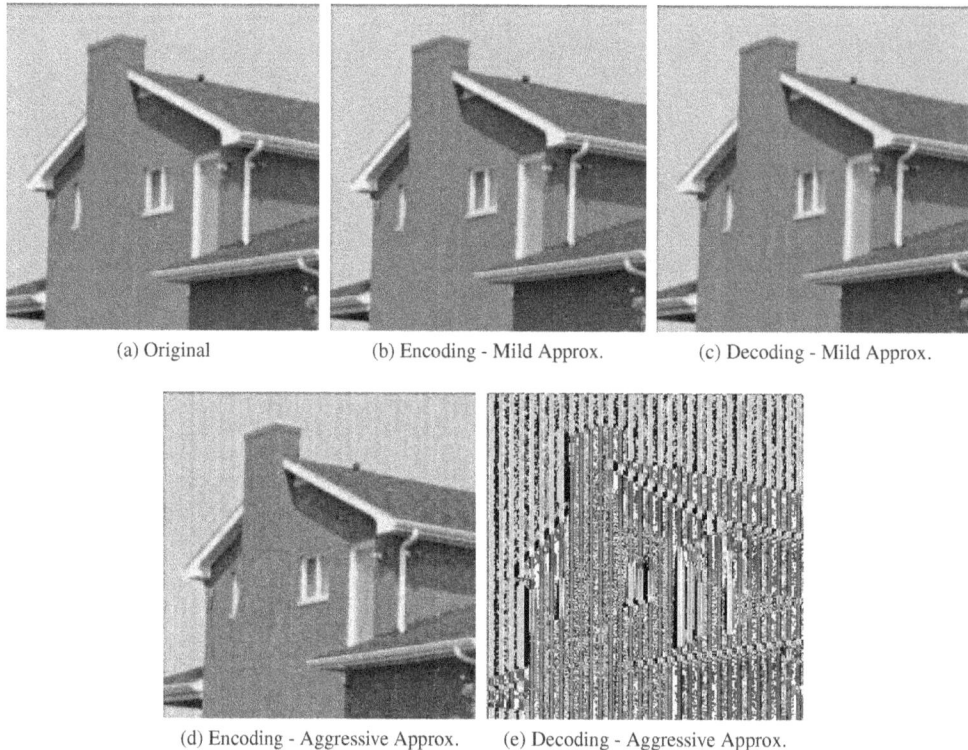

(a) Original   (b) Encoding - Mild Approx.   (c) Decoding - Mild Approx.

(d) Encoding - Aggressive Approx.   (e) Decoding - Aggressive Approx.

Figure 6: JPEG benchmark with various level of approximations separately in *Encode* and *Decode* stages. Image (a) is the original image. Images (b) and (c) are result of introducing mild approximation (in 30% of the variables). Images (d) and (e) are result of introducing aggressive approximation (in all the variables that are approximable).

There are many popular applications in commercial embedded devices that do not require a strict QoS as long as they meet an acceptable threshold [15]. Building on this idea, approximate computing has gained much attention. It allows programs to relax their accuracy in order to save on energy consumption. There are also many works focused on mitigating soft-errors in programs [13, 15, 26].

6.1 Approximation in Programs

Recently there has been proposals on how to allow a disciplined approximation to relax the accuracy of a program and reduce energy consumption as a consequence [2, 9, 16, 23, 24, 31]. Approximation is achievable at different levels of abstraction such as code approximation, program approximation, approximate computer architectures and device level approximations.

Baek et.al. [2] pioneered the idea of this trade-off by proposing a loop and function approximation framework. In this, the programmers are expected to provide multiple versions of a function or a loop structure. The framework consists of a calibration that generates a QoS model and allows a graceful QoS loss during runtime to save energy. However, this solution places a demand on the programmer's expertise and involvement. With the popularity of open-source application development for embedded devices, it is generally not feasible to request multiple versions of a code to allow approximate computing. In addition, compiling (or re-compiling, in case of legacy softwares) a program with extra versions of functions and loops would result in code bloat and larger executables which is not suitable for tight budget and low power devices.

In EnerJ, Sampson et.al. [23] proposes a type-qualifier based programming paradigm to facilitate approximation of program data. This ensures safety in terms of maintaining a distinction between approximate and precise computation of program data. Only with explicit programmer's endorsements, a conversion from precise to approximate or vice-versa is allowed. It provides an exclusive compiler to generate instructions for the underlying dynamic voltage scaling-based hardware called "Truffle" to switch between high and low power modes [9].

Carbin et.al. [4] proposed a technique that classifies code regions into approximable and critical by a training method that uses fuzzed input data. Depending on the program path taken by different inputs, it is able to identify critical program regions and approximable regions. Many works propose program transformations and code generation techniques to allow approximate computation. The motivation in these works is to save computation power i.e. loop iterations, floating point operations etc. One such method is known an "loop perforation" where loop iterations are skipped in order to save computation which results in approximation in the output [27]. Misailovic et.al. [18, 30] proposes probabilistic accuracy tests to allow for program level approximations. However, in most of the above mentioned works, one common drawback is the programmer's involvement, and the lack of scalability. ASAC tries to alleviate both.

6.2 Approximation in Hardware Devices

There are many other works investigating and designing architectural or device level approximation infrastructures [5, 7, 29]. Chippa et.al. [8] presented a work on characterizing error resilience in applications based on approximate adders. They also proposed "Impact", an approximate adder circuit that saves energy by approximating addition operations [10]. Liu et.al. [16] proposed a

DRAM refresh mechanism that protects critical data and approximates non-critical data to save refresh energy. There has also been research works exploring program level error resilience that allows safe approximation. Shafique et.al. [25] proposes a technique to discover errors that are masked by program flow and operations on data. This indicates an inherent error resilience and approximation capability of a program. However, this is based on static code analysis and thus is not accurate as a whole program optimization framework. Error concerning only statically allocated data and compile-time inferable computation is exposed to this technique. Program data that are dynamically allocated or are influenced by runtime computations are hard to analyse. ASAC is a software testing based framework and thus, is able to analyse all kinds of program variables.

(a) Encoding - Mild Approx.   (b) Decoding - Mild Approx.

Figure 7: JPEG benchmark with errors in data that are marked as "Precise" by ASAC.

7. Conclusion

In this paper, we present ASAC, a framework to automatically classify internal program data as approximable and non-approximable. We propose a novel sensitivity analysis that makes use of statistical sampling in performing a controlled perturbation based program testing. We are able to achieve 86% accuracy in identifying approximable data as compared to a manually annotated baseline. We also show that ASAC is scalable, and is able to analyze large applications such as JPEG and H.264. To the best of our knowledge, our work is the first to propose such an automated framework for approximate computing.

Our experimental results show that using our annotations to approximate program data resulted in program outputs that are within the acceptable QoS thresholds. ASAC is easy to adapt in either a compilation or a software testing framework. In addition, it can be used to provide suggestive annotations for large-scale programs that are difficult to annotate manually.

As a part of future work, ASAC can be extended to comprise more complex analysis and study sensitivity of program data across software versions. We expect ASAC to be a key contribution as the first automatic framework to classify program data in the field of approximate computing, which will grow as energy efficiency demands become more prevalent.

Acknowledgments

The research reported here was supported in part by the Singapore Ministry of Education Tier 2 Research Grant MOE2010-T2-1-075, and the A*STAR PSF Research Grant 102-101-0028. We also thank Manmohan Manoharan for valuable reviews.

References

[1] J. Ansel, Y. L. Wong, C. Chan, M. Olszewski, A. Edelman, and S. Amarasinghe. Language and compiler support for auto-tuning variable-accuracy algorithms. In *Proceedings of the 9th Annual IEEE/ACM International Symposium on Code Generation and Optimization*, CGO '11, pages 85–96, Washington, DC, USA, 2011. IEEE Computer Society. ISBN 978-1-61284-356-8. URL http://dl.acm.org/citation.cfm?id=2190025.2190056.

[2] W. Baek and T. M. Chilimbi. Green: A framework for supporting energy-conscious programming using controlled approximation. In *Proceedings of the 2010 ACM SIGPLAN Conference on Programming Language Design and Implementation*, PLDI '10, pages 198–209, New York, NY, USA, 2010. ACM. ISBN 978-1-4503-0019-3. . URL http://doi.acm.org/10.1145/1806596.1806620.

[3] F. Benz, A. Hildebrandt, and S. Hack. A dynamic program analysis to find floating-point accuracy problems. In *Proceedings of the 33rd ACM SIGPLAN Conference on Programming Language Design and Implementation*, PLDI '12, pages 453–462, New York, NY, USA, 2012. ACM. ISBN 978-1-4503-1205-9. . URL http://doi.acm.org/10.1145/2254064.2254118.

[4] M. Carbin and M. C. Rinard. Automatically identifying critical input regions and code in applications. In *Proceedings of the 19th International Symposium on Software Testing and Analysis*, ISSTA '10, pages 37–48, New York, NY, USA, 2010. ACM. ISBN 978-1-60558-823-0. . URL http://doi.acm.org/10.1145/1831708.1831713.

[5] V. Chippa, A. Raghunathan, K. Roy, and S. Chakradhar. Dynamic effort scaling: Managing the quality-efficiency tradeoff. In *Proceedings of the 48th Design Automation Conference*, DAC '11, pages 603–608, New York, NY, USA, 2011. ACM. ISBN 978-1-4503-0636-2. . URL http://doi.acm.org/10.1145/2024724.2024863.

[6] V. K. Chippa, D. Mohapatra, A. Raghunathan, K. Roy, and S. T. Chakradhar. Scalable effort hardware design: Exploiting algorithmic resilience for energy efficiency. In *Proceedings of the 47th Design Automation Conference*, DAC '10, pages 555–560, New York, NY, USA, 2010. ACM. ISBN 978-1-4503-0002-5. . URL http://doi.acm.org/10.1145/1837274.1837411.

[7] V. K. Chippa, D. Mohapatra, A. Raghunathan, K. Roy, and S. T. Chakradhar. Scalable effort hardware design: Exploiting algorithmic resilience for energy efficiency. In *Proceedings of the 47th Design Automation Conference*, DAC '10, pages 555–560, New York, NY, USA, 2010. ACM. ISBN 978-1-4503-0002-5. . URL http://doi.acm.org/10.1145/1837274.1837411.

[8] V. K. Chippa, S. T. Chakradhar, K. Roy, and A. Raghunathan. Analysis and characterization of inherent application resilience for approximate computing. In *Proceedings of the 50th Annual Design Automation Conference*, DAC '13, pages 113:1–113:9, New York, NY, USA, 2013. ACM. ISBN 978-1-4503-2071-9. . URL http://doi.acm.org/10.1145/2463209.2488873.

[9] H. Esmaeilzadeh, A. Sampson, L. Ceze, and D. Burger. Architecture support for disciplined approximate programming. In *Proceedings of the Seventeenth International Conference on Architectural Support for Programming Languages and Operating Systems*, ASPLOS XVII, pages 301–312, New York, NY, USA, 2012. ACM. ISBN 978-1-4503-0759-8. . URL http://doi.acm.org/10.1145/2150976.2151008.

[10] V. Gupta, D. Mohapatra, S. P. Park, A. Raghunathan, and K. Roy. Impact: Imprecise adders for low-power approximate computing. In *Proceedings of the 17th IEEE/ACM International Symposium on Low-power Electronics and Design*, ISLPED '11, pages 409–414, Piscataway, NJ, USA, 2011. IEEE Press. ISBN 978-1-61284-660-6. URL http://dl.acm.org/citation.cfm?id=2016802.2016898.

[11] M. R. Guthaus, J. S. Ringenberg, D. Ernst, T. M. Austin, T. Mudge, and R. B. Brown. Mibench: A free, commercially representative embedded benchmark suite. WWC '01, 2001.

[12] H. Hoffmann, S. Sidiroglou, M. Carbin, S. Misailovic, A. Agarwal, and M. Rinard. Dynamic knobs for responsive power-aware computing. In *Proceedings of the Sixteenth International Conference on Architectural Support for Programming Languages and*

Operating Systems, ASPLOS XVI, pages 199–212, New York, NY, USA, 2011. ACM. ISBN 978-1-4503-0266-1. . URL http://doi.acm.org/10.1145/1950365.1950390.

[13] J. Hu, F. Li, V. Degalahal, M. Kandemir, N. Vijaykrishnan, and M. J. Irwin. Compiler-assisted soft error detection under performance and energy constraints in embedded systems. *ACM Trans. Embed. Comput. Syst.*, 8(4):27:1–27:30, July 2009. ISSN 1539-9087. . URL http://doi.acm.org/10.1145/1550987.1550990.

[14] J. Lee and A. Shrivastava. Static analysis to mitigate soft errors in register files. In *Proceedings of the Conference on Design, Automation and Test in Europe*, DATE '09, pages 1367–1372, 3001 Leuven, Belgium, Belgium, 2009. European Design and Automation Association. ISBN 978-3-9810801-5-5. URL http://dl.acm.org/citation.cfm?id=1874620.1874949.

[15] K. Lee, A. Shrivastava, I. Issenin, N. Dutt, and N. Venkatasubramanian. Mitigating soft error failures for multimedia applications by selective data protection. In *Proceedings of the 2006 International Conference on Compilers, Architecture and Synthesis for Embedded Systems*, CASES '06, pages 411–420, New York, NY, USA, 2006. ACM. ISBN 1-59593-543-6. . URL http://doi.acm.org/10.1145/1176760.1176810.

[16] S. Liu, K. Pattabiraman, T. Moscibroda, and B. G. Zorn. Flikker: Saving dram refresh-power through critical data partitioning. In *Proceedings of the Sixteenth International Conference on Architectural Support for Programming Languages and Operating Systems*, ASPLOS XVI, pages 213–224, New York, NY, USA, 2011. ACM. ISBN 978-1-4503-0266-1. . URL http://doi.acm.org/10.1145/1950365.1950391.

[17] M. D. McKay, R. J. Beckman, and W. J. Conover. A comparison of three methods for selecting values of input variables in the analysis of output from a computer code. *Technometrics*, 42(1):55–61, Feb. 2000. ISSN 0040-1706. . URL http://dx.doi.org/10.2307/1271432.

[18] S. Misailovic, D. Kim, and M. Rinard. Parallelizing sequential programs with statistical accuracy tests. *ACM Trans. Embed. Comput. Syst.*, 12(2s):88:1–88:26, May 2013. ISSN 1539-9087. . URL http://doi.acm.org/10.1145/2465787.2465790.

[19] T. Naughton, W. Bland, G. Vallee, C. Engelmann, and S. L. Scott. Fault injection framework for system resilience evaluation: Fake faults for finding future failures. In *Proceedings of the 2009 Workshop on Resiliency in High Performance*, Resilience '09, pages 23–28, New York, NY, USA, 2009. ACM. ISBN 978-1-60558-593-2. . URL http://doi.acm.org/10.1145/1552526.1552530.

[20] S. Palaniappan, B. Gyori, B. Liu, D. Hsu, and P. Thiagarajan. Statistical model checking based calibration and analysis of bio-pathway models. In A. Gupta and T. Henzinger, editors, *Computational Methods in Systems Biology*, volume' 8130 of *Lecture Notes in Computer Science*, pages 120–134. Springer Berlin Heidelberg, 2013. ISBN 978-3-642-40707-9. . URL http://dx.doi.org/10.1007/978-3-642-40708-6-10.

[21] R. Pozo and B. Miller. Scimark 2.0. www.math.nist.gov/scimark2/.

[22] F. M. Quintao Pereira, R. E. Rodrigues, and V. H. Sperle Campos. A fast and low-overhead technique to secure programs against integer overflows. In *Proceedings of the 2013 IEEE/ACM International Symposium on Code Generation and Optimization (CGO)*, CGO '13, pages 1–11, Washington, DC, USA, 2013.

IEEE Computer Society. ISBN 978-1-4673-5524-7. . URL http://dx.doi.org/10.1109/CGO.2013.6494996.

[23] A. Sampson, W. Dietl, E. Fortuna, D. Gnanapragasam, L. Ceze, and D. Grossman. Enerj: Approximate data types for safe and general low-power computation. In *Proceedings of the 32Nd ACM SIGPLAN Conference on Programming Language Design and Implementation*, PLDI '11, pages 164–174, New York, NY, USA, 2011. ACM. ISBN 978-1-4503-0663-8. . URL http://doi.acm.org/10.1145/1993498.1993518.

[24] A. Sampson, J. Nelson, K. Strauss, and L. Ceze. Approximate storage in solid-state memories. In *Proceedings of the 46th Annual IEEE/ACM International Symposium on Microarchitecture*, MICRO-46, pages 25–36, New York, NY, USA, 2013. ACM. ISBN 978-1-4503-2638-4. . URL http://doi.acm.org/10.1145/2540708.2540712.

[25] M. Shafique, S. Rehman, P. V. Aceituno, and J. Henkel. Exploiting program-level masking and error propagation for constrained reliability optimization. In *Proceedings of the 50th Annual Design Automation Conference*, DAC '13, pages 17:1–17:9, New York, NY, USA, 2013. ACM. ISBN 978-1-4503-2071-9. . URL http://doi.acm.org/10.1145/2463209.2488755.

[26] A. Shrivastava, J. Lee, and R. Jeyapaul. Cache vulnerability equations for protecting data in embedded processor caches from soft errors. In *Proceedings of the ACM SIGPLAN/SIGBED 2010 Conference on Languages, Compilers, and Tools for Embedded Systems*, LCTES '10, pages 143–152, New York, NY, USA, 2010. ACM. ISBN 978-1-60558-953-4. . URL http://doi.acm.org/10.1145/1755888.1755910.

[27] S. Sidiroglou-Douskos, S. Misailovic, H. Hoffmann, and M. Rinard. Managing performance vs. accuracy trade-offs with loop perforation. In *Proceedings of the 19th ACM SIGSOFT Symposium and the 13th European Conference on Foundations of Software Engineering*, ESEC/FSE '11, pages 124–134, New York, NY, USA, 2011. ACM. ISBN 978-1-4503-0443-6. . URL http://doi.acm.org/10.1145/2025113.2025133.

[28] SPEC-CPU2006. Spec benchamrks. www.spec.org/cpu2006/.

[29] S. Venkataramani, V. K. Chippa, S. T. Chakradhar, K. Roy, and A. Raghunathan. Quality programmable vector processors for approximate computing. In *Proceedings of the 46th Annual IEEE/ACM International Symposium on Microarchitecture*, MICRO-46, pages 1–12, New York, NY, USA, 2013. ACM. ISBN 978-1-4503-2638-4. . URL http://doi.acm.org/10.1145/2540708.2540710.

[30] Z. A. Zhu, S. Misailovic, J. A. Kelner, and M. Rinard. Randomized accuracy-aware program transformations for efficient approximate computations. In *Proceedings of the 39th Annual ACM SIGPLAN-SIGACT Symposium on Principles of Programming Languages*, POPL '12, pages 441–454, New York, NY, USA, 2012. ACM. ISBN 978-1-4503-1083-3. . URL http://doi.acm.org/10.1145/2103656.2103710.

[31] Z. A. Zhu, S. Misailovic, J. A. Kelner, and M. Rinard. Randomized accuracy-aware program transformations for efficient approximate computations. In *Proceedings of the 39th Annual ACM SIGPLAN-SIGACT Symposium on Principles of Programming Languages*, POPL '12, pages 441–454, New York, NY, USA, 2012. ACM. ISBN 978-1-4503-1083-3. . URL http://doi.acm.org/10.1145/2103656.2103710.

em-SPADE: A Compiler Extension for Checking Rules Extracted from Processor Specifications

Sandeep Chaudhary

School of Computer Science
University of Waterloo, Canada
skchaudh@uwaterloo.ca

Sebastian Fischmeister

Electrical and Computer Engineering
University of Waterloo, Canada
sfischme@uwaterloo.ca

Lin Tan

Electrical and Computer Engineering
University of Waterloo, Canada
lintan@uwaterloo.ca

Abstract

Traditional compilers ignore processor specifications, thousands of pages of which are available for modern processors. To bridge this gap, em-SPADE analyzes processor specifications and creates processor-specific rules to reduce low-level programming errors. This work shows the potential of automatically analyzing processor- and other hardware specifications to detect low-level programming errors at compile time.

em-SPADE is a compiler extension to automatically detect software bugs in low-level programs. From processor specifications, a preprocessor extracts target-specific rules such as register use and read-only or reserved registers. A special LLVM pass then uses these rules to detect incorrect register assignments. Our experiments with em-SPADE have correctly extracted 652 rules from 15 specifications and consequently found 20 bugs in ten software projects. The work is generalizable to other types of specifications and shows the clear prospects of using hardware specifications to enhance compilers.

Categories and Subject Descriptors   D.2.5 [*SOFTWARE ENGI-NEERING*]: Testing and Debugging;   B.5.3 [*REGISTER-TRANSFER-LEVEL IMPLEMENTATION*]: Reliability and Testing—Error-checking

General Terms   Bug Detection, Specification, Experimentation, Performance

Keywords   Embedded systems, LLVM, static analysis, compiler

1.   Introduction

Building embedded systems is time-consuming and it is hard to fix bugs in embedded systems after deployment. Therefore, helping developers build such systems is key to the development process. Because of this reason, automated techniques for bug detection are of great use for embedded software.

Embedded system developers have to write software at low level. This means that they directly program different types of hardware, such as registers, memory, timers, interrupt controllers, I/O controllers, and other peripheral controllers. Developers have to initialize hardware and have to work at the register level. Knowing what to do depends on the processor specification and varies between processors. This variability between processors becomes a likely source of bugs. Bugs might occur for a variety of reasons such as—developers' unawareness of such constraints, insufficient knowledge, human errors, etc. Compiler will be unable to catch these bugs, because they are not syntactical issues.

Embedded system devices possess specifications that state constraints and requirements for these devices. Developers should strictly adhere to the rules and constraints mentioned in the specification to use the device and the associated hardware. As mentioned earlier, because of variability between devices, incorrectly modifying registers is a likely scenario.

Thus, it is imperative to utilize specifications to detect inconsistencies in embedded software. Our analysis demonstrates that it is possible to extract such invariant rules from specifications and use the rules to automatically check for bugs in embedded software.

Thousands of microcontrollers are currently available and each microcontroller has its own specification. Specifications are large and can extend over one thousand pages. Reading the specification before programming a microcontroller is a laborious and tiresome activity. Large volume of information in specifications can cause unintentional mistakes. While analyzing 15 ATMEL AVR specifications, we found 72 registers on average in each specification. With these many registers, one can expect register-related constraints to be many-folds the number of registers.

We manually studied processor specifications to understand what rules are available in processor specifications and how to extract these rules. The focus of this study was on the processor specifications for the AVR family of microcontrollers, which are embedded devices manufactured by ATMEL corporation. To understand the generality of extracting rules from processor specifications, we also studied a specification for NXP semiconductors qualitatively. This qualitatively study demonstrated that rules across different line of devices remain generic to a good extent; thus, it is possible to build a general rule extractor.

The main focus of this project was on extracting and verifying two common types of constraints: (1) access (read/write only), and (2) reserved bits. These rules are in the context of registers. Register bits can be read-only, write-only, or read/write bits. Some bits in registers can be reserved which requires that users do not set reserved bits to one. The implemented rule extractor automatically extracts such rules from processor specifications.

Our tool, em-SPADE, is a static analysis based checker which compares the source code against the extracted rules to automatically detect bugs. Currently em-SPADE checks the validity of register assignments in underlying source code.

The novelty of this paper is that em-SPADE is able to automatically make use of information present in specifications to perform

LCTES '14,   June 12–13, 2014, Edinburgh, UK.
Copyright © 2014 ACM 978-1-4503-2877-7 /14/06... $15.00.
http://dx.doi.org/10.1145/2597809.2597823

static analysis. This paper demonstrates that the large volume of the information in specifications can be leveraged for bug detection.

The rule extractor of em-SPADE currently uses simple heuristics to automatically deduce rules from specifications. In the future, we plan to incorporate natural language processing techniques to extract more complex rules from, for instance, English sentences. This will increase the utility of em-SPADE.

We performed experiments for the family of AVR microcontrollers from ATMEL. To test em-SPADE, we collected code from two sources: (1) application notes from ATMEL for their AVR microcontrollers, and (2) github repository. em-SPADE found inconsistencies for several AVR microcontrollers.

We evaluated em-SPADE on 15 specifications and ten open source embedded software projects. em-SPADE extracted a total of 409 read-write only rules with an accuracy of 99.20% and a total of 243 reserved bit rules with an accuracy of 94.88%. We used em-SPADE to check these rules against the source code of the projects, and found 16 warnings related to read-only rules and 4 errors related to reserved bit rules. These bugs are important because writing to a read-only bit or reserved bits might lead to unintended side effects. While such actions might be fine with one revision of the chip, future revisions might alter the use of, for instance, the reserved bits and consequently introduce subtle bugs in previously functionally correct code.

Organization of the rest of the paper is as follows. Section 2 describes the problem statement in detail. Section 3 discusses related work. Section 4 describes the idea and approach of em-SPADE in detail. Section 5 discusses experimental methods. Section 6 discusses the bugs detected by the LLVM [9] checker and the rules extracted by the rule extractor. In Section 7, we describe the performance of em-SPADE. Section 8 discusses some important points about em-SPADE. Finally, in Section 9, we make concluding remarks and discuss future work.

2. Problem Statement

em-SPADE bridges the gap between device specifications and the source code that executes on the device. As described in Section 1, specifications detail requirements and constraints that developers need to follow. However, since the volume of this information is vast, it is probable that developers unknowingly violate some constraints. For example, the specification for ATUC128L3U [27] has 964 pages. If developers want to write some code for the ATUC128L3U, they will need to read the entire document. This tedious task creates a likely scenario of making mistakes.

The goal of em-SPADE is to provide reliability by doing cross-validation of embedded software with the corresponding specification. To demonstrate the usefulness of em-SPADE at a basic prototype level, we are only looking at two types of constraints specified in documents. These constraints are related to value assignment to a different register bits. The first type is about register bits designated as read-only or write-only. If a register bit is read-only and developers write to it, then em-SPADE will issue a warning for this because writing to a read-only register bit might change register behavior. We will use *RO-Writes* to refer to writes to read-only register bits.

The other type is related to reserved bits in registers. If some bit is designated as a reserved bit, developers should not write one to it. If it is present in the source code, then em-SPADE will report an error for this violation. Reserved bits might get some functionality in future versions of the device, so incorrectly writing to them might disrupt some intended future functionality. We will use *Reserved-Writes* to refer to writes to reserved register bits.

In specifications, it is standard to use ':' between two register bits to represent a range. For example, "Bits 4:0" represents five bits i.e., 4, 3, 2, 1 and 0. We will use this notation throughout the paper.

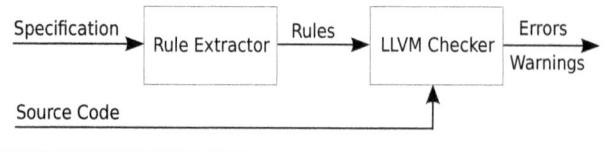

Figure 1. General framework of em-SPADE

In the following, we present one example of each type of rule for the ATmega640/V microcontroller:

1. *"TCCR5C—Timer/Counter 5 Control Register C*
   Bit 4:0—Reserved Bits
   These bits are reserved for future use. For ensuring compatibility with future devices, these bits must be written to zero when TCCRnC is written." [24]

2. *Bits 7, 6, 4 are read-only bits in the Timer/Counter 1 Interrupt Mask Register (TIMSK1).* [24]

Therefore, em-SPADE is addressing the problem of improper value assignment to register bits. The goal of em-SPADE is to provide reliability with respect to two types of probable issues: (1) RO-Writes, and (2) Reserved-Writes. RO-Writes and Reserved-Writes are likely scenarios in the context of microcontroller code. em-SPADE achieves this goal by cross-checking microcontroller code with corresponding rules in the specification. Since specifications are proses in English language, em-SPADE needs to employ heuristics to automatically extract rules of interest. We discuss the heuristics in detail in Section 4. Our aim is to automate the entire toolchain including the rule extractor. Though, several natural language processing techniques are available for extracting rules, em-SPADE is using simple heuristics for now.

3. Related Work

To the best of our knowledge, em-SPADE is the first to automatically analyze processor specifications for automatic bug detection.

Our work consists of two parts: (1) extracting invariants from device specifications, and (2) applying the invariant rules to find bugs in embedded software. Therefore, we discuss work related to rule extraction from natural language documents, and work related to static analysis based bug detection in embedded software.

Fehnker et al. [7] present an automatic bug detection tool which uses static analysis to find bugs in microcontroller software. They examine three types of issues: (1) incorrect-interrupt-handling check; (2) incorrect-timer-service check; and (3) register-to-reserved-bits check. The last check detects similar bugs as em-SPADE. However, the idea of their paper is different from em-SPADE. They manually create rules in the form of CTL formulae for these three types, and their static analysis tool detects bugs based on the rules. Although the bug detection process is partially automatic, automating the rule extraction process is unaddressed, which is exactly the main contribution of em-SPADE.

Dinesh et al. [5] present techniques to extract formal specifications from legal documents, which, are in natural language. They derive CTL specifications from the document which model checking tools can use for verification of models. The specifications are obtained with the use of intermediate semantic representation of different sentences. On the similar line of work, Pandita et al. [17] discuss about extracting formal method specification from natural language text of API documents.

iComment [29] proposes to detect bugs by analyzing comments in the code. They use Natural Language Processing (NLP), statistical and machine learning techniques to analyze comments in source code. The paper presents the novel idea of automatically analyzing comments to extract programming rules. iComment uses the extracted rules to automatically detect inconsistencies between comments and source code. Based on the analysis, the tool indicates either bugs or bad comments. On the similar line of work, Padioleau et al. [16] discuss the taxonomies and characteristics of comments in operating system (OS) codes. Empirical data presented in the paper shows that comments in OS code are not merely explanations and it is possible to exploit comments for software bug detection.

PR-Miner [11] extracts general programming rules from large software projects and uses them to automatically detect violations in the code. It uses a data mining technique called frequent itemset mining to extract implicit programming rules. AccMon [36] presents automatic detection of memory related bugs using program counter based invariants. Alattin [30] is an alternative pattern mining technique for detecting neglected conditions. RRFinder [32] automatically mines resource-releasing specifications for API libraries. Xie et al. [33, 34] discuss mining techniques for software engineering and program source code data.

Our implementation of rule checker is static which uses LLVM to issue warnings or errors at compile time. The rule checker can be implemented at run-time as well. Csallner and Xi [4], and Smaragdakis and Csallner [21] discuss about combined static and run-time approaches. Engler et al. [6] discuss concepts that lay the foundation of static analysis. The originality of their paper is that they extract the checking information from the code itself and use them to find inconsistencies in the code. The tool can be used to find bugs in source code without any prior knowledge of the system. Hallem et al. [8] describe a framework for performing system specific static analysis.

4. The Framework

This section describes the two components of em-SPADE: (1) Rule extractor, and (2) LLVM checker. The idea of em-SPADE is to extract invariant rules from specifications and use them to detect inconsistencies in embedded software. Therefore, these are related to the two components of em-SPADE respectively. em-SPADE follows the static analysis approach by issuing warnings or errors at compile time to indicate bugs. The automatic approach of extracting rules from specifications is based on heuristics and does not involve any natural language processing.

Figure 1 presents a schematic view of em-SPADE. The first component of em-SPADE, i.e., the rule extractor, takes a microcontroller specification as input and gives the extracted rules in XML format as output. The second component of em-SPADE, i.e., the LLVM checker, takes the XML rules and software code as input and produces errors and warnings as output. We discuss the two components in detail in following subsections.

4.1 Rule Extractor

To gather preliminary data, we first performed an extensive study of four specifications to understand the types of rules. Three of the specifications are for AVR microcontrollers (i.e., ATtiny4 [25], ATmega640/V [24], and ATUC256L3U [27]) and one is for the ARM-M3 based microcontrollers (i.e., UM10360 [28]). The ATtiny4 and ATmega640/V are 8-bit AVR microcontrollers with different sizes of in-system programmable flash. ATUC256L3U is 32-bit Atmel AVR Microcontroller. LPC17xx family are ARM Cortex-M3 based microcontrollers. Section 4.1.1 presents examples of manually extracted rules for ATmega640/V [24] and ARM-M3 processors.

4.1.1 Rules to Extract

While this paper, for now, focuses only on the two mentioned types of rules, the initial study investigated more types of constraints. Consequently, some rules listed below fall outside the category of access type and reserved bit type of rules. These rules show the great potential of generalizing our approach to other types of rules. Some rules from ATmega640/V [24] are:

1. *"XMCRB—External Memory Control Register B; Bit 6:3—Res: Reserved Bits; These bits are reserved and will always read as zero. When writing to this address location, write these bits to zero for compatibility with future devices."*

2. *"ACSR—Analog Comparator Control and Status Register; When changing the ACD bit (i.e., bit 7), the Analog Comparator Interrupt must be disabled by clearing the ACIE bit in ACSR. Otherwise an interrupt can occur when the bit is changed."*

3. *Bits 6:4 in the Clock Prescale Register (CLKPR) are read-only bits.*

4. *"ADCSRB—ADC Control and Status Register B: Bit 7—Res: Reserved Bit; This bit is reserved for future use. To ensure compatibility with future devices, this bit must be written to zero when ADCSRB is written."*

5. *"Bit 0—EERE: EEPROM Read Enable; When the correct address is set up in the EEAR Register, the EERE bit must be written to a logic one to trigger the EEPROM read."*

Some rules from the NXP UM10360 [28] are as follows:

1. *"Reset Source Identification Register (RSID—0x400F C180); 31:4—Reserved, user software should not write ones to reserved bits. The value read from a reserved bit is not defined."*

2. *Bit PLL0STAT in the PLL0 register is read-only and Bit PLL0FEED in the PLL0 register is write-only.*

3. *"PLL1 Status register (PLL1STAT—0x400F C0A8); 31:7—Reserved, user software should not write ones to reserved bits. The value read from a reserved bit is not defined."*

4. *"PLL1 Feed register (PLL1FEED—0x400F C0AC); 31:8 — Reserved, user software should not write ones to reserved bits. The value read from a reserved bit is not defined."*

5. *"External Interrupt Flag register (EXTINT - address 0x400F C140); 31:4—Reserved, user software should not write ones to reserved bits. The value NA read from a reserved bit is not defined."*

Processor specifications follow similar in structure and content across chip vendors. The first specification is for an ATMEL based microcontroller whereas second specification is for microcontrollers from NXP semiconductors. Although these specifications are from different vendors, yet the extracted rules are substantially analogous. Therefore, if it is possible to build a tool to extract rules from AVR microcontrollers, the tool should be able to extract rules from other line of microcontrollers with small or no modifications.

4.1.2 How to Extract the Rules

After this study showed that processor specifications are similar in structure and content, we started creating the automatic rule extractor primarily for the AVR family of microcontrollers. The rule extractor is based on the following observations:

1. The register description layout allows us to get information about the specific bits. Figure 2 shows one such example for Power Control Register 1 (PRR1). Bits 7 and 6 in this register are designated as read-only bits while the rest of the bits are all read and write bits.

2. Register names are in uppercase letters with few numeric characters. Lowercase letters, if any, appear after the first three characters in the name. Also, register name are acronyms with a

Bit	7	6	5	4	3	2	1	0	
(0x65)	–	–	PRTIM5	PRTIM4	PRTIM3	PRUSART3	PRUSART2	PRUSART1	PRR1
Read/Write	R	R	R/W	R/W	R/W	R/W	R/W	R/W	
Initial Value	0	0	0	0	0	0	0	0	

Figure 2. Layout of PRR1 register in ATmega640/V

given acronym description. Timer/Counter Control Register A (TCCR0A) is an example from the ATmega640/V specification. USARTn Control and Status Register B (UCSRnB) is another example from ATmega128 specification.

3. Reserved bits in registers have descriptions. We are able to look up these with keyword searches. For example, EECR register in the ATmega640/V specification has the following description about some reserved bits: "Bits 7:6 — Res: Reserved Bits. These bits are reserved bits and will always read as zero." We have observed this kind of description in all AVR specifications and the NXP UM10360 specification.

Based on these observations, the rule extractor applies the following heuristics to extract the reserved bit and read- and write-only rules:

Heuristics for Reserved Bit Rules – The extraction of reserved bit type of rules starts with identifying the sentences that describe the reserved bits in registers. For this, the rule extractor goes through the sentences and looks for related words such as 'reserved' and 'unused'. Sentences of this type are converted to concrete checkable rules if reserved bit numbers and the register name can both be found. Since the sentence describing the bits is placed as per the bit numbers, it is easy to find the bit numbers given the sentence. The extractor needs only look at the beginning of the sentence, and find the bit number or range of bits. For an example, "Bits 5..0 Res: Reserved Bits - These bits are reserved bits in the ATmega103(L) and will always read as zero." is a description for reserved bit range 5 to 0 in 'SPSR' register in ATmega103. Note that the extractor uses regular expression such as "\\Bit[\\s+s][\\s0-9:,.]*" for matching the bit numbers. This is a 'Boost' [20] based regular expression which requires an extra backslash before any escape sequence involving a backslash such as '\s'.

Extraction of the register name is simple. Unlike bit numbers, the register name might not be available at the beginning of the sentence. However, the name is present in close vicinity of the bit description. Based on our observation, the rule extractor looks at the preceding 100 characters for the register name. Register names are alphanumeric with all letters in capital. Also, the name is based on the acronym of words which are also available along with the name. For example, "ADC Control and Status Register - ADCSR" in ATmega103. One can observe that the register name 'ADCSR' is an acronym of 'ADC Control and Status Register'. One can use this observation to confirm the validity of the extracted register name.

Heuristics for Read- and Write-only Rules – Extraction of read- and write-only rules is based on the register description layout such as the layout shown in Figure 2. One can observe that each bit in this register is designated as 'R', 'W' or 'R/W'. 'R' represents a read-only bit, 'W' represents a write-only bit and 'R/W' represents a read-write bit. For read-only and write-only rules, we need the bit numbers which are read-only or write-only along with the register name.

The rule extractor uses regular expression matching technique for identifying the register description. It looks for the bit description pattern in the document, and then uses this pattern to find the read-only or write-only category of each bit. The regular expression used is - "[R/W]*\\s[R/W]*\\s[R/W]*\\s[R/W]*\\s[R/W] \\s[R/W]*\\s[R/W]*\\s[R/W]*". This is again a 'Boost' [20] based regex with an extra backslash before the escape sequence '\s'. The eight occurrences of 'R/W' in the above regular expression correspond to the eight register bits which are marked as either 'R' or 'W'. This regex identifies register bits from register layouts such as the one in Figure 2. Note that extraction of the register name is same as it is for reserved bit rules.

The tool applies a combination of above mentioned heuristics and uses some stop words, such as MCU and AVR, to extract the rules. Specifications of processors are generally in PDF format. em-SPADE first converts it into text format using a free PDF-to-text tool called pdftotext [19]. For comparison, we also tried other available tools such as pdftxt, ebook-convert, pdf2ps, ps2ascii and ps2txt. pdftotext is better than all of these in terms of preserving format and information. Once em-SPADE gets the text form of the specification, it reshapes the text by getting rid of empty lines and merging some lines to get the original register description layout. The tool relies on the Boost regular expression libraries [20] to search for patterns and uses C++ containers available in Standard Template Library (STL) to manipulate the intermediate data during rule extraction. The rule extractor writes the rules into a simple text file, which the next module of the tool converts to rules in XML format. The LLVM checker in em-SPADE leverages these extracted rules directly to detect bugs.

```
1   <?xml version = '1.0'?>
    <!DOCTYPE rules SYSTEM 'rules.dtd'>
3   <rules>
     <equals>
5     <l>
        <bit_id = 'XMCRB'
7        location = '6' />
      </l>
9     <r>
         0
11    </r>
     </equals>
13  </rules>
```

Figure 3. An example of reserved bit rule in XML

4.1.3 Conversion of Rules to XML Format

em-SPADE uses XML to store extracted rules from specifications. The rules XML file is an input to the LLVM checker along with the software code. Figure 3 shows an example of a reserved bit rule in XML. The rule corresponds to bit 6 in External Memory Control Register B (XMCRB) of ATmega640/V [24] microcontroller. In this example, the register name is present in line 6 in Figure 3. The next line lists the location of the reserved bit in the register. Figure 3 shows only the XML expression for the 6th bit of the XMCRB register. Similar expressions can be written for other bits, i.e., 5:3.

4.2 LLVM Checker

This subsection describes the static checker implemented in LLVM [9]. LLVM stands for Low Level Virtual Machine. It is a compiler infrastructure that allows users to perform a variety of optimizations on the source code with the help of LLVM passes. Building a pass creates a shared object, which users can load using the LLVM optimizer tool *opt* [9]. *Opt* can load LLVM specific bitcode files and perform optimizations written in the pass. Using LLVM passes, we can also do static analysis of the source code. The checker of em-SPADE is an implementation of an LLVM pass.

The pass implemented for em-SPADE performs static analysis based on the XML rules file. Since, the rules of interest only have reserved bits and access type of rules, the pass looks at assembly statements, which are assignments to some registers. The pass parses the XML rules using *libxml2* and verifies the validity of assignments. Assignments become store instructions in LLVM intermediate representation (IR) of the program, so the LLVM checker specifically looks at store instructions in the LLVM IR.

If it finds inconsistencies in assignments based on the rules file, it will produce warnings and/or errors. Since, writing one to a reserved bit can cause problems for a future versions of the device, em-SPADE reports reserved bit violations as errors. However, violations of access type of rules produce warnings. It is important to mention that register names in *avr-libc* are present as macros. Therefore, the tool does not find the register names in the IR of the program. This necessitates another small module in em-SPADE which creates a mapping of register names and corresponding macro values. It does the mapping by parsing the specification header file in the library. Header files for all AVR microcontrollers are available in *avr-libc*, which is a part of the *avr-gcc* toolchain. This small module creates this mapping in an simple text file which the LLVM pass reads while going through the IR of the program. These changes do not affect LLVM binaries as the changes are only limited to mapping register name macros from headers files to text files.

em-SPADE compiles the program under test with debug options to get more information about the instructions. Thus, em-SPADE is able to provide sufficient information about the warnings and errors that it reports. This helps developers in locating bugs in the program. Currently, em-SPADE only examines one-line instructions in LLVM intermediate representation, and does not handles cases where writes to reserved or read-only bits are data-dependent or conditional.

In summary, we have implemented em-SPADE in C++ that uses LLVM as back-end for performing static analysis. em-SPADE uses `pdftotext` to parse specification PDF documents in text form. Additionally, it uses C++ standard template library, Boost regex library and *libxml2* library. em-SPADE uses Clang as a front end to get the LLVM bitcode from the source.

5. Experimental Method

This section discusses the experimental method under the following four subsections:

5.1 Subjects & Design

To test technical feasibility and understand how em-SPADE works in practice, we experimented with several AVR processors from ATMEL. To experiment with the rule extractor of em-SPADE, we randomly selected ten specifications for training. After training the rule extractor, we randomly selected another set of five specifications for evaluating the rule extractor of em-SPADE.

For evaluating em-SPADE's capabilities of finding bugs, we looked at application notes [14] and source from ATMEL. Application notes are general application programs for ATMEL based mi-

crocontrollers. The application notes span over different domains such as automotive, home appliances, industrial automation, mobile electronics, PC peripherals. em-SPADE analyzed 81 application notes downloaded from ATMEL website. Source code of these application notes contain 50 to 500 lines of code. Apart from this, em-SPADE also analyzed projects for ATMEL AVR microcontrollers available at github.

The 15 specifications in the training and evaluation set cover a wide variety of microcontrollers. They represent three subfamilies: (1) ATmega, (2) ATtiny, and (3) AT90S. These 15 specifications dictate requirements and constraints for 39 AVR microcontrollers. With 39 microcontrollers spanning over three subfamilies, the training and evaluation set becomes representative of AVR microcontrollers. Therefore, the selected set of 15 specifications representing 39 AVR microcontrollers provides a good variability and scale for testing em-SPADE. The 15 specifications are the following:

1. AT90S2313 – 8-bit AVR Microcontroller with 2K Bytes of In-System Programmable Flash

2. AT90S8515 – 8-bit AVR Microcontroller with 8K Bytes In-System Programmable Flash

3. ATmega169, ATmega169V – 8-bit AVR Microcontroller with 16K Bytes In-System Programmable Flash

4. ATtiny25/V, ATtiny45/V, ATtiny85/V – 8-bit AVR Microcontroller with 2/4/8K Bytes In-System Programmable Flash

5. ATtiny24, ATtiny44, ATtiny84 – 8-bit AVR Microcontroller with 2/4/8K Bytes In-System Programmable Flash

6. ATmega103, ATmega103L – 8-bit AVR Microcontroller with 128K Bytes In-System Programmable Flash

7. ATmega8, ATmega8L – 8-bit AVR Microcontroller with 8K Bytes In-System Programmable Flash

8. ATmega128, ATmega128L – 8-bit Atmel Microcontroller with 128KBytes In-System Programmable Flash

9. ATtiny13, ATtiny13V – 8-bit AVR Microcontroller with 1K Bytes In-System Programmable Flash

10. ATmega48/V, ATmega88/V, ATmega168/V – 8-bit Atmel Microcontroller with 4/8/16K Bytes In-System Programmable Flash

11. ATmega640/V, ATmega1280/V, ATmega1281/V, ATmega2560/V, ATmega2561/V – 8-bit Atmel Microcontroller with 64K/128K/256K Bytes In-System Programmable Flash

12. ATtiny4, ATtiny5, ATtiny9, ATtiny10 – 8-bit AVR Microcontroller with 512/1024 Bytes In-System Programmable Flash

13. ATmega48PA, ATmega88PA, ATmega168PA, ATmega328P – 8-bit AVR Microcontroller with 4/8/16/32K Bytes In-System Programmable Flash

14. AT90S8535, AT90SL8535 – 8-bit AVR Microcontroller with 8K Bytes In-System Programmable Flash

15. ATtiny261/V, ATtiny461/V, ATtiny861/V – 8-bit AVR Microcontroller with 2/4/8K Bytes In-System Programmable Flash

5.2 Apparatus

We performed the experiments on a Lenovo T420 machine which has an Intel Core i5-2520M processor running at 2.50 GHz. It has 4.0 GB RAM memory and is running Ubuntu 12.10 which has 3.5.0-26-generic version of the Linux kernel.

We manually collected the data about the rule extractor by inspecting the generated rules file for each specification. Then, we compared these rules with the manually extracted rules to calcu-

Table 1. Summary of detected bugs

Project	Total	Reserved-Writes	RO-Writes
Optiboot	1	1	0
Libpolulu	3	3	0
AVR064	2	0	2
AVR130	3	0	3
AVR132	3	0	3
AVR312	2	0	2
AVR314	2	0	2
AVR318	1	0	1
AVR319	1	0	1
AVR441	2	0	2
Aggregate	**20**	**4**	**16**

late different metrics. Source codes of AVR based software were downloaded from ATMEL AVR and github websites.

5.3 Measures

We use the following metrics about the extracted rules from different specifications in the training and evaluation set: (1) Actual Total Rule, (2) True Positives (TP), (3) False Positives, (4) False Negatives, (5) Precision, (6) Recall, and (7) F_1 score. Actual Total Rule gives the number of manually extracted rules from the specifications. True positives (TP) are the correct rules reported by em-SPADE. False positives (FP) are the incorrect rules reported by em-SPADE which are not actual rules. False negatives (FN) are the rules that em-SPADE missed to report.

Precision (P) is the fraction of extracted rules that are correct. Precision is defined as:

$$P = \frac{TP}{TP + FP}$$

Recall (R) is the fraction of correct rules that em-SPADE extracts. It is defined as:

$$R = \frac{TP}{TP + FN}$$

F_1 score is a measure of accuracy which takes both precision and recall into account:

$$F_1 = 2 * \frac{P * R}{P + R}$$

F_1 score reaches its best value at one and worst value at zero.

5.4 Procedure

We performed the testing by categorizing the software code according to the specifications in the training and evaluation set. For example, to test microcontroller software for bugs against the AT-tiny13 specification, we first extracted the rules from this specification. em-SPADE took the same rules file as input to perform bug detection test on the set of all ATtiny13 software. Therefore, we needed to vary the specification and the LLVM specific bitcode file of the microcontroller software for testing em-SPADE. We generated the LLVM specific bitcode file using the LLVM front-end tool *Clang*.

6. Results

This section discusses the bugs, i.e., errors and warnings, that em-SPADE reported, and the rules that rule extractor of em-SPADE extracted from the AVR family of microcontroller specifications. In the first subsection, we provide a detail description of the errors and warnings that em-SPADE found for some application note projects and github projects.

6.1 Errors and Warnings Detected

em-SPADE found a total of 20 errors and warnings in ten projects. An overall summary of these bugs is available in Table 1. Table 1 lists four columns: (1) Project, (2) Total, (3) Reserved-Writes, and (4) RO-Writes. The first column lists the name of the project. The second column tells the total bugs (errors and warnings) found in the particular project. Third and fourth columns tell the number of Reserved-Writes and RO-Writes bugs found in the project respectively. An elaborate discussion on these two type of bugs is available as follows:

6.1.1 RO-Writes

em-SPADE found 16 RO-Writes type of bugs in eight projects which are application notes published by ATMEL. Although writing to read-only bits might not cause a program to fail, it is bad programming practice and can cause new bugs in future revisions. Therefore, we consider RO-Writes as bugs. These bugs correspond to three specifications, i.e., ATmega169, ATtiny13 and ATtiny24. In all these cases, specifications dictate that the registers have read-only bits that are initialized with 0 but developers incorrectly write 1 to those register bits. The next two paragraphs provide two examples of RO-Writes bugs which em-SPADE found.

Assignment "TIFR1 = 0xFF;" in Main.c in AVR064 project sets all eight bits in TIFR1 register to one. Project AVR064 is intended for the ATmega169 microcontroller and the corresponding specification dictates that bits 7:6 and 4:3 in Timer/Counter1 Interrupt Flag Register (TIFR1) are read-only bits. Hence, setting bits 7:6 and 4:3 to one in TIFR1 register is a violation of the read-only rule and, therefore, the assignment is a bug.

Another example is the assignment "PORTB = 0xFF;" in Wake-upTimer/main.c in AVR132. This assignment sets are eight bits in PORTB register to one. The project is intended for the ATtiny13 microcontroller. The ATtiny13 specification dictates that bits 7:6 in Port B Data Direction Register (PORTB) are read-only bits. Hence, setting bits 7:6 to one in PORTB register is a violation of the read-only rule and, therefore, the assignment is a bug.

6.1.2 Reserved-Writes

em-SPADE found one Reserved-Writes type of bug in Optiboot [15]. Optiboot is an optimized bootloader for Arduino [2], and is a quarter of the size of the default bootloader. It allows larger Arduino programs and makes Aurduino programs upload faster. Therefore, it plays an important part as Aurduino bootloader. Optiboot has two target MCUs, i.e., ATtiny84 [26] and ATmega168/V [23]. In both these specifications, bits 7:6 and 4:3 in Timer/Counter1 interrupt flag register (TIFR1) are reserved. However, bynase.c in Optiboot sets all these bits in TIFR1 register to one. This is a violation of the above mentioned reserved bit rule for ATtiny84 and ATmega168/V microcontrollers.

em-SPADE found three Reserved-Writes type of bugs in a library called libpolulu0-avr [12]. The Pololu AVR Library is a collection of support functions for programming AVR-based Pololu products or for using Pololu products with AVRs. It is designed for use with the free *avr-gcc* compiler. Most of the library can also be used together with the Arduino environment. This project targets the following microcontrollers—ATmega48pa [22], ATmega88pa [22], ATmega168pa [22], ATmega328p [22], AT-mega48/V [23], ATmega88/V [23] and ATmega168/V [23].

For all these microcontrollers, bits 7:3 in Pin Change Interrupt Flag Register (PCIFR) are reserved. However, in two files in libpolulu project i.e., PololuWheelEncoders.cpp and Orangutan-PulseIn.cpp, these bits are set to one as "PCICR = 0xFF;". This is a violation of the reserved bits rule for all seven microcontrollers. Therefore, the mentioned assignment is a bug for libpolulu-avr project. In these specifications, bits 7:6 and 4:3 in Timer/-

Table 2. Data about extracted rules from training specifications

Specification	Reserved bit rules							Read-write only rules						
	Actual	Tool	FP	FN	P (%)	R (%)	F_1	Actual	Tool	FP	FN	P (%)	R (%)	F_1
AT90S2313	15	12	0	3	100.00	80.00	0.89	18	15	0	3	100.00	83.33	0.91
AT90S8515	12	12	0	0	100.00	100.00	1.00	16	13	0	3	100.00	81.25	0.90
ATmega169 ATmega169V	12	11	1	1	91.67	91.67	0.92	46	39	0	7	100.00	84.78	0.92
ATtiny25/V ATtiny45/V ATtiny85/V	16	15	1	1	93.75	93.75	0.94	29	27	1	2	96.43	93.10	0.95
ATtiny24 ATtiny44 ATtiny84	18	18	0	0	100.00	100.00	1.00	29	25	0	4	100.00	86.21	0.93
ATmega103 ATmega103L	14	12	1	2	92.31	85.71	0.89	21	14	2	7	87.50	66.66	0.76
ATmega8 ATmega8L	10	8	1	2	88.89	80.00	0.84	29	20	0	9	100.00	68.96	0.82
ATmega128 ATmega128L	14	13	3	1	81.25	92.86	0.87	30	23	0	7	100.00	76.67	0.87
ATtiny13 ATtiny13V	17	15	0	2	100.00	88.24	0.94	23	22	0	1	100.00	95.65	0.98
ATmega48/V ATmega88/V ATmega168/V	33	28	1	5	96.55	84.85	0.90	45	44	0	1	100.00	97.78	0.99
Aggregate	**161**	**144**	**8**	**17**	**94.74**	**89.44**	**0.92**	**286**	**242**	**3**	**44**	**98.78**	**84.61**	**0.91**

Table 3. Data about extracted rules from evaluation specifications

Specification	Reserved bit rules							Read-write only rules						
	Actual	Tool	FP	FN	P (%)	R (%)	F_1	Actual	Tool	FP	FN	P (%)	R (%)	F_1
ATmega640/V ATmega1280/V ATmega1281/V ATmega2560/V ATmega2561/V	20	19	1	1	95.00	95.00	0.95	54	53	0	1	100.00	98.15	0.99
ATtiny4 ATtiny5 ATtiny9 ATtiny10	24	24	2	0	92.31	100.00	0.96	34	31	0	3	100.00	91.18	0.95
ATmega48PA ATmega88PA ATmega168PA ATmega328P	33	27	1	6	96.43	81.82	0.88	46	42	0	4	100.00	91.30	0.95
AT90S8535 AT90SL8535	17	16	0	1	100.00	94.12	0.97	23	18	0	5	100.00	78.26	0.88
ATtiny261/V ATtiny461/V ATtiny861/V	16	13	1	3	92.86	81.25	0.87	28	23	0	5	100.00	82.14	0.90
Aggregate	**110**	**99**	**5**	**11**	**95.19**	**90.00**	**0.92**	**185**	**167**	**0**	**18**	**100.00**	**90.27**	**0.95**

Counter1 interrupt flag register (TIFR1) are reserved. However, in OrangutanServos.cpp, the assignment "TIFR1 = 0xFF;" sets all the register bits to one which violates the requirement of reserved bits 7:6 and 4:3 in TIFR1 register. Therefore, this statement is also buggy.

The reported 20 bugs in Reserved-Writes and RO-Writes category span across ten AVR projects and 13 different AVR microcontrollers. It is evident that such bugs are prevalent in microcontrollers codes. Therefore, em-SPADE is useful in detecting register assignment bugs in microcontroller software.

6.2 Specification Analysis Results

Table 2 shows the data about extracted rules for the ten specifications in the training set. Similarly, Table 3 shows the data about extracted rules for the five specifications in the evaluation set. Table 2 and 3 list the same metrics for access and reserved-bits types of rules.

Reserved bit rules and read-write only rules are present separately in both tables. Each row in these tables starts with the specification name followed by data about reserved bit rules and read-write only rules. Within reserved bit rules and read-write only rules, the tables list seven entries. Within *reserved bit rules* and *read-write only rules* multicolumns, column "Actual" reports the number of manually extracted rules. Column "Tool" reports the number of correct rules that em-SPADE extracted. In the next two columns, the tables show the number of false positives (FP) and the number of false negatives (FN). The next two columns report precision (P) and recall (R) in percentage. The last column lists the F_1 score which is a collective measure of precision and recall. The range of F_1 score in the tables is from zero to one.

Table 2 shows that the overall precision is 94.74–98.78% and the overall recall is 84.61–89.44% for reserved bit rules and the read-write only rules in the training set. Table 3 shows that the overall precision is 95.19–100.00% and the overall recall is 90.00–90.27% for reserved bit rules and read-write only rules in the evaluation set. The F_1 score of reserved bit rules is 0.92 for both training and evaluation set. The F_1 score of read-write only rules is 0.91 for the training set and 0.95 for the evaluation set. The F_1 score of higher than 0.9 for training and evaluation set indicates that the rule extractor of em-SPADE is accurate, precise, and effective. In addition, it indicates that the rule extractor works accurately for specifications outside of the training set.

Table 2 and 3 show the number of false positives and false negatives for rules extracted from all the specifications. The main reason attributed to both, the false positives and false negatives, is the failure of the heuristics in some cases. In majority of the observed cases, the heuristics fail due to conversion of PDF specifications to text form by `pdftotext`. While converting, `pdftotext` sometimes produces unordered lines or misaligned text for register description layouts. This type of incorrect conversion negatively affects the rule extractor heuristics, which results in false positives and false negatives. In the future, we can use advanced conversion tools or analyze the manufacturers' source files of specifications to reduce false positives and false negatives.

7. Performance

We discuss the performance of em-SPADE in terms of overhead caused by the LLVM pass, overhead caused by the rule extractor. We also discuss the scalability of em-SPADE in with respect to large concatenated specifications.

7.1 Rule Extractor Overhead

Overhead caused by the rule extractor of em-SPADE is not important because rule extraction is a one time task for each processor specification. Once em-SPADE extracts the rules from a particular specification, the LLVM checker can use the same rules file to detect bugs in any software intended for the processor. However, we recorded the one time overhead that the rule extractor causes while extracting the rule. For all the 15 specifications in training set and evaluation set, the rule extractor produced a mean overhead of 4.52 seconds. It took 4.41 seconds of mean CPU time.

7.2 LLVM Checker Overhead

To get data about overhead produced by the LLVM pass implementation, we ran em-SPADE on four projects using rules from the 15 specifications individually. For all these 60 trials, the LLVM checker produced a mean overhead of 1.87 seconds. The checker produced a CPU overhead of 1.79 seconds.

7.3 Scalability of em-SPADE

We tested the scalability of em-SPADE with respect to large specification. To test the scalability of the rule extractor, we combined 15 specs using pdftk [18] to get one large combined PDF file of 3857 pages. The rule extractor completed the extraction in 24.25 seconds. It took 24.10 seconds of CPU time. The mean overhead caused by LLVM checker of em-SPADE in this case was 2.29 seconds. It produced a CPU overhead of 2.22 seconds.

8. Discussion

In this section, we discuss four important points about em-SPADE which provide details about the limitation, effectiveness and generality of em-SPADE. In below subsections, we discuss the following specific points:

8.1 The Need to Modify the Source Code to Get LLVM Bitcode

As mentioned earlier, we have implemented the checker as a LLVM pass. Building the pass creates a shared object which the LLVM optimizer tool can load. The pass works on the LLVM specific binary bitcode file of the source code under inspection. em-SPADE needs to compile the source code using clang to get the LLVM binary. Clang is the front end for LLVM compiler infrastructure. Clang needs 'emit-llvm' option to generate the LLVM specific bitcode output. Most of the projects em-SPADE analyzed were for *avr-gcc* [3] compiler. Avr-gcc is a port of GCC which creates binaries for AVR [14] processors. To compile such source codes using clang, we manually need to make some changes such as adding the required header files in the code, providing the path to the include directory of avr library and commenting out a few lines if required. However, in doing so we make sure that none of the changes made put em-SPADE at an advantage in any way as far as finding errors and warnings are concerned.

8.2 False Positives & False Negatives

em-SPADE did not find any false positives while analyzing the embedded software projects. However, since the rule extractor reports false positives, it is probable that em-SPADE may report false positive bugs if the register corresponding to the false rule is assigned some value in the software.

Since the rule extractor is based on heuristics, em-SPADE does not guarantee that it extracts all the rules from specifications. Low recall, specially for ATmega103/ATmega103L and ATmega8/ATmega8L, in Table [1] suggests that em-SPADE misses some actual rules. Inspecting these specifications and the tool heuristics, we found that the limitation comes from `pdftotext` [19]. Pdftotext fails to preserve the register description layout in the text format which negatively affects the heuristics. Following the current line of work such as [1], [10], [13], [31] and [35], em-SPADE seeks a balance between false positives and false negatives.

8.3 Incorrect Data in Specifications

The underlying assumption in the context of em-SPADE is that specifications contain correct rules. If there is incorrect data in the specification, then em-SPADE might report false bugs or miss bugs. If developers reference the specification to develop a project, then em-SPADE will not report any bugs because of the consistency between the project code and specification, even though the data in specification is incorrect. However, if developers write projects with the help of their prior knowledge or experience about the device, then em-SPADE will report the bug caused by the inconsistency between project code and the specification. Since specifications act as standard reference guide for developers, it is reasonable to assume their correctness.

8.4 Generality of em-SPADE to other Specifications

Since the rule extractor in em-SPADE makes no specific assumption about ATMEL AVR specifications, em-SPADE should be generalizable to other type of specifications. The heuristics used to extract rules from specifications are applicable to other families of microcontrollers. Our study of NXP LPC17xx microcontrollers gives credence to this belief. Some example rules from these microcontrollers are present in Section 4. One can observe that these rules are similar to the extracted rules from ATmega640/V [24] which have been listed earlier.

9. Conclusion and Future Work

In this paper, we propose a new approach to extract rules from processor specifications automatically and check source code against these rules to detect bugs in embedded systems automatically. We build the prototype em-SPADE, which automatically extracts 652 rules correctly from 15 specifications with precisions of 95.19–100.00% and recalls of 90.00–90.27%. em-SPADE detects 20 bugs in ten ATMEL and AVR software projects automatically, which demonstrates the effectiveness of the approach.

In the future, we plan to employ data mining and natural language processing techniques to extract more complex rules which will generalize em-SPADE and boost the usefulness of em-SPADE. We would accordingly need to enhance our static checker so that it can following type of complex rules:

1. *"To enter any of the three sleep modes, the SE bit in MCUCR must be set (one) and a SLEEP instruction must be executed."*

2. *"The SE bit must be set (one) to make the MCU enter the sleep mode when the SLEEP instruction is executed.".*

3. *"This bit must be set (one) when the WDE bit is cleared, Otherwise, the Watchdog will not be disabled."*

4. *"When changing the ACD bit, the Analog Comparator interrupt must be disabled by clearing the ACIE bit in ACSR."*

5. *" The Stack Pointer must be set to point above $60."*

The idea is to automatically classify such sentences into different categories. Once such classification of sentences is available, it would be easy to extract required information which can be turned to concrete checkable rules.

In addition, we plan to express the extracted rules in LTL formulae to help us categorize the rules. The rules of interest are correctness properties which LTL formulae can express in well defined categories. Once we have categorized the rules, we could convert the LTL formuale directly to XML format. XML is expressive enough to accommodate the extracted rules from specifications. To further improve the precision and recall of the rule extractor, we can use advanced PDF-to-text conversion tools or analyze the manufacturers' source files of PDF specifications. In addition, we plan

to port em-SPADE to gcc framework to avoid the issues of generating LLVM IR e.g., mapping of register names and corresponding macro values for generating IR. Another possible future extension is detecting assignment violations involving function calls.

Acknowledgements

This research was funded through grants provided by the Natural Sciences and Engineering Research Council of Canada.

References

[1] P. Anderson. Detecting bugs in safety-critical code. In *Dr. Dobb's Journal*, 2008.

[2] Arduino. http://www.arduino.cc/.

[3] Avr-gcc. http://gcc.gnu.org/wiki/avr-gcc.

[4] Christoph Csallner and Tao Xie. DSD-Crasher: A hybrid analysis tool for bug finding. In *ISSTA*, pages 245–254. ACM, 2006.

[5] Nikhil Dinesh, Aravind Joshi, Insup Lee, and Bonnie Webber. Extracting Formal Specifications from Natural Language Regulatory Documents. In *Proceedings of the Fifth International Workshop on Inference in Computational Semantics*, 2006.

[6] Dawson Engler, David Yu Chen, Seth Hallem, Andy Chou, and Benjamin Chelf. Bugs as Deviant Behavior: A General Approach to Inferring Errors in Systems Code. In *Proceedings of the Eighteenth ACM Symposium on Operating Systems Principles*, SOSP '01, pages 57–72, New York, NY, USA, 2001. ACM.

[7] Ansgar Fehnker, Ralf Huuck, Bastian Schlich, and Michael Tapp. Automatic Bug Detection in Microcontroller Software by Static Program Analysis. In *Proceedings of the 35th Conference on Current Trends in Theory and Practice of Computer Science*, SOFSEM '09, pages 267–278, Berlin, Heidelberg, 2009. Springer-Verlag.

[8] Seth Hallem, Benjamin Chelf, Yichen Xie, and Dawson Engler. A system and language for building system-specific, static analyses. In *Proceedings of the ACM SIGPLAN 2002 Conference on Programming Language Design and Implementation*, PLDI '02, pages 69–82, New York, NY, USA, 2002. ACM.

[9] The LLVM Compiler Infrastructure. http://llvm.org/.

[10] Holger M. Kienle, Johan Kraft, and Thomas Nolte. System-Specific Static Code Analyses: A Case Study in the Complex Embedded Systems Domain. *Software Quality Control*, 20(2):337–367, June 2012.

[11] Zhenmin Li and Yuanyuan Zhou. PR-Miner: Automatically Extracting Implicit Programming Rules and Detecting Violations in Large Software Code. In *Proceedings of the 10th European Software Engineering Conference held jointly with 13th ACM SIGSOFT International Symposium on Foundations of Software Engineering*, ESEC/FSE-13, pages 306–315, New York, NY, USA, 2005. ACM.

[12] Pololu AVR Library. http://www.pololu.com/docs/0J20.

[13] Shan Lu, Soyeon Park, Chongfeng Hu, Xiao Ma, Weihang Jiang, Zhenmin Li, Raluca A. Popa, and Yuanyuan Zhou. MUVI: Automatically Inferring Multi-variable Access Correlations and Detecting Related Semantic and Concurrency Bugs. In *Proceedings of Twenty-first ACM SIGOPS Symposium on Operating Systems Principles*, SOSP '07, pages 103–116, New York, NY, USA, 2007. ACM.

[14] Atmel AVR Microcontrollers. http://www.atmel.com/products/microcontrollers/avr/default.aspx.

[15] Optiboot. https://code.google.com/p/optiboot/.

[16] Yoann Padioleau, Lin Tan, and Yuanyuan Zhou. Listening to Programmers—Taxonomies and Characteristics of Comments in Operating System Code. In *Proceedings of the 31st International Conference on Software Engineering*, ICSE '09, pages 331–341, Washington, DC, USA, 2009. IEEE Computer Society.

[17] Rahul Pandita, Xusheng Xiao, Hao Zhong, Tao Xie, Stephen Oney, and Amit Paradkar. Inferring Method Specifications from Natural Language API Descriptions. In *Proceedings of the 2012 International Conference on Software Engineering*, ICSE 2012, pages 815–825, Piscataway, NJ, USA, 2012. IEEE Press.

[18] Pdftk. http://www.pdflabs.com/tools/pdftk-the-pdf-toolkit/.

[19] Pdftotext. http://linux.die.net/man/1/pdftotext.

[20] Boost Regex. http://www.boost.org/doc/libs/1_53_0/libs/regex/doc/html/index.html.

[21] Yannis Smaragdakis and Christoph Csallner. Combining static and dynamic reasoning for bug detection. In *Proc. 1st International Conference on Tests And Proofs (TAP)*, pages 1–16. Springer, 2007.

[22] ATMEL ATmega48PA/ATmea88PA/ATmega168PA/ATmega328P specification document.

[23] ATMEL ATmega48V/ATmea88V/ATmega168V specification document.

[24] ATMEL ATmega640/V specification document.

[25] ATMEL ATtiny4 specification document.

[26] ATMEL ATtiny84 specification document.

[27] ATMEL ATUC256L3U/ATUC128L3U specification document.

[28] NXP UM10360 specification document.

[29] Lin Tan, Ding Yuan, Gopal Krishna, and Yuanyuan Zhou. /*iComment: Bugs or Bad Comments?*/. *SIGOPS Oper. Syst. Rev.*, 41(6):145–158, October 2007.

[30] Suresh Thummalapenta and Tao Xie. Alattin: Mining alternative patterns for detecting neglected conditions. In *Proceedings of the 2009 IEEE/ACM International Conference on Automated Software Engineering*, pages 283–294. IEEE Computer Society, 2009.

[31] Ferdian Thung, Lucia, David Lo, Lingxiao Jiang, Foyzur Rahman, and Premkumar T. Devanbu. To What Extent Could We Detect Field Defects? An Empirical Study of False Negatives in Static Bug Finding Tools. In *Proceedings of the 27th IEEE/ACM International Conference on Automated Software Engineering*, ASE 2012, pages 50–59, New York, NY, USA, 2012. ACM.

[32] Qian Wu, Guangtai Liang, Qianxiang Wang, Tao Xie, and Hong Mei. Iterative mining of resource-releasing specifications. In *Automated Software Engineering (ASE), 2011 26th IEEE/ACM International Conference on*, pages 233–242. IEEE, 2011.

[33] Tao Xie, M. Acharya, S. Thummalapenta, and K. Taneja. Improving software reliability and productivity via mining program source code. In *Parallel and Distributed Processing, 2008. IPDPS 2008. IEEE International Symposium on*, pages 1–5, April 2008.

[34] Tao Xie, Jian Pei, and A.E. Hassan. Mining software engineering data. In *Software Engineering - Companion, 2007. ICSE 2007 Companion. 29th International Conference on*, pages 172–173, May 2007.

[35] Wei Zhang, Junghee Lim, Ramya Olichandran, Joel Scherpelz, Guoliang Jin, Shan Lu, and Thomas Reps. ConSeq: Detecting Concurrency Bugs Through Sequential Errors. In *Proceedings of the Sixteenth International Conference on Architectural Support for Programming Languages and Operating Systems*, ASPLOS XVI, pages 251–264, New York, NY, USA, 2011. ACM.

[36] Pin Zhou, Wei Liu, Long Fei, Shan Lu, Feng Qin, Yuanyuan Zhou, Samuel Midkiff, and Josep Torrellas. AccMon: Automatically Detecting Memory-Related Bugs via Program Counter-Based Invariants. In *Proceedings of the 37th annual IEEE/ACM International Symposium on Microarchitecture*, MICRO 37, pages 269–280, Washington, DC, USA, 2004. IEEE Computer Society.

VOBLA: A Vehicle for Optimized Basic Linear Algebra

Ulysse Beaugnon[1,2]   Alexey Kravets[1]   Sven van Haastregt[1]   Riyadh Baghdadi[2]   David Tweed[1]
Javed Absar[1]   Anton Lokhmotov[1]

[1]ARM, United Kingdom
firstname.lastname@arm.com

[2]INRIA and École Normale Supérieure, France
firstname.lastname@inria.fr

Abstract

We present VOBLA, a domain-specific language designed for programming linear algebra libraries. VOBLA is compiled to PENCIL, a domain independent intermediate language designed for efficient mapping to accelerator architectures such as GPGPUs. PENCIL is compiled to efficient, platform-specific OpenCL code using techniques based on the polyhedral model. This approach addresses both the programmer productivity and performance portability concerns associated with accelerator programming.

We demonstrate our approach by using VOBLA to implement a BLAS library. We have evaluated the performance of OpenCL code generated using our compilation flow on ARM Mali, AMD Radeon, and AMD Opteron platforms. The generated code is currently on average $1.9\times$ slower than highly hand-optimized OpenCL code, but on average $8.1\times$ faster than straightforward OpenCL code. Given that the VOBLA coding takes significantly less effort compared to hand-optimizing OpenCL code, we believe our approach leads to improved productivity and performance portability.

Categories and Subject Descriptors   D.1.3 [*Programming Techniques*]: Concurrent programming

General Terms   Algorithms, languages, performance

Keywords   linear algebra; GPU; domain-specific language; parallel; sparse matrix; BLAS

1. Introduction

Programming accelerators such as (GP)GPUs is accomplished today using rather low-level Application Programming Interfaces (APIs) such as OpenCL, which raises concerns from the programmer productivity and performance portability perspectives. *Programmer productivity* is affected because low-level APIs distract the programmer from the actual problem. *Performance portability* is affected because code optimized for a particular accelerator often underperforms on a different accelerator. We present the compilation flow depicted in Figure 1 that aims to address both concerns for the domain of linear algebra. This compilation flow includes VOBLA, a novel Domain-Specific Language (DSL) for linear algebra, which is the key focus of this paper.

LCTES '14,   June 12–13 2014, Edinburgh, United Kingdom.
Copyright is held by the owner/author(s). Publication rights licensed to ACM.
ACM 978-1-4503-2877-7/14/06...$15.00.
http://dx.doi.org/10.1145/2597809.2597818

VOBLA provides basic operations and traversals of array types while hiding implementation and layout details. This allows a programmer to describe an operation at the domain level in an intuitive way, avoiding to deal with low-level memory allocation and layout. The result is compact, readable, and maintainable code. This addresses the concern of programmer productivity.

VOBLA is compiled into PENCIL, a C99-based platform-neutral compute intermediate language [1], while retaining sufficient information for generating efficient accelerator code. PENCIL is then compiled into OpenCL code optimized for a specific accelerator using polyhedral compilation techniques that make use of the retained information. This addresses the concern of performance portability.

The main contributions of our paper can be summarized as follows:

- VOBLA: A DSL that can compactly represent linear algebra operations, separating functional semantics from implementation details such as storage layouts. Any parallelism inherent in the function is not obscured by implementation details, enabling parallel code generation.

- A Basic Linear Algebra Subprograms (BLAS) implementation in VOBLA to prove the advantages of VOBLA and of our compilation flow.

- A compilation flow that links domain-specific languages such as VOBLA to the performance-portable intermediate language PENCIL, and the compilation of PENCIL to optimized OpenCL. The VOBLA and PENCIL tools are available as open-source software [8].

The rest of this paper is organized as follows. Section 2 outlines our solution approach. Section 3 motivates our choice for a new DSL and compares other approaches to obtain linear algebra libraries. Section 4 introduces PENCIL and Section 5 introduces VOBLA. Section 6 describes how user-defined matrix layouts are described and handled in VOBLA. Section 7 describes a VOBLA implementation of a BLAS library, and Section 8 reports performance results of VOBLA BLAS routines.

2. Solution Approach

The compilation flow in Figure 1 depicts our solution to the problems of programmer productivity and performance portability. Our flow starts with the domain of linear algebra, covering a wide range of operations on vectors and matrices. While one could program linear algebra solutions directly in OpenCL, it would be cumbersome with no guarantee of good performance across different GPUs. Depending on which platform the code is written for and which platform the code is running on, the performance will vary. So even though direct OpenCL programming gives some degree of functional portability, performance portability is lacking.

The last step of our compilation flow translates PENCIL code to OpenCL code. In this step we use the Polyhedral Parallel Code

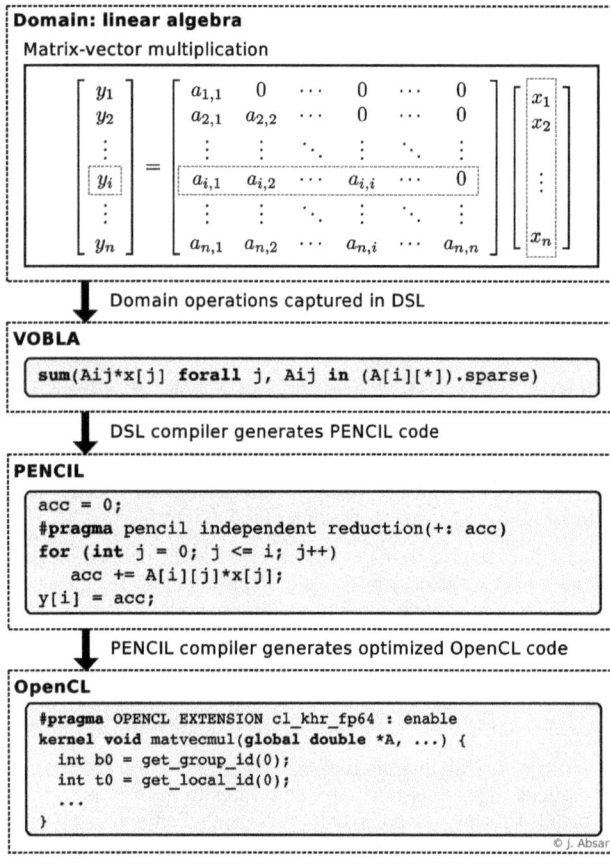

Domain: linear algebra

Matrix-vector multiplication

$$\begin{bmatrix} y_1 \\ y_2 \\ \vdots \\ y_i \\ \vdots \\ y_n \end{bmatrix} = \begin{bmatrix} a_{1,1} & 0 & \cdots & 0 & \cdots & 0 \\ a_{2,1} & a_{2,2} & \cdots & 0 & \cdots & 0 \\ \vdots & \vdots & \ddots & \vdots & \ddots & \vdots \\ a_{i,1} & a_{i,2} & \cdots & a_{i,i} & \cdots & 0 \\ \vdots & \vdots & \ddots & \vdots & \ddots & \vdots \\ a_{n,1} & a_{n,2} & \cdots & a_{n,i} & \cdots & a_{n,n} \end{bmatrix} \begin{bmatrix} x_1 \\ x_2 \\ \vdots \\ \\ \vdots \\ x_n \end{bmatrix}$$

↓ Domain operations captured in DSL

VOBLA

```
sum(Aij*x[j] forall j, Aij in (A[i][*]).sparse)
```

↓ DSL compiler generates PENCIL code

PENCIL

```
acc = 0;
#pragma pencil independent reduction(+: acc)
for (int j = 0; j <= i; j++)
    acc += A[i][j]*x[j];
y[i] = acc;
```

↓ PENCIL compiler generates optimized OpenCL code

OpenCL

```
#pragma OPENCL EXTENSION cl_khr_fp64 : enable
kernel void matvecmul(global double *A, ...) {
    int b0 = get_group_id(0);
    int t0 = get_local_id(0);
    ...
}
```

© J. Absar

Figure 1. Compilation Flow.

Generator (PPCG) [16] which is a tool that employs polyhedral compilation techniques to generate parallel GPU code. Polyhedral compilation techniques are effective in improving parallelism and locality for codes that involve array accesses inside loop nests where the access functions for the array indices are affine combinations of loop iterators. Not all codes can be optimized easily by polyhedral compilation techniques. For example, irregular codes such as tree and graph traversals are more difficult to analyze. Our compilation flow is specially suited for the domains that we call *polyhedral-friendly* such as linear algebra, scientific computation, and image processing domains.

3. Related Work

In this section, we review work on domain-specific language development and work on implementation of linear algebra libraries. In particular, we focus on linear algebra libraries for GPUs.

3.1 Domain-Specific Languages

Domain-specific languages have existed for a long time. The programmable looms and the playable piano scrolls are probably the earliest examples of domain-specific languages. Even some of the early general programming languages were essentially domain-specific such as COBOL (COmmon Business-Oriented Language) and Fortran (FORmula TRANslation) as they were designed with a specific class of applications in mind. Then there was an era of general-purpose programming languages (1970-2000) which saw many flavors – imperative, declarative, object-oriented, logic and functional – and combinations of them develop and flourish.

In the last decade, there has been a renaissance in DSLs. Van Deursen et al. [15] give a survey of the literature on domain-specific languages. They list 75 key publications, at the time of their publication in 2000, with a brief description for each. While van Deursen et al. list best practices in DSL design, Kelly et al. [7] present "what NOT to do", based on an analysis of 76 Domain-Specific Modeling (DSM) languages spanning 15 years, four continents, and around 100 language creators. They present worst practices in DSL development, in the order DSL developers would encounter them over the life of their project. Some of the interesting ones they list are:

- Poor domain understanding – Insufficiently understanding the problem domain (17%) or the solution domain (5%).
- Sacred at birth – Viewing the initial language version as unalterable (12%).
- Theoretically great – Wanting the language to be theoretically perfect, leaving implementation as secondary concerns (8%).
- Poor use case – Ignoring largely the language's usage (42%).

We do not claim that we have avoided all mentioned pitfalls. But we have tried to avoid many by coding a key domain application, that is, a BLAS library, in our VOBLA DSL.

Many papers and books classify DSLs into external and internal [3]. An *external* DSL is a domain-specific language that has a syntax different from the programming language implementing the DSL. For example, a MATLAB compiler may be written in C; the language syntax and semantics of MATLAB are quite different from C's syntax and semantics. An *internal* DSL is a language represented within the syntax of a general purpose language. Powerful functional languages like Haskell and Scala provide stylized use of the language to present the look and feel of a separate DSL to a domain programmer. Internal DSL are referred in most literature as *embedded* DSLs, but we, like Fowler et al. [3], prefer the term internal since embedded has an unintended connotation of embedded systems. Typically, an external DSL requires more work to build compared to an internal DSL. For an external DSL, one needs to define the grammar and implement the entire compiler framework.

Delite [5] uses a hybrid approach of internal and external DSLs. They use the concept of *language virtualization* to characterize a host language (Scala) that lets them implement embedded DSLs that are virtually indistinguishable from stand-alone DSL. The virtualized host language provides the front-end that the DSL can use, while letting the DSL leverage meta-programming facilities to build and optimize an IR. However, the Delite approach does not leverage the polyhedral framework and we are looking to see if Delite output could be channeled to generate PENCIL code which could then leverage our compilation framework.

The Halide DSL language and compiler [11] targets image processing algorithms. Halide uses an interval analysis technique which, as the authors put it, *"is simpler and less expressive than polyhedral model, but more general in the class of expressions it can analyze"*.

3.2 Linear Algebra Libraries

In addition to developing VOBLA, we have used VOBLA to implement BLAS. Due to its extensive use in industry and academia, many tuned implementations of BLAS have been developed in the past. Some examples of industry tuned BLAS are Apple's Accelerate framework for MAC OS X and iOS; AMD's Accelerated Parallel Processing Math Libraries (APPML); Microsoft's C++ AMP BLAS [2], leveraging C++ AMP language for GPU programming; and Intel's Math Kernel Library (MKL).

The main difference between these implementations and our implementation is that our implementation has been coded in a high-level DSL, whereas the other implementations have been coded and hand-optimized and so are not performance portable. Other notable examples of implementations of BLAS include Automatically Tuned Linear Algebra Software (ATLAS) [18], which provides APIs in C and Fortran; Kazushige Goto's BLAS [6] which is tuned for x86 and AMD64 processor architectures by means of handcrafted assembly code; and GNU Scientific Library [4], which provides generic BLAS implementation for GNU/Linux.

OoLaLa (Object Oriented anaLysis And design of numerical Linear Algebra) [10] models matrices in terms of properties and storage formats similar to VOBLA, e.g. using iterators to scan sparse matrices. Since it is Java based, the linear algebra function implementations are not as compact as the same coded in VOBLA. But the key difference is that the VOBLA compiler generates PENCIL which is passed through polyhedral optimization to generate parallel OpenCL code, while OoLaLa executes the code in a Java virtual machine, which makes it portable but not performance-oriented.

The Vienna Computing Library [14] addresses specifically the performance and portability of linear algebra codes for GPUs. It proposes device-specific OpenCL code generation at runtime, through use of common code templates and supplemented by an auto-tuning framework for portable performance. Many of the elements of ViennaCL, such as auto-tuning, can be integrated into our approach for efficient OpenCL code generation, while still taking advantages of programmer productivity of VOBLA.

uBLAS [17] is another high-level portable BLAS library. It is a C++ template class library and provides BLAS level 1, 2, 3 functionality for dense, packed, and sparse matrices.

4. PENCIL

PENCIL (Platform-Neutral Compute Intermediate Language) is an intermediate language for accelerator programming [1]. It is a C99-based language that uses a strict subset of C constructs with additional annotations provided by the programmer or a DSL compiler to capture meta information about the program. The following are three key characteristics of PENCIL.

First, the language itself does not specify which parts of the program must be executed on an accelerator device. Such decisions are intended to be made by device-specific compilers instead. Second, every PENCIL program can be considered as a semantically equivalent sequential C program, by ignoring the annotations. This helps for example in debugging of PENCIL programs. Third, all meta information in PENCIL is optional.

Any C program that uses only the allowed subset of C constructs is a valid PENCIL program with the same semantics.

4.1 Restrictions

Pointers, jumps, global non-constant variables, unions, and bitfields are forbidden in PENCIL. These restrictions make the code analyzable by polyhedral compilation techniques.

PENCIL also imposes some restrictions on the allowed C constructs:

* *A* **for***-loop must be a counted loop with a constant stride:*
```
for (int iter = 0; iter < N; iter += step) {
  //Body
}
```

* *A compound assignment cannot be part of an expression:*
```
int i = 2;
int j = i += 2; //Forbidden in PENCIL.
```

This eliminates constructs with undefined behaviour such as:

```
int j = i++ + ++i;
```

This restriction enables PENCIL compilers to apply loop transformations using polyhedral compilation techniques.

* *An array argument must be declared using the C99 variable-length array syntax and using the* **restrict***,* **const***, and* **static** *type qualifiers:*
```
void foo(int n, int m,
  float a[static const restrict n * m]) {}
```

This restriction simplifies memory access domain analysis, since the shape of the array is known at compile time.

* *Calling external C functions is forbidden.*

These restrictions make it possible to represent PENCIL in the polyhedral model, while keeping PENCIL expressive enough to represent irregular algorithms. For irregular code, whose properties cannot be directly extracted from the implementation code, PENCIL meta information should be used to provide such information.

4.2 PENCIL Meta Information

PENCIL provides various ways for a DSL compiler or programmer to provide program meta information that cannot be captured in regular program code.

Loop annotations

A PENCIL loop can be annotated with a pragma to mark high-level loop properties:

* Independent pragma: this pragma specifies that there are no dependences between iterations of a loop:
```
#pragma pencil independent
for (i = 0; i < n; i++) {
  B[T[i]] = foo(i);
}
```

* Reduction pragma: extends the independent pragma to specify that a loop does not contain loop-carried dependences except for dependences through a reduction variable:
```
#pragma pencil independent reduction(+: result)
for (i = 0; i < n; i++) {
  B[T[i]] = foo(i);
  result += A[i];
}
```

Inline memory access information

Additional memory access information can be provided for every PENCIL statement to specify memory access information that cannot be derived from the code.

```
#pragma pencil access\
  {USE(A); USE(B); DEF(A);}
for(int i = 0; i < N; i++) {
  A[B[i]] *= 2;
}
```

USE and DEF are polymorphic built-in functions and can be used to mark the usage (read access) or definition (write access) of individual locations, that is, variables or elements of an array.

Summary functions

Alternatively, additional memory access information can be provided in the form of a summary function:

```
void
summary1(int N, int A[const static restrict N],
         int B[const static restrict N]) {
  USE(A);USE(B);DEF(A);
```

```
}
#pragma pencil access {summaryl(N, A, B);}
for(int i = 0; i < N; i++) {
  A[B[i]] *= 2;
}
```

Built-in functions

PENCIL provides a set of built-in functions which capture program meta information:

- **void** ASSUME(cond): specifies that a PENCIL compiler can assume that the expression cond is true at the given program point. ASSUME proves to be useful in situation where otherwise conservative conclusion by the compiler would lead to insufficient optimization. For example, using the assume information below, a compiler can infer that there is no dependence present between the read and write to the same array.

  ```
  ASSUME(m > n)
  for (i = 0; i < n; i++) {
    D[i] = D[i+m];
  }
  ```

- **void** KILL(loc): marks its argument as dead at this point, that is, it is not used after this point.

5. VOBLA

VOBLA is designed for implementing linear algebra libraries like BLAS [12] or LAPACK [13]. Unlike some other DSLs like MATLAB, VOBLA only provides a small set of built-in functions. It focuses on providing a generic and compact representation of basic linear algebra algorithms that can be compiled into highly efficient code for GPUs, and allowing to use the accelerated code in existing software.

Compactness is achieved using template functions that are instantiated for different data types, floating-point precisions, and array storage formats. Ease of programming is achieved by using a restricted set of vector operators and iterators over arrays. Code performance is achieved by annotating the PENCIL code with information essential for generating efficient GPU code. In addition, we ensure that access patterns remain compatible with the polyhedral model such that advanced compilation techniques can be used to obtain efficient GPU code. Compatibility with existing software is enabled both by allowing generic functions that can be adapted to existing data formats and by ensuring existing libraries can be expressed in VOBLA.

5.1 General Description

VOBLA functions are defined using an imperative programming style to match the semantics of existing libraries written in C or Fortran. VOBLA provides three control flow operators: **for**, **if**, and **while**. The **if** and **while** operators have semantics similar to their counterparts in the C and PENCIL languages. The **for** operator has the following three key features.

First, the programmer can specify that iterations of a loop are independent of each other by using the **forall** keyword instead of **for**. A loop without **forall** can still be parallelized by a downstream PENCIL compiler but this requires more analysis by the downstream compiler.

Second, a **for** or **forall** loop specifies a multi-dimensional iteration space instead of a single-dimensional iteration space. A multi-dimensional iteration space is specified by a comma-separated list of single-dimensional iteration spaces. A single-dimensional iteration space specifies a scalar range or array to iterate over. A scalar

$\langle assignment \rangle$	::= $\langle expr. \rangle$ $\langle assign \rangle$ $\langle expr. \rangle$
$\langle assign \rangle$	::= '=' | '+=' | '-=' | '*=' | '/='
$\langle op \rangle$	::= '+' | '-' | '*' | '/'
$\langle len \rangle$	::= 'len' '(' $\langle expr. \rangle$ ')'
	| 'len' '(' $\langle expr. \rangle$ ',' $\langle int \rangle$ ')'
$\langle expr. \rangle$	::= $\langle expr. \rangle$ $\langle op \rangle$ $\langle expr. \rangle$
	| '-' $\langle expr. \rangle$
	| '(' $\langle expr. \rangle$ ')'
	| 'sum' '(' $\langle expr. \rangle$ 'forall' $\langle iter.\ space \rangle$ ')'
	| $\langle function\ call \rangle$
	| $\langle array\ access \rangle$
	| $\langle len \rangle$
	| $\langle builtin\ call \rangle$

Figure 2. Partial grammar of VOBLA expressions

range can be of the form $\langle lb : ub \rangle$, where lb and ub are the inclusive lower and upper bounds. Iterating over dense or sparse arrays will be explained in Section 5.4. The following loop iterates over a 3-dimensional space, with each iteration being independent of the other iterations.

```
forall(i in 0:n-1, j in 0:i-1, k in j:i-j) {
  <body>
}
```

Third, VOBLA provides a compact way to express loops over assignments. The following statement assigns i to X_i for $0 \le i < n$:

```
X[i] = i forall i in 0:n-1;
```

5.2 Expressions

A partial grammar of VOBLA expressions is shown in Figure 2. The basic operators are also available for vector and vector-scalar operands, as we will describe in Section 5.5. The **len** operator returns the size of the different dimensions of an array. The **sum** operator provides a compact notation to sum a sequence of scalars, an operation that is often needed in the linear algebra application domain. As an example of the **sum** operator, the following statement computes $\sum_{x \in X} x \cdot x$ and assigns it to norm2:

```
let norm2 = sum(x*x forall _, x in X);
```

Given that X is a one-dimensional array, the **forall** keyword is followed by a comma-separated pair of the iterator and a variable holding the values of X. We do not use the iterator value in the above computation, so we discard the iterator using the _ symbol.

VOBLA provides the **Conjugate**, **Re** (real part) and **Im** (imaginary part) built-in functions, as well as built-in functions for real and integer scalars such as sqrt that have direct OpenCL counterparts.

5.3 Template Functions

Linear algebra libraries often implement many versions of the same function that only differ in the data type, the floating-point precision, or the way arrays are stored. VOBLA addresses this characteristic using template functions. Inside template functions, only generic types are used. The VOBLA compiler generates different versions of the template function with different types. Template functions improve the ease of programming and compactness of the code by hiding details and exposing only the algorithm. Template functions also help the compiler since they allow better analysis of the function as the high-level structure of the algorithm is not obfuscated by implementation details.

Functions are either automatically instantiated when called from another VOBLA function or explicitly instantiated with an **export** statement as follows:

```
function scal(a: Value, out X: Value[]) { ... }

export scal<Complex Double>(X is Column) as zscal;

export scal<Float>(X is Reversed Column) as sscal;
```

The first export statement exports a version of scal that operates on double-precision complex numbers and treats X as a plain array. The second export statement exports a version of scal that operates on single-precision real numbers and treats X as a reversed array.

5.3.1 Scalar Types

VOBLA provides a generic scalar type **Value** that is specialized to **Real** or **Complex** during template function instantiation. The **Real** and **Complex** types are still generic, as these can be specialized into single-precision (**Float** and **Complex Float**) and double-precision (**Double** and **Complex Double**) types. The specialization of **Value** operates at the function level such that **Value** can be treated as a standard type inside a function. VOBLA provides the **Index** type for integer types.

5.4 Array Access Patterns

To hide the complexity of storage formats, provide genericity, and simplify code generation, arrays can only be accessed through access patterns. VOBLA provides three built-in access patterns:

- **Iterate**: This access pattern enumerates the elements of an array in an undefined order. For example, to compute

$$A_{i,j} \leftarrow i \cdot j \quad \forall\, 0 \leq i < m,\, 0 \leq j < n$$

for an $m \times n$ matrix A (where A can be a sparse matrix, meaning elements which are zero are not stored) using the Iterate access pattern, one writes the following VOBLA code:

```
Aij = i * j forall i, j, Aij in A;
```

The Iterate access pattern is useful for repeating an operation on each element of an array. The Iterate access pattern should be used when it is impossible to access a specific element efficiently from its indices, which is the case for most sparse matrix formats.

- **Sparse Iterate**: This access pattern operates similar to Iterate, but skips the elements of the array that are known to be zero at compile time. For example, for a lower-triangular matrix, we know at compile time which elements are zero. Some zero elements might still be enumerated if their locations are not known at compile time. Thus, this access pattern can only be used if the zero elements have no effect on the result. The following VOBLA code computes $\sum x \cdot x$ for all elements $x \in X$ known to be non-zero at compile-time:

```
let norm2 = 0;
norm2 += Xi * Xi for _, Xi in X.sparse;
```

- **Indexed**: This access pattern allows accessing an element from its indices. The Indexed access pattern is more expressive than the Iterate and Sparse Iterate access patterns, but it cannot be implemented for every storage format. For example, it is impossible to efficiently access an element given its coordinates for most of the sparse matrix formats. This access pattern is necessary when multiple arrays are involved, as it is impossible to iterate over multiple arrays at once. The following VOBLA code accesses a 1-dimensional array X using the Sparse Iterate

access pattern, which yields the index i. This index is then used to access an array y using the Indexed access pattern.

```
let dot = 0;
// y is accessed using Indexed access
dot += xi * y[i] forall i, xi in X.sparse;
```

The Sparse Iterate access pattern can be implemented using the Iterate access pattern by not skipping any zero elements. The Iterate access pattern can be implemented using the Indexed access pattern by accessing all the elements one-by-one. Thus, any array implementing Iterate also implements Sparse Iterate and any array implementing Indexed implements both Iterate and Sparse Iterate.

We believe these three access patterns are expressive enough to cover a wide range of storage formats in linear algebra. This assumption has been confirmed by the implementation of BLAS described in Section 7. Custom access patterns can be defined as well, for example to iterate over the rows of a matrix instead of iterating over the scalar elements. Defining custom access patterns is discussed in Section 6. A current limitation of VOBLA is that custom access patterns cannot be used with built-in operators.

5.5 Array Operators

VOBLA allows a compact representation of basic array operations such as element-wise scaling. They make use of the different access patterns described in Section 5.4. The VOBLA compiler translates array operators into equivalent scalar code using iterators. The scalarized code iterates over one array and uses the Indexed access pattern on the other array. Therefore, one of the operands must implement the Indexed access pattern.

As an example, consider the following VOBLA code that computes

$$X_i \leftarrow X_i + 2Y_i, \quad \forall\, 0 \leq i < n,$$

where n equals the number of elements in X and Y:

```
X += 2*Y;
```

The assignment to X is scalarized by accessing X using the Indexed access pattern and accessing Y using the Sparse Iterate access pattern. This yields the following equivalent VOBLA code:

```
X[i] += 2*Yi forall i, Yi in Y.sparse;
```

Operations on two arrays require the arrays to have the same dimensionality and size. When possible, our VOBLA compiler uses the Sparse Iterate access patterns for array operations such that zero-elements are skipped. When the compiler has to choose on which array to iterate, it currently picks an arbitrary one. As a future optimization, the compiler could choose the array with the least number of non-zero elements to apply Sparse Iterate to.

5.6 Array Views

Certain linear algebra operations such as matrix transposition can be performed by only changing the way an array is accessed, avoiding expensive copy operations. Since the algorithm is decoupled from the way the array is stored in VOBLA, we leverage this for the following operations:

- **Conjugate**, **Re** (real part), and **Im** (imaginary part) for arrays.

- **Transpose**, **Diagonal**, and **AntiDiagonal** for dense matrices.

- Extraction of array substructures for dense arrays, such as:

```
X[2:4] // Take elements of X between 2 and 4
A[*][2] // Take the third column of A
```

For example, the following transposition of matrix A in VOBLA

```
let a = Transpose(A)[i][j];
```

is translated into the following PENCIL code:

```
float a = A[j][i];
```

The operations listed above can also be applied to function arguments. Instead of applying the operation before calling the function, a new version of the called function is generated that accesses the data according to the operation. This helps reducing the number of unnecessary array copy operations at the expense of a larger code size. Arrays are only copied when it is specified explicitly using the assignment operator:

```
B = Transpose(A);      // A is copied
foo(Transpose(A));     // A is not copied
```

6. User Defined Access Patterns

By default, VOBLA provides the Iterate, Sparse Iterate, and Indexed access patterns defined in Section 5.4. VOBLA allows defining new access patterns and storage formats to cope with user defined access patterns and storage layouts. We use four different objects to define new access patterns. They are defined below and explained in detail in the remainder of this section.

- **Interface**: An Interface object defines the type representing an array when declaring a function. It specifies which access pattern is implemented by the array.

- **Storage**: A Storage object contains the storage layout for an array. Storage objects do not contain information on how to access data.

- **Layout**: A Layout object describes how to access data for a given storage format. A Layout object implements an interface.

- **View**: A View object describes layouts in terms of existing ones using inheritance, enabling reuse of layout definitions.

6.1 Interfaces

Interface objects allow a VOBLA programmer to declare arrays in function headers. They represent the different ways an array can be used. Interface objects only exist to implement the type system and do not contain any information on how the array data is accessed. During compilation, each array will have a layout implementing its interface specifying how to access the array data.

Interface objects can be considered as an object-oriented feature. They declare the access methods that the Interface provides. Only the prototypes of Interface methods are defined in an Interface object; the method implementations are defined in Layout objects. Interface objects can inherit from other Interface objects.

6.1.1 Interface Methods

To access an array, a method defined by an Interface object is called. Unlike real object-oriented languages, the methods of an Interface are only used to access the array data. They are not meant to perform computations and cannot have side effects. The built-in access patterns defined in Section 5.4 are also defined using Interface objects. Array accesses using a particular interface are made through the methods described in Table 1.

Access Pattern	Method	Interface
Iterate	iterate	Iterable
Sparse Iterate	sparse	SparseIterable
Indexed	[<**Index**>]	Accessible

Table 1. Built-in access patterns, methods, and interfaces.

Methods can return a reference to an element of the array. This is the only way to modify an array. References are denoted by & and can only be used in method return types. The following VOBLA code declares a method prototype named access for accessing a 1-dimensional array:

```
access(i: Index): &Value;
```

Methods can return a range of elements. In such a case, the method can only be used as an iterator in a **for** or **forall**. Ranges may contain references such that all elements in the range can be modified. The following VOBLA code declares a method prototype named iterate that returns a range of references:

```
iterate(): range<Index, &Value>;
```

Methods can also return an Interface object representing a different view of the same data. No data is copied in such a case, only the way the data is accessed is changed. The following VOBLA code declares a method prototype named re that returns the Accessible interface specialized for **Real** types:

```
re(): Accessible<Real>[];
```

6.1.2 Interface Specialization

Interfaces are not used directly for array type declarations. They are first optionally specialized by a scalar type and an optional read-only qualifier. The scalar specialization replaces **Value** by a type such as **Complex** or **Real**, or retains **Value**. The read-only qualifier **in** replaces any reference types by their equivalent non-reference types and makes returned views read-only. The following function argument declaration declares argument A as a read-only argument inheriting the SparseIterable interface on the generic **Value** type:

```
in A: SparseIterable<Value>[m][n]
```

This means **Value** can be specialized when exporting the declared function.

The read-only qualifier enables optimizations in the downstream PENCIL compilation process by flagging PENCIL arrays as **const**. A non-read-only interface can always be casted to a read-only interface. Read-only interfaces can also be casted to the same interface with a weaker scalar type specialization. For example, a constant array of **Real** can be casted to a constant array of **Complex** with the same interface.

6.1.3 Interface Inheritance

When defining a new interface, one or more interfaces can be specified as a base interface. The defined interface then inherits the access patterns of the base interfaces. The following VOBLA code defines a new interface for triangular matrices. The triangle method returns the non-zero triangular part of the matrix. The diagonal method returns the diagonal of the matrix.

```
interface TriangularMatrix[][]
        implements SparseArray<Value>[][] {

  triangle(): Triangle<Value>[][];
  diagonal(): Array<Value>[];
}
```

Every type implementing this interface must implement the methods of the base interface SparseArray, and the triangle and diagonal methods specified in this TriangularMatrix interface.

Types implementing the derived interfaces also implement all base interfaces. Thus, any object which type implements the TriangularMatrix interface can be passed to a function expecting a SparseArray<Value> interface.

Inherited interfaces must be specialized. This restricts the derived interface to only implement the specific version of the base interface. For example, the interface for complex sparse matrices can be defined as follows:

```
interface ComplexSparse[][]
            implements SparseArray<Complex>[][] {
}
```

6.2 Storages

The data storage layout of an array is described using a storage object. A storage object does not describe how the data is accessed and the data in the same storage may be accessed in different ways. Thus, a storage object represents the part of an array that is independent of the way an array is accessed. A storage object contains array fields that hold the array elements, and scalar fields that hold data such as the sizes of the array fields. The VOBLA code below defines a storage object for a sparse matrix in the coordinate list (COO) sparse format.

```
storage CooStorage {
  nRows: Index;
  nCols: Index;
  nNonZeros: Index;
  rowIdx: Index[nNonZeros];
  colIdx: Index[nNonZeros];
  data: Value[nNonZeros];
}
```

The COO format stores a matrix as a list of tuples (row index, column index, value). The nRows and nRows fields store the matrix dimensions and the nNonZeros field stores the number of stored tuples. The rowIdx and colIdx fields contain the row and column indices of the actual matrix elements in the data field.

6.3 Layouts

A layout object defines how the fields of a storage are accessed. A layout definition contains the following information:

- The name of a storage object. The fields of the storage can be accessed inside the implementation of layout's methods. Different layouts can use the same storage object.

- A list of interfaces that are implemented by the layout.

- Scalar read-only parameters specific to a particular access pattern. An access pattern cannot be modified and always accesses data in the same way. Parameters can be used to define variations of a given access pattern that iterate over a different number of rows for example.

- An implementation for each of the methods defined in the interface(s).

The following layout defines an access pattern for the COO format:

```
layout Coo: CooStorage implements
            SparseIterable<Value>[][] {
  parameter:
  interface:
    getLen1(): Index { return nRows; }
    getLen2(): Index { return nCols; }

    sparseIterate(): range<Index, Index, &Value> {
      yield rowIdx[k], colIdx[k], data[k]
            forall k in 0:nNonZeros;
    }
}
```

This Coo layout refers to the CooStorage format defined in Section 6.2 and implements the builtin SparseIterable interface. The layout above defines three methods: two getLen methods that return the dimensions of the matrix and a sparseIterate method that returns the row and column indices and matrix data.

6.3.1 Methods

Layout methods returning scalars or interfaces look similar to regular VOBLA functions. Methods must contain exactly one return statement at the end of the body in the current implementation of our VOBLA compiler.

Methods of a layout can be called in the method itself via the **this** keyword. For example, the iterate method below invokes the access method defined elsewhere in the layout to obtain the element at position i.

```
iterate(): range<Index, &Value> {
  yield i, this.access(i) forall i in 0:n-1;
}
```

Inside layout methods, the **yield** keyword is available. Each execution of **yield** causes the next tuple of the iteration to be returned.

VOBLA enforces typing rules on methods to ensure they have no side effects. All variables except local variables in a method are read-only. Inside a **return** or **yield** statement, the arrays defined in the storage become writable such that references can be returned. References to local variables cannot be returned.

6.4 Views

Layouts allow user-defined types but have two shortcomings. First, the user has to define all access patterns for each layout, while some could be reused from other layouts. For example, the iterate method of an Iterable interface can be implemented from the [<int>] and **len** methods of an Accessible interface. Second, some layouts can be implemented by calling another layout's method in a different way. For example, a layout representing a transposed matrix can be implemented from the layout of the non-transposed matrix by swapping row and column indices.

VOBLA provides views to solve both issues. A view acts as a wrapper around a layout. Instead of being based on a storage, a view is based on an interface called the *base interface*. Methods from the base interface can be accessed using the keyword **base**. The view can be used with any layout implementing the base interface to create a new layout. The following VOBLA code defines a view named TransposedMat that has base interface Accessible. The access method is implemented by calling the access method from the base interface.

```
view TransposedMat: Accessible<Value>[][]
  implements Accessible<Value>[][] {

  access(i: Index, j: Index): &Value {
    return base.access(j, i);
  }
}
```

This view can then be used in an export statement, to for example obtain a function that accesses a transposed sparse matrix in the COO format:

```
export gemm<Float>(A is TransposedMat(COO), ...
```

6.5 VOBLA Compilation

We have implemented a VOBLA compiler that generates PENCIL code. A key challenge for the VOBLA compiler is that PENCIL does not support pointers or references. To handle references created in interface methods, we inline the interface methods and replace reference variables by the actual memory access they represent. Iterators are compiled in a similar fashion. For example, an iterate method defined as follows:

```
iterate(): range<Index, &Value> {
  yield i, data[i] forall i in 0:n-1;
}
```

and used in a VOBLA function as follows:

```
x = i*i forall i, x in X;
```

is translated into the following PENCIL code:

```
#pragma pencil independent
for(int i=0; i<n; i++) {
  data[i] = i*i;
}
```

Since all method calls and iterators are inlined, there is no performance penalty caused by virtual method dispatch overhead. This requires a different version of the function to be generated for each storage format, which allows the PENCIL compiler to separately optimize each function. Although this increases the overall code size, we believe the ability to separately optimize each functions outweighs the code size increase. To enable more optimizations, the VOBLA compiler keeps track of aliasing between function arguments and creates a different version of a function when two arguments are the same.

7. BLAS Library

We have implemented a complete BLAS (Basic Linear Algebra Subprograms) library [9, 12] to demonstrate the practical use of VOBLA. A BLAS library provides basic operations on vectors and matrices such as vector scaling (scal), triangular matrix equation solving (trsv), and general matrix-matrix multiplication (gemm). BLAS functions are commonly used as building blocks for more complex algorithms (*e.g.* LAPACK [13]). BLAS functions are grouped into three levels: level 1 provides vector-vector operations, level 2 provides matrix-vector operations, and level 3 provides matrix-matrix operations. In this section, we show how VOBLA deals with the following two properties of the BLAS interface:

- **Storage layout**: The level 2 and 3 BLAS functions support dense matrix storage layouts and a predefined set of compressed matrix storage layouts such as triangular or symmetric layouts.

- **Substructures**: The BLAS interface allows efficient access to matrix substructures such as rows, diagonals, or submatrices. This is accomplished by providing an increment parameter that selects on which matrix elements a BLAS function iterates.

7.1 Storage Layout

Besides regular dense matrices, the BLAS interface supports a predefined set of compressed matrix storage layouts. For example, the BLAS interface provides symmetric matrix multiplication (symm) and hermitian matrix multiplication (hemm). These variants differ from gemm only in the storage layout of the first input matrix. The matrix multiplication algorithm is identical for each variant. A user first defines these symmetric and hermitian storage layouts in VOBLA, as detailed in Section 6, and then exports the symm and hemm functions from the gemm definition.

To demonstrate the benefits of separating data type, access pattern, and storage layout information from the algorithm, we consider the following generic description of matrix multiplication:

```
function gemm(alpha: Value,
           in A: SparseIterable<Value>[m][k],
           in B: Value[k][n],
           beta: Value,
           out C: Value[m][n]) {
  Cij *= beta forall _, _, Cij in C.sparse;
  C[i][j] += alpha*Ail*B[l][j]
           for i, l, Ail in A.sparse, j in 0:n-1;
}
```

We then use 50 export statements to obtain all BLAS variants for gemm, symm, and hemm from this generic description.

7.2 Substructures

The standard BLAS interface allows efficient access to substructures (such as a row, column, diagonal, or sub-matrix) of a matrix across functions without the need to duplicate matrix elements. The Fortran reference implementation supports such substructures by relying on all matrix elements being stored contiguously in memory as a one-dimensional array. In a such layout, the i-th element of a row, column, diagonal, or sub-matrix is stored at location $offset + i \cdot incr$ of the matrix storage. Here, *offset* is the offset of the first element of the substructure from the beginning of the matrix, and *incr* selects the elements corresponding to the substructure. For example, setting *offset* = 2 and *incr* = m yields all elements of the second column of an $m \times n$ matrix stored in row-major order. In the reference implementation, *offset* is added to the pointer representing the matrix and *incr* is the increment of a loop iterating over the desired substructure.

Since PENCIL does not support pointers, passing an arbitrary subrange of an array to a function without copying the array data is not trivial. The VOBLA compiler solves this by passing the offset explicitly as an argument, and supporting only row, column, (anti)diagonal, and rectangular submatrix substructures. This solution avoids pointers and array copying, at the expense of not supporting every possible matrix substructure. All information needed to access a substructure is stored in a PENCIL structure that is passed alongside every matrix argument. The PENCIL structure is invisible at the VOBLA level and is generated automatically when a substructure is used in VOBLA.

8. Results

To demonstrate the practical use of VOBLA, we have realized a tool flow to compile our VOBLA BLAS to OpenCL code. We use this tool flow to assess the performance of our BLAS implementation.

8.1 Performance of VOBLA-generated BLAS OpenCL code

We have compiled the VOBLA code for selected BLAS functions into PENCIL code using our VOBLA compiler. We have compiled this PENCIL code into OpenCL code using the PPCG [16] OpenCL backend. A summary of the used BLAS functions and the input data sizes are given in Table 2. All of these BLAS matrix functions operate on dense matrices.

Figure 3 shows the normalized execution time for seven commonly used BLAS functions, on an Arndale board containing an ARM Mali-T604 GPU running at 533 MHz. We compare the VOBLA-default and VOBLA-autotuned implementations to a naive implementation and a hand-optimized implementation. The naive implementations compute one vector or matrix element per work-item and do not incorporate any hand-coded optimizations such as tiling, vectorization, or unrolling. The hand-optimized implementations leverage a range of techniques such as loop tiling, loop fission, and vectorization. Obtaining a hand-optimized implementation requires the programmer to iterate over the source code, gradually improving its execution time while maintaining functional correctness of the code. This is a non-trivial task, and getting good performance requires a thorough understanding of the algorithm, its memory access patterns, and the accelerator platform.

We compare single-precision (32-bit) and double-precision (64-bit) real and complex floating-point implementations for each of the seven BLAS functions. Obtaining the VOBLA-default and VOBLA-autotuned implementations for both data types requires negligible effort, as the programmer only needs to write the desired data type in the **export** statement. In contrast, obtaining a hand-optimized implementation for a different data type requires considerable effort. We have found that the optimal implementation for one data

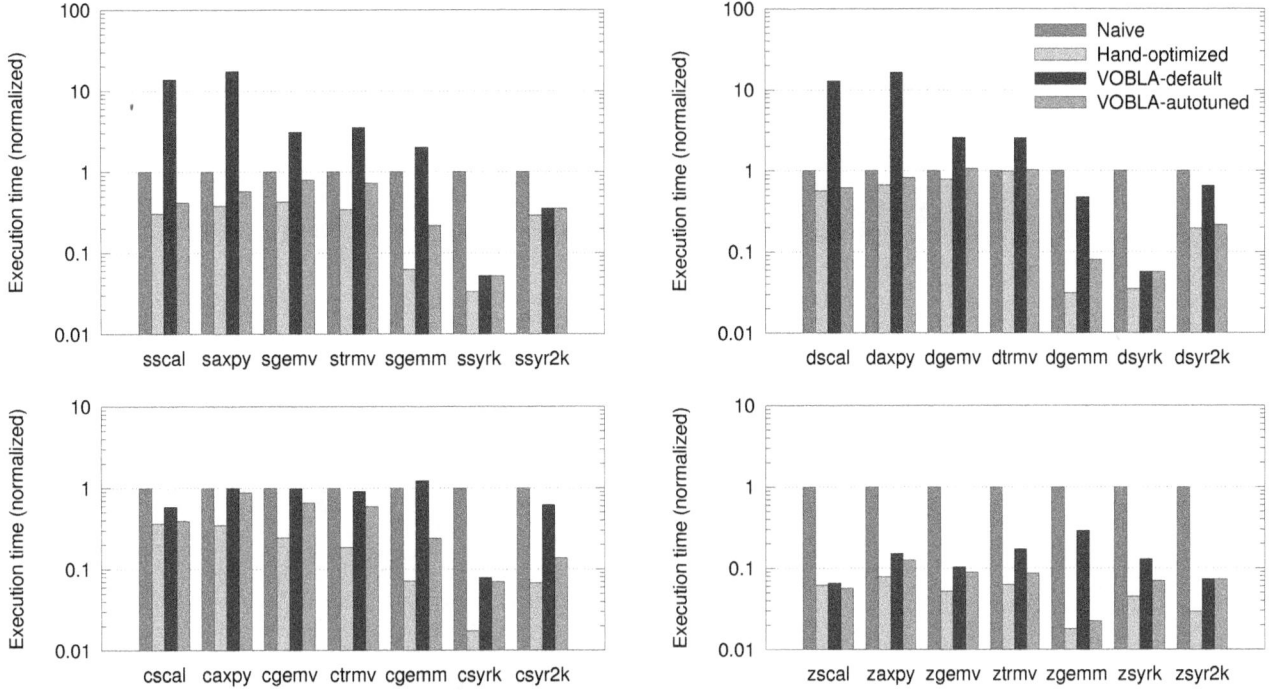

Figure 3. Execution times on an ARM Mali GPU for single-precision (top left), double-precision (top right), complex single-precision (bottom left), and complex double-precision (bottom right) BLAS primitives, normalized to a naive implementation. The VOBLA-default implementations are obtained from PPCG with default parameter values. The VOBLA-autotuned implementations are obtained from PPCG with tuned parameter values found using automated exploration.

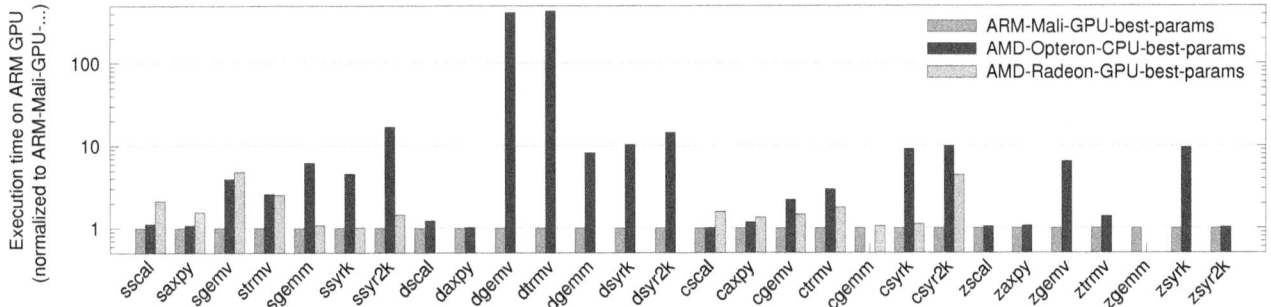

Figure 4. The performance portability problem: the optimal PPCG-generated OpenCL for a particular platform (*e.g.* AMD Radeon GPU or AMD Opteron CPU) is not optimal for another platform (*e.g.* ARM Mali GPU). Results for the double-precision functions (prefixed with d and z) on the AMD Radeon GPU are missing due to lack of double-precision floating point support on that device.

type is not the optimal implementation for a different data type, as for example the different data size affects cache behaviour considerably. This requires the programmer to iterate over the source code again to obtain an optimized implementation for the new data type.

Currently, the OpenCL backend of PPCG is still under development. In particular, PPCG does not take characteristics of our chosen GPU into account and does not perform vectorization or reduction optimizations. Despite this, we are already able to obtain results competitive with hand-optimized implementations. The hand-optimized implementations currently outperform any of the PPCG-generated implementations on average by a factor of $1.9\times$, with an extremal case of $4\times$ (csyrk). But the programmer effort needed for the hand-optimized implementations is considerably larger than

the effort needed for the VOBLA implementations. Moreover, hand-optimized implementations require skills which are not necessarily available to a linear algebra domain expert.

8.2 Performance Portability

Figure 4 illustrates the performance portability problem across three different platforms: an ARM Mali-T604 GPU, an AMD Radeon HD 5670 GPU, and an AMD Opteron 12-core 6164HE CPU. For each BLAS function on each platform, we determine PPCG parameters that result in the lowest execution time. We then generate OpenCL implementations using PPCG with these parameters, and run the OpenCL implementations on a single platform. Figure 4 shows that the best parameters for a particular platform do not give the best performance on another platform. Moreover, the

BLAS Function	Data size	Description
*scal (level 1)	10485760	Vector scale
*axpy (level 1)	10485760	Vector scale and add
*gemv (level 2)	1024×1024	Matrix-vector multiply
*trmv (level 2)	1024×1024	Triangular mat-vec mult.
*gemm (level 3)	1024×1024	Matrix-matrix multiply
*syrk (level 3)	1024×1024	Symmetric rank-1 update
*syr2k (level 3)	1024×1024	Symmetric rank-2 update

Table 2. BLAS Function descriptions.

	Our work	Ref. [12]	uBLAS [17]
Language	VOBLA	Fortran	C++
Passes full test suite	Yes	Yes	Yes[1]
Function count	26	150	24
Total line count	1714	16086	45908
∟ BLAS functionality	248	16086	158
∟ Data structures	434	-	45750
∟ Export statements	1032	-	-

Table 3. Source code statistics for BLAS implementations.

best cgemm and zgemm implementations for the AMD CPU could not be run on the ARM GPU due to tighter resource constraints.

8.3 Productivity

Table 3 shows a comparison of source code statistics for our VOBLA BLAS implementation and two reference implementations [12]. All implementations provide the three levels of the BLAS interface. We break down the line count for the VOBLA implementation into lines describing the core functionality of BLAS functions; lines defining (reusable) data structures such as triangular matrices; and lines containing export statements such that all functions constituting the BLAS interface are generated from the 26 generic VOBLA functions. The VOBLA implementation requires about nine times less lines than the Fortran reference implementation. This is mainly because of the higher level of VOBLA compared to Fortran, and because of the use of generic functions in VOBLA. The line count comparison is even more favourable for VOBLA when omitting the export statements needed to obtain a library conforming to the legacy Fortran BLAS interface.

We also compare the VOBLA implementation to uBLAS, which is a more modern object-oriented BLAS implementation based on C++ templates [17]. Like VOBLA, uBLAS hides the storage format specific operations under the hood, keeping the BLAS functionality code small and clean. However, the data structure definitions require about one hundred times more lines of code than the VOBLA data structure definitions. Although code conciseness is not a guarantee for improved programmer productivity, we believe the significant differences do strengthen our productivity claim.

9. Conclusions

In this paper, we described our work towards solving the *programmer productivity* and *performance portability* concerns for GPUs. We presented VOBLA, a DSL for efficient linear algebra programming. A VOBLA compiler compiles VOBLA programs into PENCIL code. PENCIL has special constructs to carry meta-data that help

the polyhedral code generator to generate efficient OpenCL code. We implemented the compilation flow and used it to code the entire BLAS libary in VOBLA. The results showed the VOBLA based BLAS implementation performs $8.1\times$ better than straightforward OpenCL code, although it is still $1.9\times$ slower than hand-optimized OpenCL code for a particular GPU.

Acknowledgments

This work was partly supported by the EU FP7 STREP project CARP (project number 287767).

References

[1] R. Baghdadi, A. Cohen, S. Guelton, S. Verdoolaege, J. Inoue, and T. Grosser. PENCIL: Towards a Platform-Neutral Compute Intermediate Language for DSLs. *Workshop on Domain Specific Languages, WOLFHPC'12*, 2012.

[2] A. Faucher, C. Fu, D. Callahan, K. Spagnoli, and P. Nagpal. C++ AMP BLAS. http://ampblas.codeplex.com/, 2013.

[3] M. Fowler and R. Parsons. *Domain-Specific Languages*. Addison Wesley, 2011.

[4] GNU Project. GSL: GNU Scientific Library. http://www.gnu.org/software/gsl/, 1996-2013.

[5] H. Joong, K. J. Brown, A. K. Sujeeth, and H. Chafi. Implementing Domain-Specific Languages for Heterogeneous Parallel Computing. *IEEE Micro*, 31:42–53, October 2011.

[6] K. Goto. GotoBLAS: Texas Advanced Computing Center Software. http://www.tacc.utexas.edu/tacc-software/gotoblas2, 2013.

[7] S. Kelly and R. Pohjonen. Worst Practices for Domain-Specific Modelling. *Software, IEEE*, 26(4):22–29, Aug. 2009.

[8] A. Kravets, S. van Haastregt, U. Beaugnon, D. Tweed, J. Absar, and A. Lokhmotov. VOBLA and PENCIL tools. https://github.com/carpproject, 2014.

[9] C. Lawson, R. Hanson, D. Kincaid, and F. Krogh. Basic Linear Algebra Subprograms for Fortran Usage. *ACM Trans. Math. Softw.*, 5(3):308–323, September 1979.

[10] M. Luján, T. L. Freeman, and J. R. Gurd. OoLALA: an Object Oriented Analysis and Design of Numerical Linear Algebra. In *Proceedings of the conference on Object-oriented programming, systems, languages, and applications*, OOPSLA '00, pages 229–252, 2000.

[11] J. Ragan-Kelley, C. Barnes, A. Adams, S. Paris, F. Durand, and S. Amarasinghe. Halide: a Language and Compiler for Optimizing Parallelism, Locality, and Recomputation in Image Processing Pipelines. In *Proceedings of the conference on Programming Language Design and Implementation*, PLDI '13, pages 519–530, 2013.

[12] The Netlib. BLAS – Basic Linear Algebra Subprograms. http://www.netlib.org/blas/, 1979.

[13] The Netlib. LAPACK – Linear Algebra Package. http://www.netlib.org/lapack/, 1992.

[14] P. Tillet, K. Rupp, and S. Selberherr. An Automatic OpenCL Compute Kernel Generator for Basic Linear Algebra Operations. In *Proceedings of the Symposium on High Performance Computing*, HPC '12, pages 4:1–4:2. Society for Computer Simulation International, 2012.

[15] A. van Deursen, P. Klint, and J. Visser. Domain-Specific Languages: an Annotated Bibliography. *SIGPLAN Not.*, 35(6):26–36, June 2000.

[16] S. Verdoolaege, J. Carlos Juega, A. Cohen, J. Ignacio Gómez, C. Tenllado, and F. Catthoor. Polyhedral Parallel Code Generation for CUDA. *ACM Trans. Archit. Code Optim.*, 9(4):54:1–54:23, Jan. 2013.

[17] J. Walter and M. Koch. uBLAS: Basic Linear Algebra Library. http://www.boost.org/doc/libs/1_54_0/libs/numeric/ublas/doc/index.htm, 2013.

[18] R. C. Whaley, A. Petitet, and J. J. Dongarra. Automated Empirical Optimization of Software and the ATLAS Project. *Parallel Computing*, 27:2001, 2000.

---

[1] Passes internal Boost testsuite for uBLAS, instead of Fortran test suite.

A Framework to Schedule Parametric Dataflow Applications on Many-Core Platforms

Vagelis Bebelis[†,‡]   Pascal Fradet [†]   Alain Girault [†]

INRIA [†]
Univ. Grenoble Alpes, F-38000, Grenoble, France
STMicroelectronics [‡]
first.last@inria.fr

Abstract

Dataflow models, such as SDF, have been effectively used to program streaming applications while ensuring their liveness and boundedness. Yet, industrials are struggling to design the next generation of high definition video applications using these models. Such applications demand new features such as parameters to express dynamic input/output rate and topology modifications. Their implementation on modern many-core platforms is a major challenge.

We tackle these problems by proposing a generic and flexible framework to schedule streaming applications designed in a parametric dataflow model of computation. We generate parallel as soon as possible (ASAP) schedules targeted to the new STHORM many-core platform of STMicroelectronics. Furthermore, these schedules can be customized using user-defined ordering and resource constraints.

The parametric dataflow graph is associated with generic or user-defined specific constraints aimed at minimizing timing, buffer sizes, power consumption, or other criteria. The scheduling algorithm executes with minimal overhead and can be adapted to different scheduling policies just by adding some constraints. The safety of both the dataflow graph and constraints can be checked statically and all schedules are guaranteed to be bounded and deadlock free. We illustrate the scheduling capabilities of our approach using a real world application: the VC-1 video decoder for high definition video streaming.

Categories and Subject Descriptors   D.3.2 [*Language Classifications*]: Data-flow languages; D.4.1 [*Process Management*]: Scheduling; D.2.4 [*Software/Program Verification*]: Formal methods

General Terms   Algorithms, Languages, Verification

Keywords   Dataflow, Manycore, Scheduling, Liveness, Boundedness

LCTES '14,   June 12–13, 2014, Edinburgh, UK.
Copyright is held by the owner/author(s). Publication rights licensed to ACM.
ACM 978-1-4503-2877-7 /14/06... $15.00.
http://dx.doi.org/10.1145/2597809.2597819

1. Introduction

Dataflow models of computation, such as SDF [13], provide analyses to guarantee the boundedness and liveness of an application. However, they generally lack the expressivity needed by modern streaming applications such as next generation video codecs. *Parametric* dataflow models such as PSDF [6], VRDF [22], SADF [21], SPDF [8] or BPDF [3] allow more dynamicity while preserving liveness and boundedness guarantees.

The target for streaming applications is often modern embedded platforms which typically use many-core architectures with network-on-chip interconnection. Yet, the parallel implementation of parametric dataflow applications on such platforms remains a major challenge.

In this paper, we propose a framework for effectively producing parallel schedules for the next generation of streaming applications. We consider Boolean Parametric Data Flow (BPDF) [3] model of computation and the STHORM (formerly, P2012) [4] many-core platform by STMicroelectronics. BPDF is a very expressive parametric dataflow model that combines integer and boolean parameters allowing dynamic data rates and graph topology changes while providing static guarantees. STHORM is a leading-edge, cluster-based, many-core architecture, designed to support the future high definition video and augmented reality embedded applications.

We focus on the parallel scheduling of applications expressed as BPDF graphs. A BPDF graph consists of actors linked by dataflow edges (FIFOs), each actor producing a parametric number of tokens. Each edge may also have a boolean guard that enables or disables the edge at runtime. We consider *coarse-grain* BPDF applications, where actors are large blocks of C code, typically video codec filters. High-definition video codecs require very fast execution times, for this reason each actor is implemented as a hardware processing element or executes as software on a dedicated core.

We rely on a *slotted* scheduling model compatible with STHORM, such that, in each slot, several actors are scheduled to execute. Since each actor is a separate processing element, their execution can proceed concurrently. When all fired actors have terminated, new actors can then be scheduled in the next slot. This scheduling scheme is general enough and it can be used by other many-core platforms. This slotted scheduling contrasts with other existing multi-processor scheduling methods where the execution time of each actor plays a central role to determine the shortest schedule.

In applications such as video decoding, the complexity of filters depends on data and precise timing information cannot be known statically. In such a context, an ASAP execution of the available tasks is the best strategy[20]. When precise timing information is available, slotted scheduling should strive to minimize slack between slots. Techniques such as retiming [15] can be used for that purpose.

Our scheduling procedure starts by deriving from the graph a set of graph constraints representing data dependencies. They express the partial ordering of the firings of the actors.

Additional ordering constraints can be added to tune the scheduling policy. For instance, constraints can be used to enforce properties inherent to the execution platform or optimize various criteria, such as buffer size or power consumption. Furthermore, it can be checked that these constraints preserve liveness.

Along with ordering constraints, our framework also supports resource constraints. These constraints filter the fireable actors at each slot to accommodate physical mapping on the platform or to take into account timing and power consumption. Resource constraints are expressed as a set of rules that regulate the parallel execution of actors.

In many cases, constraints can be statically simplified and scheduling entails only a minimal dynamic overhead. The scheduling algorithm finds, at each slot, the set of actors whose constraints are satisfied and can thus be fired. This amounts to an ASAP quasi-static slotted schedule. Static analyses guarantee that it exists and that it is bounded. The scheduler is executed in parallel with the previously issued actors so the overhead remains minimal.

Constraints make the approach *flexible* since the same scheduling algorithm can take into account a new platform or new optimization criteria just by modifying the set of constraints. Our approach focuses on flexibility, enabling easy manipulation and fine-tuning of the schedule for various platforms and optimizing criteria. In summary, our contributions consist in

- a flexible framework to schedule parametric dataflow applications on many-core platforms;

- several kinds of constraints (ordering and resource constraints) to specify optimized and tailor-made scheduling policies;

- a correct-by-construction approach that guarantees bounded and deadlock free schedules.

The paper is organized as follows. In Section 2, we introduce the technical context, namely BPDF and STHORM. In Section 3, we present the scheduling framework composed of different kinds of constraints and a simple ASAP scheduler. In Section 4, we illustrate our approach using the well-known VC-1 video codec [14]. Section 5 compares our approach to related work. Finally, Section 6 summarizes our contribution and hints at future research directions.

2. Background and Context

Our scheduling technique considers the recent Boolean Parametric Data Flow (BPDF) model [3] and a modern many-core platform (STHORM) [4].

2.1 Boolean Parametric Data Flow Model

BPDF can be described as a parametric extension of the SDF (Synchronous Data-Flow) model [13] that also allows dynamic changes of the topology. In SDF, an application is defined as a directed graph of *actors*. Each actor represents a functional unit and has *ports* connected by *edges* implemented as FIFO channels. Each time an actor executes (*fires*), it consumes data tokens from its incoming edges (its *inputs*) and produces data tokens on its outgoing edges (its *outputs*). The number of tokens produced and consumed are specified by *rates* associated with each port. In SDF, all rates are constant and known at compile time.

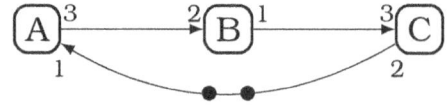

Figure 1. A consistent SDF graph

The *state* of an SDF graph is the number of tokens stored at each edge at a given instant. An edge can have zero or more tokens at any instant. The initial tokens at each edge specify the initial state of the graph.

A major advantage of SDF is that, if it exists, a bounded schedule can be found statically. Such a schedule ensures that each actor is eventually fired (ensuring *liveness*) and that the graph returns to its initial state after a certain sequence of firings (ensuring *boundedness* of the FIFOs). Such sequence is called an *iteration*, obtained by solving the so-called system of *balance equations*. This system is made of one equation per edge (X_1, X_2) of the form

$$\#X_1 \cdot r_1 = \#X_2 \cdot r_2 \qquad (1)$$

where $\#X_1$ and $\#X_2$ indicate the number of firings of actors X_1 and X_2 for one iteration and r_1 and r_2 the rates of the equivalent ports.

A graph is *consistent* if its system of balance equations has non-trivial solutions. The repetition vector is the minimal solution of the balance equations. That vector represent the number of firings of each actor per iteration.

A simple SDF graph is shown in Fig. 1. The graph is consistent, has the repetition vector $[A^2 \, B^3 \, C^1]$ and the initial state $[0\,0\,2]$ for edges (A, B), (B, C) and (C, A) respectively. A sample schedule for an iteration is: $A\,B\,A\,B\,B\,C$.

BPDF extends SDF by allowing rates to be parametric and edges to be annotated with a boolean condition. BPDF port rates are products of positive integers (k) or symbolic variables (p). They are defined by the grammar:

$$\mathcal{R} \quad ::= \quad k \mid p \mid \mathcal{R}_1 \cdot \mathcal{R}_2 \qquad \text{where } k \in \mathbb{N}^* \text{ and } p \in \mathcal{P}_i$$

with the set of symbolic variables $\mathcal{P}_i$ denotes the integer *parameters*.

Each BPDF edge is annotated by a boolean condition which deactivate the edge when it evaluates to *false*. These boolean expressions are defined by the grammar:

$$\mathcal{B} \quad ::= \quad true \mid false \mid b \mid \neg\mathcal{B} \mid \mathcal{B}_1 \wedge \mathcal{B}_2 \mid \mathcal{B}_1 \vee \mathcal{B}_2$$

where b belongs to the set of symbolic variables $\mathcal{P}_b$ denoting boolean parameters.

Unlike the rates of SDF graphs that are fixed at compile time, the parametric rates of a BPDF graph can change dynamically between iterations. This change can be performed by a single actor or a centralized scheduler. Moreover, each boolean parameter is modified by a single actor called its *modifier*. A modifier may change a boolean parameter within an iteration using the annotation $b@\alpha$ where b is the boolean parameter to be set and α is the *writing period*. The period of a boolean parameter b is the exact (possibly symbolic) number of firings of its modifier between two changes. Depending on the graph (rates, modifiers, users, ...) some writing periods are invalid. BPDF checks that periods are safe *i.e.,* that the graph returns to its initial state after each iteration.

The actors that have a boolean parameter on any of their edges are called *users* of that parameter. Users read new parameter values periodically. This period is measured in number of firings of the user and is called *reading period*. It is easily computed from the writing period and the number of firings of the user and modifier. The number of different values produced for a parameter is called its *frequency*. BPDF guarantees that the users will use properly all the produced boolean values within an iteration.

Intuitively, a BPDF actor reads and/or writes boolean parameters at specific periods. When it fires, it first evaluates the condition of its edges according to the current value of the boolean parameters. Then, it produces (resp. consumes) tokens on its outgoing (resp. incoming) edges that are annotated by a *true* condition only. It implies that a completely disconnected actor, *i.e.,* whose edges are all annotated by *false*, fires (at least conceptually) but does not read nor write any channel except for reading or writing boolean parameters.

Figure 2 shows a simple BPDF graph where actors have constant or parametric rates (*e.g.,* p for the output rate of A). Omitted rates and conditions equal to 1 and *true* respectively. The symbolic solution of the balance equations gives a repetition vector which can be noted as $[A^2 \ B^{2p} \ C^p \ D^{2p} \ E^{2p}]$. The actor B is the modifier of b with a writing period of 2. The actors (C, D, E) are users of b. Intuitively, the writing period of b is safe because the global iteration can be seen as $A^2 S^p$ where S is the sub-iteration $B^2 C D^2 E^2$. The modifier (resp. the users) writes (respread) b at each such sub-iteration *i.e.,* after each 2 firings for $B \ D \ E$ and after each firing for C. Note that a period of p would have been safe whereas 1 or 3 would have been invalid

The edges (B, D), (B, C) and (C, E) are *conditional*. They are present only when their condition (here b or $\neg b$) is *true*. A sample iteration of the graph is the following. First, p is set and sent to users; A fires and produces p tokens on edge (A, B). Then B fires and starts by setting the value of the boolean parameter b.

- If b is *true*, B produces one token on (B, C) and does not produce tokens on (B, D). As the edge is disabled, D fires twice without consuming tokens and producing 2 on (D, E). Actor B fires a second time without changing the value of b enabling C to fire once and producing 2 token on (C, E). Finally, E can fire twice to consume the tokens produced by C and D.

- If b is *false*, C is disconnected and it will fire once without producing or consuming tokens. B will fire twice producing 2 tokens on (B, D) that will be consumed by two firings of D. The actor E will fire twice to consume the tokens produced by D since the edge (C, E) is disabled.

This sub-iteration continues until each actor has fired a number of times equal to its repetition count (as in SDF).

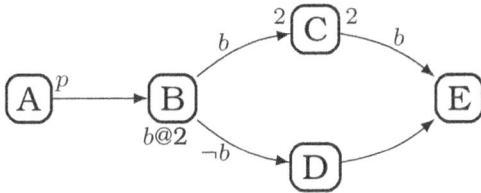

Figure 2. A simple BPDF graph with integer parameter p and boolean parameter b

BPDF combines parametric rates and frequent topology reconfigurations as no other dataflow model. This makes its scheduling on many-core platforms quite challenging. We show in the next sections that our scheduling framework is expressive and flexible enough to produce various parallel schedules for BPDF applications.

2.2 The STHORM Platform

The platform we target is STHORM by STMicroelectronics [4], which is representative of a modern many-core platform. It is com-

posed of a set of clusters (currently up to 32) in a GALS design and connected with an asynchronous Network-on-Chip.

Each cluster contains up to 16 software processing elements (SWPE), as a general purpose RISC Processor, and a set of dedicated hardware processing elements (HWPE). In our implementation, each BPDF actor is implemented in a separate (hardware or software) processing element and the execution of the application (*i.e.,* the scheduling of the BPDF graph) is controlled by a processor.

Moreover, STHORM includes a native programming model that simplifies the parallel implementation of streaming applications. This programming model uses *filters* to implement applications. A filter can be:

- A *primitive filter* which applies a well defined function to a set of input data in order to produce a set of output data. It is the building block of STHORM's native programming model. We implement BPDF actors as primitive filters. A filter can execute on a HWPE or a SWPE.

- A *controller* which schedules the firing of the filters and controls configuration parameters for each filter.

We focus on the generation of the controller that controls the execution of each BPDF actor.

The native programming model uses the notion of *slots* to schedule the firing of the filters. At the beginning of a slot, the controller selects several filters to be fired, and their execution takes place concurrently. When all previous executions are completed, the next slot starts. The controller can execute concurrently with the filters and therefore the hardware pipeline is not slowed down by the controller.

We produce slotted schedules which can be directly implemented using this model. We believe that such a scheduling model can also be used by other state-of-the-art many-core platforms. For instance, modern Graphical Processing Units (GPUs) support a similar execution model. In mainstream GPU programming models such as CUDA [17] and OpenCL [16], the host processor, equivalent to the controller of STHORM, creates a task group, loads it on the GPU, and get the results when the latter has finished execution. In parallel with the execution of the task group, the host processor may determine tasks to be executed next.

Although, we rely on the STHORM platform, our scheduling framework can easily adapt to produce non slotted schedules as discussed in Sec. 3.4. Moreover, we assume that each actor is mapped on a separate processing element but the framework can handle any other kind of static assignment, where actors may share resources as shown in Sec. 3.2.

3. Scheduling Framework

Our scheduling framework takes as input an application (specified as a BPDF graph) and a set of user-defined constraints, and produces the ASAP slotted schedule meeting the constraints. An overview of the scheduling framework is presented in Fig. 3.

The constraints belong to two distinct types: *Ordering constraints* that restrict individual actor firings, and *resource constraints* that control parallel execution (*e.g.,* limiting the level of parallelism). The two types of constraints are presented in detail in Sec. 3.1 and 3.2.

Ordering constraints can derive either from the *application* expressing the data dependencies of the dataflow graph, or from the *user* expressing platform specificities or optimizing some criteria. Application constraints can only be ordering constraints. User-defined constraints can be both resource and ordering constraints.

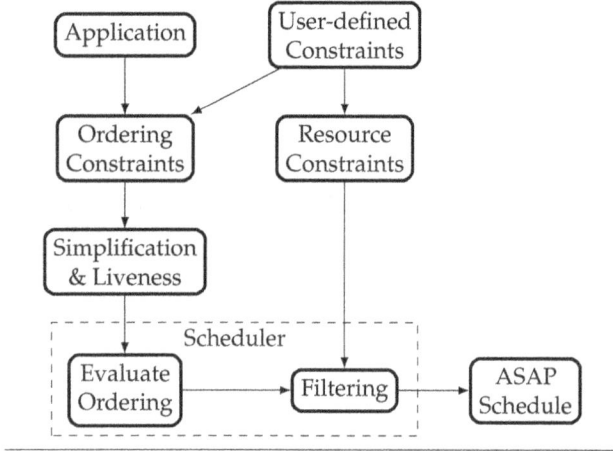

Figure 3. Scheduling Framework.

Inconsiderate user-defined constraints may introduce deadlocks. To guarantee liveness, such constraints are automatically detected and rejected (see Sec. 3.3). The valid constraints can then be simplified and taken into account by the scheduler as described in Sec. 3.4.

3.1 Ordering Constraints

An ordering constraint is a relationship between the firings of two actors of the form:

$$A_i > B_{f(i)}$$

where A_i denotes the ith firing of actor A and $B_{f(i)}$ denotes the $f(i)$th firing of actor B (where f is any total function from $\mathbb{N}^*$ to $\mathbb{Z}$). A null or negative $f(i)$ means that instance A_i does not depend on $B_{f(i)}$. Some ordering constraints are derived from the application and additional ones can be given by the user.

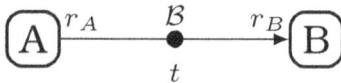

Figure 4. A generic BPDF edge.

3.1.1 Application constraints

Application constraints (or dataflow constraints) are automatically derived from data dependencies between actors. For each edge between actors A and B with production/consumption rates r_A and r_B respectively, initial tokens t, and boolean guard $\mathcal{B}$ (see Fig. 4), the following data constraint is generated

$$B_i > A_{f(i)} \quad \text{with} \quad f(i) = \left\lceil \frac{r_B \cdot i - t}{r_A} \right\rceil \quad (2)$$

If actor A has fired $\left\lceil \frac{r_B \cdot i - t}{r_A} \right\rceil$ times, it has produced $\left\lceil \frac{r_B \cdot i - t}{r_A} \right\rceil \cdot r_A$ tokens, which is greater than or equal to the number of tokens required to fire actor B i times, that is $r_B \cdot i - t$. Therefore, after $f(i)$ firings of A and $i-1$ firings of B, there remains enough tokens in the FIFO to fire B for the ith time.

Equation (2) does not depend on the boolean guard $\mathcal{B}$. However, the scheduler takes boolean guards into account by disregarding data constraints of disabled edges.

Boolean parameters introduce constraints due to the communication of their values between modifiers and users. A user needs to read a new value according to its reading period (π_r). The modifier

produces a new value according to its writing period (π_w). Therefore, we get the following ordering constraint for each user (U) - modifier (M) pair:

$$U_i > M_{f(i)} \quad \text{with} \quad f(i) = \pi_w \cdot \left\lfloor \frac{i-1}{\pi_r} \right\rfloor + 1 \quad (3)$$

This states that the ith firing of U requires the boolean value that is produced on the $f(i)$th firing of M. U will use this value for its next π_r firings. The constraint restricts the user to wait for the production of a boolean value but does not restrict the modifier. Indeed, the modifier may produce a new boolean value (or all the boolean values) before the user has finished using the previous one. The user will use the new values later, based on its reading period, when they are needed.

3.1.2 User constraints

User constraints are typically used to optimize various criteria (*e.g.,* power consumption, buffer size) or express platform specificities (*e.g.,* resource limitations). They are defined by the programmer for a specific application or platform. Consider again the simple BPDF graph of Fig. 4.

The repetition vector is $[A^{r_B} B^{r_A}]$ and A will fire r_B times without constraints[1]. Since A fires r_B times consecutively, if B does not consume enough tokens, there will be an accumulation of tokens on the edge buffer.

If the programmer wants to restrict the buffer to be of size, say k, it can restrict the execution of A so that it fires only when there is enough space left on the buffer thanks to the constraint:

$$A_i > B_{g(i)} \quad \text{with} \quad g(i) = \left\lceil \frac{r_A \cdot i + t - k}{r_B} \right\rceil \quad (4)$$

If only application constraints are used, the dataflow analyses guarantee liveness and the existence of a valid schedule. When additional constraints are considered, they may introduce a deadlock if they are not compatible with the application constraints. For instance, in the previous example, it should be checked that k is large enough so that A can trigger all r_A firings of B. This verification step is done using a deadlock detection algorithm presented in Sec. 3.3.

3.2 Resource Constraints

Resource constraints are used to regulate the parallel execution of actors. Such constraints can be used to limit the degree of parallelism or to enforce mutual exclusion between (groups of) actors. They can be seen as filter functions applied to the set of enabled (fireable) actors and returning a subset. Any such function f satisfies the two following conditions:

$$\forall \mathcal{S}. \ f(\mathcal{S}) = \mathcal{T} \Rightarrow \begin{cases} \mathcal{T} \subseteq \mathcal{S} & (C_1) \\ \mathcal{T} \neq \emptyset & (C_2) \end{cases}$$

Condition (C_1) ensures that the function is safe (only enabled actors can be selected), while (C_2) ensures that it preserves liveness (at least one actor is selected to be fired).

Many languages can be used to express such constraints. Since they are functions over finite domains, one may even consider expressing them exhaustively as tables. Here, we use rewrite rules on sets inspired from the Gamma formalism [1]. The general form of a resource constraint is:

$$\textbf{replace } S_A \textbf{ by } S_B \textbf{ if } condition \quad (5)$$

where S_A and S_B are nonempty sets of enabled actors such that $S_B \subseteq S_A$. It can be read as "replace S_A by S_B if *condition* is

---

[1] This repetition vector assumes that r_A and r_B are coprimes.

128

true". When the *condition* is always true it can be omitted. For example, the rule

$$\textbf{replace } A, B \textbf{ by } A \qquad (6)$$

can be read as "if the actors A and B are in the set (of enabled actors), then replace them by A". It prevents actors A and B to be fired together and gives priority to A.

Rewrite rules can use pattern variables to match arbitrary actors. For instance, the rule

$$\textbf{replace } x, y, z \textbf{ by } x, y \qquad (7)$$

can be read as "select three arbitrary enabled actors and suppress one of them". It limits the level of parallelism to 2. Indeed, rewriting rules apply until no match can be found. Rule (7) above applies as long as there are more than two enabled actors.

Rules can also depend on a condition. For instance, assuming that the two predicates *short* and *long* denote whether an actor takes a short or long time to execute, the rule

$$\textbf{replace } x, y \textbf{ by } x \textbf{ if } short(x) \wedge long(y) \qquad (8)$$

prevents short and long actors to be fired within the same slot (priority is given to short ones). This rule may improve the overall computation time. Indeed, if S is a "short" actor while L_1 and L_2 are two "long" actors such that S and L_1 are enabled at the same slot and firing S enables L_2, then it is better to fire first S alone and then L_1 and L_2 in parallel.

Several rules can also be combined in sequence or in parallel. The semantics of parallel composition enforces that rules applied in parallel act on disjoint sets of actors. Rules are applied repeatedly and terminate when no match can be found. For example, the sequential combination of rule (8) followed by rule (7) limits the possible parallel firings to one actor, two short actors, or two long actors. Additional examples of resource constraints are presented for the VC-1 decoder application in Sec. 4.

When actors are mapped on the same processing elements, resource constraints can be used to express their mutual exclusion. For instance, rule 6 can be used when actors A and B share the same processor. Although rule 6 gives priority to actor A, a condition can be added to express a more complex usage of the shared processor.

It is very easy to check that such rules preserve boundedness and liveness. If the *rhs* of Rule (5) is a non empty subset of its *lhs*, then the rule obeys conditions (C_1) and (C_2), and is, therefore, safe. For each application, they are statically compiled according to the set of actors into constant time selection operations.

3.3 Liveness analysis

User-defined ordering constraints may introduce deadlocks. For this reason, they must be checked statically for liveness. A set of ordering constraints may prevent liveness when they imply (by transitivity) a constraint of the form:

$$(A_i > A_j) \wedge (i \le j) \qquad (9)$$

which requires that the ith firing of an actor A must take place after the jth firing where j is a future firing ($j > i$). All cyclic constraints from an actor to itself must be checked. To ensure liveness, it must be shown that the deadlock condition in (9) is false for each cycle of the form:

$$A_i > B_{f_1(i)} > \cdots > C_{f_n(i)} > A_{f_{n+1}(i)}$$
$$\Rightarrow A_i > A_{f_1(\cdots(f_n(f_{n+1}(i))))}$$

hence that

$$i > f_1(\cdots(f_n(f_{n+1}(i)))) \qquad (10)$$

We consider all ordering constraints to detect such cycles. Typically, the expression $f_1(\cdots(f_n(f_{n+1}(i))))$ contains parameters and ceiling functions. In general, only an upper bound can be computed. Parameters are replaced by their maximum or minimum values and ceilings $\lceil \frac{a}{b} \rceil$ by $\frac{a}{b}+1$ (or $\frac{a}{b}-1$) depending on their sign and position. The expression $f_1(\cdots(f_n(f_{n+1}(i))))$ can then be simplified to get an upper bound. If Equation (10) is true for all cycles, then the liveness of the schedule is guaranteed.

Figure 5. A simple BPDF graph

Consider, for instance, the simple BPDF graph in Fig. 5 where the user wants to limit the edge buffer to k tokens. In practice, such a limit (k) as well as the maximum values of parameters (p_{max}, q_{max}) are actual integers. Here, we illustrate the verification process using symbolic values. The graph constraint is:

$$B_i > A_{f(i)} \quad \text{with} \quad f(i) = \left\lceil \frac{q \cdot i}{p} \right\rceil$$

and the user constraint that limits the buffer size to k is:

$$A_i > B_{g(i)} \quad \text{with} \quad g(i) = \left\lceil \frac{p \cdot i - k}{q} \right\rceil$$

Together they form a cyclic constraint:

$$A_i > A_{f(g(i))}$$

To ensure liveness we must verify that:

$$
\begin{aligned}
i > f(g(i)) \quad &\Leftrightarrow \quad i > \left\lceil \frac{q \cdot \left\lceil \frac{p \cdot i - k}{q} \right\rceil}{p} \right\rceil \\
&\Leftarrow \quad i > \frac{q \cdot (\frac{p \cdot i - k}{q} + 1)}{p} + 1 \\
&\Leftarrow \quad i > i + \frac{q - k}{p} + 1 \\
&\Leftarrow \quad k > p + q \\
&\Leftarrow \quad k > p_{max} + q_{max}
\end{aligned}
$$

So, if the limit placed on the buffer size k is greater than $p_{max} + q_{max}$, a live schedule is ensured. This is only a *sufficient* condition, because of the approximation incurred by removing the ceiling functions.

In general, if there exists a cycle that does not satisfy Equation (10), then user constraints involved are rejected. Actually, this cycle condition can be relaxed by taking boolean guards into account. Indeed, if the constraints occurring in the cycle depend on contradictory boolean guards, then the cycle is live as it cannot be formed.

3.4 Scheduler

When all the constraints are defined and checked for liveness, a scheduler is used to produce the slotted ASAP schedule for one iteration of the graph. The total number of firings of each actor must be equal to the solution of the balance equations. Two kinds of schedules can be distinguished:

Static schedules which are a finite sequence of actor instances, each repeated a constant number of times $(1, 2, ...)$. For instance, $A(B|C)^2$ is a static schedule which starts by firing A then B and C in parallel twice (where '|' denotes parallel firings within one slot).

Quasi-static schedules which depend on the values of the integer or boolean parameters. For instance, $(A(b? B : C))^p$ is a quasi-static schedule that depends on both an integer and a boolean parameter. Actor A is fired followed by B (resp. C) if b (resp. $\neg b$), and this sequence is iterated p times.

In general, the ASAP schedule of a BPDF graph can vary a lot in complexity, even when boolean parameters are absent. For example, the simple graph in Fig. 5 produces parametric constraints whose ceilings cannot be removed statically. The repetition vector is $[A^q\ B^p]$ and the ASAP scheduling of this simple graph must consider several cases:

Case p $\geq$ q: The slotted schedule is $A(A|B)^{q-1}B^{p-q+1}$. Indeed, once A has fired the first time, there are enough tokens to fire B at least once, because $p \geq q$. For each subsequent slot, A will fire in parallel with B until it has fired a total of $\#A = q$ times. This totals to $q-1$ firings of B so there remains to fire B another $p - (q - 1)$ times.

Case q $>$ p: Then, two sub-cases must be considered:

Sub-case q $=$ k.p: If q is a multiple of p, then the slotted schedule is $A(A^{k-1}(B|A))^{p-1}A^{k-1}B$, where each firing of B occurs after k firings of A. The total number of firings of A is $1 + (k - 1 + 1).(p - 1) + k - 1 = k.p = q$, while the total number of firings of B is $p - 1 + 1 = p$.

Sub-case q $=$ k.p + r with 0 $<$ r $<$ p: Otherwise, the slotted schedule cannot be expressed by a regular formula as in the other cases. Indeed, it starts with the sequence $A^{k+1}B$, at which point there are $p - r$ tokens remaining in the edge. So, if $p \geq 2r$, then only k firings of A are necessary before B can be fired again, leaving $p - 2r$ tokens; otherwise, A must be fired $k + 1$ times before B can be fired, leaving $2p - 2r$ tokens, and so on.

In general, we use a scheduler that evaluates the scheduling constraints at runtime. However, there are many cases where the scheduler can be simplified and implemented in a static or quasi-static way.

The scheduler takes as input the set of actors, the repetition vector, the writing/reading periods as well as the ordering and resource constraints. It processes the constraints and produces a schedule in a per slot manner (see Fig. 6). The scheduler stops when an iteration is finished and is reset to begin the next iteration.

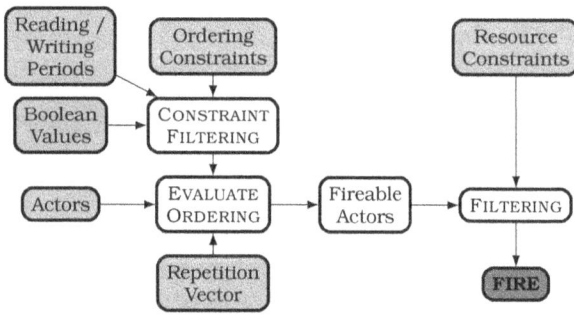

Figure 6. Scheduler overview

At the beginning of an iteration, the scheduler gets the values of integer parameters and possibly new boolean values if there are modifiers producing. Since all the reading periods are known, the scheduler can deduce which boolean value corresponds to which user firing (user firings may lag behind modifiers). Then, the scheduler filters out the set of ordering constraints based on the current values of the boolean parameters: data dependencies from disabled edges are not taken into account. Then, the set of remaining constraints is evaluated and a set of fireable actors is produced. Finally,

the resource constraints evaluate the fireable set and select a subset of actors to fire. The scheduler reaches the end of the current iteration when the set of fireable actors is empty.

The scheduler is composed of three main functions: One function that filters out data dependencies based on the current boolean values (CONSTRAINT FILTERING), one function that evaluates the ordering constraints and produces a set of fireables actors (EVALUATE ORDERING), and finally one function that filters the set of fireable actors to a subset based on the resource constraints (FILTERING).

The filtering of the data dependencies (CONSTRAINT FILTERING) takes as input the set of ordering constraints ($\mathcal{C}$) and the values of the boolean parameters ($\mathcal{B}$). Then, it evaluates the boolean guards of each edge, and if the guard is false, the corresponding data dependency is removed from the set of ordering constraints. The procedure produces a reduced set of ordering constraints ($\mathcal{C}'$).

The evaluation of ordering constraints (procedure EVALUATE ORDERING in Fig. 7) takes as input a set of actors $\mathcal{A}$, a set of constraints $\mathcal{C}$, the repetition vector R and a status vector depicting the number of past firings per actor V_s. The output of the algorithm is the fireable vector V_f that flags the fireable actors for the current slot.

procedure EVALUATE ORDERING($R, \mathcal{C}, \mathcal{A}, V_s$)
    $V_f \leftarrow \vec{0}$
    for $\forall X \in \mathcal{A}$ **do**
        if (EVAL($\mathcal{C}(X), V_s$)) $\wedge$ ($V_s[X] < R[X]$) **then**
            $V_f[X] \leftarrow 1$
        end if
    end for
    return(V_f)
end procedure

Figure 7. Evaluation of ordering constraints.

We denote $R[X]$ the number of firings of actor X required by the iteration and $\mathcal{C}(X)$ the set of constraints imposed on X (i.e., all constraints of the form $X_i > \ldots$).

The core of the algorithm is the evaluation of constraints represented by the function EVAL, which evaluates the constraints of an actor ($\mathcal{C}(A)$) according to the current status vector (V_s). More precisely, for each constraint

$$X_i > Y_{f(i)}$$

the EVAL function simply checks whether:

$$f(V_s[X] + 1) \leq V_s[Y]$$

which corresponds to the satisfaction of the data dependency. Indeed, $V_s[X] + 1$ represents the index of the next firing of X and $f(V_s[X] + 1)$ represents the number of firings that actor Y should have achieved before we can fire $X_{V_s(X)+1}$ due to the $X_i > Y_{f(i)}$ constraint. If the current number of firings of Y (i.e., $V_s[Y]$) is greater than the index of the next firing of X (i.e., $f(V_s[X] + 1)$) then the constraint

$$X_i > Y_{f(i)} \text{ with } i = V_s[X] + 1$$

is satisfied. If all the constraints on X are satisfied, then EVAL returns true and X is allowed to be fired in the next slot. Otherwise, it returns false and X will not be fired.

Apart from the ordering constraints, the repetition vector is also checked, ($V_s[X] < R[X]$), to determine whether the actor needs to be fired again in the current iteration. If both conditions are satisfied, $V_f[X]$ is set to 1. After all actors have been considered, the fireable vector is produced. The deadlock detection algorithm ensures that the inner loop always terminates.

Since each actor is selected as soon as its constraints are met, the procedure produces an ASAP schedule *w.r.t.* constraints. We choose ASAP scheduling because it produces highly parallel schedules. Actually, without timing information, it can be shown to be the most parallel slotted schedule. Moreover, it ensures a minimal schedule length in terms of number of slots.

When the fireable vector has been produced, it is used as input, along with the resource constraint matrix $\mathcal{G}$ by the FILTERING procedure. FILTERING is just a lookup procedure that finds V_f in the constraint table and returns the entry of the table for that vector, so we do not provide its pseudo code. The output of FILTERING is a new firing vector $V_f' \subseteq V_f$ containing all the actors to be fired in the current slot that also updates the status vector V_s.

Our scheduler is summarized in Fig. 8. The inputs are the set of actors $\mathcal{A}$, the two sets of constraints ordering and resource $(\mathcal{C}, \mathcal{G})$ and the repetition vector R.

procedure SCHEDULER($\mathcal{A}, \mathcal{C}, \mathcal{G}, R$)
    while true **do**
        READ INTEGER VALUES()
        $V_s \leftarrow \vec{0}$
        $F \leftarrow \vec{0}$
        while $V_s \neq R$ **do**
            $\mathcal{B} \leftarrow$ READ BOOLEAN VALUES()
            $\mathcal{C}' \leftarrow$ CONSTRAINT FILTERING($\mathcal{C}, \mathcal{B}$)
            $V_f \leftarrow$ EVALUATE ORDERING($R, \mathcal{C}', \mathcal{A}, V_s$)
            $V_f' \leftarrow$ FILTERING($V_f, \mathcal{G}$)
            $V_s \leftarrow V_s + V_f'$
            fire(F)
        end while
    end while
end procedure

Figure 8. Scheduler algorithm.

The SCHEDULER procedure is structured as an outer infinite loop and an inner loop that iterates over the iteration of the graph. As both functions, EVALUATE ORDERING and FILTERING, guarantee to fire at least one actor as long as the the repetition vector is not reached, the inner loop terminates when the iteration is complete. The outer loop resets the auxiliary vectors and repeats the iteration.

Actors are scheduled and fired one slot at a time. While actors execute, the SCHEDULER procedure concurrently evaluates constraints to find the actors that must be fired at the next slot.

The slotted scheduling model may introduce a lot of slack in the produced schedule because of the explicit synchronization after every slot. This is inherent to the model but can be mitigated using constraints to group actors with similar timings in slots (see Sec. 4).

The slotted model was prescribed by our target platform but we should point out that our framework can also be used to produce non slotted schedules. In our context, where each actor is a separate processing element, the ASAP non-slotted schedule is optimal *w.r.t.* to time and constraints. The scheduler main-loop needs to be adjusted so that the status vector is updated each time an actor ends its firing (instead of at the end of each slot). The scheduler re-evaluates constraints each time an actor ends, finds new enabled actors and fires them. An extra vector recording the active (*i.e.,* currently executing) actors is also needed. It is used to prevent executing actors to be considered during constraint evaluation and also to evaluate resource constraints which now apply on enabled *and* already active actors.

3.5 Constraint simplification

Scheduling can be optimized in several cases. For an SDF graph (*e.g.,* without parameters), all constraints can be solved statically by considering the constraints for each individual firing (thus getting rid of the index i). Then, the scheduling algorithm boils down to a sequence of firings.

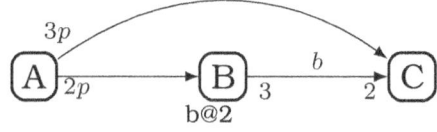

Figure 9. BPDF graph with constraints that can be solved symbolically

Even for parametric graphs, it is often possible to solve ordering constraints symbolically. Consider the graph in Fig. 9, whose iteration is $AB^{2p}C^{3p}$ and whose dataflow constraints are:

$$B_i > A_{\lceil \frac{i}{2p} \rceil}, \quad C_i > B_{\lceil \frac{2i}{3} \rceil}, \quad C_i > A_{\lceil \frac{i}{3p} \rceil}$$

plus the implicit $X_i > X_{i-1}$ for all actors. Moreover, actor C, as a user of the boolean parameter b, is constrained by (from Eq. 3):

$$C_i > B_{2\lfloor \frac{i-1}{3} \rfloor + 1} \quad \Rightarrow \quad C_i > B_{2\lceil \frac{i}{3} \rceil - 1}$$

Knowing that there is only one firing of A in each iteration, and that A is unconstrained, we schedule A in the first slot and we get $A_1 = 1$. For actor B, the constraint becomes:

$$B_i > A_1 \quad \Rightarrow \quad B_i > 1$$

Since B_i should be fired as soon as the constraints are satisfied, its constraints are rewritten into the equation:

$$B_i = max(B_{i-1}, 1) \text{ for } i \in [1..2p]$$

which can be solved to $B_i = i + 1$ indicating that the ith firing of B will fire in the $i + 1$th slot. Finally, for actor C we have three constraints:

$$C_i > A_{\lceil \frac{i}{3p} \rceil} \quad \Rightarrow \quad C_i > 1$$

$$C_i > B_{\lceil \frac{2i}{3} \rceil} \quad (11)$$

$$C_i > B_{2\lceil \frac{i}{3} \rceil - 1} \quad (12)$$

which form the equation:

$$C_i = max(A_1, B_{\lceil \frac{2i}{3} \rceil}, B_{2\lceil \frac{i}{3} \rceil - 1}, C_{i-1}) \text{ for } i \in [1..3p] \quad (13)$$

The two constraints on actor B dominate the one on actor A and the data dependency (11) dominates over the modifier - user dependency (12) as $\lceil \frac{2i}{3} \rceil \geq 2\lceil \frac{i}{3} \rceil - 1$. So, Equation (13) yields:

$$C_i = max(B_{\lceil \frac{2i}{3} \rceil}, C_{i-1}) + 1 \text{ for } i \in [1..3p]$$

However, when the boolean parameter b is set to *false*, the data dependency is not taken into account and Equation (13) yields:

$$C_i = max(B_{2\lceil \frac{i}{3} \rceil - 1}, C_{i-1}) + 1 \text{ for } i \in [1..3p]$$

In both cases, the solution for actor C is found to be $C_i = i + 2$, so the value of the boolean parameter does not influence the schedule. The resulting schedule can be expressed as regular expressions:

$$A \; B \; (B|C)^{2p-1} \; C^{p+1}$$

Such schedules can be implemented as standard quasi-static schedules. However, in general, resource constraints and boolean parameters entail some dynamic checks in the scheduler.

131

4. Case studies

4.1 The VC-1 decoder

The VC-1 decoder [14] is a good example of a demanding codec. Its resemblance with the more recent and widely used H.264 [14] and with future generation codecs like HEVC, makes it especially relevant. The BPDF implementation of VC-1 is shown in Fig. 10.

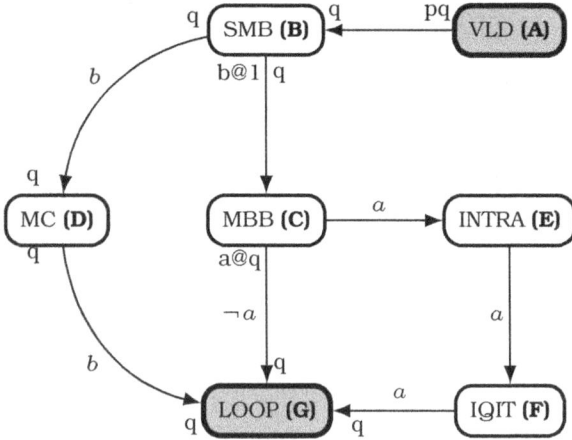

Figure 10. BPDF capture of VC-1 decoder

The decoder is composed of two main pipelines, the inter and the intra. The inter pipeline is composed of actor MC (Motion Compensation), while the intra pipeline is composed of actors MBB (MacroBlock to Block), INTRA (Intra prediction), and IQIT (Inverse Quantization and Inverse Transform). These two paths are combined and produce the final decoded slice in the LOOP (Loop filter). Actors SMB (Slice to MacroBlock) and MBB are auxiliary actors that are used as modifiers of the boolean parameters. For easier reference, each actor is assigned a letter (shown in "()").

The inter pipeline reconstructs data based on motion between different frames. For this, it fetches data from previous or future frames and, based on motion vectors, compensates the motion for the current macroblock. The intra pipeline reconstructs the data that depends on macroblocks in the neighborhood of the decoding macroblock. The intra prediction actor calculates coefficients based on this information, the IQIT applies inverse transformations to complete the decoding of the data. Finally, the residues of both pipelines are combined and smoothed in the loop filter.

The decoder makes use of two integers and two boolean parameters. The integer parameters are p, which encodes the slice size in macroblocks, and q, which encodes the macroblock size in blocks. Each iteration of the graph processes a single slice. The boolean parameters capture whether a block is using intra (a) or inter (b) information. With these two boolean parameters, three possible modes of operation can be distinguished:

$$a \wedge \neg b : \quad \text{Intra only}$$

$$\neg a \wedge b : \quad \text{Inter only}$$

$$a \wedge b : \quad \text{Intra and Inter}$$

In the *Intra only* case, the value of the current block depends only on the values of the surrounding blocks. The inter pipeline is disabled. In the *Inter only* case, the value of the current block depends on the value of another block from a previous frame, as defined with a motion vector. Only the inter pipeline is used. Finally, in the *Intra and Inter* case, both pipelines are used.

By solving the balance equations, we get the repetition vector

$$[A B^p C^{pq} D^p E^{pq} F^{pq} G^p]$$

The graph is first scheduled, with no additional constraints, as explained in the previous section.

Actor	Execution Time (Cycles/Firing)	ASAP Sequences
VLD (A)	7400	$\mathcal{F}$
SMB (B)	10	$\mathcal{E}\mathcal{F}^p$
MBB (C)	10	$\mathcal{E}^2 \mathcal{F}^{pq}$
MC (D)	1937	$\mathcal{E}^2 \mathcal{F}^p$
INTRA (E)	288	$\mathcal{E}^3 \mathcal{F}^{pq}$
IQIT (F)	365	$\mathcal{E}^3 \mathcal{R}_F(pq)$
LOOP (G)	4074	$\mathcal{E}^3 \mathcal{R}_G(p)$

Table 1. ASAP sequences of VC-1

The resulting schedule cannot be expressed as a single sequence using the notation introduced in Section 3.4. It is possible though, to express the schedule using individual execution sequences for each actor as shown in Table 1 (third column). Each one represents the sequence of slots of the iteration where either the actor is fired (written $\mathcal{F}$) or it remains idle (written $\mathcal{E}$). The possible idle slots after the last firing of actors are omitted.

In the case of actors IQIT and LOOP, the schedule is depending on the boolean value of a and shows increased dynamicity. To express the sequence of firings, we use two recursive functions $\mathcal{R}_F$, for IQIT and $\mathcal{R}_G$ for LOOP defined as follows:

$$\mathcal{R}_F(n) = a ?\ \mathcal{E}\ \mathcal{F}^n\ :\ \mathcal{F}^q\ \mathcal{R}_F(n-q)$$

$$\mathcal{R}_G(n) = a ?\ \mathcal{E}^{q+1} \mathcal{F}\ \mathcal{R}_T(n-1)\ :\ \mathcal{E}^{q-1} \mathcal{F}\ \mathcal{R}_G(n-1)$$

$$\mathcal{R}_T(n) = a ?\ \mathcal{E}^{q-1} \mathcal{F}\ \mathcal{R}_T(n-1)\ :\ \mathcal{E}^{q-3} \mathcal{F}\ \mathcal{R}_F(n-1)$$

$$\mathcal{R}_F(n) = a ?\ \mathcal{E}^{q+1} \mathcal{F}\ \mathcal{R}_T(n-1)\ :\ \mathcal{E}^{q-1} \mathcal{F}\ \mathcal{R}_F(n-1)$$

The sequence associated to IQIT (F) means that IQIT remains idle in the first 3 slots, and then if a is *true*, it waits one more slot and fires consecutively until he finishes its iteration. If a is *false*, IQIT fires for q slots and then checks again the value of a.

The execution sequence of LOOP (G) is a more complex one, as it depends not only on the boolean values but also on their sequence. For this reason, the functions $\mathcal{R}_T$ and $\mathcal{R}_F$ are used for when the boolean is *true* and *false* respectively. The complete schedule is the parallel combination of all execution sequences. It exhibits a high level of parallelism and a sample execution starts as

$$(A)\ (B)\ (B|C|D)\ (B|C|D|E)\ (B|C|D|E|F)\ \ldots$$

The total span of the produced schedule has a maximum of $pq + 5$ slots and a minimum of $pq + 3$ slots. By adding user-constraints, we can modify the ASAP schedule to improve it or satisfy some given criteria. In the following, examples of ordering and resource constraints are given. To evaluate the decoder's performance we reused the VC-1 performance on STHORM based on the implementation presented in [2]. The execution time of each actor's firing is shown in Table 1 (second column).

4.2 Ordering constraint examples

The inter-prediction path processes one macroblock at a time whereas the intra-prediction path processes one block at a time. Consequently, actors in the intra-prediction are fired a total number of pq times, whereas D fires only p times. This results into D firing in the early slots and producing a lot of tokens on the edge (D, G). However, G cannot consume these tokens because it is blocked by the intra-prediction pipeline.

Using additional constraints, we can limit the buffer size of the edge (D, G) and prevent the accumulation of data in the inter-prediction path. To produce the alternative schedule, we delay the inter-prediction path by constraining the (D) actor to wait until (G) has consumed q tokens. Using the constraint from (4) we get:

$$D_i > G_{\lceil \frac{q \cdot i - q}{q} \rceil} \Rightarrow D_i > G_{i-1} \tag{14}$$

The constraint adds idle intervals of $q - 1$ slots between the firings of D. This redistribution of the firings of D has the additional benefit of a more evenly distributed power consumption, and subsequently a smaller temperature. Although the schedule span of actor D increases, we observed only a slight increase of 2% to the total schedule time, so the total schedule span effectively remains the same.

This significant change on the graph schedule is achieved by adding a single constraint. It demonstrates the flexibility of our scheduling framework.

4.3 Resource constraint examples

When slotted scheduling is used, the goal is to minimize the introduced slack because of the synchronization after each slot. For this reason, we try to cluster together the more cycle-demanding actors. In Table 1, we notice that, apart from A that fires only once, the most costly actors are D and G. An obvious optimization is to fire them in the same slots.

We can use a resource constraint to achieve this goal. By looking at the actors' schedule streams of Table 1, we see that all firings of D, after the first one, are fired in parallel with E. The following constraint can be used:

$$\textbf{replace } D, E \textbf{ by } E \textbf{ if } \neg \texttt{fireable}(G) \tag{15}$$

This constraint suppresses D when G is not present, effectively clustering the two actors together. This extra constraint led to an improvement of 15% in the total schedule time. A non-slotted schedule (optimal *w.r.t.* timing in our context) would improve the total execution time by an additional 30%.

Resource constraints can also be used to restrict concurrency and power consumption of the VC-1 application. For instance, if we want to limit its parallelism to at most 3 concurrent actors, we can use the following resource constraint:

$$\textbf{replace } w, x, y, z \textbf{ by } w, x, y \tag{16}$$

We may additionally want to limit the power consumption of the chip during a slot. Assuming two predicates that classify actors into high (H) or low (L) power consumers, we can limit power consumption by firing at most one H actor either alone or along with at most one L actor. The following set of rules implements such a limitation:

$$\textbf{replace } x, y \quad \textbf{by } x \quad \textbf{if } H(x) \wedge H(y)$$
$$\textbf{replace } x, y, z \quad \textbf{by } x, y \quad \textbf{if } H(x) \wedge L(y) \wedge L(z)$$

With precise information about actors (that we do not currently have), total power consumption could be better controlled, *e.g.*, bounded by a specified limit). Further experimentation is needed to demonstrate the way VC-1's schedule can be altered and optimized using the above constraints, however the platform is not readily available to us yet.

4.4 Scheduler overhead evaluation

Temporal Noise Reduction (TNR) is an algorithm applied after the video decoding process to reduce the noise of each frame. We implemented TNR on the STHORM platform using BPDF and used the scheduling framework to schedule it. The BPDF graph of TNR processes one frame per iteration. We measured the average cycles used by the processor that schedules the graph for each frame.

We consider three different cases: the original manual implementation of the scheduler for TNR (*Manual Sched.*), our BPDF scheduler without any simplification of constraints(*BPDF no opt.*) and our BPDF quasi-static schedule produced after simplification of constraints (*BPDF opt.*). Table 2 shows the number of cycles taken by the scheduler at each frame (line 2) and the maximum QoS (in terms of fps) the scheduler or actors could meet (line 3). For comparison, column 2 shows the corresponding numbers for the faster actor of TNR. We can see that the dynamic scheduler

	Best Actor Performance	BDPF no opt.	BPDF opt.	Manual Sched.
Cycles / frame	2.140.000	1.100.000	360.000	340.000
FPS	187	363	1111	1176

Table 2. Schedule overhead for different schedules of TNR

introduces a large overhead (almost three times more costly than the manual schedule). Once the constraints are simplified and the schedule is reduced to a quasi-static one, the overhead is comparable with that of the manual schedule. For VC-1, the required quality of service is 30 Frames/sec and in the best case an actor is much more costly than the scheduler. So, in the best case, although the unoptimized scheduler introduces large overhead, since it runs in parallel with such coarse grain actors, the required QoS is still achieved. In that context, a dynamic scheduler is realistic and allows the use of additional constraints to optimize various criteria.

5. Related Work

Parallel scheduling of data flow graphs is an old problem that has been dealt with for many years. In the case of SDF [13], it typically involves the transformation of the graph to a homogeneous SDF (HSDF) format where all actors produce or consume a single token [12]. It exposes parallelism and allows to use popular techniques like list scheduling. The hierarchical scheduling framework proposed in [18] uses a clustering technique to prevent the actor explosion that occurs when SDF is transformed into HSDF. These approaches apply only to SDF graphs however, and although there is a suggestion of a scheduler to optimize the schedule, it has never been explored.

SDF graphs are fully compatible with our framework. In the case of a SDF graph, all constraints can be resolved statically. Scheduling can be resolved at compile time and produce a static ASAP parallel schedule for the SDF graph. Different scheduling strategies can be expressed using specific user-defined constraints. Such constraints can be checked and integrated in the static schedule.

When the expressiveness of data flow models increases, so does the complexity of their scheduling. To deal with switch actors and conditional execution, Lee proposed quasi-static schedules [11] expressed with iterations and conditionals which must be evaluated at run-time. A similar approach has been explored further by Ha & Lee [9], where quasi-static schedules for data-dependent data flow graphs are produced. They consider schedules that have the same frontier regardless the presence of switch actors (expressing conditional execution) or actors with an iteration based on the data. In our case though, we explore the production of self-timed schedules using a different scheduling model based on slots.

Bhattacharya & Bhattacharyya [5] explore the use of quasi-static scheduling to produce schedules for parameterized dataflow applications captured in the PSDF model [6]. A clustering technique is used to produce parameterized looped schedules. In [19] the approach is generalized to schedules expressed using generalized schedule trees. However, these schedules are sequential.

In [10], the use of generalized scheduling trees along with an analysis that minimizes buffers is used to produce quasi-static schedules for parameterized cyclo-static dataflow graphs [7]. The expressiveness of the approach is reduced because of restrictions of the clustering mechanism and limitations of the schedule representation. Finally, there is no flexibility to alter the schedule nor any liveness guarantees. Our framework is compatible with these scheduling techniques as it can express such parameterized looped schedules using the appropriate constraints.

6. Conclusions

We have presented a framework to specify and implement bounded, live and highly parallel schedules for boolean parametric dataflow graphs. Scheduling is made flexible by the use of user constraints that allow the framework to adapt to new execution platforms, express optimizations and regulate parallel firings. Static checks can ensure that constraints preserve the existence of bounded and live schedules.

The approach was used to schedule two streaming applications (VC-1 and TNR) on the STHORM platform demonstrating the feasibility and flexibility of the approach. The framework facilitates the automatic production of complex schedules that can be as efficient as the manual ones, which are often hard to produce and error-prone.

The main aim of our framework is not to produce the optimal quasi-static schedule but to propose a flexible and correct by construction approach that can easily express different schedules and scheduling strategies. The framework can then be used to explore the various scheduling possibilities and to optimize the schedule *w.r.t.* various criteria.

Although we only considered BPDF, our framework can be adapted to schedule other data flow models as long as their data flow constraints can be expressed in our constraint language. We believe that the framework can also accommodate other models of computation such as Petri nets and process networks. Similarly, if the framework was designed with slotted scheduling in mind, it can easily be converted to non-slotted models without compromising its flexibility.

As future work, we have the following mid-term objectives:

- Make use of constraints to optimize bi-criteria scheduling, specifically power consumption vs. throughput;

- Design a high-level language to express scheduling policies that can be automatically compiled into constraints, which can in turn be taken into account by the scheduler.

References

[1] J.-P. Banâtre and D. Le Métayer. Programming by multiset transformation. *Comm. of the ACM*, 36(1):98–111, Jan. 1993.

[2] M. Bariani, P. Lambruschini, and M. Raggio. Vc-1 decoder on stmicroelectronics p2012 architecture. In *Proc. of 8th Annual Intl. Workshop 'STreaming Day'*, Sept 2010. .

[3] V. Bebelis, P. Fradet, A. Girault, and B. Lavigueur. BPDF: A statically analyzable dataflow model with integer and boolean parameters. In *ACM Int. Conf. Embedded Software, EMSOFT'13*, pages 1–10, Montreal, Canada, Sept. 2013.

[4] L. Benini, E. Flamand, D. Fuin, and D. Melpignano. P2012: Building an ecosystem for a scalable, modular and high-efficiency embedded computing accelerator. In *Design Automation and Test in Europe, DATE'12*, pages 983–987, 2012.

[5] B. Bhattacharya and S. S. Bhattacharyya. Quasi-static scheduling of reconfigurable dataflow graphs for DSP systems. In *IEEE International Workshop on Rapid System Prototyping*, pages 84–89, 2000.

[6] B. Bhattacharya and S. S. Bhattacharyya. Parameterized dataflow modeling for DSP systems. *IEEE Trans. on Signal Processing*, 49 (10):2408–2421, 2001.

[7] G. Bilsen, M. Engels, R. Lauwereins, and J. Peperstraete. Cyclo-static dataflow. *IEEE Trans. on Signal Processing*, 44(2):397–408, 1996.

[8] P. Fradet, A. Girault, and P. Poplavko. SPDF: A schedulable parametric data-flow MoC. In *Design Automation and Test in Europe, DATE'12*, pages 769–774, 2012.

[9] S. Ha and E. A. Lee. Compile-time scheduling and assignment of data-flow program graphs with data-dependent iteration. *IEEE Trans. Computers*, 40(11):1225–1238, 1991.

[10] H. Kee, C.-C. Shen, S. S. Bhattacharyya, I. Wong, Y. Rao, and J. Kornerup. Mapping parameterized cyclo-static dataflow graphs onto configurable hardware. *Signal Processing Systems*, 66(3):285–301, 2012.

[11] E. A. Lee. Recurrences, iteration, and conditionals in statically scheduled block diagrams languages. In *VLSI Signal Processing III*, chapter 31, pages 330–340. IEEE Press, 1988.

[12] E. A. Lee and D. G. Messerschmitt. Static scheduling of synchronous data flow programs for digital signal processing. *IEEE Trans. Computers*, 36(1):24–35, 1987.

[13] E. A. Lee and D. G. Messerschmitt. Synchronous data flow. *IEEE Trans. Computers*, 36(1):24–35, 1987.

[14] J.-B. Lee and H. Kalva. *The VC-1 and H.264 Video Compression Standards for Broadband Video Services*. Springer, 2008.

[15] C. E. Leiserson and J. B. Saxe. Retiming synchronous circuitry. *Algorithmica*, 6(1):5–35, 1991.

[16] A. Munshi. *The OpenCL Specification*. Khronos OpenCL Working Group, 1.1 edition, June 2011.

[17] *NVIDIA CUDA Programming Guide*. NVIDIA Corp., 4.1 edition, 2012.

[18] J. L. Pino, S. S. Bhattacharyya, and E. A. Lee. A hierarchical multiprocessor scheduling framework for synchronous dataflow graphs. Tech. report UCB/ERL M95/36, Univ. of California at Berkeley, May 1995.

[19] W. Plishker, N. Sane, and S. S. Bhattacharyya. A generalized scheduling approach for dynamic dataflow applications. In *Design Automation and Test in Europe, DATE'09*, pages 111–116, Nice, France, Apr. 2009.

[20] S. Sriram and S. S. Bhattacharyya. *Embedded Multiprocessors: Scheduling and Synchronization*. Marcel Dekker, Inc., New York, NY, USA, 1st edition, 2000. ISBN 0824793188.

[21] B. Theelen, M. Geilen, T. Basten, J. Voeten, S. Gheorghita, and S. Stuijk. A scenario-aware data flow model for combined long-run average and worst-case performance analysis. In *International Conference on Formal Methods and Models for Codesign, MEMOCODE'06*, pages 185–194, Napa Valley (CA), USA, July 2006. ACM-IEEE.

[22] M. H. Wiggers, M. J. G. Bekooij, and G. J. M. Smit. Buffer capacity computation for throughput constrained streaming applications with data-dependent inter-task commnication. *ACM Trans. Embedded Comput. Syst.*, 10(2):17, 2010.

Improving Performance of Loops on
DIAM-based VLIW Architectures

Jinyong Lee   Jongwon Lee
Yunheung Paek *
Seoul National University
jylee@sor.snu.ac.kr/jwlee@sor.snu.ac.kr/ypaek@sor.snu.ac.kr

Jongeun Lee
Ulsan National Institute of Science and Technology
jlee@unist.ac.kr

Abstract

Recent studies show that very long instruction word (VLIW) architectures, which inherently have wide datapath (e.g. 128 or 256
bits for one VLIW instruction word), can benefit from dynamic implied addressing mode (DIAM) and can achieve lower power consumption and smaller code size with a small performance overhead.
Such overhead, which is claimed to be small, is mainly caused by
the execution of additionally generated special instructions for con-
veying information that cannot be encoded in reduced instruction
bit-width. In this paper, however, we show that the performance
impact of applying DIAM on VLIW architecture cannot be over-
looked expecially when applications possess high level of instruction level parallelism (ILP), which is mostly the case for loops because of the result of aggressive code scheduling. We also propose
a way to relieve the performance degradation especially focusing
on loops since loops spend almost 90% of total execution time in
programs and tend to have high ILP. We first implement the original DIAM compilation technique in a compiler, and augment it
with the proposed loop optimization scheme to show that ours can
clearly alleviate the performance loss caused by the excessive number of additional instructions, with the help of slightly modified
hardware. Moreover, the well-known loop unrolling scheme, which
would produce denser code in loops at the cost of substantial code
size bloating, is integrated into our compiler. The experiment result
shows that the loop unrolling technique, combined with our augmented DIAM scheme, produces far better code in terms of performance with quite an acceptable amount of code increase.

Categories and Subject Descriptors   C.1.1 [*PROCESSOR AR-
CHITECTURES*]: Single Data Stream Architectures-*Pipeline processors; RISC/CISC, VLIW architectures*; D.3.4 [*Programming
Languages*]: Processors-*Code generation; Compilers; Optimization*

Keywords   VLIW architecture; reduced bit-width ISA; Dynamic
Implied Addressing Mode; code size; performance; loop; loop unrolling

---

* Corresponding author

LCTES '14,   June 12–13, 2014, Edinburgh, UK.
Copyright © 2014 ACM 978-1-4503-2877-7 /14/06... $15.00.
http://dx.doi.org/10.1145/2597809.2597825

1. Introduction

Today's design requirements of embedded processors demand system architects to consider strict constraints such as high performance, small area, and low energy consumption all simultaneously.
To meet these requirements, Very Long Instruction Word (VLIW)
architectures are widely adopted in modern embedded system-on-
chip (SoC) designs [29]. VLIW processors are designed to enhance
performance by executing multiple instructions in parallel within a
single VLIW packet statically determined at compile time. Such
delegation of extracting Instruction Level Parallelism (ILP) onto
compilers is what makes VLIW processors simpler, smaller, and
more power-efficient than superscalar processors, which normally
wield complex and expensive hardware components to extract ILP
dynamically. On the other hand, to achieve higher performance,
VLIW architectures often increase the number of issue slots, consequently extending the length of a VLIW packet. This can contribute
to significantly lower code density and increased code size, which
may also negatively affect the chip area [35, 36]. Furthermore, the
wider VLIW packets consume higher power on instruction fetch,
and increase the per-access energy of the instruction cache if a
larger cache is required.

To address these issues, Lee et al. [19] have proposed a VLIW
architecture with a reduced bit-width instruction set, where each instruction of a VLIW packet can have a 16-bit representation in addition to the original 32-bit format. Normally a reduced bit-width instruction set contains only a small subset of the original instruction
set due to the reduced encoding space. However, using Dynamic
Implied Addressing Mode (DIAM) [37] excessive information that
cannot be encoded within the reduced bit-width, such as a register number or an immediate value, can be specified as a separate
instruction, and at runtime dynamically combined with the matching instruction. This hardware-assisted approach allows for 100%
equivalent behavior as the original instruction sequence, while providing important benefits such as code size reduction (41% on average) and reduced energy consumption ($8 \sim 16\%$ on average) on a
4-way VLIW processor for a set of compute-intensive kernels [19].

However, the DIAM-based instruction encoding, especially
when applied to VLIW processors, can incur a significant overhead in terms of runtime. Experimental results in [19] attest that
the execution time increase can be up to 40%, and 10% on average,
for the same set of kernels. Therefore to make the DIAM-based
VLIW architecture more practical, the performance overhead must
be minimized.

Fundamentally, the runtime increase in the above case is caused
by the new instructions inserted into the code to provide the extra information necessary for DIAM. Those extra instructions may
in turn lead to extra VLIW packets, which, when fetched and
executed, result in increased execution cycles. Such performance

degradation is aggravated in loops as opposed to straight-line code, since in loops extra instructions are more likely to generate extra VLIW packets. While simply upping the average instruction fetch rate may be enough to negate the effect of extra instructions in the case of a single-issue processor [37], the changes made to VLIW packets by extra instructions are more permanent and much harder to reverse at runtime. In this paper to address the runtime overhead we present a revised DIAM-based instruction encoding scheme for VLIW processors. The main idea is that the extra information due to DIAM does not change dynamically, thus if it is needed in a loop, it can be *reused* rather than *re-fetched* in every iteration. In the original DIAM-based VLIW architecture, if an instruction holding the extra information is in a loop, it must be fetched along with the rest of the packet and executed repeatedly in all iterations, even though the extra information may already be found in a hardware buffer provided to support DIAM. In the modified scheme, such instructions are executed only once prior to the loop entry, which can drastically reduce the runtime overhead. We also present the new architecture, especially that of the hardware buffer for DIAM, which can retain necessary DIAM information during loop execution. Our experiments using a 4-way VLIW architecture with 32-bit instructions as a baseline architecture demonstrate that our revised DIAM-based VLIW architecture can effectively reduce the runtime overhead of loops, and also, if used with loop unrolling, can further increase the performance of loops with quite an acceptable code size increase.

The rest of the paper is organized as follows. In Section 2, we review the background. After describing the motivation of this work in Section 2.3, we explain the hardware architecture modification and also how loop unrolling works together with the architecture in Section 3. The experimental results are presented in Section 4. After discussing related work in Section 5, we conclude in Section 6.

2. Background and Motivation

In this section we briefly review DIAM and the original DIAM-based instruction bit-width reduction scheme for VLIW architectures.

2.1 Dynamic Implied Addressing Mode (DIAM)

To fully convert a given 32-bit ISA into an equivalent 16-bit one, we need to overcome the limited encoding space of the 16-bit ISA. Assuming that 7 bits and 4 bits are assigned for opcode and one register operand, respectively (the number of registers is 16), an instruction holding distinct three register operands cannot be encoded within a 16-bit word as illustrated in Figure 1(a). The excessive information, which is `r10`, one of the register operands in our example, is called *remote operand*. An instruction is called a *partial instruction* if it requires one or more remote operands after being converted into the 16-bit format; otherwise, it is called *complete instruction* (see Figure 1(b)). The strategy of DIAM is to use a special storage, called *remote operand array (ROA) buffer*, to store on demand remote operands which are delivered by a special instruction, called *ROA instruction*. An ROA instruction consists of 4-bit opcode and 12-bit remote operands which can contain register operands or a part of immediate value. Figure 2 illustrates the conceptual behavior of DIAM. Once a single ROA instruction is executed, the ROA buffer entries are updated with the remote operands. These remote operands, whenever necessary for partial instructions, are retrieved in sequence from the ROA buffer automatically by the hardware. Thus by using DIAM, a partial instruction and its corresponding remote operands can be dynamically assembled to form a complete instruction for execution, which makes it possible to build a 16-bit ISA without loss of information from an original 32-bit ISA.

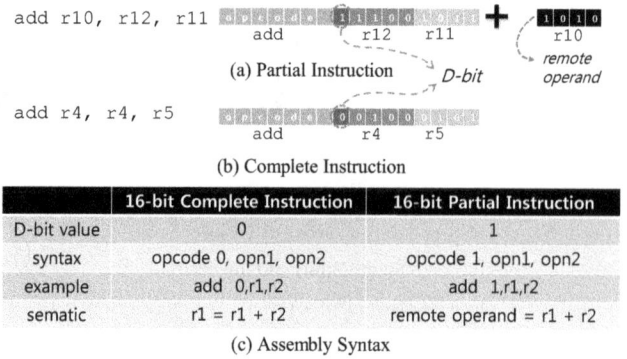

Figure 1. Examples of partial and complete instructions, and a remote operand [19]

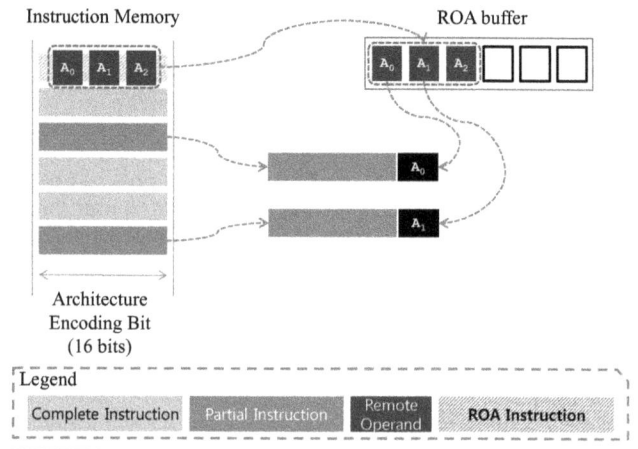

Figure 2. A conceptual view of a processor with DIAM

2.2 DIAM on VLIW Architecture

Figure 3 illustrates with an example how a DIAM-based VLIW architecture works. First, each issue slot is given a fixed priority for accessing the ROA buffer, which is shared among all the issue slots. In this example we assume that the leftmost slot (slot 0) has the highest priority while the rightmost one (slot 3) has the lowest. Now, as a VLIW packet containing two ROA instructions is decoded (Figure 3(a)), the ROA instructions at slots 0 and 1 write their remote operands sequentially into the ROA buffer (Figure 3(b), (c)). The first partial instruction at slot 2, "`add 1,r1,r2`", is then decoded, and the first remote operand 3 is extracted from the ROA buffer and interpreted as a register operand `r3` which is integrated with the instruction to form a complete instruction, "`add r1,r2,r3`" (Figure 3(d)). Finally, the second partial instruction at slot 3 is decoded, and the remote operand ('abcd') is extracted from the buffer, since an opcode `lw` requires a 16-bit immediate value to form a complete instruction (Figure 3(e)). Once all partial instructions in the VLIW packet are combined with proper remote operands during the decode stage, every instruction in the packet becomes a complete instruction, ready for execution. Note that the above-mentioned decoding process for a single VLIW packet is finished within the timing bugdet of the decode stage(s) with the support of special hardware, as explained in [19].

2.3 Code Conversion for DIAM-based VLIW

Figure 4 shows an example of converting VLIW code in a 32-bit ISA into that of a 16-bit ISA for a DIAM-based VLIW proces-

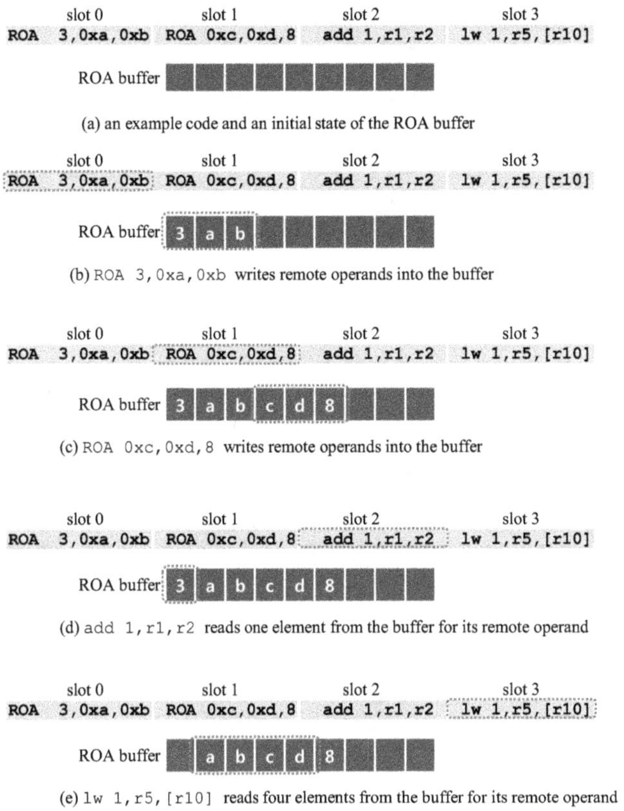

(a) an example code and an initial state of the ROA buffer

(b) ROA 3,0xa,0xb writes remote operands into the buffer

(c) ROA 0xc,0xd,8 writes remote operands into the buffer

(d) add 1,r1,r2 reads one element from the buffer for its remote operand

(e) lw 1,r5,[r10] reads four elements from the buffer for its remote operand

Figure 3. An example of accessing ROA buffer at run time in DIAM-based VLIW architecture

(a) 32-bit ISA VLIW code

(b) 16-bit ISA VLIW code

Figure 4. An example of converting 32-bit ISA VLIW code into 16-bit one with DIAM (memory access instructions: slot 0,1; expensive instructions: slot 2,3)

sor. We assume that arithmetic logic unit (ALU) instructions such as add and sub can be assigned to all slots, but memory instructions (lw, sw) and expensive ones (mul, div) are restrictively allocated to slots 0 and 1 and to slots 2 and 3, respectively. We also assume that the ROA buffer can hold 9 ROA buffer words; one ROA buffer word is four bits, so a 4-bit register operand consists of one ROA buffer word and a 16-bit immediate value is composed of four ROA buffer words. In this example, through the ISA conversion, we can achieve about 40% of code size reduction (the size of the 32-bit code: 32 bits × 4 slots × 8 lines = 1024 bits; the size of the 16-bit code: 16 bits × 4 slots × 10 lines = 640 bits). Notice, however, that the number of VLIW packets is increased mainly due to the newly generated ROA instructions. While some ROA instructions fill previously unoccupied (NOP) slots, many others help generate new VLIW packets (see Line 5 in Figure 4(b) for example). Because of the extra VLIW packets, the 16-bit ISA DIAM-based VLIW processor takes more cycles to execute than the original 32-bit ISA VLIW processor.

The performance overhead due to the extra VLIW packets becomes more prominent in loops. To make this analysis simple, let us assume in this section that each VLIW packet takes one cycle and there is no stall of any kind. Hence, the number of execution cycles is equal to the number of VLIW packets executed. Now, for the example of Figure 4, if the loop's iteration count is 1,000, the total number of execution cycles of the 16-bit code is 2,000 higher than that of the 32-bit code, due to the two additional VLIW packets of the 16-bit code, which is about 25% overhead compared to the 32-bit code. However, if the additional VLIW packets can be generated outside of the loop, the cycle count increase will essentially become zero when considering the rest of the code of the application. Next we present how to realize this low performance overhead

for loops, which is centered on reusing the information in the ROA buffer.

3. Our Approach

3.1 Loop-invariant ROA Instruction

The role of an ROA instruction is to provide appropriate remote operands for partial instructions. Each ROA instruction writes three ROA buffer words into the ROA buffer, from which partial instructions can later retrieve remote operands as needed. The buffer works as a circular FIFO queue, so when a new ROA instruction writes its remote operands into the buffer, they are sequentially inserted at current rear of the buffer. Due to the limited size of the buffer, each entry of the buffer will be overwritten multiple times by ROA instructions during the execution. If an entry of the buffer is overwritten with a new remote operand before it is read by the corresponding partial instruction, the partial instruction will read a wrong remote operand, causing incorrect execution. Therefore, ROA instructions and their corresponding partial instructions must be carefully scheduled not to violate the original semantics of the code. This scheduling should be done by the compiler with the constraint of the limited buffer size.

However, if the size of the ROA buffer is large enough to simultaneously maintain all the remote operands of the ROA instructions in a fragment of code, such as a loop, then the ROA instructions can be freely scheduled in the loop or even moved out of the loop, as long as the relative ordering of the ROA instructions is kept. In other words, the ordering between ROA instructions and their corresponding partial instructions need not be taken into account in scheduling. Therefore, the partial instructions can be scheduled independently without considering the scheduling of the associated ROA instructions. In that case, we say that the ROA instructions are *loop-invariant*.

In the example of Figure 4(b), if the ROA buffer has enough entries for at least 10 ROA instructions, all the 10 ROA instructions shown in the figure can become loop-invariant. By generating three extra VLIW packets that contain all the 10 ROA instructions outside of the loop (just before the loop entry), we can make the loop body scheduled in 8 cycles, just like that of Figure 4(a), when the 16-bit version has the same performance as the 32-bit version, except for the three extra VLIW packets.

3.2 Hardware Modification

Based on the idea of making the ROA instructions loop-invariant, we present a modified DIAM-based VLIW architecture that can improve the overall performance by reducing the overhead caused by the ROA instructions in loops. Contrary to the original architecture where ROA instructions are located in a loop and therefore repeatedly executed for the number of loop iterations, our modified architecture executes them only once prior to entering the loop by introducing a novel single-write multiple-read (SWMR) ROA buffer. Before entering a loop, as many remote operands as the capacity of the SWMR ROA buffer can allow, are copied into the buffer. This copy operation is the only write operation to the buffer until the end of the loop. Then, when the loop executes, partial instructions access the SWMR ROA buffer only to retrieve their remote operands, which means that many read operations are performed on the SWMR ROA buffer during the loop execution, hence the name single-write multiple-read.

Since the SWMR ROA buffer has a limited capacity, it may not be able to accommodate all the remote operands of a loop. In this case, the remaining remote operands of the loop are processed in the same way as in the original DIAM-based VLIW architecture. For each remaining remote operand in the loop, a pair of corresponding ROA instruction(s) and partial instruction(s) iteratively write and read to/from the existing ROA buffer. For this reason, the existing ROA buffer is called single-write single-read (SWSR).

The code generation must reflect the modified architecture. Figure 5 illustrates an example code for the modified DIAM-based VLIW architecture. The first two lines (line 1 and 2) are sequential code that is executed only once before entering the loop. The rest of the lines (line 3 ∼ 10) are the loop code. In the sequential code, a new instruction mode_set is added to signal the start of ROA instruction to the SWMR ROA buffer. The mode_set instruction can only appear in Slot 0, to simplify decoding and its handling. At the instruction fetch stage, detecting the mode_set instruction causes the following ROA instructions to write their remote operands into the SWMR ROA buffer during the decode stage. In the example of Figure 5, the capacity of the SWMR ROA buffer is assumed to hold 21 ROA buffer words, which can be delivered by 7 ROA instructions. In our example, the sequential code consists of a total of 7 ROA instructions as shown in Figure 5. Executing the sequential code makes the remote operands of these 7 ROA instructions copied into the SWMR ROA buffer.

Next, when the loop code executes, the remote operands in the SWMR ROA buffer are referenced and read-accessed by partial instructions; every read access increases the SWMR buffer index by one, and branch instruction at the end of the loop decides whether to reset the index or not. Note that the contents of the SWMR ROA buffer are not updated repeatedly. On the other hand, three ROA instructions in the loop code (lines 3 and 7) cannot be moved out of the loop due to the limited size of the SWMR ROA buffer. These three ROA instructions write their remote operands into the SWSR buffer for every iteration, which are read by partial instructions in a few cycles later for every iteration. Note that the SWSR buffer is referenced in a loop only after the index of SWMR buffer reaches the end of the buffer. The position of the index indicates the follows: a loop might contain more ROA instructions than SWMR buffer can take, and all the entries in SWMR buffer has been referenced. When this happens, remaining partial instructions in a loop read remote operands from the SWSR buffer like partial instructions in normal straight-line code do. Upon the exit of a loop, the position of the index of SWMR buffer is moved to the end of the SWMR buffer and remain the same until mode_set instruction, which resets the index, is encountered. In doing so, the hardware control unit can simply distinguish when to use the proper buffer by observing the index of the SWMR buffer; if the index is positioned at the end of

	Slot 0	Slot 1	Slot 2	Slot 3
1	mode_set	ROA 0xf,0,6	ROA 0,0xf,4	ROA 4,8,1
2	ROA 2,6,7	ROA 8,9,10	ROA 4,11,0xf	ROA 8,3,0
L1:				
3	lw 1,r2,[r1]	lw 1,r3,[r1]	ROA 0xf,0xc,1	ROA 8,1,3
4	lsa 1,r4,r2	lsa 1,r5,r3	mul 1,r2,r3	div 1,r2,r3
5	add 1,r4,r5	sub 0,r5,r4	mul 1,r3,r3	mul 1,r2,r2
6	sub 1,r8,r6	add 0,r9,r10	sub 1,r9,r10	add 0,r5,r7
7		ROA 8,8,0	div 0,r4,r9	div 0,r5,r11
8	sw 1,r4,[r1]	sw 1,r5,[r1]	add 0,r1,1	
9	cmpne 1,r2,r1			
10	bne r2,L1			
	16 bits	16 bits	16 bits	16 bits

Figure 5. An example code for the modified DIAM-based VLIW architecture.

the buffer, no matter where program counter lies, the SWSR buffer is referenced.

Similar to the example of Figure 4, if we assume that the loop has many iterations (say, a thousand), then the performance overhead of two extra VLIW packets is negligible. Further, since this code has now 8 VLIW packets only in the loop body, its performance is almost identical to that of the original 32-bit version in Figure 4(a), demonstrating that the performance overhead of the DIAM-based VLIW architecture can be minimized by moving ROA instructions outside of the loops.

3.3 Applying Loop Unrolling

	Slot 0	Slot 1	Slot 2	Slot 3
L1:				
1	lw r2,[r1,0xf060]	lw r3,[r1,0xf448]		
2	lsa r4,r2,#1	lsa r5,r3,#2	mul r6,r2,r3	div r7,r2,r3
3	add r8,r4,r5	sub r5,r5,r4	mul r9,r3,r3	mul r10,r2,r2
4	sub r4,r8,r6	add r9,r9,r10	sub r11,r9,r10	add r5,r5,r7
5	lw r2,[r1,0xf064]	lw r3,[r1,0xf44c]	div r4,r4,r9	div r5,r5,r11
6	sw r4,[r1,0xf830]	sw r5,[r1,0xfc18]	lsa r4,r2,#1	lsa r5,r3,#2
7	add r8,r4,r5	sub r5,r5,r4	mul r6,r2,r3	div r7,r2,r3
8	sub r4,r8,r6	add r5,r5,r7	mul r9,r3,r3	mul r10,r2,r2
9	add r9,r9,r10	sub r11,r9,r10		
10			div r4,r4,r9	div r5,r5,r11
11	sw r4,[r1,0xf834]	sw r5,[r1,0xfc1c]	add r1,r1,2	
12	cmpne r2,r1,0x1388			
13	bne r2,L1			
	32 bits	32 bits	32 bits	32 bits

(a) 32-bit ISA code with 2X unrolling

	Slot 0	Slot 1	Slot 2	Slot 3
L1:				
1	ROA 0xf,0,6	ROA 0,0xf,4	ROA 4,8,1	
2	lw 1,r2,[r1]	lw 1,r3,[r1]	ROA 2,6,7	ROA 8,9,10
3	lsa 1,r4,r2	lsa 1,r5,r3	mul 1,r2,r3	div 1,r2,r3
4	add 1,r4,r5	sub 0,r5,r4	mul 1,r3,r3	mul 1,r2,r2
5	ROA 4,11,0xf	sub 1,r8,r6	add 0,r9,r10	sub 1,r9,r10
6	ROA 0,6,4	lw 1,r2,[r1]		ROA 0xf,4,4
7	ROA 0xc,0xf,8	lw 1,r3,[r1]	div 0,r4,r9	div 0,r5,r11
8	ROA 3,0,0xf	sw 1,r4,[r1]	ROA 0xc,1,8	ROA 1,2,8
9	sw 1,r5,[r1]	lsa 1,r4,r2	lsa 1,r5,r3	add 1,r4,r5
10	sub 0,r5,r4	ROA 6,7,4	mul 1,r2,r3	div 1,r2,r3
11	sub 1,r8,r6	ROA 9,10,11	mul 1,r3,r3	mul 1,r2,r2
12	add 0,r9,r10	sub 1,r9,r10	add 0,r5,r7	div 0,r4,r9
13	ROA 0xf,8,3	ROA 4,0xf,0xc	div 0,r5,r11	ROA 1,0xc,1
14	sw 1,r4,[r1]	sw 1,r5,[r1]	ROA 3,8,8	add 0,r1,2
15	cmpne 1,r2,r1			
16	bne r2,L1			
	16 bits	16 bits	16 bits	16 bits

(b) 16-bit ISA code with 2X unrolling

Figure 6. An example code after loop unrolling by a factor of two.

Loop unrolling is a loop optimization technique that replaces the body of a loop with several copies of it and adjusts the loop-control code accordingly [25]. The number of copies is called the unrolling factor. The purpose of loop unrolling is to improve the performance of the loop by reducing the frequency of branches at the expense of the code bloating due to the multiple copies of the loop body. The code bloating problem of loop unrolling would be better mitigated in 16-bit ISA code as compared to the 32-bit one, since, generally

	Slot 0	Slot 1	Slot 2	Slot 3
1	mode_set	ROA 0xf,0,6	ROA 0,0xf,4	ROA 4,8,1
2	ROA 2,6,7	ROA 8,9,10	ROA 4,11,0xf	ROA 0,6,4
L1:				
1	lw 1,r2,[r1]	lw 1,r3,[r1]	ROA 0xf,4,4	ROA 0xc,0xf,8
2	lsa 1,r4,r2	lsa 1,r5,r3	mul 1,r2,r3	div 1,r2,r3
3	add 1,r4,r5	sub 0,r5,r4	mul 1,r3,r3	mul 1,r2,r2
4	sub 1,r8,r6	add 0,r5,r7	add 0,r9,r10	sub 1,r9,r10
5	lw 1,r2,[r1]	lw 1,r3,[r1]	div 0,r4,r9	div 0,r5,r11
6	ROA 3,0,0xf	sw 1,r4,[r1]	ROA 0xc,1,8	ROA 1,2,8
7	sw 1,r5,[r1]	lsa 1,r4,r2	lsa 1,r5,r3	add 1,r4,r5
8	sub 0,r5,r4	ROA 6,7,4	mul 1,r2,r3	div 1,r2,r3
9	sub 1,r8,r6	ROA 9,10,11	mul 1,r3,r3	mul 1,r2,r2
10	add 0,r9,r10	sub 1,r9,r10	add 0,r5,r7	div 0,r4,r9
11	ROA 0xf,8,3	ROA 4,0xf,0xc	div 0,r5,r11	ROA 1,0xc,1
12	sw 1,r4,[r1]	sw 1,r5,[r1]	ROA 3,8,8	add 0,r1,2
13	cmpne 1,r2,r1			
14	bne r2,L1			
	16 bits	16 bits	16 bits	16 bits

Figure 7. An example code after loop unrolling by a factor of two in the modified DIAM-based VLIW architecture with the SWMR ROA buffer.

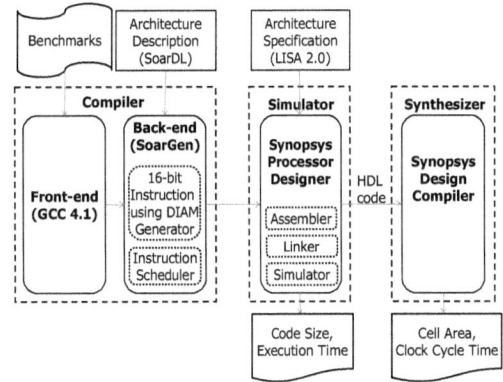

Figure 8. Our experiment framework.

speaking, the amount of code is smaller in the 16-bit code than in the 32-bit one.

Figure 6 shows the resulting code after applying loop unrolling by a factor of two to the code in Figure 4 (a) and (b). As shown in Figure 6(a), the code size is increased to 13 VLIW packets. The increase due to loop unrolling is 5 packets, whose bit length is 640 bits (32 bits × 4 slots × 5 packets). On the other hand, in the 16-bit code of Figure 6(b), loop unrolling generates 6 more VLIW packets, which are apparently more than 5 packets of the 32-bit case but, at just 384 bits (16 bits × 4 slots × 6 packets), are actually smaller in terms of the number of bits due to the reduced instruction bit-width. Thus, the DIAM-based 16-bit ISA VLIW architecture can also make loop unrolling more appealing in terms of code size as well as from the performance perspective.

Let us quantify the performance of 32-bit vs. 16-bit code with/without loop unrolling, given an original loop with 1,000 iterations. The result is summarized in Table 1, which provides a high-level comparison in terms of code size, runtime (dynamic packet count), and expected IF (instruction fetch) power dissipation among different configurations. A configuration is defined by i) whether DIAM is applied or not, ii) if DIAM is applied, whether it is with or without the SWMR ROA buffer, and iii) whether loop unrolling is applied or not. There are six configurations in all, which are listed in the second column of the table.

Without loop unrolling, the *dynamic packet count* of the 32-bit original code is 8,000 (= 8 × 1,000), while that of the 16-bit code on the DIAM-based VLIW architecture is 10,000 (= 10 × 1,000) if the SWMR ROA buffer is not used, or 8,002 (= 2 + 8 × 1,000) otherwise (see Figure 4 and Figure 5). With loop unrolling, the dynamic packet counts of the 32-bit unrolled code and the 16-bit one are 6,500 (= 13 × 500) and 8,000 (= 16 × 500), respectively (see Figure 6). Note that here the number of iterations is halved. We can also apply loop unrolling to the code for the modified DIAM-based VLIW architecture with the SWMR ROA buffer to gain more performance. Figure 7 shows a schedule after 2X loop unrolling. The dynamic packet count is 7,002, which is almost 1,000 less than without the SWMR ROA buffer.

It is straightforward to calculate the code size for the configurations using Figures 4 through 7. The IF power is significantly reduced only when DIAM is used.

From Table 1, we can see that Configuration 2 is the best in terms of code size while Configuration 4 is the best (i.e., least) in terms of runtime. However, Configuration 2 is also the worst in terms of runtime, and Configuration 4 is the worst in terms of code size. Thus neither Configuration 2 nor Configuration 4 may be the best if we are concerned with both code size and runtime,

which is typically the case. On the other hand, Configuration 6 gives the result that is inbetween, representing a very useful design point when both performance and code size must be optimized for. Also, Configuration 6 has the second-lowest runtime only next to Configuration 4. Further, though the table shows the code size for a loop only, at the application level, the code size difference between Configuration 6 and Configuration 2 may be small, as they differ only in loops, which means small code size for Configuration 6.

4. Experiments

4.1 Setup

Figure 8 illustrates our experiment framework for compilation, simulation, and synthesis, which is based on Synopsys Processor Designer [30]. Software tools including an assembler, a linker, and a simulator have been generated by Synopsys Processor Designer from an architecture description in LISA 2.0. With more detailed LISA description, RTL code is also generated by the same tool for all the VLIW processors used in the experiments. RTL code is then synthesized using Synopsys Design Compiler, with 130nm technology in our experiment, to obtain hardware implementation results such as clock cycle time and cell area. Our extensions such as DIAM and SWMR ROA buffer are also successfully described in LISA, driving the generation of software tools and RTLs used in our experiments.

The compiler for the proposed VLIW processor is generated by a retargetable compiler platform, SoarGen [1]. Given a description in architecture description language called SoarDL [1], SoarGen generates the compiler for the target processor.

In our experiments, we have selected as the baseline configuration the 16-bit ISA 4-way DIAM-based VLIW processor, which was proposed and evaluated in the previous work [19]. The ISA of the baseline processor follows a typical RISC-style such as MIPS ISA [31]. The baseline processor is augmented with the SWMR ROA buffer as explained in Section 3.2, which is our proposed VLIW processor. Key architectural parameters of the baseline and proposed processors are listed in Table 2. The only difference between the two processors is the existence of a SWMR ROA buffer and relevant control units. The size of the SWMR ROA buffer is determined by the average number of ROA instructions generated in the loops found in benchmark code used in our experiments. Even though the size of the buffer is set as 19 throughout the experiment, a sensitivity test of various buffer size is conducted in Section 4.3.

We have used Livermore Loops [23] and DSPstone kernels [38][1] to evaluate the effectiveness of our approach. Livermore Loops is

---

[1] In order to conduct experiments with conventional complex benchmark suite such as SPEC2006, full support for standard library is mandatory.

Table 1. High-level comparison of six configurations (original loop iteration count: 1000, unroll factor: 2)

No.	Configuration	Code Size (bits)	Runtime (#packets)	IF Power
1	32-bit original code (Figure 4(a))	1024	8000	unchanged
2	16-bit code with DIAM (Figure 4(b))	640	10000	reduced
3	16-bit code with DIAM and SWMR ROA buffer (Figure 5)	768	8002	reduced
4	32-bit unrolled code (Figure 6(a))	1664	6500	unchanged
5	16-bit unrolled code (Figure 6(b))	1024	8000	reduced
6	16-bit unrolled code with DIAM and SWMR ROA buffer (Figure 7)	1024	7002	reduced

Table 2. VLIW processors used in the experiments

	Baseline VLIW processor	Modified VLIW processor
# of way	4-way	
instruction bit-width	16 bits	
data bit-width	32 bits	
# of pipeline stages	5 (IF,DC,EX,MEM,WB)	
size of SWSR ROA buffer	9 ROA buffer words (3 ROA instructions)	
size of SWMR ROA buffer	x	57 ROA buffer words (19 ROA instructions)

a benchmark suite for parallel architectures and consists of a set of loop kernels in numerically intensive applications. DSPstone is a kernel benchmark suite consisting of code fragments or functions which are commonly used in DSP algorithms.

To evaluate the efficiency of our proposed architecture, Section 4.2 presents the code size and execution time results, measured using the software tools. To estimate the overhead of our proposed architecture, the cell area and clock cycle time are reported in Section 4.3.

4.2 Code Size and Execution Time

We estimate the code size and the execution time for each benchmark program in every possible configuration from whether DIAM is applied or not, whether the SWMR ROA buffer is introduced or not, and whether loop unrolling is applied or not. The configurations are summarized in Table 3. The compiler must generate appropriate code corresponding to each configuration. The code for Configuration 1 and 4 has 32-bit instruction format since DIAM is not applied. The difference is that loop unrolling is applied only to Configuration 4. The code from Configuration 2,3,5, and 6 is all together 16-bit ISA code since DIAM is applied to all of them. They are classified by whether or not the SWMR ROA buffer and loop unrolling are used.

4.2.1 Effectiveness of SWMR ROA buffer

Figure 9 and Figure 10 show the code size and the execution cycles of each configuration normalized to those of Configuration 1, respectively. Similar to the results of the previous paper [19], the code size reduction due to DIAM is about 38.6% on average as seen by the comparison between Configuration 1 and 2. From the same comparison, however, the performance is degraded by about 10.8% on average. Hence, eliminating the 10.8% performance overhead would be the goal of our SWMR ROA buffer.

To reduce the performance overhead, the SWMR ROA buffer is introduced in our proposal. The net effect of the SWMR ROA buffer is found in the comparison between Configuration 2 and 3. Compared to Configuration 2 (the previous DIAM-based VLIW ar-

chitecture without the SWMR ROA buffer), Configuration 3 shows that the code size is increased by 4.8% on average, while the performance improves by about 4.9%, which achieves almost a half of the goal of eliminating the performance overhead. Since the purpose of introducing the SWMR ROA buffer is to help the previous DIAM-based VLIW architecture, it is essential to see the effect of both applying DIAM and the SWMR ROA buffer compared to the original 32-bit ISA VLIW architecture. Compared to Configuration 1 (the original 32-bit VLIW processor without loop unrolling), applying both DIAM and the SWMR ROA buffer (Configuration 3) can yield code size reduction of about 35.7% at the expense of performance degradation of about 6.81%. Thus, Configuration 3 (DIAM with the SWMR ROA buffer) still gives substantial code size reduction with less performance overhead compared to Configuration 2 (DIAM without the SWMR ROA buffer).

The above comparisons among Configuration 1, 2, and 3 deal with the cases that loop unrolling is not applied. From the comparisons among Configuration 4, 5, and 6, we can also see the net effect of the SWMR ROA buffer. From the comparison between Configuration 4 and 5, due to DIAM, the code size is reduced by about 37.7% while losing about 13.7% in performance. Thus it is also the goal of the SWMR ROA buffer to remove the 13.7% performance overhead in the case that loop unrolling is applied.

Compared to Configuration 5 (DIAM without the SWMR ROA buffer and with loop unrolling), Configuration 6 shows that the code size is increased by 3.4% on average, while the performance is improved by about 6.3%, which is also almost a half of the goal of removing the performance overhead. Compared to Configuration 4 (the original 32-bit VLIW processor with loop unrolling), we can see the effect of applying both DIAM and the SWMR ROA buffer with loop unrolling (Configuration 6), which shows that the code size is reduced by about 35.5% at the expense of performance degradation of about 8.7%. Thus Configuration 6 (DIAM with the SWMR ROA buffer and loop unrolling) still gives substantial code size reduction with less performance overhead compared to Configuration 5 (DIAM without the SWMR ROA buffer and with loop unrolling).

4.2.2 Effectiveness of loop unrolling

From Section 4.2.1, we can see that the SWMR ROA buffer improves the performance of loops in the DIAM-based VLIW architecture. In addition to the SWMR ROA buffer, loop unrolling can also result in performance improvement. Three comparisons

---

However, our VLIW architecture is a custom-designed circuit generated with the help of Synopsys tool-sets and therefore the standard library is not fully supported. Thus, DSPstone and Livermore Loops have been selected as our benchmark suite since they have been widely used and can cover vast range of applications from parallel computing to digital signal processing.

Table 3. Configurations in terms of DIAM, SWMR ROA buffer, and loop unrolling in the experiments

Configurations	DIAM	SWMR ROA buffer	Loop unrolling
1	x	x	x
2	o	x	x
3	o	o	x
4	x	x	o
5	o	x	o
6	o	o	o

between Configuration 1 and 4, between Configuration 2 and 5, and between Configuration 3 and 6 show the effect of loop unrolling when it is only applied regardless of whether the SWMR ROA buffer is used. With loop unrolling, the performance improves by about 34.3% at the expense of the code size increase of about 30.5%. As seen by this result, the substantial code bloating is a critical disadvantage of loop unrolling. However, if loon unrolling is applied with DIAM, the penalty of the code bloating can be considerably resolved mainly due to the reduced instruction bit-width, which halves the instruction packet size from 16 bytes to 8 bytes.

Apart from this seemingly obvious reason, there is another factor that is worth noting. Consider Configuration 2 and 3, and Configuration 5 and 6 in Table 1. Since the SWMR buffer has been implemented, the performance of Configuration 3 and 6 has increased compared to those of Configuration 2 and 5, respectively. However, the code size of Configuration 3 is slightly bigger than that of Configuration 2 while such a tendency is not seen in Configuration 6. The reason for this slight size change can be attributed to the aggressive ROA instruction scheduling for loops that have relatively low/modest level of instruction level parallelism (ILP). The original scheduler for DIAM, which does not consider loops, tries to replace as many NOPs with ROA instructions as possible to hide the performance overhead caused by these additional instructions; therefore, in a loop, some ROA instructions substitute for NOPs in existing packets while others generate extra VLIW packets. Contrary to the original scheme, the augmented scheduler tries to make as many ROA instructions as loop-invariant VLIW packets possible so that it can move such packets outside the loop to improve the performance. During the step, NOPs which have been replaced by ROA instructions will be revealed again. The generated loop-invariant VLIW packets will be inserted to the front of the loop as seen in Section 3, thus improving performance but slightly increasing the overall code size.

In such a case, loop unrolling can be applied. By doing so, most NOPs existing in a loop can be removed, thus compensating the aforementioned side effect of increased code size while achieving performance improvement. In Figure 9 and Figure 10, a comparison between Configuration 1 and 6 shows the combined effect of our enhanced DIAM-based VLIW architecture with the SWMR ROA buffer and loop unrolling, which is, on average, the code size reduction of about 17.4% and the performance increase of about 25.0%.

To summarize, our scheme is benefited from loop unrolling in terms of code size and performance because of the removed NOPs and loop control code, respectively. Loop unrolling, on its part, can gain advantage in terms of code size because of the reduced bit-width provided by DIAM technique. Therefore, in the DIAM-based 16-bit ISA VLIW architecture, loop unrolling can be more appealing optimization technique in terms of code size as well as from the performance perspective than in the 32-bit ISA VLIW architecture, and both technique should be applied simultaneously to reach the maximum performance.

4.3 Hardware cost

An important issue in the design of the modified VLIW processor is to determine the size of the SWMR ROA buffer. The larger the SWMR ROA buffer, the higher the achievable performance, as more ROA instructions of a loop can be moved to the SWMR ROA buffer. However, having or adding to the SWMR ROA buffer could have a negative side effect of having another register file. Therefore, we should consider the effect of the SWMR ROA buffer on the hardware cost and the cycle time.

The size of the SWMR ROA buffer is represented by the number of ROA instructions that can be contained in the SWMR ROA buffer. The amount of additional code for writing ROA instructions into the SWMR ROA buffer depends on the size of the SWMR ROA buffer. For example, in the case that the size of the SWMR ROA buffer is seven in 4-way VLIW processor, two extra lines of VLIW packets including one *mode_set* instruction and seven ROA instructions have to be newly generated (1 *mode_set* + 7 ROA instructions = 4-way × 2 packets). If the size of the SWMR ROA buffer is eleven, a total of three lines of VLIW packets should be newly generated as sequential code (1 *mode_set* + 11 ROA instructions = 4-way × 3 packets). Thus we evaluate the hardware cost for a sequence of increasing SWMR ROA buffer sizes, in steps of four ROA instructions, which comprise one VLIW packet in 4-way VLIW processor (e.g. 7, 11, 15, etc.).

Table 4 shows the cell area of each VLIW processor for different sizes of the SWMR ROA buffer. The total cell area is the sum of combinational area and non-combinational area. The overhead of the total cell area is about 7% per one step of the SWMR ROA buffer size increase (i.e., four ROA instructions). This non-negligible overhead results from the fact that the SWMR ROA buffer is basically a register file. In particular, since our VLIW architecture has 4-issue slots, it requires four read/write ports, and the cell area of a register file is roughly proportional to the number of read/wirte ports. Furthermore, unlike the original SWSR ROA buffer whose capacity is just 36 bits (4 bits × 9 ROA buffer words), the SWMR ROA buffer requires more bits (e.g., 7 ROA instructions: 84 bits, 11 ROA instructions: 132 bits, 15 ROA instructions: 180 bits, etc.). The combined effect of many read/write ports and the big capacity of the SWMR ROA buffer incurs non-negligible overhead due to the SWMR ROA buffer in terms of the cell area.

Table 5 shows the clock cycle time of each VLIW processor for different SWMR ROA buffer sizes. Unlike the cell area, the clock cycle times are almost constant within the margin of error. This means that the increasing the SWMR ROA buffer size, or even the introduction of the SWMR ROA buffer itself, hardly affects the critical path delay of the VLIW processors used in the experiment.

5. Related Work

Much research has been conducted on reducing the loop overhead with software techniques. Loop strength reduction with basic induction variable elimination is one of them [25]. It replaces expensive operations, such as multiplications and divisions, with cheap ones, such as additions and subtractions, so that the latency of an iteration in a loop can be minimized. As mentioned in Section 3.3, loop unrolling is a software technique that replaces the body of a loop with several copies of the body and adjusts the loop-control code accordingly [25]. Even though loop unrolling can improve the performance of loops, it suffers from the increased code size because of the duplicated loop bodies. However, as demonstrated in the experiment results, loop unrolling can be applied on our DIAM-based VLIW architecture with relatively low cost in terms of code size because of the reduced bit-width while attaining certain level of performance improvement.

Software pipelining is a software technique that reduces the execution time of a loop by overlapping the execution of successive iterations of the loop [2–5, 7–10, 12, 13, 15, 18, 24, 26–28, 33, 34]. While delivering higher level of ILP thus improving the overall performance, it also increases the code size due to the compensation

Code size (normalized to config. 1)

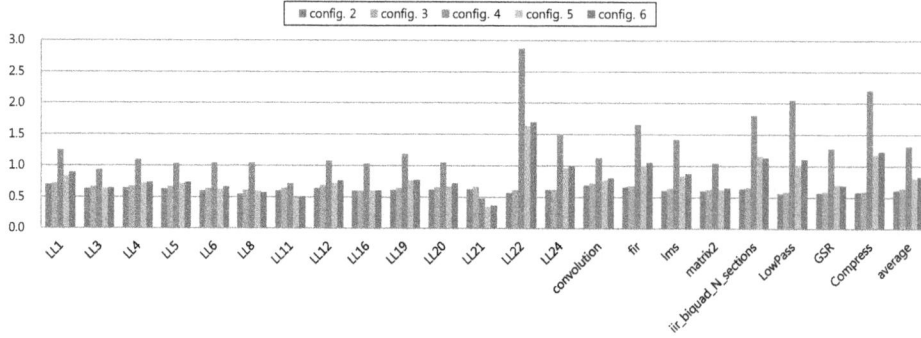

Figure 9. Code size of each configuration (normalized to 32-bit without unroll)

Execution time (normalized to config. 1)

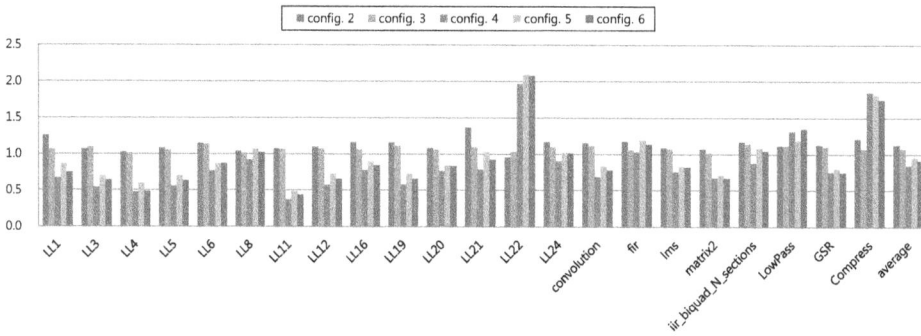

Figure 10. Execution time of each configuration (normalized to 32-bit without unroll)

Table 4. Cell area of each VLIW processor for varied SWMR ROA buffer size (unit: μm^2)

size of SWMR ROA buffer (# of ROA instructions)	0 (baseline)	7	11	15	19	23
Combinational area	541613.94	617155.03	655537.40	698770.55	749064.89	784043.40
Non-combinational area	66774.96	72319.80	75494.32	78700.52	81918.79	85058.60
Total cell area	608388.90	689474.83	731031.71	777471.07	830983.68	869102.00

Table 5. Clock cycle time of each VLIW processor for varied SWMR ROA buffer size (unit: ns) (32VLIWP: 32-bit ISA original VLIW processor)

	32VLIWP		0		7		11		15		19		23	
Point	Incr.	Path	Incr.	Path	Incr.	Path	Incr.	Path	Incr.	Path	Incr.	Path	Incr.	Path
Clock clk_main(rise edge)	2.00	2.00	2.00	2.00	2.00	2.00	2.00	2.00	2.00	2.00	2.00	2.00	2.00	2.00
Library setup time	-0.05	1.95	-0.07	1.93	-0.06	1.94	-0.07	1.93	-0.05	1.95	-0.07	1.93	-0.05	1.95
Data required time		1.95		1.93		1.94		1.93		1.95		1.93		1.95
Data arrival time		-3.71		-3.64		-3.66		-3.68		-3.69		-3.60		-3.66
Slack		-1.76		-1.71		-1.71		-1.75		-1.74		-1.67		-1.71

code such as prolog and epilog code derived from kernel code. Similarly to loop unrolling, even if the results are not presented, software pipelining can also be applied with small code size increase on the DIAM-based VLIW architecture. In other words, the drawback of both loop unrolling and software pipelining in terms of code size can be alleviated if these techniques are applied on the DIAM-based VLIW, while similar performance improvement can be achieved in both the DIAM-based VLIW architecture and normal 32-bit ISA VLIW architecture.

There has been a rich body of research that tries to improve, not only for loops but also for the overall code, the overall performance while minimizing code size of VLIW by applying aggressive inter-block scheduling, such as trace scheduling, superblock scheduling and hyper-block scheduling [11, 16, 22]. Even though these techniques and our approach have the same goal of providing better performance with minimal code size, their techniques are in fact complementary to ours and can be integrated into our compilation environment so as to further improve code quality.

NOP compression techniques [6] [17] and instruction compression techniques [20] [36] are another interesting approach. They try to fulfill their goal of reducing code size by substituting a set of instructions with a new code word or eliminating NOP instructions in VLIW packets. It has been reported in [19] that NOP compression technique can help DIAM architecture to achieve smaller code size and consume less power. Even though loops are less likely to benefit from the technique as they tend to have higher code density in the loop body because of the aforementioned advanced scheduling techniques such as loop unrolling and software pipelining, yet we believe that the compression technique will still be able to help reduce the overall code size if applied to DIAM architecture.

Another interesting approach is introduced in [14] that tries to reduce code size by packing instructions in an *instruction register file* (IRF). In the work, they proposed the IRF, which is a special register file of 32 entries each of which can contain an instruction word selected by profiler. Up to 32 most frequently executed instructions are chosen during profiling phase and loaded into the IRF before running an application. At runtime, the instructions can thus be fetched from either the IRF by a simple indexing scheme or the memory by regular addressing. In doing so, they could reduce the number of memory accesses which in turn saves the overall performance and power consumption. In order to support the approach, the machine provides *packed* instructions that can reference up to five instructions in the IRF by their indices. H.Lin, et al [21] further extended the concept so that VLIW architectures can benefit from the technique. In their work, for each slot, most frequently occurring instructions are first selected and loaded into the IRF. In such a case, synchronization among the issue slots must be guaranteed. To avoid the issue, they introduced new instruction formats and modified micro-architecture.

Their approach has resemblance to ours in that both use a special type of buffer to store instructions. However, the goal and the contents stored in the buffers of both approaches are quite different. The first one, IRF-based approach stores normal instructions in the buffer to reduce the number of memory accesses and corresponding power consumption. Therefore, the number of instructions need to be executed at runtime is unchanged. Ours, on the contrary, stores redundant ROA instructions in the buffer to prohibit these instructions from being executed repeatedly, thus reducing the number of instructions executed during runtime. Therefore, the two approaches are quite orthogonal and might be integrated into a unified environment to attain higher performance and lower power consumption.

In [32], they introduced zero overhead loop buffer (ZOLB) to mainly increase the performance of loops by providing a hardware feature that requires relatively little overhead in terms of area and power consumption. ZOLB is a buffer that can hold a fixed number of instructions to be executed for a specified number of times. By executing special load instructions, code fragment of the innermost loop is loaded into the ZOLB, from which the stored instructions are fetched faster at runtime without needing to be loaded from caches or main memory. Moreover, the ZOLB does not require any instructions related to loop indexing, since the hardware supports automatic loop iteration counting, thus removing all overhead caused by these instructions. Thus, significant performance improvement can be achieved through the ZOLB with negligible area and power overhead. The ZOLB is the most similar architectural feature to our proposed SWMR ROA buffer, as it stores instructions to a dedicated buffer to improve loop performance. However, both techniques have different means to attain the goal and in fact orthogonal to each other; ZOLB removes the necessity of loop indexing by loading a whole loop into the buffer while ours only loads a set of ROA instructions from the loop in an attempt to remove the overhead caused by executing redundant ROA instructions repeatedly. In fact, our scheme and ZOLB can be combined together to achieve higher performance.

There has been another attempt that seeks to reduce the performance degradation caused by ROA instructions. In [37], Youn et al. introduced a mechanism that can conceal the overhead of executing ROA instructions in a single-issue RISC architecture. The idea is relatively simple. The problem comes with the fact that ROA instructions are treated as normal instructions thus consuming all the cycles for fetching and executing, causing non-negligible performance overhead and wasting valuable resources. ROA instructions are, in fact, nothing but a special type of operation that can be executed in parallel with any type of instructions because the main goal of ROA instructions is to merely fill in remote operands to the special buffer. Inspired by this fact, Youn et al. suggested to fetch two instructions every cycle at the fetch stage. Then the decode stage checks whether there is an ROA instruction between the two. If both are found to be normal instructions, then the two are decoded one after the other, and the fetch stage is stalled by one cycle. If an ROA instruction is found between the two, the two instructions are decoded at the same time. Since executing an ROA instruction does not need any functional units, the two pair of instructions can safely be executed at the same cycle and performance overhead caused by ROA instruction is avoided.

Unfortunately, however, this mechanism is not scalable and therefore cannot be directly applied to VLIW architectures since, unlike a single-issue processor where individual normal instruction and ROA instruction can easily be scheduled to maximize the benefit of hiding ROA instructions, for VLIW architecture, one chunk of instructions, so called VLIW packet, has a mixture of normal instructions and ROA instructions and thus cannot be scheduled in a way that explained priori. The only possible case that enables the optimization is when a VLIW packet consists purely of ROA instructions. However, such a case rarely occurs and scheudling to generate more of these packets might seriously impact on code quality. Moreover, even in the existence of such packets, fetching two packets would negate benefit in power consumption gained from the adoption of DIAM.

6. Conclusion

Previously proposed DIAM-based VLIW architecture failed to prevent performance degradation resulting from executing extra VLIW packet generated mainly due to delivering ROA instructions. As we showed in this paper, such extra packets can seriously hamper the overall performance if these packets are generated and inserted in loops. In this work, we propose a modified DIAM-based VLIW architecture to reduce the performance degradation by introducing a SWMR ROA buffer. Instead of repeatedly writing and reading remote operands of ROA instructions in a loop to/from the existing SWSR ROA buffer, our proposed architecture moves as many the number of remote operands to the SWMR ROA buffer as possible only once prior to entering the loop. Since this mechanism eliminates the need of performing redundant write operations to the ROA buffer during the loop execution, the performance overhead can be sufficiently reduced. Further, we also show that loop unrolling is more attractive optimization technique for the DIAM-based 16-bit ISA VLIW architecture since the size of the generated code for DIAM is far smaller compared to the original 32-bit one, while both architectures are achieving almost the same level of performance improvement.

Acknowledgments

This work was supported by the Engineering Research Center of Excellence Program of Korea Ministry of Science, ICT & Future Planning(MSIP) / National Research Foundation of Korea(NRF) (Grant NRF-2008-0062609), the IT R&D program of MSIP/KEIT [K10047212, Development of homomorphic encryption supporting arithmetics on ciphertexts of size less than 1kB and its applications], the IDEC, and the Basic Science Research Program through the National Research Foundation of Korea

(NRF) funded by the Ministry of Science, ICT and Future Planning(2013R1A1A1005534)

References

[1] M. Ahn and Y. Paek. Fast code generation for embedded processors with aliased heterogeneous registers. In *Transactions on High-Performance Embedded Architectures and Compilers II*, pages 149–172. Springer, 2009.

[2] A. Aiken and A. Nicolau. *Optimal loop parallelization*, volume 23. ACM, 1988.

[3] A. Aiken and A. Nicolau. A realistic resource-constrained software pipelining algorithm. *Advances in Languages and Compilers for Parallel Processing*, pages 274–290, 1991.

[4] V. H. Allan, R. B. Jones, R. M. Lee, and S. J. Allan. Software pipelining. *ACM Computing Surveys (CSUR)*, 27(3):367–432, 1995.

[5] P.-Y. Calland, A. Darte, and Y. Robert. Circuit retiming applied to decomposed software pipelining. *Parallel and Distributed Systems, IEEE Transactions on*, 9(1):24–35, 1998.

[6] T. M. Conte, S. Banerjia, S. Y. Larin, K. N. Menezes, and S. W. Sathaye. Instruction fetch mechanisms for vliw architectures with compressed encodings. In *Microarchitecture, 1996. MICRO-29. Proceedings of the 29th Annual IEEE/ACM International Symposium on*, pages 201–211. IEEE, 1996.

[7] K. Ebcioğlu. A compilation technique for software pipelining of loops with conditional jumps. In *Proceedings of the 20th annual workshop on Microprogramming*, pages 69–79. ACM, 1987.

[8] K. Ebcioglu and A. Nicolau. A global resource-constrained parallelization technique. In *Proceedings of the 3rd international conference on Supercomputing*, pages 154–163. ACM, 1989.

[9] A. E. Eichenberger, E. S. Davidson, and S. G. Abraham. Optimum modulo schedules for minimum register requirements. In *Proceedings of the 9th international conference on Supercomputing*, pages 31–40. ACM, 1995.

[10] P. Feautrier. Fine-grain scheduling under resource constraints. In *Languages and Compilers for Parallel Computing*, pages 1–15. Springer, 1995.

[11] J. A. Fisher. Trace scheduling: A technique for global microcode compaction. *Computers, IEEE Transactions on*, 100(7):478–490, 1981.

[12] F. Gasperoni and U. Schwiegeishohn. Scheduling loops on parallel processors: a simple algorithm with close to optimum performance. In *Parallel Processing: CONPAR 92VAPP V*, pages 625–636. Springer, 1992.

[13] R. Govindarajan, E. R. Altman, and G. R. Gao. Minimizing register requirements under resource-constrained rate-optimal software pipelining. In *Proceedings of the 27th annual international symposium on Microarchitecture*, pages 85–94. ACM, 1994.

[14] S. Hines, J. Green, G. Tyson, and D. Whalley. Improving program efficiency by packing instructions into registers. In *ACM SIGARCH Computer Architecture News*, volume 33, pages 260–271. IEEE Computer Society, 2005.

[15] R. A. Huff. Lifetime-sensitive modulo scheduling. In *ACM SIGPLAN Notices*, volume 28, pages 258–267. ACM, 1993.

[16] W.-M. W. Hwu, S. A. Mahlke, W. Y. Chen, P. P. Chang, N. J. Warter, R. A. Bringmann, R. G. Ouellette, R. E. Hank, T. Kiyohara, G. E. Haab, et al. The superblock: an effective technique for vliw and superscalar compilation. *the Journal of Supercomputing*, 7(1-2):229–248, 1993.

[17] S. Jee and K. Palaniappan. Performance evaluation for a compressed-vliw processor. In *Proceedings of the 2002 ACM symposium on Applied computing*, pages 913–917. ACM, 2002.

[18] M. Lam. Software pipelining: An effective scheduling technique for vliw machines. In *ACM Sigplan Notices*, volume 23, pages 318–328. ACM, 1988.

[19] J. Lee, J. M. Youn, D. Cho, and Y. Paek. Reducing instruction bit-width for low-power vliw architectures. *ACM Transactions on Design Automation of Electronic Systems (TODAES)*, 18(2):25, 2013.

[20] C. Lefurgy, P. Bird, I.-C. Chen, and T. Mudge. Improving code density using compression techniques. In *Microarchitecture, 1997. Proceedings., Thirtieth Annual IEEE/ACM International Symposium on*, pages 194–203. IEEE, 1997.

[21] H. Lin and Y. Fei. Harnessing horizontal parallelism and vertical instruction packing of programs to improve system overall efficiency. In *Proceedings of the conference on Design, automation and test in Europe*, pages 758–763. ACM, 2008.

[22] S. A. Mahlke, D. C. Lin, W. Y. Chen, R. E. Hank, and R. A. Bringmann. Effective compiler support for predicated execution using the hyperblock. In *ACM SIGMICRO Newsletter*, volume 23, pages 45–54. IEEE Computer Society Press, 1992.

[23] F. H. McMahon. The livermore fortran kernels: A computer test of the numerical performance range. Technical report, Lawrence Livermore National Lab., CA (USA), 1986.

[24] S.-M. Moon and K. Ebcioglu. An efficient resource-constrained global scheduling technique for superscalar and vliw processors. In *Microarchitecture, 1992. MICRO 25., Proceedings of the 25th Annual International Symposium on*, pages 55–71. IEEE, 1992.

[25] S. Muchnick. Advanced compiler design and implementation. 1997.

[26] J. Ramanujam. Optimal software pipelining of nested loops. In *Parallel Processing Symposium, 1994. Proceedings., Eighth International*, pages 335–342. IEEE, 1994.

[27] B. R. Rau and J. A. Fisher. Instruction-level parallel processing: history, overview, and perspective. *The journal of Supercomputing*, 7(1-2):9–50, 1993.

[28] B. R. Rau and C. D. Glaeser. Some scheduling techniques and an easily schedulable horizontal architecture for high performance scientific computing. In *ACM SIGMICRO Newsletter*, volume 12, pages 183–198. IEEE Press, 1981.

[29] Y. Shan and L. Bill. Stream execution on embedded wide-issue clustered vliw architectures. *EURASIP Journal on Embedded Systems*, 2008, 2009.

[30] *Design Compiler Reference Manual*. Synopsys Inc., Mountain View, CA, 2001.

[31] M. Technologies. *MIPS32 Architecture for Programmers Volume IV-a: The MIPS16 Application Specific Extension to the MIPS32 Architecture*. 2001.

[32] G.-R. Uh, Y. Wang, D. Whalley, S. Jinturkar, C. Burns, and V. Cao. Effective exploitation of a zero overhead loop buffer. In *ACM SIGPLAN Notices*, volume 34, pages 10–19. ACM, 1999.

[33] V. H. Van Dongen, G. R. Gao, and Q. Ning. A polynomial time method for optimal software pipelining. In *Parallel Processing: CONPAR 92VAPP V*, pages 613–624. Springer, 1992.

[34] N. J. Warter, G. E. Haab, K. Subramanian, and J. W. Bockhaus. Enhanced modulo scheduling for loops with conditional branches. In *ACM SIGMICRO Newsletter*, volume 23, pages 170–179. IEEE Computer Society Press, 1992.

[35] V. M. Weaver and S. A. McKee. Code density concerns for new architectures. In *Computer Design, 2009. ICCD 2009. IEEE International Conference on*, pages 459–464. IEEE, 2009.

[36] Y. Xie, W. Wolf, and H. Lekatsas. Code compression for embedded vliw processors using variable-to-fixed coding. *Very Large Scale Integration (VLSI) Systems, IEEE Transactions on*, 14(5):525–536, 2006.

[37] J. M. Youn, J. Lee, Y. Paek, J. Kim, and J. Cho. Implementing dynamic implied addressing mode for multi-output instructions. In *Proceedings of the 2010 international conference on Compilers, architectures and synthesis for embedded systems*, pages 87–96. ACM, 2010.

[38] V. Zivojnovic, J. M. Velarde, C. Schlager, and H. Meyr. Dspstone: A dsp-oriented benchmarking methodology. In *Proc. of ICSPAT*, volume 94, 1994.

Superoptimization of Memory Subsystems *

Joseph G. Wingbermuehle   Ron K. Cytron   Roger D. Chamberlain

Washington University in St. Louis

{wingbej,cytron,roger}@wustl.edu

Abstract

The disparity in performance between processors and main memories has led computer architects to incorporate large cache hierarchies in modern computers. Because these cache hierarchies are designed to be general-purpose, they may not provide the best possible performance for a given application. In this paper, we determine a memory subsystem well suited for a given application and main memory by discovering a memory subsystem comprised of caches, scratchpads, and other components that are combined to provide better performance. We draw motivation from the *superoptimization* of instruction sequences, which successfully finds unusually clever instruction sequences for programs. Targeting both ASIC and FPGA devices, we show that it is possible to discover unusual memory subsystems that provide performance improvements over a typical memory subsystem.

Categories and Subject Descriptors   C.3 [*SPECIAL-PURPOSE AND APPLICATION-BASED SYSTEMS*]: Real-time and embedded systems; B.1.4 [*CONTROL STRUCTURES AND MICRO-PROGRAMMING*]: Optimization

Keywords   Superoptimization; Cache

1. Introduction

Memory accesses are the primary bottleneck for many applications [34]. In an effort to alleviate this bottleneck, modern computers typically use large cache hierarchies between compute resources, such as general-purpose processors or field-programmable gate arrays (FPGAs), and main memory. These cache hierarchies form a memory subsystem that connects the compute resources to the main memory with the goal of improving the performance of an application by exploiting common properties of memory accesses, such as temporal and spatial localities.

Most memory subsystems built today are designed to be general-purpose by providing good overall memory performance for a wide variety of applications. This is exemplified by the fact that most computers today have a fixed cache hierarchy. However, because of this generality, such memory subsystems do not necessarily provide the best possible performance for a particular application and

main memory. Further, a general-purpose cache may use more on-chip resources than necessary for a particular application. With this in mind, we set out to investigate whether it is possible to design application-specific memory subsystems that provide better performance than a general-purpose memory subsystem. Such memory subsystems could take advantage of specific properties of both the application and main memory to provide better performance than might be possible with a general-purpose memory subsystem.

In addition to the improved performance, if it were possible to discover a good memory subsystem automatically, the manual and laborious process of optimizing an application for a particular memory subsystem may not be necessary. Although both cache-aware [28] and cache-oblivious [9] algorithms and data structures exist, it remains a relatively difficult task to make an arbitrary application perform well for a given memory subsystem and main memory.

Rather than focus exclusively on selecting cache parameters for a fixed cache hierarchy, we widen the search space to include components other than caches, such as scratchpad memories and address transformations, which are not typically found in memory subsystems. In addition, we consider total access time rather than relying solely on cache misses. This allows us to customize the memory subsystem to take advantage of certain properties of the main memory, such as burst behavior.

This work draws motivation from superoptimization [20], which has been used successfully in GCC to find short instruction sequences [13]. More recently, the concept of superoptimization has been extended using stochastic search to explore larger code segments [27]. The concept of *superoptimization* in those works is to try many instruction sequences with the hope of discovering a new sequence that is shorter or faster than other, functionally equivalent, instruction sequences. However, rather than superoptimizing instruction sequences, we are interested in superoptimizing memory subsystems.

Unfortunately, modern computer systems do not have configurable memory subsystems. Indeed, even in the embedded space, there are often limitations on how much a memory subsystem can be modified. However, it is conceivable that general-purpose computers might introduce more memory subsystem flexibility in the future, especially if such flexibility were able to provide a significant performance advantage. Moreover, flexible memory subsystems exist today for applications deployed on FPGAs and application-specific integrated circuits (ASICs).

In this work, we target both an FPGA and an ASIC process. The FPGA we target is a Xilinx Virtex-7 running at 250 MHz. An FPGA is a type of reconfigurable hardware consisting of configurable logic gates (formed from look-up tables), registers, and a routing matrix. In addition, modern FPGAs typically have additional resources, such as block RAMs and hardware multipliers. Block RAMs are configurable memories, which make it possible to implement diverse memories efficiently on an FPGA device. These

* This work is supported by the National Science Foundation under grants CNS-09095368 and CNS-0931693.

block RAMs are of particular interest to us since we can use them in our memory subsystems.

Block RAMs are typically some fixed size in terms of storage bits, but with a configurable aspect ratio. For example, on our target device, block RAMs are 72 bits wide and 512 entries deep. Such a block RAM can be used to implement other aspect ratios, such as 36 bits by 1024 entries, 18 bits by 2048 entries, etc. By using multiple block RAMs, one can create larger memories as well.

To demonstrate the generality of our approach, we target a 45 nm ASIC process in addition to the FPGA target. In both the FPGA and ASIC cases, we assume a DDR3 main memory, however, we note that designing custom main memory models for our superoptimizer is straightforward.

To superoptimize a memory subsystem for an application, we use a memory address trace from a representative run of the application. We then generate candidate memory subsystems from a neighborhood of memory subsystems around the previous proposal and simulate the address trace. Finally, we either accept or reject the proposed memory subsystem based on its performance. This process repeats until we give up searching.

Here we build upon earlier work on application-specific memory subsystems [33] by evaluating a wider variety of benchmark applications, using a different approach to meta-heuristic optimization, performing an explicit model validation, and including support for an ASIC target. In addition, we use a more realistic model for the main memory. Finally, we show that it is possible to exploit information available in the memory traces to discover better memory subsystems faster.

The remainder of this paper is organized as follows. Section 2 discusses related work. Section 3 describes how we perform the optimization and as well as the experimental setup. Section 4 shows our experimental results. Section 5 provides a discussion of the results and what they mean. Finally, Section 6 concludes.

2. Related Work

Although there is much related work on design space exploration [16, 19], the ability to change completely the memory subsystem for a specific application and main memory subsystem distinguishes this work from most previous work.

Techniques for improving the performance of memory subsystems at the software level include a profiling approach used to guide the placement of variables in the virtual address space to decrease cache conflicts and improve locality [3]. Compiler optimizations have been used to improve data locality across loop iterations [4]. Reorganization and cache-conscious memory allocation have been explored [7]. Finally, splitting and reordering of structures have been explored in the interest of improving cache behavior [6]. These approaches do not consider altering the memory subsystem at the hardware level.

At a higher level, there are approaches to application design that focus on improving cache performance. In particular, cache-aware algorithms [28] attempt to take advantage of a particular cache structure. Likewise, the performance of cache-oblivious algorithms [9] is asymptotically optimal on an ideal cache hierarchy. Unfortunately, ideal cache hierarchies do not exist and, further, these techniques are specific to a very small set of algorithms.

Much related work exists with respect to tuning the parameters of a fixed memory subsystem dynamically. Methods to change the size and associativity of a cache hierarchy dynamically have been explored [2, 29] and the ability to disable various levels of a multi-level cache in the interest of reducing latency and reducing power consumption has been considered [5]. Finally, adjusting the size of cache lines dynamically to lower the cache miss rate has been considered [31]. Unlike our method, these approaches are dynamic, but limited in the amount of variation supported by the memory subsystem. Techniques such as these are complementary to our work as they could be added to the set of memory subsystem components that our optimizer has at its disposal.

There are also many approaches to tuning cache parameters statically. A method for selecting cache parameters analytically has been described for a single-level cache [10]. In addition, heuristic methods for selecting the parameters of a two-level cache have been presented [11, 12]. Unlike our approach, these approaches consider a much smaller search space. However, we note that it may be possible to use such techniques to speed up the superoptimization process.

Non-traditional memory subsystems have been proposed. For example, a victim cache [17] cache is a small, fully-associative cache structure used to store recently evicted items from a larger cache with low associativity. The use of such caches in embedded applications has been explored [35]. The combination of a scratch-pad and cache has been considered [23, 25]. Further, the combination of multiple caching techniques including split caches has been considered [21]. Each of these works presents a particular memory subsystem. Our work, on the other hand, attempts to discover memory subsystems with arbitrary structure. Therefore, it is possible that our superoptimizer would discover similar structures if provided the necessary memory subsystem components.

Finally, there is complementary work in the area of hardware synthesis. For example, LEAP scratchpads [1] provide multiple logical memories to an FPGA backed by a single main memory. In such a system, our work could be used to discover the best use of the on-chip memory resources to improve performance. Likewise, our system could be used to find more suitable memory subsystems in high-level synthesis tools such as CHiMPS [24] and ScalaPipe [32].

3. Method

Our goal is to discover a memory subsystem that offers the best possible performance for a given application and main memory. To do this, we propose and evaluate candidate memory subsystems. We can then view the discovery of good memory subsystems as a classical optimization problem with an objective function and constraints. Here, we seek to minimize the total memory access time constraining the on-chip memory used. It would be possible to use other objective functions, however, such as minimization of energy use or minimization of writes to main memory.

We consider both an FPGA device and an ASIC process for deployment. When targeting an FPGA device, we constrain the optimization by specifying the maximum number of block RAMs (BRAMs) that can be used in the memory subsystem as well as the minimum operating frequency. During the optimization process, we synthesize each component individually and store the results so that they can be reused. The optimization proceeds assuming that, when combining memory components, the maximum clock frequency does not change and that the number of block RAMs is added together. Although the assumption about the number of required block RAMs is conservative, the assumption about the frequency remaining the same is not conservative. Therefore, once the optimization is complete, we validate that the discovered memory subsystem will run at the target frequency and fit on the target device by synthesizing the complete memory subsystem.

When targeting an ASIC process, we constrain the optimization by specifying the maximum chip area dedicated to the memory subsystem and assume that the system runs at a fixed clock frequency. We use the CACTI [30] program to determine the access time, cycle time, and area required for each memory component. Full synthesis, however, is not performed for the ASIC target.

Component	Description	Parameters ($n \in \mathbb{Z}_+$)	Latency (cycles)
Cache	Parameterizable cache	Line size ($word\_size \times 2^n$) Line count (2^n) Associativity ($1 \ldots line\_count$) Replacement (LRU, MRU, FIFO, PLRU) Write policy (write-back, write-through)	3
Offset	Address offset	Value ($\pm n$)	0
Prefetch	Stride prefetcher	Stride ($\pm n \times word\_size$)	0
Rotate	Rotate address transform	Value ($\pm n$)	0
Scratchpad	Scratchpad memory	Size ($word\_size \times 2^n$)	2
Split	Split memory	Location ($n \times word\_size$)	0
XOR	XOR address transform	Value (n)	0

Table 1. Memory Subsystem Components

3.1 Address Traces

We use address traces to evaluate the performance of a particular memory subsystem for an application. We consider two types of traces: traces gathered from real applications and traces gathered from custom kernels. To gather the address traces for the application benchmarks, we use a modified version of the Valgrind [22] *lackey* tool. This allows us to obtain concise address traces for applications that contain only data accesses (reads, writes, and modifies). We ignore instruction accesses since the instructions would likely be stored in a separate memory.

For both the application benchmarks and kernel benchmarks, we ignore the notion of processing time in the trace; our focus is exclusively on memory performance. Because there is no notion of processing time, however, certain memory subsystem components, such as prefetchers, are unlikely to be useful. Introducing processing time is possible, but to do so would require a specific implementation of the application, which would make the results less general.

All of the address traces contain virtual (instead of physical) addresses and are gathered for 32-bit versions of the benchmark applications. To evaluate a general-purpose memory subsystem, the physical addresses are important since some levels of cache use physical addresses to avoid problems when context switching. However, we note that our memory subsystem is specific to the application and, therefore, using virtual addresses is appropriate. We leave the problem of sharing the same memory resources among multiple applications or kernels as future work.

3.2 Simulation

Given an address trace for an application and a candidate memory subsystem, we use a custom memory system simulator to determine how many cycles are spent performing memory accesses. Our simulator is capable of simulating the memory subsystem components shown in Table 1, which also shows the latency in cycles required for the FPGA implementation.

For caches, the simulator supports four replacement policies. The supported policies include least-recently used (LRU), most-recently used (MRU), first-in first-out (FIFO), and pseudo-least-recently used (PLRU). The PLRU policy approximates the LRU policy by using a single *age* bit per cache way rather than $\lg n$ age bits, where n is the associativity of the cache. With the PLRU policy, the first way where the age bit is not set is selected for replacement. Upon access, the age bit for the accessed way is set and when all age bits are set for a set, all but the accessed age bit are cleared.

The offset, rotate, and xor components in Table 1 are address transformations. The *offset* component adds the specified value to the address. The *rotate* component rotates the bits of the address that select the word left by the specified amount (the bits that select

Parameter	Description	Value
Frequency	The I/O frequency of the DRAM	400 MHz
CAS	Cycles select a column	5
RCD	Cycles from opening to read/write	5
RP	Cycles required to precharge a row	5
Page size	Size of a page in bytes	1024
Page count	Number of pages per bank	65536
Width	Channel width in bytes	8
Burst size	Number of columns per access	4
Page mode	Open or closed page mode	open
DDR	Double data rate	true

Table 2. Main Memory Parameters

the byte within the word remain unchanged). Note that for a 32-bit address with a 4-byte word, $32 - \lg 4 = 30$ bits are used to select the word. Finally, the *xor* component inverts the selected bits of the address.

Other supported components include prefetch and split. The *prefetch* component performs an additional memory access after every memory access to the prefetch. This additional access reads the word with the specified distance from the original word that was accessed. Finally, the *split* component divides memory accesses between two memory subsystems based on address.

The communication between each of the memory components as well as the communication between the application and main memory is performed with 4-byte words. The bytes within the word are selected using a 4-bit mask to allow byte-addressing. The address bus is 30 bits, providing a 32-bit address space.

As presented here, the optimizer supports seven distinct subsystem components. However, adding additional components is simply a matter of adding a synthesizable HDL model of the component and a simulation model for the optimizer. Likewise, additional parameters can be added to the existing components. Unfortunately, adding additional components can make the optimization process take longer since more steps will be required.

In addition to simulating memory subsystems, our memory simulator is capable of simulating main memories with various properties, shown in Table 2. As is the case with the memory subsystems, it is possible to model main memories with other properties if required. For our purposes, we consider a DDR3-800D memory, whose properties are shown in Table 2.

3.3 Optimization

To guide the optimization process, we use a variant of *threshold acceptance* [8] called *old bachelor acceptance* [15]. Old bachelor acceptance is a Markov-chain Monte-Carlo (MCMC) stochastic hill-climbing technique similar to simulated annealing [18].

Using stochastic hill-climbing, one typically selects an initial state, $s_t = s_0$, and then generates a *proposal* state, s^*, in the neighborhood of the current state. The state is then either accepted, becoming s_{t+1}, or rejected. With threshold acceptance, the difference in cost between the current state, s_t, and the proposal state, s^*, is compared to a threshold, T_t, to determine if the proposal state should be accepted. Thus, we get the following expression for determining the next state:

$$s_{t+1} = \begin{cases} s^* & \text{if } c(s^*) < c(s_t) + T_t \\ s_t & \text{otherwise} \end{cases}$$

For our purposes, the state is a candidate memory subsystem and the cost function, $c(\cdot)$, is the total access time in cycles that the application will experience from memory accesses.

With threshold acceptance, the threshold is initialized to some relatively high value, $T_t = T_0$. The threshold is then lowered according a cooling schedule. The recommended schedule in [8] is $T_{t+1} = T_t - \Delta T_t$ where $\Delta \in (0, 1)$. Old bachelor acceptance generalizes this, allowing the threshold to be lowered when a state is accepted and raised when a state is not accepted. This allows the algorithm to escape areas of local optimality more easily. For our experiments, we used the following schedule:

$$T_{t+1} = \begin{cases} T_t - \Delta T_t & \text{if } c(s^*) < c(s_t) + T_t \\ T_t + \Delta T_t & \text{otherwise} \end{cases}$$

Because the evaluation of a state involves simulating a memory subsystem for an address trace, each state evaluation can take several minutes or even longer depending on the size of the trace. Further, to discover a good memory subsystem, the total number of states visited can be large, which can make the optimization process take a prohibitively long time.

To reduce the time required for superoptimization, we employ two techniques to speed up the process. First, we memoize the results of each state evaluation so that when revisiting a state we do not need to simulate the memory trace again. The second improvement is that we allow multiple superoptimization processes to run simultaneously sharing results, thereby allowing us to exploit multiple processor cores.

3.4 Neighborhood Generation

Our memory subsystem optimizer is capable of proposing candidate memory subsystems comprised of the structures shown in Table 1. These components can be combined in arbitrary ways leading to a huge search space limited only by the constraints. Recall that for the FPGA target, the constraints include the minimum clock frequency and the maximum number of BRAMs for the memory subsystem. For the ASIC target, the constraint is the area as reported from the CACTI tool.

Given a state, s_t, we compute a proposal state s^* by performing one of the following actions:

1. Insert a new memory component to a random position,

2. Remove a memory component from a random position, or

3. Change a parameter of the memory component at a random position.

With MCMC algorithms such as simulated annealing and threshold acceptance, it is necessary that the generated proposal states be *ergodic*. Ergodicity means that it is possible to reach every state from any given state in a finite number of steps. It is easy to see that the above process is ergodic as actions 1 and 2 are capable of canceling each other and action 3 can cancel itself.

To ensure that any discovered memory subsystem is valid, we reject any memory subsystem that exceeds the constraints. How-ever, there are other ways a memory subsystem may be invalid. First, because we support splitting between memory components by address, any address transformation occurring in a split must be inverted before leaving the split. To handle this, we always insert (or remove) both the transform and its inverse when inserting (or removing) an address transformation.

Another situation that can lead to an invalid memory subsystem is when a complex memory subsystem prevents the subsystem from achieving the required clock frequency on the FPGA device. Note that for an ASIC device we increase the number of cycles required to access the memory component. Although we synthesize each component for the FPGA target separately to prevent this, it is still possible that a combination of components prevent the complete memory subsystem from achieving the required clock frequency.

To prevent the optimizer from generating a memory subsystem that is unable to run at the required clock frequency, the optimizer keeps a rough estimate on the longest combinational path and prevents the path from becoming too long. Nevertheless, it is still possible that a particular superoptimized memory subsystem may not achieve the required clock frequency. Therefore, for the FPGA results, we synthesize the superoptimized memory subsystems to validate them.

3.5 Offset Selection Heuristic

Because the search space is so large, arbitrarily selecting addresses to segment the address space in a split component can be problematic. Therefore, rather than proposing arbitrary addresses for split offsets, we restrict the set of addresses to values that actually exist in the address trace. We do this by recording the address ranges that are used during the first evaluation of the trace for the initial state. To further improve these results, the addresses we generate are weighted such that those addresses at the ends of address ranges are more likely to be selected.

Given an address range of length n that starts at a, addresses used for splits are selected according to the following algorithm:

$$A(a, n) = \begin{cases} a & \text{w.p. } 1/8 \\ a + n - 1 & \text{w.p. } 1/8 \\ A(a, \lceil n/2 \rceil) & \text{w.p. } 3/8 \\ A(a + \lfloor n/2 \rfloor, \lceil n/2 \rceil) & \text{w.p. } 3/8 \end{cases}$$

Here *w.p.* stands for "with probability". Thus, there is a 12.5% chance of selecting the first address in the range, a 12.5% chance of selecting the last address, and a 75% chance of selecting an address between these two extremes.

3.6 Model Validation

To validate the simulation model used during the optimization process, our optimizer generates synthesizable VHDL that has the characteristics shown in Table 1. By synthesizing the VHDL, we can ensure that the discovered memory subsystem is able to run at the required frequency and fit on our target device. The synthesis targets a Xilinx Virtex-7 running at 250 MHz.

3.7 Benchmarks

We use a collection of six benchmarks from the MiBench benchmark suite [14] as well as four kernels for evaluation purposes. The MiBench benchmark suite contains single-threaded benchmarks for the embedded space that target a variety of application areas. For some benchmarks, the MiBench suite contains large and small versions. We chose the large version in the interest of obtaining larger memory traces.

The locally developed kernels include a kernel that performs random lookups in a hash table (hash), a kernel that performs

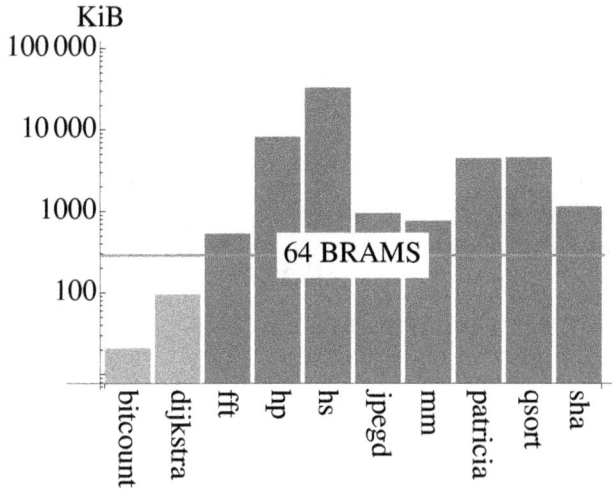

Figure 1. Working-Set Sizes

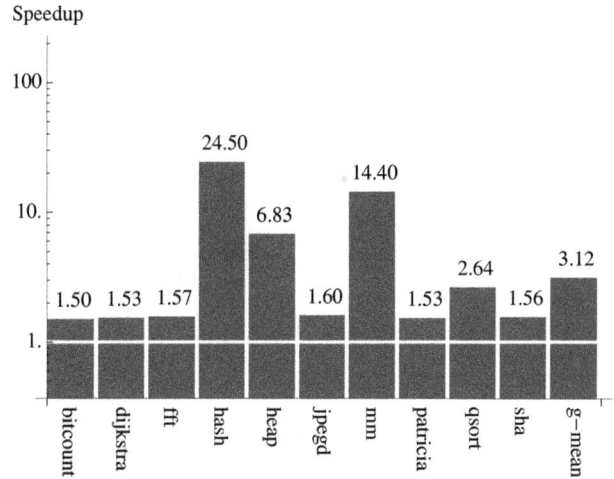

Figure 2. Best-case FPGA Speedup (Log Scale)

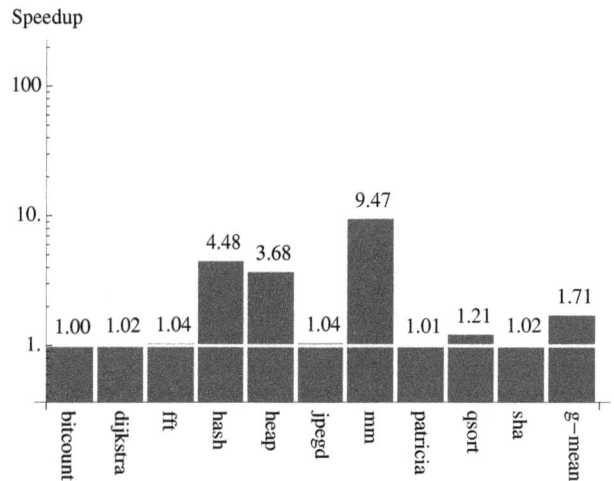

Figure 3. Realized FPGA Speedup (Log Scale)

matrix-matrix multiply (mm), a kernel that inserts and then removes items from a binary heap (heap), and a kernel that sorts an array of integers using the Quicksort algorithm (qsort). Rather than implement an application to perform these operations and use Valgrind to capture the address trace, the addresses traces for these kernels are generated directly during a simulation run, which allows us to avoid processing large trace files for the kernels.

Because we are optimizing the memory subsystem, the amount of memory accessed by each benchmark is important. If a particular benchmark accesses less memory than is available to the on-chip memory subsystem, then it should be possible to have all memory accesses occur in on-chip memory, though such a design may require clever address transformations. A graph of the total working-set size for each benchmark is shown in Figure 1.

In Figure 1, we see that there are two benchmarks, bitcount and dijkstra, that are small enough that all memory accesses could be mapped into 64 BRAMs, which is 2,359,296 bits, or 294,912 bytes. All of the other benchmarks are too large to fit completely within 64 BRAMs, which is the constraint on BRAMs we consider for the FPGA target.

For the 45nm ASIC process with an area constraint of $1mm^2$, we can store a total of 379,392 bytes in a scratchpad according to our CACTI model. This means that, as with the FPGA, both the bitcount and dijkstra benchmarks are small enough to be mapped into a scratchpad, but all of the remaining benchmarks require too much memory.

4. Results

To evaluate the performance of our superoptimized memory subsystems, we compare the performance of the superoptimized memory subsystems against a baseline cache. For our baseline cache, we selected a cache that closely resembles the data cache in a Raspberry Pi [26]. This is a 64 KiB, 4-way set-associative writeback cache with 32-byte lines and a PLRU replacement policy. The FPGA implementation of this cache uses 16 BRAMs and meets our 250 MHz target frequency. According to CACTI, the 45nm ASIC implementation is $0.18mm^2$ with a 1-cycle access time and a 3-cycle cycle time.

4.1 FPGA Results

For the first set of experiments, we target a Xilinx Virtex-7 with a target frequency of 250 MHz and a constraint of 64 BRAMs

maximum. The main memory is assumed to be the DDR3 device whose properties are shown in Table 2.

The first question we attempt to answer is: how much better might we make the memory subsystem than the baseline cache? To determine this, we compare the performance of each benchmark to a "best-case" access time. For the best-case access time, we assume that all memory accesses hit in the fastest memory component available for each of our targets. For the FPGA target, this means that all accesses hit in a scratchpad and, therefore, take two cycles to complete. This best-case speedup for our benchmarks running on the FPGA target is shown in Figure 2.

The *g-mean* bar in Figure 2 represents the geometric mean. Assuming that we could somehow arrange for all of the memory accesses to hit in the scratchpad we would get a $3.12\times$ speedup over the baseline cache for the FPGA target. Note that, in reality, such a speedup is not possible since we do not have enough resources available to make all of the accesses hit in a scratchpad.

Figure 3 shows the speedup that the superoptimized memory subsystem provides over the baseline memory subsystem. Across the set of benchmark applications, the performance gain varies

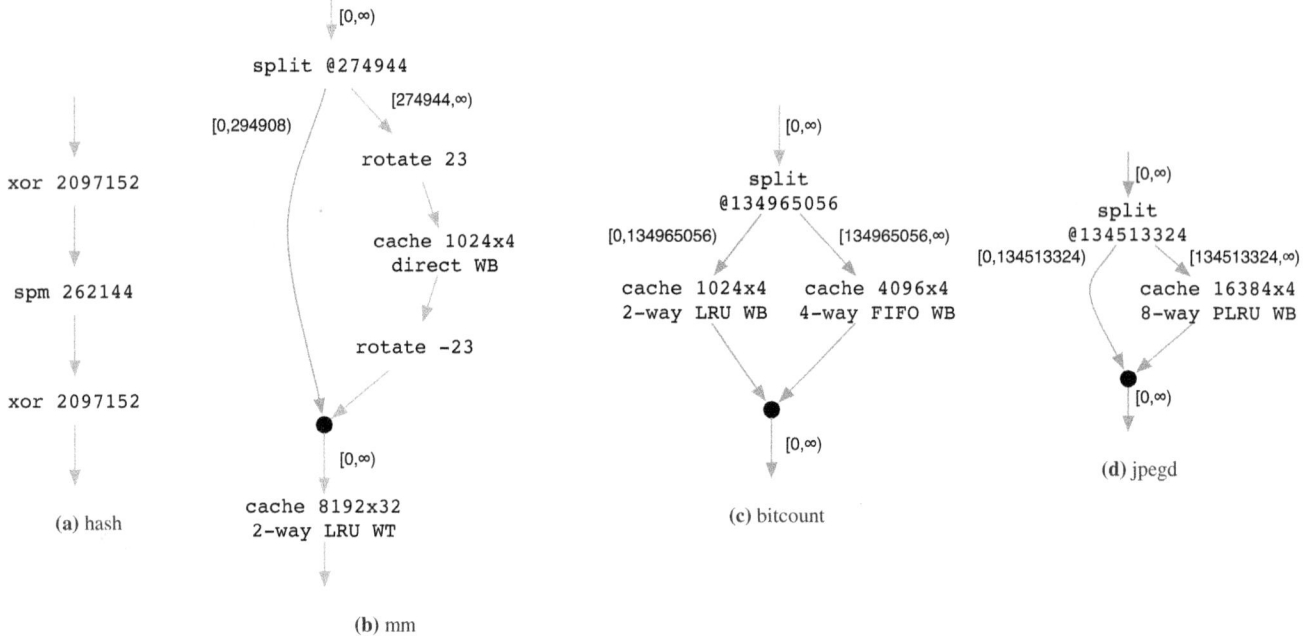

Figure 4. Superoptimized Memory Subsystems for the FPGA Target

from very little to over 9× with a geometric mean speedup of 1.71×.

Although the results are not much better than the baseline memory subsystem, we note that for all of the benchmarks there was some improvement, though less than 1% in a few cases. There are a few benchmarks, however, that exhibit substantial performance gain. The matrix-matrix multiply shows the best speedup of over 9×. Because the main memory is not much slower than the cache structures running on a 250 MHz FPGA fabric, we do not anticipate substantial gains for all of the applications (see Figure 2). A number of the discovered memory subsystems are, however, worth considering in more detail.

The first interesting memory subsystem we consider is the superoptimized memory subsystem for the hash benchmark, shown in Figure 4a. The hash benchmark performs random probes into a hash table containing 8,388,608 entries, each 4-bytes. This type of access pattern causes problems for caches due to the lack of locality. In Figure 4a, memory accesses enter the top and accesses to main memory come out the bottom. There are two address transformations and a 262,144-byte scratchpad. The first address transformation toggles a bit of the address. The transformed address then enters the scratchpad. The second transformation reverses the first transformation so that the addresses remain unchanged as they enter the main memory (recall that address transformations are always inserted and removed in pairs).

The reason that the address transformation is beneficial for the hash benchmark is due to the random accesses to the hash table being slightly unbalanced. Removing the address transformation results in a very slight decrease in performance. If we remove the scratchpad completely, there is again only a slight decrease in performance. Here we note that the speedup is primarily due to the removal of the cache, which serves only to cause overhead when there is no locality. The scratchpad speeds up some of the accesses, but only a small fraction.

Another interesting memory subsystem, which also provides the greatest performance improvement, is discovered for mm: the matrix-matrix multiply benchmark. This benchmark performs a

matrix-matrix multiply using the naive $O(n^3)$ algorithm with 256-by-256 matrices. Each element of the matrix is 4 bytes. The superoptimized memory subsystem for this benchmark is shown in Figure 4b. In the superoptimized memory subsystem for the mm benchmark, memory accesses enter the top and are then split, with accesses below address 274944 going directly to a 262,144-byte cache at the bottom of Figure 4b and accesses to addresses above and including 274944 going to a separate memory subsystem before going to the 262,144-byte cache. For accesses to addresses above and including 274944, first the bits of the address that select the word are rotated left by 23 bits. The accesses then enter a 4,096-byte, direct-mapped cache, and finally, the address is rotated right by 23 bits before entering the larger cache.

To understand why the memory subsystem for the mm benchmark provides such good performance, we consider the way the memory is organized for the benchmark. There are 3 matrices: two sources and a destination. The first source matrix, which is accessed in row-major order, is stored in addresses 0 through 262140. The second source matrix, which is accessed in column-major order, is stored at addresses 262144 through 524284. Finally, the destination matrix is stored at addresses 524288 through 786428.

With this memory organization in mind, we note that the address split moves most accesses for the second source matrix as well as the destination matrix into a separate memory subsystem. Within this subsystem, the addresses are transformed and then routed to a cache. Given that the second source matrix is accessed in column-major order, for the first column, we access $00040000_{16}, 00040400_{16}, \ldots 0007FC00_{16}$ for the first column, then $00040004_{16}, 00040404_{16}, \ldots 0007FC04_{16}$ for the second column, and so on. However, after the split and address transformation, the addresses from the perspective of the 1024 entry cache look about like this: $00000000_{16}, 00000008_{16}, \ldots 00000FF8_{16}$ for the first column, $01000000_{16}, 01000008_{16}, \ldots 01000FF8_{16}$ for the second column, and so on. The result is that each column of the matrix is cached and can be reused 256 times before the next column is required.

150

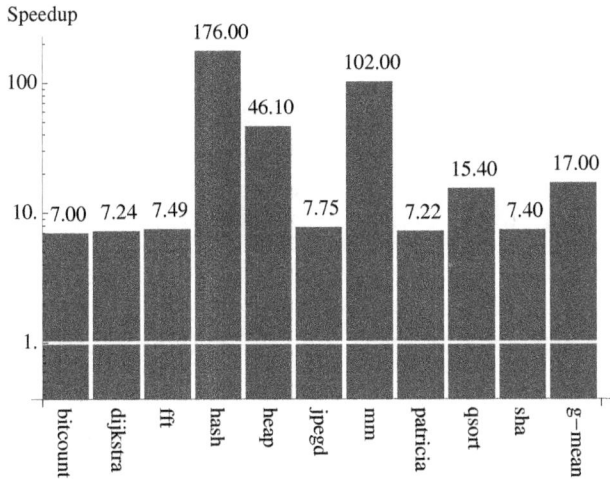

Figure 6. Best-case ASIC Speedup (Log Scale)

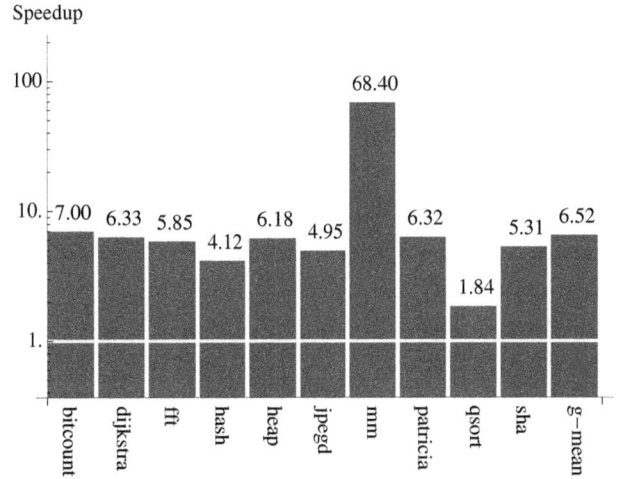

Figure 7. Realized ASIC Speedup (Log Scale)

Note that due to the layout of the matrices, one would expect that the ideal address for the split would be 262144 instead of 274944. Indeed, changing the split address results in a 0.46% improvement in performance. Thus, running the superoptimizer longer would likely result in an even better memory subsystem. Further, this implies that there may be better ways to propose offsets for splits.

A final observation about the memory subsystem for the mm benchmark is the large cache after the split. This cache has 32-byte cache lines, which allows it to prefetch values for the source matrix. Also, the cache is write-through rather than write-back, which prevents cache pollution due to writes to the destination matrix.

The memory subsystem discovered for the bitcount benchmark is shown in Figure 4c. This memory subsystem only provides a small performance improvement over the baseline (a speedup of less than 1%), but it also uses fewer block RAMs than the baseline memory subsystem (9 instead of 16). This feat is accomplished by splitting the address space between two caches. The first cache handles accesses to heap allocations whereas the second cache handles accesses to the stack. This type of split is common for the benchmarks that have accesses to a separate stack and heap.

Finally, we consider the memory subsystem for the jpegd benchmark, shown in Figure 4d. For the jpegd benchmark, the superoptimizer selected a split memory subsystem where only memory accesses to addresses 134513324 and higher go to a cache. This causes accesses to the program stack to be cached, but not accesses to heap allocations.

Of the superoptimized memory subsystems for the FPGA target, none contained only a single-level cache component. Five of the memory subsystems contained splits (bitcount, fft, jpegd, mm, and sha), five contained scratchpads (dijkstra, hash, heap, patricia, and qsort), and five contained address transformations (dijkstra, hash, mm, patricia, and qsort). Further, all of the superoptimized memory subsystems performed better than the baseline memory subsystem, even if only marginally better in some cases.

4.2 ASIC Results

The best-case speedup for the ASIC target is shown in Figure 6. For the ASIC target, we assume that, in the best case, all memory accesses hit a scratchpad with a 1-cycle access time and cycle time. Here we see that the geometric-mean best-case speedup is 17×. As

in the FPGA case, it is not necessarily possible to achieve such a speedup.

The superoptimizer is able to get more impressive speedups for the ASIC than the FPGA for two reasons. First, the ASIC is assumed to be running at a higher clock frequency than the FPGA (1 GHz versus 250 MHz), making a miss in the memory subsystem have a greater impact. Second, there are more trade-offs for the ASIC memory components. In particular, when targeting an ASIC, the optimizer uses the access time and cycle time results from CACTI rather than using a fixed access time and cycle time as is done for the FPGA. Figure 7 shows the speedup that the optimized memory subsystem provides over the baseline memory subsystem. The geometric mean speedup is 6.52×.

The greatest increase in performance is again seen for the mm benchmark, whose memory subsystem is shown in Figure 5b. This memory subsystem has two sets of address rotations. The rotation by 27 bits causes every eighth entry of the first source matrix for 16384 entries to be stored in the first scratchpad, which has a cycle time of 1 cycle. Another 65536 entries of the first source matrix are stored in the second scratchpad, which has a cycle time of 3 cycles. Finally, the second set of rotations causes columns of the second source matrix to be cached in a way similar to the memory subsystem for the FPGA. Although the first address rotation may seem unnecessary, by reducing conflict misses in the cache, it actually improves the performance of the memory subsystem.

The memory subsystem for the hash benchmark targeting the ASIC is shown in Figure 5a. As is the case with the mm benchmark, the subsystem for the hash benchmark is similar to the subsystem for the FPGA. However, rather than an xor transform, this subsystem uses a rotate. In addition, this subsystem incorporates two scratchpads instead of one.

The memory subsystem discovered for the bitcount benchmark, shown in Figure 5c, is similar to the memory subsystem discovered for the bitcount for the FPGA target, shown in Figure 4c. Note that the split offset is only slightly different. However, here we have a cache before the split rather than on the left side of the split.

The last memory subsystem we consider in detail is the memory subsystem for the jpegd benchmark, shown in Figure 5d. This memory subsystem is one of the most complex memory subsystems discovered. The split causes access to the memory in the stack space to be mapped to a 4-level cache. Finally, accesses to both the stack and heap are backed by a smaller cache. The four levels of cache in the split each have slightly different properties and

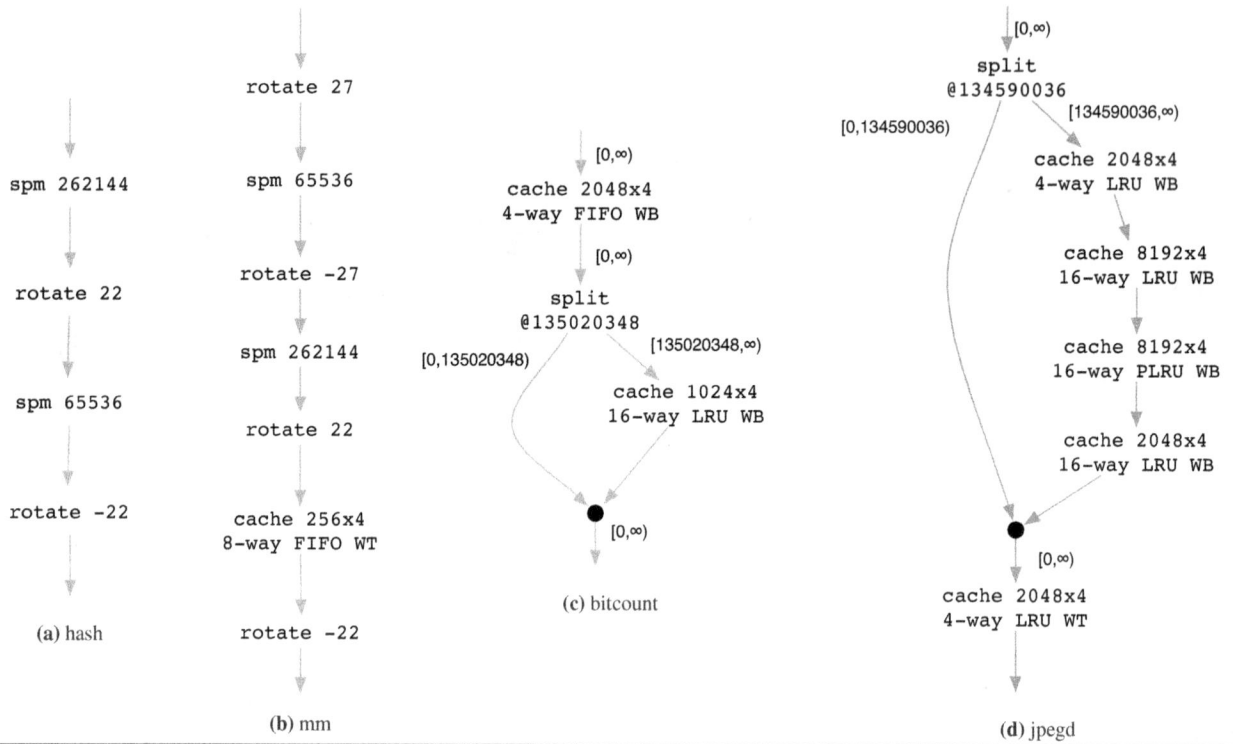

Figure 5. Superoptimized Memory Subsystems for the ASIC Target

removing any one of the caches causes a decrease in performance. Having separate, smaller caches such as this can be beneficial since smaller caches are faster than larger caches.

As is the case with the FPGA target, none of the superoptimized memory subsystems for the ASIC target contained only a single-level cache component. Four of the memory subsystems contained splits (bitcount, jpegd, patricia, and sha), six contained scratchpads (dijkstra, fft, hash, heap, mm, qsort) and six contained address transformations (dijkstra, fft, hash, heap, mm, and qsort). Further, like the FPGA target, all of the superoptimized memory subsystems performed better than the baseline memory subsystem.

4.3 Memory Subsystem Specificity

Finally, we consider how specific each of the memory subsystems is to the application for which the subsystem was superoptimized. Figure 8 shows a heat map comparing the results of running each of the 10 benchmarks with each of the 10 superoptimized memory subsystems for the FPGA target. The results are computed by dividing the total access time of each benchmark running with each memory subsystem by the total access time of the benchmark running with the memory subsystem that was superoptimized for that benchmark. In the figure, darker colors represent better performance.

In Figure 8, we see that the mm and heap benchmarks appear to run well only on the memory subsystems that are superoptimized for them. For the mm benchmark, the performance improvement from the rotate in the memory subsystem is significant enough to prevent any of the other memory subsystems from approaching the performance of the mm memory subsystem. The heap benchmark contains only a scratchpad, which causes accesses to the start of the heap, which are most frequent, to be fast. However, such a structure is suboptimal for the other benchmarks, though the hash benchmark performs fairly well with the memory subsystem for the heap benchmark. In all cases, the memory subsystem that was superop-

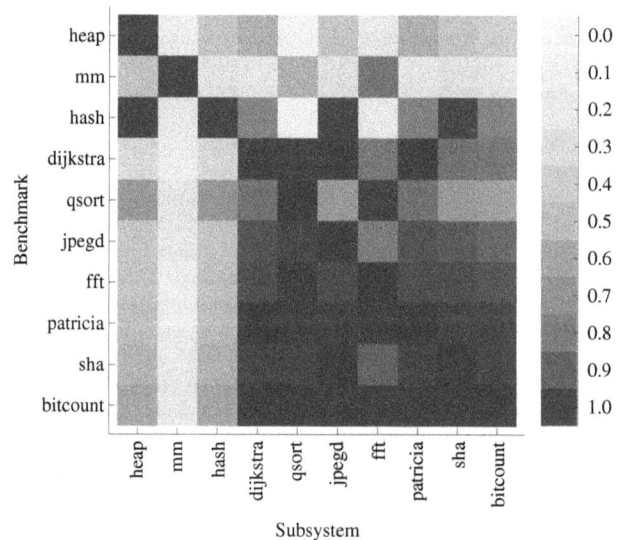

Figure 8. FPGA Memory Subsystem Specificity

timized for a particular benchmark provides the best performance for that benchmark.

Figure 9 shows a heat map comparing the results of running each of the 10 benchmarks with each of the 10 superoptimized memory subsystems for the ASIC target. As is the case with the FPGA results, the benchmarks all perform best with the superoptimized memory subsystem for the particular benchmark. In fact, the results are more specific for the ASIC target than for the FPGA tar-

152

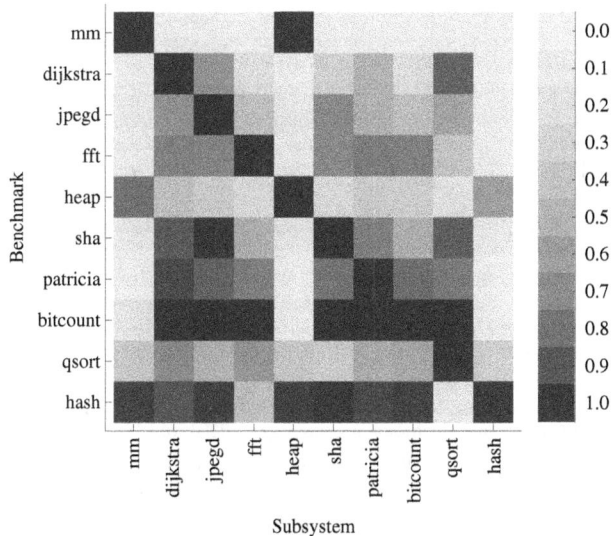

Figure 9. ASIC Memory Subsystem Specificity

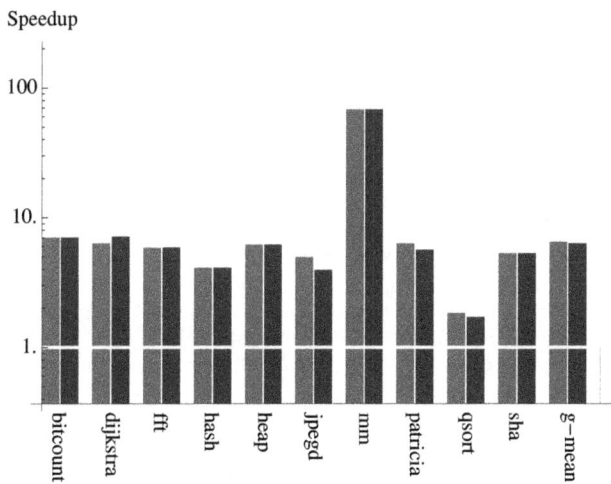

Figure 10. Speedup with Different Inputs

get, which is likely due to the fact that the ASIC target runs faster and has a more complex search space.

Given that the superoptimized memory subsystems are specific to the benchmark for which they were superoptimized, we note that the memory subsystem may further be specific to a particular run of the benchmark. To investigate this, we used a different input data set of the same size for each of the benchmarks for the ASIC target. For example, for the jpegd benchmark, a different input image of the same dimensions as the original was chosen. A comparison of the speedups over the baseline memory subsystem for the original data set and the new data set is shown in Figure 10.

In Figure 10, the lighter bars (on the left) show the speedup of the superoptimized memory subsystem over the baseline memory subsystem for the original data set and the darker bars (on the right) show the speedup for the modified data set. For many of the benchmarks there is little or no difference and in one case (dijkstra), the speedup actually improved. Overall, the geometric mean dropped from $6.43\times$ to $6.27\times$. Although its impossible to

draw anything conclusive from these results, it appears that the effects of over-fitting are minimal.

5. Discussion

When there are enough resources available on the target device (FPGA or ASIC) to contain the complete memory image of a benchmark, one might expect that a scratchpad memory would be the ideal choice. However, the addresses from these traces is do not necessarily start at 0 nor are they contiguous due to the memory layout of the application. Therefore, for such benchmarks, we might expect to see address transformations to move the bulk of the memory references into a scratchpad.

Unfortunately, the number of address transformations needed to move all memory accesses into a scratchpad can make it unlikely the optimizer will discover such a memory subsystem. In addition, the overhead, either in terms of area or BRAMs, of having many small scratchpads may prevent the optimizer from dividing up the memory addresses perfectly. Thus, a cache structure is often selected instead of a scratchpad. This is why, for example, the discovered memory subsystem for the bitcount benchmark uses caches for both the FPGA and ASIC targets despite the fact that the memory image of the bitcount benchmark could fit easily within a memory subsystem afforded by the constraints.

Despite the limitations of placing scratchpads, the optimizer uses such a technique for several of the benchmarks, most notably, the hash and heap benchmarks. By doing so, certain addresses that occur frequently can be accessed faster. Further, accesses that hit in a scratchpad that is before a cache avoid cache pollution.

An observation when comparing the superoptimized memory subsystems for the ASIC target against those for the FPGA target is that, for a particular benchmark, the overall structure is similar, though the memory subsystems for the ASIC target are typically more complex. We expect that the memory subsystems would have similar properties since the benchmark and main memory are held constant. Further, we expect that there would be some variation due to the different properties of the memory subsystem components when deployed on our target devices.

As a last point of discussion, we note that these memory subsystems are specific not only to an individual application, but also a particular run of that application. Although Section 4.3 demonstrates that this effect can be minimal, it is quite possible that some superoptimized memory subsystems could be overly-specific. Obviously, this can be bad in some cases. For example, when traversing a graph, we likely do not want the memory subsystem to have good performance only for a particular graph. On the other hand, when the memory accesses are not data dependent or when we expect the data to be similar from run to run (biased accesses into a hash table, for instance), it may be acceptable or even beneficial for a memory subsystem to be highly optimized for a particular access pattern.

6. Conclusion

We have shown that it is possible to superoptimize memory subsystems for specific applications that out-perform a general-purpose memory subsystem. Unlike previous work, the memory subsystems that our superoptimizer discovers can be arbitrarily complex and contain components other than simple caches. To superoptimize a memory subsystem, we use a form of threshold acceptance. We are then able to improve the discovery process by using information from the address trace.

This work targets both an FPGA as well as an ASIC process. For the FPGA target, we have validated the discovered memory subsystems by generating VHDL for each of the subsystems. The VHDL was then synthesized to ensure that the discovered memory subsystems are realizable at the required frequency. For the ASIC process, we used the CACTI [30] tool to get area and time estimates for each of the memory components.

In the future, we would like to extend this work to speed up the superoptimization process and support more memory subsystems. We would also like to investigate ways to find a representative trace signature for multiple runs of the same application to avoid discovering memory subsystems that are specific to a particular run. In addition, we would like to explore application-specific memory subsystems for parallel applications.

7. Acknowledgments

We thank our colleagues and the EIT staff for the use of the Engineering Cloud Cluster.

References

[1] M. Adler, K. E. Fleming, A. Parashar, M. Pellauer, and J. Emer. LEAP scratchpads: automatic memory and cache management for reconfigurable logic. In *Proc. of 19th ACM/SIGDA Int'l Symp. on Field Programmable Gate Arrays*, pages 25–28, 2011.

[2] R. Balasubramonian, D. H. Albonesi, A. Buyuktosunoglu, and S. Dwarkadas. A dynamically tunable memory hierarchy. *IEEE Trans. on Computers*, 52(10):1243–1258, Oct. 2003.

[3] B. Calder, C. Krintz, S. John, and T. Austin. Cache-conscious data placement. In *Proc. of 8th Int'l Conf. on Architectural Support for Programming Languages and Operating Systems*, pages 139–149, 1998.

[4] S. Carr, K. S. McKinley, and C.-W. Tseng. Compiler optimizations for improving data locality. In *Proc. of 6th Int'l Conf. on Architectural Support for Programming Languages and Operating Systems*, pages 252–262, 1994.

[5] J. Chang, P. Ranganathan, D. A. Roberts, M. A. Shah, and J. Sontag. Data storage apparatus and methods, Mar. 2012. US Patent App. 2012/0131278.

[6] T. M. Chilimbi, B. Davidson, and J. R. Larus. Cache-conscious structure definition. In *Proc. of ACM SIGPLAN Conf. on Programming Language Design and Implementation*, pages 13–24, 1999.

[7] T. M. Chilimbi, M. D. Hill, and J. R. Larus. Cache-conscious structure layout. In *Proc. of ACM Conf. on Programming Language Design and Implementation*, pages 1–12, 1999.

[8] G. Dueck and T. Scheuer. Threshold accepting: a general purpose optimization algorithm appearing superior to simulated annealing. *Journal of Computational Physics*, 90(1):161–175, 1990.

[9] M. Frigo, C. E. Leiserson, H. Prokop, and S. Ramachandran. Cache-oblivious algorithms. In *Proc. of 40th Symp. on Foundations of Computer Science*, pages 285–297, 1999.

[10] A. Ghosh and T. Givargis. Cache optimization for embedded processor cores: An analytical approach. *ACM Trans. on Design Automation of Electronic Systems*, 9(4):419–440, Oct. 2004.

[11] A. Gordon-Ross, F. Vahid, and N. Dutt. Automatic tuning of two-level caches to embedded applications. In *Proc. of the Conf. on Design, Automation and Test in Europe*, page 10208, 2004.

[12] A. Gordon-Ross, F. Vahid, and N. Dutt. Fast configurable-cache tuning with a unified second-level cache. In *Proc. of Int'l Symp. on Low Power Electronics and Design*, pages 323–326, 2005.

[13] T. Granlund and R. Kenner. Eliminating branches using a superoptimizer and the GNU C compiler. In *Proc. of ACM SIGPLAN Conf. on Programming Language Design and Implementation*, pages 341–352, 1992.

[14] M. R. Guthaus, J. S. Ringenberg, D. Ernst, T. M. Austin, T. Mudge, and R. B. Brown. MiBench: A free, commercially representative embedded benchmark suite. In *Proc. of 4th Int'l Workshop on Workload Characterization*, pages 3–14, 2001.

[15] T. C. Hu, A. B. Kahng, and C.-W. A. Tsao. Old bachelor acceptance: A new class of non-monotone threshold accepting methods. *ORSA Journal on Computing*, 7(4):417–425, 1995.

[16] E. Ïpek, S. A. McKee, R. Caruana, B. R. de Supinski, and M. Schulz. Efficiently exploring architectural design spaces via predictive modeling. In *Proc. of 12th Int'l Conf. on Architectural Support for Programming Languages and Operating Systems*, pages 195–206, 2006.

[17] N. P. Jouppi. Improving direct-mapped cache performance by the addition of a small fully-associative cache and prefetch buffers. In *Proc. of 17th Int'l Symp. on Computer Architecture*, pages 364–373, 1990.

[18] S. Kirkpatrick, C. D. Gelatt, and M. P. Vecchi. Optimization by simmulated annealing. *Science*, 220(4598):671–680, 1983.

[19] B. C. Lee and D. M. Brooks. Accurate and efficient regression modeling for microarchitecture performance and power prediction. In *Proc. of 12th Int'l Conf. on Architectural Support for Programming Languages and Operating Systems*, pages 185–194, 2006.

[20] H. Massalin. Superoptimizer: a look at the smallest program. In *Proc. of 2nd Int'l Conf. on Architectural Support for Programming Languages and Operating Systems*, pages 122–126, 1987.

[21] A. Naz. *Split Array and Scalar Data Caches: A Comprehensive Study of Data Cache Organization*. PhD thesis, Univ. of North Texas, 2007.

[22] N. Nethercote and J. Seward. Valgrind: a framework for heavyweight dynamic binary instrumentation. In *Proc. of ACM SIGPLAN Conf. on Programming Language Design and Implementation*, pages 89–100, 2007.

[23] P. Panda, N. Dutt, and A. Nicolau. Local memory exploration and optimization in embedded systems. *IEEE Trans. on Computer-Aided Design of Integrated Circuits and Systems*, 18(1):3–13, 1999.

[24] A. Putnam, S. Eggers, D. Bennett, E. Dellinger, J. Mason, H. Styles, P. Sundararajan, and R. Wittig. Performance and power of cache-based reconfigurable computing. *ACM SIGARCH Computer Architecture News*, 37(3):395–405, 2009.

[25] P. Ranjan Panda, N. D. Dutt, A. Nicolau, F. Catthoor, A. Vandecappelle, E. Brockmeyer, C. Kulkarni, and E. De Greef. Data memory organization and optimizations in application-specific systems. *IEEE Design & Test of Computers*, 18(3):56–68, 2001.

[26] Raspberry Pi. http://www.raspberrypi.org.

[27] E. Schkufza, R. Sharma, and A. Aiken. Stochastic superoptimization. In *Proc. of 18th Int'l Conf. on Architectural Support for Programming Languages and Operating Systems*, pages 305–316, 2013.

[28] S. Sen, S. Chatterjee, and N. Dumir. Towards a theory of cache-efficient algorithms. *Journal of the ACM*, 49(6):828–858, Nov. 2002.

[29] K. T. Sundararajan, T. M. Jones, and N. P. Topham. Smart cache: A self adaptive cache architecture for energy efficiency. In *Proc. of Int'l Conf. on Embedded Computer Systems*, pages 41–50, 2011.

[30] S. Thoziyoor, N. Muralimanohar, J. H. Ahn, and N. P. Jouppi. CACTI 5.1. *HP Laboratories*, 2, Apr. 2008.

[31] A. Veidenbaum, W. Tang, R. Gupta, A. Nicolau, and X. Ji. Adapting cache line size to application behavior. In *Proc. of 13th Int'l Conf. on Supercomputing*, pages 145–154, 1999.

[32] J. G. Wingbermuehle, R. D. Chamberlain, and R. K. Cytron. ScalaPipe: A streaming application generator. In *Proc. of 2012 Symp. on Application Accelerators in High-Performance Computing*, pages 244–254, July 2012.

[33] J. G. Wingbermuehle, R. K. Cytron, and R. D. Chamberlain. Optimization of application-specific memories. *Computer Architecture Letters*, Apr. 2013.

[34] W. A. Wulf and S. A. McKee. Hitting the memory wall: Implications of the obvious. *ACM SIGARCH Computer Architecture News*, 23(1): 20–24, Mar. 1995.

[35] C. Zhang and F. Vahid. Using a victim buffer in an application-specific memory hierarchy. In *Proc. of Design, Automation and Test in Europe Conference and Exhibition*, pages 220–225, 2004.

Lightweight and Block-level Concurrent Sweeping for JavaScript Garbage Collection

Hongjune Kim   Seonmyeong Bak   Jaejin Lee

Department of Computer Science and Engineering, Seoul National University, Seoul, Korea

{hongjune, seonmyeong}@aces.snu.ac.kr   jlee@cse.snu.ac.kr

http://aces.snu.ac.kr

Abstract

JavaScript is a dynamic-typed language originally developed for the purpose of giving dynamic client-side behaviors to web pages. It is mainly used in web application development and because of its popularity and rapid development style it is now also used in other types of applications. Increasing data processing requirements and growing usage in more resource-limited environments, such as mobile devices, has given demands for JavaScript implementations to handle memory more efficiently through garbage collection.

Since aggressive use of time consuming operations in garbage collection can slow down the JavaScript application, there is a trade-off relationship between the effectiveness and the execution time of garbage collection.

In this paper, we present a lightweight, block-level concurrent sweeping mechanism for a mark-and-sweep garbage collector. The sweeping process is detached to an additional thread to eagerly collect free memory blocks and recycle it. To minimize the overhead that comes from the synchronization between the mutator thread and the new sweeping thread, we have chosen a course grained block-level collecting scheme for sweeping. To avoid contention that comes from object destruction, we execute the object destruction phase concurrently with the foreground marking phase.

We have implemented our algorithm in JavaScript Core (JSC) engine embedded in the WebKit browser that uses a variant of mark-and-sweep algorithm to manage JavaScript objects. The original garbage collection implementation performs lazy sweeping that cannot reuse the free blocks. We evaluate our implementation on an ARM-based mobile system and show that memory utilization of the system is significantly improved without performance degradation.

Categories and Subject Descriptors D.3.4 [*Processors*]: Memory management (garbage collection), Run-time environments

General Terms Languages, Performance, Algorithms

Keywords concurrent; garbage collection; JavaScript; memory management

LCTES '14, June 12–13, 2014, Edinburgh, UK.
Copyright © 2014 ACM 978-1-4503-2877-7/14/06...$15.00.
http://dx.doi.org/10.1145/2597809.2597824

1. Introduction

JavaScript[9] is a dynamic-typed language designed to script the behavior of a web page in the client side. It gives programmability to the web page, and this makes the browser to become a popular platform for running system-independent and network-enabled applications. These days JavaScript is a core component of various web application development technologies. Because of its popularity and rapid development style, it is now also used outside the browser in network server applications, desktop applications, and application components developed in other languages.

Web-based applications has been widely spread from desktop computers to various new computing platforms including mobile and embedded devices because of their portability and ubiquity. Some of newly developed mobile platforms use JavaScript and other standard web technologies as their main application development tools[11, 17, 20].

To catch up with the performance demand of web-based applications, there has been an increasing demand for high-performance JavaScript. Most of the widely-used JavaScript engines now compile the time consuming parts of an application into native instructions just-in-time rather than interpreting them directly.

In addition to the execution speed, memory consumption has been a major issue in JavaScript engines because of increasing data processing requirements in web applications and memory restriction in mobile platforms. To meet these requirements, memory spaces allocated to JavaScript objects should be managed efficiently. As a result, various garbage collection and memory management techniques have been applied to JavaScript implementations. In many modern programming languages, dynamic memory management is done by the language runtime. Garbage collector in the language runtime checks for unused objects and enable it to be recycled for further allocation.

WebKit[28] is one of the most widely used browser engines. Its JavaScript implementation is called JavaScript Core (JSC). JSC has a garbage collection scheme for the JavaScript object heap space. It is a variant of the mark-and-sweep algorithm[15]. Garbage collection algorithms typically have a trade-off between memory usage and execution speed. Even if aggressive or frequent garbage collection frees more memory spaces, it may diminish throughput and user responsiveness.

Multicore processors have widely spread from servers to desktops and now mobile platforms. But there is only a limited number of applications to take advantage of multicores available in mobile platforms. Additional cores are not exploited most of the time in mobile devices. Consequently, improving the memory usage and execution performance of JavaScript engines by exploiting these additional cores will give the users better browsing experiences.

In this paper, we propose a lightweight concurrent garbage collection technique that uses an extra thread for memory block sweeping and object destruction. To take advantage of the multi-core processor, these two critical phases of garbage collection are passed to an extra thread, and executed concurrently with the normal script execution. To prevent the slowdown of the foreground execution and waste of energy, we carefully choose the target, degree and timing of the sweeping and destruction operation. Due to the ahead of time sweeping process, the collected free blocks can be used for the object class of a different size. This is particularly effective when adapting to the memory access pattern changes in the application. Our approach achieves significant memory space reduction with comparable performance.

When the free memory space gets scarce, original JSC stops execution and only performs the mark phase to reduce the pause time caused by the garbage collection. The sweeping process is done lazily by processing a single memory block at a time when more free memory cell space is needed. This lazy sweeping prevents from freeing blocks with no marked cells after the mark phase. We present a novel design to hide this sweep process execution time using a background thread. It asynchronously and eagerly collects memory block as soon as possible without blocking the foreground thread. The actual object destruction is done concurrently with the foreground marking phase to avoid synchronization overheads. The runtime or operating system can reuse the freed memory blocks for other types of memory allocations or other programs in the system. Consequently the total memory requirement of the JavaScript engine can be reduced without any performance degradation. Moreover the total computation of all cores required for garbage collection is minimally increased. This is especially important for embedded devices with low clock speed and limited energy capacity.

The major contributions of this paper are as follows:

- We propose a lightweight and block-level concurrent garbage collection scheme. It is based on the mark-and-sweep collection that performs a course-grained sweeping phase at the block-level concurrently with the mutator thread. This course-grain approach has much less contention between threads and computation resource usage than the cell-based, fine-grained sweeping approach.

- To minimize the synchronization overhead with the mutator thread, we separate the destruction step of objects from sweeping phase and execute it concurrently with the marking phase.

- We show the effectiveness of our approach by implementing the block-level concurrent garbage collection scheme in JSC and evaluating the implementation with three representative JavaScript benchmark suites.

The rest of the paper is comprised as follows. We describe the original JSC garbage collection mechanism in Section 2. Our design and implementation of concurrent sweeping is described in Section 3. Our implementation is evaluated in Section 4. Section 5 describes previous studies to improve the efficiency of memory management. Finally, section 6 concludes this paper.

2. Memory Management in JSC

In this section, we describe the memory management mechanism used in JSC.

2.1 Heap Space Allocation

When more memory space in the heap is required for object allocation, JSC obtains a *memory block* of 64KB size from the memory allocator. Memory blocks are managed in two different spaces; *marked space* and *copied space*. In the marked space, each memory block is evenly divided into *cells* to which an allocated object

is mapped. Objects whose size is smaller than or equal to 2KB is placed in the marked space.

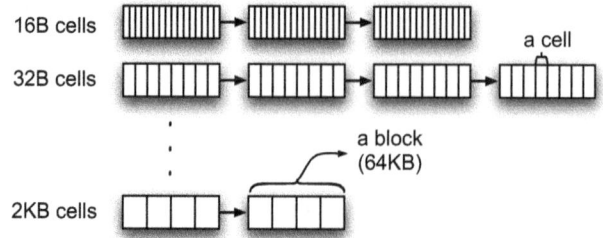

Figure 1: Memory block lists in the marked space (32-bit machine).

Figure 1 shows how the memory blocks are managed in the marked space. Lists of memory blocks are maintained. Each list has a fixed cell size and each memory block in the list is divided into the cells with the fixed size. The cell size is different from list to list. The maximum cell size is 2KB. Machines with 32-bit addresses, the minimum cell size is 16B. Machines with 64-bit addresses, it is 32B. The cell size varies from the minimum cell size to 256B by an increment of the minimum cell size. It varies from 256B to 2KB with an increment of 256B.

For each block list, the memory allocator maintains a current block pointer that points to a block who has free cells. It also maintains a free cell list in each block list.

To allocate memory space for an object of size S, the memory allocator chooses a block list whose cell size is greater than or equal to S and closest to S. Then, it allocates to the object the first free cell in the free cell list.

Cells in the marked spaces are marked in the marking phase of garbage collection. Sweeping each block and recycling cells is done lazily by the memory allocator, on demand when there is a request for object allocation.

Objects whose size is larger than 2KB or changes over time are placed in the copied space. The blocks in the copied space do not have cells. Objects are greedily allocated in a block and non-marked blocks are freed right after the marking phase in the copied space.

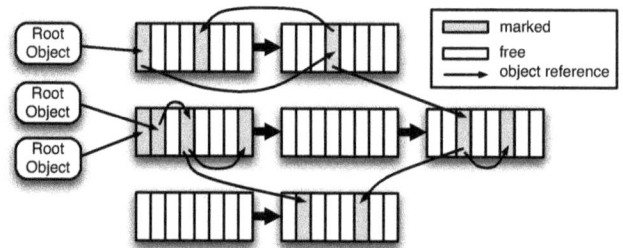

Figure 2: Marking used cells in JSC.

2.2 Garbage Collection

JSC uses a variant of the mark-and-sweep garbage collection scheme[15] for the object heap space. The memory allocator accumulates the sizes of allocated cells after last garbage collection. If the sum exceeds a predefined limit, execution stops and the mark phase of garbage collection starts. Figure 2 illustrates the mark phase of the block lists in the marked space. Starting from root object references, objects are traversed and all live cells are marked. JSC does this marking in a parallel manner exploiting multiple cores available in the target platform. Then, the current block pointers are reset to point to the first blocks in the block lists. At the end of marking phase, the limit for the next garbage collection is determined. Its value is proportional to the size of current live objects. Unmarked cells are neither collected nor recycled at this time.

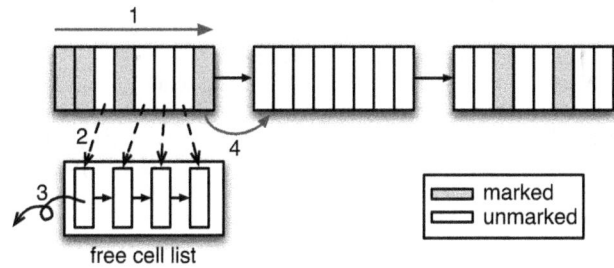

Figure 3: Sweeping a block list in JSC.

The sweep phase is responsible for finding unmarked cells to destroy and to reuse. As mentioned before, the sweep phase is done lazily when there is a memory request, one block at a time. Figure 3 illustrates the sweep process of JSC. When a new cell is requested for object allocation, the block list with the corresponding cell size is visited. If there is no free cell left in the current block's free cell list, the block is swept (step 1 in Figure 3).

Each unmarked cells in the block is destroyed (by invoking the destructor of the corresponding object) and put into the free cell list (step 2 in Figure 3). The first cell in the free cell list is popped and returned for the allocation request (step 3 in Figure 3). If the free cell list of the current block is empty, then the next block becomes the current block and gets swept (step 4 of Figure 3).

The block allocator in JSC maintains a pool of *free blocks*. A free block is a block with no live object on it, and a non-free block is a block that contains at least one live cell. These free blocks can be reused for object allocation in JSC or released to the operating system after some amount of time. The block allocator resides between the JSC heap space and the system memory allocator. If the free cell list of the last block in the matching block list is empty, a new block is allocated from the block allocator and attached to the block list. All the cells in this block are added to the free cell list without the destruction step.

Since only one block is swept at a time, current policy of JSC can never release free blocks from the marked space to the block allocator in normal JavaScript execution; it is only done by a special request from the browser (e.g., when loading a new web page). This implies that unused memory blocks from the marked space are never freed for a normal JavaScript execution within a web page, and free blocks are not exchanged between different block lists in the marked space.

Moreover, with the current memory allocation policy of JSC, an object may be allocated to a free cell in a free block even though a free cell exists in a non-free block. Note that it is desirable to reuse a free cell in a non-free block and to return free blocks to the block allocator for better memory space utilization.

2.3 Incremental Sweeping

Because of the lazy sweeping policy of JSC, the marked block list is swept for only one block at a time. Only the cells in this block and objects referenced by them are destroyed and freed. If memory requests to the marked space are rarely occur, it takes long time to free the unmarked cells residing in blocks far from the head of a block list. If these cells reference other objects outside the marked space (including dynamic browser objects, such as DOM objects), these objects are not freed either.

To free these objects, there is an additional sweeping mechanism in WebKit called *incremental sweeper*. The procedure of call-

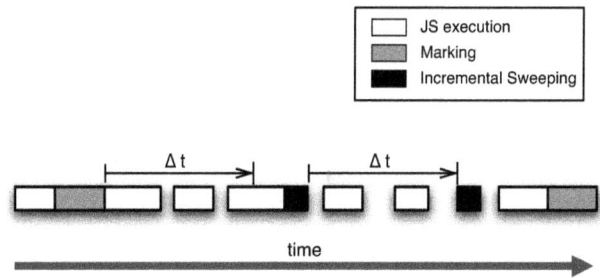

Figure 4: Incremental sweeping in JSC.

ing the incremental sweeper is described in Figure 4. If the marking phase has not been called for a certain amount of time (Δt in Figure 4), WebKit engine fires the incremental sweeper. The incremental sweeper traverses the marked space and destroys unmarked objects and objects referenced by them. The sweeper also releases the free blocks from the block list so that they can be reused by other block lists. The running time for a single incremental sweeping process is limited to guarantee responsiveness and not to harm execution performance excessively.

Unlike JSCs internal mark-and-sweep GC scheme, which is triggered by the JSC engine preemptively in the mutator thread, the incremental sweeper must be exclusively invoked from the mutator thread. The mutator thread cannot be preempted for incremental sweeping. The browser event handler routine triggers the incremental sweeper between executions of the mutator thread. In Figure 4, the first incremental sweeper call is delayed because of the mutator thread execution. The incremental sweeper is invoked for a limited amount of time not to degrade the performance of the mutator thread. In some cases, the amount of time is not sufficient for destroying all unmarked objects and those objects referenced by them.

3. Block-level Concurrent Sweeping

In this section, we present the design and implementation of our lightweight, block-level concurrent sweeping mechanism.

When a JavaScript application has a large data set with a short lifetime, a large portion of the marked space is left unmarked after the GC phase, resulting in many free blocks. Our experimental result indicates that half of the benchmark applications have, more than 88.9% of the blocks free during execution. We propose a lightweight and concurrent sweeping mechanism to reuse these free blocks.

In the following subsections, *semi-free blocks* are the blocks whose cells are all unmarked, but the cells and objects referenced by the cells are not destructed yet.

3.1 Key Idea

The three key ideas of our approach are as follows:

- We collect free *blocks*, not free cells.
- We collect semi-free blocks concurrently with the mutator thread.
- We destroy the cells in semi-free blocks and objects referenced by them concurrently with the mark phase.

The reason why we collect only semi-free blocks, not every unmarked cell, is that collection at the block level is highly efficient, and only the entirely free blocks can be reused by other block lists.

As the original JSC does, sweeping at cell level requires checking every cells in a block and constructing a free cell list, which costs large amount of time and memory space compared to block level sweeping. Even if this sweeping process is done concurrently, the synchronization overhead could lead to noticeable slowdown of the mutator thread.

On the other hand, block level sweeping could be simply done by checking the bitmap of a block to see if it is free, and moving it to a separate list. This process incurs minimal synchronization overhead between threads, because only removing a single block from the original block list requires synchronization.

Aside from discovering unmarked cells, the actual destruction of objects also requires complicated synchronization mechanisms between the mutator and the destruction thread. This includes an atomic access to reference counters on global data structures. We avoid these overheads by delaying the destruction phase until the next marking phase of the main thread. By destructing objects concurrently with the marking phase, there is almost no overhead introduced because the marking phase dose not access these shared data structures.

Since our sweeper collects these semi-free blocks eagerly, the resulting free blocks can be assigned to another block list when the block list lacks free blocks. This prevents the block allocator from requesting more blocks from the system, or reducing the frequency of invoking the mark phase in the mutator thread. Both are adverse to performance. The effect of our approach is similar to compaction. Since free blocks are returned to the block allocator, further allocation occurs using the free cells in non-free blocks first.

3.2 Block-level Sweeping Mechanism

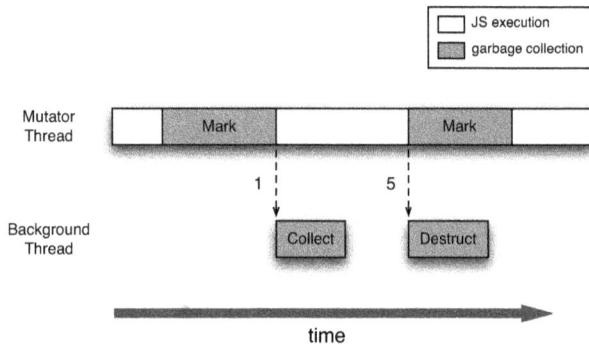

(a) Invocation of the concurrent sweeping

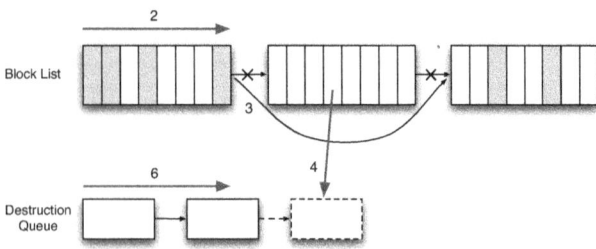

(b) Steps in the concurrent sweeper

Figure 5: Concurrent sweeping.

Figure 5a illustrates the invocation of concurrent sweeper, and Figure 5b shows the steps in *collect* and *destruct* stages of the concurrent sweeper.

After the mark phase, our concurrent sweeper is triggered (1). It runs concurrently with the main JavaScript execution. The sweeper traverses the block lists in the marked space and looks for a semi-free block (2). If a semi-free block is found, it is removed from

the list (3) and inserted to the destruction queue (4). The destruction queue contains those blocks that do not contain any marked cells. However, the objects referenced by the cells have not been destructed yet. Destruction of the objects in the blocks occurs in the next mark phase concurrently (5). During the mark phase, the background thread that is in charge of destruction traverses the destruction queue and performs destruction (6).

When the background thread is collecting semi-free blocks in step 2 and 3, there is a bitmap of cells in each block that can be used for checking if the entire cells are free. Thus checking each cell in the block is not required. This makes the block level sweeping far more lightweight than sweeping each cell in the block.

In step 6, destructing objects is executed concurrently with the mark phase. This is because if the destruction process is overlapped with the mutator thread, some global data structures, such as string literal table, should be locked, resulting in slowdown of the mutator thread. On the contrary, no synchronization is required between the mark phase and the destruction step because the cells in the block and the contents of objects being destructed are not touched in the mark phase. Note that all the cells in a semi-free block are unmarked cells from the previous mark phase, and the current mark phase does not touch these cells.

3.3 Using the Incremental Sweeper

Since long-lived unused cells (these can be found in long-running server-side JavaScript applications) in non-free blocks may cause the system a noticeable memory reduction or performance degradation, we use the original incremental sweeper complementary to our concurrent sweeper. Even in this case, since most of the free cells belong to free blocks when the occupancy ratio is low, large portion of the unused free objects are freed by our concurrent sweeper before the incremental sweeper frees them. Hence, the interval and duration of the incremental sweeper need to be adjusted shorter.

4. Evaluation

In this section, we implement the block-level concurrent sweeping mechanism and evaluate its effectiveness.

4.1 Evaluation Environment

Table 1: The platform used for evaluation

Platform	ARM
Processor	Exynos C210
Number of cores	2
Main memory	800MB
Operation system	Tizen 2.0

We evaluate our implementation on an ARM-based mobile platform. The specification of the system is shown in Table 1. The operating system is Tizen[17]. Tizen[17] is based on Linux and uses WebKit as a core part of the system. Its physical memory size is highly restricted (800MB) compared to desktop computers. We implement our scheme in the JSC engine and WebKit packaged in Tizen.

In the following subsections, JSC stands for the original JSC with the incremental sweeper and CS stands for our block-level concurrent sweeper.

4.2 Benchmark Applications

We use applications from 3 benchmark suites for our evaluation: V8[12], Kraken[21] and Dromaeo[19]. V8 and Kraken are benchmark suites to measure the performance of JavaScript engine and can be executed with any pure JavaScript execution environment. On the contrary, DOM-core tests in Dromaeo perform excessive browser Document Object Model (DOM) operations through JavaScript handlers, and they can be executed only with a full browser environment. We evaluate our approach for both computational workload (V8 and Kraken) and browser based applications (Dromaeo-DOM).

For each benchmark suite, we measure the execution time of the entire suite as well as the execution time of each application in the suite. Running the entire suite, i.e., running all the applications in the suite sequentially one by one, is more close to the real browser experience. We refer this type of execution as *chained execution* in this section.

We also use the Sunspider benchmark suite[28] but do not report the result because it consists of very simple tests on JavaScript functionality, and most of the applications do not trigger the garbage collection phase. Some of benchmark applications in V8 and Kraken do not trigger garbage collection either. In the V8 suite, one (richards) out of eight, and in Kraken, nine (ai-astar, audio-oscillator, imaging-darkroom, imaging-desaturate, imaging-gaussian-blur, json-parse-financial, json-stringify-tinderbox, stanford-crypto-ccm, and stanford-crypto-sha256-iterative) out of fourteen applications do not trigger garbage collection. These applications have a lower memory footprint than the predefined allocation limit. We exclude these applications for stand-alone execution, but include them in the chained execution.

The driver program of the V8 benchmark suite executes each of the benchmark application repeatedly until a predefined timing condition is met. Then, a total score is calculated based on the number of iterations and execution time. For a fair comparison when each benchmark application is independently executed, we fix the iteration number for each application to match the number of iterations obtained when it runs inside the suite.

However the Kraken suite runs each application in a separated HTML iframes. It creates a new instance of JavaScript engine to guarantee independence between applications and iterations. To make the applications in Kraken run in a chained manner, we concatenates application sources.

Although all applications but Dromaeo-DOM can be executed with the shell-based JSC runtime, we use the full blown Tizen browser to see the effects of the interaction between the browser and the garbage collector in JSC.

4.3 Heap Space Occupancy after Garbage Collection

To show the effectiveness of freeing non-used blocks (i.e., returning them to the block allocator), we inspect occupancy of marked cells in the heap after the original mark phase by counting the number of marked cells for each cell size, the number of all blocks in the marked space, and the number of free blocks. Assume the block lists are enumerated by the increasing order of their cell size. After every mark phase, we can compute the occupancy ratio R_{occ} and free block ratio R_{free} as follows:

$$R_{occ} = \sum_i \frac{C_i \times S_i}{B_i \times 64KB}$$

$$R_{free} = \frac{\sum_i F_i}{\sum_i B_i}$$

where C_i is the number of marked cells, S_i is the size of a cell, F_i is the number of free blocks, and B_i is the number of blocks in block list i.

By obtaining R_{occ} and R_{free} periodically during the execution of each application and calculating the geometric mean of these

Table 2: Heap space occupancy and free block ratio of JSC

Suite	Benchmark	Cell Occupancy	Free Blocks
V8	deltablue	0.42%	93.67%
	crypto	5.42%	32.97%
	raytrace	0.38%	96.65%
	earley-boyer	2.09%	91.01%
	regexp	6.07%	75.53%
	splay	56.88%	0.11%
	navier-stokes	54.61%	4.21%
Kraken	audio-beat-detection	1.20%	95.03%
	audio-dft	92.48%	0.00%
	audio-fft	1.11%	95.24%
	stanford-crypto-aes	15.37%	59.00%
	stanford-crypto-pbkdf2	0.74%	88.90%
Dromaeo	dom-attr	0.81%	83.19%
	dom-modification	1.71%	89.84%
	dom-query	1.12%	84.24%
	dom-traverse	21.15%	7.69%
Geomean		3.75%	36.06%
Chained	v8	3.08%	71.95%
	kraken	40.73%	50.54%
	dromaeo-dom	1.07%	84.69%

values, we obtain an average occupancy ratio and an average free block ratio for the application.

Table 2 summarizes the experimental result with the original JSC engine. We see that the occupancy ratio of an application is inversely proportional to its free block ratio. For example, in splay, navier-stokes and audio-dft that has more than half of its heap space objects marked after GC (occupancy ratio is higher than 50%), there are almost no free blocks left (less than 5%). In deltablue, raytrace, earley-boyer, audio-beat-detection, audio-fft, stanford-crypto-pbkdf2, dom-attr, dom-modification and dom-query, their occupancy ratio is less than 3% and more than 83% of the blocks are free.

Half of the applications have more than 88.9% of free blocks. Our block-level concurrent sweeper potentially free these blocks. On average, the applications show 3.75% of the cells are occupied and 36.06% of blocks are free after GC.

When we execute all applications in the chained manner, over 50% of blocks are free for V8 and Kraken. Over 84% of blocks are free for Dromaeo. Our algorithm is able to reclaim these free blocks to the block allocator or to the operating system eagerly. This increases memory utilization and reduces the amount of memory consumed by the system.

4.4 Memory Footprint

To see the memory savings by our approach, we measure the total size of the used JSC heap space and full memory footprint of the browser application. The JSC heap space consists of the marked space, the copied space and blocks in the destruction queue. To see the actual effect of freeing blocks and memory objects referenced by the blocks, we also measure the resident set size (RSS) of the browser process.

We choose two applications, earley-boyer from V8 and dom-query Dromaeo, which have noticeable memory footprint changes over time. Figure 6 and Figure 7 show the memory usage over time for earley-boyer and dom-query, respectively.

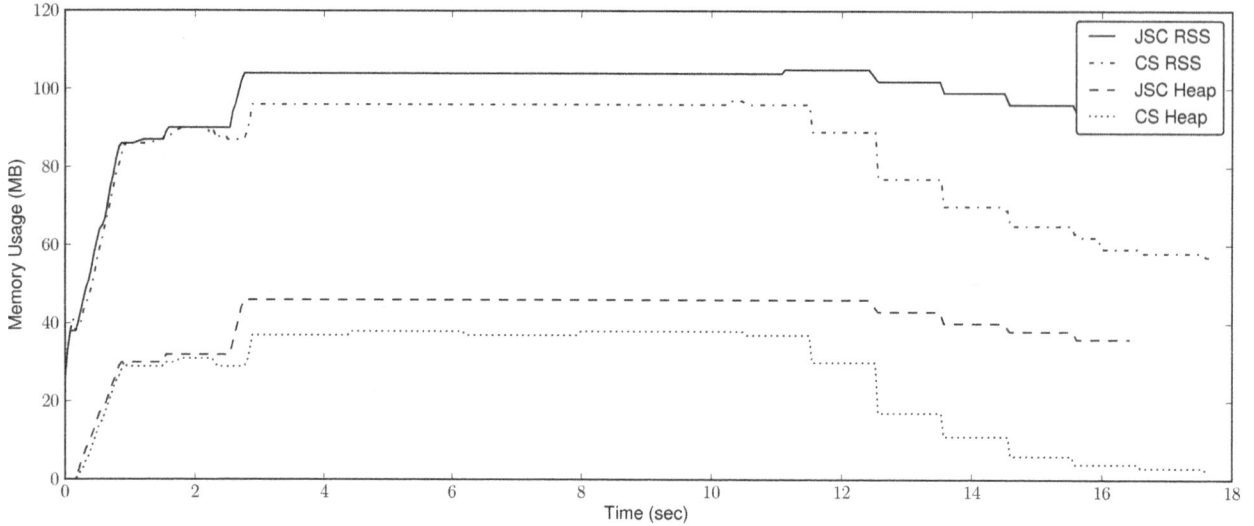

Figure 6: Memory footprint of V8 earley-boyer

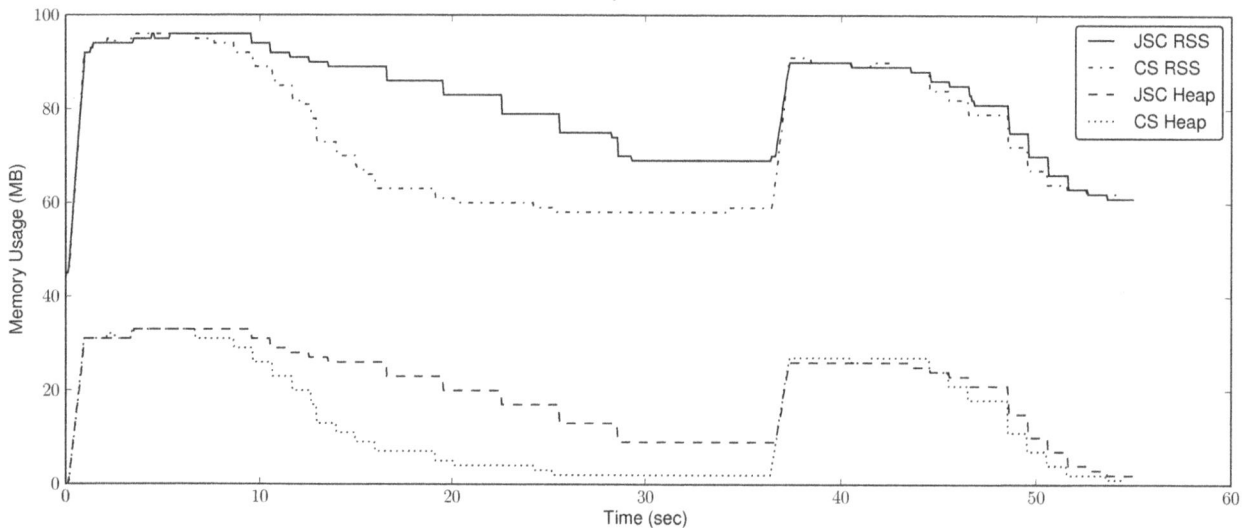

Figure 7: Memory footprint of Dromaeo dom-query

The average memory usage over time is defined as follows:

$$\frac{\sum_i \Delta t \cdot m_i}{T} \tag{1}$$

where m_i is the memory space used at the sampling point i, Δt is the sampling interval, and T is Δt multiplied by the number of sampling point. That is, T is the execution time of the application excluding the garbage collection time. If the sampling rate is fixed, then the value is equal to the arithmetic mean of m_i. The above equation implies that the area under the curve is proportional to the average memory usage.

For both of earley-boyer and dom-query, we see that CS is more effective than JSC. CS reduces memory footprint significantly compared to JSC.

In earley-boyer, the differences between JSC and CS for both of RSS and heap are almost the same over time. This implies that

memory management in the heap space has minimal effect on the browser memory space. This is because the V8 benchmark suite has no interaction with browser objects during execution.

Unlike earley-boyer, in the case of dom-query, the difference between JSC and CS for RSS is bigger than that for heap. This is because destroying unmarked cells in the marked space triggers destroying browser DOM objects referenced by the unmarked cells if it is the last reference. Thus, the bigger the data (e.g., images, audio, video, etc.) associated with the browser object are, the more browser memory space will be freed by our algorithm.

To see memory management in applications that have more complicated phases, we analyze the chained execution of each suite. Figure 8, Figure 9 and Figure 10 show the memory usage over time for the V8, Kraken and Dromaeo benchmark suites, respectively.

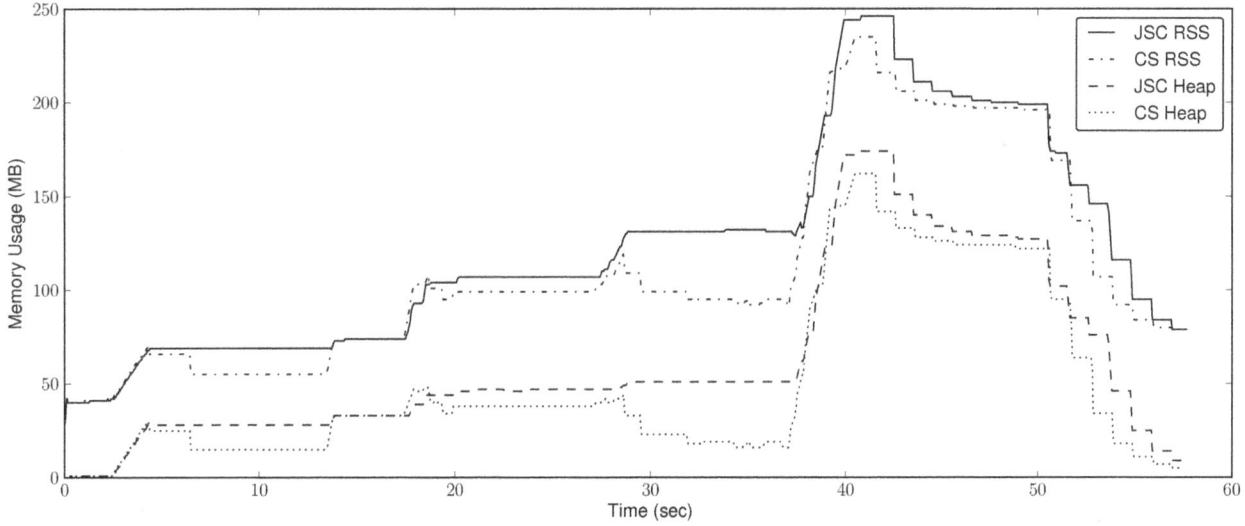

Figure 8: Chained execution of V8

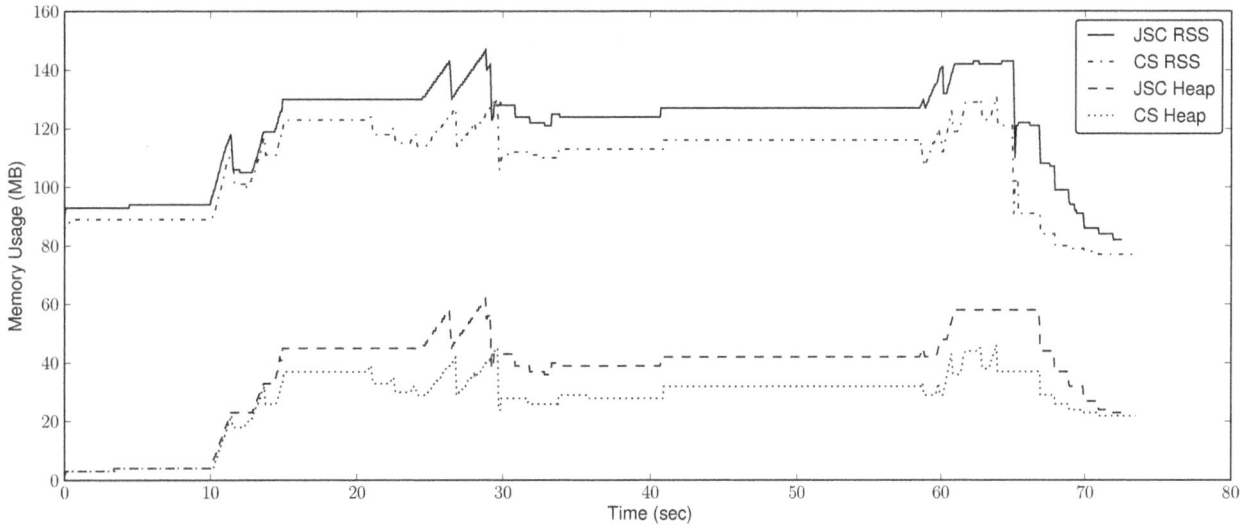

Figure 9: Chained execution of Kraken

In the V8 suite, the peak memory usage is reduced by CS and there are some large memory saving phases during execution. This is because free blocks from the previously executed application is recycled eagerly by our sweeper. Since the V8 benchmark suite has no browser interaction, the shape of RSS curve is almost identical to the shape of heap curve. The trend of the Kraken suite is similar to the case of the V8 suite.

In the Dromaeo suite, the heap space garbage collection in CS triggers freeing more browser objects. Note that the gap between JSC RSS and CS RSS is much bigger than that between JSC Heap and CS Heap.

4.5 Memory Savings

Table 3 presents the memory usage for each individual application and chained execution. Memory usage of CS is normalized to JSC.

For the cases of individual applications, the peak memory usage of CS does not differ from JSC significantly. The geometric mean of peak heap memory usage across applications is 97.44% and that of the peak RSS memory usage is 97.06%. This is because a typical benchmark application keeps iterating the same loop that allocates objects until it reaches the garbage collection limit. This limit becomes the peak value. But in earley-boyer, regexp, and splay, the peak memory reduction is quite significant.

For many individual applications, the average heap memory usage of CS is significantly reduced from that of JSC. However, the RSS values show less reduction even if the heap values show significant reduction. This is because RSS includes many unaffected memory spaces by the garbage collection. These memory spaces include static code region, spaces for dynamically loaded libraries, spaces for many browser-created objects that are unrelated to JavaScript, etc.

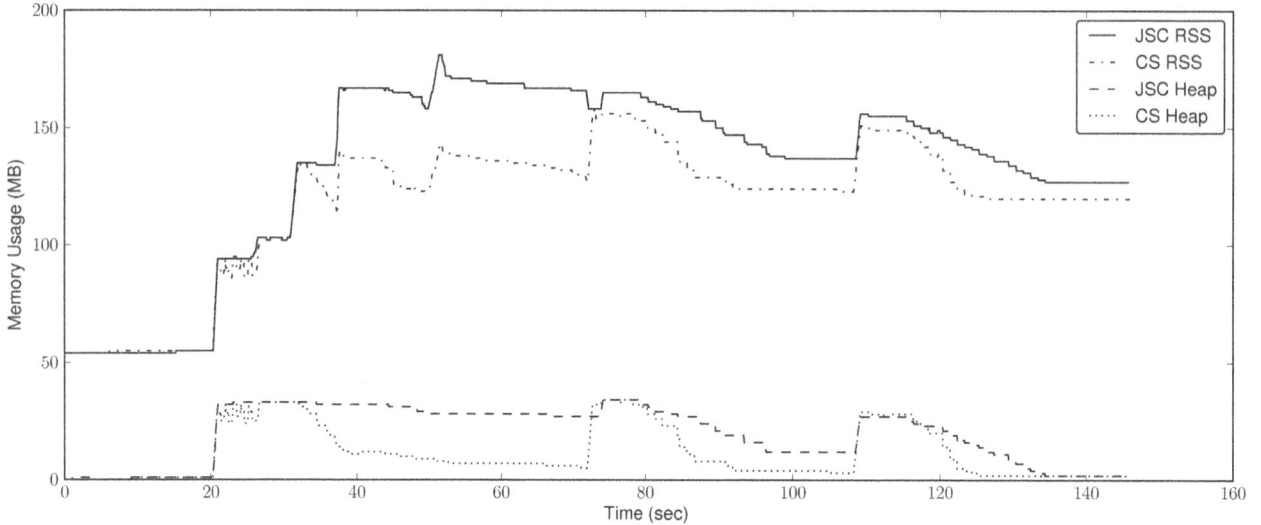

Figure 10: Chained execution of Dromaeo-DOM

Table 3: Memory usage of CS

Suite	Benchmark	RSS Peak	RSS Average	Heap Peak	Heap Average
V8	deltablue	99.35%	99.30%	98.60%	96.58%
	crypto	99.63%	98.83%	104.03%	85.95%
	raytrace	99.97%	100.24%	99.95%	100.16%
	earley-boyer	90.41%	92.28%	80.93%	83.69%
	regexp	82.15%	83.93%	93.83%	85.90%
	splay	88.70%	92.98%	86.15%	90.87%
	navier-stokes	100.15%	100.41%	100.00%	100.01%
Kraken	audio-beat-detection	99.67%	96.01%	100.00%	89.50%
	audio-dft	100.34%	100.38%	100.00%	100.04%
	audio-fft	99.67%	95.74%	100.00%	89.09%
	stanford-crypto-aes	99.89%	99.26%	100.00%	96.41%
	stanford-crypto-pbkdf2	99.81%	93.16%	100.00%	85.61%
Dromaeo	dom-attr	99.97%	100.69%	100.00%	101.78%
	dom-modification	95.53%	90.91%	98.57%	76.42%
	dom-query	99.60%	89.00%	99.81%	65.92%
	dom-traverse	100.56%	100.55%	100.00%	99.41%
Geomean		97.06%	95.73%	97.44%	89.91%
Chained	v8	87.26%	85.77%	86.66%	78.38%
	kraken	92.82%	91.86%	81.84%	77.00%
	dromaeo-dom	80.21%	82.75%	98.90%	58.62%

As mentioned before, chained execution is close to the real execution environment. The different memory usage patterns across different applications in the chained execution give more chances to the block-level concurrent sweeper to free unused blocks. The average heap memory usage is reduced to 78.38%, 77.00% and 58.62% of JSC for V8, Kraken, and Dromaeo, respectively. The reduction in heap memory usage also affects the reduction in RSS memory usage significantly.

4.6 Performance Comparison

To evaluate the performance of our approach, we measure the total execution time of each benchmark suite.

Table 4 and shows the execution time of CS normalized to the execution time of JSC. Since the V8 suite provides a score to measure performance, we use this number as a performance metric for V8 for chained execution. The score is inversely proportional to the execution time. Thus, it is possible to obtain relative execution time from the score. Overall, the execution time of CS is comparable to JSC and CS does not degrade the performance of an application in general.

5. Related Work

Previous studies focus on shortening the garbage collection time by parallelizing the algorithm itself, which is called parallel garbage collection, or by hiding the pause time by running garbage col-

Table 4: Normalized execution time of CS to JSC

Suite	Benchmark	Execution Time
V8	deltablue	100.35%
	crypto	100.03%
	raytrace	99.45%
	earley-boyer	99.55%
	regexp	101.08%
	splay	100.74%
	navier-stokes	101.63%
Kraken	audio-beat-detection	99.36%
	audio-dft	99.67%
	audio-fft	98.84%
	stanford-crypto-aes	99.38%
	stanford-crypto-pbkdf2	101.29%
Dromaeo	dom-attr	100.26%
	dom-modification	100.83%
	dom-query	100.63%
	dom-traverse	101.24%
Geomean		100.27%
Chained	v8	99.92%
	kraken	101.21%
	dromaeo-dom	101.50%

lection concurrently with the mutator thread, named concurrent garbage collection.

Boehm et al.[6] propose a parallel collector that uses the virtual memory hardware to check for a dirty page. This work parallelizes most parts of garbage collection to minimize the pause time. Based on this work, studies including [14], [10] and [24] proposed concurrent GC without explicit synchronizations.

Hudson and Moss[13] has presented concurrent GC algorithm named Sapphire. They suggested a mechanism on copying collection to flip one thread per a time from old copies to new copies to reduce the stopped number of threads in copying process. Since this is an optimization on copying phase, it is not applicable on engines that do not rely on copying phase such as JSC.

There also have been many studies on concurrent garbage collection. Base studies including Steele[25], Dijkstra et al.[8] and Lamport[16] have shown that garbage collection can run in parallel with proper computation. Many concurrent garbage collection algorithms have been proposed since then[1–3, 29]. Vechev et al.[27] have shown that these concurrent algorithms could be formally described and converted to another one using a set of transformations without losing their correctness.

Blackburn[5] have presented that distributed garbage collection algorithm can be derived from a distributed termination algorithm and a centralized garbage collector.

Most of the concurrent garbage collection algorithms focuses on parallelizing the algorithm itself and give less attention to the effect on applications. Many of these techniques have been implemented in Java Virtual Machines. Commercial JVMs such as JRockit[22], HotSpot[26], which both are acquired by Oracle, and IBM's JVM[4] have implemented multiple instances of prior concurrent and parallel garbage collectors. But unlike parallel collection, the concurrent collection is not enabled by default, because the performance gain is not stable and sometimes give high overheads on mutator threads [7].

JavaScript has many dynamic features in language design[23], so there are many difficulties in optimizing the virtual machine. Most of the widely used JavaScript engines use mark-and-sweep based implementation in garbage collection. There are some ongo-

ing efforts to parallelize the engine, and JavaScriptCore has parallelized the mark phase in the mark-and-sweep garbage collection. Our approach does not prevent from being used together with parallel marking.

But all of the previous studies do not focus on the fact that in embedded platforms, fine grain parallelizing hurts the execution performances in many cases. Moreover, less effort has been taken analyzing the computation and resource usage of the background thread, which is also important in embedded systems.

Studies that have comparable goal with ours is the studies that focuses on reducing GC pause time on concurrent execution using schemes without primitive lock-based synchronization.

Click et al.[7]'s work on implementing pauseless GC used special read barrier hardware instruction to implement fully parallel GC. This mechanism requires special hardware implementation and was focused on systems with large parallel processors, executing large number of multiple virtual machine threads.

The work of McGachey et al.[18] focuses on close issue from our work. They used concept of transactional memory to overcome the synchronization overhead between the mutator thread and the garbage collection thread. But they focuses on reducing pause time, and there are no evaluation of total execution time. This is an interesting approach, but implementation of transactional memory is complex, and also the commit process on mutator thread takes time. So it would take more research on using transactional approach for reducing the total execution time. And due to transaction logging and rollback, this approach needs more CPU computation and memory interaction than our approach, which is likely to consume more power and bandwidth related resources on embedded platforms.

Our lightweight sweeping approach could be used together with other concurrent and parallel techniques, and reduce the load on more heavy, fine-grained collection.

6. Conclusion

In this paper we have presented the design and implementation of block-level concurrent mark-and-sweep garbage collection scheme in the JavaScript runtime. Sweeping is done at the block level to return free blocks to the system. It is concurrent to the mutator thread. The object destruction in these blocks are concurrently done with the marking phase. We have implemented the policy in the JavaScriptCore engine, and evaluated our approach on a Tizen mobile platform. Experimental results indicate that half of the benchmark applications have more than 88.9% of the blocks free during execution, on average. This implies that our coarse-grained block reusing mechanism is effective. We use the V8 and Kraken benchmark suites to see memory footprint improvement for general JavaScript execution, and used the Dromaeo-DOM benchmark suite to see the improvement in browser-interfacing applications. The evaluation results show that average heap footprint reduces to 89.9% when executing a single benchmark application. When the entire applications in each benchmark suite are executed sequentially one by one, the heap usage is reduced more to 78.4%, 7.0% and 58.6% for V8, Kraken and Dromaeo-DOM, respectively. This shows our approach has more effective for long-running applications that have multiple phases. The experimental result also indicates that the performance of our implementation is comparable to the original JSC.

For further study, we would like to apply our algorithm to other garbage collection systems. The idea of how we concurrently execute the mutation, marking, sweeping and object destruction phases with minimal synchronization overhead could be applied to systems that use a different memory layout from the block and cell based allocation. We are also planning to study on how our scheme could be applied to other types of garbage collection algorithms, such as generational garbage collection and compaction based algorithms.

Acknowledgements

This work was supported by the National Research Foundation of Korea (NRF) grant funded by the Korea government (MSIP) (No. 2013R1A3A2003664). ICT at Seoul National University provided research facilities for this study.

References

[1] H. Azatchi, Y. Levanoni, H. Paz, and E. Petrank. An on-the-fly mark and sweep garbage collector based on sliding views. In *Proceedings of the 18th Annual ACM SIGPLAN Conference on Object-oriented Programing, Systems, Languages, and Applications*, OOPSLA '03, pages 269–281, New York, NY, USA, 2003. ACM.

[2] D. F. Bacon, C. R. Attanasio, H. B. Lee, V. T. Rajan, and S. Smith. Java without the coffee breaks: A nonintrusive multiprocessor garbage collector. In *Proceedings of the ACM SIGPLAN 2001 Conference on Programming Language Design and Implementation*, PLDI '01, pages 92–103, New York, NY, USA, 2001. ACM.

[3] D. F. Bacon, P. Cheng, and V. T. Rajan. A real-time garbage collector with low overhead and consistent utilization. In *Proceedings of the 30th ACM SIGPLAN-SIGACT Symposium on Principles of Programming Languages*, POPL '03, pages 285–298, New York, NY, USA, 2003. ACM.

[4] K. Barabash, Y. Ossia, and E. Petrank. Mostly concurrent garbage collection revisited. In *Proceedings of the 18th annual ACM SIGPLAN conference on Object-oriented programing, systems, languages, and applications*, OOPSLA '03, pages 255–268, New York, NY, USA, 2003. ACM.

[5] S. M. Blackburn, R. L. Hudson, R. Morrison, J. E. B. Moss, D. S. Munro, and J. Zigman. Starting with termination: A methodology for building distributed garbage collection algorithms. In *Proceedings of the 24th Australasian Conference on Computer Science*, ACSC '01, pages 20–28, Washington, DC, USA, 2001. IEEE Computer Society.

[6] H.-J. Boehm, A. J. Demers, and S. Shenker. Mostly parallel garbage collection. In *Proceedings of the ACM SIGPLAN 1991 conference on Programming language design and implementation*, PLDI '91, pages 157–164, New York, NY, USA, 1991. ACM.

[7] C. Click, G. Tene, and M. Wolf. The pauseless gc algorithm. In *Proceedings of the 1st ACM/USENIX International Conference on Virtual Execution Environments*, VEE '05, pages 46–56, New York, NY, USA, 2005. ACM.

[8] E. W. Dijkstra, L. Lamport, A. J. Martin, C. S. Scholten, and E. F. M. Steffens. On-the-fly garbage collection: an exercise in cooperation. *Commun. ACM*, 21(11):966–975, Nov. 1978.

[9] ECMA. *ECMA-262: ECMAScript Language Specification*. ECMA (European Association for Standardizing Information and Communication Systems), third edition, Dec. 1999.

[10] C. Flood, D. Detlefs, N. Shavit, and C. Zhang. Parallel garbage collection for shared memory multiprocessors. In *Usenix Java Virtual Machine Research and Technology Symposium (JVM01)*, Monterey, CA, 2001.

[11] Google Inc. Chrome os. http://www.chromium.org/chromium-os.

[12] Google Inc. V8 benchmark suite. http://v8.googlecode.com/svn/data/benchmarks/current/run.html, 2008.

[13] R. L. Hudson and J. E. B. Moss. Sapphire: Copying gc without stopping the world. In *Proceedings of the 2001 Joint ACM-ISCOPE Conference on Java Grande*, JGI '01, pages 48–57, New York, NY, USA, 2001. ACM.

[14] L. Huelsbergen and P. Winterbottom. Very concurrent mark-&-sweep garbage collection without fine-grain synchronization. In *Proceedings of the 1st international symposium on Memory management*, ISMM '98, pages 166–175, New York, NY, USA, 1998. ACM.

[15] R. Jones and R. D. Lins. *Garbage Collection: Algorithms for Automatic Dynamic Memory Management*. Wiley, August 1996.

[16] L. Lamport. Garbage collection with multiple processes: an exercise in parallelism. In *Proceedings of the 1976 International Conference on Parallel Processing*, pages 50–54.

[17] Linux Foundation. Tizen. http://www.tizen.org.

[18] P. McGachey, A.-R. Adl-Tabatabai, R. L. Hudson, V. Menon, B. Saha, and T. Shpeisman. Concurrent gc leveraging transactional memory. In *Proceedings of the 13th ACM SIGPLAN Symposium on Principles and Practice of Parallel Programming*, PPoPP '08, pages 217–226, New York, NY, USA, 2008. ACM.

[19] Mozilla Foundation. Dromaeo javascript testing. http://dromaeo.com/.

[20] Mozilla Foundation. Firefox OS. https://developer.mozilla.org/en/docs/Mozilla/Firefox_OS.

[21] Mozilla Foundation. Kraken javascript benchmark. http://krakenbenchmark.mozilla.org/.

[22] Oracle/BEA. Bea jrockit: Java for the enterprise, 2003.

[23] G. Richards, S. Lebresne, B. Burg, and J. Vitek. An analysis of the dynamic behavior of javascript programs. In *Proceedings of the 2010 ACM SIGPLAN conference on Programming language design and implementation*, PLDI '10, pages 1–12, New York, NY, USA, 2010. ACM.

[24] F. Siebert. Concurrent, parallel, real-time garbage-collection. In *Proceedings of the 2010 international symposium on Memory management*, ISMM '10, pages 11–20, New York, NY, USA, 2010. ACM.

[25] G. L. Steele, Jr. Multiprocessing compactifying garbage collection. *Commun. ACM*, 18(9):495–508, Sept. 1975.

[26] Sun Microsystems Inc. Memory management in the java hotspot virtual machine, 2006.

[27] M. T. Vechev, E. Yahav, and D. F. Bacon. Correctness-preserving derivation of concurrent garbage collection algorithms. In *Proceedings of the 2006 ACM SIGPLAN Conference on Programming Language Design and Implementation*, PLDI '06, pages 341–353, New York, NY, USA, 2006. ACM.

[28] WebKit Project. Sunspder javascript benchmark. http://www.webkit.org/perf/sunspider/sunspider.html, 2008.

[29] T. Yuasa. Real-time garbage collection on general-purpose machines. *J. Syst. Softw.*, 11(3):181–198, Mar. 1990.

Author Index

Absar, Javed 115

Asavoae, Mihail 43

Baghdadi, Riyadh 115

Bak, Seonmyeong 155

Ballabriga, Clément 33

Beaugnon, Ulysse 115

Bebelis, Vagelis 125

Bhandarkar, Pranav 85

Cardoso, João M. P. 63

Carlsson, Mats 23

Castañeda Lozano, Roberto 23

Chamberlain, Roger D. 145

Chandramohan, Kiran 73

Chaudhary, Sandeep 105

Chong, Lee Kee 33

Cytron, Ron K. 145

Dasgupta, Anshuman 85

Delbem, Alexandre C. B. 63

Edler von Koch, Tobias J.K. 85

Fischmeister, Sebastian 105

Fradet, Pascal 125

Franke, Björn 3, 85

Girault, Alain 125

Guo, Minyi 83

Henry, Julien 43

Hjort Blindell, Gabriel 23

Kim, Hongjune 155

Krall, Andreas 13

Kravets, Alexey 115

Lee, Jaejin 155

Lee, Jinyong 135

Lee, Jongeun 135

Lee, Jongwon 135

Lezuo, Roland 13

Lokhmotov, Anton 115

Maïza, Claire 43

Marques, Eduardo 63

Martins, Luiz G. A. 63

Monniaux, David 43

Nobre, Ricardo 63

O'Boyle, Michael F.P. 73

Paek, Yunheung 135

Paulweber, Philipp 13

Ray, Rajarshi 95

Roy, Pooja 95

Roychoudhury, Abhik 33

Schulte, Christian 23

Spink, Tom 3

Tan, Lin 105

Topham, Nigel 3

Tweed, David 115

van Haastregt, Sven 115

Wagstaff, Harry 3

Wang, Chundong 95

Whalley, David 1

Wingbermuehle, Joseph G. 145

Wong, Weng Fai 95

Wu, Hui 53

Zheng, Wenguang 53

www.ingramcontent.com/pod-product-compliance
Lightning Source LLC
Chambersburg PA
CBHW081533220326
41598CB00036B/6423